THE OXFORD HISTORY OF ENGLISH LITERATURE

General Editors

JOHN BUXTON, NORMAN DAVIS,
BONAMY DOBRÉE, *and* F. P. WILSON

X

THE OXFORD HISTORY OF
ENGLISH LITERATURE

Certain volumes originally appeared under different titles (see title-page versos).
Their original volume-numbers are given below.

THE AGE OF JOHNSON
1740–1789

JOHN BUTT

edited and completed by
GEOFFREY CARNALL

CLARENDON PRESS · OXFORD

Oxford University Press, Walton Street, Oxford OX2 6DP

Oxford New York Toronto
Delhi Bombay Calcutta Madras Karachi
Petaling Jaya Singapore Hong Kong Tokyo
Nairobi Dar es Salaam Cape Town
Melbourne Auckland
and associated companies in
Berlin Ibadan

Oxford is a trade mark of Oxford University Press

Published in the United States by
Oxford University Press, New York

© *Oxford University Press 1979*

First published 1979
Reprinted 1980, 1990

Originally published as volume VIII with the title The Mid-
Eighteenth Century (*ISBN 0-19-812212-8*)

British Library Cataloguing in Publication Data
data available

Library of Congress Cataloging in Publication Data
data available
ISBN 0-19-812236-5

Printed in Great Britain by
Courier International
Tiptree, Essex

PREFACE

IT distresses me that I should have taken so long to complete the present volume. Among John Butt's friends some who would have been his most keenly appreciative readers have themselves died, and others, I fear, must occasionally have given up hope of ever seeing the work published. The patience of the Oxford University Press has been strained to the limit, and perhaps beyond it. I am sorry that this should have been so, and sorry too that in the end my attempts to include a substantial portion of Butt's draft of a chapter on the historians should have proved abortive. He was working on Chapter VII during the last months of his life, and considering how severely he was handicapped by illness, the text he composed is extraordinarily attractive. It remains a first draft, however, and one that eventually I found myself compelled to abandon, with the exception of the first paragraph of the chapter, and a few isolated sentences elsewhere.

In addition to Chapter VII, I am responsible for the following sections of the book: Chapter VIII, except for the final section, dealing with Boswell's *Life of Johnson*; the section on dialogue in Chapter IX; the section on Sterne in Chapter X (except for a paragraph on page 444); Chapters XI and XII; and the chronological tables. Butt had drafted parts of the bibliography, and wherever practicable I incorporated his wording into my own text. His hand may be detected in some thirty-three author bibliographies, including those for Burke, Burns, Chatterton, Cowper, Junius, Macpherson, Percy, Samuel Richardson, and Smollett.

In the remainder of the book, the text has been left unchanged as far as possible, though some minor revisions were necessary to remove occasional obscurities and avoid loose ends and omissions. In this delicate operation I was greatly assisted by Professor G. S. Rousseau, who read all Butt's chapters and made a considerable number of comments and suggestions. I should also like to thank Mr. John Buxton, the general editor especially concerned with this volume, for his many helpful observations on the text submitted to him.

I am grateful, too, to Professor R. W. Hepburn and Dr. N. T. Phillipson, who read portions of what I wrote myself, and allowed me to benefit from their wide knowledge of the period. As for the bibliography, Mr. Alan Bell and Miss Ann Matheson kindly checked the sections dealing with general bibliographies and with the book trade, Mrs. V. G. Salmon suggested some of the titles in the section on language, and Dr. Roger Savage greatly improved the section on the drama. It would be impracticable to name all those colleagues and students whose conversation has stimulated and enlightened me: but I have been very fortunate in my associates.

John Butt himself wished to acknowledge his indebtedness for information on specific points to Professor D. C. Bryant, the late Professor D. B. Horn, Professor K. H. Jackson, and Professor C. J. Price. He often discussed his work with such friends as the late Professor W. L. Renwick and Professor James Sutherland, and was particularly grateful to those who had read and commented on chapters or sections in draft: Professor J. T. Boulton, Professor A. F. Falconer, Professor John Mac-Queen, Professor C. J. Rawson, and the late Professor Geoffrey Tillotson. He expressed warm appreciation of the former general editors of the series, the late Professor F. P. Wilson and the late Professor Bonamy Dobrée, recalling their encouragement, their forbearance, and their excellent advice.

John Butt also wished to thank the staffs of the four libraries which he had principally used: the National Library of Scotland, and the University Libraries of Edinburgh, Newcastle upon Tyne, and Yale. He mentioned particularly Professor William Beattie, Mr. E. R. S. Fifoot, Mr. D. M. Lloyd, Mr. W. Park, Miss W. C. Donkin, Miss J. M. Gladstone, and Miss Marjorie Wynne. I should like to make a similar acknowledgement, adding a special word of thanks to the staff of the Cambridge University Library, whose courtesy and helpfulness I have appreciated for many years. Obviously I am much indebted to the staffs of the Edinburgh libraries, and should like to mention particularly Mr. C. P. Finlayson of the University Library.

I must thank the University of Edinburgh for allowing me three terms of sabbatical leave, without which this volume would certainly never have been completed.

Portions of the text have already appeared in print. Butt

first developed his views on Johnson as a writer of poetical 'imitations' in a lecture delivered to the Johnson Society of London, published in *The New Rambler* in 1959, and reprinted by the Yale University Press in the same year in *New Light on Dr. Johnson*, edited by F. W. Hilles. Johnson as biographer is considered in the second of the Ewing Lectures which Butt delivered at the University of California, Los Angeles, in 1962, published there in 1966 as *Biography in the hands of Walton, Johnson, and Boswell*. An abbreviated version of Chapter V was published in a volume of essays presented to Professor F. A. Pottle, entitled *From Sensibility to Romanticism*, edited by F. W. Hilles and H. Bloom, Oxford University Press, New York, 1965. The section on Boswell's *Life of Johnson* in Chapter VIII is taken from the third of the Ewing Lectures. A few paragraphs from the section on Richardson in Chapter X appeared as an introduction to the Everyman Library edition of *Clarissa*. The section on Fielding is slightly adapted from a pamphlet in the British Council series 'Writers and their Work'. The section on Smollett was published in *Tobias Smollett: Bicentennial Essays presented to Lewis M. Knapp*, edited by G. S. Rousseau and P. C. Boucé, New York, 1971. I am grateful to the editors and publishers for making it possible to reprint.

These acknowledgements would not be complete without a word of thanks to Miss E. M. Davidson, who typed much of the volume both for Professor Butt and for myself, and whose interest and concern were appreciated by both of us. Mrs. Margot Butt's help and encouragement over the years of painfully slow progress have meant more to me than I can well express. I am deeply grateful, too, to my wife. She compiled the index, and my part of the text owes much to her sympathetic criticism.

G. C.

CONTENTS

I

INTRODUCTION

ALL divisions of time in literary history are artificial and
arbitrary, but 1740 is as convenient a year to choose as
any for the beginning of a new period. It is true that in
the later 1730s there is not that sense of an epoch ending which
Dryden had observed and so successfully conveyed in *The
Secular Masque* of 1700; nor does anyone declare that a literary
reign was drawing to a close, as Dryden himself had announced
in his verse epistle to Congreve (1694); but in 1740 no writer
could match Dryden in authority and prestige and in the
sway he exerted. Addison's rule at Button's Coffee-house had
come to an end with his death in 1719, and there was no one
left who by temperament and achievement could aspire to that
succession. Swift and Pope, the only two great survivors of the
wits of a former age, had each made his private retreat. By
1740 Swift was in failing health; though he was to linger for
another five years, they were to be years of increasing mental
distress, and he had delivered his testament in the *Verses on the
Death of Doctor Swift* at the end of 1731. Pope had still one major
work to complete, *The New Dunciad* (1742), or *The Dunciad*,
Book IV, as we are more accustomed to call it; but he too, in
the remaining four years of his life, was more concerned with
revising old works than with writing new. His great satirical
activity had been virtually brought to a close with the *Epilogue
to the Satires* of 1738: 'This', he tells us, 'was the last poem of the
kind printed by our author, with a resolution to publish no
more.' One other man of letters had established a solid reputation by his work in the 1730s: James Thomson had completed
his *Seasons* and had published the four parts of *Liberty*, besides
producing three tragedies. In 1740 he was no more than forty
years old, and he had still to write a masque, *Alfred*, two more
tragedies, and *The Castle of Indolence*; but by disposition he was
too acquiescent for a leader, and he was to die in 1748, his
body oppressed, as his friend Armstrong said, 'with a great
load of materials for a disease'.

In 1740 a different kind of reign was coming to an end. Sir Robert Walpole had been in power with only a brief interval since 1721. His influence had been diminishing since 1737, but he retained office until 1742, three years before his death. Certain aspects of his rule had offered a fair field for satire in prose and verse and on the stage. Stage attacks were easily suppressed by the Licensing Act of 1737, which closed all theatres but Drury Lane and Covent Garden, and brought all plays under the censorship of the Lord Chamberlain; and a plain warning was given to verse satirists when Paul Whitehead was summoned before the House of Lords in 1739 to answer for libels discovered in his *Manners*. The close of Walpole's career may therefore be said to have brought all writers who cared for political issues into closer relation with government, either through the need to exercise more discretion in attack or by the prospect of greater rewards in defence. Walpole's removal at the beginning of our period drew the teeth of some Tory satire, but it did not provide an occasion for rescinding the Licensing Act. The most notable sufferer was Henry Fielding, to whose energies the stage was now closed. But what the drama suffered by his compulsory retirement, the novel was to gain. One remote consequence of the uneasy close of Walpole's rule was therefore to help in making the 1740s the first great decade of the novel, a new form (or largely new) in which new or largely new writers—Richardson, Fielding, Smollett, and later, Sterne—were to found their reputations.

The same decade was to see new reputations made in verse. In 1740 Edward Young, an older man than Pope, was already fifty-seven and well known as a satirist and tragic dramatist. After more than seven years' silence, he began to publish in 1742 a series of meditations in blank verse 'on Life, Death, and Immortality', *The Complaint: Or, Night-Thoughts*, which brought him an entirely different, more lasting, and more widespread popularity, one more appropriate to his cloth, and as characteristic of the mood of the mid-century as his satirical reputation had been characteristic of an earlier period.

Apart from Fielding, Young, and John Dyer—whose *Grongar Hill* had appeared as long ago as 1726, and who was now to begin writing verse in a different manner—there are no other instances in our period of new reputations made by men who had earned different reputations amongst the Augustans;

but there were several younger writers beginning to publish at the end of the 1730s whose development a perceptive and sympathetic critic might have watched with interest. This critic would eventually have been forced to admit that Richard Glover had done nothing better than *Leonidas*, published in 1737 at the age of twenty-five, though the ballad *Admiral Hosier's Ghost* (1740) has undoubted merits; he might have expected more from the lyrical talents of George Lyttelton than was eventually to appear. Thanks to his perceptiveness, he might have discerned in an unintentionally bawdy poem, *The Oeconomy of Love* (1736), which John Armstrong published at the age of twenty-seven, at least one passage approaching eloquence, as well as signs of other qualities to reach maturity in *The Art of Preserving Health* (1744). He could have been forgiven if he had seen no signs of unusual talent in Mark Akenside's *A British Philippic* (1738) or even in the crude earliest version of William Shenstone's *The Schoolmistress* (1737); but if, like Pope, he had inquired about the author of *London: a Poem, in Imitation of the Third Satire of Juvenal* (1738) and had been told that 'his name was Johnson, and that he was some obscure man', he ought to have replied, like Pope, 'He will soon be *déterré*.'

Each of these writers was to enjoy some esteem for his poetry, but with the exception of that last great name, none of them seemed to offer so much as the new poets of the 1740s. Gray was to begin writing in 1742, and by 1750 he had finished his *Elegy*, which was to be published the following year. Smart had begun about the same time, though not in a manner to forecast *A Song to David* (1763). Collins had published his *Persian Eclogues* in 1742, and his schoolfellow Joseph Warton wrote a provocative poem *The Enthusiast, or the Lover of Nature*, which appeared in 1744. The two friends happened to meet at Guildford races in 1746, and began to plan a volume of odes which was evidently intended by both of them as a *Lyrical Ballads* of experiment and reform. In the event they were to publish their odes separately later the same year.

In other branches of literature, the 1740s mark a turning-point. In classical scholarship it is the end of Bentley's long reign. His *Manilius* was published in 1739, three years before his death, and no one of comparable fame arose to take his place until Porson began to write at the very end of our period. By

1765 Joseph Priestley could venture on the claim that antiquity had come to occupy only a small part of general conversation, which was now preoccupied with modern history, policy, arts, manufactures, and commerce. 'A hundredth part of the time which was formerly given to criticism and antiquities, is enough in this age to gain a man the character of a profound scholar.' In Anglo-Saxon scholarship, too, the achievements of the previous period were not adequately sustained. On the other hand, antiquarianism of a more miscellaneous kind flourished, and helped to shape a new historical consciousness. That painstaking antiquary, William Oldys, was in the middle of his long and fruitful career. In 1740 he was acting as librarian to the Earl of Oxford, whose huge library was bought in 1742 by the bookseller Thomas Osborne. Osborne employed Oldys and Samuel Johnson to prepare a catalogue of the library (1743), and the two men were later engaged upon the eight-volume selection of pamphlets from the library entitled *The Harleian Miscellany* (1744–6). It was this great library, whose treasures Oldys and Johnson helped to unfold, that became one of the three principal collections in the library of the British Museum, opened in 1759. But Oldys's main interest was in biography. He had been associated with Thomas Birch in the supplement to Bayle's *Dictionary*, which Birch finished in 1741, and he was soon to begin work on *The Biographia Britannica* (6 volumes, 1747–66), which served as *The Dictionary of National Biography* of the eighteenth century. This is the scholarly context in which more popular and abiding biography was written, the lives written by Johnson for publication in *The Gentleman's Magazine* at the beginning of this period, the biographical work of Goldsmith in the middle, and *The Lives of the Poets* and Boswell's *Life of Johnson* at the end.

Scholarly and antiquarian activity lend a tone to the literature of the period in other ways. It was in this decade that Johnson began to plan his edition of Shakespeare and his *Dictionary of the English Language*, both of which summarized the best work of the past in each kind and so provided a basis of revision for future editors and lexicographers. The period was also to be one of great achievements in historiography. The work of the older men had been brought to a close with Carte's *General History of England* (4 volumes, 1747–55), and in 1740 Gibbon was only three years old. But Hooke began to publish his *Roman History* in 1738; and Robertson, though still in his early twenties, set to work in the middle of the decade upon his *History of Scotland* (2 volumes, 1759). Hume relates that he did not form the plan of writing his *History of Great Britain* until 1752, and in 1740 he was little known. His *Treatise of Human Nature*, published in 1739, had fallen 'dead-born from the press, without reaching such distinction as even to excite a murmur among the zealots'. The beginning of his philosophical career therefore lies just outside our period, but it was early in the new decade, with the publication of the first volume of his *Essays Moral and Political* in 1741, that his work began to obtain a favourable reception.

Much of the best writing of these fifty years still lay well out of sight. In 1740 Adam Smith was a university student; the Revd. Laurence Sterne was already a Prebendary of York, but was otherwise unknown to fame; Smollett had just gone to London, Goldsmith, Cowper, and Burke were at school, and Boswell was a babe in arms; Blake, Burns, Crabbe, and Sheridan were as yet unborn. But it is possible to detect enough evidence of changes in the making, with old careers ending and new careers beginning, to justify the convenience of opening a new volume at 1740.

The interest of the literary scene in the 1740s might even suggest the propriety of organizing this volume by surveys of each decade. It is true that the 1750s is not a remarkable period except in the careers of Johnson, who completed his *Dictionary* and wrote the *Rambler*, the *Idler*, and *Rasselas* as well, and of Hume, who besides his *History of England* published his *Enquiry concerning the Principles of Morals*, his *Political Discourses*, and his *Four Dissertations*; but no student of eighteenth-century literature should fail to observe the peculiar character of the 1760s. Though the decade is notable for the revival of satire in Churchill's meteorically bright and short career, it is more particularly marked by the unusual range of scholarly study of earlier literature, and the reflection of this in the imaginative literature of the day. In 1760 Edward Capell published his *Prolusions*, and thus made readily accessible the text of the play of *Edward III*. In 1761 Thomas Percy published the first Chinese novel to be translated into English (see p. 100), an authentic and substantial corrective to contemporary taste for chinoiseries. He had long been at work collecting and selecting English and Scottish ballads, to be published at last as *Reliques of Ancient English Poetry* in 1765; and the care he took in presenting *Five Pieces of Runic Poetry* in 1763 was to defend himself from the suspicion with which many readers greeted Macpherson's Ossianic translations (1760–3). Welsh poetry was beginning to be explored (in Evan Evans's *Specimens of the Poetry of the Ancient Welsh Bards*, 1764) as well as Norse, and both were to inspire one of Thomas Gray's last publications containing 'The Descent of Odin' and 'The Triumphs of Owen', 1768. Two important books published during this decade contributed greatly to a better understanding of Elizabethan and earlier literature, namely Hurd's *Letters on Chivalry and Romance* (1762) and Farmer's *Essay on the Learning of Shakespeare* (1767). At the same time the boy Chatterton was fabricating his medieval romances, the first of which, 'Elinoure and Juga', was published in 1769. Lastly the novel, whose biographical structure had been turned upside down in *Tristram Shandy*, 1760–7, was reunited to the romance in Horace Walpole's 'Gothic' tale, *The Castle of Otranto*, 1764.

Johnson took an important part in this renascence of learning. His sympathetic understanding of Percy's work is shown in the 'dedication' to the Countess of Northumberland that he wrote for the *Reliques*; and in the same year he published his long-expected edition of Shakespeare, the best edition that had so far appeared. He was now beginning to take life a little more easily, and had been granted a pension in 1762. But as late as the 1770s, a decade which might otherwise seem most notable for a revival of comedy in *She Stoops to Conquer* and the plays of Sheridan, it was the old pensioner who still dominated the literary scene with his four political pamphlets, his *Journey to the Western Islands of Scotland*, and the first volume of his *Lives of the Poets*. In fact Johnson's is the only great literary career that overspreads the whole period. He is alone amongst his contemporaries, or almost alone—Goldsmith is his closest rival here—in attempting a large variety of literary kinds. That is why the habit may be approved of borrowing his name for the title of this age, why his achievement is summarized at the beginning of this volume, and why his work alone has been accorded a chapter to itself.

A history of the literature of this period could be written on different principles and with different emphasis from those to be found in this volume. Apart altogether from a survey of the period by decades, it would be possible to write a history of the intellectual movements of the age. This would rightly have given more prominence to Hume, who might then have become the subject of the second chapter. A history interested principally in literature as a reflection of society might properly have promoted to a higher rank some minor talent such as that of Horace Walpole; and a historian with his eye on the achievements of the early nineteenth century might have been embarrassed in the choice of a suitable forerunner—Akenside, or Gray, or Cowper, or (with increasing desperation) Macpherson—as a banner-holder. But the choice of Johnson serves to emphasize that this is a history undertaken upon more purely literary principles. Intellectual movements, the face of society, economic and political developments, have not been neglected; but care has been taken not to isolate them in separate chapters from purely literary discussion. As to the literary future, that will be observed as opportunity offers; for this, like all other ages, was an age of transition. The great figures of Wordsworth and Coleridge, Scott, Byron, Shelley, and Keats will be descried at the end of many a vista, but the positions they will be found to occupy are in no sense Messianic.

This was the last age in which writers were seriously affected by the doctrines associated with the traditional literary 'kinds'. Though it seems to have been felt that the epic was no longer entirely suited to the age—only one was written (Wilkie's *Epigoniad*)—it could be adapted, as Fielding was to show in his novels, and Gibbon in the *Decline and Fall*. Other adaptations scarcely less ingenious gave new life to the pastoral, the georgic, the satire, and the ode. In the pages that follow it will be seen how new 'kinds' derive from old by different processes, imitative or parodic, to which the biological term 'mutation' may be applied. Nor are the traditional 'kinds' alone in attracting the attention of the imitator and the parodist, as the sections devoted to the ballad and the letter will show. It is within the 'kinds', then, that the achievements of the age are to be considered and assessed.

II

SAMUEL JOHNSON

THOUGH Johnson[1] had worked as a journalist and translator in Birmingham and had occupied a schoolmaster's leisure at Edial in writing his tragedy *Irene*, it was not until he went to London in 1737 that his literary career may be said to have begun. He went there to try the fate of his tragedy and to get some employment in journalism and translating; but 'what first displayed his transcendent powers', in Boswell's words, was his *London: a Poem, in Imitation of the Third Satire of Juvenal*, published in May 1738, within a few days of the first dialogue of Pope's *One Thousand Seven Hundred and Thirty-Eight* (the *Epilogue to the Satires*).

The form he had chosen, the Imitation, was well established. It had sprung from the paraphrastic manner of translation admired in the mid-seventeenth century, and advocated by Denham and Cowley. 'If Virgil must needs speak English,' Denham had said in the preface to his *Destruction of Troy* (1656), 'it were fit he should speak not only as a Man of this Nation, but as a Man of this Age.' It is not a far cry from such an expression of policy to Oldham's determination, when rendering Horace's *Ars Poetica*, 'to alter the scene from *Rome* to *London*, and to make use of *English* names of Men, Places, and Customs, where the Parallel would decently permit' (1681). Poets were quick to take the hint, and the last thirty years of the seventeenth century can show numerous Imitations, ranging from the loosest of paraphrases to modernized translations running more or less in parallel with their originals. Creech reports that when translating Horace (1684) he had been

---

[1] Samuel Johnson, 1709–84, was the son of a Lichfield bookseller, and was educated at Lichfield Grammar School and Pembroke College, Oxford, which he left without a degree. After an unsuccessful period as a schoolmaster, when David Garrick was one of his pupils, he went to London and worked for the *Gentleman's Magazine*. He undertook a great variety of literary projects, including his *Dictionary*, published in 1755. He became the centre of a brilliant literary circle which eventually constituted itself into 'The Club', 1764. In 1762 he received a state pension, and thereafter lived in a more leisurely fashion, recorded in detail by Boswell. He was given an LL.D. at Oxford in 1775.

advised to 'turn the *Satyrs* to our own Times', since '*Rome* was now rivall'd in her Vices, and Parallels for Hypocrisie, Profaneness, Avarice and the like were easie to be found'. He resisted the temptation; but there were many who seized their opportunity. The finest examples belong to Johnson's lifetime. In 1713–14 Swift published *Part of the Seventh Epistle of the First Book of Horace Imitated*, *The First Ode of the Second Book of Horace Paraphras'd*, and *Horace, Part of the Sixth Satire of the Second Book Imitated*. In each instance he courted comparison with his originals by printing the Latin parallels; and in this he was followed by Pope, whose splendid series of *Imitations of Horace*, eleven in all, appeared between 1733 and 1738.

This was the tradition that Johnson inherited, and adapted, at the very climax of its reputation. What he knew of the tradition at the beginning of his career is uncertain. In later years he was to show himself characteristically well informed: in *The Lives of the Poets* (Life of Pope) he says that 'this mode of imitation . . . was first practised in the reign of Charles the Second by Oldham and Rochester, at least I remember no instances more ancient'. But it was sufficient for his present purposes that he knew what Pope had done, whose most significant contribution had been to use the form for political satire. A compliment to statesmen 'out of place' in the first *Imitation* and a reflection upon Walpole's Excise Bill in the second might show where Pope's political sympathies lay; but it was only in the later *Imitations*—the ironic *Epistle to Augustus*, the *Imitation of the Sixth Epistle of the First Book*, where moneyed interests and rigged elections are attacked, and the *First Epistle of the First Book* reverentially addressed to the Government's arch-enemy Bolingbroke—that Pope unmistakably directed this form to a political target. All three poems were published within the twelve months preceding the publication of *London*; and by following in their wake Johnson shows that he recognized the latest development in political attack, namely, the enlisting of a classical moralist in the struggle. In the last few months Pope had enlisted Horace in the Tory party; Johnson was now to make a Tory champion of Juvenal as well.

But in spite of similarities, so intentional and so well-marked as to provoke comparison with Pope, there are almost equally well-marked differences in substance and treatment. The choice of Juvenal seems pointed and deliberate; and its appropriateness was confirmed, in the most authoritative manner, when *The Vanity of Human Wishes* was published in 1749. The choice of classical satirist to some extent conditioned the manner of attack. Horace's doctrine of contentment with a moderate competence was well suited to oppose the mercenariness and display of a mercantile government's supporters, and Horace's 'polite, insinuating style' was easily adapted to the voice of the elder statesman of poets, conscious of his own superiority in breeding and of the superiority of the noble friends with whom he is conversing. But this would have been an entirely inappropriate attitude for the young Samuel Johnson, unknown, with no influential friends, and with a radically different, indeed rawer experience of life. In so far as he and Pope may both be said to have belonged to the Tory party—the phrase itself is anachronistic—they belonged, in modern parlance, to different wings. Both are agreed in their diagnosis: moral standards have become tainted by a widespread lust for money. Pope can utter his condemnation from a position of modest affluence, but Johnson does not possess even that. His is the rancour of unrecognized merit, the indignation of one who scorns to learn the art of currying favour, but suffers for not practising it. Juvenal had taken this stance before him; but Johnson seems to have recognized the appropriateness of the stance to his own position.

Unlike a translator, an imitator is not in duty bound to find a parallel for every phrase in his original. He may select; and the extent to which Johnson exercised the privilege can be roughly indicated by measurements of length. In spite of the greater conciseness of the Latin language, *London* is sixty lines shorter than the original, and *The Vanity of Human Wishes* is about the same length as the Tenth Satire. Dryden, with every phrase on his conscience, had needed 503 lines of English verse to render the 322 lines of the Third Satire; even Oldham, who had set himself a task similar to Johnson's, required 477 lines; and Pope exceeded his originals every time by amounts varying from 42 lines to 149. Johnson's brevity can be attributed in part to the skill with which he packs his verse. Thus the famous line 'Slow rises worth, by poverty depress'd' (l. 177) distils a line and a half of Juvenal:

> Haud facile emergunt, quorum virtutibus obstat
> Res angusta domi.

Partly it can be attributed to Johnson's habits in composition, for he appears to have worked without the book in front of him, relying on his memory of the Latin, and composing as much as seventy lines at a time without committing them to paper. Partly also it can be attributed to his difficulty in finding parallels, for 'between Roman images and English manners', as he was to complain in the *Life of Pope*, 'there will be an irreconcilable dissimilitude'. In this respect he was not so successful as either Oldham or Pope had been. 'To vote a patriot black, a courtier white' (l. 52) is a happy topical application of 'maneant qui nigrum in candida vertunt'; and there are many more. But Johnson gives the impression of not troubling to exert himself in this way, of disliking unnecessary particulars, and of preferring to condense. Both Oldham and Dryden enlarge upon the taunts and jests made at the expense of the poorly clothed citizen. Oldham has:

> If his apparel seem but overworn,
> His stocking out at heel, or breeches torn,
> One takes occasion his ripped shoe to flout,
> And swears 't has been at prison-gates hung out;
> Another shrewdly jeers his coarse cravat,
> Because himself wears point; a third his hat,
> And most unmercifully shows his wit,
> If it be old, or does not cock aright.

Dryden mentions 'the torn Surtout' and 'the tatter'd Vest';

> The greasie Gown, sully'd with often turning,
> Gives a good hint, to say The Man's in Mourning:
> Or if the Shoo be ript, or patches put,
> He's wounded! see the Plaister on his Foot.

But Johnson is content with sufficient direction to encourage the reader to supply his own particulars:

> The sober trader at a tatter'd cloak,
> Wakes from his dream, and labours for a joke;
> With brisker air the silken courtiers gaze,
> And turn the varied taunt a thousand ways. (ll. 162–5)

The Vanity of Human Wishes (1749) enabled Johnson to yield more fully to his bent towards generalization and his dislike of unnecessary particulars. The original was a philosophical satire that did not necessarily require illustration with contemporary detail. Johnson in fact chose two instances within recent memory: when he wrote that 'Swift expires a driv'ler and a show', he was describing, in too sensational terms, what had happened four years previously; and it was in the same year 1745 that his 'bold Bavarian', Charles VII, stole 'to death from anguish and from shame'. But the force of these examples is not derived from their contemporaneity, nor is the force of his application of Juvenal's Sejanus lost by his turning back two centuries for his parallel to Wolsey. His *exempla* are universal figures, independent of contemporary detail, and they are built up without recourse to those vivid camera shots with which Pope entertains us as he composes his satiric characters. Johnson even neglects such opportunities as Juvenal offered. Thus it is Dryden that describes the young scholar as

> So small an Elf, that when the days are foul,
> He and his Satchel must be borne to School;

and it is Dryden that asks of Juvenal's Hannibal, Johnson's Charles XII of Sweden:

> Ask what a Face belong'd to this high Fame;
> His Picture scarcely wou'd deserve a Frame:
> A Sign-Post Dauber wou'd disdain to paint
> The one Ey'd Heroe on his Elephant.

But the absence of picturesque detail is not to be regretted if it has served to draw attention to Johnson's skill in defining the general situation so forcibly as to incite each reader to supply his own particular version. It is as though he was already cautious of committing the fault he was to ascribe to Cowley, 'that of pursuing his thoughts to their last ramifications, by which he loses the grandeur of generality'. That grandeur he attains in his best poetry; the pursuit of his thoughts to their last ramifications is the challenge he leaves with his readers.

A purist might have complained that Johnson was misusing the Imitation, inasmuch as its point consists in the ingenious exchange of English detail for Roman. In *London* Johnson's political purpose had ensured that he paid some deferential regard to tradition; but even there he saw his opportunity of leaving the detail and capturing the spirit of his original. In *The Vanity of Human Wishes* his disregard of detail and his

apparent determination to temper the sarcasm and vitupera-
tion of his original resulted in his producing, not an Imitation
as Pope understood the form, but rather a compassionate
variation upon a theme of Juvenal.

Johnson easily dropped into verse. After *The Vanity of Human
Wishes* he was to write numerous poems that serve to illustrate
several moods of his mind, the judicious *Prologue . . . Spoken at the
Opening of the Theatre in Drury-Lane 1747*, the satirical *Short Song
of Congratulation* (to Sir John Lade, 1780), the gay impromptu
To Mrs. Thrale, on her Completing her Thirty-fifth Year (1776),
the deeply-moved and deeply-moving verses *On the Death of
Dr. Robert Levet* (1782); and the best of them exhibit once more
his remarkable power of lifting the particular to the general,
of rising, as Imlac is made to say in *Rasselas*, Chapter X, 'to
general and transcendental truths, which will always be the
same'. But he was never again to submit himself to the discipline of composing in a recognized poetic form.

The bent for generalization, so marked in Johnson's poetry,
is also apparent in the more menial tasks that he undertook to
earn his living, and in none is it so striking as in the first substantial body of prose from his pen, his versions of the Parliamentary Debates. The *Gentleman's Magazine* and its rival, the
London Magazine, had been reporting debates in parliament
since 1732; but when in 1738 the House of Commons resolved
that such publication was a notorious breach of privilege, the
magazines were reduced to subterfuges. The *London* represented
that its reports were the proceedings of a political club of young
noblemen and gentlemen; the *Gentleman's*, more fancifully, pretended to offer accounts sent by Captain Gulliver's grandson of debates in the Senate of Lilliput. Johnson had written
from Birmingham offering his services to the proprietor of the
Gentleman's, Edward Cave, as early as 1734, and he seems to
have got into touch with him soon after his arrival in London
in 1737. His first contribution appeared in March 1738, a
Latin poem *Ad Urbanum*, defending Cave from his competitors'
attacks; and in subsequent years he took over much of the
editorial work, besides contributing reviews, short biographies,
and apparently some theatrical criticism. In addition he was
given the assignment of 'composing' the Parliamentary Debates from November 1740 till February 1743. Attendance in

either House was not required of him. At best he was furnished with scanty notes of what had happened; sometimes, as he told Boswell, 'he had nothing more communicated to him than the names of the several speakers, and the part which they had taken in the debate'.

In the circumstances an accurate report could be neither expected nor intended. If sometimes the order of speakers was followed and their main arguments recorded, more often Johnson was left to his own invention on a known topic of debate, and then he seems to have taken the opportunity of shaping miscellaneous arguments into unified essays, setting before his readers opposing views on those issues which were then dividing the nation. He shows little interest in such detail as his notes may have given him. As Birkbeck Hill remarked, in one of the appendices to his edition of Boswell's *Life of Johnson*, 'Had Defoe been the composer, he would have scattered over each speech the most ingenious and probable matters of detail, but Defoe and Johnson were wide as the poles asunder.' Johnson does indeed find room for some energetic exchange of invective, as for example the famous retort to the elder Horace Walpole which he credited to Pitt:

Sir, The atrocious Crime of being a young Man, which the honourable Gentleman has with such Spirit and Decency charged upon me, I shall neither attempt to palliate, nor deny, but content myself with wishing that I may be one of those whose Follies may cease with their Youth, and not of that Number, who are ignorant in spite of Experience;

but he prefers to seize such opportunity as the debate offers to present the topic in a wider context. The same debate that provoked Pitt's exchange with Walpole—a bill for manning the fleet in the war against Spain, and for regulating seamen's wages—shows members appealing throughout to general principles, such as those of contract and of supply and demand:

Is it reasonable [asks the Attorney General] that any Man should rate his Labour according to the immediate Necessities of those that employ him? Or that he should raise his own Fortune by the Publick Calamities? If this has hitherto been a Practice, it is a Practice contrary to the general Happiness of Society, and ought to prevail no longer.

This was journeyman work, but it provided occasion for Johnson's generalizing bent; and in indulging it he necessarily adapted the debate, making of it a new form with clear affinities to the philosophical dialogue, the oration, and the essay.

The complete extent of the work that Johnson undertook for the booksellers during these early years in London may never be fully known, although new attributions are constantly being made. That which has been recognized is uniform in character. Whether he is writing an expository introduction to a Medicinal Dictionary, or endowing with words the purposes of a dedicator, or compiling a set of Proposals to invite subscriptions for a literary project, it is his custom to drive for first principles. Boswell tells a story about a preface written some years later for a Dictionary of Trade and Commerce by one Richard Rolt (1756). Did he know much of Rolt, and of his work, Boswell asked; and the reply came:

Sir, I never saw the man, and never read the book. The booksellers wanted a Preface to a Dictionary of Trade and Commerce. I knew very well what such a Dictionary should be, and I wrote a Preface accordingly.

This was the spirit in which he wrote a Preface for Dodsley's *The Preceptor: containing a General Course of Education* (1748), an introduction to *The World Displayed: or, a Curious Collection of Voyages and Travels* (1759) and to Macbean's *Dictionary of Ancient Geography* (1773), proposals for the Catalogue of the Harleian Library (1742), and many more. Even in these scattered pieces he may be said to have exemplified the principle which a relative impressed upon him in early youth and which he was to recall to Mrs. Thrale: 'Learn the leading Precognita of all things—no need perhaps to turn over leaf by leaf; but grasp the Trunk hard only, and you will shake all the Branches.'

Besides this hack work his mind was full of larger designs. His failure to secure the performance of *Irene*—it was not staged until 1749—had not altogether deflected his thoughts from a dramatist's career, for in the autumn of 1742 he was preparing a play about Charles XII of Sweden: it came to nothing, the subject being reserved for *The Vanity of Human Wishes*. A letter to Cave written about the same time mentions a 'Historical

Design' to be printed 'in Numbers', and a resolution to write the Life of Savage, published the following year. A remarkable list of projects may belong to the same period. Besides editions of Chaucer, Oldham and Roscommon, and numerous translations from Greek and Latin, it mentions a 'History of Criticism, as it relates to judging of Authours, from Aristotle to the present age', a 'History of the Heathen Mythology', a 'History of the Revival of Learning in Europe, containing an account of whatever contributed to the restoration of literature', a 'Treatise on the Study of Polite Literature', and a 'Poetical Dictionary of the English Tongue'. None was to be fulfilled; but on the other hand the list does not mention the two projects begun in this decade that constitute Johnson's greatest contributions to literary scholarship, his *Dictionary of the English Language* and his edition of Shakespeare.

When Johnson began work on his Shakespeare, the field was held by Theobald's edition of 1733, reissued in 1740. He designed to show his qualifications for the task by publishing some 'Miscellaneous Observations' on *Macbeth* together with proposals for a new edition. The *Miscellaneous Observations* were published in April 1745 with some remarks appended on Sir Thomas Hanmer's edition which had appeared in the meantime. The immediate effect of the publication was a letter from Tonson the bookseller, stating his claim to the copyright of Shakespeare's plays, and this had the effect of stopping work upon the edition. It was not published until twenty years later. How soon his mind turned, or was directed by the booksellers, towards the *Dictionary* cannot be determined. But within twelve months of Tonson's letter he had written 'A Short Scheme for compiling a new Dictionary of the English Language', a first draft of *The Plan of a Dictionary of the English Language*, published the following July (1747). The 'Scheme' itself could have been written in a day or two, but it is clearly the product of prolonged thought. It shows that he was well acquainted with lexicographical practice both here and abroad, and that he understood what needed doing to bring an English dictionary up to the level of achievement attained in the great dictionaries of France and Italy.

English dictionaries of the seventeenth century had for the most part been content to provide lists of 'hard' words with their 'easy' equivalents; but in the dictionaries of Kersey and Bailey in the first quarter of the eighteenth century the scope was widened to include common words as well as learned and technical terms, and to explain their derivations. Nathan Bailey's *Universal Etymological English Dictionary* was published in 1721, and passed through more than twenty-five editions during the next eighty years. The folio version, *Dictionarium Britannicum* (1730), and Benjamin Martin's *Lingua Britannica Reformata* (1749) are the most distinguished of Johnson's predecessors. The *Dictionarium* contains some 48,000 entries; stress accents are supplied, derivations given, different meanings are distinguished and occasionally expanded into articles of encyclopedic length; proper names are also included. Martin was content with half the number of entries in Bailey's *Dictionarium*, but he seems to have taken advantage of Johnson's *Plan* to provide the first dictionary in which the meanings of a word are presented in a systematic order.

Johnson's work shows once more his capacity for appreciating first principles and for modifying a traditional form. He subjected both the theory and practice of his English predecessors to criticism in the light of his understanding of continental achievements in lexicography. The first matter for decision was the choice of words. 'The chief intent', he wrote in the *Plan*, 'is to preserve the purity, and ascertain [establish] the meaning of our English idiom.' This implied neither a dictionary of 'hard' words, nor a universal dictionary, but in broad terms a dictionary of standard usage, containing 'words and phrases used in the general intercourse of life, or found in the works of those whom we commonly style polite writers'. This had been the stated ideal of the French and Italian dictionaries; and Johnson shows his awareness both of the ideal itself and of the need for modifying it in practice by pointing to the experience of the French, who first rejected 'terms of science' and later found that such terms must be permitted to 'settle themselves amongst the natives'. His intention, therefore, was to profit by French experience and admit a generous selection from the terms used in various branches of learning as well as those used in the professions.

From the idea of a dictionary of standard usage, it was a short step to the idea of fixing the language. The step had been taken by his continental predecessors, and Johnson was prepared at least to consider it. The intention of preserving the purity of idiom, mentioned at the beginning of the *Plan*, is reiterated in the summary. But even at this stage of his task, he permitted himself some expression of doubt; for he had observed that words, like those that speak them, are generally losing strength when they are not gaining it. The doubt was to be expressed more forcibly in the Preface when, at the end of his labours, experience had convinced him of linguistic change: a lexicographer may be derided, he declares, if he imagines 'that his dictionary can embalm his language, and secure it from corruption and decay'; or (the Great Moralist characteristically adds) 'that it is in his power to change sublunary nature, and clear the world at once from folly, vanity, and affectation'. But though the language may not be fixed by a dictionary, standard usage may still be determined by settling orthography and pronunciation, by accuracy of definition, by appropriate selection of words for admission, and by citing examples taken from writers of the first reputation.

Of Johnson's theory and practice in orthography and pronunciation nothing need be said. He made little or no advance upon Bailey. On his definitions he expected 'malignity most frequently to fasten', and he was right: several were stigmatized as either incorrect, prejudiced, or verbose; Boswell has been responsible for securing and perpetuating attention to the explanations of *pastern, network, tory, whig, pension, oats,* and *excise,* although this section of Johnson's work provided in Boswell's opinion 'astonishing proofs of acuteness of intellect and precision of language'. It is so; and a comparison with Bailey immediately reveals Johnson's superiority. Bailey's tacit assumption is that his readers understand the meaning of common words. Thus *net* is defined by him as 'a device for catching fish, birds, &c.' and *needle* as 'an instrument for sewing'; but Johnson, with his customary search after exactness, offers for *net* 'a texture woven with large interstices or meshes, used commonly as a snare for animals', and for *needle* the satisfying precision of 'a small instrument pointed at one end to pierce cloath, and perforated at the other to receive the thread, used in sewing'. Nor is it always Johnson who is verbose: he gives the primary meaning of *thirst* as 'the pain suffered from want of drink: want of drink'; it is Bailey who defines it as 'a Dryness of the Throat, a painful Sensation occasioned by

a preternatural Vellification of the Nerves of the Throat or
Fauces, and producing a Desire of drinking'.

Standard usage may be prescribed in a dictionary either by
controlling the admission of words or by remarking upon words
admitted. Johnson practised both methods. Bailey's dictionary
had reached some 60,000 words in the edition of 1736; but
though Johnson claimed to have 'much augmented the vocabulary', his dictionary includes only some 40,000. The reduction
was made at the expense partly of obsolete and technical terms,
partly of proper names and adjectives formed from them—he
instances in the Preface the omission of *Arian, Socinian, Calvinist,
Benedictine, Mahometan*—and partly of compound words, such
as *coachdriver*, whose 'primitives contain the meaning of the
compounds', and of 'words arbitrarily formed by a constant
and settled analogy', like diminutive adjectives in *-ish*, adverbs
in *-ly*, and substantives in *-ness*. But he took upon himself to
admit words found only in dictionaries, and others without
authority which might yet prove their use. At the same time
he did not hesitate to include vulgar terms and unnecessary
innovations, his reason being presumably that the man who
would write English undefiled should be warned against them.
Thus *banter, bamboozle*, and *sham*, already reprobated by Swift
in *Tatler*, No. 230, are stigmatized afresh: *banter* is 'a barbarous
word, without etymology, unless it be derived from *badiner*,
Fr.'; *bamboozle* is 'a cant word not used in pure or in grave
writings'; and *sham*, like *splutter*, is 'a low word'. *Bite*, in the
sense of *cheat*, though found in the poetry of Pope—a passage
that Johnson imperfectly recollected and did not trouble to
check—was pronounced to be 'a low phrase'; and *shabby*,
quoted from Swift, is castigated as 'a word that has crept into
conversation and low writing; but ought not to be admitted
into the language', though *stinkard* ('a mean stinking paltry
fellow') is allowed to pass without censure.

His objection to innovations was less to Latinisms than to
Gallicisms. 'Whoever knows the *English* tongue in its present
extent', he had declared in the *Rambler*, No. 208, 'will be able
to express his thoughts without further help from other nations.'
The same point was made in the Preface to the *Dictionary*:

Our language, for almost a century, has, by the concurrence of many
causes, been gradually departing from its original Teutonick character, and deviating towards a Gallick structure and phraseology,

from which it ought to be our endeavour to recal it, by making our ancient volumes the ground-work of style, admitting among the additions of later times, only such as may supply real deficiencies, such as are readily adopted by the genius of our tongue, and incorporate easily with our native idioms.

These are the principles which will prevent us from being 'reduced to babble a dialect of France'. In accordance with them, *ruse* (not found in Bailey) is censured as 'a French word neither elegant nor necessary'; and a subsidiary meaning of *transpire*, not recognized by Bailey, 'to escape from secrecy to notice', is reprobated as 'a sense lately innovated from *France*, without necessity'. *Finesse* too is 'an unnecessary word which is creeping into the language', and *fraischeur* is 'a word foolishly innovated by Dryden'. Others which were brought over at about the same time, such as *chagrin, fatigue, grimace, incontestable* (all found in Bailey) are accepted without stricture, and may be presumed to have been 'readily adopted by the genius of our tongue', while *sublime* is recognized as 'a Gallicism, but now naturalized'.

In appending illustrative quotations to his definitions Johnson was following the practice of Greek and Latin lexicographers, of the Accademia della Crusca, and of others. This was his most impressive contribution to English lexicography. The possibility had been discussed between Pope and Warburton, and Spence records in his *Anecdotes* the names of nine poets and twenty prose authors whom they regarded as authoritative. The list appears to have been handed to Johnson, since he acknowledges in his *Plan* that it had formed the basis of his own list.

Passages were to be selected, not merely for their use in definition of words, but also to 'give pleasure or instruction, by conveying some elegance of language, or some precept of prudence, or piety'. Practice was to show that 'this accumulation of elegance and wisdom' needed severe pruning; but enough was left to 'intersperse with verdure and flowers the dusty deserts of barren philology'. Johnson was determined that his dictionary might be read as well as consulted, and read with profit and pleasure. Pleasure may be derived from turning to *pitchforks*, and finding, on Swift's authority,

An old lord in Leicestershire amused himself with mending *pitchforks* and spades for his tenants gratis;

profit from what he has picked out of Tillotson and Sprat on *zeal*:

Good men often blemish the reputation of their piety by over-acting some things in their religion; by an indiscreet *zeal* about things wherein religion is not concerned.   *Tillotson*

True *zeal* seems not to be any one single affection of the soul; but rather a strong mixture of many holy affections; rather a gracious constitution of the whole mind, than any one particular grace, swaying a devout heart, and filling it with all pious intentions; all not only uncounterfeit, but most fervent;   *Sprat*

and a blend of both in a brief fable from L'Estrange under *lapidary*:

As a cock was turning up a dunghill, he espied a diamond: Well (says he) this sparkling foolery now to a *lapidary* would have been the making of him; but, as to any use of mine, a barley-corn had been worth forty on't.

Numerous passages might be cited which are of little or no service in defining the word in question and extend much beyond the strict purpose of illustration. Behind these extensive quotations there often lies unresolved a dispute about the frontiers of a dictionary and an encyclopedia. Bailey (following previous practices) had many encyclopedic features, such as historical and statistical information, and illustrative woodcuts; while Ephraim Chambers's *Cyclopaedia* (1728) served partly as a dictionary. In fact it was upon Chambers's definition of *tussis* that Johnson framed his notorious definition of *cough*: 'A convulsion of the lungs, vellicated by some sharp serosity'. In the *Plan* Johnson debated this question and decided that he would supply 'explanations real as well as verbal'; thus he would not only define *barometer* but spend a few lines upon its invention, construction, and principles. Experience was to show him that his scope was too large, and in a famous passage of his Preface he told his reader how from the 'dreams of a poet' he was doomed at last 'to wake a lexicographer'. Yet the encyclopedic character of the *Dictionary* remains distinct, though it is subordinated to the lexicographical. The few lines to be spent on the principles of the barometer extended to a full half-column, the longest article in the book; Philip

Miller's *Gardeners Dictionary* (1731–9) yielded him more than 350 descriptions of plants; and in a notable appendix to *electricity* he sketched the developments in that science of the previous thirty years. It was lexicographically unnecessary, yet a signal contribution to his readers' benefit. The distinction between dictionary and encyclopedia lay unresolved. The form is impure, but the blend is remarkably happy.

The *Dictionary* was published on 5 April 1755. During the progress of the work Johnson had spent all the money advanced to him from the booksellers and he needed another large project to support him. He returned to his abandoned edition of Shakespeare and issued fresh *Proposals* in June 1756, promising that the edition would be ready by the following Christmas; but it was not until the autumn of 1765 that the edition appeared. Since he had first begun to work on Shakespeare in the early 1740s, the editions of Hanmer (1744) and Warburton (1747), and a Scottish edition (1753), had been added to those of Rowe (1709), Pope (1725), and Theobald (1733), yet without presenting Shakespeare as he should be presented. The text was still needlessly corrupt, partly through editors' failure to appreciate the reasons for corruption, partly owing to their negligence in collation; and difficulties of interpretation still abounded, which an editor might hope to solve who had read the books his author read. These aims are concisely set out in Johnson's *Proposals*, and they constitute the first rational study of Shakespeare's text, as well as an additional instance of Johnson's capacity for getting down to first principles. If the account he gives of the transmission of the text may need adjusting in the light of modern knowledge, he correctly appreciated the basic reasons for corruption and understood the difference between the textual criticism of printed texts and that of classical manuscripts. His work upon the *Dictionary* had given him, as he admitted, 'some degree of confidence' in explaining obsolete and peculiar diction; from his knowledge of Elizabethan literature he hoped to explain the unintelligible, and to show that what was no longer current idiom had been acceptable in Shakespeare's day. 'My opinion is', he wrote

that very few of his lines were difficult to his audience, and that he used such expressions as were then common, though the paucity of contemporary writers makes them now seem peculiar.

He had long been convinced that 'in order to make a true estimate of the abilities and merit of a writer, it is always necessary to examine the genius of his age, and the opinions of his contemporaries': this is the first sentence of his *Miscellaneous Observations on the Tragedy of Macbeth* (1745), introducing a note on the doctrine of witchcraft. It amounted to a new critical instrument, similar indeed to the historical method developed independently at much the same time by Robert Lowth in his *Lectures on the Sacred Poetry of the Hebrews* (see Chap. XII, pp. 498, below). Johnson's approach is clearly explained in a letter of commendation he wrote to Thomas Warton on the publication of his *Observations on the Faerie Queene* (16 July 1754):

You have shown to all who shall hereafter attempt the study of our ancient authours the way to success, by directing them to the perusal of the books which those authours had read. Of this method Hughes and Men much greater than Hughes [presumably Warburton] seem never to have thought. The Reason why the authours which are yet read of the sixteenth Century are so little understood is that they are read alone, and no help is borrowed from those who lived with them or before them. Some part of this ignorance I hope to remove by my book which now draws towards its end.

In one other respect Johnson proposed to improve upon his predecessors. He would put his reader outside the reach of editorial caprice by printing all textual variants and all that was valuable of the notes of previous commentators. It had previously occurred to 'the Scots editor' (generally believed to have been Hugh Blair) to supply an index of conjectures and alterations and to select and abridge the notes of his predecessors. But Johnson was the first to present a reasoned case for a variorum edition, and in some measure to achieve what he set out to do. A series of subsequent editions was based on Johnson's, including the version of Edmond Malone's edition brought out by James Boswell the younger in 1821. This proved to be the standard complete edition for the rest of the nineteenth century.

If the edition itself did not fulfil all that the *Proposals* promised, at any rate the text was better than previous texts; and of the notes, it has been well said that 'in all those passages where scholarship and historical knowledge fail to give us their aid there is still no more helpful guide than he'. They also occasionally embody an estimate of the play and a brief study of a character, a form of criticism then beginning to be practised and one that was to be given extensive treatment in the hands of Thomas Whately, William Richardson, and Maurice Morgann in the next decade, though not to be systematically pursued until the following century.

But the crowning virtue of the edition is its Preface. Text and character-study look forward to new advances in the understanding of Shakespeare; the Preface summarizes the old. Yet even here the reader may be helped to appreciate the mastery of Johnson's achievement if he sees it in the context of a contemporary reader's expectations. When Johnson's old schoolfellow, Tom Newton, published his edition of Milton's poems in 1749, he remarked that it had 'almost become a custom' to prefix the life of an author to a new edition of his works. The life constitutes the bulk of Newton's prefatory material; he wrote as well an account of his procedure and some comment upon the work of his predecessors, but for a critique upon his author he was content to reprint Addison's papers on *Paradise Lost* from the *Spectator*. John Hughes in the preface to his *Spenser* (1715), John Urry in the preface to his *Chaucer* (1721), and Thomas Birch in the preface to his edition of Milton's prose works (1738) proceed in essentially the same way; they tell their reader what he may expect, but their prefaces are primarily biographical, though Birch interpolates a few critical comments at appropriate moments, and Hughes appends a long essay on allegorical poetry with 'remarks' on Spenser's writings.

Rowe had had a similar view of his prefatory task when he introduced the earliest of eighteenth-century editions of Shakespeare. 'It seems to be a kind of respect due to the memory of excellent men,' he began, 'especially of those whom their wit and learning have made famous, to deliver some account of themselves, as well as their works to posterity.' Accordingly he fancied that 'some little account of the man himself may not be thought improper'. This was the first systematic biography of Shakespeare, and it remained the standard account throughout the eighteenth century. Pope set the tradition of reprinting an abbreviated version of it, a tradition followed by all but Theobald amongst subsequent editors, including even James

Boswell the younger, who did not discard it in the great 'third variorum' edition of 1821, though he there printed the new life, by Malone, which superseded it.

Rowe had disclaimed the intention of writing a 'large and complete criticism' of Shakespeare's works, but he had offered a few observations on some of the things that had most pleased him. Pope had been equally modest in his disclaimer, but his reflections are set down less haphazardly than the remarks of Rowe; his preface is primarily a brief essay on Shakespeare's literary and dramatic character, to which is appended an account of the corruption of the text and the manner of correcting it.

Theobald, Hanmer, Warburton, and Blair, the four succeeding editors, reveal their unwillingness to compete with Rowe and Pope in biography and critical appreciation, even though they may not announce it. Theobald, indeed, begins with some wretched pretence at biography and criticism; but his preface and those of his successors are mainly devoted to a statement of editorial policy and a more or less misleading account of how it has been carried out. The acknowledgement paid by all of them but Theobald to the merits of Rowe and Pope takes the form of reprinting their prefaces.

Such was the peculiar state of a preface to Shakespeare when Johnson took up the task. He bowed to tradition by reprinting Rowe's preface, and thus absolved himself of writing a new life. He also reprinted the prefaces of Pope, Theobald, Hanmer, and Warburton, but he did not regard himself as thereby excused from all but an account of his own labours. He tells indeed what he has done, and what had been done before him, expressing himself in his most trenchant manner, delighting the scholar by the vigorous common sense applied to the mysteries of textual criticism, and engaging the confidence of the youngest student by assuring him that though 'notes are often necessary . . . they are necessary evils': if he would 'feel the highest pleasure that the drama can give', let him 'read every play, from the first scene to the last, with utter negligence of all his commentators'. But this is an appendix to the body of his preface, just as a parallel account had been an appendix to Pope's. He had warmly commended Pope's preface: it was 'a general criticism on his author, so extensive that little can be added, and so exact that little can be disputed'; and in his own preface he was to present once more, but also for the last time, a general estimate of Shakespeare's literary character, without regard to his performance in particular plays.

Like Pope, Johnson took as his model Dryden's account of Shakespeare in his *Essay of Dramatic Poesy* (1668). It was, he said in *The Lives of the Poets,* an 'epitome of excellence', 'a perpetual model of encomiastick criticism'. Dryden had determined the principal topics of discussion: Shakespeare as a poet of Nature, the question of his learning, the imperfections of his comic and serious wit. These topics were resumed by Rowe and Pope (and also by Dennis), but they offered a fair opportunity for expansion in Johnson's hands. Thus in discussing Shakespeare as the poet of Nature, he argued vigorously against Dennis and Rymer on behalf of the generic nature of Shakespeare's characters, claiming that

Shakespeare always makes nature predominate over accident; and, if he preserves the essential character, is not very careful of distinctions superinduced and adventitious. His story requires Romans or kings, but he thinks only on men.

The same topic, for it is very wide in interpretation, allowed him to review the old discussion, recently revived in Joseph Warton's *Essay on the Writings and Genius of Pope* (1756), whether love is a proper subject for tragedy. Upon every other stage, he observed, the universal agent is love, and 'for this, probability is violated, life is misrepresented, and language is depraved';

But love [he continues] is only one of many passions; and as it has no great influence upon the sum of life, it has little operation in the dramas of a poet, who caught his ideas from the living world [i.e. from Nature], and exhibited only what he saw before him.

Even more striking is his defence of Shakespeare from the charge of neglecting the dramatic unities, a defence conveniently presented as part of the discussion of his learning. The gravamen of Rymer's charge against Shakespeare, as against his fellow Elizabethans, was of 'ignorance or negligence of these fundamental Rules and Laws of Aristotle'; this was the occasion of the manifold absurdities they committed. But even in his own day Rymer's insistence upon the unities was unusually illiberal, and subsequent criticism might be regarded as a retreat from Rymer on this issue. Dennis might 'shew, that for want of the Poetical Art, *Shakespear* lay under very great Disadvantages. At the same time', he admitted, 'we must own to his Honour, that he has often perform'd Wonders without it.' In short, he was 'naturally learned', as Dryden had said long before; 'he needed not the spectacles of books to read Nature'. Rowe's view was similar:

> If one undertook to examine the greatest part of these [plays] by those rules which are established by *Aristotle*, and taken from the model of the *Grecian* stage, it would be no very hard task to find a great many faults; but as *Shakespear* lived under a kind of mere light of nature, and had never been made acquainted with the regularity of those written precepts, so it would be hard to judge him by a law he knew nothing of.

The point was to be made more epigrammatically by Pope:

> To judge . . . of *Shakespear* by *Aristotle*'s rules, is like trying a man by the Laws of one Country, who acted under those of another.

Although Pope's context does not warrant the deduction, it might seem that he is propounding the doctrine of the relativity of the poetical kinds: a critic must first determine what kind his author is pursuing and formulate his judgement in the light of that kind. Pope seems not to have been prepared for such an extension of his thinking. It is applied to Spenser by Richard Hurd in his *Letters on Chivalry and Romance* (1762), a book which Johnson may have had in mind when he said that Hurd was one who accounted for everything systematically:

for instance, it has been a fashion to wear scarlet breeches; these men would tell you, that according to causes and effects, no other wear could at that time have been chosen.

The warning is appropriate, but the doctrine itself is implicit in Johnson's Preface (1765). It is implied in the passage where Johnson justifies the tragi-comedies as 'compositions of a distinct kind', conducted contrary to the rules of criticism; the histories too, 'being neither tragedies nor comedies, are not subject to any of their laws'. But instead of showing that no other kind of play could at that time have been written, Johnson practises the sort of criticism that Warburton had advocated before him: 'such as judgeth our Author by those only Laws and Principles on which he wrote, NATURE and COMMON SENSE'. Like Kames, who had considered the whole question in his *Elements of Criticism* (1762), Johnson appealed to the experience of the audience in the theatre. Kames, indeed, has a stronger sense of the impression of reality that a play can make. Johnson attacks the unities of time and place so robustly that the reader fears for the whole case of dramatic make-believe. Certainly the spectator who 'can be once persuaded, that his old acquaintance are *Alexander* and *Caesar*, that a room illuminated with candles is the plain of *Pharsalia*, or the bank of *Granicus* . . . is in a state of elevation above the reach of reason'; but he came to the theatre for more than 'to hear a certain number of lines recited with just gesture and elegant modulation', and he may not feel altogether satisfied by being told that his pleasure in the drama enacted was owing to 'a just picture of a real original'. But if he is dissatisfied, he can at least feel that fundamental issues are being clarified. In this instance Kames provides a more acceptable answer to the difficult philosophical questions posed, just as Richard Farmer's *Essay on the Learning of Shakespeare* (1767) provides a fuller account of the extent of Shakespeare's reading; but in all these matters Johnson was presenting with an unequalled trenchancy answers to questions that had been mooted for the past hundred years. The case for the denigrators of Shakespeare was beginning to look much weaker; the future lay with the idolators.

For twenty years Johnson was occupied with these two great tasks, his dictionary and his edition of Shakespeare, but it is not to be supposed that all his available time was spent upon them. He had his living to earn, and this he procured partly by such commissions from the booksellers as have been described on an earlier page, and partly by more extended undertakings. Of these the *Rambler*, a periodical essay published twice a week from 20 March 1750 to 14 March 1752, was the most impressive. Nearly forty years had elapsed since the publication of the *Spectator* without the appearance of any effective imitation, and a change in public manners had opened the way for a new censor. But Johnson made no attempt to court a close comparison. If he began with a settled purpose, he did not choose to announce it. The first four papers, all dealing with literary topics, might be thought to predict a somewhat restricted field, and one lying closer to the boundaries than to the centre of the *Spectator*'s territory. It was only in the next four, each concerned with mental activity, that the *Rambler* showed what were to prove his distinguishing qualities, and declared somewhat parenthetically his intention; 'my purpose', he tells the reader in No. 8, 'is to consider the moral discipline of the mind.' The tone was more severe than that of either the *Tatler* or the *Spectator*, and signs of restiveness began to appear amongst his readers. 'The number of correspondents . . . increases every day upon me', he remarks in No. 10. The four imaginary letters published in this number are known to have all been written by Hester Mulso, later Mrs. Chapone; but there is no reason to suppose that real letters had not been received, and it is worth remarking that two of the imaginary ones are critical; one begs for 'some papers of a gay and humorous turn', and the other reminds him that the essayist's business should be with the manners of the age. Numbers 12, 15, and 16 give some redress to both objections; but the murmurings of readers can be detected once again in No. 23. The *Rambler*, it seems, had received several remonstrances: he was too 'solemn', too 'serious', too 'dictatorial'; he was not sprightly; he did not, like his eminent predecessor, have an eye to the coffee-houses of London; he had 'neglected to take the ladies under his protection', and his naked moral precepts were thought to need setting off with examples and characters. Still later in his career the *Rambler* confesses to having been charged with too much uniformity (No. 107), and another imaginary correspondent (No. 109) excuses his contribution with the wry observation that 'though you seem to have taken a view sufficiently extensive of the miseries of life, and have employed much of your speculation on mournful subjects, you have not yet exhausted the whole stock of human infelicity'.

Johnson would not have admitted to these remonstrances if he had not thought that there was some substance in the criticism, yet the compensating merits were sufficiently clear to a small but respected band of readers. He had recourse to few of the arts by which Addison had recommended himself. There is little variety in the forms his essays take. No. 3 is the first of nine allegorical fables (invariably the most tedious of his imaginative strokes), and the first of half a dozen eastern fables is No. 38. It was not until No. 18 that he used the character; but thereafter characters abound, sometimes three or four being used in a paper to illustrate a single point (No. 18), sometimes in more extended form as in the masterly Prospero (No. 200), said to have been based upon David Garrick. These characters bear a close relation to another favourite form, the imaginary letter in which a correspondent relates the outstanding events in a mis-spent or unfortunate life, or chooses one or two prominent episodes to illustrate unhappiness. Though the *Rambler*'s dominant mode is meditative, one paper in three contains more or less extended passages of narrative such as these. This is the full range of Johnson's artifice. The imaginary club, though club life was no less important in his day than in Addison's, is entirely disregarded; the 'vision' had little appeal; and the *Spectator*'s simple ironies are recaptured only in No. 100, a paper by Elizabeth Carter, recommending encouragement to dissipation.

The types of subject treated are also limited in range. 'I have never complied with temporary curiosity, nor enabled my readers to discuss the topick of the day', he remarks in the last *Rambler* (No. 208). He seems to have overlooked No. 107, the first part of which was prompted by the prospect of calendar reform, and it is possible that a diligent student might discover some other topicalities, such as the mitigation of the death sentence, so wisely pleaded in No. 114; but so strict was his normal rule that even the hysterical response to prophecy of a third earthquake in April 1750—expected to be a devastating climax to the shocks already felt in London in the two previous months—evoked no comment from the *Rambler*. Apologies for lack of attention to the ladies are found in papers 34 and 126, and an explanation is offered: 'masculine duties afford more room for counsels and observations, as they are less uniform, and connected to things more subject to vicissitude and change.' But their peculiar concerns were recalled from time to time; at least ten per cent of the papers have them prominently in view. In his last number he admits to having allotted a few papers to 'the idle sport of imagination', and some to 'disquisitions of criticism'. In the first category even such an idle frolic as No. 199, on the virtues of an Arabian magnet supposed capable of testing a woman's chastity, carries moral overtones. In the second category lie papers on subjects as varied as the modern novel (No. 4), biography (No. 60), Spenserian imitations (No. 121), historiography (No. 122), comedy (No. 125), plagiarism (No. 143), the letter (No. 152), the rules of art

(Nos. 156, 158), decorum in poetic diction (No. 168), and the poetry of Milton (Nos. 86, 88, 90, 92, 94, 139, 140).

The occurrence of critical papers is not frequent—it is one paper in ten, compared with the *Spectator*'s one in nine—but mere frequency represents very imperfectly the literary cast of the *Rambler*'s work. Johnson was essentially a man of letters. He does not indeed reflect upon the great work that was then engaging him, except to draw a rueful illustration:

> The task of every other slave has an end. The rower in time reaches the port; the lexicographer at last finds the conclusion of his alphabet. (No. 141)

But he shows in paper after paper his appreciation of the troubles incident to a life of letters. The poet who had traced the young scholar's career so searchingly, and yet so sympathetically, in *The Vanity of Human Wishes* a year or two earlier reverts to a theme of which he had intimate knowledge. In his poem he had cautioned his young enthusiast lest 'Praise relax, [or] Difficulty fright'. In the *Rambler* each clause receives extended treatment, the first in No. 111, the second in No. 25. And there are other pitfalls in the path of steady application. The most recluse are not necessarily the most vigorous prosecutors of study:

> Many impose upon the world, and many upon themselves, by an appearance of severe and exemplary diligence, when they, in reality, give themselves up to the luxury of fancy, please their minds with regulating the past, or planning the future. . . . There is nothing more fatal to a man whose business is to think, than to have learned the art of regaling his mind with those airy gratifications.
>
> (No. 89)

Another type of indiscipline is attempting to accomplish too much, gratifying 'our minds with schemes which we know our lives must fail in attempting to execute' (No. 17):

> The fate of learned ambition is a proper subject for every scholar to consider; for who has not had occasion to regret the dissipation of great abilities in a boundless multiplicity of pursuits, to lament the sudden desertion of excellent designs, upon the offer of some other subject made inviting by its novelty, and to observe the inaccuracy and deficiencies of works left unfinished by too great an extension of the plan?

A life spent too much with books will render a man liable to certain diseases of the personality as well as of the mind. The advice rendered to the young scholar in *The Vanity of Human Wishes* was:

> Deign on the passing world to turn thine eyes,
> And pause awhile from letters to be wise.

Gelidus, in No. 24, is a great philosopher, 'insensible to every spectacle of distress, and unmoved by the loudest call of social nature, for want of considering that men are designed for the succour and comfort of each other'. 'He that can only converse upon questions, about which only a small part of mankind has knowledge sufficient to make them curious', is reminded in No. 137, that he 'must lose his days in unsocial silence, and live in the crowd of life without a companion'. The experience of the young heir in No. 177 was similar. He had decided to retire from the world to his library, but had found his mind contracted and stiffened by solitude after some years, his ease and elegance sensibly impaired, and his quickness of apprehension and celerity of reply entirely lost; and the young man fresh from college is given some excellent counsel in No. 173, when he is dismayed to find that the world at large considers him a highbrow.

But even he who brings his work to a successful conclusion may be robbed of what he considers his due reward, for literary fame is a possession of very uncertain tenure (No. 21), and hope of it 'is necessarily connected with such considerations as must abate the ardour of confidence, and repress the vigour of pursuit' (No. 146); 'there are, indeed, few kinds of composition from which an author, however learned or ingenious, can hope a long continuance of fame' (No. 106).

This view of the troubles in the life of a man of letters has been set out in some detail so as to show in a particular instance Johnson's concern with the moral discipline of the mind. This is how we ail, he points out relentlessly, and this is how we may effect a cure, or at least improve ourselves. Above all we must endeavour to rid our minds of desire for 'some imaginary state of happiness unknown and unattainable' (No. 66), for 'all human happiness has its defects' (No. 203). He would no doubt have wished to be numbered amongst those 'very useful monitors, [who] have left many proofs of strong reason, deep penetration, and accurate attention to the affairs of life, which it is now our business to separate from the foam of a boiling imagination, and to apply judiciously to our own use' (No. 66).

Towards the end of December 1751 Johnson was already led to confess that he found 'the irksomeness of his task rather increased than lessened by every production' (No. 184), and in the following March he decided to abandon it on completing his second year. Arthur Murphy, in his 'Essay on the Life and Genius of Dr. Johnson', reports that 'the number sold on each day did not amount to five hundred: of course the bookseller [Johnson's old friend, Edward Cave], who paid the author four guineas a week, did not carry on a successful trade'. But no periodical essay in recent years had lasted so long, and its merits were increasingly recognized as the years went by. Already in 1752, Charlotte Lennox was declaring in *The Female Quixote* that it contained 'the finest system of ethics yet extant'; re-reading the *Rambler* in 1760 Shenstone found Johnson 'one of the most *nervous*, most *perspicuous*, most concise, and most harmonious prose-writers I know'; and in 1764, Smollett, at the pinnacle of his literary eminence, when editor of the influential *Critical Review*, could say that Johnson, though inferior to none in his other work, stood 'foremost as an essayist, justly admired for the dignity, strength, and variety of his stile, as well as for the agreeable manner in which he investigates the human heart, tracing every interesting emotion, and opening all the sources of morality'.

By that time the *Rambler*'s success, restricted as it had been, had already acted as sufficient encouragement for others to follow. Of these the *World* (1753–6), the *Connoisseur* (1754–6), Goldsmith's 'Chinese Letters' (1760–1), and the two Edinburgh periodicals, the *Mirror* (1779–80) and the *Lounger* (1785–7), have most claim upon our attention, and will be mentioned again later (pp. 314–23). The *Rambler*'s first successor was the *Adventurer*. This periodical was conducted by John Hawkesworth on the same bi-weekly plan that Johnson had adopted for the *Rambler*. Hawkesworth had wisely decided not to undertake the work alone; but when after a few months his partner withdrew from the scheme, he succeeded in enlisting the help of Johnson, who seems to have already sent an occasional contribution, and, through Johnson, Joseph Warton. Johnson's letter to Warton (8 March 1753) inviting his assistance has survived, and shows that the essayists' tasks had been methodically distributed, one taking 'Pieces of Imagination' as his province, others collaborating in 'pictures of Life', and another—it was Warton—being responsible for 'the Province of Criticism and Literature'.

Thus little more than a year after completing the *Rambler*, Johnson was once more at work as a periodical essayist, writing mainly 'pictures of Life'. Nor was this the last occasion. In 1758 his friend John Payne, who had published the *Adventurer*, started a weekly newspaper, the *Universal Chronicle, or Weekly Gazette*. He seems to have engaged Johnson to provide a weekly essay for a period of two years, and in the second number the *Idler* began publication. It may be thought that the changes in Johnson's policy were the result of his experiences with the *Rambler* and the *Adventurer*. Hawkins tells us that not only was the *Rambler* begun without any desire of assistance, but that 'his most intimate friends seemed to think it would have been presumptuous to offer it', and Cave, the proprietor, is known to have complained of Johnson's not admitting correspondents. In fact he admitted a few: besides those that have been already mentioned, the second letter in No. 15 is supposed to have been written by Garrick, No. 30 by Catherine Talbot, No. 44 by Elizabeth Carter, No. 97 by Richardson, and the second letter in No. 107 by a young lawyer called Joseph Simpson. But the *Idler* begins with a cordial invitation to such as will 'enable him to please without his own labour': 'he excludes no style, he prohibits no subject'. The number of contributions thought fit to use was not to be large, but at least it amounted to one paper in ten; and three of them by Sir Joshua Reynolds on painting (Nos. 76, 79, and 82), because they lay well outside Johnson's range, helped to give the impression of variety in the *Idler* that the *Rambler* had lacked.

Another distinction between the *Idler* and the *Rambler* is that the *Idler* permitted that discussion of topics of the day which the *Rambler* had so sternly refused. The capture of Louisburg and of Quebec provided a subject for two (Nos. 20, 81) of the six papers prompted by the war with France; the *Idler* finds one subject in the publication of Clarendon's autobiography (No. 65), and another in 'the rainy weather, which has continued the last month' (No. 17); still another (No. 6) is prompted by an item of news that would have been more surprising two hundred years ago than it would be today: 'the lady who had undertaken to ride on one horse a thousand miles in a thousand hours has completed her journey in little more than two-thirds of the time stipulated, and was conducted through the last mile with triumphal honours'; the *Idler* need not have been careful to add for the information of posterity that the lady's incitement was to win her wager.

In other respects the *Idler* follows the *Rambler*'s lead, except that here there is happily no place for allegory. For the first twelve months it seemed that he had dispensed with critical essays; but in his second year he made up for his neglect by several papers, among which Nos. 60 and 61, with the character of Dick Minim, the retailer of trite critical commonplaces, No. 84 on autobiography, No. 97 on the writing of travel books, No. 101 on literary biography, and Reynolds's three contributions are of particular interest. Once more he relies heavily upon characters and fictitious autobiography, in which it is noticeable that the affairs of women, more particularly those of humble life, receive increasing attention. Boswell's verdict on the *Idler* was that it had 'less body and more spirit' than the *Rambler*, and 'more variety of real life'. Such papers as No. 40, on the art of advertising, and No. 56, a meditation on attending an auction sale, justify Boswell's opinion. He also thought that the *Idler* was the work of the same mind which produced the *Rambler*; and except that the *Idler* papers tend to be a little shorter, several (such as No. 23, on the uncertainty of friendship, No. 27, on conquering evil habits, and No. 89, on physical evil the cause of moral good) might have been written for the earlier periodical. But though clouds gather here and there, the sky is appreciably lighter, and we should no longer expect the imaginary correspondent of *Rambler* No. 109 to remark, 'whatever be your subject, melancholy for the most part bursts in upon your speculation'.

Rasselas is appropriately mentioned in this section, not merely because it followed the *Idler* so rapidly—the last *Idler* appeared on 5 April 1759, and *Rasselas*, which had been written in the previous January, was published on 19 April—but because in form and content it is so closely related to the two periodicals. Hawkins reports it as a fact that, finding the eastern tales of the *Rambler* and the *Adventurer* so well received, Johnson had for some time been meditating an eastern tale of greater length as a vehicle for his views on human life, and that the necessity of finding money to pay for his mother's funeral urged him to compose the tale. There is nothing inherently improbable in this. He may, though we cannot be certain, have read the Persian Tales that Ambrose Philips 'turned' for half-a-crown a time, he may even have read Voltaire's *Zadig* (though he cannot yet have had an opportunity of reading *Candide* which so closely resembles *Rasselas*); but since those early days when he had translated Father Lobo's *Voyage to Abyssinia*, he had, like so many of his fellow countrymen, suffered his imagination to dwell upon the near east, a vast tract of country which differed from the west as a setting for a story only in that riches could be more opulently displayed, power more imperially exercised, and sages and hermits more frequently discovered and patiently attended to. In each eastern tale told by the *Rambler* there is a man—in every instance but one, a young man—with power at his command, who sets out to provide himself with happiness, and learns by experience how happiness cannot be procured; in three of the tales a 'genius', a sage, or a hermit points the moral, while in the remainder the protagonist can discover the moral for himself. In each moral there is a vanity to be learned, of insatiable desires (No. 38), of solacing our disquiet with sensual gratification (No. 65), of 'idle hopes' and 'fallacious appearances' (No. 120); Abouzaid in No. 190 confesses that he has 'now learned the vanity of those labours that wish to be rewarded by human benevolence', and Seged at the end of No. 205 bequeathed his narrative to 'future generations, 'that no man hereafter may presume to say, 'This day shall be a day of happiness'' '.

It will be seen that the conduct of the story of *Rasselas* had already been practised by Johnson in the eastern tales told by the *Rambler*, and that the characters of the prince himself and Imlac lay there ready to hand. Much more illustrative detail was needed for the expansion; but this could be provided without much difficulty by a writer who had accustomed himself in numerous essays to inventing such autobiographical narratives as Imlac and the hermit relate to point his morals. For the discussion of marriage and the single life he returned to a form which he had practised in the Parliamentary Debates; but the other great passages of exposition and reflection do not call upon essentially different powers from those exercised in the *Rambler*. Several of the topics of *Rasselas* had already been discussed there, the 'glimpse of pastoral life' in Chapter XIX, for example; the essence of Imlac's dissertation upon poetry in Chapter X could have appeared as a periodical essay, though it must be admitted that its existing context permits a delicate note of irony that the *Rambler*'s critical dissertations do not contain; and Imlac's remarks on the astronomer's disordered imagination could have been taken from the *Rambler* without much change. The difference here, if difference there is, is that which distinguishes *Rasselas* as a whole from the *Rambler* as a whole; it is not so much a difference of theme or of formal elements as of intensity and compendiousness. Already in his second paper the *Rambler* was cautioning his readers against 'suffering the imagination to riot'. The powerful image is used again in No. 89 ('this invisible riot of the mind, this secret prodigality of being'), and others no less powerful appear elsewhere ('the foam of a boiling imagination', No. 66). It was appropriate for a writer whose purpose was the moral discipline of the mind to issue these warnings. But what if riot takes entire control? This is what Johnson has faced in *Rasselas*. 'Of the uncertainties of our present state', says Imlac, 'the most dreadful and alarming is the uncertain continuance of human reason.' It was a dread that Imlac shared with his creator, who was also afflicted with 'the dangerous prevalence of imagination'; and while he faces the possibility and describes the symptoms, Johnson follows the custom that had guided him in the *Rambler* of prescribing medicaments. But the prescription here has a peculiarly telling effect. When Imlac advises the astronomer not only to 'fly to business and to Pekuah' but also to remember that he was 'only one atom in the mass of humanity', the sweep of the narrative is broadened immensely. A fresh perspective opens on the succession of disenchantments that has battered at the resilience implicit in the quest for a 'choice of life'. Part of the enduring appeal of *Rasselas* is that the resilience, though battered, persists throughout, right up to the deliberately enigmatic 'conclusion in which nothing is concluded'. The gloom of the discourse of the old man in Chapter XLV— so transparently autobiographical—is corrected by its position in the narrative, near the end, but not at the end. The effect, exceedingly austere, is far from despairing.

The travel book was a form with sufficiently marked characteristics to allow of such different parodies as *Gulliver's Travels* and *A Sentimental Journey*, though its rules could be expressed only in the most general terms. Johnson had often complained of finding himself disappointed by books of travel. 'Those whose lot it is to ramble can seldom write,' he once told Mrs. Thrale, 'and those who know how to write very seldom ramble.' The first qualification was a well-stored mind; 'books of travel', he told Boswell, 'will be good in proportion to what a man has previously in his mind; his knowing what to observe; his power of contrasting one mode of life with another . . . A man must carry knowledge with him, if he would bring home knowledge.' But being able to write meant a prior exercise in discrimination, so as to avoid on the one hand 'such general accounts as leave no distinct ideas behind them', and on the other 'such minute enumerations as few can read with either profit or delight' (*Idler*, No. 97). The great object of remark is human life; but the traveller, like other writers of the time, would deserve praise by his manipulation of detail in the service of some broader truth, by his intelligent relation of the particular to the general.

Johnson's solitary performance in this kind is *A Journey to the Western Islands of Scotland* (1775). This famous tour, in which he was accompanied by Boswell, lasted from 14 August 1773, when he arrived in Edinburgh, until 22 November, when he left for England. His wish to visit the Hebrides had been formed many years before, but it was not until he reached Glenshiel on the nineteenth day of his journey that the thought occurred to him of writing his narrative. The form adopted by contemporaries for their published travels seems to have depended upon the form their materials had taken. Thus Sharp and Brydone claimed to have prepared for the printer letters that were not originally intended for the public eye (*Letters from Italy*, 1766; *A Tour through Sicily and Malta*, 1773), whereas Pennant seems to have relied upon his journal. Johnson favoured neither of these popular forms. He had read the journal Boswell kept, but he seems not to have had it by him to assist his memory. Mrs. Thrale had kept the long letters he wrote her; but though he frequently turned to them, he did not base his narrative upon them. He also kept what he calls 'a book of remarks', that has not been found. Perhaps it was this book which conditioned the form of his narrative; but even without its evidence, we can see that neither a daily and factual record nor a less regular account of fleeting impressions would have suited his purpose. 'I suspect some mistakes,' he wrote to Boswell, after sending his manuscript to the printer, 'but as I deal, perhaps, more in notions than facts, the matter is not great.' It was 'notions' he had sought to arrange and clarify.

Although nearly half his time was spent upon the mainland, his title rightly emphasizes the objective of his journey. 'I have now the pleasure of going where nobody goes, and of seeing what nobody sees', he had written to Mrs. Thrale, shortly after landing in Skye. It was a pardonable exaggeration. Bishop Pococke had been to Iona and Mull in 1760, but his account of his tour was not published until 1887; and in the year before Johnson's visit, Pennant[1] on his second trip to Scotland had been to Skye as well, where he had met several people Johnson was to meet, and (in spite of being an undeserving Whig) had even preceded Johnson in the Young Pretender's bed at Flora Macdonald's house. Though he had looked across the sound at Raasay and had sailed close to Coll, he had not landed, thus leaving to Johnson the distinction of being the first traveller from the south to publish an account of those islands.[2]

The country was still, as Pennant said in his *Literary Life* (1793), 'as little known to its southern brethren as *Kamtschatka*'. At Inverness the travellers were about 'to enter a country upon which perhaps no wheel has ever rolled', and Mrs. Thrale was reminded in a letter that there were not 'to be any more towns or Inns'. Furthermore they were visiting the islands in a particularly wet and stormy autumn, when they were frequently at the mercy of winds and were more than once in some danger. The fortitude shown by an elderly man of letters, whose proper environment was the clubs of London, appeals to every imagination; but this was to be Boswell's theme, not Johnson's. These

---

[1] Thomas Pennant, 1726–98, was educated at Queen's College, Oxford, and travelled widely in Europe and in the British Isles. He was a zoologist of distinction.

[2] When Pennant came to publish his *Tour* two years later, the fame of Johnson's visit was sufficiently widespread (though the *Journey* was not yet in print) to permit a reference to it: 'Coll was celebrated', said Pennant, 'for being the place where Doctor *Samuel Johnson* had long and woeful experience of oats being the food of men in *Scotland*, as they are of horses in *England*.' The witticism had no basis in fact, and Pennant was therefore rebuked in the *Journey* for his 'fit of simple credulity'.

details of the journey were no more than the setting for his inquiry; 'our business', he wrote, 'was with life and manners'. The life and manners he saw were very different from those he was accustomed to, but there is evidence that they did not differ so much as he had expected. 'To find simplicity and wildness, and all the circumstances of remote time or place, so near to our native great island, was an object within the reach of reasonable curiosity'; that is how Boswell expresses their intention. He does not say that they were disappointed, but Johnson has to admit before even reaching Raasay that they came 'too late to see what we expected, a people of peculiar appearance, and a system of antiquated life'. Thereafter he inquires 'after the reliques of former manners', as in Ulva, and regrets that they had had no opportunity of visiting the Roman Catholic islands of Eigg and Canna, for 'we . . . who came to hear old traditions, and see antiquated manners, should probably have found them amongst the Papists'.

They had come too late by thirty years, since the subjection of the clans after the rebellion of 1745 had made rapid changes in the economy of the islands, which were then suffering from an epidemic of emigration. Johnson responded to the circumstances he found: the use of travelling, he told Mrs. Thrale, 'is to regulate imagination by reality, and instead of thinking how things may be, to see them as they are'; but enough remains of what he expected to see. In that same letter to Mrs. Thrale (15–21 September 1773), he tells her 'you are perhaps imagining that I am withdrawn from the gay and the busy world into regions of peace and pastoral felicity, and am enjoying the reliques of the golden age'; what he was really doing, he goes on to say, was very different. He was making once more the contrast so often made in the *Rambler* and *Rasselas* between things as they are and things as we fondly imagine them to be. A phrase in another letter to Mrs. Thrale (30 September 1773) suggests that he had gone hoping to instruct himself 'in the whole system of pastoral life', and that recent changes had partially defeated him. But enough remained, certainly enough to expose false notions of a golden age: 'in pastoral countries the conditions of the lowest rank of people is sufficiently wretched'. Already in the Great Glen he had entered a typical Highland hut and allowed his description of its incommodiousness to stand for itself with only the bare comment, 'such is the general structure of the houses in which one of the nations of this opulent and powerful island has been hitherto content to live'. The diet of the family is as barely described, but it is noted that 'with the true pastoral hospitality' their hostess asked them to sit down and drink whisky. The same tale is told in the islands, of meagre subsistence, of agriculture 'laborious, and perhaps rather feeble than unskilful', where 'the climate is unkind, and the ground penurious', and of vulgar superstitions:

The traveller who comes hither from more opulent countries, to speculate upon the remains of pastoral life, will not much wonder that a common Highlander has no strong adherence to his native soil; for of animal enjoyments, or of physical good, he leaves nothing that he may not find again wheresoever he may be thrown.

This was the condition of the lowest orders, and Johnson is at pains to inquire why their life was no better; the climate, the relation of landlord and tenant, the rigour of puritanism, the want of money as a medium of exchange, the effect of the subjection of the clans, all are passed in review. But pastoral society includes the higher orders as well as the lower. Here too there had been change. The lairds had lost their military importance and Johnson feared that, 'divested of their prerogatives, [they] necessarily turned their thoughts to the improvement of their revenues, and expect more rent, as they have less homage'. He was faced with a difficult task in trying to strike a balance between losses and gains from the results of 1745; he could not be expected to do more while the changes were not yet complete. But here and there he recognized some relics of the golden age, notably on Raasay where the travellers found nothing but civility, elegance, and plenty, an oasis of pastoral charm the more delightful for the contrariety of images it evoked:

Without is the rough ocean and the rocky land, the beating billows and the howling storm: within is plenty and elegance, beauty and gaiety, the song and the dance. In Raasay, if I could have found an Ulysses, I had fancied a Phæacia.

The modern visitor from the south, when he is not attracted by the opportunities of sport, has an eye for the beauties of the scene. Johnson was not entirely oblivious of these beauties. He responded to the sublime, even though moorland repelled him; he liked to step aside to visit a waterfall or such curious rock formations as the Buller of Buchan and the basalt pillars on the Ross of Mull, and was sorry not to have been treated to a storm when he looked across the ocean from Slanes Castle, on the north-east coast. But he did not belong to the school of picturesque travellers, and in so far as we now demand of all travellers a proper deference to picturesque beauties, Johnson must disappoint. For some readers a single letter from Gray to Wharton, that of 30 September 1765 in which he describes with exactness of detail his wanderings amongst the beauties of Perthshire, will be thought to show more proper respect than the whole of Johnson's *Journey*. But this is to allow a romantic prejudice to blind us to Johnson's success not only in presenting a civilization in process of change and in defining standards for evaluating that change, but in organizing the detail that he thought significant. It is rarely picturesque, or scientific, or antiquarian. For such detail he is apt to show some impatience: he brought away some 'rude measures' of the sacred buildings on Iona, but he did not trust them and refers his reader to Pennant instead; and as for geological detail, 'there are so many more important things, of which human knowledge can give no account, that it may be forgiven us, if we speculate no longer on two stones in Col'. But detail of human significance was another matter. The use of the quern and the crooked spade, the manufacture of brogues, how windows are made and how they are opened, these are topics that excite all his attention. The manner of opening windows happily leads him to return to the important question raised in *Idler* No. 97 about the subordination of the particular to the general. He fears that some readers may think his observations on Highland windows too diminutive. But they should remember that 'life consists not of a series of illustrious actions, or elegant enjoyments; the greater part of our time passes in compliance with necessities, in the performance of daily duties, in the removal of small inconveniences, in the procurement of petty pleasures; and we are well or ill at ease, as the mainstream of life glides on smoothly, or is ruffled by small obstacles and frequent interruption'. The inference is that such details as he chooses to record will help us to estimate in what conditions life is lived in the Highlands. But the argument is taken one step further to claim that we estimate the true state of a nation not when we pay attention to the life of the rich but to the life of people in the streets and villages, in the shops and farms.

As they approach to delicacy, a nation is refined; as their conveniences are multiplied, a nation, at least a commercial nation, must be denominated wealthy.

There is some defect in the argument, since for all we are told to the contrary the windows of cottages and palaces opened in the same way. But apart from that, the passage is important in two respects: it clearly announces one of the standards by which Johnson encourages his readers to judge Highland life, a standard whose importance was increasingly recognized in the eighteenth century, and it defines the relationship between the particular and the general that informs Johnson's thinking on biography, which is the subject of the following section.

Johnson's biographical writings cover a period of over forty years. The earliest is his life of Father Paul Sarpi published in the *Gentleman's Magazine* for November 1738, his latest *The Lives of the Poets*, publication of which was not completed until 1781. Between these dates lie nine more lives appearing in the *Gentleman's* (Boerhaave, 1739; Admiral Blake, 1740; Drake, 1740–1; Barretier, 1741; Burman, 1742; Sydenham, 1742; Roscommon, 1748; Cave, 1754; Cheynell, 1775; one (Frederick the Great, 1756–7) written for the *Literary Magazine*; some short lives contributed to Dr. Robert James's *Medicinal Dictionary* (1743–5); some prefatory biographies (to editions of Browne's *Christian Morals*, 1756, *The English Works of Roger Ascham*, 1761, and Zachary Pearce's commentary on the Four Evangelists, 1777); a brief account of Collins contributed to Fawkes's *Poetical Calendar* (1763), and a separately published life of Savage (1744), the last two being reprinted in *The Lives of the Poets*.

It is not surprising that a learned man, much of whose livelihood depended upon executing commissions for the booksellers, should have written so many biographies at a time when the public appetite for biography was insatiable. But this was also Johnson's favourite pursuit. Even if we did not have Boswell's word for it, we might have guessed as much from the way in which his mind so easily turned, when engaged on the *Rambler* and the *Idler*, to episodes in imaginary biographies and autobiographies. The imaginary autobiographies occur in those periodicals more frequently than biographical episodes. Of course the convention of the letter from the imaginary correspondent lent itself more easily to the autobiographical form. But this apparent preference also accorded with his critical opinions. 'Those relations are commonly of most value', he remarked in *Idler*, No. 84, 'in which the writer tells his own story', the reasons being that he who writes his own life is more likely to tell the truth and to reveal the man that lies behind the public figure.

Biographical truth is important because biographies teach men the art of living. The man who looks back upon his own life, as so many of the *Rambler*'s imaginary correspondents had done, could readily see what episodes were most instructive. Thus when the Revd. William Dodd had been convicted of forgery and lay under sentence of death, Johnson wrote to one whom he used as a go-between, telling him to urge upon Dodd the duty of autobiography:

If his remissions of anguish, and intervals of devotion leave him any time, he may perhaps spend it profitably in writing the history of his own depravation, and marking the gradual declination from innocence and quiet, to that state in which the law has found him. Of his advice to the Clergy or admonitions to Fathers of families there is no need; he will leave behind him those that can write them. But the history of his own mind, if not written by himself, cannot be written, and the instruction that might be derived from it must be lost. This therefore he must leave, if he leaves anything.

But whether a man relates the story of his own life or that of another, he must do it without fear or favour. The failings of his subject should not be concealed from a sense of piety, for 'if we owe regard to the memory of the dead, there is yet more respect to be paid to knowledge, to virtue, and to truth' (*Rambler*, No. 60). There may be some danger in mentioning that good men like Addison and Parnell drank too freely, for a man might be led to indulge in drinking from reading this. On the other hand, 'if nothing but the bright side of characters should be shewn, we should sit down in despondency, and think it utterly impossible to imitate them in *any thing*'. This is reported in 1782 on the authority of Malone, and would seem to be Johnson's final opinion.

The truth must also condescend to quite small detail, as discussion of the *Journey to the Western Islands* has already shown. Some discretion must be exercised in the choice of detail. It is no advantage to be told that Addison was distinguished from the rest of mankind by the irregularity of his pulse; but when Sallust reports of Catiline that 'his walk was now quick, and again slow', we are given a valuable indication of 'a mind revolving something with violent commotion'. The reason for this attention to detail is similar to that given in the *Journey*. 'It is by studying little things', he told Boswell, 'that we attain the great art of having as little misery and as much happiness as possible.' The same point is made in a letter written to Langton on the death of the elder Langton:

> We must now endeavour to preserve what is left us, his example of Piety, and economy. I hope you make what enquiries you can, and write down what is told you. The little things which distinguish domestick characters are soon forgotten, if you delay to enquire you will have no information, if you neglect to write, information will be vain.

> His art of life certainly deserves to be known and studied. He lived in plenty and elegance upon an income which to many would appear indigent and to most, scanty. How he lived therefore every man has an interest in knowing.

These were good enough reasons for a life (never to be written) of the elder Langton, even though he was not to be found in the walks of fame. Johnson's preference is often expressed for lives that lay outside those walks, and the preference is ultimately moral: 'few are engaged in such scenes as give them opportunities of growing wiser by the downfal of statesmen or the defeat of generals'; on the contrary, 'the mischievous consequences of vice and folly . . . are best discovered by those relations which are levelled with the general surface of life'. These are the main features of Johnson's theory of biography; but the theory was not altogether maintained in practice.

His preference for autobiography was indulged not only in the fictions of the *Rambler* and the *Idler* but in authentic form. How much he wrote it is no longer possible to say. In the last week of his life he burnt many papers, amongst which in

Boswell's opinion there were 'two quarto volumes, containing a full, fair, and most particular account of his own life'. A few other records have survived: the 'Annales', in which he briefly recorded in Latin at the age of twenty-five the most important events of his life; an *Account* in English written sometime subsequent to 1765, and preserved from burning by Johnson's servant, Francis Barber; and various fragments of diaries, amongst which must be grouped the *Prayers and Meditations* published shortly after Johnson's death by the Revd. George Strachan. Though it is unsafe to argue the character of what is lost from what survives, it seems unlikely that we have lost a regular composition, a work of art to compare with Gibbon's autobiography. The *Prayers and Meditations* bear distressing testimony to the neurotic illness that afflicted him for many years, and show as well his attention to the significance of small detail; thus on Good Friday, 1775 he records:

> Boswel and I went to Church, but came very late. We then took tea, by Boswels desire, and I eat one bun, I think, that I might not seem to fast ostentatiously.

In the *Annals*, too, details both significant and insignificant jostle together: 'these little memorials sooth my mind', he wrote. There is evidence of ample power in self-analysis—that was the function of a journal, in his opinion—but there is no attempt made at artistic organization.

Though in theory he was prepared to argue a preference for lives spent in an even tenor, three of his biographies, and those not the least valuable, are lives of men of action—he also projected lives of Alfred the Great and Cromwell—and all his sixty-three subjects were men of some distinction; there was not an elder Langton amongst them. Many too had lived at such a distance of time as to deny him the use of illustrative detail. Furthermore he was often restricted to working in miniature without opportunity for ample development of his theories. None of his lives is a full-scale performance, and the majority provide little or no more scope than a newspaper obituary or 'profile' of today. His scale at most is that of *Eminent Victorians*, never that of *Queen Victoria*.

To some extent, both scope and choice lay outside his control. He was the servant of the booksellers, and they supplied a public that liked to read biography in handfuls. It was an age of encyclopedic collections, not only great enterprises like Birch's *General Dictionary* in ten massive folios (1734-41) and the *Biographica Britannica* in seven, but collections more modest in scope and character such as Cibber's *Lives of the Poets* (1753), and Horace Walpole's *Catalogue of the Royal and Noble Authors of England* (1758). Johnson in the pages of the *Gentleman's Magazine* was catering for the same taste. It seems probable that the war with Spain suggested to his editor the suitability of short lives of Admiral Blake and Sir Francis Drake, although it was doubtless the leanings of his own mind that prompted accounts of the lives of learned men, and particularly of physicians. The poets whose lives he wrote were mostly chosen for him. It was the booksellers who wished to protect their copyright, and saw that a new edition of the poets from Chaucer to the present day would be greatly recommended by prefaces from Johnson's hand; and it was they who subsequently contracted their designs by beginning with Cowley instead of Chaucer, and who appear to have been forced by copyright trouble to exclude Goldsmith, and perhaps Churchill too. Thus the choice of lives was the booksellers', except that they agreed to Johnson's recommendation of four or five that lay within their design, namely Blackmore, Watts, Pomfret, Yalden, and apparently Thomson as well. And the scope was theirs, for Johnson was engaged, he told Boswell, 'to write little lives, and little Prefaces, to a little edition of the English Poets'. That is what they remain. Though they were not at first to be bought separately—the purchaser of the first four volumes of *Lives* in 1779 had to buy fifty-six volumes of *Poets* as well—ultimately (in 1781) they were to appear in four volumes, and in this form they took their place as the most famous of eighteenth-century biographical collections.

Johnson's character as a biographer was determined in the days of the *Gentleman's Magazine*. His custom, inherited from seventeenth-century practice, was to append to his narrative a short character-sketch, and if his subject was an author, to add a bibliography of his writings. The exceptions are the lives of Drake and Cheynell, which are almost purely narrative, and the life of Ascham, for which no bibliography was needed because it prefaced a collection of Ascham's writings. The lives of Sydenham and Savage are also exceptional. In the first Johnson was dealing with a career encrusted with dubious anecdote, and was led by his natural scepticism to what is largely an extended critical examination of the evidence. In the *Savage*, which was partly commemorative and partly moral, the writings were not isolated for separate treatment; it was his province, he thought, 'rather to give the history of Mr Savage's performances, than to display their beauties'.

This form, established in his early lives, is repeated in *The Lives of the Poets*. In that work too there are exceptions to his rule, for of some of his subjects so little was known as to preclude any estimate of character. But most of the *Lives* observe the pattern of the early lives of Boerhaave and Burman. To the narrative is appended a character, which proceeds in the larger lives from a description of personal appearances and domestic habits to an examination of the mind. Lastly the bibliography of the early lives is expanded, not into a critical dissertation, but into a series of remarks upon the principal poems rehearsed in chronological order.

The tidiness of the form has its convenience for a work of reference; the reader of the *Poets* could readily find his way to Johnson's estimate of an individual poem, or his account of an important episode, or his appreciation of a poet's character. But there were several disadvantages. The form encouraged repetition and discouraged the formulation for each major poet of such a general critical estimate as Johnson had made of Shakespeare, and it necessarily separated the character from any important stage in the subject's career. It seems unlikely that Johnson, who frequently expressed his admiration for Izaak Walton's *Lives*, cannot have observed how effectively Walton leads his subject to some place of important activity— Wotton at Eton, Hooker at Bishopsbourne, Herbert at Bemerton—and there pauses to describe his appearance and draw his character; but artistry had to yield, we must suppose, to convenience of reference.

For his narratives Johnson could frequently rely on some previously printed biographies—Birch and Derrick for Dryden, Ruffhead for Pope, Mason for Gray—and his dependence upon them can be shown to extend to a phrase as well as to a fact. He had not much time for what we now call research, and he found it irksome, as he reveals in the *Life of Dryden*:

to adjust the minute events of literary history is tedious and troublesome; it requires indeed no great force of understanding, but often depends upon enquiries which there is no opportunity of making, or is to be fetched from books and pamphlets not always at hand. But it would be a grave mistake to suppose that he was content with a secondary source, even though he had to struggle with a sluggish temperament and the printer was pressing him for fresh copy. 'If it rained knowledge I'd hold out my hand; but I would not give myself the trouble to go in quest of it': this was spoken in a moment of exasperation with Boswell, who had been over-officious in securing him an introduction to Pope's friend, Lord Marchmont; but the sequel shows that he called upon Marchmont, and the *Life of Pope* is enriched by what Marchmont told him. Several other *Lives* show the effect of inquiries conducted at first or at second hand, of documents inspected, and of information recollected sometimes over a great many years. Thus he recalled his father (who died in 1731) mentioning the large sale of *Absalom and Achitophel* and describing Burnet and Sprat preaching before the House of Commons; a story of Addison as a schoolboy organizing an end-of-term 'rag' was 'told me when I was a boy by Andrew Corbet of Shropshire'; and the manuscript of Spence's *Anecdotes of Pope*, not published till 1820, was borrowed for him from the Duke of Newcastle, and was put to use in no fewer than eight *Lives*.

Nor did either haste or inertia prevent him from criticizing his sources. His inherent scepticism is evident as early as the life of Boerhaave, where he declines to tell stories of Boerhaave's egregious skill in diagnosis: 'I mention none of them, because I have no opportunity of collecting testimonies, or distinguishing between those accounts which are well proved, and those which owe their rise to fiction and credulity'; and in the life of Barretier, he is tempted to suppress part of a letter, 'being unwilling to demand the belief of others to that which appears incredible to myself'. This scepticism is put to use in weighing evidence. The life of Sydenham, as has already been mentioned, provides an extended example, and many other instances can be collected from *The Lives of the Poets*. Thus Davenant was said by Betterton to have saved Milton from prosecution at the Restoration in return for Milton's pleading for his life ten years earlier. We shall all agree that 'here is a reciprocation of generosity and gratitude so pleasing that the tale makes its own way to credit'. But have we any justification for believing it?

The danger of Davenant is certain from his own relation; but of his escape there is no account. Betterton's narration can be traced no higher; it is not known that he had it from Davenant. We are told that the benefit exchanged was life for life, but it seems not certain that Milton's life ever was in danger.

This is not simply to break a butterfly upon a wheel. The truth is more important than a pleasing or a wonderful story; and why he was sceptical is partly revealed in a sentence which concludes his correction of the story of Pope's Man of Ross:

Narrations of romantick and impracticable virtue will be read with wonder, but that which is unattainable is recommended in vain; that good may be endeavoured, it must be shewn to be possible.

It is at such moments as this that we discern Johnson's descent from the seventeenth-century tradition of moral biography, and begin to understand what he meant by hoping his lives were written 'in such a manner, as may tend to the promotion of Piety'.

This essentially moral view of biography is what prompts him to such frequent comments on the behaviour of his subjects.

Ever attentive to the more important aspects of mankind, and sensible that biography ought to be a lesson of virtue, Dr. Johnson never omits to intersperse, amongst the different parts of his narration, either maxims of prudence or reflexions on the conduct of human life.

So wrote the *Monthly Review* in 1779. It is here that the *Life of Savage* is so impressive, with its keen yet sympathetic treatment of this wasted life, and its firm presentation of the moral of mistaking the love for the practice of virtue. Unlike his predecessors in the seventeenth century, Johnson is not given to hagiography; there are times, indeed, when one is disposed to wonder whether he is not indulgent to an eighteenth-century taste for the lives of rogues and scoundrels. Certainly there is often an acidulous flavour in his reflections, as when he writes in the life of Frederick the Great that 'Princes have this remaining of humanity, that they think themselves obliged not to make war without a reason'; or on the exchange of compliments between Sir Thomas Browne and Sir Kenelm Digby, 'the reciprocal civility of authors is one of the most risible scenes in the farce of life'; and the recollections of his own early experience at Edial School evoke an echo in every teacher's breast as he dismisses the stories of Milton's success as a schoolmaster:

Every man that has ever undertaken to instruct others can tell what slow advances he has been able to make, and how much patience it requires to recall vagrant inattention, to stimulate sluggish indifference, and to rectify absurd misapprehension.

Something has already been said of the value Johnson attached to 'those minute peculiarities which discriminate every man from all others'. His choice did not satisfy all his readers. 'Can it be of any importance to us to be told how many pair of stockings the author of the Essay on Man wore?' exclaims one exasperated critic; and it has to be admitted that a tale is sometimes told purely for the love of anecdote. We learn no more of Rowe from the story of his discomfiture at the hands of the Earl of Oxford.[1] But the Lives are full of strokes both vivid and illuminating: Collins saved from the bailiffs by an advance of money from a publisher—'he shewed me the guineas safe in his hand'; Addison, at the first performance of Cato, wandering 'through the whole exhibition behind the scenes with restless and unappeasable solicitude'; Pope reading one of Cibber's attacks and remarking, 'his features writhen with anguish, These things are my diversions'; Thomson on his first visit to London with his letters of recommendation tied up in his handkerchief, but with his attention so much distracted by what he saw that 'his magazine of credentials was stolen from him'; Thomson, again, sitting in the upper gallery at the first night of his Agamemnon, accompanying the players 'by audible recitation, till a friendly hint frighted him to silence': all these, and many more, are recorded for the first time in The Lives of the Poets. The life of Thomson, indeed, is one of the minor successes of that empirical approach that Johnson's own biographer was later to adopt: the details are assembled with an appearance of casualness yet they succeed in showing us the man.

---

[1] Rowe had applied to him for some public employment, and had been enjoined to learn Spanish. 'When, some time afterwards, he came again, and said that he had mastered it, Oxford dismissed him with this congratulation, "Then, Sir, I envy you the pleasure of reading Don Quixote in the original." '

But it is for the critical essays that most readers today value *The Lives of the Poets*. In this section too it must not be forgotten that Johnson was originally engaged to write 'little Prefaces, to a little edition'. Though quite early in his work he admits to being drawn to a greater length than he intended, yet his scope remained too small to permit formal treatises. Very occasionally he took an opportunity of discussing a poetical kind or a school of writers; thus Waller's 'Sacred Poems' permitted him to explain in seven paragraphs why devotional poetry cannot often please, and the life of Cowley provided an appropriate occasion for his acute analysis of metaphysical wit. A poem of the outstanding importance of *Paradise Lost* demanded methodical treatment, and received what the *Monthly Review* called a 'truly excellent analysis and criticism . . . executed with all the skill and penetration of Aristotle, and animated and embellished with all the fire of Longinus'. It is discussed under the traditional headings of fable, characters, sentiments, and language that Addison had already used for his examination of the poem in the *Spectator*; in fact Johnson had Addison's papers open in front of him as he wrote, just as in the life of Pope he kept an undeviating eye upon Warton's *Essay* to stimulate his argument. But such treatment of a poem is exceptional and serves to emphasize, by contrast, the almost casual nature of Johnson's work. He throws off hints and observations, but rarely stops to elaborate them: 'Milton, being well versed in the Italian poets, appears to have borrowed often from them', he remarks, and leaves it to twentieth-century scholarship to show how right he was.

Criticism conducted in accordance with the 'rules' of poetry he could write when occasion demanded. But he distrusted it.

The questions, whether the action of the poem be strictly *one*, whether the poem can be properly termed *heroick*, and who is the hero, are raised by such readers as draw their principles of judgement rather from books than from reason.

Such criticism is not empirical enough; it does not appeal to a reader's experience. He also recognized and could use that type of criticism which undertakes the historical development of a poetical kind. Once again, it has been left for modern scholars to elaborate the few remarks he offered in the life of

Pope on the origin and development of the poetical imitation. But he did not trouble to pursue this type of criticism, or rather the occasion did not warrant the pursuit. Nor did he think it appropriate to make a considered statement in the *Lives* about what he looked for in poetry, though his demands are implicit in all he says.

He looked to poetry, as all neoclassical critics did, to give him both profit and pleasure, and was at one with Dennis in thinking that, though the end of poetry is moral, poetry will not improve us unless it has first attended to the subordinate aim of giving pleasure. And so he complains that in Denham's *Cooper's Hill* 'the morality is too frequent', that in *Comus* (a poem he greatly admired) the moralizing of the Attendant Spirit is unacceptably presented—'the auditor therefore listens as to a lecture, without passion, without anxiety'—and that 'a long poem of mere sentiments easily becomes tedious'.

But what was it that pleased him? 'Smooth metre', certainly, as he confesses in the life of Pomfret. Irregular verse gave him no delight, for 'the great pleasure of verse', he declares in the life of Cowley, 'arises from the known measure of the lines and uniform structure of the stanzas'. This accounts in part for his displeasure with the verse of *Lycidas*, and perhaps with blank verse also; like the odes of Pope and Dryden, they wanted 'the essential constituent of metrical compositions, the stated recurrence of settled numbers'.

Nor did poetry entirely satisfy him unless it moved his passions. He regrets that Waller is 'never pathetick, and very rarely sublime', that Dryden 'with all his variety of excellence is not often pathetick', and he rejoices that though there is little opportunity for the pathetic in *Paradise Lost*, what little there is has not been lost.

But above all else the chief pleasure that poetry could give him was a display of imagination or 'invention'. When poetic pleasure is mentioned in *The Lives of the Poets*, the reader usually finds it associated with one of these qualities. The definitions of poetry attempted in the lives of Milton and Waller imply this association. 'Poetry', Johnson writes, in the first of those lives, 'is the art of uniting pleasure with truth, by calling imagination to the help of reason'; and in the second of them, 'the essence of poetry is invention; such invention as, by producing something unexpected, surprises and delights'. The distinction between 'invention' and 'imagination' is explained in the life of Pope, where we are told that invention is the faculty 'by which new trains of events are formed and new scenes of imagery displayed... and by which extrinsick and adventitious embellishments and illustrations are connected with a known subject', and that imagination is that 'which strongly impresses on the writer's mind and enables him to convey to the reader the various forms of nature, incidents of life, and energies of passion'.

For Johnson, therefore, the poet is a creator by virtue of his inventive and imaginative power, and the evidence of that creative ability is to be found in the poet's imagery. When he is pleased with a poet's work, his first words of commendation are usually given to the imagery. Thus Akenside's *Pleasures of Imagination* 'has undoubtedly a just claim to a very particular notice as an example of great felicity of genius and uncommon amplitude of acquisitions, of a young mind stored with images, and much exercised in combining them'. Of *Comus* he writes that 'a work more truly poetical is rarely found', and in amplification of the judgement he immediately remarks that 'allusions, images, and descriptive epithets embellish almost every period with lavish decoration'. And the first quality of Gray's *Elegy* to deserve his notice is that 'the *Churchyard* abounds with images which find a mirrour in every mind'.

It may seem surprising that criticism which can be represented as so eminently reasonable and acceptable, and which was widely applauded, should nevertheless have also roused so much controversy. Cowper was neither the first reader nor the last to feel like threshing Johnson's 'old jacket till I made his pension jingle in his pocket'. It was the lives of Milton, Swift, Gray, Hammond, and Lyttelton that caused most offence at the time, and the life of Cowley, which Johnson considered his best, has caused most people to stumble in our own day. The *Lives* were attacked partly for the denigration encountered in the biographical sections, and partly for the vigorous and even intemperate expressions of what were regarded as critical prejudices. To say of *Lycidas* that 'its form is that of a pastoral, easy, vulgar, and therefore disgusting', even though the last two epithets bore less harsh senses then than they do today, was to ask for trouble; and Johnson expected it. He knew that in censuring *Lycidas* and Gray's two Pindaric Odes he was opposing himself to the taste of the time, and as often happened in conversation, he expressed himself the more vigorously in anticipation of attack. But though he might be spoiling for a fight, he was not departing in any significant degree from the critical premises described above. The pastoral seemed to him to involve tediously repeated fiction, without reference to life as it is lived and without the opportunity of using fresh images; and as well as finding unsuitable language in Gray's Pindaric Odes, he is once more offended by unhappy fiction remote from a reader's experience. In criticizing the metaphysical poets, Johnson was not opposing himself to a regrettable aberration in contemporary taste; Cowley, as he mentioned to a friend, 'never had any critical examination before'. But as with *Lycidas* and the Pindaric Odes, his criticism was based on premises which are made familiar in the other *Lives*; truth and freshness of imagery in such metaphysical poetry as he chose for censure were not rooted in human passion and human experience.

Comparison between Johnson's criticism and Dryden's shows what changes had come about in the intervening years. Dryden's criticism is the criticism of an artist attempting to explain how his work was done. When he writes about Shakespeare or Jonson, Horace or Juvenal, he writes as a fellow craftsman examining the work of other men confronted with similar problems; and he addresses a limited society of noble patrons, men whom he assumes to be his equals in culture, whose judgements are already formed. After Dryden's time critics, assuming a much wider audience, addressed themselves to the formation of the judgement; and perhaps it was in consequence that they began to inquire into the causes of poetic pleasure.

We find these new inquiries in the critical work of Dennis and Addison. They attempted to give reasons for the pleasures they found in poetry and for the critical judgements they made. At their best they judge not by book but by an appeal to reason. Rules there are, but the authority for those rules is to be found not in Aristotle but from where Aristotle drew them, 'from the bottom of the most profound philosophy, and the deepest knowledge of the heart of man'. It is in this tradition that Johnson worked. He was a poet, and no doubt his experience as a poet assisted his criticism; but he did not write, like

Dryden, as an artist examining another artist's methods. He wished to form his readers' judgements, to qualify their minds to think justly about poetry, and his appeal is therefore to the hearts and minds of his readers and not to the authority of books.

III

POETRY, 1740–1760

THE most convenient way of examining the state of English poetry at the death of Pope is to turn over the pages of Dodsley's *Collection of Poems. By Several Hands*, first published in three volumes in 1748. The editor and publisher[1] was himself a poet and a man of taste. As a publisher he had won the confidence of Pope, and had sponsored the work of four new poets, Akenside, Gray, Johnson, and Shenstone. Through Pope he had come to know Lord Lyttelton and Spence, men who with Horace Walpole were prepared to solicit poems for him and to guide him in his selection. The moment was favourable for such a venture, especially since the last collection of poetry in several volumes—Tonson's revision of Dryden's *Miscellany*—had appeared some thirty years earlier. Tonson furthermore had printed many poems more than a hundred years old, whereas Dodsley had decided to take his with few exceptions from the present day, particularly those poems, as he explained in his preface, 'which seemed to merit a longer rememberance than what would probably be secured to them by the MANNER wherein they were originally published'. Thus the work of Dryden and his contemporaries as well as of most of the Augustans was excluded on principle. Tickell, Bramston, Matthew Green, and a few others from the recent past, were found a place because their poems had not yet appeared in collected editions; but for the most part Dodsley and his advisers drew upon the work of men and women still alive.

The three volumes were received with considerable approval, and Dodsley immediately set about revising and adding to them with the assistance of Shenstone. A second and revised edition appeared the same year, a fourth volume was added in 1755, and two more in 1758. 'To extend it further', he explained to a contributor, 'would make both the collection and the

---

[1] Robert Dodsley, 1703–64, was first a footman. He set up a bookseller's shop in 1735 and became one of the leading publishers of the age. He also enjoyed a mild success as poet and dramatist.

price too large'; but the six volumes were reissued six times in the later years of the century, and received the tribute of editorial notes from the hands of the antiquary Isaac Reed in the last edition of 1782. The work had achieved the status of a classic.

It was to be expected that Pope's publisher, assisted by two of Pope's closest friends and admirers, should print at least some poetry in the manner of Pope's last years. 'Jovi Eleutherio: Or, an offering to Liberty' sets out to show that the Supreme Being has provided us with as much liberty as can be safely enjoyed; it was the work of Gloster Ridley, a Winchester friend of Spence. Another Winchester poet, Edward Rolle, is represented by a 'moral essay' on the Duty of Employing One's Self, and by a Horatian epistle, whose opening lines testify to the limits of his skill in mimicking Pope's *Epilogue to the Satires*, a poem barely ten years old:

> What, sir,—a month and not one line afford?
> 'Tis well:—how finely some folks keep their word!
> I own my promise.—But to steal an hour,
> 'Midst all this hurry—'tis not in my pow'r.

These poems, and such others as 'The Danger of Writing Verse' by William Whitehead, a future Poet Laureate, and 'An Essay on Conversation' by Benjamin Stillingfleet, friend of that remarkable circle of cultivated ladies known as 'the Blue Stockings',[1] are addressed to men and women interested in fostering the morals and graces that sweeten social relationships: precisely the audience, in fact, to which the *Rambler* was soon to appeal. The standards of behaviour invoked are beyond reproach, but it was beginning to be felt that these were unadventurous paths for a poet to explore.

In what other directions could he move? He could take Spenser or Milton as his model, or he could succeed in rivalling the ancients, where so many had patently failed, by writing lyric poetry, not simply songs and ballads, but the greater or the lesser ode.

The admiration that Spenser excited in eighteenth-century readers shows how ready they were to enjoy poetry which made

---

[1] See entries in the bibliography for Elizabeth Carter, Hester Mulso Chapone, and Elizabeth Montagu.

substantial demands upon the understanding and upon neo-classical standards of taste. Spenser's diction is far removed from the language of the age, and his stanza encourages diffuse-ness of expression as much as Pope's couplet encourages conciseness; but these could be excused in a poet of such 'warm and boundless Fancy', whose 'Embellishments of Description are rich and lavish . . . beyond Comparison'. This was the view taken by John Hughes, a minor poet, who produced the first modern edition of Spenser (6 volumes, 1715); and no doubt Pope would have agreed, for he commended the remark of an old lady, who told him that in reading Spenser to her he had been showing her a gallery of pictures. Not all Spenser's pic-tures are gorgeous; several are homely, even trite, and others are gross and horrible, calculated to excite a sense of loathing and contempt. These were the pictures which seem to have caught the attention of two precocious boys, Pope and Aken-side. 'The Alley' and 'The Virtuoso', written while each was still in his teens, show how fascinated these two young poets were by what must have seemed to them the naïvety of Spen-ser's syntax and diction and the childlike innocence of his manner of description. 'The Alley', which was first published in 1727, may have affected Akenside: it certainly affected Shen-stone,[1] who confessed when he bought Spenser first, he

read a page or two of the Fairy Queen, and cared not to proceed. After that, Pope's Alley made me consider him ludicrously [i.e. sportively]; and in that light, I think, one may read him with pleasure. I am now . . . from trifling and laughing at him, really in love with him. I think even the metre pretty (though I shall never use it in earnest); and that the last Alexandrine has an extreme majesty.

At the time of writing that letter (June 1742) Shenstone had recently completed a revision of *The Schoolmistress*, a poem which had originally appeared in 1737 and was to be revised once more in 1748. In this idyll of a village dame-school Shen-stone said that he was paying particular regard to Spenser's *Language*, his *Simplicity*, his manner of *Description*, and a pecu-liar *Tenderness* of *Sentiment*, remarkable throughout his *Works*.

[1] William Shenstone, 1714-63, was a contemporary of Johnson at Pembroke College, Oxford. In 1724 he inherited the estate of The Leasowes, Halesowen, near Birmingham, which he spent the remainder of his life in cultivating and adorning. He was regarded as a leading exponent of landscape gardening and as arbiter of taste in his generation.

The tenderness of sentiment was well suited to the spirit of the age. Here for the first time we find that affectionate yet condescending treatment of village life which was to receive more notable expression in Goldsmith's *Deserted Village* (1770) and George Morland's genre paintings at the end of the century. Shenstone dwells with loving particularity upon the dame's cap, 'far whiter than the driven snow, Emblem right meet of decency . . .', her apron 'dy'd in grain, as blue, I trowe, As is the hare-bell that adorns the field', her russet stole and kirtle, and her elbow chair. With Spenser as authority he could devote a whole stanza to

> One ancient hen she took delight to feed,
> The plodding pattern of the busy dame;
> Which, ever and anon, impell'd by need,
> Into her school, begirt with chickens, came;
> Such favour did her past deportment claim:
> And if neglect had lavish'd on the ground
> Fragment of bread, she would collect the same;
> For well she knew, and quaintly could expound,
> What sin it were to waste the smallest crumb she found.

His letters show how anxious he was to avoid misunderstanding, and he must therefore explain and defend so unusual a venture. In a letter to Lady Luxborough of 1 June 1748 he points out that his poem is

somewhat more grave than Pope's Alley, and a good deal less than Mr. Thomson's Castle etc. At least I meant it so, or rather I meant to skreen the ridicule which might fall on so *low* a subject (tho' perhaps a *picturesque* one) by *pretending* to *simper* all the time I was writing.

Certainly *The Castle of Indolence* (1748) is more grave than *The Schoolmistress*; yet Thomson, like Shenstone, felt the need of apology, and made his defence on the grounds that an imitation of Spenser must employ 'obsolete words, and a simplicity of diction in some of the lines which borders on the ludicrous'. In spite of this emphasis upon the 'ludicrous', that is not the main impression the reader is left with. He will recognize the 'ludicrous' in stanza liv of Canto I describing the 'puzzling sons of party' who 'whispered close, now shrugging reared The important shoulder', but when at last they are 'pushed up to power . . . In comes another set, and kicketh

them downstairs', and he will find it again in the last stanza
of the poem; but h e will see too that Thomson is more concerned to imitate Spenser the allegorist. The first and better of
the two cantos is an eighteenth-century anticipation of 'The
Lotos-Eaters', and was evidently inspired by Spenser's description of the Bower of Bliss in *The Faerie Queene*, Book II. Thomson's Spenser is much closer than Shenstone's to the romantic
dreamer admired by nineteenth-century critics; witness his
fiends

> Who hurl the wretch as if to hell outright
> Down, down black gulfs where sullen waters sleep,
> Or hold him clambering all the fearful night
> On beetling cliffs, (I. xlvi)

or the wood

> Of blackening pines, ay waving to and fro [that]
> Sent forth a sleepy horror through the blood,
>   (I. v)

or the picture of the 'pleasing land of drowsyhed . . .

> Of dreams that wave before the half-shut eye;
> And of gay castles in the clouds that pass,
> For ever flushing round a summer sky. (I. vi)

Every reader recognizes how widely this poetry differs from
the characteristic note of *The Seasons*; it is, in general terms,
a difference between the sublime and the voluptuous. It shows
what the imitation of Spenser might help to release in a poet.

None of the Spenserian poems hitherto mentioned is a
narrative poem and none suggests the appeal of a medieval
setting; but readers of Dodsley's *Collection* would have found
several poems that pretended to imitate Spenser in just those
ways, notably Gilbert West's 'On the Abuse of Travelling',
and his 'Education: a poem in Two Cantos, Written in
Imitation of the Style and Manner of Spenser's Fairy Queen'
(1751); Gloster Ridley's 'Psyche: Or, The Great Metamor-
phosis' (1747); and Moses Mendez's 'The Squire of Dames. A
Poem. In Spenser's Stile' (1751). When West[1] first published
his 'Abuse of Travelling' in 1739, he called it 'A Canto of the

---

[1] Gilbert West, 1703-56, was educated at Eton and Christ Church, Oxford. His
translations of Pindar and other poems were undertaken in the intervals of his
duties as a civil servant. He became clerk to the Privy Council and Paymaster of
Chelsea Hospital.

Fairy Queen, Written by Spenser, Never Before Published'. He may well have succeeded in deceiving the unsophisticated, for his characters are allegorical figures involved in appropriate adventures, whose appearance and setting are described in glowing colours. The same is true of Mendez; and though Ridley's theme is classical, he too indulges in rich and elaborate description. Each poet seems to have recognized that this species of imitation required or justified a leisurely voluptuousness of manner not associated with other contemporary verse forms; and it is clear that each was at pains to learn a verse rhythm differing in many respects from what was normally permitted in the closed couplet, and to enlarge the diction of poetry with words that had fallen out of use.

The subsequent history of the Spenserian poem may be traced conveniently at this point. The idyll still continued to be written—Fergusson's 'The Farmer's Ingle' (see p. 156) and Burns's 'The Cotter's Saturday Night' (see p. 162) owe something to *The Schoolmistress*—but it was the opportunities for narrative that made the stronger appeal, whether for a didactic poem on a modern topic, such as Mickle's *The Concubine* (1767; renamed *Syr Martin* in the fifth edition of 1777), or for a historical poem like Chatterton's spirited 'Battle of Hastynges' (written in 1768), or for Beattie's *Minstrel* (1771-4).

Beattie's poem[1] proved to possess a greater contemporary appeal than he had expected or than a modern reader can easily credit. Like Wordsworth in *The Prelude*, he set out to trace the growth of a poet's mind; and like Wordsworth, the mind he chose was his own. It is obvious that Beattie possessed neither psychological curiosity nor enough power of imaginative reconstruction for his task; but he recognized what variety of experience had made him the man he was, and he seems to have felt that to convey this variety the Spenserian stanza was well suited. Writing to Blacklock on 22 September 1766 about his recent occupations, he mentions 'a poem in the style and stanza of Spenser', begun not long ago. In it, he says,

I propose to give full scope to my inclination, and be either droll or pathetic, descriptive or sentimental, tender or satirical, as the

[1] James Beattie, 1735-1803, Professor of Moral Philosophy and Logic at Marischal College, Aberdeen, 1760. His *Essay on Truth*, 1770, in which he attempts to confute Hume, was rewarded by an honorary Doctorate of Civil Law from the University of Oxford, and a pension from the King.

humour strikes me; for, if I mistake not, the manner which I have
adopted admits equally of all these kinds of composition. I have
written one hundred and fifty lines, and am surprised to find the
structure of that complicated stanza so little troublesome. I was
always fond of it, for I think it the most harmonious that ever was
contrived. It admits of more variety of pauses than either the couplet
or the alternate rhyme; and it concludes with a pomp and majesty
of sound, which, to my ear, is wonderfully delightful.

So might several other poets have described their response to
the stanza, and so in fact did Byron, who follows the eighteenth-
century custom of explanation and apology in his preface
to the first and second cantos of *Childe Harold's Pilgrimage*. He
was aware of the tradition he had inherited, and Keats was,
too; Keats seems to have been rereading Beattie in December
1818, for in a letter written in that month he confesses that
though *The Minstrel* 'once delighted me—now I see through
[it]'. This was just before beginning work on *The Eve of St.
Agnes*, a poem which combines, while it surpasses, so many
features of eighteenth-century Spenserian poems—their medieval setting, their glowing colours, their diction redeemed from
the past or invented on half-understood analogies—while in
one detail of Porphyro's encounter with Angela we recognize
a momentary trace of Shenstone's 'simpering' style:

> Feebly she laugheth in the languid moon,
> While Porphyro upon her face doth look,
> Like puzzled urchin on an aged crone
> Who keepeth clos'd a wond'rous riddle-book,
> As spectacled she sits in chimney nook.

The history of the Spenserian poem provides one more example
to show that the Romantic poets were not cut off from their
predecessors.

The story of how Milton's blank verse was first burlesqued
and then adopted for nobler purposes has been told in the
previous volume. Blank verse was much used in this period too,
mainly by poets with a 'georgic' theme. But their inspiration
was less strictly Miltonic than Virgilian; Miltonic blank verse
seemed to lie convenient to their hands as the English measure
closest in its dignity to the Virgilian hexameter. Perhaps
because of its length or because of its ready accessibility, the

English georgic was completely neglected by Dodsley and his advisers, even though they published other work by the georgic poets. A discussion of this genre is therefore postponed until later in this chapter (pp. 86-9).

By comparison with *Paradise Lost*, Milton's minor poems were little studied during the early years of the century; but by the 1740s several writers had recognized the opportunities they seemed to offer of a wider range of poetical forms. Thus when Gilbert West decided to celebrate the Institution of the Garter, he turned to *Comus* for a model, introduced his Etherial Spirit to speak a prologue in octosyllabics (a measure also appropriated to his Druids), and modulated into blank verse at the entry of Edward III and his court. The sonnet had not been written for sixty years; but in the 1740s William Mason, Thomas Edwards, Benjamin Stillingfleet, and Thomas Warton began to use it for the purposes of brief meditation and address, and Gray used it to memorialize his friend West. (Its popularity at the end of the period is discussed in the next chapter, pp. 131-3.) Even the unrhymed stanza that Milton had used for his translation of Horace's 'Ode to Pyrrha' appealed to two young Winchester poets, Joseph Warton and William Collins, as a suitable form for odes on the subject of Evening, Shooting, and The Happy Life. *Lycidas*, too, began to attract attention. Out of several monodies written at this time, Dodsley chose two that made some attempt to copy Milton's elegy in development of theme, in transition, and in phrasing. These are Richard West's 'Monody on the Death of Queen Caroline' and William Mason's 'Musæus: A Monody to the Memory of Mr. Pope'. Both poets had their admirers, and it is still possible to discern in each, as Gray remarked to Walpole, 'the promise at least of something good to come'.

Of these attempts to escape from the charmed circle of Augustan verse forms—all of them represented in Dodsley's *Collection*—only one, the sonnet, was to become increasingly popular before the end of the century. Apart from the sonnet and blank verse, Milton's influence was exerted chiefly through 'L'Allegro' and 'Il Penseroso'. Numerous poems in octosyllabics show how much these works were admired, even in the early years of the century, before Handel had set them to music and added a chairman to their tuneful dispute, named 'Il Moderato'. In spite of this encouragement to recognize the two pieces as a diptych or as the twin sides of a coin, only two poets seem to have written octosyllabic poems in more than one part; Mason as an undergraduate (1744) contrasted 'Il Bellicoso' and 'Il Pacifico', and John Gilbert Cooper divided his 'Estimate of Life' between the reflections of 'Melpomene: or, the Melancholy', 'Calliope: or, the Chearful', and 'Terpsichore: or, the Moderate'. The mood of 'Il Penseroso' proved to be the more congenial. Pope's friend Parnell, who died in 1718, was the first poet to meditate at night, in octosyllabics, in the solitude of a country churchyard. Forty years later Shenstone, on looking into the fourth volume of Dodsley's *Collection*, exclaimed that 'Milton's *Il Penseroso* has drove half our Poets crazy', but he allowed that it had 'produced some admirable Odes to *Fancy*'. Solitude at dusk encouraged fanciful excursions, attempts to explore a world beyond the range of the senses. Thus the Revd. James Merrick, a friend of Joseph Warton, was encouraged to describe what he thought he had seen and heard, 'wild music wand'ring in the air', for example, and

> the Fairy band
> Dancing on the level land,
> Now with step alternate bound,
> Join'd in one continu'd round,
> Now their plighted hands unbind,
> And such tangled mazes wind
> As the quick eye can scarce pursue.

Merrick agreed with his friend Warton in calling his octosyllabics an ode. Neither of them seemed to have been deterred by Milton's not using the term for 'Il Penseroso', since there was no structural form which the lesser ode was required to obey. So much metrical variety was permitted, indeed, that one obscure poet named Barnett ventured to write the greater part of an ode in blank verse and defended himself by the analogy of recitative in music.

More important were considerations of manner and subject. The descriptive ode was found to offer an attractive escape from didactic poetry and essays on moral subjects. It was frequently regarded as a poem, not unlike 'Il Penseroso', in which some abstract quality was personified and endowed with suitable attributes of feature, dress, and habitation. Chearfulness and Sleep were invoked by Akenside; Superstition, Liberty, Fancy, Solitude, and Despair by Joseph Warton; Wisdom by

Elizabeth Carter; Solitude again by Grainger; Memory, Independency, and Melancholy by Mason; Wisdom and Despair once more by James Scott; and Virtue, Content, Ambition, Melancholy, Envy, Health, and Hope by the Revd. Richard Shepherd. A longer list could be made, but it would not add much variety of topic; the poets were attracted either to L'Allegro's pole or to Il Penseroso's, though most of them preferred to dwell in the Penseroso hemisphere. It was justly claimed by Joseph Warton,[1] in the advertisement to his *Odes on Various Subjects* (1746), that ode-writing gave opportunities to 'the chief Faculties of a Poet . . . Invention and Imagination'; and yet it is to be remarked how similar are the haunts of these abstractions. Wisdom's seat in Mrs. Carter's ode lies close to a 'time-shook tow'r' inhabited by the owl,

> Where, shelter'd from the blaze of day,
> In philosophic gloom he lay,
> Beneath his ivy bow'r.

A ruined tower is also the abode of Warton's Despair,

> Who, on that ivy-darken'd ground,
> Still takes at eve his silent round,

conditions equally well appropriated to Solitude and to Melancholy, as both Gray and Thomas Warton were able to show. Milton had given a lead in inventing suitable companions for the poet's favoured abstractions, as well as unsympathetic characters who must keep aloof: Grainger's Solitude is sought by

> Sage Reflection bent with years,
> Conscious Virtue void of fears,
> Muffled Silence, wood-nymph shy,
> Meditation's piercing eye,

and several others; while James Scott's Wisdom avoids

> Mirth that Thought and Care derides,
> And 'Laughter holding both his Sides';
> And jeering Wit, the time beguiling,
> And Ignorance for ever smiling.

---

[1] Joseph Warton, 1722–1800, the elder son of an Oxford Professor of Poetry, and brother of the first historian of English poetry, was educated at Winchester, of which he subsequently became headmaster (1766–93), and at Oxford. Poetry gave way to works of criticism and scholarship which won the respect of Samuel Johnson.

By 1760 the form had become so widespread as to invite parody
at the hands of Boswell's friend, Andrew Erskine, who published two clever odes in 1762, entitled *To Indolence and to
Impudence*, in which these unheroic figures are suitably poised in
appropriate scenery; and the following year William Cowper—
the initials appended to the essay suggest that the poet may
have been responsible—wrote a satiric 'Dissertation on the
Modern Ode' for the *St. James's Magazine* (April 1763),
recommending 'a description in at least fourteen lines, of the
person and dwelling of no matter whom, . . . with some observations upon her equipage and attendance, no matter what',
advising assiduous reading of Milton's minor poems with an
eye to their epithets, and reminding the tiro that 'oaks must
be bound in *Ivy-chains*, and a Tower will make a very insignificant appearance that is not *moss-grown* as well as *cloud-capt*'.

Though allegory became the favourite form of the descriptive ode, it was not the only form. The brothers Warton both
wrote odes evoking a typical mood or scene. Thus Joseph
Warton in his 'Ode to Evening' observes how

> To the deep wood the clamorous rooks repair
> Light skims the swallow o'er the wat'ry scene,
> And from the sheep-cotes, and fresh-furrow'd field,
> Stout ploughmen meet to wrestle on the green;

and Thomas,[1] confined to his college rooms for some disciplin-
ary offence on a summer morning in 1745, imagines how

> The pensive poet through the green-wood steals
>   Or treads the willow'd marge of murmuring brook;
>   Or climbs the steep ascent of airy hills;
>   There sits him down beneath a branching oak,
>   Whence various scenes, and prospects wide below,
> Still teach his musing mind with fancies high to glow.

This tradition should be borne in mind when reading Collins's *Odes on Several Descriptive and Allegoric Subjects* (1747).[2]

---

[1] Thomas Warton, 1728-90, educated like his elder brother at Winchester and
Oxford, spent most of his life as a don and became, like his father, Professor of
Poetry (1757-67) at Oxford. He was also Camden Professor of Ancient History
(1785-90) there. His scholarship is shown in his learned *History of English Poetry*
and his edition of Milton's minor poems; and in poetry he achieved sufficient
renown to be rewarded with the laureateship (1785).

[2] William Collins, 1721-59, was educated at Winchester and Oxford. He lived
in London for a few years as a literary adventurer (Dr. Johnson's phrase) before
succumbing to acute melancholia.

The range of his abstractions is wider than custom had led the reader to expect: Liberty and Evening he shared with his friend Joseph Warton (the two young men had once thought of publishing their odes in a joint volume); but Pity, Fear, Simplicity, Mercy, and Peace were less often chosen. Collins was not afflicted by the pedantry that led to the timid plagiarism of Milton which so displeased Cowper; he was a devoted disciple whose study of the master can be traced at every step, yet what he learned he made his own. Thus like his contemporaries he discovered in 'L'Allegro' and 'Il Penseroso' the opportunities for allegorical description; but the organization never follows Milton's pattern precisely, while the painting itself is always individual. The Madonna-like appearance of Pity is entirely appropriate:

> Long, *Pity*, let the Nations view
> Thy sky-worn Robes of tend'rest Blue,
> And Eyes of dewy Light!

Memories of Raphael or perhaps of Guido Reni may have inspired this figure; and it may have been to Guido in more theatrical mood that Collins turned for inspiration when describing Vengeance, who

> in the lurid Air,
> Lifts her red Arm, expos'd and bare.

Certainly he was already accustomed to modelling his figures on the designs of Raphael, as appears in his *Verses Humbly Address'd to Sir Thomas Hanmer. On his Edition of Shakespear's Works*, 1743.

Metrically, too, Collins shows a large measure of independence. While others were content with the 'L'Allegro' measure, he preferred to use it in association and for contrast with other lyric metres. The 'Nativity Ode' stanza served as a model for the 'Ode to Simplicity', but it was slightly adapted for the purpose. Only the unrhymed stanza of the 'Pyrrha' Ode, which had already been used by the elder Thomas Warton and his son, Joseph, was taken over unchanged. It was used for his 'Ode to Evening', a poem not altogether devoid of allegorical figures; yet apart from the posthumous 'Ode on the Popular Superstitions of the Highlands of Scotland', it is Collins's nearest approach to the purely descriptive ode. The unrhymed stanza helps to convey a deliberate lack of definition: where

Warton in depicting Evening had presented a succession of
distinct and generalized pictures, Collins seems to have aimed
at a Corot-like indistinctness:

> Or if chill blustring Winds, or driving Rain,
> Prevent my willing Feet, be mine the Hut,
>   That from the Mountain's Side
>   Views Wilds, and swelling Floods,
> And Hamlets brown, and dim-discover'd Spires,
> And hears their Simple Bell, and mark o'er all
>   Thy Dewy Fingers draw
>   The gradual dusky Veil.

In a much-quoted passage of his 'Life of Collins', Johnson
remarked that 'while he was intent upon description, he did
not sufficiently cultivate sentiment'. Not sufficiently, perhaps;
but it is his cultivation of sentiment that distinguishes him
from contemporary ode-writers. Though he was 'eminently
delighted', in Johnson's words, 'with those flights of imagination
which pass the bounds of nature', he seems to have entertained
them largely for the purpose of awakening the minds of others
to social and moral virtues by presenting them in unusual lights.
Of the twelve odes published in 1747, five are patriotic, one of
which, the longest and perhaps the most spirited of all, traces
the descent of Liberty at a time when liberty was in danger.
More characteristic of Collins's disposition, however, is the
tenderness which invokes Mercy for those involved in the 1745
Rebellion, which prays (though with less than his usual inventive power) for the return of Peace with Honour, and celebrates in two closely related odes those who have died for
their country and are mourned by a shadowy concourse of
beings whose appropriateness appeals to the imagination:

> By Fairy Hands their Knell is rung,
> By Forms unseen their Dirge is sung;
> There *Honour* comes, a Pilgrim grey,
> To bless the Turf that wraps their Clay,
> And *Freedom* shall a-while repair,
> To dwell a weeping Hermit there!

The odes placed at the beginning of the volume indicate
other ambitions. They are addressed to Pity and Fear, and
suggest that Collins was studying to be a tragic dramatist.

Certainly he aspired to be not only a poet of retirement and meditation but also a poet of society. In his *Verses . . . to Sir Thomas Hanmer* (1743) he had appeared as a young critic seeking his place in a world of men and books; that also is the character of 'The Manners, An Ode', probably written at about the same time, and forecasting the greater opportunities that London would present over Oxford for humorous observation of 'Life's wide Prospects'; and some fragments of verse discovered and published in 1956 reveal an unfinished sketch of our stage history, as well as an ambitious satirical dissertation on nature, art, and original composition. Furthermore the 'Ode to Simplicity', which follows the 'Ode to Fear', is to be read as in some sort a manifesto and as a dedication to pastoral poetry, presumably to chaster pastorals than the exotic *Persian Eclogues* (1742) already published; while the obscure 'Ode on the Poetical Character', which follows the 'Ode to Simplicity', seems to declare his devotion to writing poetry at once truthful, imaginative, and rapturous. The claim has in fact been made that the odes all bear a close thematic relationship to one another, and are all meditations on the poet's art or on his social responsibilities. It is as well to recall these varied aspirations in the work of a man whose career was untimely cut short. They give promise of a greater variety than he managed to accomplish, though it is only in the ode that he has survived.

The discussion has been confined so far to the lesser ode, but most poets attempted the greater ode as well. Of these Collins wrote four. The most famous practitioner of all time in the greater ode was Pindar. This was acknowledged by everyone; but even those who read him in the original Greek, as Collins did, were generally agreed that the best way of writing an English Pindaric was to follow the practice of Cowley, which permitted an irregular number of stanzas, an irregular number of lines to the stanza, and an irregular number of stresses to the line.

Dryden had imposed some order upon this anarchy by declaring that 'the ear must preside, and direct the judgment to the choice of numbers'. His own odes had shown how 'the cadency of one line must be a rule to the next'; but they remain irregular, and their prestige helped to ensure the popularity of the irregular ode, in spite of Congreve's attempt to persuade

the public of the beauty of symmetry and harmony attained
when strophe is answered exactly by antistrophe and is contrasted by epode, and in spite of Gilbert West's insistence that
an irregular Pindaric could only be a monstrous and distorted
likeness of the original.

Collins was not persuaded. He preferred to work within the
maximum of metrical licence permitted by Dryden, and, in
his own ode for music, seemed indeed to challenge comparison
with him in adapting the measure to each passion. Much admired by Collins's contemporaries was the violent and abrupt
abbreviation of the measure in the fifth and sixth lines of the
'Ode to Fear',

> Thou, to whom the World unknown
> With all its shadowy Shapes is shown;
> Who see'st appall'd th'unreal Scene,
> While Fancy lifts the Veil between;
> Ah *Fear*! Ah frantic *Fear*!
> I see, I see Thee near.

This calculated appeal to terror had become popular, and was
generally known by those investigating the aesthetics of the
subject as the sublime. His theme in this ode offered Collins
ample opportunity of cultivating the sublime, and he put his
fancy to work in brief allegorical descriptions designed to chill
the blood. Such is the figure of Vengeance quoted on p. 68,
and such is his Danger,

> Who stalks his Round, an hideous Form,
> Howling amidst the Midnight Storm,
> Or throws him on the ridgy Steep
> Of some loose hanging Rock to sleep.

All but a few of these sublimities have lost their power to move
the reader; but they were felt to have a special appropriateness
in the greater ode whose function was less to please than to
astonish, and to rouse the mind from ordinary pursuits to contemplate what is elevated or what lies beyond the round of
everyday experience. It has been well said that the great odes
of this period are 'specimens of the art of adding magnificence
to objects already splendid in attribute and accomplishment'.

Of ode writers in this tradition no one at this time, not even Collins, was more accomplished than Gray.[1] His earliest poems, printed in the second volume of Dodsley's *Collection* within six years of their composition, are pleasing specimens of the lesser ode. The 'Ode on the Spring', the 'Ode on a Distant Prospect of Eton College', as well as the unfinished and posthumous 'Ode on the Pleasure arising from Vicissitude', are all descriptive odes, but the description is even less 'pure' than in Collins's; that is to say, it is not undertaken simply for its own sake. The lines in the 'Vicissitude' ode,

> But chief the Sky-lark warbles high
> His trembling thrilling ecstasy
> And, less'ning from the dazzled sight,
> Melts into air and liquid light,

testify as clearly as many passages in Gray's letters to the keen-ness of his powers of observation; but in the context of the poem they support the argument from that contrast between winter past and coming spring which lies behind the title. Even the less charming colours of the radiant 'Ode on the Spring' and the nostalgic, distant view of children at play in the 'Eton College' ode serve an equally clear moral purpose, although Gray with his exquisite sense of tact is diffident about pressing the moral too seriously.

In the seventh stanza of the 'Eton College' ode Gray pays his tribute to what may be called the allegorical tradition in ode-writing, but in this poem his abstractions are given the merest vestige of description. His only contribution to the allegorical ode is the 'Hymn to Adversity', written at the same time as the other odes in 1742 but not included in Dodsley's *Collection* till the fourth volume, 1755. The stanza form (which Wordsworth was to adopt for his 'Ode to Duty') helps to conceal its derivation from 'Il Penseroso'; but like Milton, and like so many contemporary ode-writers, Gray has organized his poem on what is essentially the Penseroso pattern of relating first the birth and attributes of Adversity, then listing those who avoid her company and those who keep it. His descriptions are

---

[1] Thomas Gray, 1716-71, was educated at Eton and Peterhouse, Cambridge. He accompanied Horace Walpole on the Grand Tour from 1739 to 1741, and in 1742 returned to Cambridge, where he lived for the remainder of his life. He was appointed Regius Professor of Modern History in 1768.

neither so dynamic nor so romantic as Collins's; his beings are
not fantastic, fairy creatures; instead they have the static composure and appropriateness of figures in the Bologna school
of painting that Gray and some of his contemporaries admired
so much:

> Wisdom in sable garb array'd
> Immers'd in rapt'rous thought profound,
> And Melancholy, silent maid
> With leaden eye, that loves the ground.

In the penultimate stanza of the 'Adversity' ode, in which
he begs to be spared from the Goddess's 'Gorgon terrors', from

> screaming Horror's funeral cry
> Despair, and fell Disease, and ghastly Poverty,

he begins to exercise himself in the sublime. But, like Collins,
he seems to have recognized that the sublime belongs to the
greater ode; the 'Hymn to Adversity' for all its solemnity falls
clearly into the lesser category. Not long after arranging for its
publication, Gray wrote to Walpole in July 1752 suggesting
that he might soon offer Dodsley 'an ode to his own tooth, a
high Pindarick upon stilts, which one must be a better scholar
than he is to understand a line of, and the very best scholars
will understand but a little matter here and there'. The poem
was to be 'The Progress of Poesy'. Self-depreciatory and whimsical as Gray's manner is in referring to the unfinished work,
it is obvious that he considered it a somewhat different kind of
composition from the odes he had already written. Learned
they are, even the mock-heroic 'Ode on the Death of a Favourite
Cat', but they carry their learning lightly; the two companion
poems, 'The Progress of Poesy' and its successor, 'The Bard', are
altogether more substantial works.

Gray recognized Congreve's logic about the structure of the
Pindaric ode, though as one of the best Greek scholars of his
time he did not need Congreve's help in making the observation. In his two Pindaric odes there are three triads, in each of
which a strophe is answered by an antistrophe and contrasted
with an epode. In 'The Progress of Poesy' he devised a strophe
of twelve lines and in 'The Bard' one of fourteen, taking for
his model, as Milton had done in 'At a Solemn Music' and his
poems on Time and the Circumcision, the *canzoni* of Petrarch.

So long a stanza was at variance with the sensible observation he made at the time in a letter to Wharton (9 March 1755):

methinks it has little or no effect upon the ear, which scarce perceives the regular return of Metres at so great a distance from one another. To make it succeed, I am persuaded the Stanza's must not consist of above 9 lines each at most.

The objection is valid. It is difficult to retain the stanzaic pattern of the strophes in the memory, and even more difficult to recall from triad to triad the pattern of the epode which, in 'The Progress of Poesy', consists of seventeen lines, and in 'The Bard' of as many as twenty. But there is no doubting the broad contrast in measure that the epode provides. In 'The Progress of Poesy' the change from strophe and antistrophe is marked by a shift in the first eleven lines of the epode from rising to falling rhythm; but as the measure of the verse grows longer in the last six lines, the rhythm reverts once more to an iambic beat. It will also be noticed that, in each epode of this poem, the return from falling to rising rhythm takes place at an important point in the argument. No less care was expended over the epode of 'The Bard'. Thus internal rhymes are employed in the fifteenth and seventeenth lines, a 'double cadence' which Gray claimed to have introduced at that point 'not only to give a wild spirit and variety to the Epode; but because it bears some affinity to a peculiar measure in the Welch Prosody, called Gorchest-Beirdh, i.e. the *Excellent of the Bards*'.

The diction is as highly wrought as the versification. Gray himself pointed out in notes to the poems the passages from Pindar and later poets upon which he had modelled some of his most striking phrases. 'He pass'd the flaming bounds of Place and Time' is a line from his celebration of Milton in 'The Progress of Poesy'; but as though feeling that such boldness of expression required to be supported by the authority of a great poet, Gray accordingly draws the reader's attention to his source in Lucretius, 'flammantia moenia mundi'. 'The crested pride of the first Edward' in the first strophe of 'The Bard' was modelled upon 'the crested adder's pride' in Dryden's *Indian Queen*, a fact which would have been difficult to discover without the poet's help, and which is yet required knowledge if the reader is to appreciate the sinister power of Edward I poised to strike. After mentioning several other instances in a letter to

Bedingfield (27 August 1756), Gray comments

> Do not wonder therefore, if some Magazine or Review call me
> Plagiary: I could shew them a hundred more instances, which they
> never will discover themselves;

and he continues,

> There is a certain measure of learning necessary, and a long ac-
> quaintance with the good Writers ancient and modern . . . without
> [which readers] can only catch here and there a florid expression,
> or a musical rhyme, while the Whole appears to them a wild obscure
> unedifying jumble.

He implies in this passage a theory of diction expressed more
boldly in a letter to Richard West, written at the beginning of
his career (8 April 1742):

> The language of the age is never the language of poetry; except
> among the French . . . Our poetry, on the contrary, has a language
> peculiar to itself; to which almost every one, that has written, has
> added something by enriching it with foreign idioms and deriva-
> tives: Nay sometimes words of their own composition or invention.
> Shakespear and Milton have been great creators this way; and no one
> more licentious than Pope or Dryden.

The pleasure which the texture of Gray's poetry offers, in the
Elegy no less than in the Pindaric Odes, is one which it shares
with Milton's and Pope's, and in the twentieth century with
T. S. Eliot's; nor is it absent from Wordsworth's and Keats's.
It is a sophisticated pleasure derived from observing a great
master in emulation of his predecessors, profoundly aware of
a treasury of word and phrase that they have bequeathed him,
using it with distinction in a new context, or giving final expression to what oft was thought.

The two odes, on which Gray had lavished so much metrical
and linguistic skill, bear the same relationship to each other as
Dryden's 'Ode on St. Cecilia's Day' to 'Alexander's Feast'.
The first celebrates the history and influence of lyric verse,
and the second employs a legend to illustrate its power. 'The
Progress of Poesy', like the 'Ode on St. Cecilia's Day', is both
a highly animated performance and a model of organization.
The three triads are quite distinct in topic, yet perfectly related
in theme; and in each are found broad and effective contrasts,

between the types of lyric and the types of dance in the first triad, between the sorts of comfort that the Muse can provide in the second, and between the respective triumphs of Shakespeare, Milton, and Dryden in the third. Though Gray's theory of versification precluded him from attempting to match Dryden's representations of different instruments, he has succeeded within the stricter measures of his verse in representing at one moment impetuosity, and at another such frolic measures as made Mrs. Garrick, the prima ballerina of her day, exclaim that Gray was the only poet that understood dancing; while at a third he achieves, if only momentarily, something of the pride and

> ample pinion
> That the Theban Eagle bear
> Sailing with supreme dominion
> Thro' the azure deep of air.

'The Bard' shows, more than any other composition of its length, that calculated appeal to terror already observed in some of the odes of Collins. Contemporary interest in the sublime reached a new climax while Gray was at work on this poem. Burke's *Philosophical Enquiry into the Origin of Our Ideas of the Sublime and Beautiful* was published in 1757, a few months before 'The Bard'. There the interested reader would find a convenient list of the most powerful causes of the sublime, most of which he would be able to discover reflected in the poem, from the abruptness of the opening to the violence of the conclusion. He would find terror, obscurity, and gloomy pomp in ample measure, besides horrid phantoms and visions of annihilation, all listed by Burke; he would even find a calculated juxtaposition of the beautiful and the sublime in the concluding lines of the first antistrophe which describe the magnificence of Richard II's reign:

> Fair laughs the Morn, and soft the Zephyr blows,
> While proudly riding o'er the azure realm
> In gallant trim the gilded Vessel goes;
> Youth on the prow, and Pleasure at the helm;
> Regardless of the sweeping Whirlwind's sway,
> That, hush'd in grim repose, expects his evening-prey.

A model response was provided by a certain Mr. Butler, who sent his observations to Gray in December 1757; Gray found them 'not nonsense', and fragments of them were printed by Mason in his edition of the *Poems*. One remark in particular, directed to the second strophe, conveys the tone of mysterious rapture to which it is no longer easy to respond:

Can there be an image more just, apposite, and nobly imagined than this tremendous tragical winding-sheet? In the rest of this stanza the wildness of thought, expression, and cadence are admirably adapted to the character and situation of the speaker, and of the bloody spectres his assistants. It is not indeed peculiar to it alone, but a beauty that runs throughout the whole composition, that the historical events are briefly sketched out by a few striking circumstances, in which the Poet's office of rather exciting and directing, than satisfying the reader's imagination, is perfectly observed. Such abrupt hints, resembling the several fragments of a vast ruin, suffer not the mind to be raised to the utmost pitch, by one image of horror, but that instantaneously a second and a third are presented to it, and the affection is still uniformly supported.

Though the modern reader is not so easily rocked from his composure by these carefully contrived frenzies, he may still admire Gray's control over this difficult form, the nicely adjusted transitions from one triad to the next, and the movement from a dreary present to a glorious future that gradually breaks upon the old bard's prophecy.

Gray's pindarics occupy the last pages of Dodsley's last volume—two *tours de force* chosen for a proud position—and an engraving of the bard in the act of taking his final plunge suggests that no further bays were to be earned in that kind. Gray himself published three more odes in 1768, but they were intentionally primitive in form and subject; they serve to illustrate the awakening of interest in northern antiquities at the time, which is touched on in a later chapter (pp. 214–17). So far as the great ode was concerned, the majority of poets in the second half of the century were content to use the looser form: for the most part that was what had to satisfy George III when his poets laureate celebrated his birthday and the coming of a new year, though William Whitehead occasionally presented him with a strict pindaric; and it was the looser form that Coleridge and Wordsworth preferred when they recovered the fortunes of the ode forty years later. Gray's friend Mason[1] practised the stricter form. It is of some interest to

[1] William Mason, 1724–97, was educated at St. John's College, Cambridge. Besides being a poet and a dramatist, he became a chaplain to the King, 1757, and

observe that when there was a prospect in 1747 of his returning to a Cambridge fellowship for which Gray had been supporting him, he composed a strict pindaric on the occasion. Almost certainly Gray was given it to read, and though its merits are not remarkable, it may have drawn Gray's attention to the possibilities of the form. Mason wrote several other strict pindarics, some of which were incorporated as choric odes in his tragedies, *Elfrida* (1751) and *Caractacus* (1759). But he was a poet of limited powers. He could write a mellifluous line, but he had little force of imagination and none of Gray's architectonic skill. He is at his best in the lesser ode, such as the 'Ode to a Water-Nymph', published in Dodsley's third volume, where he can lament with some play of fancy the false taste of a modern landscape gardener.

It was not until 1768 that Gray consented to a collected edition of his poems; till then the general reader would have known them largely from Dodsley's *Collection*. In the two editions of 1768, published simultaneously in London and Glasgow, he excluded one poem, 'A Long Story', because he regarded it simply as an explanation of the engravings with which it had first appeared. The volume thus became a volume of odes apart from one important exception, 'Elegy written in a Country Church-yard', the best poem in the book. Gray might have included a few more trifles already written, for he was somewhat concerned, as he told Horace Walpole, 'lest *my works* should be mistaken for the works of a flea, or a pismire'; but altogether they would scarcely have amounted to half an ounce of snuff on his own reckoning, and there were objections to publishing what looked like the merest ephemerae. Later critics, who have admired the powerful character of 'Tophet' and the imaginative 'Impromptu' on Lord Holland's seat, have wished that Gray had shown more indulgence to his gift for satire. Perhaps he felt discouraged at failing to complete his 'Hymn to Ignorance' (1742), a fragment too closely imitative of *The Dunciad*; perhaps he recognized that a more conscious direction to satire would have been at odds with his main intellectual pursuits.

The *Elegy* for all its familiarity is a puzzling work in the

a Canon Residentiary and Precentor of York Minster, 1762. As Gray's literary executor, he edited his poems and letters, and wrote his life.

context of Gray's poetry. We do not know for certain when or
at what impulse it was written. Except for 'A Long Story' it
is the only poem he brought to completion that is not a lyric.
Yet what is it? In an age when writings either conformed to the
recognized kinds or avoided them with due calculation, Gray
himself seems to have wondered how he should describe the
poem. 'Stanzas wrote in a Country Church-yard' is the title
in the Eton College manuscript, an early draft; it was Mason,
so he claimed, who persuaded Gray 'first to call it an *Elegy*,
because the subject authorized him so to do', and he added, in
justification, 'the alternate measure, in which it was written,
seemed peculiarly fit for that species of composition'. But
whatever Gray's reasons for hesitating, Mason seems to have
removed them—'the Title must be, Elegy . . .' he wrote to
Walpole, when giving him directions for the printer—and
though he may not have been aware of this when he began the
poem, his work was in tune with contemporary elegiac practice. If, as Mason was inclined to believe, the *Elegy* was begun
in 1742, Gray would not have known the *Love Elegies* of James
Hammond, published posthumously at the end of that year,
though according to the title-page written ten years earlier.
These poems are adaptations of the elegies of Tibullus, a
favourite poet of Gray's close friend, Richard West. To represent Tibullus' alternate hexameters and pentameters (elegiac
couplets), Hammond had chosen another alternate measure,
the quatrain. Dr. Johnson might shake his head over so obtuse
a choice, for

the character of the elegy is gentleness and tenuity; but this stanza
has been pronounced by Dryden [in the preface to *Annus Mirabilis*] whose knowledge of English metre was not inconsiderable, to
be the most magnificent of all the measures which our language
affords.

But the choice commended itself to Shenstone, who defended
it in a prefatory essay to his 'Elegies in Hammond's Meter',
written about 1743 but not published till 1764, as well as to
Percy, who found it 'peculiarly suited to the plaintive turn
of Elegy', and to Grainger, who when translating Tibullus
considered that its 'solemnity and kind of melancholy flow'
provided the nearest correspondent to the Latin measure. Presumably Gray also concluded that the quatrain was the best

equivalent to the elegiac couplet, and it seems at least possible that he reached that conclusion independently.

As a classical scholar he would know that the range of themes open to the Roman elegiac poet was very wide; yet recognizing that love eventually became the dominant theme of Latin elegy, he might well hesitate to mislead the reader's expectations by using the term in his title. But he would also know that Tibullus, besides telling us of his loves, is full of moral reflection, that he expresses his contentment in country life and his interest in the labours of the countryman; and with West's version of the fifth elegy of the third book before him, how could he forget Tibullus' melancholy? In short, he could determine to write a type of Latin elegiac poem and yet feel diffident in calling it an elegy before he received Mason's assurance.

To Gray, as much as to Pope, the incentive of writing in a classical form was to make that form a denizen of England, to show that Nature is unchanged, and thus to put modern life into a wider context of time. The echoing corridors of his memory supplied him with numerous instances from a remote past to place within an English village setting. The curfew itself he said he drew from a bell in Dante's *Purgatorio* that from far off seemed to lament the dying day, though he must also have recalled it sounding in 'Il Penseroso',

> Over some wide-water'd shore,
> Swinging slow with solemn roar.

He could not resist adopting Lucretius' pity for the dead house-holder—a vignette that was later to appeal both to Collins and to Burns (p. 162)—and as he re-expressed it in the sixth stanza of the *Elegy*, he shows by a touch here and there that he recalled both Dryden's translation and Thomson's adaptation of it in *Winter*. Virgil helped him to shape a passage in the eleventh stanza, and Petrarch a passage in the twenty-third, while the traces of more recent poets, Drummond, Milton, Pope, Parnell, and Gay amongst them, are evident elsewhere, though whether Gray consciously recalled them we cannot tell. Yet not for a moment do we gain the impression of a clever piece of mosaic work. Had Gray claimed for his *Elegy* what Shenstone claimed for his—

If he describes a rural landscape, or unfolds the train of senti-ment it inspired, he fairly drew his picture from the spot, and felt very sensibly the affection he communicates—

we should have had no hesitation in believing him. Even without such a claim, we are persuaded that the 'nodding Beech that wreathes its old fantastic Roots so high' was one of the trees that still grow so peculiarly at Burnham Beeches, and (with less probability) that the poem was written in the churchyard at Stoke Poges close by; while it seems fitting that the names who replaced the 'Village Cato' and the 'mute inglorious Tully' of the Eton College draft should have been the names of Buckinghamshire worthies. An observant countryman may stumble over the confusion of two sheep-farming systems in the eighth line of the poem (for 'if the sheep are folded there is no need for a bell-wether'), but for the rest of us who know the area everything seems to be in keeping. Yet the illusion of a particular scene was all that was required, and in fact Gray was at some pains to draw in as many contemporary readers as possible by representing to them their familiar backcloth of moonlit ivy-mantled ecclesiastical ruin for pensive meditation. The scene is as skilfully placed in the literature of the day as it is in the South Buckinghamshire countryside.

Shenstone thought that an elegiac poet should communicate the affection he feels. This is the impression that many readers have received from Tibullus; and if what Gray had in mind to write was an elegy of this kind, there is no reason to think that he would have shrunk from some measure of personal application. The 'Ode on the Spring', the 'Hymn to Adversity', and 'The Progress of Poesy' all turn upon the poet in conclusion, and the traditions of elegy made such an application entirely fitting. In the original draft of twenty-two stanzas the proportions of general and particular are much the same as in the odes. It is the expansion of three stanzas about the poet to nine that troubles the reader, as indeed does the entire revision.

The plan of the original draft is clear enough. It is an extended meditation upon the difference in human lot between the humble and the mighty. Their birth and station deprive the village worthies of fame and glory, but there are compensations that make the settled order acceptable. If 'Chill Penury had damp'd their noble Rage' and 'their struggling Virtues' had been circumscribed, their lot had also confined their crimes, forbidden them

> to wade thro' Slaughter to a Throne,
> And shut the Gates of Mercy on Mankind,

The struggling Pangs of conscious Truth to hide,
To quench the Blushes of ingenuous Shame,
And Crown the Shrine of Luxury and Pride
With Incense kindled at the Muse's Flame.

So the argument proceeds until the seventy-second line of the
poem, and Gray summarizes it in a stanza which he later
removed:

The thoughtless World to Majesty may bow
Exalt the brave, and idolize Success
But more to Innocence their Safety owe
Then Power and Genius e'er conspired to bless.

Three concluding stanzas address the poet himself and apply
the moral to him, as was customary in elegy and as the moral
had been applied in the 'Ode on the Spring' and the 'Hymn
to Adversity'. When deciding to revise, Gray expanded the
argument in five stanzas of mounting pathos (ll. 73-92), and
dramatized the conclusion by introducing a 'kindred Spirit' to
inquire the poet's fate from 'some hoary-headed Swain' and to
point to his epitaph. It is possible to prefer the restraint of the
original version and its relative freedom from ambiguity, and
to sympathize with the perplexity of those who wonder whether
the poet himself is still intended in the character of the romantic
solitary presented in the final verses; but it is not possible to
doubt that the sentimental appeal was immeasurably strengthened in the revision.

Two more 'graveyard poets' may be mentioned at this point,
Robert Blair[1] and Edward Young. The popularity their works
enjoyed has long since waned, but it is still possible to recognize the power they exerted over more than one generation of
readers. Though *The Grave* was not published until 1743, Blair
claimed to have written it before his ordination in 1731, and
hoped that there was nothing in it unbecoming his profession
as a minister of the gospel. So little is there unbecoming that
the poem has been regarded as a popular sermon on mortality.
But this is to argue from his subsequent career. Nothing suggests

---

[1] Robert Blair, 1701-46, was educated at Edinburgh University. He was
ordained minister of Athelstaneford, East Lothian, in 1731, a charge in which he
was succeeded by another poet, John Home, author of *Douglas*.

that Blair was taking the sermon as his form, in spite of the
appeals to repentance, the attempts to awaken the sluggish
imagination, the reminders of the consolations of a well-spent
life, all apparently indicative of a writer accustomed to the
arts of pulpit oratory.

The poem may be described more confidently as a dramatic
address, though scarcely as an excerpt from an imaginary play.
The sense of an audience and of a precise location are not
consistently maintained, but the reader is made aware throughout of a speaker formulating his passing thoughts into words,
interrupted by what happens to catch his eye, and continually
urged to reflect and to exclaim. There is plenty of evidence
from diction and syntax of Blair's admiration for *Paradise Lost*,
yet his blank verse is less Miltonic than dramatic. *The Grave*
belongs to no well-established kind· of poem, but its closest
affinity is with the dramatic soliloquy, of which it forms a commendably original variation.

Young's *Complaint: or, Night-Thoughts on Life, Death, and
Immortality* is a more substantial work—literally, as well as
metaphorically, for it extends to more than ten thousand lines
of blank verse. The dramatist and satirist of the Augustan
period[1] had taken orders, and after ten years' silence had begun
when nearly sixty to publish this immense and immensely
popular philosophical poem in nine parts or 'Nights' over a
period of four years (1742-6). Its affinities, philosophical and
poetical, are quite clear. It belongs to a tradition of Christian
apologetics which set out to confute atheism and deism, the
one by demonstrating the being and nature of God from the
works of creation, and especially from that most popular source
of evidence, the starry universe, and the other by asserting the
truths of Christian revelation, and in particular by demonstrating that man is assured of immortality. From this point of
view *Night-Thoughts* differs little in its thinking from the works
of Derham and the Boyle lecturers expounded in the previous
volume (pp. 20 ff.). And as a poem it had some famous prototypes in the literature of the previous eighty years. Milton,
Thomson, and Pope had taken different ways to 'assert eternal
providence', Milton with the help of a story, Thomson with the
help of natural description, and Pope on a more abstract level
of reasoning. There is no narrative in *Night-Thoughts*; but the

---

[1] For a biographical note on Young see the previous volume, pp. 249-50.

sense of an occasion that motivated the poem was strong
enough to excite many readers to inquire what episode it was
in Young's life that prompted it, who were Lucia, Narcissa,
and Philander for whom

> The Grave, like Fabled Cerberus, has op'd
> A triple Mouth,

and whether gossip was correct in claiming Young's son as the
model for Lorenzo, the infidel voluptuary with whom Young
maintains his long-drawn argument. Croft, who wrote the
account of Young in Johnson's *Lives of the Poets*, was able to
prove convincingly that the attribution was false, and no evidence of a real episode or of actual prototypes has survived,
perhaps because there never was any. But these misguided
inquiries do at least serve to show that though *Night-Thoughts*
is closer in kind to the *Essay on Man* than to either *Paradise Lost*
or *The Seasons*, Young relies more than Pope does on a sense
of occasion and upon a dramatic manner of developing his
argument.

It is remarkable that a poet who had learned to command
the couplet for his satires and whose early work bespoke his
admiration for Pope should turn to blank verse at so advanced
an age for a poem which resembles the *Essay on Man* in kind and
which, like the *Moral Essays*, requires an imagined attendant
on the poet's sermon. It has been suggested that he had been
impressed by the new instrument which Thomson had lately
been demonstrating in *The Seasons*. But Young's manner of
expounding his theme is less like Thomson's than Pope's, and
his blank verse never reminds us of Thomson, nor indeed of
Milton, for very long. It is in fact almost all his own; it gives
him the opportunity of speaking with an individuality of voice
that makes his principal claim to originality. His characteristic
manner is exclamatory and epigrammatic. He had observed
that Pope did not need the full scope of the couplet for turning
such epigrams as 'A little learning is a dang'rous thing' and
'Hope springs eternal in the human breast'. The limits of the
blank verse line were enough, and even more than enough.
'Procrastination is the thief of time', 'All men think all men
mortal but themselves', 'Man wants but little, nor that little
long': in the gnomic wisdom of these lines, Young takes a
momentary position with Shakespeare, Pope, and only a few

other poets, in the national consciousness. These proverbs
deserve to survive. And Young also showed that blank verse
could be broken down to units even more terse and no less
sententious:

> Throw years away?
> Throw empires, and be blameless. Moments seize;
> Heaven's on their wing: A moment we may wish,
> When worlds want wealth to buy. Bid day stand still,
> Bid him drive back his car, and reimpose
> The period past, regive the given hour.
> Lorenzo, more than miracles we want;
> Lorenzo—O for yesterdays to come!

So generally acceptable was this Senecan abruptness of ejacula-
tion that Joseph Warton was led to propose a new punctuation
for the first line of Gray's Elegy:

> The curfew tolls! The knell of parting day!

But though this 'impatient colloquialism', as it has well been
called, is Young's staple manner, he recognized the value of
variety in rhythm and could conclude a series of rapidly formed
questions and replies with such well-turned and imaginative
phrasing as

> And can eternity belong to me,
> Poor pensioner on the bounties of an hour?

His range is perhaps best exhibited in the first 250 lines of
'Night IX', which opens with a long Miltonic simile showing
a quite different control of blank verse within his power. In his
vision of the Last Day he once more demonstrates that he has
learnt what Milton could teach him so as to heighten his appeal
to the contemporary taste for the sublime:

> At the destin'd hour
> By the loud trumpet summon'd to the charge
> See, all the formidable sons of fire,
> Eruptions, earthquakes, comets, lightnings, play
> Their various engines; all at once disgorge
> Their blazing magazines; and take, by storm
> This poor terrestrial citadel of man.

But this scarcely deserves a place beside an earlier and much more imaginative vision of the Deluge:

> Of one departed world
> I see the mighty shadow; oozy wreath
> And dismal sea-weed crown her; o'er her urn
> Reclin'd, she weeps her desolated realms,
> And bloated sons; and, weeping, prophesies
> Another's dissolution, soon, in flames.

Even more surprising is that a poet capable of this:

> Our lean soil,
> Luxuriant grown, and rank in vanities,
> From friends interr'd beneath; a rich manure!

should have been able to proceed within five lines to this:

> Where is the dust that has not been alive?
> The spade, the plough, disturb our ancestors;
> From human mould we reap our daily bread.

The fact is that Young had never learnt what his friend Pope could have taught him, 'the last and greatest Art, the Art to blot'. Blessed as he was with unusual powers of imagination, with great facility in the use of words, and with something like rhythmical virtuosity, he seems nevertheless to have been quite incapable of distinguishing between first-rate and third-rate; and having no sense of organization, he was unable to dispose the forces of his argument or manage a climax. The consequence is that though his voice is easily distinguishable from the crowd, it is a voice we soon grow tired of hearing. Yet the reader who threads his way through the wilderness of *Night-Thoughts* will join with Dr. Johnson in the reluctant admission that Young 'with all his defects . . . was a man of genius and a poet'.

Virgil's *Georgics*, said Addison, in his prefatory essay to Dryden's translation (1697), 'are a subject which none of the critics have sufficiently taken into their consideration', yet none of his poems is more perfect and exquisite, more diverting to the understanding and appealing to the imagination. Though, unlike his young friend Tickell, he did not invite his contemporaries to compose modern georgics, Addison provided a convenient scheme of rules for any who should try. The success of

John Philips in *Cyder* (1708) and William Somerville in *The Chace* (1735) has been discussed in the previous volume. They showed some of the opportunities offered in this kind, and they set a challenge in the adaptation of Virgilian detail to the English scene; but many further experiments were possible. The appeal, indeed, was obvious. If the poet could recognize his kinship to the natural philosopher, it was to be expected that the technologist, no less than Newton, would 'demand the Muse'; for the discoveries he was making were scarcely less far-reaching and had produced effects which could appeal to a poet's imagination. Virgil's poem had shown that the welfare of Italy depended on its agriculture; it was no less evident that Britain's welfare depended on the management of its natural resources.

This seems to have been the theme that Dodsley set himself in his unfinished poem *Public Virtue*, of which only the first book, 'Agriculture' was published (3 cantos, 1753). Shenstone remarked that the poem was 'infinitely beyond what they cou'd reasonably *expect* from him', but the note of condescension betrays the fear Dodsley himself had expressed in his preface, that 'the projected building' was too great for the abilities of the architect. He follows timidly in Virgil's footsteps commending the dignity of labour, conscientiously adapting Virgil's instructions to 'the love of fair *Berkeria*'s Son (the late Mr. Tull, of Shalborne in Berkshire)', recommending the enclosure of fields and showing how it could best be effected, distinguishing the merits of different native timbers, listing the points to be looked for in a breeding-ram, a hunter, and a war-horse, and describing rural merry-making. But his muse was pedestrian; he showed no sense of phrasing, and he had no imaginative grasp of the implications of his theme.

'The Hop-Garden' by Christopher Smart, published in his *Poems on Several Occasions* (1752), but probably written several years earlier, is even less commendable. It is obviously an attempt to do for Kent what Philips had done for Herefordshire. But what is done is offered with apology; these are 'tasks indelicate'; given greater poetic powers, says Smart, 'no peasants' toil, no hops Shou'd e'er debase my lay'. So radical a failure in sympathy for the Virgilian impulse prevented him from pondering the problems of the georgic, and accordingly he manages to please only in a note or two of local patriotism and the description—itself lifted from Virgil—of the signs of an approaching storm.

Dyer's *Fleece* (1757) and Grainger's *Sugar-Cane* (1764) are more considerable performances. Grainger's[1] merits are largely due to a happy choice of theme, whose Virgilian opportunities he was quick to exploit. In an age which valued the novelty of a poet's description, Grainger could scarcely fail to please with all the exotic richness of West Indian life at his command: lemon, lime, and orange 'amid their verdant umbrage countless glow'; 'yellow plantanes bend the unstain'd bough With crooked clusters, prodigally full'; but since this is a georgic dealing with life as it is, and not a pastoral, the poet is forced to admit that 'cockroaches crawl displeasingly abroad', and that the devastations of a West Indian hurricane are cruel. Unlike the cockroaches, however, the hurricane offers the poet a grand occasion for invoking the sublime. Advice on the salient points of an animal had been required of a georgic poet ever since Virgil had described a stallion in his third book; but even here Grainger has an advantage in the novelty of his theme, for he can offer advice (excellent, no doubt) on what to look for when buying slaves, which African tribes to prefer, and which to avoid ('Worms lurk in all: yet pronest they to worms, Who from Mundingo sail'). But he is as humane in his treatment as his British audience would require, and he modulates by an easy transition to one more exotic variation upon a Virgilian episode, the negro choral dance.

Dyer[2] too owed much to a happy choice of theme; but whereas Grainger's choice led to at best a freakish success, a *tour de force* with more than a touch of the absurd, Dyer chose the care of sheep with full recognition of its wide potentialities. It is the ingenuity of Grainger's Virgilian parallels that laughingly reconciles us to the sedulous ape; but in Dyer we recognize a poet possessed by the importance of a great theme, with many ramifications, that happens to be Virgilian, and we willingly allow that such a poet might attend to the lessons of the master. Dyer's theme is the co-operation of labour that sustains the greatness of his country; he sings not merely 'the care of sheep'

---

[1] James Grainger, 1721?–66, was educated at Edinburgh University. He spent some years as an army surgeon before settling in London, where he practised as a physician and a man of letters. He emigrated to the West Indies (St. Christopher) in 1759 and died there.

[2] See Vol. VII, p. 477 n.

but 'the labors of the Loom, And arts of Trade', and his appeal is therefore made to all degrees, to farmers and their shepherds, to the new manufacturers and their hands, and to merchants and those who man their fleets. Thus his theme expands from the pastures of England and Wales in his first book to a vision of a Pax Britannica in his fourth, where Britannia shall

> fold the world with harmony, and spread,
> Among the habitations of mankind,
> The various wealth of toil.

It is both a learned and an innocent poem. Dyer's own practical experience enabled him to speak with confidence on major points of sheep-farming, to pick the breeding-stock best adapted to the soil, to urge the duty of enclosure, and to assure any artisan who might be listening that the new machinery, whose ingenuity gives the poet so much pleasure to describe, brought no danger of over-production:

> Nor hence, ye nymphs, let anger cloud your brows;
> The more is wrought, the more is still requir'd:
> Blithe o'er your toils, with wonted song, proceed:
> Fear not surcharge; your hands will ever find
> Ample employment.

To read *The Fleece* is to believe, for the moment at least, that this was the idyllic period of the Industrial Revolution. No premonition of the iniquities of child-labour clouds his vision as he describes how younger hands

> Ply at the easy work of winding yarn
> On swiftly-circling engines, and their notes
> Warble together, as a choir of larks;

and he can discern no Dickensian Coketown in his distant view of

> Th' increasing walls of busy Manchester,
> Sheffield, and Birmingham, whose redd'ning fields
> Rise and enlarge their suburbs;

for one ecstatic poet, mankind is about to re-enter Eden. Such is Dyer's innocent benevolence; and such, incidentally, is the range of verse that so various a theme required.

Two other didactic poems may be considered here, Akenside's *Pleasures of Imagination* in three books and Armstrong's

Art of Preserving Health in four, both published in 1744. *The Pleasures of Imagination* is a very remarkable performance for a young man of barely twenty-two. Akenside[1] set out with the intention of describing the constitution of the mind and characterizing 'those original forms or properties of being, about which it is conversant' and which in various combinations are a source of pleasure to it. He prepared himself for his task by extended reading in ancient and modern philosophy, and particularly in the work of Shaftesbury and Hutcheson. He was aware of at least some of the difficulties of treating the subject in verse; and like Mason, when contemplating his tedious georgic *The English Garden* (1772–81), he felt divided between Virgilian and Horatian models. The familiar epistle, as he rightly allowed, admits 'a greater variety of stile . . . and, especially with the assistance of rhyme, leads to a closer and more concise expression'; moreover, there lay before him 'the example of the most perfect of modern poets'. But since his intention was less to give precept and to argue than—in direct anticipation of Shelley—'to enlarge and harmonize the imagination, and by that means insensibly dispose the minds of men to a similar taste and habit of thinking in religion, morals, and civil life', he determined upon Virgil as his model, and blank verse as his medium. A subject that tended almost constantly to admiration and enthusiasm seemed to demand, he felt, 'a more open, pathetic, and figured style'. He might have invoked the recent authority of Thomson, whose *Seasons* is no less founded on philosophy and tends no less to admiration and enthusiasm; he could not foresee that he was setting a precedent for a later and greater poet who was also to make the mind of man his haunt and the main region of his song. Yet though Wordsworth's success seems to justify the propriety of an 'open' style for such a subject, Akenside might have done better with a measure that helped to curb his verbosity and his anxiety to soar beyond his powers. As Johnson noted:

His images are displayed with such luxuriance of expression that they are hidden, like Butler's Moon, by a 'Veil of Light'; they are forms fantastically lost under superfluity of dress . . . The words are

[1] Mark Akenside, 1721–70, was born at Newcastle upon Tyne. He studied medicine at Edinburgh University and at Leyden University, and practised in London, where he became physician to Christ's and St. Thomas's Hospitals, 1759.

multiplied till the sense is hardly perceived; attention deserts the mind and settles in the ear.

He must always interest those who like to trace Coleridge's theory of the imagination in writers of the previous century—they must attend particularly to the long passage (iii. 312–436) which begins by expounding the doctrine of association and proceeds to speculate upon the processes of poetic creation—and he still has a passing appeal for those who are attracted by anticipations of Wordsworth, not merely in the conviction he expresses at the conclusion of his third book that 'not a breeze Flies o'er the meadow . . . but whence his bosom can partake Fresh pleasure' and that Nature forms a court of appeal from 'the forms of servile custom' and 'sordid policies', but especially in one passage of the fragmentary fourth book (ll. 20–58), published posthumously in 1772, where he seeks

> the secret paths
> Of early genius to explore: to trace
> Those haunts where Fancy her predestin'd sons
> . . . doth nurse
> Remote from eyes profane,

and evokes nostalgically the spirits of the dales of Tyne and Wansbeck where his early years were spent.

Yet for all that, it is *The Art of Preserving Health* which provides the greater pleasure, as Smollett, a champion of the poem and no amateur in matters of literary taste, well knew. In treating such a subject Armstrong[1] could scarcely eschew precept, as Akenside had done; on the contrary instruction is an important point in his design, and he shows some measure of originality in offering his precepts not in couplets but blank verse, driving them home sometimes with gnomic force and sometimes in tones of genial expostulation. But every didactic poet recognized that straight instruction can better be conveyed in prose; it is the wider implications of his subject that the poet must ponder, he must eye its walks and 'try what the open, what the covert yield', and above all he must appeal to the emotions. The range of topic he springs and the variety of style at his command is some measure of Armstrong's success.

---

[1] John Armstrong, 1709–79, studied medicine at Edinburgh University. He held the posts of physician to the Hospital for Sick Soldiers in London, 1746, and physician to the British army in Germany, 1760. He was a close friend of Smollett, and of Thomson, who describes him in *The Castle of Indolence*, c. 1, st. 60.

He can rise as a blank-verse poet was expected to rise, and his description of the home of the Naiads (ii. 352 ff.) gives him his opportunity; but he can also describe in more genial vein the scene that has a peculiar appeal to every Scottish poet, the warmth of the hearth on a winter evening (iii. 136–57). The topic of exercise offers, amongst other sports, fishing; and that in turn suggests a favourite topic of poets from Ausonius through Spenser, Drayton, and Milton, to Pope: the roll-call of rivers, which Dyer too was to adopt in *The Fleece* in the interests of trade and navigation. Armstrong's survey ends with his own native stream, which he uses, as Akenside and Wordsworth were to do, for evoking the sports and wanderings of boyhood. But as Joseph Warton remarked in the 'Reflections on Didactic Poetry' contributed to his *Works of Virgil in Latin and English* (4 volumes, 1753), 'a stroke of passion is worth a hundred of the most lively and glowing description', and it is on the moving theme of mutability that Armstrong writes best. Dyer treated it in *The Ruins of Rome*, a passage that Wordsworth had commended as 'a beautiful instance of the modifying and investive power of imagination', and which he seems to have recalled in one of his finest sonnets, on 'Mutability'. The conclusion of Armstrong's second book (ii. 535 ff.) scarcely deserves less praise:

> What does not fade? The tower that long had stood
> The crush of thunder and the warring winds,
> Shook by the slow but sure destroyer Time,
> Now hangs in doubtful ruins o'er its base.
> And flinty pyramids, and walls of brass,
> Descend: the Babylonian spires are sunk;
> Achaia, Rome, and Egypt moulder down.
> Time shakes the stable tyranny of thrones
> And tottering empires rush by their own weight.
> This huge rotundity we tread grows old;
> And all those worlds that roll around the sun,
> The sun himself, shall die; and ancient Night
> Again involve the desolate abyss.

IV

POETRY, 1760–1789

THE period 1740–60 offered little opportunity for the discussion of satire and verse narrative. One great satire was written, Johnson's *The Vanity of Human Wishes* (1749), but it stands almost alone. The reasons for the decline in a form that had so recently attracted writers great and small will be examined later in this chapter, for the spectacular career of Churchill in the early 1760s and the work of Cowper, Crabbe, and others towards the end of this period suggest some revival of interest in it. The 1760s also exhibit a revival of interest in narrative verse.

The only narrative poems mentioned in the last chapter were a few written in the Spenserian mode. The novelty of this experiment bears witness to some dissatisfaction with old-established forms. 'Epic poetry', wrote Walpole to Mason on 25 June 1782, 'is the art of being as long as possible in telling an uninteresting story; and an epic poem is a mixture of history without truth, and of romance without imagination . . . Epic poetry . . . is not suited to an improved and polished state of things.' Critics were still ready to discuss it, however, but poets seemed reluctant to write it. Several poets from Butler to Pope had shown what might be done with the mock-heroic poem, but apart from such little *jeux d'esprit* as Smart's *Hilliad* (1753), their only successor on a similar scale in this period was Richard Owen Cambridge, who felt that the form had not yet been perfectly realized. His *Scribleriad* (1751) achieved the modest success of three editions in two years, but the calculated sobriety of his wit and imagery—his incidents are fantastic enough—has damned it in the eyes of all but those who are interested in the subject of false learning. As for the 'classical' epic, the stubbornness of a Scot seemed now required to bring one to fruition. *The Epigoniad, A Poem* in nine books (1757) received tributes from brother Scots, who professed to have found a Scottish Homer in William Wilkie to match the Scottish Shakespeare they had just discovered in John Home, whose

Douglas was first performed in the same year; but south of the border its reception was cool: 'too antique to please one party, and too modern for the other' was Goldsmith's verdict in the *Monthly Review*, and Shenstone told Percy that he wholly declined to read it: 'Rhime seems *actually* to have lost much ground in all Poems of this Nature; and were Pope's Homer to make it's first appearance now, he would be *greatly* blam'd for making use of it.' Yet Wilkie was not without some talent for Homeric imitation, though he is never likely to be read again, as Henry Mackenzie recommended for those without Greek in his own day, to discover what Homer is like in the original. His mistake was in failing to recognize a change in taste which deprived him of readers amongst his contemporaries.

'The public has seen all that art can do,' wrote Shenstone to MacGowan on 24 September 1761, 'and they want the more striking efforts of wild, original, enthusiastic genius.' The needs of the public were discussed with equal assurance by Thomas Percy and Thomas Warton a year later. Percy wrote to Warton on 16 August urging him to complete Chaucer's Squire's Tale: 'It is a task worthy of your Genius', he remarked; and added,

> The novelty of such a performance would be a means of recovering to poesy that attention, which it seems in great measure to have lost. The appetite of the public is so palled with all the common forms of poetry, that some new Spencer seems wanting to quicken and revive it.

Warton's reply on 4 September expressed his interest in this idea:

> I thank you for thinking me qualified to complete Chaucer's *Squiers Tale*. The Subject is so much in my own Way, that I do assure you I should like to try my hand at it. You are certainly right in thinking that the Public ought to have their attention called to Poetry in new forms; to Poetry endued with new Manners and new Images. How goes on the Collection of ancient Ballads? I hope we shall have it in the Winter.

In spite of several reminders Warton never finished the Squire's Tale; his only attempts in poetry to reconstruct aspects of the medieval scene, which as a scholar he was doing so much to illuminate, were two poems published in 1777, 'The Crusade' and 'The Grave of King Arthur'. In the one he imagines the song that the minstrel Blondel sang under the window of Richard I's prison as he was searching for his hidden master; and in the other he invents the odes chanted by Welsh bards before Henry II on his way to the Irish wars, telling him of the burial of King Arthur at Glastonbury. Both poems were written in the loose octosyllabics with which Warton was familiar from his Middle English studies. The modern reader of these poems is bound to reflect that *The Lay of the Last Minstrel* lies not far ahead in time. It may also occur to him to wonder whether Wordsworth was acquainted with them, and whether the impulse for 'Song, at the Feast of Brougham Castle' was derived, in part at least, from 'The Grave of King Arthur'.

'The Collection of ancient Ballads', to which Warton referred—Percy's *Reliques of Ancient English Poetry*—was to provide much of what the public was thought to require, though the Forms, Manners, and Images were not so much 'new' as newly discovered and persuasively presented.

Twentieth-century scholars have thrown light on the revival of interest in the ballads, but it still remains and must necessarily remain an obscure and confusing subject. In 1760 ballad-collecting had been going on for a century or more. The type of ballad collected was the broadside ballad hawked about the London streets and sold at provincial fairs. It was topical in nature and dealt in wonders, or prognostications, or in the dying moments of criminals, or in recent political events. It was written in a recognized song-measure advertised in its title, and was performed by its vendors. What we now call traditional ballads, that is, ballads that were transmitted by word of mouth in remoter parts of the country, also appeared on broadsides, as well as ballads of sentiment and love-making. The distinctions between these types that we endeavour to make today were scarcely recognized in the eighteenth century. All appear in *A Collection of Old Ballads* (3 volumes, 1723–5), though the collector, once believed to be Ambrose Philips, was more interested in the historical type; and all are represented once again in Percy's *Reliques*, as they had been in the seventeenth-century folio manuscript collection which formed the basis of Percy's publication and affected its balance.

It was in these types that simple, uneducated folk expressed their feelings and had their feelings moved. The ballads therefore lent themselves to propaganda; by lucky imitations people

could be persuaded to political or to moral action. A famous
instance is 'Lillibulero', attributed to the Marquis of Wharton,
which 'slight and insignificant as [it] may now seem'—so
Percy wrote when including it in the *Reliques*—'had once a more
powerful effect than either the Philippics of Demosthenes, or
Cicero; and contributed not a little towards the great revolution in 1688'. And there were many more, in which Prior,
Pulteney, Swift, and others had a hand, written during the
early years of the eighteenth century. The traditional anonymity of the ballad was so far maintained that even the well-
informed were not always aware of the authorship. Swift tells
Stella of dining with his printer and giving him 'a ballad made
by several hands, I know not whom. I believe lord treasurer
had a finger in it; I added three stanzas; I suppose Dr. Arbuth-
nott had the greatest share' (4 January 1712). Quite apart from
the seriousness of political controversy, there was a large element of fun in this. Imitation had become a game amongst
the wits, a means of diverting intimate friends, an activity
whose bastard productions need not be acknowledged, and
which certainly lay apart from the legitimate issue of a poet's
brain. So Pope treated his ballad progeny, 'Duke upon Duke.
An excellent new Ballad. To the Tune of Chevy Chase', 'The
Discovery: or, The Squire turn'd Ferret. An Excellent New
Ballad. To the Tune of High Boys! up go we; Chevy Chase;
Or what you please,' commemorating the fraudulent Mary
Tofts, 'the rabbit breeder', and the like; it is only by the pedantry of his editors that such things are admitted to the canon of
his works.

Once the game begins to appeal, it does not matter what
types of ballad are imitated. Political issues put a premium on
the production of political ballads, but other types were fair
sport, and as already mentioned all were apt to be gathered
without differentiation of origin into the poetical garlands of the
day. One type exerted a particular appeal; it may be called the
Sentimental Ballad, and its subject was the distresses of young
lovers owing to separation, desertion, insensitivity, or infidelity.
The game was played by the earliest imitators of this type with
the greatest of delicacy. Should we have known that Gay's
"'Twas when the seas were roaring' was intended as a parody, if
he had not described it as a 'sad ballad . . . bought at a fair'
and included it in his 'tragi-comi-pastoral farce' *The What d'Ye*

Call It (1715)? And how were we intended to take his 'Sweet William's Farewell to Black-Ey'd Susan' (1720), which has no dramatic context to guide us? A shadow of doubt—was the poet inviting us to laugh?—hangs over Rowe's 'Colin's Complaint', written about 1715. This poem describes the humble shepherd-poet lying in despair beside a stream and voicing his lament at being abandoned by some high-born beauty for a more wealthy rival. It is lyrical rather than narrative in mode, and its characters are not the common folk of Gay's ballads but those of the pastoral convention, yet its publication in an undated broadside of about 1715 shows how easily (and confusingly) ballad imitation could make use of strands which to later eyes appear separate and distinct. The new form that derives from the union of old forms is highly characteristic of eighteenth-century art.

But there is no ambiguity of response in a sentimental ballad of slightly later date, Mallet's 'William and Margaret' (1724). Mallet seems to have known an old ballad, 'Fair Margaret and Sweet William', that was circulating in broadside form. His own account (in *Plain Dealer*, No. 46, 1724) reads:

These Lines, naked of Ornament, and simple as they are, struck my Fancy. I clos'd the Book, and bethought myself that the unhappy Adventure I have mentioned above, which then came fresh into my mind, might naturally raise a Tale, upon the Appearance of this Ghost.—It was then Midnight. All, round me, was still and quiet. These concurring Circumstances work'd my Soul to a powerful Melancholy. I could not sleep; and at that Time I finish'd my little Poem.

Mallet's rewriting was thorough. He eliminated the bride for whom William had forsaken Margaret, and he had nothing to say about William's account of his dream or his colloquy with Margaret's brother. He laid emphasis instead upon the appearance of Margaret's ghost at William's bedside; and the single stanza she is given to speak in the original ballad was expanded to nine. It is clear that these alterations were made with an eye to invoking terror and pity. The mischievous Sir Charles Hanbury Williams could see what hilarious opportunities they offered for political balladry, when he introduced the 'grimly ghost' of Sir Joseph Jekyll, author of the Gin Act, at the bedside of Sandys, the Chancellor of the Exchequer who had recently repealed this humane Act to increase the revenue; but upon the purer sensibilities of one reader at least they had their intended effect. Aaron Hill, whose extravagant admiration for Richardson's *Pamela* indicates his taste in literature, announced his discovery of the ballad in *Plain Dealer*, No. 36 (24 July 1724). He supposed it to be ancient, and pleased himself 'with an Imagination that this *Sonnet* might be one of Shakespear's. A hundred worse are imputed to him.' He then proceeded to commend the author's judgement in detaining his reader with an exquisitely imaginative description of the ghost before her speech is opened with a sharp and startling summons. Thereupon we are touched by the noble tenderness of her reproach, and the '*Erotema*, or figure of *Questioning*', that is 'pursued with the most pathetic Emphasis, and, at last, broken off with an *Aposiopesis* so natural and so moving, that I have seldom seen a Beauty more distinguishable'. In short, Mallet's ballad evokes the sort of praise (four years before the publication of *The Dunciad*) that Wordsworth would have appreciated for his ballads seventy-five years later:

It is a plain and noble Masterpiece of the *natural* way of Writing, without Turns, Points, Conceits, Flights, Raptures, or Affectation of what Kind soever. It shakes the Heart by the mere Effect of its own Strength and Passionateness, unassisted by those flaming Ornaments which as often *dazzle* as *display* in Poetry. This was owing to the Author's Native Force of Genius; for they who conceive a Thought distinctly, will, of Necessity, express it plainly.

So much needed to be said about one of the most popular poems of the century—'William and Margaret' was reprinted at least twenty-five times before 1800—partly for the influence it exerted and partly for the response it excited. Mockery of the ballad, both affectionate and satiric, would still continue: in fact the most affectionate mockery ('John Gilpin') and the most contemptuous parody ('I put my hat upon my head and walk'd into the Strand') were still to come; but the imitation as a serious form was now as firmly established in the south of Britain as it was established—a theme for the next chapter—in the north. When Tickell published his 'Colin and Lucy' as an anonymous broadside in the following year (1725), he already found it worth recommending as 'Written in Imitation of William and Margaret', and at least nine other professed imitations or parodies appeared before the end of the century, besides many other ballads where the influence is perceptible.

Some were printed in Percy's *Reliques*; but the principal collection is *Old Ballads, Historical and Narrative, with some of Modern Date*, the second edition of 1784 in four volumes, published by Thomas Evans, who announced his trust that 'the Modern Ballads will not be displeasing to the Reader, When he sees among them the productions of a Goldsmith, a Percy, a Blacklock, a Mickle, and others of distinguished merit'. There is admittedly some variety in story and climax; sometimes, as in Mallet's second ballad 'Edwin and Emma' (1760), the lovers are faithful, but are separated by disapproving parents; or one is drowned and the other dies distracted; or one kills another by accident, as in Percy's *Hermit of Warkworth* (1771); or both die in grief because the lover has inadvertently slain his mistress's father, as in Helen Maria William's 'Edwin and Eltruda' (1782); or the survivor laments perhaps her lover's execution, as in Shenstone's 'Jemmy Dawson' (1748), or perhaps her discovery of his wounded corpse with a raven drinking the blood, as in Jerningham's 'Alicia'. A happy ending is rare, though the discovery of a lost lover in disguise is the climax of two of the most popular ballads of the century, Goldsmith's 'Edwin and Angelina', written in 1764, and Percy's 'Friar of Orders Gray' (1765). So unseemly was a happy ending considered that in Mrs. Hampden Pye's version of 'Childe Waters' (1771), the conclusion of the old story, by which the wife's faith receives its reward after severe testing, is discarded in favour of a conclusion more to the taste of the time:

> And dost thou know at length my heart?
> Then have I well been tried;
> I only liv'd to prove my faith:—
> She grasp'd his hand, and died.

There is also some variety of setting. The timeless, pastoral setting used by Rowe and Tickell becomes more rare. Instead, we are led to believe that such a tale as Mallet has to tell in 'Edwin and Emma' could have taken place only in the remoteness of the North Riding; and even stranger tales needed distancing in time as well as place. Thus Helen Maria Williams's ballad of lovers divided by the hostility of their families is set in the time of the Wars of the Roses, and Percy's learned notes to *The Hermit of Warkworth* ('a Northumberland ballad') testify to a story of the early fifteenth century; while William Julius

Mickle, whose 'Ballad of Cumnor Hall' was set in the reign of
Elizabeth, as every reader of Scott's *Kenilworth* knows, went
back to the period of the Saxon invasions for a ballad of 'Hengist
and Mey'.

Here then was an attempt to offer 'new Manners' blended
with the sentiment of the earlier imitation ballad, and the
inspiration of these poets was in large measure Percy's *Reliques
of Ancient English Poetry* (3 volumes, 1765). We have seen that
the *Reliques* was not so much the beginning of ballad-collection,
and the imitation of the ballad which accompanied collection,
as the first climax in a well-established movement that suited
the taste and temper of the age. The *Reliques* exercised so powerful an influence partly because the age was ready for it and
partly because its contents were exceptionally well arranged
and were edited with anxious care.

Thomas Percy[1] was no mere antiquary. He was a man,
Johnson wrote to Boswell on 23 April 1778, 'out of whose company I never go without having learned something. . . . So much
extension of mind, and so much minute accuracy of enquiry, if
you survey your whole circle of acquaintance, you will find so
scarce, if you find it at all, that you will value Percy by comparison. . . . Percy's attention to poetry has given grace and
splendour to his studies of antiquity. A mere antiquarian is
a rugged being.' His favoured project was a collection to be
called 'Specimens of the ancient Poetry of different nations',
for which, he wrote to Evan Evans on 14 August 1762, he had
'gleaned up specimens of *East-Indian Poetry: Peruvian Poetry:
Lapland Poetry: Greenland Poetry*'. His inquiring mind had also
led him into other strangely varied studies, Spanish, Icelandic,
Hebrew, and Chinese. In 1761 he published *Hau Kiou Choaan,
or The Pleasing History*, and thereby became responsible for the
first translation of a Chinese novel into a European language.
Percy himself knew no Chinese; his source was a manuscript
three parts of which were in English and the fourth in Portuguese.
The work appeared at the height of the Chinese vogue, but no

---

[1] Thomas Percy (born Piercy), 1729–1811, the son of a Shropshire grocer, was
educated at Bridgnorth Grammar School and Christ Church, Oxford. The demands
of his country living at Easton Maudit, Northamptonshire (1753–82), and his
chaplaincy to the Duke of Northumberland and to the King allowed him opportunity to pursue his antiquarian and literary interests. These did not interfere
with his advancement in the Church, for he was appointed Dean of Carlisle in
1778 and Bishop of Dromore in 1782.

one would guess as much from turning over its pages. 'That there is a littleness and poverty of genius in almost all the Works of taste of the Chinese, must be acknowledged by capable judges': such is Percy's opinion. But leaving questions of taste aside, he offered the translation as 'a curious specimen of Chinese literature' and as 'a faithful picture of Chinese manners'; and that it might the better serve its purposes, it was accompanied by ample annotation, a bibliography of sources, and an index by which the curious might satisfy their interest in, for example, 'Beds of the *Chinese*; Beheading, how performed; Bells of the *Chinese* described; Betrothing, how practised; Birds-nests eaten; Birth-day, how celebrated'. To the novel Percy added, amongst other things, some fragments of Chinese poetry. He seems to have taken them from Du Halde's *Description de la Chine*, translated by Green and Guthrie (2 volumes, 1738–41), and to have made such improvements in rhythm as readers who admired Ossian's metrical prose would require. The reader of taste is not to expect much, since the Chinese show too great a fondness for affectation and little conceits, and they lack 'that noble simplicity, which is only to be attained by the genuine study of nature, and of its artless beauties'. Yet amongst so much affectation, Percy seems to have found at least one piece of evidence of such 'genuine study', and he proceeded to render it 'in the same kind of stanza with the original'. It is an 'elogium on the willow tree', and perhaps it was the more appreciated by its translator for the 'newness' of its imagery:

> Scarce dawns the genial year: its yellow sprays
> The sprightly willow cloaths in robes of green.
> Blushing with shame the gaudy peach is seen;
> She sheds her blossoms and with spleen decays.
> Soft harbinger of spring! What glowing rays,
> What colours with thy modest charms may vie?
> No silkworm decks thy shade; nor could supply
> The velvet down thy shining leaf displays.

This is a small but illuminating instance of the way in which Percy's taste and skill as a poet graced his antiquarian pursuits. For the most part the antiquary had been in charge, though restrained by the man of taste; and the same is true of his *Five Pieces of Runic Poetry Translated from the Islandic Language* (1763).

In that work the antiquary had had to mind his step, since comparison with the Ossianic fragments was inevitable; and while any doubt remained about their authenticity, it behoved Percy 'to be as exact as possible' in translation. But Icelandic poetry had suffered neglect because it had hitherto fallen into the hands of mere antiquaries interested solely in illustrating the history and antiquities of the country; whereas Percy's book should serve to 'unlock the treasures of native genius', present 'frequent sallies of bold imagination', and show 'the workings of the human mind in its almost original state of nature'.

But it is the *Reliques* that most clearly demonstrates this turning of Percy's mind on the poles of poetical taste and antiquarian learning. As an antiquary he was not only well equipped himself, but also kept in touch with all who could give him the best assistance: Richard Farmer, whose knowledge of Elizabethan literature was unrivalled, Thomas Warton, who was exceptionally well versed in medieval studies, Sir David Dalrymple (Lord Hailes), the best informed of the Scottish antiquaries, and several others, while Edward Lye, the greatest Anglo-Saxon scholar of the day, was a close neighbour. Johnson too sympathized with this aspect of Percy's work, recommended publication of Percy's precious folio manuscript upon which the *Reliques* was based, and wrote the dedication. In that dedication the nature of Johnson's interest is unmistakably clear, and it is one which Percy had expressed in the preface to his *Five Pieces of Runic Poetry*. Johnson wrote:

These poems are presented... not as labours of art, but as effusions of nature, shewing the first efforts of ancient genius, and exhibiting the customs and opinions of remote ages ... No active or comprehensive mind can forbear some attention to the reliques of antiquity: It is prompted by natural curiosity to survey the progress of life and manners, and to inquire by what gradations barbarity was civilized, grossness refined, and ignorance instructed.

But Percy was also a poet of the school of Shenstone. His imitation of a Scottish song and other little pieces sent to Shenstone for his miscellany show that he shared his mentor's taste for 'simplicity'; and it was Shenstone who insisted on keeping the balance in the *Reliques*. He was afraid that Percy's 'fondness for antiquity should tempt him to admit pieces that have no other sort of merit', and even that he might publish his ballads

without the 'improvements' needed to render them acceptable
to modern taste. But there was in fact no cause for anxiety.
Percy entertained a decent respect for Shenstone's taste and
judgement; he gave him a right of veto, and he listened to his
views on the arrangement of the contents: thus the assembling
of the Mad Songs in a group was Shenstone's idea. The folio
manuscript offered Percy, as he told Hailes, 'an infinite farrago
of ancient Songs, Ballads, Metrical Romances, Legends in verse
and poems of the low and popular kind: Some pretty correct,
others extremely mutilated and inaccurate'. In selection he
exercised good judgement. Not all the ballads in the folio manuscript were suitable for print, but of those that were he excluded
very few; and he followed his source book in admitting poems
of other kinds into each of his three series for the sake of contrast.
Some of these were 'modern attempts in the same kind', such
as 'William and Margaret', 'Jemmy Dawson', 'Colin and Lucy',
already mentioned, and some compositions of his own: 'The
Friar of Orders Gray', his pretty piece of patchwork, made from
Shakespearian fragments, to conclude the section of 'Ballads
that illustrate Shakespeare', and two verse translations he had
made from the Spanish, which he included to show that the
English were not the only people distinguished for their ancient
ballads. Other pieces included were 'little elegant pieces of the
lyric kind', many of them dating back to the sixteenth century.
A rigorous standard in editing Elizabethan texts had recently
been set by Edward Capell in his *Prolusions* (1760), and here
Percy took the greatest pains to secure the best text available.
Any reader of the *Reliques* who was fond of songs would have
been familiar with most of the Elizabethan lyrics Percy printed,
for they had appeared time and time again in modernized form
in the song books of the day; but this was the first time they had
appeared in their original freshness. His methods were different,
however, in preparing the texts of his ballads. What appeared
'extremely mutilated and inaccurate' called for plastic surgery.
About half the ballads he selected were printed more or less as
he found them, but in at least nine he made very substantial
alterations to which he drew attention in prefatory notes. His
methods were in keeping with contemporary practice, for it was
not until Joseph Ritson got busy at the end of this period that
the editorial standards of a Capell were extended to the ballad.
It might even be said that the nearer a ballad-collector drew to

the living source, the more likely he was to find it sophisticated, especially in Scotland where the ballad was still on the lips of cultivated people, who might reasonably feel it as much within their discretion to do their best by a ballad or a song as by a good story that had been told them. This question is raised again in the next chapter (see p. 153); for the present it is enough to say that Percy suspected Hailes of bestowing beauties on 'Edom of Gordon' and 'Gill Morris': it was 'not only an allowable freedom . . . but absolutely necessary to render them worth attention', and he encouraged both Hailes and Warton to assist in the surgery that he and Shenstone were practising.

There can be little doubt that they were justified in what they did for the contemporary reader; for as Shenstone said, 'trivial amendments in these old compositions often render them highly striking, which would be otherwise quite neglected'. What was printed must be complete, clear, and readable; and so, for example, the abruptness Percy found in 'Sir Aldingar' is removed by the insertion of nine stanzas (numbers 24 to 32 in the *Reliques* text) describing the journey made by 'one of the queenes damsèlles' to find a champion for her wronged mistress and her meeting with 'a tinye boye . . . all clad in mantle of golde', four stanzas (numbers 37 to 40) describing the preparations for burning the queen at the stake and the herald's announcement, and finally of two more (stanzas 53 and 54) to complete the narrative.

His additions to 'Sir Cauline' and 'The Child of Elle' were even more extensive, for here he was faced with two remarkable fragments which needed expansion if they were to be used at all. His principal invention in 'Sir Cauline' (the first sixteen and the last seventeen stanzas of the second part) shows once more the taste for a story of true lovers divided who find reunion only in their deaths, though in writing a conclusion for the unfinished 'Child of Elle' he allows the knight's valour its sentimental reward. In each the story proceeds without the abrupt transitions so typical of the old ballads; chivalrous ceremonies are added, and the crudely or tersely related episodes of the fragments are heightened in the interest of emotional effect. It surely makes for better story-telling that the Giant should at last be defeated by a 'stranger knighte', who turns out to be Sir Cauline in disguise, than that Sir Cauline should have been present all the time to rise and take up his sword at the King's

first request; but it is no longer possible to sympathize with the
search for simple emphasis that removed from 'The Child of
Elle' this imaginative vision of the lovers' parting:

> He leaned ore his saddle bow
> To kisse this Lady good;
> The teares that went them two between
> Were blend water and blood,

and substituted

> And thrice he clasped her to his breste,
> And kist her tenderlie:
> The teares that fell from her fair eyes
> Ranne like the fountayne free.

Later scholars have demurred. But it should not be forgotten
that it was precisely these two ballads that were particularly
admired by Percy's contemporaries and by the next generation.
'The Child of Elle' was singled out by the *Scots Magazine* in
reviewing the *Reliques* for 'the curious display of ancient manners, the affecting simplicity, and beautiful strokes of nature
and passion'; and 'Sir Cauline', from which Coleridge took
more than the name Christabelle, was commended by Wordsworth for its 'true simplicity and genuine pathos'.

The ballad was not the only form of narrative in vogue that
drew its inspiration from the past. 'It seems to be a very favourable era for the appearance of such irregular poetry' was Shenstone's comment when his friend MacGowan sent him from
Edinburgh a copy of what he called 'the Erse fragments'. These
were translations, or what purported to be translations, from
the Gaelic done by James Macpherson in 1759 at the request of
John Home to give him some impression of the nature and
quality of Gaelic poetry.[1] Home had shown the fragments to
Hugh Blair who was then preparing his first course of lectures

---

[1] James Macpherson, 1736–96, was a native of Inverness-shire who had studied
at Aberdeen and Edinburgh. His Ossianic adventures belonged to his youth, but
he was never free from the controversy about the authenticity of his Gaelic originals
even though he had long since passed on to other affairs. He engaged in historical
writing, 1771–9, wrote in defence of Lord North's ministry, and served both as
Member of Parliament for Camelford, 1780–96, and as agent to the nabob of
Arcot, 1781.

on Rhetoric and Belles-Lettres at Edinburgh University, and
Blair had been so much impressed by them as to persuade
Macpherson to publish them in 1760, to write an introduction
to the book himself, and to promote a subscription in Edinburgh
for Macpherson's expenses in travelling to remote parts of Scotland in search of more. Macpherson, who was then a young
man of twenty-four, set off on his travels and returned to Edinburgh in a few months' time with the 'epic' he had discovered
in the north. He took lodgings close to Blair, translated it, and
published it in 1762 with the title, *Fingal, an Ancient Epic Poem,
in Six Books: together with several other poems, composed by Ossian the
son of Fingal, Translated from the Galic Language.*

There was plenty of Gaelic ballad poetry to be found in the
Highlands by anyone sufficiently well equipped for the task.
Some eight or nine manuscript collections existed, of which the
best known is the Book of the Dean of Lismore compiled in the
early sixteenth century; and ballads also survived on the lips
of singers, some of them attributed to Oiséan (Ossian), who
recalled in his old age the mighty deeds of his father Fionn
(Fingal), 'a champion great and swift, nimble on a battlefield;
a hawk bright and wise, a sage in every art'. Furthermore it was
a great age of Gaelic poetry. Alasdair Mac Mhaighstir Alasdair
(Alexander Macdonald) had published a volume of his poems at
Edinburgh in 1751 proudly entitled *Aiseiridhna Sean Chanoin
Albannaich* (The Resurrection of the Ancient Scottish Language)
—it was the first book to be printed in Gaelic—and he had
declared in the preface, written in English, that his intention was
not merely to raise a desire of learning a language which contains 'in its bosom the charms of poetry and rhetoric', but 'to
bespeak, if possible, the favour of the public, to a greater collection of poems of the same sort . . . from those of the earliest
composition to modern times . . . with a translation into *English*
verse, and critical observations on the nature of such writings'.
Macdonald's project came to nothing, but another attempt was
soon begun. Jerome Stone, a graduate of St. Andrews and
Rector of Dunkeld Academy, wrote to the *Scots Magazine* on
15 November 1755, drawing attention to 'a great number of
poetical compositions in [the *Irish* language] . . . some of them
of very great antiquity, whose merit intitles them to an exemp-
tion from the unfortunate neglect, or rather abhorrence, to
which ignorance has subjected that emphatic and venerable

language in which they were composed'. He goes on to commend them for

sublimity of sentiment, nervousness of expression, and high-spirited metaphors . . . hardly to be equalled among the chief productions of the most cultivated nations. Others of them breathe such tenderness and simplicity as must be greatly affecting to every mind that is in the least tinctured with the softer passions of pity and humanity.

To this encomium is appended a translation, for which Stone begged an apology if any reader were offended by 'the uncommon turn of several expressions' and 'the seeming extravagance in some of the comparisons' that he had attempted to preserve. The 'old tale, translated from the Irish' by Stone and by him entitled 'Albin and the Daughter of Mey' exists in many versions. Whoever cares to compare Stone's rendering with the modern prose translation of Dr. Neil Ross, in his edition of *Heroic Poetry from the Book of the Dean of Lismore* (No. xxix), will recognize how faithfully Stone has followed his source, though the unlucky choice of a ten-line stanza of interlinking rhymes encouraged expansion of phrase and luxuriance of sentiment, qualities more appropriate to a Spenserian imitation than to a ballad. If Stone had continued, the English reader might eventually have had as scholarly a version of the Ossianic ballads as the times allowed; but his early death in 1756 prevented this. The future lay with the more reckless genius of Macpherson.

Macpherson undoubtedly knew some Gaelic. He travelled widely and had transcripts made of ballads that he heard. He may even have handled the Book of the Dean of Lismore, though its palaeographical obscurities have taxed more patient and better equipped investigators. When he returned to Edinburgh to write *Fingal*, he can be proved to have had more than a dozen ballads before him. It has been shown that he combined two to provide himself with the outline of his plot, and that he drew upon three more for his main episodes. It has also been shown that he misread his sources and misrepresented them in many respects. But he was certainly responsive to the melancholy of a battlefield such as that of Gabhra; a sight which led the bard to exclaim that he had never since closed his eyes in sleep nor ceased to heave a sigh by night or day. His versions, too, show that he relished such peculiarly vivid word-painting as when the bard claims that his warrior was swifter than a river's cascade, or a hawk swooping upon a bird-flock.

Macpherson's motives cannot be established with any confidence. He lived in an age when men of taste and learning, like Shenstone and Percy, felt they were justified in dressing the work of a past age so as to appeal to modern sensibilities, arguing on the analogy of a sculptor who supplies an antique statue with a missing limb. It was an age, too, in which men and women amused themselves with imitating ancient workmanship, and were ready to pass off a fabricated ruin as a tasteful and modish jest, or even to pretend (as Chatterton was to do) that a fabricated poem was a genuine discovery. It is reasonable to suppose that Macpherson was similarly affected. Perhaps ignorance and excessive confidence combined to encourage his claim in the preface to his first volume, *Fragments of Ancient Poetry . . . translated from the Gaelic* (1760), that 'the translation is extremely literal'; but even in that volume there is evidence of still another shading in his motivation. 'Though the poems now published appear as detached pieces in this collection, there is ground to believe that most of them were originally episodes of a greater work which related to the wars of Fingal', and a work furthermore that 'deserved to be styled an heroic poem'. When additional ballads relating to Fingal were discovered on his travels, it is easy to imagine him deceiving himself into supposing that the hand of Time had mangled a work that had once been as coherent as the *Iliad*, and that it was not beyond his powers to restore it. Thus his business was, in the words of the summary reached by Henry Mackenzie's committee of investigation in 1805,

to supply chasms, and to give connection, by inserting passages which he did not find, and to add what he conceived to be dignity and delicacy to the original composition, by striking out passages, by softening incidents, by refining the language, in short by changing what he considered as too simple or too rude for a modern ear, and elevating what in his opinion was below the standard of good poetry.

In his second Ossianic epic, *Temora* (1763), he seems to have felt more confidence. Subsequent investigators have not been able to discover more than one Gaelic ballad which he used as source material. By this time he was moving more freely in a world of his own imagining, a world of bravery and loss in battle, of tender sentiments and romantic love, set in a scene where torrents descend from mist-clad mountains to a rocky wind-swept shore.

The standard by which he wanted his workmanship judged is obvious both in the preface and in the notes to *Fingal*. 'How far it comes up to the rules of the epopœa, is the province of criticism to examine' he remarks in the preface, adding with brazen impudence 'it is only my business to lay it before the reader, as I have found it'; in the notes he draws attention to parallels in the imagery of Homer, Virgil, and Milton that he had been at pains to introduce.

The reconstruction in *Fingal* had been done in accordance with the best critical principles of the time. When Blair came to examine it, he was delighted to find 'the fire and the enthusiasm of the most early times, combined with an amazing degree of regularity and art'. How gratifying to discover that one's native country had produced a genius comparable with Homer! 'Examined even according to Aristotle's rules, it would be found to have all the essential requisites of a true and regular epic': that was Blair's judgement, and the initial astonishment that the Celtic bard should appear so well versed in Aristotle vanished before the sound neo-classical reflection: 'Aristotle studied nature in Homer. Homer and Ossian both wrote from nature. No wonder that among all the three, there should be such agreement and conformity.'

But more satisfying to Blair than the regularity of *Fingal* was the primitivism of its sentiments. It was written in an early age of the world when imagination was known to predominate over understanding and refinement. Here indeed was the fierceness expected at such a time; but how remarkable and how delightful to discover an even greater degree of tenderness and delicacy of sentiment! Ossian's poetry

breathes nothing of the gay and cheerful kind; an air of solemnity and seriousness is diffused over the whole . . . He moves perpetually in the high region of the grand and the pathetic. One key-note is struck at the beginning, and supported to the end; nor is any ornament introduced, but what is perfectly concordant with the general tone or melody. The events recorded are all serious and grave; the scenery throughout, wild and romantic. The extended heath by the seashore; the mountain shaded with mist; the torrent rushing through a solitary valley; the scattered oaks, and the tombs of warriors overgrown with moss; all produce a solemn attention in the mind, and prepare it for great and extraordinary events . . . His poetry, more perhaps than that of any other writer, deserves to be styled, *The poetry of the Heart.* It is a heart penetrated with noble sentiments, and with sublime and tender passions; a heart that glows, and kindles the fancy; a heart that is full, and pours itself forth.

There were disbelievers, of course: doubting Thomases, like Dr. Johnson, who wanted to handle the original manuscript, critics like Hurd, who regarded Macpherson's citation of parallel passages as evidence of what he had foisted on the reader, and Beattie, who looked in vain for the distinguishing traits of character to which Homer had accustomed him. The controversy indeed became very stormy. But Blair's encomium represents the response of many readers. They seemed able to overlook the rhapsody and incoherence, the gravest of Macpherson's artistic faults, in favour of the tenderness and pathos, and of his intoxicating display of the sublime:

Weep on the rocks of roaring winds, O maid of Inistore! Bend thy fair head over the waves, thou lovelier than the ghost of the hills,—when it moves, in a sun beam, at noon, over the silence of Morven! He is fallen! thy youth is low! pale beneath the sword of Cuthullin! No more shall valour raise thy love to match the blood of kings. Trenar, graceful Trenar, died, O maid of Inistore! His grey dogs are howling at home; they see his passing ghost. His bow is in the hall unstrung. No sound is in the hill of his hinds!

Heady stuff, which seemed to supply just that new source of manners and imagery that was felt to be lacking in the poetry of the day! It was Macpherson's distinction to have fixed upon the minds of English readers, and indeed of European readers, an image of Celtic twilight that has been very difficult to eradicate.

The heat of the Ossianic controversy had not abated before another dispute arose. Some poems, believed to be the work of Thomas Rowley, a fifteenth-century monk, and his associates, were said to have been discovered by Thomas Chatterton[1] in

---

[1] Thomas Chatterton, 1752-70, was the posthumous son of a Bristol schoolmaster. At fourteen and a half he was apprenticed to an attorney, and soon after began to create pedigrees and coats of arms for his acquaintances, and to supply the credulous local antiquaries with documents relating to the history of Bristol which he said he had found with other manuscripts in a chest in St. Mary Redcliffe.

a chest in St. Mary Redcliffe church at Bristol. Chatterton himself had committed suicide in August 1770 at the age of seventeen. Before his death he had offered some of these poems to
Dodsley and Walpole, but he had secured the publication of
only one of them, 'Elinoure and Juga', which appeared in *The
Town and Country Magazine* in May 1769. The remaining Rowley
poems survived in Chatterton's manuscript or in transcript in
the hands of two Bristol acquaintances to whom Chatterton
had disposed of them. One, *Bristowe Tragedy*, was separately
published in 1772; the remainder were collected and carefully
edited in 1777 by Thomas Tyrwhitt, who two years earlier had
begun to publish his important edition of the *Canterbury Tales*.
It says much for the excitement of the supposed discovery that
a distinguished Chaucerian scholar should step aside to edit
them. Gray, Warton, and Percy immediately recognized that
the poems were fabrications; but Tyrwhitt was at first inclined
to believe in their authenticity, and to the unscholarly it
seemed incredible that such things should be the work of a lad
of sixteen or less.

To the modern reader the Rowley poems present a rather
different response to the Middle Ages from anything previously
mentioned in this chapter. Warton and Percy worked from the
plenitude of their erudition. Percy was so deeply conversant
with ballad literature that he was convinced he could supply
what was lacking in a fragmentary text; Warton re-created
historical situations, and put into the mouths of singers modern
words to represent the thoughts they might have expressed.
Macpherson satisfied what seems to have been his wish, to
present in a recognizably coherent form a Scottish epic based
upon some of the fragments he discovered. Chatterton lived
more freely than any of them in a little world of his own
imagining. His poetic impulse came less from a world which the
study of books and manuscripts revealed to him, than from
a world whose relics he could see and touch, a church and its
furniture, parchment, and black letter. He read, of course;
and his poems show how he responded to his reading; but he
learned less from the poets of the age he pretended to inhabit

---

The earliest poems attributed by Chatterton to Rowley seem to date from 1764. In
1768 he offered copies to Dodsley without response. In 1770 he decided to seek
his fortunes in London as a free-lance writer, and committed suicide there a few
months later, seemingly in despair over his poverty.

than from Spenser and from Spenser's contemporaries, from Dryden, and even from Collins and Gray.

His notion of the Middle Ages was derived primarily from St. Mary Redcliffe, in whose shadow his youth was spent. It is a church which in size and splendour is calculated to create awe and delight. That was enough; no knowledge of the history of architecture was needed to observe that the church had been restored in the fifteenth century by William Canynges, a merchant and five times mayor of Bristol, whose fine alabaster monument still survives. It was a small step to raise Canynges to Medicean stature, to make of him a patron of all the arts, including poetry, and to imagine him at the centre of a society, provincial indeed, but heroic in impulse and magnificent in display, with a poet, Thomas Rowley, to appreciate it and record it for posterity.

This was the young Chatterton's dream. As Rowley, he can testify in verse picked up from Percy's *Reliques* to the processional splendour in the streets of Bristol as Syr Charles Bawdin is led to execution; he can also sympathize in his assumed character with the sufferings of the common people in 'the Baronnes warre', and look back regretfully on the simple pleasures of peace:

> The swote ribible dynning yn the dell,
> The joyous daunceynge ynn the hoastrie court;

and he can endow his fifteenth-century poet with an eighteenth-century sensibility that responds to the sublime in describing the thunderstorm in Rowley's best poem, 'An Excelente Balade of Charitie':

> Liste! now the thunder's rattling clymmynge sound
> Cheves slowlie on, and then embollen clangs,
> Shakes the hie spyre, and losst, dispended, drown'd,
> Still on the gallard eare of terroure hanges;
> The windes are up; the lofty elmen swanges;
> Again the levynne and the thunder poures,
> And the full cloudes are braste attenes in stonen showers—

lines which show, incidentally, that Chatterton can use his fabricated vocabulary with the vigour and conviction of a modern Scottish poet writing in Lallans.[1]

[1] Chatterton glosses the following words in the passages quoted above: ribible = violin; dynning = sounding; hoastrie = inn, or public-house; clymmynge = noisy; cheves = moves; embollen = swelled, strengthened; gallard = frighted; braste = burst.

But though he chose the fifteenth century for the period when most of his poems were written, his principal characters, Rowley and his patron Canynge (as Chatterton prefers to call him), are themselves inspired by the deeds of earlier days. Canynge meditating beside the Avon recalls 'how onne the bankes thereof brave Ælla foughte . . . who ever and anon made Danes to blede', Ælla, whose death is celebrated in Rowley's longest and most ambitious piece, 'Ælla: a tragycal enterlude, or discoorseynge tragedie . . . plaiedd before Mastre Canynge, atte hys howse nempte the Rodde Lodge'. Remarkable as this interlude is in its metrical virtuosity—the 'mynstrelles songe' fully deserves the place it has gained in so many anthologies—its heroics too plainly derive from the gestures of characters on the modern stage; and though it is clear that the author of the 'Songe to Ælla' is living in a medieval world of his own imagining, he has been helped to express it by poets of a later time. Drayton gives him a hint at one point, and Collins guides him at another both in phrase and rhythm. But Chatterton had his answer ready to the objection that his versification owed much to the Elizabethans and their successors: 'the Stanza Rowley wrote in, instead of being introduc'd by Spenser was in use 300 Years before'; and doubtless he would have made a similar answer to those who were surprised to find a fifteenth-century poet writing interludes and Elizabethan eclogues. To put his argument on a broader basis, it was Rowley who first taught later poets their trade. This is a child's argument; but it serves to show how possessed he was of his own dream-world, and the readiness with which he was prepared to meet a mere antiquarian attack upon it.

Chatterton lived long enough to write in another manner, more easily recognizable by contemporary readers. Nothing of Rowley's genius spills over into these poems, and they merely indicate how completely the boy had been able to withdraw into a world whose characters, their life, language, and rhythm, were utterly familiar to him. It is not a purely medieval world; it is a world with some medieval features improved upon by a writer with eighteenth-century sensibilities. If he had been born forty years later, Chatterton might have written his 'Eve of St. Agnes' without attempt at deceit. But he seems to have recognized that contemporary interest in the Middle Ages was antiquarian; readers were ready to accept new documents, but in that enlightened age they were reluctant to contemplate an artist seeking his inspiration in the barbarity of the past, except by way of jest, or to provide a touch of rococo decoration, or to procure a melancholy but picturesque reminder of the passage of time. In those circumstances Chatterton could only offer his poems as genuine antiquarian relics. It was an impossible situation. He was doomed to be detected, and at the end of his short life he was already waking from his Rowleyan dream.

It is not surprising that when Chatterton turned to writing poetry of a modern cast he should have modelled himself upon Churchill, for no other poet of the day could have seemed more obviously brilliant, energetic, and fertile. In his chosen field of satire, he commanded an individuality of voice that had not been heard, except in *The Vanity of Human Wishes*, since the death of Pope.

It is a limitation of the literary historian that in his concern to trace originality in venture, he passes rapidly over scores of able writers who were content to handle the measures of their immediate predecessors. This is especially noticeable when we come to consider satirists writing in the middle of the century. 'Not to go back, is somewhat to advance': that was a maxim of Pope's that satirists may be said to have adopted as they meditated upon the achievements of Pope and Prior. But the literary historian's maxim is the reverse of theirs: 'not to advance, is somewhat to go back'; and in that sense, but in that sense only, he must record a decline in verse satire at this time. The form itself retained its appeal not merely to writers concerned in political controversy, but to all who took an interest in contemporary society and in the behaviour of their fellow men. If this were a history of manners or of taste, writers such as James Cawthorn, Christopher Anstey, or Churchill himself would figure largely. Their eyes were open, and their wits were supple. Between them they present us with a varied and complex image of contemporary society. We see members of the aristocracy laying out their grounds in accordance with the newest taste, disporting themselves at gaming tables and losing vast stakes at Newmarket, patronizing poets, and employing chaplains; we see the middle classes aping their social superiors, retiring into the country, admiring the latest *chinoiserie*,

recovering their battered healths at watering-places and falling
victims to the spongers who infested those towns; we have the
peculiar habits of Methodists drawn to our attention, and are
taught to recognize the professional incompetence of doctors,
lawyers, clergymen, and actors.

The social historian has also a legitimate interest in the
writers who provide a variety of perspectives upon contemporary society. Some, like poor Chatterton, lived in Grub Street;
others, like James Cawthorn and Robert Lloyd, were school-
masters; the two Whiteheads possessed sufficient means to live
without depending upon what they wrote; while Soame Jenyns,
Christopher Anstey, and Richard Owen Cambridge were men
of substance who lived a cultivated life on their country estates,
representatives of a second 'Mob of Gentlemen who wrote with
Ease'. Cambridge's son, a prebendary of Ely, tells us—what
indeed we might deduce from the poet's verse—that his father[1]
was 'rather an elegant than a profound scholar'; nevertheless
'there were few works of the ancients of any reputation, with
which he was not conversant'. Like Pope, 'he was fond of shewing the uniformity of human nature in all ages, by the ready
application of passages in ancient writers to modern manners
and the most recent events'; and in witness of this we may
read and enjoy his 'Dialogue between a Member of Parliament
and his Servant, in Imitation of the 7th Satire of the Second
Book of Horace' (1752) and 'The Intruder. In Imitation of
Horace, Book I, Satire IX' (1754), where a descendant of
Horace's insufferable bore attaches himself to the poet on a
walk to Lambeth. In the first of these there is a brief character
of Prue, a female Methodist,

> Who gives the morning church its due,
> At noon is painted, drest and curl'd,
> And one amongst the wicked world:
> Keeps her account exactly even
> As thus: Prue, Creditor with heaven,
> By sermons heard on extra days:
> Debtor: To masquerades and plays.
> Item: By Whitfield, half an hour:
> Per Contra: To the Colonel, four.

[1] Richard Owen Cambridge, 1717–1802, a gentleman of independent means,
lived on his estates in Gloucestershire, and later, near Twickenham. He was one of
the most valued contributors to Moore's lively periodical, the *World*.

This is enough to justify the Prebendary in remarking that his father's 'insight into men was correct, judicious, and acute; he viewed with the eye of a philosopher the influence of the passions, not only in the great and leading points of human conduct, but in the trifling incidents of common life'. He assures us, however, though the reader of Cambridge needs little assurance, that 'the follies of mankind excited his mirth rather than his spleen . . . his vein of comic humour was ever regulated by that native benevolence, which would not allow him voluntarily to inflict the slightest pain'. The life of such a man, who was also a good landlord and a hospitable host, provides an amiable testimony to the society that produced him.

But the literary critic, rigorously exercising his function, is obliged to express some measure of dissatisfaction. He responds, for example, to the liveliness of Cawthorn's[1] picture of the invasion of *haute cuisine* upon the English table (*c.* 1755):

> Time was, a wealthy Englishman would join
> A rich plumb-pudding to a fat sirloin;
> Or bake a pasty, whose enormous wall
> Took up almost the area of his hall:
> But now, as art improves, and life refines,
> The demon Taste attends him when he dines;
> Serves on his board an elegant regale,
> Where three stew'd mushrooms flank a larded quail;
> Where infant turkeys, half a month resign'd
> To the soft breathings of a southern wind,
> And smother'd in a rich ragout of snails,
> Outstink a lenten supper at Versailes.
> Is there a saint that would not laugh to see
> The good man piddling with his fricassee;
> Forc'd by the luxury of taste to drain
> A flask of poison, which he calls champagne!
> While he, poor idiot! though he dare not speak,
> Pines all the while for porter and ox-cheek.

There is no questioning the appropriateness in choice of verse form, and the couplets are handled with practised competence, derived from careful study of Pope, whose *Imitations of Horace*

---

[1] James Cawthorn, 1719–61, completed a career in school-teaching by becoming Headmaster of Tonbridge School, *c.* 1743.

are persistently echoed in phrase and rhetorical structure. We might believe that this was Pope repeating himself at a level below his best.

Nor is there any question of Robert Lloyd's[1] propriety in choosing the octosyllabic to tell his amusing little story ('The Cit's Country Box', 1757) of the city merchant who bought a small place in the country and had to submit to his wife's redecorating it in the latest fashion. There

> The trav'ler with amazement sees
> A temple, Gothic, or Chinese,
> With many a bell, and tawdry rag on,
> And crested with a sprawling dragon;
> A wooden arch is bent astride
> A ditch of water, four foot wide,
> With angles, curves, and zigzag lines,
> From Halfpenny's exact designs.

Clearly Lloyd has learned almost all that Prior could teach him about the art of making the octosyllabics of *Hudibras* suave and genteel. But he has learned little more, and was perfectly content, as his friend Wilkes said of him, 'to scamper round the foot of Parnassus on his little Welch poney'.

The Dunciad seemed to offer an admirable model for excursions into burlesque and for exercises in self-defence. So it was used, entertainingly, by Paul Whitehead in *The Gymnasiad: or, Boxing Match* (1744) to describe in mock-epic terms a contest between Stephenson the Coachman and Broughton the Waterman, and by Christopher Smart in *The Hilliad* (1753) to ridicule the follies of Dr. John Hill, a notorious quack and hack writer. But it would be vain, and perhaps absurd, to expect in either any trace of concern for those larger issues by whose treatment *The Dunciad* is distinguished.

But in Churchill's[2] work there is a difference. It is obvious that he was well read both in Dryden, whom he commends, and in Pope, whom he professes to depreciate. The generous

---

[1] Robert Lloyd, 1733-64, after a short career as a schoolmaster, became an unprosperous professional author.

[2] Charles Churchill, 1732-64, succeeded his father as curate of St. John's, Westminster, in 1758 and resigned in 1763. His friendship with Wilkes engaged him in political controversy, and together they shared the responsibility for attacks upon the government in the *North Briton*.

tones of Dryden are heard in the vigorous opening of *An Epistle to William Hogarth* (1763):

> Amongst the sons of men how few are known
> Who dare be just to merit not their own!

While the peculiar turns of Pope's rhetoric and the echoes of his phrases appear so frequently as to be illustrated three times within thirty lines of one poem (*The Apology*, 1761):

> How doth it make judicious readers smile,
> When authors are detected by their stile . . .
> What had I done, that angry *Heaven* should send
> The bitt'rest Foe, where most I wish'd a Friend . . .
> Rude and unskilful in the Poet's trade,
> I kept no Naiads by me ready-made . . .

all of which have their origin in the *Epistle to Dr. Arbuthnot*. Furthermore *The Rosciad* (1761), the first of his poems to take the town by storm, has some obvious affinities with *The Dunciad* (though more with that favourite form, 'the Session of the Poets'), and in *The Conference* (1763) the poet who most closely resembles Pope in the employment of a poetical *persona* adopts the device of dialogue for self-justification that Pope had used so successfully in the *Epilogue to the Satires*. In fact, there is much in Churchill that is merely traditional, and in a writer so prolific much that is not deeply considered. He affected a carelessness for poetic art. Thus in *Gotham* (1764) he declared (ii. 165 ff.) that

> Had I the pow'r, I could not have the time,
> Whilst spirits flow, and Life is in her prime,
> Without a sin 'gainst Pleasure, to design
> A plan, to methodize each thought, each line
> Highly to finish, and make ev'ry grace,
> In itself charming, take new charms from place.

But even this passage shows an attempt to explore rhythms beyond the bounds of the closed couplet. The epigram held little appeal for him; he preferred to organize his work loosely over a series of paragraphs, throwing off parenthetical asides as he wrote. He seems to have admired the method he discerned in the apparent confusion of *Tristram Shandy*, then in course of publication,

> Where each *Digression*, seeming vain
> And only fit to entertain,
> Is found, on better recollection,
> To have a just and nice Connection,
> To help the whole with wond'rous art,
> Whence it seems idly to depart,

and attempted to apply it to his own work (*The Ghost*, iii. 971ff.). He knew how to condense his writing to a brief character, as *The Rosciad* amply testifies, and as he shows to even better purpose in these devastating lines from *The Author* (1763):

> Grown old in villainy, and dead to grace,
> Hell in his heart, and *Tyburne* in his face;
> Behold, a Parson at thy Elbow stands,
> Low'ring damnation, and with open hands
> Ripe to betray his Saviour for reward;
> The Atheist Chaplain of an Atheist Lord.

But he preferred a more loosely controlled organization, apparent in the *Epistle to William Hogarth* with its gradually mounting indignation exploding at last upon Hogarth's name (l. 309), a brilliant rhetorical structure. An even more favourable specimen of this is *The Candidate* (1764), a mock-panegyric on the vicious Lord Sandwich, who was standing for election as High Steward of the University of Cambridge. The former topics of the poet's satire are dismissed in turn with a paragraph for each—enough of actors, authors, critics, Scotland, self-styled patriots—while he woos panegyric in extended irony. In this poem he adopted the unusual device of a character setting out the profligacy of his protagonist under the name of Lothario, whom he contemptuously dismisses with the reflection that Nature

> having brought *Lothario* forth to view
> To save her credit, brought forth *Sandwich* too.

This is a device which could scarcely be repeated, and in his last and best poem, the posthumously published 'Dedication' to Bishop Warburton of a volume of *Sermons* (1765), Churchill wrote an even more masterly mock-panegyric without recourse to it. In this poem too he shows what an interesting effect may be achieved by leaving open a couplet that convention might

tempt to close. The melancholy afterthought appended to the
third couplet in the following passage has been justly admired:

> Bred to the Law, you wisely took the gown,
> Which I, like Demas, foolishly laid down.
> Hence double strength our Holy Mother drew;
> Me she got rid of, and made prize of you.
> I, like an idle Truant, fond of play,
> Doting on toys, and throwing gems away,
> Grasping at shadows, let the substance slip.

One can scarcely doubt that Pope would have contented
himself with the couplet, and that Dryden would have extended
the last line to an alexandrine rhyming with its two predecessors; in either case the note of pathos would have been less
distinct.

The loosening of the couplet's precision in Churchill's
verse is one sign of the cultivation of a less elegant manner in
satire that becomes more apparent as the century proceeds.
There is no need to spend time on Anstey's *New Bath Guide*
(1766).[1] It was fashionable to admire it: even so fastidious a
reader as Gray could commend its 'original kind of humour',
though now it seems the merest fribble. But the anacreontic
measure is not unsuitable for retailing the gossip of a country
squire's visit to Bath, and its popularity no doubt contributed
to the relaxation in satiric form which we are noticing. Its
rhythm may have been ringing in Garrick's head when he
produced that mock-epitaph on Goldsmith which provoked
Retaliation (1774) to the selfsame tune:

> Here lies Nolly Goldsmith, for shortness call'd Noll,
> Who wrote like an angel, but talk'd like poor Poll;

but we should recollect that by this time the spirited verses
that Gray had written in 1764 on 'sly Jemmy Twitcher's'
candidature for the High Stewardship of Cambridge University had begun to circulate, showing better than Anstey could
what merits the anacreontic line possessed for sketching characters.

The opportunities offered by the ballad for political propaganda and satire have already been mentioned (pp. 95-6), and

---

[1] Christopher Anstey, 1724-1805, made his reputation by his *New Bath Guide*,
and went to live permanently in that city in 1770.

it has been shown how susceptible the form had become both
to sentimental and to ironic treatment. The same fate befell the
great ode. Its sublimities could no more escape mockery than
admiration; and in the wake of parody followed satire. No
form lent itself so readily to use at a time of relaxation in satirical modes. Gray's 'Bard', 'The Progress of Poesy', and Mason's
Odes seemed to invite parody, and they received it from Robert
Lloyd and George Colman the elder who collaborated in *Two
Odes, To Obscurity* (directed chiefly at Gray) and *To Oblivion*
(directed at Mason), 1760. The mockery has no political complexion; but it was not long before Mason himself was using
the ode for this very purpose. Most of his satires, written between 1773 and 1779, are a reversion to the manner of Pope,
from whose poems he filches a phrase or two from time to
time. They are a good deal more lively than the rest of Mason's
verse, and excited much attention at the time, but they need
not detain us. More original are the quizzical *Ode to Mr.
Pinchbeck, upon his newly invented patent candle-snuffers* (1776), and
Ode to the Naval Officers of Great Britain (1779), a laboured
experiment in invoking the sublime in the service of satire.

The *Ode to the Naval Officers* prompted no imitation, but the
Ode to Mr. Pinchbeck was a portent of what was to come. When
the Poet Laureate, William Whitehead, died in 1785, the
wits who had happily promoted one ingenious frolic in *Criticisms on the Rolliad, a Poem* (1784),[1] collaborated in another.
They imagined a kind of session of aspirants for the vacant
laureateship, all of whom—such was the intensity of the struggle
to succeed to Whitehead's honours—were required to submit
an ode in evidence of their powers. These *Probationary Odes*
were duly collected and published in 1785, with a preliminary
discourse from a most suitable pen, that of the recent historian
of music, Sir John Hawkins, Kt. Hawkins was made to declare
that

the fire of Lyric Poesy, the rapid lightning of modern Pindarics,
were equally required to record the virtues of the Stuarts, or to
immortalize the Talents of a Brunswick, [since] on either theme there

---

[1] This was a mock-commentary, with ample illustrative extracts, from a fictitious
epic poem, *The Rolliad*, on the exploits of imaginary ancestors of John Rolle,
Member of Parliament for Devonshire. Pitt was the real target. The principal
collaborators were Joseph Richardson, Richard Tickell, French Laurence, and
George Ellis.

was ample subject for the boldest flights of inventive genius, the fullest scope for the most daring power of poetical creation, from the
free unfettered strain of liberty in honour of Charles the First, to the
kindred Genius and congenial Talents that immortalize the Wisdom
and the Worth of George the Third.

Warming to their task, the wits provided some 'thoughts on
Ode writing kindly communicated by the Revd. Thomas
Warton' (together with a true account of his ascent in a balloon
from Christ Church meadow for the purpose of composing
a sublime ode), and testimonials in favour of the candidates
from Boswell, Hannah More, Lord Monboddo, and others.
Amongst the poems contributed is found an 'Irregular Ode
by Mr. Mason' almost indistinguishable in absurdity from a
genuine Mason, a 'Duan, in the True Ossian Sublimity' by
Macpherson, an offering from Sir Nathaniel Wraxall, who
had obviously been studying 'The Bard':

> Murrain seize the House of Commons!
> Hoarse catarrh their windpipes shake!
> Who, deaf to travell'd Learning's summons,
> Rudely cough'd whene'er I spake!

and—prize exhibit—a submission from no less a candidate than
Thurlow, the formidable Lord Chancellor, a splendid specimen
of the mock-sublime:

> Damnation seize ye all,
> Who puff, who thrum, who bawl and squall!
> Fir'd with ambitious hopes in vain,
> The wreath, that blooms for other brows to gain;
>   Is Thurlow yet so little known?—
>   By G——d I swore, while *George* shall reign,
>   The seals, in spite of changes, to retain,
> Nor quit the Woolsack till he quits the Throne!
> And now, the Bays for life to wear,
> Once more, with mightier oaths, by G——d I swear!
> Bend my black brows that keep the Peers in awe,
> Shake my full-bottom wig, and give the nod of Law.

The prize nevertheless went to Tom Warton, who had then to
suffer the attention of other wits, for there was no difficulty in
learning the lesson so engagingly taught by the authors of
Probationary Odes.

Chief of these was John Wolcot,[1] who wrote under the name of 'Peter Pindar'. Peter attempted traditional forms of satire, such as the heroi-comical poem (*The Lousiad*, 1785-95, on the emotions experienced by George III at discovering a louse on his dinner-plate), and the verse epistle in couplets (*A Poetical Epistle to James Boswell, Esq. on his Journal of a Tour to the Hebrides*, 1786); but his characteristic manner is seen to best advantage in the satirical ode. Whereas the *Probationary Odes* are burlesque, Peter affects a sort of careless good-humour as he mocks at his victims. This is apparent already in the *Lyric Odes* with which he taunted the Royal Academicians in 1782 and subsequent years; but in 1787 he became more venturesome, and began to teach Warton how to do his duty as Poet Laureate.

> Know, Reader, that the *Laureat*'s Post sublime
> Is destin'd to record, in handsome Rhyme,
> The Deeds of Monarchs, twice a year:
> If *great*—how happy is the tuneful Tongue!
> If *pitiful*—(as Shakespeare says) the Song
> 'Must suckle Fools and chronicle Small Beer';

and therefore, why not record what happened when George III visited Whitbread's brewery? Peter will show the Laureate how it should be done:

> And now his curious Majesty did stoop
> To count the nails on ev'ry hoop:
> And lo! no single thing came in his way
> That full of deep research, he did not say
> 'What's this? hæ, hæ? what's that? what's this? what's
>   that?'
> So quick the words too, when he deign'd to speak,
> As if each syllable would break its neck. . . .
> Now Mr. Whitbread, serious, did declare,
> To make the Majesty of England stare,
> That he had butts enough, he knew,
> Plac'd side by side, would reach along to Kew:

---

[1] John Wolcot, 1738-1819, practised the cure of bodies and of souls first in Jamaica and later in Devon and Cornwall. He moved to London in 1778, and at the same time abandoned his professions for literature.

On which the King with wonder swiftly cry'd,
'What? if they reach to Kew then, side by side,
  What would they do plac'd end to end?'
To whom, with knitted calculating brow,
The Man of Beer mostly solemnly did vow,
  Almost to Windsor that they would extend;
On which the King, with *wond'ring* mien,
Repeated it unto the *wond'ring* Queen;

On which, quick turning round his halter'd head,
The brewer's horse with face astonish'd neigh'd;
The brewer's dog too pour'd a note of thunder,
Rattled his chain, and wagg'd his tale for wonder.

Thus a distorted image of George III is preserved for us by the almost affectionately contemptuous attention of a caricaturist. Peter's work in its rapidity, absurdity, and vitality is the literary counterpart of the etchings of his exact contemporary, James Gillray.

The dignity of Juvenalian satire was to be restored by William Gifford, whose *Baviad* (1791) and *Maeviad* (1795) are mentioned in the next volume. The laxer mode was to be continued in the *Anti-Jacobin* and the work of Byron, whose earlier satires in traditional styles (*English Bards and Scotch Reviewers, Hints from Horace, The Curse of Minerva, The Waltz*) are no better and no worse than the satires of Mason. *Beppo, The Vision of Judgment,* and *Don Juan* owe nothing to the authors of *Probationary Odes* and Peter Pindar—Byron went to school to the Italian satirists and to John Hookham Frere, the author of *Whistlecraft*—but in those great satires of Byron's maturity we see the culmination of the experiments in looser modes that had begun with Churchill and Anstey.

It is generally admitted that Cowper's satires[1] are the least

___

[1] William Cowper, 1731-1800, elder son of the Rector of Great Berkhampstead, was educated at Westminster School, where Churchill, Lloyd, Colman, and Warren Hastings were his contemporaries, and at the Inner Temple. A period of writing periodical essays and light verse was terminated by a fit of insanity brought on by the requirement to appear for examination before appointment to the post of Clerk of the Journals of the House of Lords, a lucrative sinecure, 1763. After spending many months in Dr. Nathaniel Cotton's excellent 'Collegium Insanorum' at St. Albans, Cowper was set up by his brother in lodgings at Huntingdon, 1765, and shortly after transferred to the Evangelical home of the Revd. and Mrs. Unwin. On Unwin's death Cowper and Mrs. Unwin moved to Olney, 1767, so as to live near the Revd. John Newton, a great Evangelical pastor. There he suffered

agreeable of his writings. If they continue to be read, it is because they were written by the author of *The Task*, the most popular poet of his day. Yet within the context of this history, they retain some independent interest. Technically they are undistinguished. Cowper's couplets, like those of his school-fellow Churchill, are loosely organized. Like Churchill he tended to depreciate Pope, complaining that he 'made poetry a mere mechanic art', though recalling by a turn or phrase or an echo here and there how well versed he was in Pope's satiric writing. His originality lies in what he chose to teach and, consequently, in his view of the satirist's character.

When Cowper began writing his satires in the winter of 1780, he had recently emerged from a second period of insanity, aggravated by his friend John Newton's well-intentioned efforts to distract him in the collaborative venture of *Olney Hymns*. The first raptures of his Evangelicalism were over; but he was still living in accordance with Evangelical beliefs, and those beliefs, though less heart-warming to him than they had been a few years earlier, inform each one of his satires. In the process, the norm which most satirists of the past had accepted and attempted to define was shifted perceptibly. For Pope, with his eye on Horace and Juvenal, the satirist is at one moment an easy-going fellow, not difficult to please, simple in his tastes and loyal to his friends, at another he is a man surprised at the perversities of the life he discovers around him, and at another he is a heroic figure, a very David slaying a vicious Goliath; but in any stance he adopts, the golden mean of an old Roman rectitude is more apparent than reliance upon the moral teaching of St. Paul. For Johnson, too, the satirist is less a man of religious principle than a man urged by indignation and wrapt in his own stoical sufficiency; only in the conclusion of *The Vanity of Human Wishes*, which contrasts so oddly with the nobly independent conclusion of Dryden's version of the same satire of Juvenal, is the reader aware that this is a poem written by a convinced Christian. But Cowper's Christianity, and more particularly his Evangelical Christianity, is explicit at every turn. 'The Progress of Errour', the first satire to be

another attack of insanity, 1773-4, and there he wrote his principal poems. In 1786 he and Mrs. Unwin moved to a more comfortable house in a neighbouring village, Weston Underwood. His continuing depression and the increasing debility of Mrs. Unwin (d. 1796) occasioned a move to Norfolk, where he died, at East Dereham.

written, brings man back in its conclusion to the saving truth of the Cross, which Johnson, despite his reported approval of these satires, might have thought a truth too awful to be so candidly handled in verse. The 'Truth' in the title of the following poem is, of course, scripture truth, scripture that is

> the only cure of woe;
> That field of promise, how it flings abroad
> Its odour o'er the Christian's thorny road!
> The soul, reposing on assur'd relief,
> Feels herself happy amidst all her grief,
> Forgets her labour as she toils along,
> Weeps tears of joy, and bursts into a song.

This is a new positive for the eighteenth-century satirist, and Cowper recognizes its novelty in the introductory poem, 'Table Talk', which was in fact the third to be written. 'Virtue indeed meets many a rhyming friend', he says; but she has very rarely appeared attired 'in that becoming vest Religion weaves for her'. And so, at a time when readers rightly complained that, whatever poets write, they bring forth nothing new,

> 'Twere new indeed to see a bard all fire,
> Touched with a coal from Heav'n, assume the lyre,
> And tell the world, still kindling as he sung,
> With more than mortal music on his tongue,
> That He, who died below, and reigns above,
> Inspires the song, and that his name is Love.

Satire based upon divine love offers plenty of problems to the satirist. The distinction between such love and a mere deistic notion of benevolence must be nicely drawn (in 'Charity'); and it becomes more important than ever to purify the satirist's motives as he exhibits specimens of vicious behaviour, since

> All zeal for a reform, that gives offence
> To peace and charity, is mere pretence;

and

> No works shall find acceptance in that day,
> When all disguises shall be rent away,
> That square not truly with the Scripture plan,
> Nor spring from love to God, or love to Man.

He may justifiably read the whole nation a lesson on their backslidings in 'Expostulation', pointing out that God's deal-

ings with the Israelites offer a pattern of how he will deal
with another chosen race, for Britain must recognize that
'Peculiar is the grace by thee possess'd'. But when it comes to
the satirist's traditional protest at individual misdemeanours,
Cowper's stance seems less well chosen than the Roman
stances of Pope and Johnson. The complaint has often been
made that he cannot distinguish the serious fault from the
trivial, that he reprimands, with an energy appropriate to
more notorious offences, the pipe-smoker in 'Conversation', and,
in 'The Progress of Errour', the parson who spends his Sunday
evenings at the harpsichord. There is some weight in the objection. Cowper's mental sufferings had led him to spend his days
in remotely provincial retirement, and to discover happiness
in earnest yet cordially disciplined domesticity. This afforded
him little insight into such Babylonian extravagance as the city
might afford.

But the real trouble is that in the satires he had not yet
discovered the 'objective correlatives' (the term is convenient)
for those Evangelical beliefs upon which his satire is based.
The character of the cottager (in 'Truth') offers a rare exception. In the little lace-making town of Olney, Cowper must have
seen her daily weaving

>   at her own door,
>   Pillow and bobbins all her little store;
>   Content though mean, and cheerful if not gay,
>   Shuffling her threads about the livelong day.

Though she has 'little understanding, and no wit', she yet possesses in the truth of her Bible

>   A truth the brilliant Frenchman never knew;
>   And in that charter reads with sparkling eyes
>   Her title to a treasure in the skies.

(Cowper's portraits are not unsuccessful, though he must have
reflected that the more satirical, such as the ancient prude in
'Truth', come close to offending against his doctrine of love.)
But for the most part in these satires he is content to urge that

>   Religion does not censure or exclude
>   Unnumber'd pleasures harmlessly pursued,

that 'True Piety is cheerful as the day', or that the harpsichord-playing parson should recognize that

> Love, joy, and peace make harmony more meet
> For sabbath ev'nings, and perhaps as sweet.

Perhaps; but it is not convincing. Yet it is precisely in the discovery of 'objective correlatives' that Cowper in his later poetry excels. There is a hint of this at the end of 'Retirement', his last and best satire. As he lists in periphrastic fashion the pleasures that Religion neither censures nor excludes, many of which he himself was delighted to practise, he comes at last to poetry, which employs him

> shut out from more important views,
> Fast by the banks of the slow winding Ouse.

Here at last is some promise of *The Task*. That is not only Cowper's most important poem, but also the most distinguished contribution to a kind of poetry practised in great diversity of form by many writers of the time, poetry inspired by the sentiment of place. To this we must now address ourselves.

Poetry that celebrates the sentiment of place was not by any means new in this period. There is plenty of it in classical Latin; it was familiar in the seventeenth century in England, the most famous example being Denham's *Cooper's Hill*; and writers of our period looked back with varying degrees of satisfaction upon such poems as Addison's *Letter from Italy*, Pope's *Windsor Forest*, and Dyer's *Grongar Hill* written during the first quarter of the eighteenth century. These three poems may be taken to represent three diverse examples of the poetry of place, the first where the locality visited leads to reflections upon the greatness of past achievements, the second in which the reflections are in the broadest sense of the word political, the third in which the prospect of a countryside prompts reflections that are mainly moral or sentimental.

It should be observed that in only one of these poems does natural description or a sense of landscape predominate. The reader who approaches the *Letter from Italy* or *Cooper's Hill* hoping to be reminded of Italian landscape or the beauties of the Thames valley will not merely be disappointed but may well fail to recognize the distinctive achievement of each poet;

and though Pope, who learned much from Denham, wrote one
brief passage of landscape description in *Windsor Forest*—and
remarkably skilful it is—his pictorial sense (and consequently
his descriptive power) was nourished less by Claude Lorrain
and Salvator Rosa than by Poussin and the allegorical painters
of the high Renaissance, while description throughout his poem
is subjected to the control of his political design. But in Thomson's *Seasons*, where the influence of Claude and Salvator has
perhaps been over-estimated, and in Dyer, the description of
a prospect becomes more prominent, even though it remains
clear that the description is subordinated to a moral or philosophical purpose.

Though he may frequently have had specific prospects in
mind, Thomson did not often refer to them by name. A rare
exception is the description of Hagley Park added to *Spring*
in the revision of 1744, where description of a specific locality
is skilfully combined with reflections prompted by the owner's
interests. But because this was not his practice Thomson stands
a little aside from the line of descent in the poetry of the
sentiment of place, which is essentially local. Poets in this
kind might look back to the *Georgics* in one direction, and to
the catalogue of delights that 'L'Allegro' and 'Il Penseroso'
yield in another; but as the century went on they came to
recognize quite clearly that they were contributing to what
Johnson in the 'Life of Denham' considered 'a new scheme of
poetry' and decided to name and define it as

local poetry, of which the fundamental subject is some particular
landscape to be poetically described, with the addition of such
incidental embellishments as may be supplied by historical retrospection or incidental meditation.

Although their models were literary, they were doubtless aware
of the sentiment of place apparent in contemporary painting.
Thus the poet John Langhorne, in celebrating the estate of
a prospective patron in his 'Studley Park', 1755, may perhaps
have known of two almost exactly contemporary paintings of
the demesnes of Studley Royal by Balthazar Nebot, and another
of the house, in all of which the owner and his dependants take
prominent positions in the foreground; the poets, as they
laboured up their hills from Grongar in 1726 to Lewesdon in
1788, must have had some fellow-feeling for such popular

landscape painters as George Lambert (1710–65), habitually
scaling suitable eminences to command a satisfactory prospect;
and as for sentiment, how could it be more blatantly conveyed
than by John Wootton (1668?–1765) in his view of Goodwood,
where a racehorse occupies the centre of the canvas and the
house itself can just be discerned under the attendant jockey's
outstretched arm? There are evident analogies between the
poets who so often meditated on the passage of time in the
shade of a ruined building, and painters like J. J. Schalch (c.
1760), whose ivy-covered abbeys have a romantically unkempt
appearance only to be savoured in recent years at an abbey
such as Jervaulx. Even in a poem as pedestrian as *Amwell*, by
John Scott the Quaker, there are hints of a diligent attention
to the varieties of light such as one might expect in the painters
of landscape towards the end of the century.

If one prospect poem must be chosen to represent the whole
race, let it be Richard Jago's *Edge-Hill. A Poem. In Four Books*
(1767). Jago's plan was to describe the view from the summit
of Edge Hill in different directions at various times of day;
but fearing, like so many of his brother poets, that mere description was not enough to prevent the reader's interest from
languishing, he tells us that he 'endeavoured to make [the
design] as extensively interesting as he could, by the frequent
introduction of general reflections, historical, philosophical,
and moral'. These reflections show clearly what traditions
Jago inherited. His intimate knowledge of the antiquities of his
county may serve to remind us that this was one of the great
ages of local antiquarianism in which many county histories
still regarded as standard works were produced; but the reflections incited by his antiquarian lore are those proper to
a student of *Windsor Forest* and *Night-Thoughts*. Thus the sight
of 'old Montfort's lofty seat' prompts some remarks upon the
barbarous policy of a Gothic age; hence 'open scenes, and
cultur'd fields' should teach us to hail

> Fair liberty, and freedom's gen'rous reign,
> With guardian laws and polish'd arts adorn'd.
> While the portcullis huge, or moated fence
> The sad reverse of savage times betray—
> Distrust, barbarity, and Gothic rule.

The more benign reign of Elizabeth, however, afforded a
gentler, more pensive comment upon the decay of human

grandeur as Jago regards the ruins of Kenilworth. It is a comment which Young, Dyer, Gray, and several other poets would
have been ready to record:

> No more, with plaint, or suit importunate,
> The thronged lobby echoes, nor with staff
> Or gaudy badge, the busy pursuivants
> Lead to wish'd audience. All, alas! is gone,
> And silence keeps her melancholy court
> Throughout the walls; save, where in rooms of state,
> Kings once repos'd, chatter the wrangling daws,
> Or screech owls hoot along the vaulted aisles.

Nor is the prospect any less conducive to 'philosophical'
reflections, whether it be to speculate on the geological reasons
for the contours of the scene before him, or to rejoice in the
activity of the silk-weavers of Coventry, or, supported in his
georgic theme by frequent imitations of Virgil, to describe the
metal-workers of Birmingham at their tasks.

The poem contrives to represent much that is most appealing in the civilization of mid eighteenth-century England, at
once aesthetic, enlightened, and progressive; but the more this
country clergyman enlarges upon his many-sided interests, the
more he allows the mere sentiment of place to become dissipated.
What is offered instead is a paean of local patriotism.

To evoke this mere sentiment a much more restricted form
will serve, and even the labour of description may be dispensed
with. This can be tested by considering the astonishing revival
of the sonnet during the last quarter of the eighteenth century.
When Milton put into practice the lessons he had learned
from Petrarch and Della Casa, he was experimenting in what
was already regarded as an outworn form. None of his contemporaries and immediate successors seems to have taken notice,
and the sonnet ceased to be written either in its English or its
Italian form until it partook in the revival of interest in Milton's
minor poems during this period. The first to make extensive use
of the sonnet was Thomas Edwards, who contributed a few to
Dodsley's *Miscellany* (1748) and appended some fifty to later
editions of the attack upon Warburton's edition of Shakespeare that he called *Canons of Criticism*. He told Richardson (18
July 1754) that reading Spenser's sonnets 'was the first occasion
of my writing that species of little poems'; but in most of them
he followed Italian precedent and, like Milton, wrote poetical

addresses; some too are satirical in tone, but none is distinguished. If they were read, they did not receive the compliment of imitation; nor can any higher claims be made for the sonnets which William Mason and Benjamin Stillingfleet were writing at about the same time. The principal credit for the revival of sonneteering is undoubtedly due to Thomas Warton. His admiration for Milton's work was to lead him to prepare a learned and elaborate edition of the minor poems (1785); but except in so far as his sonnets are occasional and sometimes autobiographical, he did not follow the master in the use to which the form was put. Instead he made of it in all but two of his nine sonnets a poem about the sentiment of place, a use which seems to have been rare in the previous history of the sonnet. Inspecting the artistic splendours of Wilton House makes him wonder how he can cheat the hours without them, but

> Vain the complaint; for fancy can impart
> (To fate superior, and to fortune's doom)
> Whate'er adorns the stately-storied hall;

Stonehenge raises many a question about its 'wond'rous origine'; and on returning to the river Lodon ('sweet native stream'),

> pensive mem'ry traces back the round
> Which fills the varied interval between.

The appeal was immediate and widespread. Within a few years of the publication of Warton's volume in 1777, several young poets—Bowles, Russell, Sotheby (their work is assessed in the next volume[1])—were using the sonnet to record sentiments prompted by visiting picturesque spots on tours, now undertaken with increasing frequency throughout the length and breadth of Britain. Wordsworth was to find the sonnet inadequate to convey all that he felt on revisiting a spot on the river Wye a few miles above Tintern Abbey, but he was content to follow this late eighteenth-century tradition in much of *Yarrow Revisited* (1835), 'composed during a tour in Scotland, and on the English border, in the autumn of 1831', and we are told by Cockburn of the young Francis Jeffrey, exploring his native country with an Edinburgh companion, that 'there was as much of the genuine enjoyment of nature . . . and as many

---

[1] Vol. IX, pp. 101–2.

fresh-made sonnets, in one of their foot and knapsack expedi-
tions, as in some journeys of greater pretension'.

There are three more poems in which the sentiment of place
has an important part to play: Goldsmith's *Deserted Village*
(1770), Crabbe's *Village* (1783), and Cowper's *Task* (1784). *The
Deserted Village* is in no sense a local poem. 'Sweet Auburn!
Loveliest village of the plain' was early believed to be Lissoy,
the Irish village where Goldsmith spent his boyhood; but the
very invention of the name discourages too particular identifica-
tion, and the idealized description is not so much an end in
itself as an element essential to the philosophical argument of
the poem. For both Goldsmith's major poems are philosophical.
In *The Traveller* (1764) he had conducted a geographical search
for happiness. Travel as he might in Italy, Switzerland, France,
Belgium, and Britain, he still found some evil to counterbalance
what happiness he first discovered, and was forced to conclude
in verses supplied him by Dr. Johnson:

> Vain, very vain, my weary search to find
> That bliss which only centres in the mind.

In Britain the counterbalance discovered was the lust for riches:

> Have we not seen round Britain's peopled shore,
> Her useful sons exchang'd for useless ore . . .
> Seen opulence, her grandeur to maintain,
> Lead stern depopulation in her train,
> And over fields where scatter'd hamlets rose,
> In barren solitary pomp repose?

Here is the germ of *The Deserted Village*. In developing this
theme, the idyllic happiness of the villagers at Auburn is
heightened to point the contrast with their life when driven to
begin it anew in the as yet untamed colony of Georgia. Yet
though the poem was written to attack the contemporary rage
for enclosures and the further extension of already large estates,
and still survives as a protest against luxury and the spread of
mercantile values, Goldsmith took less pains than Pope, in his
Moral Essays, to create images of luxury in the reader's mind;
what survives in the memory is Auburn.

In spite of Auburn being, strictly speaking, unlocalized, the
nostalgic recollection of an Eden once possessed is so pervasive
as to invoke a strong sentiment of place in any reader who has

spent his childhood in the country. A lost and irrecoverable
Eden is the foundation of much pastoral poetry, and Auburn is
unashamedly pastoral. The mists of memory cover whatever
was displeasing and frustrating, but serve to reveal more attractively the delights of a long summer evening in which the
inhabitants seemed continuously to live, and to colour with
affection such recollected grotesqueries as the character of the
schoolmaster, the conversation of the village statesmen, 'the
swain, mistrustless of his smutted face', and the alehouse where

> broken tea-cups, wisely kept for show,
> Rang'd o'er the chimney, glisten'd in a row.

There is not a detail that fails to ring true, but the selection
has been undertaken with an idealizing purpose. A different
selection of details no less truthful could produce an entirely
different picture, as Crabbe was to show in *The Village*.[1] He
seems to have had Goldsmith's poem in mind; but he chose
to ignore the purpose for which Auburn was described, and
directed his not inconsiderable powers of verse to writing an
anti-pastoral. He attempted no more than Goldsmith to write a
local poem: his poem seems deliberately unlocalized as though
to persuade the reader that this is the plain, unpalatable, anti-
pastoral truth to be found anywhere. He was no less successful
than Goldsmith in conveying the sentiment of place, but the
sentiment may be said to reek with strong effluvia.

Instead of the harmless evening sports in which Goldsmith's
villagers engage, Crabbe's villagers are busy smuggling; the
village alehouse is replaced by the poor-house; and in place of
Goldsmith's schoolmaster and preacher we find

> A potent quack, long versed in human ills,
> Who first insults the victim whom he kills,

and a young sporting parson. The setting too is no less ruthlessly
anti-pastoral. Nothing could be less like a lost Eden recollected
than the landscape Crabbe composes where

> Rank weeds, that every art and care defy,
> Reign o'er the land, and rob the blighted rye:
> There thistles stretch their prickly arms afar,
> And to the ragged infant threaten war:
> There poppies nodding, mock the hope of toil;

---

[1] See further Vol. IX, pp. 108–13.

There the blue bugloss paints the sterile soil . . .
O'er the young shoot the charlock throws a shade,
And clasping tares cling round the sickly blade.

From this contrast of pastoral and anti-pastoral, which in spite of being each unlocalized, so strongly evokes the sentiment of place, we may return in conclusion to a poem strictly localized. *The Task* is planted in the little town of Olney in Buckinghamshire, in an ugly, incommodious house overlooking the market square, in the long strip of garden behind it, and in the surrounding countryside; and there is no pretence that the author is 'the poet' or anyone but William Cowper himself, who would scorn to wear a mask, or adopt a *persona*. The novelty of *The Task* lies in its complete indifference to poetic 'kinds'. Cowper writes in the fullness of the knowledge of what a georgic is and what a pastoral, of how Milton had modelled the blank verse line, and how Thomson had adapted it to the descriptive poem, but he dispenses with the too prescriptive directions of a literary kind in the interest of a manner of writing that will allow ample latitude for his individual discursiveness. He will allow his mind to discover its own directions, zigzagging to and fro as one topic prompts another. One may require the patriot to exhort, another the satirist to chide. or the representative of enlightenment to reflect or the georgic poet to instruct or the lover of the countryside to observe. Yet these are not several poets but one poet, a retired country gentleman who has succeeded in adapting the blank-verse line to his speaking voice.

Charming as the first book ('The Sofa') is in its transitions— from the theme imposed upon the poet to the country walk and thence to the wretched housing of the cottagers, the contrasts of nature and art, the benefits of civilized life, and yet the disapprobation of life in cities—and entertaining as the third book ('The Garden') is with the mock-dignity of its instruction on raising cucumbers—the second book ('The Time-Piece') is virtually a reversion to his satires—it is in the fourth book ('The Winter Evening') that Cowper shows himself at his best. The book opens in excitement with the arrival of the post bearing newspapers from London. The poet is eager to get at them:

Is India free? and does she wear her plum'd
And jewell'd turban with a smile of peace,
Or do we grind her still? The grand debate,

> The popular harangue, the tart reply,
> The logic, and the wisdom, and the wit,
> And the loud laugh—I long to know them all,
> I burn to set th'imprison'd wranglers free,
> And give them voice and utt'rance once again.

And so,

> Now stir the fire, and close the shutters fast,
> Let fall the curtains, wheel the sofa round,
> And, while the bubbling and loud hissing urn
> Throws up a steamy column, and the cups,
> That cheer but not inebriate, wait on each,
> So let us welcome peaceful Ev'ning in.

The reader may lose himself momentarily in what the newspapers reveal, but it will not be long before the poet reminds us
that we are seeing the world through his eyes as he peeps at it
'through the loopholes of retreat', seeing the stir of the great
Babel without feeling the crowd, for 'I behold The tumult,
and am still'. So Cowper continually brings the theme round to
himself meditating. No less pleasing is a quieter evening spent
with only firelight to illuminate, uplifting

> The shadow to the ceiling, there by fits
> Dancing uncouthly to the quiv'ring flame,

the mind day-dreaming, while the understanding takes repose

> In indolent vacuity of thought;

till awakened by 'the freezing blast, That sweeps the bolted
shutter', the poet recalls the roughness of his morning winter
walk, and rejoices the more in the contrast of the warmth within.

The writing in these best passages is energetic; the phrasing
rarely fails to please; and in self-conscious revelation of personality the work is unparalleled since the time of Pope. But it is
the poet's relish for the sights that spring to his attention on his
country walks that has given such keen delight to generations of
readers from his day to our own. He had it in himself to see and
to enjoy, but it was Thomson who taught him how to compose
his pictures, and even on occasion what words to choose. Thus
it is to Thomson's example we owe the charming vignette in
the fifth book ('The Winter Morning Walk') of the woodman's
dog, who

with many a frisk
Wide-scamp'ring, snatches up the drifted snow
With iv'ry teeth, or ploughs it with his snout;
Then shakes his powder'd coat, and barks for joy;

but elsewhere he shows a skill in diction and phrasing that lay
well beyond Thomson's powers, as when in the sixth book ('The
Winter-Walk at Noon') he observes

The squirrel, flippant, pert, and full of play:
He sees me, and at once, swift as a bird,
Ascends the neighb'ring beech; there whisks his brush,
And perks his ears, and stamps, and cries aloud,
With all the prettiness of feign'd alarm,
And anger insignificantly fierce.

On still other occasions the detail has moments of Wordsworthian
anticipation, as when the robin

Pleas'd with his solitude, and flitting light
From spray to spray, where'er he rests he shakes
From many a twig the pendent drops of ice
That tinkle in the wither'd leaves below.

Yet the poem may be said to be too artless, and to suffer
because it cannot be related to any previous form. Its associations are too loose and casual. It is here that Cowper's admirers
in the next generation improved upon the lead he gave them.
Coleridge was to show that in shorter flights, such as 'The Eolian
Harp', 'This Lime-Tree Bower my Prison', and above all in
'Frost at Midnight', he could contrive a more logically related
sequence of topics in poems which are at once revelations of the
poet meditating and suffusions of local sentiment; and in the
longer poem Wordsworth was to build on Cowper's foundations, balancing in *The Prelude* contrasting passages of narrative,
description, and reflection—the sequence in Book I of winter
evening activity in the warm parlour and the raging frost outside is a notable improvement upon a passage of Cowper just
noticed—and adapting, particularly in Book III, Cowper's
deprecating mock-heroics towards himself, but finding in his
great theme a co-ordinating factor well beyond Cowper's
powers, yet one which reveals the mind and personality of

the poet growing from roots firmly planted in the sentiment of place.

There is one more poetic form in which this period is distinguished, the hymn. This is a form limited by the most precisely drawn restrictions. It is written not to be read but to be sung, and sung not by a soloist but a congregation. Congregations are conservative bodies with a marked reluctance for learning new tunes, and therefore hymns will tend to be written in traditional measures so as to fit the old tunes, Common Measure (8. 6. 8. 6: 'Oh for a thousand tongues to sing My dear Redeemer's praise'), Short Measure (6. 6. 8. 6: 'Soldiers of Christ arise, And put your armour on'), and Long Measure (8. 8. 8. 8: 'Forth in thy name, O Lord, I go, My daily labour to pursue'). Charles Wesley, the author of the three hymns mentioned, did not confine himself to these measures; but it will be observed that there is considerable variety even within the range of these three examples, for the first is a hymn of praise, the second a hymn of exhortation, and the third a hymn of dedication. All are essentially congregational in theme and expression; that is to say, none of them explores an unusual experience, none is meditative, and none seeks to use any but the well-established imagery of the Christian church. All are content to rely on experiences that are held in common by a body of worshippers. Thus when Wesley appears to write as a helpless individual imploring divine protection in 'Jesu, lover of my soul', his discretion tells him that the prayer, 'Let me to thy bosom fly', is one that may be pronounced with equal conviction by all Christians. Charles Wesley was the most prolific and experienced hymn-writer of the age, but the same understanding is shown, at their best, by Philip Doddridge, the author of 'Hark, the glad sound! the Saviour comes', Augustus Montagu Toplady, the author of 'Rock of ages, cleft for me' (1775), and by Newton and Cowper, joint authors of Olney Hymns (1779).

A hymn designed for congregational singing might seem the least personal form of poetry, yet it is remarkable how distinctive in personality the great hymn-writers are. Charles Wesley appears before us as a man overwhelmed by the love of God ('Love divine, all loves excelling') and impelled by the recognition to praise him ('Hail the day that sees him rise'); Newton, the author

of 'Glorious things of thee are spoken, Zion, city of our God', and
'How sweet the name of Jesus sounds In a believer's ear',
seems a man of unbounded confidence, particularly in the hymn

> Why should I fear the darkest hour,
> Or tremble at the Tempter's pow'r?
> Jesus vouchsafes to be my tow'r;

Cowper writes for the most part as one reluctantly performing
an unaccustomed task. In three or four of his contributions to
Olney Hymns, notably 'Hark, my soul, it is the Lord' and 'God
moves in a mysterious way His wonders to perform', he has
finely recognized a congregation's needs; but perhaps only in
'Oh for a closer walk with God' has he succeeded in giving
expression to that distinctive personality which is pre-eminently
the achievement of his secular poetry.

> What peaceful hours I once enjoy'd!
> How sweet their mem'ry still!
> But they have left an aching void
> The world can never fill.

This verse at least is the work of the sensitive, shrinking,
vulnerable creature who had already written 'The Shrubbery'
and was to write 'On the Receipt of my Mother's Picture out
of Norfolk', the lines 'To Mary', and 'The Castaway'. Only the
serenity of the last verse of the hymn is unusual. Yet it must be
emphasized that this sensitive poet is a poet of varied achievements, that he is the author of one of the merriest poems of the
century 'John Gilpin', and that in 'Toll for the Brave' he wrote
verses more stalwart in sentiment and better adapted to congregational singing than the majority of the *Olney Hymns*.

The most astonishing hymn-writer of the century is Christopher Smart.[1] His hymns, of one kind or another, seem all to
have been written towards the end of his life, certainly no earlier
than 1759 or 1760, when he was suffering physical restraint for
madness real or supposed. Except for *Jubilate Agno* they give
the impression of being intended as a practical contribution to
hymnody, for in verse structure they follow recognized patterns,
and they are in fact organized with the Prayer Book and the
festivals of the church in mind. Even *Jubilate Agno* itself, now

---

[1] Christopher Smart, 1722-71, was born in Kent and educated in Durham and
at Pembroke Hall, Cambridge, where he obtained a fellowship. He became a professional writer in London, but suffered from a species of religious mania and
from alcoholism.

that the surviving leaves of the manuscript have been more critically examined, appears to have been an attempt to apply the antiphonal principles of Hebrew poetry to English, the 'Let' verses ('Let Sarah rejoice with the Redwing, whose harvest is in the frost and snow') being answered by the 'For' verses ('For the hour of my felicity, like the womb of Sarah, shall come at the latter end'). Smart doubtless regarded it as an exercise, too private, too aphoristic, and too occult in its poetry for publication, though a selection from it has been used in our own day by Benjamin Britten as the libretto for a church cantata; but the exercise, in marshalling virtues and exploring the sonorities of rhyme, was put to good use when he came to write *A Song to David*. This poem, the corner-stone of Smart's poetical career, was first published in 1763 and reprinted two years later in a volume entitled *A Translation of the Psalms, &c., Hymns and Spiritual Songs for the Fasts and Festivals, &c.*, as though to draw attention to the relationship of the *Song to David* to these other more traditional pieces. The versification of the psalms is good journeyman work, at its weakest as good as the best of its kind, yet capable of rising, as in psalms XCI and CL, to meet a great opportunity. But when freed from the restriction of following the sacred text, Smart's imagination blossoms in a manner that might frequently puzzle and embarrass a congregation, though doubtless some, like Boswell, would admire the 'shivers of genius here and there'. The muse at Epiphany is bidden to

> Fill my heart with genuine treasures,
> Pour them out before his feet,
> High conceptions, mystic measures,
> Springing strong and flowing sweet;

the Feast of St. Philip and St. James, falling on 1 May, prompts him to observe how

> Couslips seize upon the fallow,
> And the cardamine in white
> Where the corn-flow'rs join the mallow,
> Joy and health, and thrift unite;

and at the Nativity

> Spinks and ouzles sing sublimely,
> 'We too have a Saviour born',
> Whiter blossoms burst untimely
> On the blest Mosaic thorn.

That hymn, like the hymn for Easter Day, rises inevitably and grandly to its conclusion, as does the even more impressive *Song to David*. That this poem was designed as an anthem or cantata to conclude Smart's labours in the service of the church seems not improbable. It celebrates the great psalmist, 'the minister of praise at large', in poetry that is at once flamboyant and structurally formal. A verse is set aside for each of David's twelve (four times three) virtues, following the order already prescribed in *Jubilate Agno*, and one is given to each of the nine (thrice three) topics of his song. Seven, another mystical number, are the pillars of the Lord, 'which stand from earth to topmost heaven', and they turn out to be letters of the Greek alphabet to which Smart attaches an occult significance:

> Gamma supports the glorious arch
> On which angelic legions march,
>   And is with sapphires pav'd;
> Thence the fleet clouds are sent adrift,
> And thence the painted folds, that lift
>   The crimson veil, are wav'd.

At stanza 50 a passage of moral exhortation ends in a command to praise; and there follows a *Benedicite omnia opera* of twenty-one (seven times three) stanzas in which the works of the Lord adore him in manners peculiar to each and lovely to the beholder: thus

> For ADORATION, incense comes
> From bezoar, and Arabian gums,
>   And on the civet's fur.

And the poem ends in rapturous contemplation, each to the limit of three stanzas, of what is sweet, strong, beauteous, precious, and glorious. The poem is unique amongst the lyrical poems of the century in its expression of religious ecstasy within the confines of the strictest formality; yet it is by no means uncharacteristic of the age. *A Song to David* is based upon Smart's practice in congregational hymn-writing, and the relationship still remains clear, even though the basic form has been so wonderfully modified. Thus it provides one more, and that a superb, example of what has frequently been observed in these two chapters, the respect for poetical kinds and the opportunities they nevertheless presented for modification and mutation.

V

SCOTTISH POETRY

No chapter in this history has been devoted to Scottish Literature since Professor Lewis surveyed the close of the Middle Ages in Scotland, and expressed his wonder at the 'sudden extinction' in the late sixteenth century 'of a poetical literature which, for its technical brilliance, its vigour and variety, its equal mastery of homely fact and high imagination, seemed "so fair, so fresshe, so liklie to endure"'. No subsequent chapter has been needed, because the best Scottish poets of the next century were absorbed into the English tradition. It was the great achievement of Ayton, Drummond, and Alexander that their work was indistinguishable from that of their English contemporaries. A few continued to write in Scots, notably Robert Sempill of Beltrees, but the language which had once been the language of a court had degenerated into a regional dialect; English was replacing it as a medium of formal communication; even the Bible was read in English.

The revival of Scottish literature, which began after the Union of the Kingdoms in 1707, was complex in character. It was manifest partly in the rediscovery of the vernacular for the purposes of poetry, and partly in the mastery over a closely related, yet still an alien, language. Though a man should speak Scots, it seemed good sense to learn how to write English, for English was now the language of Parliament as well as of the court, and was as useful in a united kingdom as Latin had been in medieval Europe. Furthermore it seemed to some Scotsmen that in the previous century, a century so crucial to the development of the arts and sciences in other lands, their country had been inhibited from growth by the unhappy political situation. The point is made by Robertson at the end of his *History of Scotland* with that sense of complacent superiority engendered by 'enlightened' views (1759):

Thus, during the whole seventeenth century, the English were gradually refining their language and their taste: in Scotland the former was much debased, and the latter almost entirely lost. In the beginning of that period, both nations were emerging out of barbarity; but the distance between them, which was then inconsiderable, became, before the end of it, immense. . . . At length, the union having incorporated the two nations, and rendered them one people, the distinctions which had subsisted for many ages gradually wear away; peculiarities disappear; the same manners prevail in both parts of the island; the same authors are read and admired; the same entertainments are frequented by the elegant and polite; and the same standard of taste, and of purity in language, is established. The Scots, after being placed, during a whole century, in a situation no less fatal to the liberty than to the taste and genius of the nation, were at once put in possession of privileges more valuable than those which their ancestors had formerly enjoyed; and every obstruction that had retarded their pursuit, or prevented their acquisition of literary fame, was totally removed.

Cogent as the argument may seem, not every Scot would have agreed with it; thus it is at once clear that if the political premises had been generally acceptable, there would have been no Jacobite rebellions. But even granted the desirability of catching up with the English and showing them that the Scots were a match for them in their own language, Robertson makes the task look altogether too easy. Fine indeed as his own achievement was, it was something of a *tour de force*. 'He writes', said Burke, 'like a man who composes in a dead language which he understands but cannot speak.' The same point was made by Alexander Carlyle when trying to explain to Lord Mansfield how it was that, in reading Robertson and Hume, Mansfield felt he was not reading English:

to every man bred in Scotland the English language was in some respects a foreign tongue, the precise value and force of whose words and phrases he did not understand, and therefore was continually endeavouring to word his expressions by additional epithets or circumlocutions, which made his writings appear both stiff and redundant.

Bishop Hurd, discoursing with Boswell's friend Temple on 16 May 1783, seems to have gained the same impression. He 'censured the prolixity and want of precision' in the Scots writers. Temple's record shows that he made an exception of Beattie; yet Beattie too felt the difficulty: 'We are slaves to the language we write,' he wrote sadly to Sylvester Douglas, 'and when an easy, familiar idiomatical phrase occurs, dare not adopt it, if we recollect no authority, for fear of Scotticisms'—a glossary of which he published in 1787 in order to 'correct Improprieties of Speech and Writing'.

The number of Scotsmen ready to run these risks is remarkable: historians, philosophers, critics, novelists, essayists. They invade the English literary scene; and, as always happens after successful invasions, the scene is not the same as before. Perhaps it might be said that in the later eighteenth century English prose became British, that the invaders contributed their influence to a shift of manner in prose writing which many contemporaries noticed and several deplored. 'Our tongue was brought to perfection in the days of Addison and Swift,' Beattie declared in the preface to his *Scoticisms*, 'but has now lost not a little of its elegance, particularly in the articles of simplicity, vivacity, and ease.' Another Scot, Hugh Blair, attributed the difference to a change in vocabulary. He detected a departure from Swift's standard of 'the strictest Purity and Propriety in the choice of words'. He continued:

At present we seem to be departing from this standard. A multitude of Latin words have, of late, been poured in upon us. On some occasions, they give an appearance of elevation and dignity to Style. But often also, they render it stiff and forced. (*Lectures on Rhetoric and Belles Lettres*, 1783; lect. X.)

Blair had Dr. Johnson in mind. Though neither Blair nor we can adequately characterize Johnson's prose so shortly, it is broadly true that Johnson, Burke, and Gibbon represent the stately periods of the latter part of the century which contrast so markedly with the colloquial ease of Dryden, Addison, Steele, and Swift; and it is because this prose is no longer based upon colloquial idiom that the Scottish writers found it relatively easy to adopt.

If writing prose in a foreign language is difficult, writing poetry in that language is surely more difficult still. Yet here equally the Scots were determined to excel. What Burke said of Robertson may also be said of Thomson, in *The Seasons* at any rate. He too 'writes like a man who composes in a dead language which he understands but cannot speak'. Yet Thomson was readily absorbed into the English tradition. He contributed to it something that was not there before, and the subsequent history of purely English poetry was affected by what he wrote. We fail to understand him as well as we might if we forget that he was a Scot, but we do him no essential injustice if we discuss him in the context of his English contemporaries. The same is true, by and large, of Mallet, Armstrong, Robert Blair, Beattie, and other poets of even smaller stature. They have been discussed in the previous chapters, but they are mentioned here to emphasize that there is an Anglo-Scottish tradition in eighteenth-century verse as well as in eighteenth-century prose. That they would have written better if they had always written in Scots is not susceptible of proof, even though Hamilton of Bangour's only memorable poem (see p. 147), and Beattie's best poem (see p. 152) in the judgement of some critics, was the only poem either poet wrote in Scots. That they did not choose to write in Scots except on rare occasions will become clearer when the state of the vernacular is considered.

The range of opportunities in poetry that the vernacular offered could best be appreciated by looking back to the poetry of earlier days. This was what James Watson, the King's Printer, provided when he published in three parts his *Choice Collection of Comic and Serious Scots Poems* (1706, 1709, 1711), 'the first of its Nature', he proudly claimed, 'which has been publish'd in our own Native *Scots* Dialect'. Not all the poems were in Scots; for Watson included Drummond's 'Polemo-Middinia' besides lyrics by Ayton and Montrose. But here was 'Christ's Kirk on the Green', the prototype of many a later poem of rustic revelry; here was Montgomerie's 'The Cherry and the Slae', whose stanza was to appeal to many an imitator, including Burns himself; here was 'Lady Anne Bothwel's Balo' and an early version of 'Old-Long-syne', to represent Scottish lyrics; here was Sempill's 'Life and Death of the Piper of Kilbarchan', better known as 'Habbie Simson', which was to prompt so many later comic elegies; and as if to show that the ancient spirit was not dead, here was a modern poet, little more than thirty years old, William Hamilton of Gilbertfield, putting Sempill's stanza to use in the first of many sentimental elegies on a dead animal, 'The Last Dying Words of Bonny Heck, a Famous Grey-Hound in the Shire of Fife'.

Watson's commendable attempt to display the resources of

the vernacular was supported by Allan Ramsay,[1] who in 1724 published both *The Ever Green, Being A Collection of Scots Poems, Wrote by the Ingenious before 1600* and *The Tea Table Miscellany*, described in a later reprint as *A New Miscellany of Scots Sangs*. The success of *The Ever Green* was modest at best, for only one more edition of it was issued during our period; but Ramsay can at least claim from it the credit for being the first to restore the work of the 'makars' of pre-Reformation Scotland. He had access to the Bannatyne MS. in the Advocates' Library and printed a generous selection of Dunbar's poetry, Henryson's 'Robin and Makyn', and, among much that was less worthy of survival, one ballad at least, the ballad of Johnny Armstrong. In commending these poems to his readers he applauds their native imagery and contrasts their 'natural strength of thought and simplicity of stile' with the 'affected Delicacies and studied Refinements' of modern writings. But though he felt assured in appealing to readers of 'the best and most exquisite discernment', he adopted a more defiant apology in the face of some who were evidently not prepared to countenance a revival of interest in the vernacular:

There is nothing can be heard more silly than one's expressing his *Ignorance* of his *native Language*; yet such there are, who can vaunt of acquiring a tolerable Perfection in the *French* or *Italian* Tongues, if they have been a Fortnight in *Paris* or a Month in *Rome*: But shew them the most elegant Thoughts in a *Scots* Dress, they as disdainfully as stupidly condemn it as barbarous . . . But this affected Class of Fops give no Uneasiness, not being numerous; for the most part of our Gentlemen, who are generally Masters of the most useful and politest *Languages*, can take Pleasure (for a Change) to speak and read their own.

Although the modern Scot is not directly urged to model himself upon his forebears, there is encouragement distinctly offered to him who will, so long as he is prepared to risk the charge of vulgarity. The glossary of old Scots words provided for modern reader and poet was more convenient than accurate; Ramsay had not even consulted the glossary compiled by Thomas Ruddiman for his edition of Douglas's *Aeneis* (1710); and his own skill, as Lord Hailes was soon to remark, 'scarcely

[1] See Vol. VII, p. 525.

extended beyond the vulgar language spoken in the Lothians at this day'.

The verse in *The Ever Green* is for the most part non-lyrical; *The Tea Table Miscellany* is a collection of lyrics meant for singing. The quality of the poetry is with a few exceptions much inferior; it places a much lighter tax upon the understanding; and it was a much more popular success. Ramsay's aim in this collection was the same that was to prompt Burns sixty years later, an enthusiasm for Scottish song. He prints no music; it was enough to provide new words to known tunes. He himself supplied more than sixty items and secured about thirty more from 'some ingenious young Gentlemen, who were so well pleased with my undertaking that they generously lent me their assistance'. As for the rest, they were 'such old verses as have been done time out of mind, and only wanted to be cleared from the dross of blundering Transcribers and Printers'. Many of the poems are uncompromisingly English and liable to censure, one might suppose, for their 'affected delicacies and studied refinements'; others reveal their northern origin by the irruption of an 'ilk' or a 'bonny' in an otherwise southern setting; but in a few others, notably 'Jocky said to Jeany, Jeany, wilt thou do't' and Hamilton of Bangour's 'Busk ye, busk ye, my bonny bonny bride', we can see the beginnings of a revival —or perhaps the reappearance at the surface—of Scottish song-writing in the vernacular which was to culminate in the work of Burns.

But the judicious reader did not need to rely for long either on Ramsay's texts or on Ramsay's selections. The makars were restored to their proper shape by Lord Hailes in his selection of *Ancient Scottish Poems. Published from the MS. of George Bannatyne* (1770), a work to which he said he had been prompted by 'the many and obvious inaccuracies of *the Evergreen*'. There seemed to be no longer any need to apologize for the older poetry. In Hailes's view its merits were self-evident; but he commended it in terms likely to appeal more to the historian than to the general public, for the volume was designed to offer 'such a selection as might illustrate the manners and history, as well as the state of the language and poetry of Scotland during the sixteenth century'.

The reader of songs and ballads was even better supplied. *The Reliques of Ancient Poetry* (1765) contained several Scottish ballads hitherto unprinted that Percy had obtained from Hailes and other Scottish correspondents (see pp. 102–4), and its success stimulated David Herd,[1] a learned and self-effacing antiquary, to publish the best of the collections he had made in a volume entitled *The Ancient and Modern Scots Songs, Heroic Ballads, &c. Now first Collected in one Body* (1769). The preface promised a further volume. This was delayed for seven years, partly because Percy had been asked for his advice and was dilatory in returning the collection. But the revised version of *Ancient and Modern Scottish Songs* (2 volumes, 1776) is much superior to the original volume. This was by far the best collection of ballads and songs that had appeared so far. Much that an amateur could reasonably require was now supplied, except for the tunes themselves. These were already beginning to appear. The way was led by a small collection of fifty, expensively published in London by William Thomson with the title *Orpheus Caledonius : or a Collection of the best Scotch Songs set to Musick* (1725), a first whet to the appetite. During the next sixty-five years more than twenty collections were published, the last of these being the first two of the six volumes of James Johnson's *The Scots Musical Museum* (1787–1803), to which Burns made such important contributions.

While the modern student of ballad and folk-song is immeasurably grateful to these early collectors, he is exasperated from time to time by their attitude to their sources. The origin of their texts is rarely stated with precision, even when such ballads as 'Sir Patrick Spens' and 'Edward' are concerned, which gave them so much delight in the discovery. Furthermore the best scholars relied heavily upon the authority of printed and manuscript sources. How much recourse was had to the living word is difficult to establish. There were collectors before the end of the century. Mrs. Anne Brown, the daughter of an Aberdeen professor, was amassing her repertoire about 1760, and was dictating to her nephew, Professor Robert Scott, some twenty years later, those ballads which so much enriched Walter Scott's *Minstrelsy of the Scottish Border*. But Herd himself seems never to have collected from the living word. He mentions in a letter to George Paton, a fellow antiquary, 'an old Ballad, which I got upwards of two years ago from one William Bell, who had picked it up in Annandale; it was all in detatched

---

[1] David Herd, 1732–1810, was a clerk in Edinburgh, and played an active part in literary society there.

scraps of paper, wrote down by himself at different times, as
he met with those who remembered anything of it—part of
these he had lost, and some of the remainder were illegible, being
chaff'd in his pocket'. Is this an unusually forlorn instance of
a normal process of transcription? It is difficult to say; and it is
impossible to guess how many William Bells in the eighteenth
century anticipated Walter Scott's 'raids' into Liddesdale. Yet
even Scott himself, though he heard the ballads in Liddesdale,
relied for the texts he published in the *Minstrelsy of the Scottish
Border* upon manuscript and printed sources.

In his two miscellanies Ramsay may be said to have displayed some of the resources of the vernacular for poetry, and
in his own verse he showed that the tradition was not broken.
His work belongs to a period covered in another volume, but
something must be said of it here. He saw that the life of the
Edinburgh streets still offered opportunities for the comic or
satiric elegy, and he showed that the stanza used by Sempill for
his elegy on Habbie Simson—'standart Habby', as Ramsay
called it, or the Burns stanza, as we more often call it today—was
still good for the purpose. Standart Habby was also found
suitable for the familiar verse epistle, and Ramsay exchanged
a series with a fellow poet, Hamilton of Gilbertfield. These
Doric Horaces send invitations to pass the day in each other's
company, and exchange compliments on each other's verse in
terms which are lacking neither in warmth nor in vigour:

> Thy raffan rural Rhyme sae rare,
> Sic wordy, wanton, hand-wail'd Ware,
> Sae gash and gay, gars Fowk gae gare[1]
> To ha'e them by them;
> Tho gaffin they wi' Sides sae sair,
> Cry,—'Wae gae by him'.[2]

Merry-making in the countryside prompts another canto of
'Christ's Kirk on the Green' in the same stanza; the 'Cherry
and the Slae' stanza is used for a Horatian poet's wish on the
theme of *Quid dedicatum poscit Apollinem Vates*; Horace's Soracte
ode is translated into an Edinburgh scene, with *'Pentland's*

---

[1] Make People very earnest. [Ramsay's note.]
[2] Tis usual for many, after a full Laugh, to complain of sore Sides, and to
bestow a kindly Curse on the Author of the Jest. [Ramsay's note.]

towring Tap Buried beneath great Wreaths of Snaw' and 'gow-
fers' prevented from 'driving their baws frae Whins or Tee'; and
the poet takes leave of his book *After the Manner of* Horace, *ad
librum suum*', hoping he will never

> see thee lye
> Beneath the Bottom of a Pye,
> Or cow'd out Page by Page to wrap
> Up Snuff, or Sweeties in a Shap.

But if Ramsay showed that the vernacular was no obstacle
to exhibiting a genial poetic personality, he made the limitations
of the vernacular seem no less clear. The implied comparison
with Horace only served to underline how far from the centre
such poetry was; and the language itself, though Ramsay had
been at pains to choose a common denominator of Scottish
dialects and lace it with English poetic diction, was seen to be
no longer one of the literary languages of Europe that Dunbar's
Scots had been. Some limited value it was generally admitted
to have. In southern ears, which had long since been tuned to
the pleasures of Scotch song, this pretty bastard Scots seemed
to enhance the freshness of Ramsay's pastorals. Here was the
modern equivalent of Doric appropriately used for a just
representation of rural manners; Percy even felt that 'the
Scotch . . . by constant attention to their grand national concern
have prevailed so far as to have the Dialect they speak to be
considered as the most proper language for our pastoral poetry'.
And if it also conveyed a suggestion of burlesque, that was no
more than readers of Gay's *Shepherd's Week* were prepared to
welcome.

Yet it is not altogether surprising that at Ramsay's death—
he survived until 1758, but seems to have written nothing in
the years that concern us—there should be few signs of wider
interest in the opportunities the vernacular offered to modern
poetry. Those Scots who, like Robertson, felt strongly the need
of catching up with the English in taste and elegance could be
expected to disdain it. 'Those who now write Scotch', Beattie
told Pinkerton in 1778, 'use an affected mixed, barbarous dialect,
which is neither Scotch nor English, but a strange jumble of
both.' Perhaps it is not surprising that the songs published
in Scotland before the time of Burns are overwhelmingly
English in number; and, to take a single instance, there is not

one Scots poem to be found in Ruddiman's *Edinburgh Magazine* for 1759 amongst its monthly 'poetical essays'. The same is true of *A Collection of Original Poems*, published in 1760 by 'The Rev. Mr. Blacklock, and other Scotch Gentlemen'. The volume contains pastoral ballads, elegies, and odes indistinguishable in effeteness from any that might have been published the same year in London; and there is not so much as a word of native Scots in the conversation of two Edinburgh (sedan-)chair men in a 'town eclogue', modelled upon Gay. Even Hamilton of Bangour, in spite of his association with Ramsay and his lofty Jacobite patriotism, could apparently see no opportunity in Scots either for the elegant compliments or the vigorously expressed reflections he wished to write. It is only for such a folksong as his ancestors and their retainers had been composing for centuries that he turned, naturally, to dialect.

A few writers followed Ramsay's lead. Alexander Nicol, teacher of English at Collace, published a volume of unpolished verse, entitled *The Rural Muse* (1753), in which standart Habby is used for verse epistles and comic elegies, and octosyllabics for pastoral dialogue. There is more merit in the work of Alexander Ross, an elderly schoolmaster of Lochlee, Angus, who was encouraged by Beattie, when he called on the professor at Aberdeen, in 1768, to publish the best of the poems he had written long ago to amuse his solitude. The most substantial of these is *The Fortunate Shepherdess, a Pastoral Tale in Three Cantos*, a somewhat tedious poem of the manners of rustic life, redeemed from time to time by descriptions of mountainous scenery. Ross tells his readers what instructions his muse had given him:

> Speak my ain leed, 'tis gueed auld Scots I mean,
> Your Southron gnaps, I count not worth a preen.
> We've words a fouth, that we can ca' our ain,
> Tho' frae them now my childer sair refrain.

The capture of Havana in 1762 could, perhaps, appropriately, inspire him to a brisk song in plain English, and elsewhere he will use Ramsay's recipe of Anglo-Scots; but in other songs, such as 'The Rock and the wee pickle Tow', which are no less brisk, he attempted to follow the tradition of *The Tea Table Miscellany* by writing new words in the Buchan dialect to old tunes.

'The dialect is so licentious', wrote Beattie to Blacklock, of Ross's volume, '(I mean it is so different from that of the south country, which is acknowledged the standard of broad Scotch), that I am afraid you will be at a loss to understand it.' This ever-nagging problem, to be discussed later, did not prevent Beattie from trying his hand in the same dialect for the limited purpose of commendatory verses addressed to Ross. It is interesting to note that he instinctively chose standart Habby for his stanza, and was surprised to find, as he admitted to Blacklock, that he could write it with ease—and, let us add, with unusual elegance and vigour. Certainly those who know him only as the author of *The Minstrel* would hardly expect his panegyric to find utterance in such terms as the following:

> Sure never carle was haff sae gabby
> E're since the winsome days o' Habby:
> O mayst thou ne'er gang clung or shabby,
>   Nor miss thy snaker!
> Or I'll ca' fortune nasty drabby,
>   And say—pox take her!

A younger contemporary of Alexander Ross was John Skinner, schoolmaster of Monymusk and Episcopalian minister of Longside, Aberdeenshire. In the late 1750s he had followed Ramsay's lead in using the stanza of 'Christ's Kirk on the Green' to describe 'the Monymusk Christmas Ba'ing', and the tradition of Hamilton of Gilbertfield's 'Bonny Heck' is revived in his sentimental elegy on 'The Ewie wi' the Crookit Horn'. Skinner was to live long enough to correspond with Burns both in prose and in standart Habby, for he had written what Burns considered 'the best Scotch song ever Scotland saw,—"Tulloch-gorum's my delight!"' Acknowledging the compliment paid to his uproarious song, Skinner explained in a letter to Burns how his daughters 'being all tolerably good singers, plagued me for words to some of their favourite tunes'.

If Ramsay could be credited with inspiring all the work of the Scottish poets who were setting new words to old tunes, he would have had a numerous progeny. But a movement so widespread could not spring from a single book, however popular *The Tea Table Miscellany* had proved to be. The very fact that Ramsay could so easily enlist 'ingenious young Gentle-men' to help him in his task suggests that the practice was already current; and indeed Lord Yester's reputed setting of words to 'Tweedside' and Lady Grizel Baillie's 'Werena my

Heart Licht' are examples earlier in time than Ramsay. The practice, of which the publication of *The Tea Table Miscellany* merely took advantage, persisted throughout the period. Thus Herd mentions in the preface to *Ancient and Modern Scottish Songs* (1776) that there were 'many of these adopted words to ancient tunes . . . being composed by eminent modern Scots poets'. More or less romantic stories were circulated about the origin of Jean Elliot's 'The Flowers of the Forest', of Mrs. Cockburn's inferior English version, and of Lady Anne Lindsay's 'Auld Robin Gray'; but all stories agree that the poet was stimulated by the haunting melody of a Scottish tune.

Most of the writers mentioned in the last paragraph came from families of noble blood. It seems that in several of these families the tradition of singing old Scots songs and ballads was still surviving. Whether it was the servants who sang them or their masters we cannot be certain; but it may be noticed that when Percy first printed the ballad of 'Edward' in the *Reliques* he had been sent that incomparable version by Sir David Dalrymple (Lord Hailes), who had already printed 'Edom of Gordon' (1755) 'as it was preserved in the memory of a lady'; and the excellent 'Sir Patrick Spens', also printed for the first time in the *Reliques*, seems ultimately to have been derived from 'an old Lady Dowager of Blantyre'. Did these noble singers do nothing to improve the versions that they inherited? Did they never invent new verses? Did they never pass upon the auditors more skilful imitations of the old traditional poems than Lady Wardlaw perpetrated in *Hardyknute*? Had Sir Walter Scott no predecessors in this art of innocent deception? Perhaps we shall never be able to answer these questions; but the evidence suggests that there existed a well-established affection for the folk-poetry and folk-song of Scotland and that it was being kept alive by imaginative reconstruction. This was the tradition that Burns inherited.

But great as his achievements were in lyrical poetry, they do not represent the full capacity of Burns's genius, and this he might never have reached had it not been for Fergusson.[1] He was always willing to acknowledge his debt: 'Rhyme . . . I had

---

[1] Robert Fergusson, 1750–74, was educated at the Royal High School, Edinburgh, and St. Andrews University. He was a clerk in the Commissary Office. He developed manic-depressive symptoms and died in the Edinburgh Bedlam.

given up,' he wrote to Dr. John Moore, on 2 August 1787; 'but meeting with Fergusson's Scotch Poems, I strung anew my wildly sounding, rustic lyre with emulating vigour.' If, as seems probable, this acquaintance dates from 1784, we can judge the excitement of the experience, when we reflect that before 1784 Burns had written nothing in Scots, apart from songs, but 'The Death and Dying Words of Poor Mailie' suggested by Hamilton of Gilbertfield's 'Bonny Heck'; it was in the three years following his discovery of Fergusson in 1784 that he wrote all but one of his great non-lyrical poems.

Fergusson showed opportunities for the poet in Scots that lay beyond Ramsay's reach. If a man may be called slow who achieved so much in a bare twenty-four years of life, Fergusson was slow in using the vernacular for verse, and he never used it exclusively. As a student he had written an irreverent elegy on one of his professors at St. Andrews; but his first appearances in Ruddiman's *Weekly Magazine* (1771) suggest his admiration for such modern masters as Shenstone, Gray, Cunningham, and John Philips. Fergusson was prepared to exercise his skill in English pastoral, ode, epigram, and mock-heroic till the end of his short career; but his poetry would have been forgotten (even his clever satire on Henry Mackenzie, 'The Sow of Feeling') if he had not been prompted to exercise in Scots the skill he had already learned in English.

'The Daft Days' was the beginning. It appeared on 2 January 1772, and must have surprised the discerning reader of the *Weekly Magazine*. It was not merely the first poem Ruddiman had published in Scots, but it plainly announced a new poet. Here was one who had mastered the rhythmical opportunities of standart Habby and had found a new use for that well-worn stave. Instead of the customary verse epistle and mock elegy, the stanza was now being used as an invitation to merry-making, and the appeal is strengthened by that unfailing traditional Scottish contrast between foul weather and warm hearths. But what might well promise most for the future was the range of diction displayed in that poem, the sheer skill in handling words. The poet seemed determined to widen the range of the vernacular. Allowing that it could be used with obvious propriety to convey the cosy and familiar ('Sma are our cares, our stamacks fou O' gusty gear') or a canny reflection ('When fou we're sometimes capernoity') or a bout of 'flyting' (scolding), it

needed strengthening to deal with a wider variety of expression,
and Fergusson can be seen blending his native Lothian speech
with words from other regions, with written Scots, obsolete
words picked from the makars, and for certain limited purposes
with thieves' argot. He even finds a place for those Latinate
words which are still spoken by Scottish lips with so much
relish; and so 'the bleer-ey'd sun' runs his race in December
days 'thro' his *minimum* of space', and 'a canty Highland reel
. . . even *vivifies* the heel To skip and dance'. Nor, if the vernacular was to hold its head in a wider context of modern British
poetry, could it avoid those admirable conventions that all
allow, such as the vivid personification; and so,

> Tho' Discord gie a canker'd snarl
>   To spoil our glee,
> As lang's there's pith into the barrel
>   We'll drink and gree.

Fergusson shows that he had already learned a lesson that Pope
and Gray could have taught him. While they delight us with
a well-placed vulgarism in a passage of otherwise elegantly
familiar verse, Fergusson delights us by his skill in placing
words from a wider British usage into a Lothian setting.

This scarcely amounted to the reconstitution of Scots as a
literary language suited to all the purposes of poetry; so much
could not be expected from one man in a bare two years' work,
which was all that was allowed to Fergusson after writing
'The Daft Days'. For certain themes and kinds of verse—the
serious elegy, the ode, the burlesque—he continued to rely
largely on English. This is not at all surprising. Twelve years
after Fergusson's death, Henry Mackenzie could write in the
Lounger (No. 97), reviewing Burns's poems, that 'even in Scotland,
the provincial dialect which Ramsay and [Burns] have used, is
now read with a difficulty which greatly damps the pleasure of
the reader', and a writer in the *Mirror* (No. 83) in 1780 assumed
that 'grave dignified composition', in poetry as much as in
prose, must necessarily be written in a manner different from
that in which the writer speaks; only if he 'descend to common
and ludicrous pictures of life' will his language approach that
of common life. Scots was still felt to have a 'hamely' tang: its
'auld-warld wordies clack In hame-spun rhime'; and though,
good patriot as Fergusson was, he saw plenty to engage his

attention in the life of Scotland, and more nearly in the manners of the Edinburgh streets, he seems to have found himself restricted when writing Scots to certain attitudes. It is to his credit that these attitudes were not exclusively 'common and ludicrous'. Some were obviously appropriate to the Doric. Thus Ramsay had already shown how favourable the vernacular was to a realistic pastoral, and Fergusson in following him extended his range. In one poem Willie advises his brother ploughman Sandie on his household troubles, and in another Geordie joins Davie in lamenting the death of a fellow shepherd, no less a man than Dr. William Wilkie, poet and natural philosophy professor at St. Andrews, but more especially interesting to his mourners for his agricultural experiments. These poems are skilfully devised mutations upon the Virgilian pastoral, and they justify Fergusson in his unfulfilled ambition of completing Gavin Douglas's work with a version of Virgil's *Eclogues* and *Georgics*. But even more original and ambitious than his two dialogues is the lovingly detailed genre-painting of 'The Farmer's Ingle'. It is a townsman's poem written for townsmen; unlike his English contemporary Crabbe, Fergusson recalls none of the ills and inconveniences of country life; but without trace of sentimentality, and with no more than a touch of patronage, the poem generates a warm admiration for the countryman's best qualities. It is just such a reinstatement of the pastoral as Johnson would have approved, and it is presented in a dignified elaborate stanza quite foreign to those that Ramsay had retrieved from the past. Fergusson might have discovered a suitable verse from amidst the manifold richness of Dunbar, but in choosing to adapt the Spenserian stanza, he showed his readiness to learn from English poetry, and not for the first time. Shenstone had employed it to describe rustic manners; but perhaps the recent success of Beattie's *Minstrel* (1771) was needed to persuade him that the stanza admitted dignity as well as simplicity of style, and that obsolete expressions, the bane of earlier poets who had used it, were not a necessary adjunct.

This dignity had already been apparent in the 'Elegy, on the Death of Scots Music', and in much of 'Auld Reekie', Fergusson's longest and perhaps his most successful poem. It demonstrates most obviously Fergusson's capacity to rise above the vulgarity with which Ramsay had associated the vernacular and its principal verse forms. Nevertheless it is the 'low'

humours of Edinburgh life that provide the staple of Fergusson's poetry. Restrictive as this topic is, it is remarkable what
range of voice lay within his control. Standart Habby is used,
for more varied purposes than ever before, to convey the good
cheer of 'Caller Oysters', the contemptuous merriment of 'The
King's Birth-Day in Edinburgh', and the ironical exposure of
citizens who judge a man's merits by the 'Braid Claith' he
wears. It is equally serviceable for perhaps the first revival of
'flyting' since the makars in 'To the Tron-kirk Bell', and for
the compliments proffered to the bonny lasses of Edinburgh in
'Caller Water'. There is more flyting in the two dialogues,
'Mutual Complaint of Plainstanes and Causey, in their Mother-
tongue' and 'A Drink Eclogue: Landlady, Brandy and Whisky',
two poems that recall Swift not only in the metrical skill and
Hudibrastic rhymes of their octosyllabics, but in the adaptation
of a rural 'kind' to city life that Swift had been the first to invent
in his two 'georgics', 'A Description of the Morning' and 'A
Description of a City Shower'. And closely related to these is
the sturdy admonishment addressed 'To the Principal and Professors of the University of St. Andrews, on their superb treat
to Dr. Johnson', where the vigour and vulgarity of the vernacular enhance the abuse.

To these poems we may add the gay descriptions of 'Hallow-
Fair' and 'Leith Races', both written in the tradition of 'Christ's
Kirk on the Green', whose stanza is intelligently adapted for
the purpose. All of them reveal a strong poetic personality,
self-confident, irreverent, outspoken, yet pithy of speech,
observant, and eminently sociable, one admirably suited to
stand up for Scottish rights, and to represent those qualities
which were felt to distinguish the Scotsman from the Englishman. If he had been able to cultivate his lyric vein—for in spite
of his close friendship with David Herd Fergusson was not
stimulated to write more than one song in Scots—he would
have qualified as the laureate poet of a small nation (with the
restriction in scope that that title implies); for even though
his work is based on city life, he could suit his lines, as an
admirer told him, 'to fock that's out about 'Mang hills and braes'.
In an exceptionally short career he had shown what could be
done in the vernacular to any who might follow him; and those
who were ready to look beyond the personality to the craftsman
could see the opportunities that Scots offered an educated poet,

one who was prepared to learn his trade from classical and modern masters, who could see where the local dialects needed strengthening, who would not be content with the limited resources of a few traditional staves, and who might rise from the local and temporal (as Fergusson scarcely succeeds in doing) to the universal.

In the years immediately succeeding Fergusson's death it is possible to find a little more Scots verse. Whereas Ruddiman had published nothing in Scots before Fergusson's arrival, in 1780 there are five poems in standart Habby in *The Weekly Magazine*. And it is even possible to claim that the quality is a little higher: Charles Keith's *The Farmer's Ha'* (1776), though obviously prompted by 'The Farmer's Ingle', is a vivid and cheerful reconstruction of a familiar scene. But in surveying this minor verse, it is impossible not to sympathize with Alexander Geddes in the 'Dissertation on the Scoto-Saxon Dialect' which he contributed to the *Transactions of the Society of the Antiquaries of Scotland* in 1792; he complains that the poets 'have not duly discriminated the genuine Scotish idiom from its vulgarisms'. Their attitude to vocabulary was, he thought, all too like the English Spenserians': 'nothing more was deemed necessary than to interlard the composition with a number of low words and trite proverbial phrases, in common use among the illiterate; and the more anomalous and further removed from polite usage those words and phrases were, so much the more apposite and eligible they were accounted.'

Geddes's dissertation deserves the attention of the modern Scots poet. It came too late for Burns[1] to consider, even if it would have appealed to him. He had his own theory of poetic diction, though he never troubled to express it. His conception of poetry and the poet required him to write, with complete self-consciousness, in an artificial language exceptionally wide in register, but one that neither he nor anyone else ever spoke, whose words were drawn, as his sense of poetical decorum dictated, from his native Ayrshire, from that common denominator of Scottish dialects that Ramsay had established whose

---

[1] Robert Burns, 1759–96, was born in Alloway, Ayrshire, and worked as a farm labourer. After the publication of the Kilmarnock edition of his poems, 1786, he lived for a time in Edinburgh, and then, after another period of farming, became an exciseman.

elements are often mere English words imperfectly disguised by Scottish spelling, and also from Southern English; while his syntax is almost invariably modelled on what is common to both languages. Southern readers may often need to consult a glossary when reading Burns; they are rarely troubled by the structure of his sentences.

When he came to publish his first volume of poems at Kilmarnock in 1786 he made a selection of forty, more than three-quarters of which he seems to have written in the preceding eighteen months. He dipped further into the past to retrieve a couple of songs and some religious pieces, for one of which the versified psalms had provided him with his model, but the majority bear witness to that excited redirection of his talents consequent upon his discovery of Fergusson's poems. The year 1785–6 was as much an *annus mirabilis* in his career as 1797–8 was in Wordsworth's. Fergusson revealed to him, as the already familiar Ramsay could not, the variety of tone attainable in Scots poetry, the range of diction that lay at his command, and the sheer professional skill that an educated poet could achieve.

The preface to the Kilmarnock edition indicates the principles on which the selection was made:

Unacquainted with the necessary requisites for commencing Poet by rule, he sings the sentiments and manners, he felt and saw in himself and his rustic compeers around him, in his and their native language.

He was concerned, then, with the image of the poet he intended to present, and with the manners he proposed to display.

The poet is a rustic poet, it seems, untaught, singing by the light of nature, for 'the Learned and the Polite' are urged to 'make every allowance for Education and Circumstances of Life'. While it is true that Burns was a farmer and the son of a farmer, he was by no means uneducated. From early days he had studied the works of Shakespeare, Locke, Pope, Addison, and the English poets of an earlier generation, and had learned to write a good formal English prose style. Furthermore, when he visited Edinburgh in 1786, he impressed his new acquaintances not only by the dignity of his bearing but by his command of educated Scots speech. Dugald Stewart wrote

Nothing, perhaps, was more remarkable among his various attainments, than the fluency, precision, and originality of his language, when he spoke in company; more particularly as he aimed at purity in his turn of expression, and avoided more successfully than most Scotchmen, the peculiarities of Scottish phraseology.

The width of his reading is apparent everywhere in his poetry, and shows that it was in no sense untaught. When taxed with this by Robert Anderson, Burns freely admitted that it was a part of the machinery, as he called it, of his poetical character to pass for an illiterate ploughman who wrote from pure inspiration. . . . He even admitted the advantages he enjoyed in poetic composition from the *copia verborum*, the command of phraseology, which the knowledge and use of the English and Scottish dialects afforded him.

He may like us to think that he was one of the 'merry, friendly, country-folks' gathered together in 'Halloween'; but in fact he stands a little apart from the rest, and there is no better evidence of his stance than the second sentence of his prefatory note to that poem:

The passion of prying into futurity makes a striking part of the history of human nature in its rude state, in all ages and nations; and it may be some entertainment to a philosophic mind, if any such should honour the author with a perusal, to see the remains of it among the more unenlightened in our own.

We may properly call the poem a piece of genre-painting, but we must not fail to recognize that the author is a man of 'the Enlightenment', who aspires to be a serious student of folklore, and writes for the attention of fellow students, as well as for those whom he said it was his strongest wish to please, 'my Compeers, the rustic Inmates of the Hamlet'.

This is but a casual sidelight on the poet. His portrait of himself is more consciously drawn in the verse epistles published in the Kilmarnock edition. Addressing 'Davie, a brother poet', he writes almost as one Theocritean shepherd to another, content with little in a humble way of life, and envying the rich nothing of their purse-proud state. It is January, and Scottish poets have never concealed the rigours of a northern winter:

> While frosty winds blaw in the drift,
>   Ben to the chimla lug,
> I grudge a wee the great-folk's gift
>   That live sae bien an' snug:
>   I tent less, and want less
>   Their roomy fire-side;
>   But hanker, and canker,
>   To see their cursed pride.

But there are blander seasons when on the braes 'we'll sit an' sowth a tune', and then with Meg and Jean they will relish 'The smile of love, the friendly tear, The sympathetic glow'. These words are the small change that every Man of Feeling carried about him at that time, and Burns can use it too; but in 'To a Mouse', he can write more realistically, with a more deeply sympathetic sense of a predicament, and yet remain recognizably in the mid-stream of eighteenth-century sentiment.

In epistles to other poets he reveals more features of his self-portrait. Lapraik is told that Burns is 'just a rhymer like by chance', that he makes no pretence to learning, asks simply for 'ae spark o' nature's fire', and hopes merely to fulfil great Nature's plan by being 'the social, friendly, honest man'. But he does in fact aspire to more, as he tells William Simson of Ochiltree: he intends to do for the rivers of Ayrshire what Ramsay and Fergusson have done for Forth and Tay; and in the very next stanza he shows that even fame as a regional poet will not content him:

> Th'Ilissus, Tiber, Thames, an' Seine,
> Glide sweet in monie a tunefu' line;
> But Willie, set your fit to mine,
>   An' cock your crest;
> We'll gar our streams an' burnies shine
>   Up wi' the best!

The lesser ambition is the burden of 'The Vision', in which he dreams he is visited by Coila, the muse of the region. She has recognized his love of nature, and has taught him his love poetry; now his fame spreads throughout her wide domains, and he must remember in all he writes to preserve the dignity of man.

In other poems where self-portraiture is less obviously intentional, he presents the character of a Scottish patriot, whose manly independence is not inconsistent with impudence of address ('The Author's Earnest Cry and Prayer', 'A Dream'), but whose jocularity and high spirits ('Address to the Deil', 'The Holy Fair') are qualified by fits of despondency ('Despondency, an Ode'), a man who detests hypocrisy ('A Dedication') and the insolence of social rank ('The Twa Dogs'), and one given to summarizing his experience of life not only in saws of peasant wisdom ('The best-laid schemes o' mice an' men

Gang aft agley'; 'O wad some power the giftie gie us To see
oursel as ithers see us') but in more extended advice ('Epistle to
a Young Friend').

The painter of the manners of his 'rustic compeers' is found
in many of the poems already mentioned, notably 'The Twa
Dogs'—that highly successful emulation of a Fergusson dialogue
which he chose for the first place in the volume—'Scotch Drink',
and 'The Holy Fair', in both of which the stimulus of reading
Fergusson is no less strongly felt. But Burns no doubt looked
upon 'The Cotter's Saturday Night' as his diploma piece in this
kind. It has not given so much pleasure in modern times as
it was certainly calculated to give to the Men of Feeling of
the day. Henry Mackenzie and John Skinner (the author of
'Tullochgorum', p. 152) were two of many who praised it
highly. The poem is one more whose original inspiration lay in
a poem by Fergusson; but whereas in 'The Farmer's Ingle' the
detail is uncompromisingly Scottish, in 'The Cotter's Saturday
Night' Burns seems to have been at pains to place his Scottish
scene in a wider setting. To this design we may perhaps attribute
the echoes of Gray in the second and third stanzas, transposed
as they are from a Buckinghamshire summer evening to the end
of a Scottish winter's day, the attempt once more at the famous
passage from Lucretius on the welcome awaiting the home-
coming labourer, and incidentally the seemingly deliberate
restraint in the use of dialect. This is Burns's way of persuading
the reader that what seems merely local has universal significance. At no point is this clearer than at the devotional climax
of the poem. The guidman, who leads his family in service,
shows a 'patriarchal grace' and re-enacts his 'priest-like' function as he reads from both testaments and offers up his prayers.
His manner is humble; its significance appears to be local; but
it is not so, and to help himself in proving it, Burns eliminates
all Scottish diction and draws upon what Beattie's *Minstrel* (pp.
62–3) had taught him about the swelling tones of the Spenserian
stanza to convey his lesson: 'From scenes like these, old Scotia's
grandeur springs.' The poem is not one of Burns's greatest, but
it has more artistry than it is often credited with, in design, in
the relation and subordination of the parts, in the control of
diction, and the use of stanza.

The poems which Burns added to his second edition (Edinburgh, 1787) did not significantly extend the range of the Kil-

marnock edition, though they included such well-loved pieces as 'Address to a Haggis' and 'Tam Samson's Elegy', one more example of the poet working in an established tradition and successfully challenging all competitors. But he was not content simply to challenge his Scottish predecessors, as two other new poems show. 'A Winter Night' is a curious experiment, an irregular Pindaric ode prefaced by half a dozen stanzas of standart Habby. Some lines from Lear's reflections on suffering humanity serve as an epigraph. The winter scene is set with remarkable economy in the opening stanzas which sympathize with the distress of birds and animals; but before the introduction is completed, Scots diction yields to English in preparation for another type of description, no less economical, the use of descriptive personification that Burns had undoubtedly learned from the odes of Collins, while echoes from the songs of Amiens in *As You Like It* prepare the transition from birds and animals suffering in winter to the theme of the descriptive ode, that no severity of climate can match the inhumanity of man to man. While it is Collins whom he challenges in 'A Winter Night', it is the dignity and energy of Gray that he masters in 'Address to Edinburgh'. These minor achievements are often overlooked or even scorned by those whose interest in Burns begins and ends with his poems in Scots, and who have never learned to take a sympathetic interest in English eighteenth-century poetry. They necessarily fail to appreciate the full range of Burns's poetical skill.

The Edinburgh edition contains two new ecclesiastic satires to support 'The Holy Fair'; these are 'The Ordination' and 'Address to the Unco' Guid'. Burns showed caution in publishing his views on church matters. He had touched on the subject in his 'Dedication' to Gavin Hamilton, but seems to have reflected that there was no point in courting controversy by placing the poem in its natural place at the head of the Kilmarnock volume, and had demoted it to a more lowly position. More significantly he did not publish the severest and most personal of these satires, 'Holy Willie's Prayer'; it was not published until after his death.[1] Thus he was never to see in

---

[1] 'The Jolly Beggars', brilliant both in its genre-painting and its varied versification, was also excluded from the Edinburgh edition at the advice of Hugh Blair. No doubt he thought it too 'low'; it could scarcely have been 'lower', yet it may be felt to have been within the limits tolerated by those who continued to respond so eagerly to *The Beggar's Opera*.

print one of his greatest poems and his most original use of standart Habby, namely for a monologue in which a representa- tive of Calvinism reveals the soul-destroying inhumanity of his creed and at the same time shows how his own personality is deeply flawed by contradictions. Compared with that poem, 'The Ordination' is a hilariously inoffensive mock-celebration of the triumphs of Burns's Calvinistic 'Auld Licht' opponents; and the 'Address to the Unco Guid' is equally inoffensive in that it avoids personalities to explain the moral basis of Burns's position; the rigidly righteous are bidden to exercise imagina- tion and charity in judging the failings of their fellow men and women, for

> Who made the heart, 'tis He alone
>   Decidedly can try us;
> He knows each chord, its various tone,
>   Each spring, its various bias:
> Then at the balance let's be mute,
>   We never can adjust it,
> What's done we partly may compute,
>   But know not what's resisted.

Burns wrote one more important non-lyrical poem after the publication of the Edinburgh edition, namely 'Tam o' Shanter' (1790). To describe an earlier encounter with infernal powers in 'Death and Doctor Hornbook' he had used, without particu- lar appropriateness, the well-accustomed rhythms of standart Habby; but for 'Tam o' Shanter' he turned for greater speed and freedom to Hudibrastic octosyllabics, whose suitability for narrative had been clearly demonstrated by Prior, Swift, and many more recent poets. His interest had been awakened by his friend Francis Grose, the antiquary, who had asked for something from the poet to accompany an engraving of Alloway Kirk in his *Antiquities of Scotland* (1790). Burns's letters to Grose, in which he tells more than one story about the ruined kirk, express the same enlightened superiority to peasant beliefs that we have already observed in his short preface to 'Halloween'; but now he took much more care to keep his 'philosophical' interests out of the poem. The narrator is obviously a crony of Tam's, ready to wag his finger at him in half-earnest reproof, or to sympathize with him, whether in 'bousing at the nappy' or in recklessly challenging those infernal powers that were a blend of popular superstition and of Auld Licht sanctions; but like the poet himself, the narrator has a command of English diction into which he can modulate when decorum requires. The poet's artistry is best shown in the brilliant repetitive effects, the shafts of light piercing the surrounding darkness, with which he binds the parts of his story together; for the 'ingle bleezing finely' in the inn at Ayr is no less representative of one sort of enjoyment than 'Kirk-Alloway in a bleeze' is of quite another sort, and each exerts its own attraction when contrasted with the discomforts of the surrounding darkness.

The two movements in eighteenth-century Scottish poetry are roughly and inadequately represented by *The Ever Green* and *The Tea Table Miscellany*; the work of Burns represents the culmination of each. *The Ever Green* movement succeeded in re-establishing part, though only part, of the tradition of writing non-lyrical poetry in Scots. The courtliness of Dunbar and the learning of Henryson were beyond recovery, and Burns had no aspirations in either direction; what he did was to extend a little the limits defined in the work of Ramsay and Fergusson, to perfect what lay within those limits, and to demonstrate once more that a Scotsman, no less than an Englishman or an Irishman, could contribute successfully to the broader stream of British poetry in the eighteenth century.

To say that Burns followed in the tradition of *The Tea Table Miscellany* would be to give no indication of the sympathy and brilliance of his workmanship. Yet he was like Ramsay and his associates, and like Herd, Hailes, Paton, and others mentioned earlier in this chapter in that he collected Scottish folk-songs—and ballads too: he found a magnificent variant of 'Tam Lin'; he repaired the words where necessary, and wrote new words to old tunes. His interest in traditional song and his attempts to write verses for music went back to the beginnings of his poetical career. He published a few of his songs in the Kilmarnock edition, and added a few more to the Edinburgh edition, but he did not devote himself to song-collecting and song-writing until the last years of his life. His interests were widened and stimulated by his experience of the musical life of Edinburgh, a city which was then full of enthusiasts, collectors, song-writers, musical antiquaries, and music publishers; and to this experience succeeded the opportunity of hearing Highland songs, strathspeys, and reels during his tour of the north. But the number of his songs would undoubtedly have been much less extensive, if he had not eagerly agreed to contribute to two collections then in course of preparation, James Johnson's *The Scots Musical Museum* (6 volumes, 1787–1803), and George Thomson's *A Select Collection of Original Scotish Airs for the voice* (6 volumes, 1793–1825).

The long series of his letters to Thomson throws light on Burns's policy and his manner of proceeding. The preservation of the tunes was his objective; words are subservient to that purpose. A dance tune may have a better chance of survival if it is equipped with words, even if the tempo must be changed in the process. An old set of words should be retained if it is worthy of the tune, but words may require anything from amendment to rewriting. Thus there is still some dispute about which amongst several versions of 'Auld Lang Syne' Burns chose to work upon, and how much therefore is certainly his; 'O whistle an' I'll come to ye, my lad' was built up from a chorus; and for the original bawdy complaint by a young wife of her old husband, Burns retained simply the first line 'John Anderson, my jo, John' and composed a gracious song in which passion has mellowed to affection.

In these circumstances it is not surprising that Burns should have published so few of his songs with his other poems, since they were less to be considered as poems than as adornments of music; and the demands of music might be so great as to over-tax the poet. Thus Thomson is told (8 November 1792) that he may have to put up with the second-rate:

There is a peculiar rhythmus in many of our airs, and a necessity of adapting syllables to the emphasis, or what I would call, the *feature notes*, of the tune, that cramps the Poet, & lays him under almost insuperable difficulties.—For instance, in the air, My Wife's a wanton wee thing, if a few lines, *smooth & pretty*, can be adapted to it, it is all you can expect,

and he enclosed something done 'extempore', which would suit 'the light-horse gallop of the air' better than anything more profoundly studied.

His custom was not to be content with the 'extempore', though always he would first 'consider the poetic Sentiment, correspondent to my idea of the musical expression'. That is to say, the character of the tune dictates the character of the words and their theme; and accordingly no response is adequate which fails to take account of the union of words and music.

The care with which words are adapted to the character of a tune may be illustrated from 'Ye banks and braes o' bonnie Doon' written for the well-known 'Caledonian Hunt's delight'. The tune is an example of simple binary form, in which the first air (repeated) plays about the keynote, rising only once and momentarily higher than a major third above; but the second tune is lifted a good deal higher, only to sink back to a repetition of the unaspiring first air in conclusion. To Burns it seems that the lift of the second air suggested a new note of urgency, which he represented in his first verse by the lines:

> Thou'll break my heart, thou warbling bird,
> That wantons thro' the flowering thorn;

while the return of the lowly first air dictates a relapse into despondency:

> Thou minds me o' departed joys,
> Departed never to return!

A similar response to the life of an air is to be noticed in several other songs, in 'Ay, waukin, O', for example. There the delicious melancholy of sleeplessness 'for thinking on my dearie' was given to him by the chorus of the old song; but for the lift of the air he devises a new theme, which leads him back in the end to his original theme as the second air echoes the last phrase of the chorus:

CHORUS: Ay, waukin, O, waukin still and wearie!
Sleep I can get nane for thinking on my dearie.

VERSE: Simmer's a pleasant time; Flowers of ev'ry colour;
The water rins o'er the heugh, And I long for my true lover.

Such songs cannot stand independently of their music. But while readers have certainly derived satisfaction from other songs treated purely as lyrics, even these lose by the divorce. Thus 'Ae fond kiss' is one of Burns's most elegant performances, and the famous fourth verse ('Had we never lov'd sae kindly . . .') is one of the greatest moments of its kind in his work. But we miss a great deal if we do not have the tune of 'Rory Dall's Port' in our memory, with its drop of a major fourth in the first line that lends such poignant emphasis to 'and thén we sever' 'Fare-thee-weel, thou first and fairest', and 'Ae farewell, alás, for ever'. This song also indicates Burns's recognition of the rhythmical variants possible in the beautiful third line of the music:

> Deep in heart wrung tears I'll pledge thee;
>
> But to see her was to love her;
>
> Never met, or never parted.

Burns's work was the culmination, but not the end of a movement. Ballads and folk-songs are still being collected today in Scotland from the lips of singers. There is a difference, however. Modern collectors use the tape-recorder, by means of which they are able to record what they hear more accurately than ever before; but is there a place for a modern Burns to ensure that these recovered songs live in people's hearts and memories?

VI

DRAMA

A HISTORIAN of late eighteenth-century literature would be irresponsible if he encouraged his readers to spend time on the tragedy, or much time on the comedy, of the day in the belief that they would derive profit or pleasure from their reading. Two or three comedies have justifiably maintained a place amongst those plays that are commonly revived; a few more may occasionally be seen from time to time; but only one tragedy, Home's *Douglas*, seems to have been performed in recent years. No other branch of eighteenth-century literature has sunk so far beyond any reasonable hopes of rescue. Yet the eighteenth-century theatre was a lively institution. It catered successfully for all social ranks, and was served by excellent actors. Some of them, notably the great mimic Samuel Foote, the character actor Charles Macklin, and that great interpreter of the passions David Garrick, wrote plays that achieved considerable success. Garrick's career at Drury Lane (1741–76) covers the greater part of our period, and his influence, rather than the influence of John Rich, his fellow actor-manager at Covent Garden, pervaded the repertoire, the encouragement of young playwrights, and the style of acting and presentation.

A period of good theatre may coincide with a period of worthless drama because, obviously, the theatre is not dependent upon the work of contemporary dramatists. Any given evening's entertainment in our period would consist, besides the main piece, of a musical prelude, a prologue, entr'actes of music and dancing, an epilogue, a procession, and an after-piece of farce, pantomime, or burletta. Where so much is offered, the importance of the main piece is necessarily depreciated; the audience might be prepared to tolerate an inadequate tragedy for the sake of a well-loved farce to follow. Furthermore there was a large repertoire of earlier plays to choose from. Dramatists found themselves, like Scottish poets in the previous chapter, competing for a hearing with the great writers of the past, writers whom they honoured and whose achievements they

imitated. But to read the tragedies of this age is not to feel
that writers were stimulated by their predecessors' work, as we
recognize when we read Fergusson and Burns, but to feel that
they had been overwhelmed: tragic themes and situations have
been largely exhausted, and the sole resource left is to endow them with the novelty of a freshly coloured setting. The
vehicle had become stereotyped, too. A blank verse, with more
feminine endings than are customary in Shakespeare, but in
other respects similar to that of his middle years in structure,
had become standard. It is true that Moore's *The Gamester*
(1753)[1] and Cumberland's *The Mysterious Husband* (1783)[2] are
written in what appears at first sight to be prose; but the elevation of the sentiments makes such irresistible demands upon
style and rhythm as to lead the dramatists back unawares to
long stretches of imperfectly concealed blank verse.

Shakespeare, adapted to suit contemporary taste, was already
well established in the repertoire before Garrick took charge
at Drury Lane. He restored some texts, and revived *Antony
and Cleopatra*, *Cymbeline*, and *Coriolanus*: but by the end of
his career the number of Shakespeare's plays in stock was
actually reduced. It has been calculated, however, that during
Garrick's reign as many as twenty-three per cent. of the main
pieces presented were by Shakespeare. If to these are added the
revivals of other still popular pre-Restoration plays, and those
of Otway, Southerne, Rowe, and later dramatists, as well as
the new comedies that were written, it will be seen that contemporary tragic writers provided only a small share of the
repertoire, in spite of the management's casting a more lenient
eye over a new tragedy than over a new comedy.

Although Shakespeare's plays were popular, and blank verse
had become the established medium of tragedy, his tragic
themes and situations were not felt to lend themselves happily
to modern imitation. An exception is Dodsley's *Cleone* (1758),
in which Sifroy, a white Othello, is persuaded of his wife

[1] Edward Moore, 1712–57, linen-draper and the author of *Fables for the Female
Sex*. Apart from his plays, he is best remembered for his editorship of a highly
successful periodical essay, *The World* (see pp. 315–19).
[2] Richard Cumberland, 1732–1811, grandson of the famous scholar, Richard
Bentley. A contemporary at Westminster School of Cowper, Churchill, and Colman. Fellow of Trinity College, Cambridge. He held various posts under government patronage, including secretaryship to the Board of Trade, which interrupted
his dramatic career (begun in 1765) between 1778 and 1782. An associate of
Garrick, Reynolds, Goldsmith, and later of Samuel Rogers.

Cleone's infidelity by one 'whose friendship, with reluctant grief, At length disclosed my shame', namely 'honest Glanville'. Sifroy maintains his right to punish his wife:

> That flower, which look'd so beauteous to the sense,
> Ran wild, grew ranker than a common weed.

But Glanville had already arranged for the murder of Cleone, her son, and the Cassio-like figure of Paulet—ineffectively, as it turns out, since his hired assassin succeeds only in murdering the little boy. But Cleone's mind is affected by the experience, and Paulet survives to attest her innocence.

The interest of this reshaping of *Othello* is that the audience's sympathies are redirected. Instead of Othello's holding the centre of the stage, it is now Desdemona. Cleone, who has no particular beauty or power of character to attract our interest, is a female in distress. It is enough that she is basely slandered and unprotected; and her madness, depicted first against a pastoral background which faintly recalls Ophelia's death, and subsequently enacted on stage before her harrowed relatives, is a bold appeal for pathos. Dodsley permits her to recover her senses a few lines before she dies.

This redirection of sympathy from a male to a female protagonist is characteristic of the tragedy of the day. It is apparent much earlier in the work of Rowe; but so pervasive a change cannot be attributed to the influence of one man. In Whitehead's reshaping of Corneille's *Horace* called *The Roman Father* (1750), the interest centres upon a conflict of loyalties in Horatia, married to a Curiatius who is chosen by the senators of the rival city for mortal combat with her brother. It centres too upon the noble-minded heroine of Murphy's *The Grecian Daughter* (1772), and upon the hapless Empress Zaphira in Brown's *Barbarossa* (1754), the captive of a usurping tyrant, forced to recognize the overwhelming odds that face her son, the rightful heir. Home's *Douglas* (1756)[1] has been praised for the character of the shepherd Norval, whom Henry Mackenzie regarded as a self-portrait of the author; but the audience's attention is drawn

---

[1] John Home, 1722–1808, was minister of Athelstaneford, East Lothian (1747–57), a leader of the broad church party, and a friend of Adam Ferguson, Adam Smith, the historian Robertson, and David Hume (a kinsman). The first performance of *Douglas* at an Edinburgh theatre, though enthusiastically received, was deeply offensive to the ruling party of the church, who initiated proceedings against the author and another minister who attended, Alexander Carlyle.

principally to Lady Randolph, brooding at the opening of the play upon the sorrows she cannot reveal to her husband, then reunited to Norval who is discovered to be the long-lost son of a concealed first marriage with Douglas, and driven at last to suicide when her son is killed by her husband in a fit of jealousy prompted by the wicked Glenalvon. And though the pre-eminence of Beverley seems intended in Moore's *The Gamester*, much turns upon the suffering he inflicts by his gaming on his noble and forgiving wife.

The Gamester was produced two years after the publication of a much more substantial and meritorious work, a novel, by Fielding, in which a noble and forgiving wife suffers for the irresponsible follies of her husband; but her pre-eminence is recognized by her name on the title-page, *Amelia*. Nor is she the only hapless female in the novels of the day, as will be seen in a later chapter. Richardson's Pamela is never seriously in danger, in spite of her hazardous isolation, Clementina in *Sir Charles Grandison* is a more nearly tragic figure who is pretty dextrously driven to madness; but *Clarissa* has a heroine as noble-minded as Mrs. Beverley, as distressed in the conflict of duties as Horatia, and as forlorn as Cleone. That novel is the one completely successful tragedy of the century, and its power lies in its control of the emotional note that so many tragic dramatists of the day were attempting to touch. Nor are Richardson and Fielding the only novelists whose work shares some common ground with the dramatists' preoccupations. We may recall the unprotected state of Charlotte Lennox's Henrietta and Fanny Burney's Evelina, and the more serious trials of her Cecilia; the treatment is sometimes comic and sometimes tragic, but it is always aimed at invoking pity for female distress. This preoccupation need cause us no surprise when we reflect that the age was the first in which women began to take a prominent position in society.

More baffling is the tragic dramatists' fondness for that old and threadbare device, *anagnorisis*, the discovery of identity. Here too there are analogies in contemporary novels, but at best—as in *Tom Jones*—it is felt to have some comic convenience, while in *Joseph Andrews* and *Humphry Clinker* its farcical character is blandly acknowledged. The devices of drama are admittedly neutral: what becomes principally associated with comedy or even farce may still be rescued for tragedy by a gifted writer.

The irony which resided in the Greek use of *anagnorisis*, when only the audience can see the fate that must overtake a character unaware of his own identity, was still available for use. Cumberland seems to have been faintly aware of this when, in *The Mysterious Husband*, he arranges for young Davenant to fall in love with the lady his father has bigamously married and abandoned. But for the most part *anagnorisis* in these tragedies serves principally to create surprise and to provide for an emotional reunion. Such is the recognition between mother and son effected in *Douglas* and *Barbarossa* already mentioned, but also in Whitehead's *Creusa* (1754), in Cumberland's *The Carmelite* (1784), and in two plays by Murphy,[1] *The Orphan of China* (1759) and *Alzuma* (1773), where Alzuma reveals himself first to his sister. A parodist might have noted that identity once revealed must then be kept secret for the sake of dramatic convenience rather than for motives that appeal to reason: thus it is only by concealing the identity of their sons that Home's Lady Randolph and Cumberland's Lady Saint Valori can arouse the jealousies of their husbands.

The emotional opportunities provided may perhaps sufficiently account for the pervasiveness of *anagnorisis* in the tragedy of the age. The explanation would certainly be in keeping with the overriding impulse of contemporary dramatists. The neatness of construction shown by even the few good structural craftsmen amongst them, such as Whitehead and Murphy, is subservient, not to story, theme, or character—they cared little for these—but to the depiction of emotion, or better still, emotional conflict; and therein lay the success of the partnership between dramatist and actor, who wanted no better opportunity for exhibiting his command of declamation and gesture. Murphy, for example, was quite frank about his motives. In the prologue to *Zenobia* (1768), he announces that he will 'waken to sentiment the feeling heart', and will try to rouse a succession of conflicting emotions:

> If in his scenes alternate passions burn,

(and he lists them: 'friendship, love, guilt, virtue')

> You'll give—'tis all he asks—one virtuous tear.

[1] Arthur Murphy, 1727–1805, was an Irish-born actor. His stage career extended from 1754, when he acted Othello at Covent Garden, till 1793 (a performance of his *The Rival Sisters*). He was a barrister, a close friend of Dr. Johnson, and later of Samuel Rogers.

Accordingly the audience is treated to displays of Roman energy and determination, and of tyrannical insolence; unimpeachable sentiments are expressed about liberty and patriotism, mercy is powerfully invoked, the pathos of a child separated from its mother is described, and the view of a battlefield demands the audience's pity though it evokes no response in the tyrant's breast—grand opportunities for star actors to declaim, with little or no need to rehearse a scene with their fellows.

In one other aspect of their work the tragic dramatists were responsive to the demands felt and expressed by other writers. Shenstone's recognition of the need for new scenes and images, mentioned in a letter to MacGowan, has been quoted in Chapter IV (p. 94). The dramatists undoubtedly felt the same. While Dodsley and Whitehead were still prepared to set their actions in Rome or ancient Greece, Murphy followed literally the advice of his friend Dr. Johnson and surveyed mankind from China (*The Orphan of China*) to Peru (*Alzuma*). Others preferred a setting in historical or legendary Britain. Brooke went back to Elizabethan times for *The Earl of Essex* (1750); Hannah More took a step or two further for the setting of *Percy* (1777), and Cumberland's *The Carmelite* opens romantically beneath a castle wall on the shores of the Isle of Wight in the reign of Henry III. Home had based *Douglas* on the Border Ballad of 'Gill Morris', but for *The Fatal Discovery* (1769) he tried, ineffectually, to invoke the melancholy splendours of Ossian. In *Elfrida* (1752) and *Caractacus* (1759) Gray's friend Mason ranged still further back to Saxon and British times. Perhaps it is not too fantastic to see in this learned clergyman a prototype of T. S. Eliot, trying to make some of the devices of Greek drama flourish in an alien setting. Endowed with less sense of theatre than his successor and much less poetical power, he marshals a chorus of maidens in a Warwickshire forest, who are at once attendants upon Elfrida, the confidantes of her joys and troubles, commentators upon the action, and ready with a rehearsed choric ode, as the exigencies of the drama require.

Thus writers of tragedy, like poets and novelists, attempt by the choice of more romantic settings to escape from themes and subjects which they felt to be restricting. But change of setting could not affect quality; what was needed was writers with a better sense of theatre, and a truer understanding of the nature of tragic drama.

The comedy of the age provides a more easily recognizable scene for the modern reader. This is not merely because he is certain to have some acquaintance with two of the most famous plays, *The Rivals* and *The School for Scandal*, but also because the dramatists themselves had been brought up on a broadly based repertory of earlier English comedy upon which the two principal London theatres relied, and because they were largely content to adapt familiar comic themes, situations, and types to the taste of the times. In his preface to *The School for Wives* (1774), Hugh Kelly[1] remarked that 'the great business of comedy [has always] consisted in making difficulties for the purpose of removing them; in distressing poor young lovers; and in rendering a happy marriage the object of every catastrophe'. Not invariably, for Kelly takes insufficient account of the comedy that springs from unhappy marriage; but a liberal interpretation of the remark covers most comedies of the age.

An early and convenient example is *The Suspicious Husband* (1747), written by Benjamin Hoadly,[2] which provided Garrick with one of his most famous parts (Ranger), and continued to be one of the most popular plays of the period. Here we find an independently minded young heiress, Jacintha, courted by the impecunious Bellamy, as Portia is courted by Bassanio, and Millamant by Mirabell. Jacintha is attended by a resourceful maidservant, as Millamant is attended by Mincing, and by Clarinda, a gay associate of her own social rank, as Etherege's Ariana is attended by Gatty in *She Would if She Could*. Ariana and Gatty are confronted by the young bachelors Freeman and Courtall, whose names lightly but sufficiently betray their roles; so Clarinda is matched by Frankly. Only Ranger, a daringly adventurous rake, is left unattached at the end of the play. Strictland, the jealous husband, and thus a descendant of Ford in *The Merry Wives of Windsor*, is Jacintha's guardian, and suspicious of the influence that she and Clarinda may exert by the freedom of their behaviour upon his entirely innocent wife. The ingredients are familiar, therefore; but they have been adapted with due regard to the ethos of a London audience

---

[1] Hugh Kelly, 1737–77, versatile writer of Irish origin. He came to London in 1760, began to write dramatic criticism, and was encouraged by Garrick, who launched him upon his dramatic career.

[2] Benjamin Hoadly, 1706–57, was the son of the famous latitudinarian Bishop of Bangor (later of Winchester). He practised as a physician in the royal households, and was a friend of Garrick.

that differed greatly from the audiences of Elizabethan and Restoration days. The most obvious difference between the gay couples of Restoration comedy and those of our period is that, however libertine the eighteenth-century couples may appear, the designs of the men are honourable and the sentiments of the women are innocent. In the first scene Bellamy puts his position beyond all doubt by declaring to Ranger that the minute he finds

a woman capable of friendship, love and tenderness, with good sense enough to be always easy, and good nature enough to like me, I will immediately put it to the trial, which of us shall have the greatest share of happiness from the sex, you or I.

To this Ranger scornfully retorts:

By marrying her, I suppose . . . My Lord Coke, in a case I read this morning [Ranger is a law student], speaks my sense. . . . What he says of one woman, I say of the whole sex, 'I take their bodies, you their minds; which has the better bargain?'

But his impudent philosophy belies him; for after gaining access to the Strictlands' house by a rope-ladder at midnight and surprising Jacintha in her bedroom, he exclaims:

I believe I make myself appear more wicked than I really am. For, damn me, if I do not feel more satisfaction in the thoughts of restoring you to my friend, than I could have pleasure in any favour your bounty could have bestowed! . . . Thou art a girl of spirit. And though I long to hug you for trusting yourself with me, I will not beg a single kiss, till Bellamy himself shall give me leave.

And Clarinda, who can tease the more prudish Jacintha by saying that 'a woman's surest hold over a man is to keep him in uncertainty. As soon as ever you put him out of doubt, you put him out of your power', eventually assures the audience that a 'little innocent gaiety' is 'the peculiar happiness of my temper', and that 'I shall not part with my mirth . . . so long as I know it innocent'. Late eighteenth-century comedy is full of such assurances.

Mrs. Strictland suffers passively from the suspicions of her husband, much as the Countess Almaviva does from the Count's. But as in *The Marriage of Figaro* Count and Countess are reunited at last, so at the end of our play Strictland declares that or the future his wife 'shall find a heart ready to love and trust you. No tears, I beg; I cannot bear them.' This becomes the customary comic solution of the maladjusted marriage. In Colman's *The Jealous Wife* (1761)[1] the shoe is on the other foot, but the termagant is eventually tamed; in Murphy's *All in the Wrong* (1761) both spouses are jealous, but both suffer a conversion in the final scene; in his *The Way to Keep Him* (1760), Mrs. Lovemore is herself to blame for the libertine behaviour of her husband, but she learns how to make home and married life more acceptable, and wins the truant back; in Kelly's *The School for Wives* (1774) Mrs. Belville must wait till the last act for Belville (who 'has a thousand good qualities to counterbalance this single fault of gallantry that contaminates his character') to recognize the error of his ways and return to her of his own free will. Thus there is plenty of variety in the treatment of maladjusted marriage, but the happy ending is not the ending invariably required by comedy: Congreve did not see fit to reconcile the Fainalls, and it is clear that at the end of *The Country Wife* Marjorie Pinchwife will continue to deceive her husband. That ending affords a striking contrast with the ending of *The School for Scandal*,[2] for Pinchwife and Sir Peter Teazle are alike in having postponed marriage until a more mature age; both have found their wives in the country; and both wives have entered social groups of which their husbands disapprove; but Wycherley's Juvenalian vision was foreign to the spirit of the later age. Both Sheridan's audience and the complexities of his plot demanded a reconciliation of man and wife.

Few comedies of the time are quite so restricted in range as *The Suspicious Husband*. Apart from a landlady and a milliner who each make a brief appearance, and apart from the necessary

---

[1] George Colman, the elder, 1732–94, son of the British ambassador at Florence, was a schoolfellow at Westminster with Cowper, Churchill, and Thornton, the last being his associate in a successful periodical essay, the *Connoisseur* (see p. 315). Called to the Bar, 1757. His dramatic career began in 1760 under the guidance of Garrick, with whom he quarrelled on becoming manager and one of the patentees at the rival theatre, Covent Garden (1767–74). Goldsmith's plays were produced there under his management. In charge of the Haymarket Theatre, 1777–85.

[2] Richard Brinsley Sheridan, 1751–1816, of Irish origin, the son of Dr. Johnson's friend Thomas Sheridan, the actor. His active career as a dramatist was limited to the years 1775 to 1779, though *Pizarro* was not performed till 1799. He succeeded Garrick as manager of Drury Lane Theatre in 1776. He held a seat in Parliament from 1780 to 1812, and was for a short time (1783) Secretary to the Treasury. His reputation as an orator stood exceptionally high, his most spectacular triumph being his speech at the trial of Warren Hastings in 1788.

servants, all the characters belong to the same social group and
to the same age group; and though they are sufficiently distinguished one from another, only Ranger can claim some measure
of individuality. Furthermore, though the play is brisk in action
and resourceful in incident, there are no comic themes other
than those already discussed. *The Way to Keep Him* is similarly
restricted in the age and social groups of the characters; but
Murphy deploys a somewhat wider range of types, including
the gay but good-hearted widow Bellmour, in whose hands the
comic reconciliations lie secure, and the fool (Sir Bashful Constant), who may no more suffer the exclusion or humiliation that
Shakespearian or Restoration comedy might require than the
libertine Lovemore may fail to be transformed into a loyal
husband. As early as the beginning of Act III the widow
Bellmour can encourage Mrs. Lovemore to believe that her
case is not bad; it is 'mere gallantry' on Lovemore's part; there
is no 'downright, sullen, habitual insensibility'; 'he still has
sentiment; and where there is sentiment, there is room to hope
for an alteration'. So, of course, it proves.

So skilful a playwright as Murphy must have been fully
aware that by thus restricting his range, he was depriving himself of two old-established comic devices. Intruders from other
walks of life had long been used to light up the dominant social
group of the play to expose its vices or its over-refinement, to
show off its graces by contrast, to provide a more extensive view
of society, or simply to present a well-known actor with an
eccentric character part. Such are Wycherley's Manly in *The
Plain Dealer*, Congreve's Foresight the astrologer and Ben the
sailor in *Love for Love*, and his country squire Sir Wilful Witwoud
in *The Way of the World*. Murphy could find a place for such
characters in his farces: Quidnunc in *The Upholsterer* (1758) is
a tradesman so deeply engrossed in what the newspapers tell
him of politics at home and governments overseas that he pays
no attention to his bankruptcy in business and to his daughter
eloping. But in his comedies Murphy eschews such characters,
reflecting perhaps that a wider view of society could be obtained
from the descriptive vignettes that he neatly inserts in his dialogue:

Don't you remember when he had chambers in Fig tree court, and
used to saunter and lounge away his time in Temple Coffee houses?
The fellow is as dull as a bill in chancery.

And he is proud to declare in the prologue to his *Know Your Own Mind* (1777):

> Here are no fools, the drama's standing jest!
> And Welchmen now, North Britons too may rest.
> Hibernia's sons shall here excite no wonder,
> Nor shall St. Patrick blush to hear them blunder.

In fact, Murphy had experimented with Irish and Scottish members of his 'Spouters' Club' in his earliest farce, *The Apprentice* (1756); but since then Irish humour in particular had become very popular, in some measure, perhaps, because of the recruitment at Drury Lane in 1759 of John Moody, an Irish actor with a gift for character parts. To an English ear the alien speech has a vitality denied the tamer excellences of correctness. Charles Macklin's Scotsmen savour their words with a peculiarly lingering enjoyment, as when Sir Archy Macsarcasm in *Love à la Mode* (1759) threatens to have Sir Theodore and Charlotte put in a play:

> I ken a lad of an honourable faimily, that understands the auncient classics in aw their perfaction: he is writing a comedy, and he shall inseenuate baith their characters intill it.

Sir Pertinax Macsycophant in *The Man of the World* (1781) remarks of lawyers that

> it is their interest that aw mankind should be at variance: for disagreement is the vary manure wi' which they enrich and fatten the land of leetegation.

With Colman's Irish press-gang recruiting officer in *The Jealous Wife* (1761) we are less conscious of the vitality than of the blunders of a raw, well-salted fellow spoiling for a fight. The harshness of the caricature was softened in Cumberland's *The West Indian* (1771), where Major O'Flaherty is presented, without a trace of brogue (in the printed version), as an honest, generous-minded, open-hearted gentleman, given to expressing such sentiments as

> upon my soul, I know but one excuse a person can have for giving nothing, and that is, like myself, having nothing to give;

and

> by my soul, there isn't in the whole creation so savage an animal as a human creature without pity.

But much of the Irish tang, for what it is worth, has been lost, just as it is lost in the loyal Irish clerk (Connolly) in Kelly's *The School for Wives*, who points proudly to the tear of sentiment glistening in his eye. If there must be stage Irishmen, perhaps Sheridan was right in reverting to an earlier type for Sir Lucius O'Trigger in *The Rivals* (1775).

The outsiders who intrude into the polite society of these comedies for the most part have little more function than to provide a good clown with an opportunity for his talents; such are Dr. Druid, the stage Welshman, in Cumberland's *The Fashionable Lover* (1772), and Bob Acres in *The Rivals*. Sir Harry Beagle, the squire in *The Jealous Wife* who prefers his stable to the lady he is to marry, does much less than Sir Wilful Witwoud to point a contrast between town and country society; but in *The Clandestine Marriage* (1766) Colman and Garrick were more successful than in the earlier play in presenting a wider range of social groups. The scene is laid in a country house recently acquired by a city merchant and his family. To it come an impecunious baronet and his noble uncle, with a group of lawyers to fix the marriage settlement. This opens the way for satire that is still entertaining upon the tasteless 'improvement' of house and grounds, while legal jargon and pedantry provide ample scope for the dramatic equivalent of the Theophrastan type-character that is almost as old as comedy itself. But audiences of the next decade who were prepared for the stage Irishman to be softened were no doubt equally receptive to Kelly's version of a lawyer, Leeson in *The School for Wives*, endowed with no pedantry and no jargon, but with the warmest of hearts.

The intruder who offers the richest dramatic opportunities is Belcour, the protagonist of *The West Indian*. Although wealthy and of English origins, he is a child of nature brought up in a simpler society, and now subjected to the different values, the injustice and the deceit, of London. His father, of whose identity he is unaware, discovers in him 'through the veil of some irregularities . . . a heart beaming with benevolence, an animated nature, fallible indeed, but not incorrigible'. If only Cumberland had possessed a little of the wit, the irony, the tact, the sense of farce and of pathos that Voltaire brought to his treatment of a similar theme in *L'Ingénu*! But Cumberland was almost entirely innocent of these qualities. There is no humour in Belcour's financial assistance to distressed gentlefolk given without a moment's inquiry, no farce in his implicit belief of the manifestly untrustworthy, no irony in the misapprehensions that the young women entertain of his all too ardent behaviour. It will be recalled that *The Suspicious Husband* and *The Way to Keep Him* are restricted to characters of a single age group. The purpose of the elder generation in comedy is normally, in Kelly's words, to 'distress poor young lovers'. The power which Egeus exerted over Hermia in *A Midsummer Night's Dream* was a fact to be reckoned with in real life throughout the eighteenth century, though English sanctions were not so dire as those of Shakespeare's Athens. It is not surprising, therefore, that the parent or guardian, male or female, at loggerheads with child or ward provides an inexhaustible source of the anti-comic. Sir Sampson Legend turns up again as Sir Antony Absolute, Lady Wishfort as Mrs. Malaprop, and later as Lady Bracknell; and in between stand many less famous examples of these roles. We need not pause to examine Russet in *The Jealous Wife*, who resembles his acknowledged prototype Squire Western only in his tyrannous treatment and pursuit of his daughter, nor Sterling and his rich, vulgar sister in *The Clandestine Marriage*, nor even Croker in Goldsmith's *The Good-Natured Man* (1768), whose tyranny is subordinate to the humour of his pessimism. Nor need the utterly ineffectual Mrs. Hardcastle in *She Stoops to Conquer* (1773) detain us, nor Sir William Honeywood in *The Good-Natured Man*, who like the Duke in *Measure for Measure* adopts a disguise the better to observe, and to mete out justice in the end. More interesting is an attempt to adapt the type to what was felt to be the more generous character of the times. In Kelly's *False Delicacy* (1768), Miss Rivers is designed by her father for Sidney. But she loves Sir Harry Newburg, who eventually manages to overcome her scruples, her devotion to her father, and her sense of filial obligation, and persuades her to elope with him. The elopement is prevented in the fourth act by her father, who first reproaches her with ingratitude, then overwhelms her by keeping his part of the bargain to endow her with a fortune of twenty thousand pounds (paid out there and then), but conjures her never to see him again. When Sir Harry turns up at the end of the act, it is not surprising that Miss Rivers should steadfastly resist the elopement. This treatment of one of the commonplaces of comedy is certainly unusual, and the sympathetic depiction both of father and of daughter is not entirely unsuccessful; but it is not comic, and the traditions of comedy do not require that it should be. It serves its purpose by contributing to the theme of a play that attempts to set 'false delicacy' in a wider context.

This survey of comic themes, situations, and types has also served to indicate a basic homogeneity in the comedy of the age. A contemporary critic would have denied this, however. He would have pointed out that no distinction had been drawn between comedy and farce. This objection may be allowed. The farce was designed as a short after-piece to the principal item of the evening's entertainment, whether tragedy or comedy. It was therefore of necessity limited to a single situation capable of development in a few scenes, such as Quidnunc in Murphy's *The Upholsterer*, oblivious to everything but the columns of the newspaper; or the stage-struck young fellow in Murphy's farce *The Apprentice*, whose memory of the theatrical parts he has learned determines his conduct and supplies him with a suitable response to all that is said to him; or Colman's *Polly Honeycombe* (1760), about a merchant's silly daughter who conducts her affairs in accordance with the novels she has read.

The critic would also have objected, especially if he had been living in the 1770s, that no distinction had been drawn between what Goldsmith[1] in a famous 'Essay on the Theatre' (1773) called 'laughing and sentimental comedy'. The distinction between satirical comedy that by sharp ridicule provokes laughter, and sympathetic comedy that may even provoke a tear, was felt so strongly and made so frequently that it has survived to perplex modern criticism. Yet at this distance of time it should be possible to see clearly what are essential and what are superficial differences. We have already noticed that the age was one of increasing humanitarianism, when men and women were especially susceptible to appeals from the distressed, whether the victims of war, want, disease, or an unjust social system. In spite of evidence to the contrary, human nature was felt to be basically good and corrigible: each of us was supposed to be equipped with a moral sense that might be blunted, but with

[1] Oliver Goldsmith, *c.* 1730–74, was educated at Trinity College, Dublin, and later pursued medical studies in Edinburgh and Leyden. He travelled through France and Italy, and, after a time of great poverty, established himself in London as a professional writer. He was one of the original members of Johnson's 'Club', and Johnson wrote the inscription for his monument in Westminster Abbey.

proper care and education could respond exquisitely to what occasions might demand and could direct the appropriate action. At a time when, as we have seen, satirical poetry began to yield to poetry that took a more optimistic view of human nature, when novel and essay were similarly affected, and when a heroine created by so robust a novelist as Fielding could declare, 'I love a tender sensation, and am willing to pay the price of a tear for it at any time' (*Tom Jones*, VI. 5), it would be surprising if at such a time comedy remained unaffected. In fact, almost all comedy of the period has sentimental strands. But sentiment and sympathy are not foreign to the traditions of comedy. It is safe to say that no audience has remained quite untouched by Hero's plight in *Much Ado about Nothing* and Beatrice's response to it, and that no audience has felt that Viola in *Twelfth Night* is an object of ridicule when she admits

> A blank, my Lord. She never told her love,
> But let concealment, like a worm i'th' bud,
> Feed on her damask cheek,

though perhaps it was only in the eighteenth century that these lines could provoke a tear. She is ridiculous, however, in the duel with Sir Andrew Aguecheek; and there is an area in the play of questionable response, of how far we laugh at Malvolio and how far we sympathize with him, and what attitude we adopt to the element of affectation in Orsino and Olivia. Thus 'laughing and sentimental comedy' need not be regarded as distinct genres; they may both contribute to a single play; the essential considerations are the treatment, the degree of more or less, and the blend.

The assumption that human nature is essentially good and corrigible has already been illustrated in two representative comedies of manners, *The Suspicious Husband* and *The Way to Keep Him*. Hoadly and Murphy prepare us for the fifth-act reform of their flirts and libertines, as the Restoration comic writers do not. Murphy would have us believe that even the scandal-monger Dashwould, in his *Know Your Own Mind*, has a good heart; and still larger drafts on human credulity are made by the last-moment conversion of the grasping Belfield, a determined bigamist, in Cumberland's *The Brothers* (1770), and by the discovery in *The Clandestine Marriage* that the two hard-boiled aristocrats, who have come to drive a tough marriage-bargain with the city merchant, are unable to resist a sentimental appeal from his younger daughter and her humble lover:

Sir John Melvil: No apologies to me, Lovewell, I do not deserve any. All I have to offer in excuse for what has happened, is my total ignorance of your situation. Had you dealt a little more openly with me, you would have saved me, and yourself, and that lady, (who I hope will pardon my behaviour) a great deal of uneasiness. Give me leave, however, to assure you, that light and capricious as I may have appeared, now my infatuation is over, I have sensibility enough to be ashamed of the part I have acted, and honour enough to rejoice at your happiness.

As a rule in these plays it is harder for city merchants and their class to reform than for those who live in the West End. Colman in *The Jealous Wife*, following the lead of *Tom Jones*, dismisses Lady (Bellaston) Freelove and Lord (Fellamar) Trinket, and it is true that no virtuous future can be discerned at the end of *The School for Scandal* for Joseph Surface and Lady Sneerwell; but there is hope for Lofty, the ridiculously boastful politician in *The Good-Natured Man*, and even for Lord Abberville in *The Fashionable Lover*, though the action has shown him to be a spendthrift and a seducer. The city merchants in the same play, however, though begging to be forgiven, are sternly rejected, and the same fate attends the Fulmers in *The West Indian*. The systematically corrupt Sir Pertinax Macsycophant, in Macklin's *Man of the World*, leaves his wife and his son with a malediction that proves him incorrigible. The playwrights lead us to suppose that this social class is beyond redemption, though a little lower in the ranks of society may be found warm-hearted clerks, a Scottish major-domo (in *The Fashionable Lover*) whose moral sense needs no educating, and even a servant (in the same play) who exclaims: 'If I don't discharge my heart, 'twill break; it is so full'.

It is precisely upon the point of how a character earns his passage that Goldsmith took issue with what he called sentimental comedy. His complaint in the essay already mentioned is that the good characters are 'lavish enough of their tin money on the stage', and 'though they want humour, have abundance of sentiment and feeling'.

If they happen to have faults or foibles, the spectator is taught not only to pardon, but to applaud them, in consideration of the goodness of their hearts; so that folly, instead of being ridiculed, is commended, and the comedy aims at touching our passions, instead of being truly pathetic.

Goldsmith may have had in mind Cumberland's *The West Indian*, performed two years before with great success—for twenty-eight nights without an after-piece was the author's proud recollection in his *Memoirs*, written over thirty years later (see pp. 287–8). Goldsmith had already discussed the theme himself in his first play, *The Good-Natured Man* (1768), where Honeywood is no less lavish of his tin money than Cumberland's Belcour yet, like Belcour, is redeemable because, as one of the characters says of him, 'all his faults are such that one loves him still the better for them'. Both plays are sentimental in theme; they differ, as has been suggested, in treatment, in the degree of more or less, and in the blend of sentiment and humour. Cumberland did not lack humour; it seems rather that he was incapable of developing a naturally thin stream, and of blending it into his presentation of Belcour. Goldsmith, however, possessed some of the Voltairian qualities needed: the sense for farce, shown in Act III when Honeywood tries to deceive Miss Richland into believing that the two bailiffs who have arrested him for debt are his close friends; and the comic irony of Act IV, where he woos Miss Richland on behalf of Lofty, believing that it was Lofty and not Miss Richland who had paid his debts. One might argue whether Honeywood or Belcour is more deeply humiliated by the course of the action, though there is no doubt that Honeywood's situation is more consistently droll. The resolution of the action, however, is the same. Belcour and Honeywood emerge as reformed characters, but the currency in which Belcour pays for his passage is a little more suspect than Honeywood's:

Bel: (to Louisa): I know I am not worthy your regard; I know I'm tainted with a thousand faults, sick of a thousand follies, but there's a healing virtue in your eyes that makes recovery certain; I cannot be a villain in your arms. . . . Whenever you perceive me deviating into error or offence, bring only to my mind the Providence of this night, and I will turn to reason and obey.

Honey: Yes, Sir, I now too plainly perceive my errors; my vanity, in attempting to please all by fearing to offend any; my meanness, in approving folly lest fools should disapprove. Henceforth, therefore, it shall be my study to reserve my pity for real distress; my friendship for true merit; and my love for her, who first taught me what it is to be happy.

The redemption of erring but essentially meritorious characters was a subject of very wide appeal at this time. In a later chapter (pp. 411–17) it will be shown to constitute one of the most important threads in *Tom Jones* and *Amelia*, and Sheridan was later to take it up in *The School for Scandal* (1777). Whether the apposition of the two brothers in that play, one with sentiments on his lips but with villainy in his heart, the other good at heart but libertine in action, was suggested to Sheridan by the apposition of Blifil and Tom; whether he derived something from Murphy's distinction between the innocent and the malicious scandalmongers in *Know Your Own Mind* (performed a few months previously); whether the famous screen scene, the most brilliantly developed catastrophe in eighteenth-century drama, owes anything to the inconvenient discovery of Belinda hiding in a sedan-chair in the last act of Murphy's *All in the Wrong* (1761): these are questions that need not concern us. It is safe to say, however, that no reasonably well-read member of the first audience could fail to recall Tom Jones and Blifil as he watched Charles and Joseph Surface. The redemption of Charles plays a smaller part in *The School for Scandal* than those of Belcour and Honeywood in the plays we have been discussing; and it is, of course, obvious that Sheridan has no space for Fielding's long and carefully developed exposition. We are inevitably asked to take much for granted in Charles's character. He is as lavish with his tin money as either Belcour or Honeywood, and like Honeywood he lavishes it before he pays his debts. He is found to be corrigible for purely sentimental reasons: he has endeavoured to raise a sum of money, part of which, in spite of his own debts, he intends for the relief of a poor relative; and he refuses to sell the portrait of his uncle Oliver because 'the old fellow has been very good to me'. Charles is made to behave as every sentimentalist would have him behave, and is readily excused his riot and dissipation. But if *The School for Scandal* is not found offensively sentimental, it is because of Sheridan's tact. The sentiment is not unduly indulged; and the scene of the sale of the portraits, undertaken in the presence of the disguised Uncle Oliver himself, is developed with great comic skill, for at every step Charles unwittingly presents a more and more damaging impression, until the whole is climactically reversed by Charles's suddenly formed sentimental whim. *The School for Scandal*, therefore, presents us once more not with a question of distinguishing 'laughing and sentimental comedy', but with an example of a nicely adjusted blend.

There is one more play that deserves mentioning in this context, Kelly's *False Delicacy* (1768), a play that has sometimes been regarded as the quintessence of sentimental comedy, and the scene in Act IV already examined (p. 181) undoubtedly has strong sentimental features. But the relationship of the principal characters seems to have been deliberately designed by Kelly for restrained farcical development, neither more nor less farcical than, say, the development in Iris Murdoch's *A Severed Head*. Lord Winworth still loves Lady Betty, who failed to recognize her love for him until he withdrew his addresses. He is too scrupulous to renew them, knowing that she is no flirt, yet feels that he may gratify her by transferring his affections to her friend Miss Marchmont. Miss Marchmont feels bound by gratitude to Lady Betty to accept the addresses of one recommended and so much respected by her friend, but would secretly prefer those of Sidney, who would return her affection if he were not engaged to the Miss Rivers whom we have already met on the point of eloping with Sir Harry Newburg. These five characters are actuated in their relations one towards another by such scruples as perplex the characters in Richardson's *Sir Charles Grandison* (see p. 402); each is confronted with a refined case of conscience, and is prepared to solve it by acting in what he or she believes to be the best interests of another person. This is more properly called honourable behaviour than sentimental; certainly Richardson's admirers (including Jane Austen) would have agreed with the character in the play who declares, 'the laws of delicacy are not trifles'. Yet readers of Fanny Burney and Jane Austen need not be reminded that scruples may at the same time be both honourable and fit for comic treatment, a paradox summarily expressed in the title *Sense and Sensibility*. That Kelly held the same opinion is abundantly clear. The situation, as already remarked, is farcical, and yet it is wrong-headedly honourable; as Mrs. Harley remarks in Act II:

Well, the devil take this delicacy; I don't know any thing it does besides making people miserable:—And yet some how, foolish as it is, one can't help liking it.

In short, one can laugh at their absurd scrupulosity, and yet love them for it, an ambivalence of attitude which has long been one of the commonplaces of Shakespearian criticism. The place of Mrs. Harley in the action is to ensure the eventual triumph of good sense over delicacy; and though, having achieved it, she 'could cry for downright joy', her attitude and that of Cecil, her accomplice in teasing out the absurd tangles of the situation, has been one of bluff common sense:

> Your people of refined sentiments are the most troublesome creatures in the world to deal with, and their friends must even commit a violence upon their nicety before they can condescend to study their own happiness.

Thus we are again confronted with a blend of laughter and sentiment, one more closely associated with Richardson and Sterne than with Fielding, but a blend entirely in keeping with the spirit of the times.

One play, *She Stoops to Conquer* (1773), stands a little apart from the homogeneity of comedy at this time. In this play Goldsmith shows no interest in comedy of manners; he displays no contemporary types, neither Irishmen, Scotsmen, nor Welshmen, not a lawyer, nor a city merchant, not even a stage country squire; and his interest in sentimental questions is extremely restricted. There is indeed a young man to be corrected, Young Marlow, but his correction is less moral than social: he learns through the course of the action to lose his bashfulness in the presence of young gentlewomen. He is already sufficiently well equipped with moral sense and proper delicacy: this point is made with praiseworthy economy. Having fallen in love with Kate Hardcastle, whom he takes to be a servant at the inn, he feels constrained to take leave of her:

> Excuse me, my lovely girl, you are the only part of the family I leave with reluctance. But to be plain with you, the difference of our birth, fortune and education, make an honourable connexion impossible; and I can never harbour a thought of seducing simplicity that trusted in my honour, or bringing ruin upon one, whose only fault was being too lovely;

on which Kate's comment (aside) is, briefly, 'Generous man! I now begin to admire him'.

The play makes use of some traditional comic material, but at every point Goldsmith shows his independence and originality. As in *The Suspicious Husband* and *Know Your Own Mind* (performed four years after *She Stoops to Conquer*) the principal young women are contrasted in character, the vivacious Kate Hardcastle setting the pace for the more demure Miss Neville; but it is only in Goldsmith's play that we gain the Shakespearian impression of the women being more than a match for the men. We also find a division in age groups; but apart from the ineffectual Mrs. Hardcastle, the two generations are agreed, the young people being at first quite willing to fall in with their parents' wishes. There is therefore nothing anti-comic in the roles of Hardcastle and Sir Charles Marlow. The action is ostensibly concerned with the pursuit and capture of the heroine, as comedy requires; but owing to Young Marlow's bashfulness, the traditional roles are reversed, and it is Kate who is forced to pursue and capture Young Marlow. Because he is at ease only in the company of maidservants, she must stoop to conquer.

Comedy occasionally makes use of a manipulator, who holds in his hands most of the strings of the plot, and contrives a happy issue to the action. Such is Don Alfonso in *Cosi fan Tutte*; such, also, are the Widow Bellmour in *The Way to Keep Him* and Mrs. Harley in *False Delicacy*. A more sentimental example is Mortimer, the elderly satirist in *The Fashionable Lover*, whose motto is 'Sheathe a soft heart in a rough case; 'twill wear the longer'. Shakespeare had little use for this role—Prospero is perhaps a special case—but when he did employ it, he showed his customary boldness in choosing an incompetent, even a bungling manipulator: such in their different ways are Puck and Dogberry. In *She Stoops to Conquer* Kate Hardcastle is in almost effortless control. She requires no assistance; but Hastings and Miss Neville need help, and it is given in ample measure by Tony Lumpkin, who is also made responsible for the initial confusion by which Young Marlow mistakes Kate for a maidservant. Goldsmith shows some Shakespearian quality in choosing for his manipulator a character as mischievous as Puck, as ignorant as Dogberry, and at times as incompetent as either in appreciating what precisely is at issue.

The play shows rather more affinity with contemporary farce than with contemporary comedy. The scope of the farce as a short after-piece placed some restriction on a writer's choice of theme. Thus Colman's *The Deuce is in Him* (1763) consists in effect of a single episode: Colonel Tamper, home from the wars, decides to test the affection of his lover Emily by pretending that he has lost a leg and an eye, but she is undeceived by what Dr. Prattle happens to say and is thereby enabled to turn the tables on Tamper. It is enough for development in two scenes. Goldsmith undoubtedly began with an equally simple situation: two travellers mistake a country house for an inn. The situation could have been developed up to the limits prescribed for a farce. But though it offered opportunities for more extended treatment, Goldsmith seems to have regarded it as sufficiently presented in about three acts. A little less than half of Acts II to V are given to the attempted elopement of Hastings and Miss Neville. The comic peripeties make this sub-plot sufficiently droll; but it is a more conventional theme, reminiscent of the sub-plot of his first play *The Good-Natured Man*—a theme, we might suspect, which Goldsmith was ready to fall back upon in a hurry—and it is in no way dependent upon the initial situation. It is on the comic invention and originality shown in developing that farcical situation that Goldsmith's reputation as a dramatist rests.

VII

HISTORY

WRITING to Hugh Blair on 28 March 1769 about their friend John Home's most recent play, David Hume remarked, 'The Success of all plays, in this Age, is very feeble; and the people now heed the Theatre as little as the Pulpit. History, I think, is the Favourite Reading.' Dr. Johnson might have been constrained to agree; but the benefit to be obtained from the study of history was not a topic on which he rejoiced to concur with the common reader. He professed to 'hate historic talk', and maintained that 'there is but a shallow stream of thought in history' (*Life*, 9 May 1772). There is more to Johnson's view of history than this, and indeed, as we shall see, he had a keen appreciation of some elements of the new historiography. But undoubtedly he felt much impatience with history as it was fashionably understood. More representative in this respect was Lord Chesterfield, who never tired in recommending historical study to his son. On 13 April 1752 he told Philip that Voltaire had sent him a copy of his 'History *du Siècle de Louis XIV*', and continued: 'It came at a very proper time; Lord Bolingbroke had just taught me how History should be read; Voltaire shows me how it should be written.'

In mentioning Bolingbroke and Voltaire, Chesterfield brought together two writers who were recognized as leading exponents of a new style in the writing of history. Voltaire's special contribution was, in part, to widen the accepted scope of historical study. He was much concerned to establish the idea that battles and court intrigues formed only part of the picture, and while such matters still figure largely in his accounts of France under Louis XIV and of Russia under Peter the Great, he pays some attention too to the development of law, commerce, and institutions. Readers of Voltaire found, moreover, that the prospect before them was not confined to Europe and the Mediterranean. The *Essai sur les mœurs* makes a valiant attempt to span the globe, and as Gibbon judiciously noted, Voltaire 'casts a keen and lively glance over the surface of history', noting unexpected affinities, stimulating fresh lines of research. Bolingbroke might appear at first sight to be more traditional in his view of the historian's task. His *Letters on the Study and Use of History*, begun in 1735, and published posthumously in 1752, is a late example of those *artes historicae* that had been much in vogue in the two previous centuries. Like them it saw history in the light of the familiar dictum of Dionysius of Halicarnassus: 'History is Philosophy teaching by examples.' Bolingbroke, however, uses the idea with a difference. When Amyot, the French translator of Plutarch's *Lives*, spoke of history as 'a certain rule and instruction, which by examples past, teacheth us to judge of things present, and to foresee things to come', one may infer that the examples had a meaning immediately plain to all. By Bolingbroke's time, a century and a half later, it was commonly felt that the historian should not rest content with what appeared on the surface, but should penetrate to more recondite springs of action and policy. René Rapin's widely read *Instructions pour l'histoire* (1677) had emphasized the importance of diving into the real sentiments of a statesman, judging him 'by those natural and unconcerted Motions that escape him, before he is aware'. It was thus that the historian could really show his mettle: 'an Action well laid open, and stript to its Causes, and a deep Counsel rightly Sounded and Fathom'd, give us a noble Idea of the Capacity of an Author.' Preoccupations of this kind help to account for the interest in memoirs and private papers that becomes apparent in the eighteenth century—material which could often throw a fresh light upon public events, as when Clarendon's autobiography (first published in 1759) gave an account of the anxieties and uncertainties that lay behind the apparently triumphant restoration of Charles II. Part of the attraction for Lord Lyttelton in writing the history of the reign of Henry II was that, in spite of the remoteness of the period, many excellent original documents were still in existence: collections of letters written by principal actors in affairs of state, or by those who enjoyed their confidence. More recent periods abounded in such materials of authentic history. Bolingbroke remarked that the sixteenth and seventeenth centuries offered the same opportunities for the modern historian that Livy enjoyed when writing the later books of his history of Rome. He would have had free access to the letters and orations of Cicero, where the principal actors in the drama could be seen without disguise. This part of Livy's work had, deplorably, been lost, but it would doubtless have shown 'in one stupendous draught, the whole progress of that government from liberty to servitude, the whole series of causes and effects, apparent and real, public and private . . . '. It is in similar terms that Voltaire congratulates himself on the excellence of the materials for his narrative of the civilizing mission of Peter the Great in Russia. In general, the founding lawgivers of the human race had had their stories obscured by absurd fictions. Peter the Great alone, marvellous though much of his career might appear to be, could be the subject of a properly attested history.

Modern European history had the further advantage of bearing directly upon the system of government with which statesmen actually had to work. The close of the fifteenth century, said Bolingbroke, marked the beginning of all those revolutions which produced 'so vast a change in the manners, customs, and interests of particular nations, and in the whole policy, ecclesiastical and civil, of these parts of the world'. It was in understanding this policy, and not in the mere conning of annals or mastering the discoveries of antiquaries, that a reader could benefit from historical study. In this way he could collect those rules of life and conduct that would form 'a general system of ethics on the surest foundation'. The quest for a 'general system' underlying the various phenomena of human nature shows the way in which Bolingbroke is representative of a new attitude—one that endeavours to rise above national partialities and prejudices, and moves towards the idiom of the physical sciences. This is particularly apparent in a passage like the following, from the sketch of the history and state of Europe with which he closes the *Letters*:

The precise point at which the scales of power turn, like that of the solstice in either tropic, is imperceptible to common observation; and, in one case as in the other, some progress must be made in the new direction before the change is perceived. They who are in the sinking scale,—for in the political balance of power, unlike to all others, the scale that is empty sinks, and that which is full rises,— they who are in the sinking scale do not easily come off from the habitual prejudices of superior wealth, or power, or skill, or courage, nor from the confidence that these prejudices inspire. They who are in the rising scale do not immediately feel their strength, nor assume that confidence in it which successful experience gives them afterwards. They who are most concerned to watch the variations of this balance misjudge often in the same manner, and from the same prejudices. They continue to dread a power no longer able to hurt them, or they continue to have no apprehensions of a power that grows daily more formidable.

Bolingbroke here formulates a law whose elegant simplicity helps to establish a clear pattern among data of great complexity.

The laws of human behaviour, however, are evidently European laws. Although Bolingbroke is not untouched by that broadening of geographical perspective that is such a striking characteristic of the period, and although he believes that a philosophical reader can profit from accounts of Peruvians or Mexicans, Chinese or Tartars, Muscovites or Negroes, the interest he expresses in these exotic races is perfunctory. In mentioning them, he may simply have been recalling the speculations of a writer who had developed a similar theme nearly half a century earlier. This was Sir William Temple. His essay 'Of Heroick Virtue', which first appeared in 1683, reads like a corrective appendix to Bossuet's eloquent *Discours sur l'histoire universelle*, published two years earlier. For Bossuet, 'universal history' was emphatically confined to the areas familiar to the writers of Greek and Roman antiquity. In interpreting it, a central place was given to the Hebrew and Christian scriptures. Temple insists, however, that there are many vast regions of the world, wrongly accounted barbarous, which may justly be brought into comparison with states more generally known to us. There are some, indeed, which 'will be found to have equalled or exceeded all the others, in the wisdom of their constitutions, the extent of their conquests, and the duration of their empires or states'. He expressed great admiration for the empire of China, 'framed and policed with the utmost force and reach of human wisdom, reason, and contrivance'. He thought that the victories of the Scythians showed that 'there was among them some force of order, some reach of conduct, above the common strain'; and he gave a strikingly sympathetic account of Mahomet—a man of mean birth and illiterate, 'but of great spirit and subtle wit'. Gibbon writes somewhere of Temple as 'that lover of exotic virtue', and the essay was perhaps generally regarded with the reserve implicit in that comment. It is clear that many eighteenth-century writers would have echoed the Earl of Shaftesbury's condemnation (in his *Advice to an Author*) of those 'Virtuosos' who prefer 'monstrous Accounts of Men and Manners' to narrations of the affairs of the wisest and most polished peoples. But as time went on, this attitude became increasingly difficult to sustain. A steady flow of books of travel, many of them reissued in massive compilations, served to bring home the fact that mankind lived under an extraordinary variety of conditions, and governed their conduct by laws and customs which differed widely, and not necessarily for the worse, from the practice of Christian Europe. The new attitude was well established by the time Richard Graves published *The Spiritual Quixote* (1773). In this novel there is a sympathetic recluse, Mr. Rivers. He lives in an old Gothic mansion, with a gloomy hall, 'the wall covered with maps and chronological tables, above which were a number of cheap prints, representing the customs and habits of the various nations of the world'. This mode of decoration implies no specialized interest on the part of Mr. Rivers. It merely hints that he is a cultivated gentleman, one who would have appreciated Bishop Percy's plan to collect specimens of the poetry of various nations, and admired the ease with which Sir William Blackstone, in his *Commentaries* (1765–9), moves from the laws of England to practices on the Guinea coast, or the laws of Genghis Khan.

Blackstone was somewhat indebted, like many of his contemporaries, to one of the largest monuments of this cosmopolitanism: the *Universal History* published, from 1736 onwards, by a group of London booksellers and printers. The 'modern part' of this work appeared in forty-four octavo volumes between 1759 and 1766. It constituted a determined, if inadequate, attempt to fulfil the promise of its title, and while nearly half of it was devoted to the various countries of Europe, much ingenuity was exercised to make the non-European histories as extensive as possible. Smollett—one of the principal contributors—once complained that he was being left with the task of 'filling up a chasm of fifteen or sixteen sheets, with a description of a country which all the art of man cannot spin out to half the number'. This was the *Terra Australis Incognita*. The empire of Monomotapa must have presented equal difficulties, the author confessing how little information he had about 'the antiquity, foundation, and regular succession of this opulent and extensive monarchy'. In some respects, obviously, the *Universal History* is a piece of hackwork. Gibbon said of Swinton's volumes on the

history of Islam and the Arabs that 'the dull mass is not quickened by a spark of philosophy or taste'; and other volumes could
be included in this censure. The sparks that occasionally
quicken the pages of the volume on Russia prove, on inspection,
to be plagiarism from Voltaire. Some of the character-sketches
in the French history (presumably by Smollett) are good of
their kind. In Charles IX, that deep dissembler who was also
'passionate to a degree of madness', one catches a glimpse of
a temperament highly congenial to the novelist, vehemently
hunting, playing tennis, and working at the forge (he was an
excellent gunsmith). 'His impetuosity appeared even in his
dancing, with which he fatigued himself and his whole court.'
Even at its best, however, the *Universal History* remains a collection of national annals. Smollett remarked, in the Swedish
history, that inconsistencies were bound to arise when 'we
deduce the history of every people from their own writers'. He
thought such inconsistencies 'easily reconciled', as perhaps they
were in this instance, when it was a question of comparing
Swedish authorities with Danish ones. The work suffers, none
the less, from the absence of a wider frame of reference. As
Goldsmith remarked, it contained 'no landscapes to· amuse nor
pleasing regions to invite, but a continued uniformity of dreary
prospects, shapeless ruins, and fragments of mutilated antiquity'.
Imperfect as it was, however, it enjoyed a European reputation,
being translated into French and German. The German edition was enlarged even beyond the size of the English by means
of supplementary dissertations. From the French translation,
on the other hand, an elegant abridgement was prepared by
Louis-Pierre Anquetil, and this in turn was translated back into
English.

Goldsmith's criticism was not entirely disinterested. He was
writing the preface to *A General History of the World* (1764–7),
a rival work written by William Guthrie and others. Perhaps
more readable than the *Universal History*, it is certainly more
limited in scope, and shows no advance in historical method.
Goldsmith's preface states an intention of tracing the progress
of arts and laws, but this is remembered in the text only fitfully.
In the seventh volume, indeed, there is an extended account of
the reign of Kublai Khan as 'the *Augustan* age of the *Moguls*',
when the arts and sciences were carried to a height almost
incredible in comparison with the barbarous state of Tartary in

the eighteenth century. This aspect of Kublai's reign was one of 'those few delightful spots upon which history delights to dwell', although it was set 'amidst the tumults of many dreadful, and some of them unsuccessful wars; which barbarous and unpleasing subject', the anonymous author adds, with a sigh almost audible, 'we are now obliged to resume'. The obligation to resume such a subject, however, was no longer felt to be as binding as it had once been. The 'ancestral voices prophesying war' were ceasing to monopolize the historian's attention. Obviously no single writer can be given the credit for this, but one name stands out above others: Montesquieu.

L'Esprit des lois (1748) is not history in the narrative sense, but its influence on historians was very great. It is a work founded on an impartially comparative natural history of human society, following a method that may be compared with that of Montesquieu's great contemporary, the naturalist Buffon. The right way to study natural history, says Buffon, is to allow the mind to range over the vast profusion of objects that the earth contains, and to do so without over-hasty theorizing. One should be willing to wait for order to emerge spontaneously from the mass. Buffon concedes that it is not easy to combine the ability to form general views with a talent for that minute attention to particulars which makes possible the detection of every nuance of the great work of nature. Montesquieu, certainly, is often vulnerable to criticism in detail. But this should not be allowed to obscure the skill with which he both conveys the bewildering variety of human societies, and explains it in terms of the interacting influence of religion, manners, political institutions, and climate. Gibbon praised the energy of style, the boldness of hypothesis, the brilliance of imagination that distinguishes Montesquieu's writings; and he seems (in the early essay on the study of literature) to have been particularly impressed by the capacity Montesquieu displayed for perceiving the wider significance of mean and apparently trivial facts. One should not underestimate the importance of Montesquieu's emancipation from narrow preconceptions of what was proper to the 'dignity of history'. On a journey from Lahore to Kashmir, the French traveller Bernier perspired copiously, and perhaps only Montesquieu could have drawn this experience into a discussion of the connection between climate and legislation. He was criticized for being over-ingenious, more anxious to make a witty than a scrupulously accurate observation. But this was an indispensable element in the agility of mind which was itself a stimulus to further study. No work, said Gibbon, had been more read and criticized in the latter half of the eighteenth century than *L'Esprit des lois*: 'the spirit of inquiry which it has excited, is not the least of our obligations to the author'. Needless to say, that spirit did not always reach conclusions flattering to *L'Esprit des lois* itself. Thus, in the course of a *Dissertation on the Languages, Literature, and Manners of Eastern Nations* (1777), John Richardson[1] the orientalist complained that Montesquieu accepted uncritically an over-simple notion of the Tartar peoples. Because Europeans referred to the 'Tartars' as though they were a clearly-defined and homogeneous group, Montesquieu assumed that they could be compared directly with the Arabs—another group whose characteristics became less easy to define the more accurately they were inspected. Arabs and Tartars alike lived among the most various kinds of environment, and included peoples who were barbaric and others who were highly civilized. The polished citizens of Mecca or Samarkand had little in common with desert plunderers or Tartar wanderers in the northern wilds. But Montesquieu had a broad antithesis in his mind which induced him to ignore stubbornly complex facts behind the all-too-convenient names. 'The *Arabs* are *free*,' says Richardson, 'and he derives their freedom from the *Rocks*: the *Tartars* he chuses to make *slaves*, and he gives them *an immense plain*.'

Montesquieu would not have written so loosely about countries in western and central Asia if they had been nearer to him. Richardson, for his part, viewed the world through Persian spectacles, denying any special significance to the battles of Marathon and Thermopylae—mere incidents connected with the collecting of tribute, or possibly even victories over Persian pirates. Oriental scholarship, indeed, did much to undermine the unconscious insularity of eighteenth-century European cosmopolitanism, and perhaps no single person did more to enlarge the scope of the historical imagination in this period than Sir William Jones.[2] His pioneer work on Sanskrit was of crucial

---

[1] John Richardson, 1741–1811, was admitted to membership of the Society of Antiquaries in 1767, and entered Wadham College, Oxford, in 1775.

[2] Sir William Jones, 1746–94, was educated at Harrow and University College, Oxford. He was a barrister and commissioner of bankrupts, and a brilliant legal

significance in developing the comparative study of languages, but this was only part of its importance at the time. The common origin of the Indo-European languages has been a familiar piece of intellectual furniture for so long that it comes as a shock to experience the first effects of perceiving the connection, as Jones enables one to do. There is an eager sense that a vast area of darkness is about to be illuminated, perhaps to disclose riches even greater than those of Greece and Rome. Sanskrit, manifestly related to both Greek and Latin, seemed to Jones to be 'more exquisitely refined than either'. Superiority in language was matched by a corresponding intellectual distinction. It was in India, after all, that the numerical characters essential to modern mathematics were invented, and their philosophers developed doctrines later taken up by the Greeks. All the metaphysics of the Academy, the Stoa, and the Lyceum, he observes in one of his addresses to the Asiatic Society of Bengal, are comprised in the principles explained in the Dersana Sastra; 'nor is it possible to read the Vedánta, or the many fine compositions in illustration of it, without believing that Pythagoras and Plato derived their sublime theories from the same fountain with the sages of India'. Jones is admittedly of more importance to the historian of ideas than to the literary reader, although it is characteristic of him that he should have been one of the earliest exponents of the view that poetry and the arts derive not from imitation, but from 'a strong and animated expression of the human passions'. His zealous appreciation of Indian civilization found at least one worthy memorial in his translation of Kalidasa's play *Sacontala* (1789). He conveys the play's tender ceremoniousness with great delicacy, and with an ease which he could have derived only from an immediate experience of Indian life and manners.

An enlarged horizon tended to diminish the individual figures in the landscape. This tendency was reinforced by the concern to discover laws of human behaviour comparable to the laws of physics. Increasing dissatisfaction came to be felt with the assumption—still very much alive in Voltaire—that a pre-eminent role was played by the great legislator in politics,

scholar. He was also a respected man of letters, and familiar with the Johnson circle. In 1783 he went to India as a High Court judge in Calcutta, where he founded the Bengal Asiatic Society.

the great innovator in arts and sciences. As James Dunbar suggested, it is all too easy to ascribe to the genius of a few superior minds what in fact arises from the efforts of many. The actions of a prominent individual are readily described; 'the efforts of the species are more remote from sight, and often too deep for our researches'. James Barry makes a similar point in his *Inquiry into the Real and Imaginary Obstructions to the Acquisition of the Arts in England* (1775). Artistic excellence, he says, is the result of a long period of improvement. The great names of a great period seem like geniuses descended from heaven, 'whilst the men, the time, and the labour that really built up this fabric of perfection, came naturally to be forgotten, and buried in obscurity'. Nor was it only the builders of the fabric who had to be taken into account. The artist needs a sympathetic and responsive audience. He cannot rely entirely on his own mental vigour. A work of genius, said Barry, is 'a complex object, and its merit or demerit depends upon the taste of the age'.

Barry himself felt that it was almost impossible to reduce the great mass of influences at work upon taste and manners to a system. Change is continuous and imperceptible. Many of his contemporaries, however, were confident that laws of social development might be discovered, and that the discovery might preserve, and perhaps improve, their own society. This was particularly true of writers in Scotland, where 'improvement' had been more startling in scale since the turn of the century than in the sister kingdom, making the survivals of unimproved clan-society the more striking by comparison. It was in Scotland that the method of Montesquieu was most eagerly and fruitfully followed, and the evolution of manners and institutions most elaborately investigated. The literary career of Henry Home, Lord Kames,[1] is representative. His interest in the historical study of law, especially in connection with the differences between Scottish and English law, led him into a much wider field of investigation. His essay on criminal law, in the *Historical Law Tracts* (1758), contains some particularly fine examples of what might be called legal psychology, with a telling use of literary evidence. He draws his readers into the feelings animating archaic penal systems with the same skill that he shows in exploring the psychology of our response to literature in

[1] Henry Home, Lord Kames, 1696–1782, was a Scottish judge and landowner, much concerned with agricultural improvement.

Elements of Criticism (1762). The main work of the latter part of his long life was a project for writing 'a history of the species, in its progress from the savage state to its highest civilization and improvement'.

He found that such an enterprise was beyond his powers, perhaps beyond the powers of any one man, but the 'few imperfect sketches' that resulted—the *Sketches of the History of Man* (1774)—provide a full and often entertaining picture of world history from the standpoint of a man of the Enlightenment. A modern reader will perhaps be most impressed by the skill with which Kames places the social and dissocial passions of mankind in the context of animal behaviour, which he observes with the experienced eye of an improving land-owner (II. 1). Tentative though his inquiries are, it is still possible to sense the cautious excitement with which he suggests the hypothesis that the concepts of attraction and repulsion may have the same kind of usefulness in the analysis of social phenomena as they do in Newtonian physics. War he sees as a necessary element in the interaction of human groups; and one excellence of the English constitution unnoted by Montesquieu is the scope it gives to the combative energies, leading to the full unfolding of mental powers and talents. The tranquil Golden Age, 'so lusciously described by poets', would in fact lead to stagnation and degeneracy. Kames is anxious that we should not struggle ignorantly against the necessary chain of causes and effects, and his solicitude to ensure his readers' acquiescence in this wisdom had, on one occasion at least, a most depressing effect upon James Boswell. 'I saw', he wrote in his journal (17 February 1781), 'a dreary nature of things, an unconscious, uncontroulable power by which all things are driven on.' He was sunk into dreadful melancholy, 'so that I went out to the wood and groaned'.

Boswell's anguish was little felt by those whose zeal for discovery buoyed them up, even when their discoveries had implications more disturbing than those suggested by Kames. This is particularly apparent in the ebulliently sombre work of John Brown,[1] author of a celebrated *Estimate of the Manners and*

---

[1] John Brown, 1715–66, was educated at Wigton Grammar School and St. John's College, Cambridge. He was ordained, but his career did not conform to the usual clerical pattern, and he had some success as a playwright. He obtained the patronage of William Warburton, and eventually became Vicar of St. Nicholas's, Newcastle upon Tyne. He hoped to visit Russia to promote a scheme of education, but his health prevented him, and he committed suicide.

Principles of the Times (1757). Inspired by the setbacks suffered by Britain in the early part of the Seven Years War, he inveighed against the effeminacy of modern manners. No one, he insisted, could altogether escape its influence, 'We might as well attempt', he said, 'to divest ourselves of the Modes of Speech, as of the Modes of Thought and Action which are peculiar to our Time and Country.' National misfortunes should not be blamed on individual misconduct, but on 'permanent and established Causes', that is, the predominant manners and principles of the age. How those manners came to be as they were was an inquiry that increasingly absorbed his attention, and the subject appears to have formed an important part of the *Principles of Christian Legislation* which he planned and went some way to completing. The manuscript now seems to be lost, but something of its scope may be inferred from a book that was closely connected with it, *A Dissertation on the Rise, Union, and Power, the Progressions, Separations, and Corruptions, of Poetry and Music* (1763).

In order to understand the function of art in the community, Brown goes back to the account of savage life given by Lafitau in his work on the North American Indians. Interest in them had been heightened by their part in the Seven Years War, and became especially topical as a result of the Indian war that followed in 1763. No nation could be less effeminate than the Iroquois, and Brown translates Lafitau's account of their song-feast with great warmth of feeling. In the song-feast, says Brown, one can see the earliest state of melody, dance, and song, all united in a simple, pure, and energetic act of celebration. Here, too, is the primitive union of legislator and musician, whose offices would tend to coalesce because 'the Chiefs are they who most signalize themselves by *Dance* and *Song*; and their *Songs* rowl principally on the *great Actions* and *Events* which concern their *own Nation*'. In this primordial celebration Brown detects the elements of poetic numbers (words being adjusted to suit the rhythm of dance and melody), and the genres of epic, ode, and tragedy. Thus, Lafitau had described how, after a war-chief had recounted the battles he had fought, 'they who are present will often rise up to dance, and represent these Actions with great Vivacity'. If to this, says Brown, 'we add the usual Exclamations of the surrounding Choir, we here behold the first *rude Form of savage Tragedy*'. Brown is impressed not only by the sheer vigour of the Indian dance, but also by its clearly defined social function. The increasing artifice of art in more sophisticated communities obscures its weightiest purpose. Music and poetry retain their excellence in Brown's eyes only so long as they continue to be an utterance of the general will, and manifest something at least of the elemental energy of the Iroquois. The force of melody does not depend on its elaborate construction but on the extent to which it exploits the passions of its hearers. It will be most powerful 'where Fear, Joy, Wonder, Terror, and Astonishment, are most easily and most frequently excited'. Hence the remarkable powers attributed to Greek music, although it had nothing of the complex structure developed since the invention of counterpoint.

With the progress of society, the various arts grow more specialized. Homer's pre-eminence as a poet itself engendered a division of labour between composers and performers, poets and rhapsodists. The trend towards virtuosity which this indicates made poetry more vulnerable to moral corruption, and the effects are conspicuous in the derivative, sophisticated literature of Rome. Horace's odes are not real hymns, but compliments to his masters, urbanely and elegantly expressed. Virgil's powers were under the constraint of servility, and he was incapable of conceiving a great original epic. The ultimate degeneracy is exhibited in the artistic career of the Emperor Nero, who in his own way restored the original union of bard and legislator:

ORPHEUS drew the barbarous Tribes from Theft, Adultery, and Murder, by his Songs and Lyre: NERO plundered his Patricians of their Estates to load his Musicians with Wealth; and amidst the forced Acclamations of a corrupted Theatre, violated a vestal Virgin on the Stage.

Modern poetry and music has been vitiated by its dependence on the Roman example, and Brown can show no convincingly restorative processes at work. He tries, but in the later part of the book the momentum of the argument is lost. The division of labour has set in motion an irreversible process of corruption: that at least is where Brown's analysis seems to point. It is, none the less, an exhilarating work, admirably illustrating Adam Smith's contention that it gives us pleasure to see apparently disconnected and various phenomena deduced from one principle and united in one chain. Brown's argument gives most pleasure when it is most pessimistic.

Adam Smith[1] himself is far removed from Brown in the tone and temper of his work. The *Inquiry into the Nature and Causes of the Wealth of Nations* (1776) is informed by just that spirit which Brown most reprobated, that of judging a nation's felicity in terms of its trade and wealth; and it is appropriate that Smith should consider the role of music in Greek education only to dismiss it as a vestigial relic of primitive times. 'Music and dancing', he says in *The Wealth of Nations*, 'are the great amusements of all barbarous nations'; and elsewhere he remarks that he once saw 'a Negro dance to his own song, the war-dance of his own country, with such vehemence of action and expression, that the whole company, gentlemen as well as ladies, got up upon chairs and tables, to be as much as possible out of the way of his fury.' An experience that for Brown would have surely been a profound illumination is for Adam Smith merely entertaining. But different as they are in such ways, Brown and Smith have something in common in their underlying procedure. Both show the workings of a basic human impulse through a wide range of types of society. With Brown it is what he calls 'the natural Passion for *Melody* and *Dance*'; with Smith, in *The Wealth of Nations*, that 'general disposition to truck, barter, and exchange' which leads to the division of labour and a consequent complication of economic and social arrangements.

The Wealth of Nations is a work which a literary historian naturally approaches with some timidity, and its significance can only be adequately assessed in terms of its contribution to economic thought. On the other hand, no account of the writing of history in the latter part of the eighteenth century can afford to leave Adam Smith out of account. *The Wealth of Nations* is clearly the work of the man whose early lectures on what may be called the philosophy of law—'the general principles which ought to run through, and be the foundation of, the laws of all nations'—inspired William Robertson's account of the progress of society in the Middle Ages, and John Millar's *Historical View of the English Government*. No work of the British

[1] Adam Smith, 1723–90, came from Kirkcaldy, and was educated at Glasgow University and Balliol College, Oxford. He then returned to Kirkcaldy, and later went to Edinburgh. In 1751 he became Professor of Logic at Glasgow, then Professor of Moral Philosophy. In 1764 he became tutor to the Duke of Buccleuch, and went to Toulouse, where he began writing *The Wealth of Nations*. In 1778 he was appointed commissioner of customs.

'Enlightenment' brings out more strikingly the way in which a growing preoccupation with the processes of society created a new perspective for the historian. The expansion of markets for goods and services comes to be seen as crucially important, for it is this expansion which provides the basis for the improvement of society, and for that vast differentiation of natural talent which is the effect rather than the cause of the division of labour. Thus, for Smith, the discovery of America, and the opening up of the sea passage to the East Indies, were 'the two greatest and most important events recorded in the history of mankind'. They were so because they made possible a market that was virtually world-wide. Henceforth the most distant parts of the globe would be able to 'relieve one another's wants, to increase one another's enjoyments, and to encourage one another's industry'.

Although Adam Smith sometimes described the historical process in such optimistic terms, he was well aware that this happy state of affairs was far from having been achieved in his own time: the non-European peoples had suffered dreadful misfortunes as a result of the opening up of their markets. In due course, however, such injustices would be corrected by an alteration in the balance of power. The oppressed peoples would grow stronger, and the Europeans weaker, thus bringing about 'that equality of courage and force which, by inspiring mutual fear, can alone overawe the injustice of independent nations into some sort of respect for the right of one another' (Book IV. vii. 3). Smith was keenly interested in the military aspect of such shifts in the balance of power, showing a firm grasp of the interaction of economic factors with the more traditional topics of historical inquiry. He argues that a society of shepherds is better adapted to military exertions than one of farmers, while in an advanced commercial state a military spirit can be expected only if it is encouraged by deliberate policy. A manufacturer or an artificer, he explains, cannot spend a single hour in martial exercises without some loss, and he will naturally tend to neglect them altogether. Accordingly, it is necessary to raise a militia, or create a specialized professional force. Like many of his contemporaries in Scotland, Smith was strongly attached to projects for a militia, believing that a martial spirit was necessary to the health of a state. He was even more impressed, however, by the effectiveness of a standing army, particularly when it came to fighting battles under modern conditions, where good order and prompt obedience were more important than dexterity in the use of weapons. He enlarges on this point in a passage which borders on the sublime:

The noise of firearms, the smoke, and the invisible death to which every man feels himself every moment exposed as soon as he comes within cannon-shot, and frequently a long time before the battle can be well said to be engaged, must render it very difficult to maintain any considerable degree of this regularity, order, and prompt obedience, even in the beginning of a modern battle. In an ancient battle there was no noise but what arose from the human voice, there was no smoke, there was no invisible cause of wounds or death . . . (Book V. i. 1)

Under any conditions, however, a well-exercised standing army is bound to gain an advantage over a militia. It is a natural consequence of the benefits necessarily derived from the division of labour. He illustrates the point in a brief survey of the great revolutions of the ancient world. Philip of Macedon overturned the Greek republics and the Persian empire by means of the professional army which he created out of his country's militia. In doing so, says Smith, he effected 'the first great revolution in the affairs of mankind, of which history has preserved any distinct or circumstantial account'. The second great revolution arose out of the contention of Rome and Carthage. The Roman militia was at first in no state to fight effectively against the professional armies of the Carthaginians, but under the stimulus of Hannibal's invasion the militia evolved into a standing army, which in turn overcame the Carthaginians, and made Rome the undisputed mistress of the Mediterranean. The third revolution was the fall of the western Empire, occasioned by the degeneration of the Roman forces into what was virtually a militia: and the militia of a civilized nation is always at a disadvantage when pitted against the militia of nations of herdsmen.

Adam Smith reduces to near-insignificance the skill of great commanders, or the policy of great statesmen. Philip of Macedon showed wisdom in taking care never to disband his militia, so that it became in effect a standing army. But having done this, he had apparently only to rely on 'the irresistible superiority which a standing army has over every sort of militia'.

If circumstances are unfavourable, human wisdom has little scope. Diocletian or Constantine may have helped on the decline of Roman military power by their policy of dispersing the legions through the provinces instead of keeping them massed on the frontier; but this policy was virtually forced on them by the danger which such a military power presented to the civil authority. The sense of man's necessary submission to an overruling power was, of course, not in the least new. It is a theme that reverberates through the closing pages of Bossuet's *Discours sur l'histoire universelle*, and it has a venerable ancestry. What is distinctive about Adam Smith's version of this theme is the connection established between the overruling power, the 'invisible hand', and people going about their daily business and pursuing their own interest, narrowly or magnanimously as the case may be. He has a keen eye for the incident from common life which proves to be an instance of some vast historical process. One of the greatest improvements in the early steam engine, he says, was the invention of a boy with a healthy love of play. His work was to open and shut a valve as the piston went up and down, and he observed that

by tying a string from the handle of the valve which opened this communication, to another part of the machine, the valve would open and shut without his assistance, and leave him at liberty to divert himself with his playfellows.   (Book I. i)

The boy had no inventive intentions; he was almost a passive instrument of progress. Equally unaware of the consequences of their actions were the great feudal proprietors, who, when the products of trade started to become available, eagerly bartered away their impregnable authority for the sake of frivolous and useless luxuries. 'The silent and insensible operation of foreign commerce and manufactures', says Smith,

gradually furnished the great proprietors with something for which they could exchange the whole surplus produce of their lands, and which they could consume themselves without sharing it either with tenants or retainers. All for ourselves, and nothing for other people, seems, in every age of the world, to have been the vile maxim of the masters of mankind. As soon, therefore, as they could find a method of consuming the whole value of their rents themselves, they had no disposition to share them with any other persons. For a pair of diamond buckles, perhaps, or for something as frivolous and useless, they exchanged the maintenance, or, what is the same thing, the price of the maintenance, of 1000 men for a year, and with it the whole weight and authority which it could give them.

(Book III. iv)

Much of the pleasure of reading *The Wealth of Nations* comes from the skill with which Smith traces the workings of man's elemental disposition to traffic in a great variety of situations. This is the clue that he follows, often with an ingenuity that one suspects was intended to startle his readers. For example, he argues that working men are more likely to need restraining from undertaking excessive labour than to need curbs on their idleness. Soldiers put on to piece-work tend to overwork themselves, driven by emulation and the lust for gain. Even the long week-ends taken by some tradesmen are pressed into Smith's argument: 'excessive application during four days of the week is frequently the real cause of the idleness of the other three, so much and so loudly complained of' (Book I. viii). The unfolding of the argument is exhilarating in its very single-mindedness, although it is clear that Smith sometimes disregards factors with which he is well acquainted. The division of labour, which at the beginning of *The Wealth of Nations* is seen as the great engine of improvement, becomes at the end a source of grave social evils. The contradiction is real, and not a mere shift in perspective. In the first chapter of Book I, Smith alludes to the period of 'sauntering' that necessarily occurs when a man passes from one type of work to another; and he draws the conclusion that in those employments where many types of work have to be performed, workpeople will be slothful and inefficient. In Book V, however, he points out that those who spend their lives in one or two simple operations will have no occasion to exert their understandings, and so will become stupid and ignorant. One feels that if he had juxtaposed the two passages, each would have had to be written somewhat differently. While this is perhaps the most extreme example, a more familiar one is the difference in outlook observable between *The Wealth of Nations* and Smith's earlier work *The Theory of Moral Sentiments* (1759). There is no strict contradiction between the two treatises, and in many ways they illuminate each other, but the earlier one shows such a keen pursuit of the varied manifestations of man's social nature, and the later is so resolutely preoccupied with man's desire of bettering his condition, that it is only with an effort that one recalls that Smith is writing about the behaviour of the same animal. A different clue again is followed in the posthumously published essay on the history of astronomy. Here what is uppermost in his mind is the desire for intellectual coherence. He examines the impulse to reduce apparently solitary and incoherent phenomena to some regular system. A man who tries to follow a game of cards without knowing the rules will soon feel confusion and giddiness coming upon him which, if persisted in, will end in lunacy and distraction. A pressure of the same kind is at work in attempts to explain the movements of the heavenly bodies. So long as it was assumed that the earth was the static centre of the universe, the planets gave unending difficulty, which increased as their movements were more carefully noted. Explanations became more and more complex, so that they defeated their own purpose for the imagination, which felt baffled by their intricacies and residual uncertainties. It was the very simplicity of Copernicus's theory that marked its superiority to what had gone before, although to attain this simplicity it was necessary, as Tycho Brahe remarked, to move the earth from its foundations, stop the revolution of the firmament, make the sun stand still, and subvert the whole order of the universe. Philosophy, said Smith,

never triumphs so much, as when, in order to connect together a few, in themselves perhaps inconsiderable objects, she has, if I may say so, created another constitution of things, more natural, indeed, and such as the imagination can more easily attend to, but more new, more contrary to common opinion and expectation, than any of those appearances themselves.

This sense of triumph is one of the main pleasures that a literary reader can still derive from the work of Adam Smith.

Smith never attempted to write a fully developed historical narrative, and would probably not have found it a congenial task. Another analyst of social processes who did, however, also try his hand at history of the traditional kind was Adam Ferguson.[1] He is remembered now mainly for his *Essay on the History of Civil Society* (1767), but his *History of the Progress and*

---

[1] Adam Ferguson, 1723–1816, was educated for the ministry in St. Andrews University and in Edinburgh, and saw active service as chaplain to the Black Watch. He became keeper of the Advocates' Library, and then successively Professor of Natural Philosophy, of Moral Philosophy, and finally of Mathematics at Edinburgh University.

Termination of the Roman Republic (1783) should not be neglected
by anyone who wants to understand the nature of 'philosophical history'. Like John Brown and many others at the time,
Ferguson was haunted by anxieties about the corruption and
decline of wealthy and complex societies. The *Essay* examines
the leading characteristics of societies in various stages of
advancement, from the rude to the polished, and the last third
of the book is devoted to the processes of decline. The most
dangerous disease of society, he thought, was the failure of
citizens to play their due part in public affairs. He placed a
special emphasis on the repudiation of individualistic theories of
man: in every part of the world, he argued, the human race has
always been represented as 'assembled in troops and companies'.
The love of society, friendship, and public affection are part of
the original character of the species, and not a late invention.
Questions about the rights of government owe more to intellectual subtlety than to any uncertainty in the feelings of the
heart.

Involved in the resolutions of our company, we move with the
croud before we have determined the rule by which its will is collected. We follow a leader, before we have settled the ground of his
pretensions, or adjusted the form of his election . . .   (I. x)

But this spontaneous sociability can be thwarted and debilitated.
The division of labour tends to withdraw individuals from the
central concerns of their society, and Ferguson is deeply concerned to warn his readers against that 'remissness of spirit, that
weakness of soul, that state of national debility, which is likely
to end in political slavery' (VI. iv). Commotion and activity
are not contrary to civil order, which is not at all the same thing
as the good order of stones in a wall. Good social order exists
in so far as men are placed 'where they are properly qualified
to act', and action includes contention and strife. 'He who has
never struggled with his fellow-creatures', says Ferguson, 'is
a stranger to half the sentiments of mankind' (I. iv).
    Ferguson's robust attitude to civil conflict owes something
to Montesquieu, more especially to the ninth chapter of the
Grandeur et décadence des Romains, where Montesquieu insists that
the dissensions of republican Rome were a necessary aspect of
its greatness. The outcome of these dissensions was admittedly not a happy one for the lovers of liberty, but the energies

displayed in the conflicts which ended in the subversion of the republic were of a sublimity unmatched elsewhere in the history of the world. The temptations to wickedness were great, but, as Ferguson remarks, 'minds that were turned to integrity and honour had a proportional spring to their exertions and pursuits'. Moreover, in spite of the loss (so much deplored by Bolingbroke) of the later books of Livy's history, these sublime exertions were very fully documented. The speeches, and still more the letters, of Cicero formed a superb record of immediate impressions, laying open, as Conyers Middleton put it, the grounds and motives of all the great events of that time:

> They breathe the last words of expiring liberty; a great part of them having been written in the very crisis of its ruin, to rouse up all the virtue that was left in the honest and the brave, to the defence of their country.   (*Life of Cicero*, sect. xii)

In composing his narrative of Roman history, Adam Ferguson appears to have had two different and not always compatible aims in view. One was to attempt a kind of expanded version of Montesquieu's *Grandeur et décadence*, showing the steps by which republican institutions were subverted and replaced by monarchical ones. The other object he proposed was to provide a detailed narrative of political struggles and military campaigns, not all of which had an immediate bearing on the constitutional issue. A reader is apt to lose himself in local details, forgetting, especially in the brisk account of Caesar's campaigns, the part which they played in the main action. But at his best, Ferguson shows considerable skill in reconstructing the circumstances in which critical measures were undertaken, and he is particularly adroit in suggesting the atmosphere of civil commotion, with its alarms and uncertainties. A fair example of this is his account of the tumults accompanying the passage of the Agrarian Law of Tiberius Gracchus (II. ii). The narrative follows Plutarch's account of the Gracchi very closely, but Ferguson has a knack of placing events within a context far more precisely visualized than in his source, and is thus able to display the various impulses and motives at work with a gratifying lucidity. He conjures up the 'feverish state of suspense and anxiety' which helped to precipitate the onslaught of the senators on the partisans of Tiberius, setting the moderation of the consul abruptly aside,

'The consul', said Scipio Nasica, 'deserts the republic; let those who wish to preserve it, follow me.' The senators instantly arose, and moving in a body, which increased as they went, by the concourse of their clients, then seized the shafts of the fasces, or tore up the benches in their way, and, with their robes wound up, in place of shields, on their left arm, broke into the midst of the assembly of the people.

It is impossible to do full justice to this passage without reading it in context, where it acquires an additional force from the confusions that preceded it. Ferguson has a manifest predilection for strong measures, and relates even the most revolting instances with an equanimity that is almost, though not altogether, unflinching. He feels able to detail and justify the bloody proscriptions of Sulla, arguing that violent remedies were needed in a populous city whose democratic institutions had to cope with the administration of many provinces. The people of Rome spurned the authority needed to govern themselves, and, equally, 'the principles of justice and order which were required to regulate their government of others. Where the gangrene spread in such a body, it was likely to require the amputation-knife' (II. vii).

Ferguson makes no pointed parallels between his own time and the period of his history. As we have seen, he is more apt to emphasize the uniqueness of the Roman commonwealth, with its unparalleled opportunities for the extremes of vice and virtue. But as he remarked in an unpublished essay on history, now preserved in the Edinburgh University Library, 'narrative history' is a means of extending experience, teaching us to 'anticipate or conjecture the Event of Transactions from their Origin and Progress'. The *Essay on the History of Civil Society* makes clear how uneasy Ferguson was at the prospect of European 'inundations' of Asia and Africa, the consequences of which were likely to be even more ruinous in their ultimate effects than the Roman conquests. One may infer that he believed that British statesmen might well find themselves in future in a situation comparable to that of Cato, Cicero, Brutus, and others. In retrospect their endeavours to preserve the republic can be seen to have been hopeless, but Ferguson is sure that they were justified. Free men will always be entitled to assert their right to liberty, and the great Romans 'must for ever receive from those who respect integrity and magnanimity the tribute of esteem, even of tenderness, which is due to their memory' (VI. i.). If *The Progress and Termination of the Roman Republic* occasionally touches distinction, it comes from Ferguson's quest for a virtue that can meet the shock of inconceivably vast political disasters.

A full picture of eighteenth-century historiography would entail consideration of many works which must be passed over lightly here, or omitted altogether. If Kames's *Sketches* merit some attention from the literary reader, so too does Lord Monboddo's treatise *Of the Origin and Progress of Language* (1773–92).[1] Like Kames, Monboddo was keenly interested in the borderland between man and the other social animals. His reputation has suffered from the undeniable credulity he displayed when the evidence of travellers suited his theories: for example, Cardinal Polignac's account of the baubacis, an animal alleged to exist in the Ukraine, displaying highly-developed powers of political and military organization. Monboddo's merits are more apparent in his clear grasp of the circumstances in which speech might be invented, and he conveys vividly to his readers the sheer difficulty of the invention: a point which one is apt to lose sight of in Adam Smith's influential essay on the formation of languages. Constant practice, says Monboddo, makes the act of articulation seem easy; but the simplest syllable involves blowing the breath with a 'tremulous concussion' of larynx and windpipe, together with a complex movement of the other organs of speech.

> But the business becomes much more difficult, when we compound vowels, making what we call *diphthongs*, and when we throw into the same syllable two or three consonants, as in the English word *strength*. In short, the more accurately and minutely we consider language, the greater the difficulty of the invention appears, and indeed the absolute impossibility of it, unless we suppose it to be invented by very slow degrees, from very small beginnings, and in a very long course of time.   (I. iii. 5)

His account of some features of the Huron language, which he takes as an example of language at an early stage of its evolution, shows considerable skill in helping the reader to enter into modes of thought very different from those of modern commercial society.

---

[1] James Burnett, Lord Monboddo, 1714–99, was a Scottish advocate, later a judge. His simplicity of life, modelled on that of 'the ancients', was remarkable.

In later volumes Monboddo considers the structure and functioning of the more polished languages, and has much to say about such matters as the appropriate style for various genres. In his vehement assertion of the superiority of the Greek and Sanskrit languages, he was consciously reacting against the tendency to minimize the role of the great legislator, or at least of the reforming élite, which, as we have seen, distinguishes much of the historical and sociological work of the time. An art like that of language, he thought, was not 'natural' to man, but 'a kind of forced production of the soil'. Such arts require as much careful tending to preserve them as to rear them; 'and if that is but a little remitted, down the stream we go to our natural state of ignorance and barbarity' (II. iii. 14). Monboddo's writings help one to understand the temper of those who felt that they were living in a corrupt and degenerate society, whose fatal influence might none the less be resisted by anyone with the necessary strength of mind. It is in this context that one must understand the 'primitivism' that is so conspicuous in Monboddo's other great work, *Antient Metaphysics* (1779–99). Polished societies have developed in such a way as to enervate the human race; but this does not mean that a more wholesome civilization is inconceivable.

A similar dissatisfaction with the manners of contemporary civil society informs much of the work of Gilbert Stuart,[1] although nothing could be further from the mood of his panegyric of the ancient Germans than the elaborately articulate philhellenism of Monboddo. Stuart is remembered now, if at all, for his scurrilous career as a reviewer, but his *Historical Dissertation concerning the Antiquity of the English Constitution* (1768), and the *View of Society in Europe* (1778), deserve attention as trenchant statements of a point of view which was an important ingredient of the 'age of sensibility'. Like John Brown, Stuart was deeply impressed by the spirit informing the manners and laws of our barbaric ancestors, before the division of labour and increasing wealth created conditions in which men could lord it over others. Here was the genuine source of democratic institutions. The freedom of speech at the old Germanic assemblies was unlimited. People were influenced by persuasion,

---

[1] Gilbert Stuart, 1742–86, was educated at Edinburgh University, and became a professional reviewer in London and Edinburgh. His attacks on William Robertson were particularly acrimonious.

not authority. 'A murmur coarse, and often rude, expressed their dissent: the rattling of their armour was the flattering mark of their applause.' No respect was paid but to merit, the poor were not crushed by proud oppressors, women played an active part in the affairs of the tribe, and the whole people 'possessed a greatness and extent of mind, which are not generally attained in more advanced ages'. Unfortunately this admirable state of affairs was so intimately bound up with a vanished state of society that Stuart's view of his own time was if anything more pessimistic than Brown's. It is in his work that one finds what is probably the most extreme statement at that time of a deterministic view of social development. In the *View of Society in Europe*, he argues that the system of chivalry was an unconscious development of the instincts, the passions, the usages of the barbarians who destroyed the Roman Empire. 'They were to build, without knowing it, a most magnificent structure. Out of the impulse of their passions, the institutions of chivalry were gradually to form themselves.' Just so the institutions established by Lycurgus and Solon merely confirmed existing custom; they were not 'projects suggested by philosophy and speculation'. One may infer that Stuart found little comfort in Monboddo's faith that a man could rise, by the assistance of philosophy, above the degenerate manners of the age. He looked back with an angry, despairing nostalgia.

In John Millar's work,[1] on the other hand, one encounters a mood closer to the buoyancy of Adam Smith. His most famous book, *Observations concerning the Distinction of Ranks in Society* (1771), considers the development of such examples of subordination as that of women to men, children to fathers, and servants to masters. Liberty, he argues, is most solidly based in a polished, complex society. A tradesman in a prosperous commercial nation has no occasion to court the favour of the great, and it follows that an English wagoner will have a more independent spirit than a man of corresponding rank in the Scottish highlands. Millar combines a tough-minded analysis of the origin of social sentiments with a genuine capacity for enabling his readers to enter into those sentiments. Perhaps more than any of his contemporaries he makes one feel both the astonishing variety of the human race, and its underlying uniformity. Some

---

[1] John Millar, 1735–1801, was educated at Glasgow University, where he became Professor of Law.

of the best instances of this capacity are to be found in his *Historical View of the English Government* (1787), a work devoted to showing the essential continuity between the primitive and the modern forms of the 'constitution'. 'The variations that have occurred in the modes of living,' he said, 'and in the condition of individuals, have been gradually accommodated to the spirit of the old institutions.' The original was a 'rude sketch'; progress has since been made in filling up the picture. Thus, although the Saxons were victims of the confusion which people commonly make between the activities of government and the personal will of the prince, royal prerogative was not unlimited. It is true that 'the sovereign, who appeared to direct, and put in motion, all the wheels and springs of government', might therefore be imagined to exercise, in his own right, powers which he in fact derived from the community. But there was, none the less, an understanding that the estate acquired by the king was the estate of the public, and as such open to interference from the Witenagemote (I. 8). Here, in an embryonic form, was the principle which later found utterance in the slogan 'No taxation without representation'. While Millar avoids making his Saxons into ninth-century Whigs, he contrives to remind his readers of common elements in greatly contrasting types of society. The achievement is a more subtle one than it may appear to be.

The Scottish contribution to the new kind of history was characteristically systematic. In England, while a sense of the expanded scope of historical studies was equally prevalent, it took shape in erudite investigation of particulars. Thus Warburton's *Divine Legation of Moses Demonstrated* (1738–41) is overloaded with a mass of exceedingly miscellaneous detail, most of which is of far greater interest than the main argument. The book is concerned to prove the divine origin of the Mosaic dispensation from its failure to rely on a future state of rewards and punishments—a sanction that all other polities have found indispensable. In support of this thesis he deploys the results of much ingenious historical research, providing (for example) an analysis of the evolution of alphabets from picture-writing. 'He carries you round and round', said Dr. Johnson, 'without carrying you forward to the point; but then you have no wish to be carried forward.' Johnson himself was certainly predisposed to appreciate Warburton's fertile genius. As the preface to the *Dictionary* shows, he was highly susceptible to the temptation of unending, shapeless inquiries. He not only dreamed of entering and ransacking the obscure recesses of northern learning, but was also an encourager of such scholarship in others. He commended Richard Farmer's project for a *History of Leicester*, and was impressed by Evan Evans's efforts to rescue from oblivion the 'remains of ancient British genius'. He wished for a better history of manners, of common life, than existed in his time, and even urged Boswell (in October 1769) to go on with his collections of Scottish words and Scottish antiquities: 'Make a large book; a folio.' BOSWELL: 'But of what use will it be, Sir?' JOHNSON: 'Never mind the use; do it.'

The collection of materials for local history, the recording of antiquities, was a pursuit that had engaged the attention of distinguished scholars since the sixteenth century, and no contemporary of Johnson's can be said to have excelled the work of Sir William Dugdale or of Thomas Hearne. It is the progressive increase in the sheer volume of such inquiries that is most striking, a fact that can be appreciated if one studies successive numbers of the *Gentleman's Magazine*. To survey the material concisely would itself make a considerable book. Increasingly it was understood that the remains of antiquity were richly available in every corner of the land. The history of Britain was an immensely complex process, every current and eddy of which had its interest and importance for the student of human nature. Tracing these currents and eddies was more profitable than premature attempts to achieve a clear outline or system. Even so, the diligent antiquary was occasionally rewarded with a completely fresh view of a historical landscape. William Clarke's treatise *The Connexion of the Roman, Saxon, and English Coins* (1767) was the result of what at the start was a very limited inquiry, but it served to illuminate not only the economic state of the Roman Empire, but also the origins of the English parliament and other national institutions. A more celebrated example is Horace Walpole's *Historic Doubts on the Life and Reign of King Richard the Third* (1768). Walpole's main concern is to examine the implications of a document that he calls Richard III's 'coronation roll':

It is the account of Peter Courteys keeper of the great wardrobe, and dates from the day of king Edward the Fourth his death, to the feast of the purification in the February of the following year. Peter Courteys specifies what stuff he found in the wardrobe, what contracts he made for the ensuing coronation, and the deliveries in consequence. The whole is couched in the most minute and regular manner, and is preferable to a thousand vague and interested histories.

Walpole argues that this document proves that the young Prince Edward walked, or was intended to walk, in his uncle's coronation procession, a fact which undermines the structure of 'mob-stories and childish improbabilities' that constitutes the received account of Richard's reign. A similar confidence in the value of the specific, well-authenticated detail underlies his *Anecdotes of Painting in England* (1762–71), and prompted such ventures as Thomas Percy's edition of the Northumberland Household Book. Of all the historical works in this period, the one that illustrates the antiquarian temper most engagingly is Thomas Warton's *History of English Poetry* (1774–81). Although preliminary dissertations sketch in a wider and earlier background, it deals with the period between the Norman Conquest and the reign of Elizabeth, exhibiting a slow, uneven progress towards 'correctness', the 'gleams of science' struggling through a barbarous and scholastic cloud. Histories of English poetry had been projected by Pope and Gray, and Warton had seen their plans. He decided to proceed in quite a different way, finding that their emphasis on schools of poets was too restrictive, and tended to 'destroy that free exertion of research with which such a history ought to be executed'. The 'complication, variety, and extent of materials' that he wished to include sometimes almost had the effect of transforming the *History* into a mere anthology with comment. A certain fitful unity does begin to emerge, however, owing to Warton's shrewd discernment of technical competence in work which Lord Kames, for one, would have found invincibly unappetizing. Thus, in admiring Lydgate's occasional command of the vivid pictorial detail, or in analysing the structural qualities which make the ballad of 'The Nut-Browne Mayde' superior to Prior's imitation, 'Henry and Emma', he gradually constructs a system of improvements which make up what his generation termed polished literature. It is true that he sometimes dallies with the view that the institutions of a primitive society were peculiarly favourable to poetry. He obviously shared Sir William Temple's

admiration of the northern destroyers of the Roman Empire,
and paraphrased Richard Hurd's regrets about the effect on
poetry of modern good sense. He even remarks that the early
'minstrels' poured forth spontaneous rhymes in obedience to
the workings of nature (XIX). Comments in this vein are apt
to come in rather awkwardly, though a synthesis is implied in
his explanation of why the age of Spenser and Shakespeare
was especially favourable to the writing of poetry. The superstitions of a primitive and passionate period survived (he argued)
in a form not too violent and chimerical. 'The Shakespeare of
a more instructed and polished age, would not have given us a
magician darkening the sun at noon, the sabbath of the witches,
and the cauldron of incantation':

> Undoubtedly most of these notions were credited and entertained
> in a much higher degree, in the preceding periods. But the arts of
> composition had not then made a sufficient progress, nor would the
> poets of those periods have managed them with so much address and
> judgment.   (LXI)

Passages like these indicate where the most enduring interest of
Warton's *History* lies. Perhaps no reader can read it through—
as a book, and not as a work of reference—unless he does so for
what it tells him of the history of manners. Given this preoccupation, which Warton could take for granted in most of his
contemporaries, almost every page will inform and entertain,
though as a series of picturesque details rather than as a coherent narrative.

The shapelessness which Warton so cheerfully accepted set
his work apart from the idea of history presented in most
theoretical discussions of the art which one finds in the eighteenth century. The theory tends to be based on conservative
assumptions, even in the hands of Adam Smith, who was
doing so much to change men's ideas of what constituted the
primary material of history. In the lectures which Smith delivered in Glasgow in the winter of 1762-3 historical narrative
and fictitious narrative are closely related in their technique. He
praises the ancients for their power of showing us 'the feelings
and agitations of mind in the actors previous to and during the
event' (XVII), and he deplores the long dissertations that
modern historians feel bound to introduce into their work, distracting our attention from the main facts, and so weakening

our concern for the issue of the affair (XVIII). Hugh Blair, in his *Lectures on Rhetoric and Belles Lettres* (1784), speaks in similar terms, placing great emphasis on unity and due connection, so that the reader may be led smoothly along, and have the satisfaction of seeing how one event arises out of another (XXXVI). Herodotus he praises in spite of his many digressions and episodes, because he avoids 'a broken and scattered narration of the principal story'. The episodes are clearly marked as such (XXXV). The influence here of Aristotle's *Poetics* is evident, and at least one critic, James Moor,[1] based his discussion of historical composition directly upon that venerable authority. His essay, published with others in a collection edited by Robert and Andrew Foulis in Glasgow in 1759, would almost certainly have been known to Smith and Blair. This traditionalist approach would direct attention away from efforts to solve the problem of assimilating the new materials to a narrative that would engage the feelings of the reader. Interest was focused rather on what Sir John Dalrymple[2] called 'that picturesque simplicity and choice of circumstances, which distinguish the historical compositions of the ancients'. Dalrymple's *Memoirs of Great Britain and Ireland* (1771–88) may be studied as a work that conforms closely to the requirements of contemporary historiographical theory, and indeed Smith and Blair were among the friends he mentions in the preface as having advised him on the style and presentation. The *Memoirs* are a narrative of events leading up to the Glorious Revolution, and an account of the years immediately following. The subject gives much scope for Dalrymple's research into secret motives and hidden transactions, but the book's most striking literary quality is its deliberately lofty manner. He has a keen eye for the subject of a 'history-painting', like Lord Russell's last farewell to his wife:

> With a deep and noble silence; with a long and fixed look, in which respect and affection, unmingled with passion, were expressed; Lord and Lady Russel parted forever; he great in this last act of his life, but she greater.   (Part I, Book i)

Johnson dismissed this style as 'the mere bouncing of a schoolboy: Great He! but greater She! and such stuff'. But Dalrymple's

---

[1] James Moor, 1712–79, was librarian of Glasgow University, and Professor of Greek there.

[2] Sir John Dalrymple, 1726–1810, was a Scottish advocate and judge, educated at Edinburgh University and Trinity Hall, Cambridge.

work gives one a vivid appreciation of the way in which his contemporaries viewed the moral sublime. A splendidly extended instance of this quality is provided by his account (Part II, Book ii) of the manners of the Scottish Highlanders. Uniting the ties of both feudal and patriarchal authority, the Highlanders embodied the essential virtues of the savage and civilized states of society alike. They had the politeness of courts without their vices; honour without folly; neither 'that excess of industry which reduces man to a machine, nor that total want of it which sinks him into a rank of animals below his own'. Music was in their society what it had been in ancient Greece, a powerful auxiliary of virtue. High sentiments were consistently inculcated by historians and bards. Their landscape provided a setting which reinforced the effects of their education: 'The vastness of the objects which surrounded them, lakes, mountains, rocks, cataracts, extended and elevated their minds.' They were naturally cosmopolitan in their sympathies, and combined refinement of sentiment with strength and hardiness of body. It was only fitting that their dress should prove to be 'the last remains of the Roman habit in Europe'.

Although Dalrymple's Highlanders are perhaps more of a romantic vision than a sober historical picture, this passage does incidentally demonstrate that he was influenced by what Blair called the 'very great improvement which has, of late years, begun to be introduced into Historical Composition', namely an attention to

laws, customs, commerce, religion, literature, and every other thing that tends to show the spirit and genius of nations. It is now understood to be the business of an able Historian to exhibit manners, as well as facts and events; and assuredly, whatever displays the state and life of mankind, in different periods, and illustrates the progress of the human mind, is more useful and interesting than the detail of sieges and battles.   (XXXVI)

Blair names Voltaire as the initiator of this improvement, and in fact the three great figures in British historiography in this period—Hume, Robertson, and Gibbon—are all profoundly affected by it. All three, however, conform to the traditional definition of history. Each has his own characteristic way of evading the limitations of the genre. Their tact and skill in doing so are a measure of their greatness.

David Hume,[1] for one, appears in the *History of England* (1754–61) to be writing a political history in the strictest sense. Although he makes a place for observations on commerce, manners, literature, and so forth, the place is at certain intervals in the narrative: they are independent of the whole, and have not been so organized as to illuminate it. Hume lacks the adroitness displayed by Gibbon when he insinuated into the second chapter of the *Decline and Fall* a brief history of ancient agriculture, in order to show how the grave disadvantages of an extended empire were attended by some compensation in diffusing at the same time the improvements of social life. None the less, Hume's political history takes place within a wider context, suggested rather than described, but insistently reminding us that changes in manners count for even more than changes in political systems. In order to appreciate this wider context, it is essential to read some of Hume's essays and dissertations on religious, moral, and political subjects. Two of these in particular deserve attention, the essay 'Of the Populousness of Ancient Nations' (first published in 1752), and *The Natural History of Religion* (1757). The former work ingeniously deploys a great variety of literary evidence to support the contention that Europe is better cultivated and better peopled in Hume's time than it was in that of Thucydides or Cicero. The essay paints an elaborately comfortless picture of a world where primitive methods of trade and agriculture, bloody factions, and an inclement climate united to produce an unenviable mode of life. While Hume was very far from disparaging the ancients, and greatly admired the unequalled eloquence and literary art of Greece and Rome, he was happy to live in eighteenth-century Britain. The inhabitants of a polished society in modern Europe would be well advised to examine the sources of their happiness rather than indulge the humour of blaming the present and admiring the past, strongly rooted though this might be in human nature. The other work mentioned, *The Natural History of Religion*, is a work of a different kind, placing

---

[1] David Hume, 1711–76, studied at Edinburgh University, and later spent three years in France, where he wrote the *Treatise of Human Nature*. He was present at the raid on Lorient in 1747, and in 1748 accompanied a military mission to Vienna and Turin. He settled in Edinburgh, and was for a time keeper of the Advocates' Library. His reputation as an unbeliever excluded him from academic appointments, but he had a brief but successful diplomatic career in Paris, 1763–5. His friendship with Rousseau ended in a celebrated quarrel.

less emphasis on the accumulation of minute historical evidence
(though this is skilfully used) than on the psychology of religious
belief. Hume's main thesis is that the most primitive form of
religion is polytheistic, and that monotheism emerges as a later
development. The most telling passages are those which embody
Hume's perceptive analyses of religious sentiment as he knew it
from personal observation, analyses which he uses to explain
features of other and more primitive states of mind. As ideas of
divinity are exalted, he remarks, it is in practice the divine
power and knowledge that are thought of, not the goodness.
Thus men's terrors increase, and since even the inmost recesses of
the mind are open to God's inspection, they must take care

not to form expressly any sentiment of blame and disapprobation.
All must be applause, ravishment, exstasy. And while their gloomy
apprehensions make them ascribe to him measures of conduct, which,
in human creatures, would be highly blamed, they must still affect
to praise and admire that conduct in the object of their devotional
addresses.

The Natural History of Religion relates such unworthy and in-
jurious notions firmly to man's anxious fear of the unknown
causes that surround him, and in explaining them thus deprives
them of their power.

All Hume's work is informed with a love of manly, steady
virtue, the 'calm sunshine of the mind'. For him perhaps the
most admirable feature of the English constitution was that it
fostered enlarged and generous sentiments. In an essay 'Of the
Protestant Succession', he declared that there was no other
instance in human history of so many millions of people, over
so long a tract of time, being 'held together, in a manner so
free, so rational, and so suitable to the dignity of human
nature'. The *History of England* was written to help his readers
understand the processes by which this agreeable condition had
been attained. The Whig myth of tyrannical Stuart kings,
tirelessly intriguing to overthrow the liberty guaranteed in the
'ancient constitution', had acquired great influence through
the patronage of the governing party in the state; but it stood
in the way of a proper understanding of the sources of political
well-being, and might be taken to justify factious violence in
which the enlarged and generous sentiments would be tram-
pled on,

Hume began his *History* with a revaluation of the four Stuart reigns (volume I, 1754; volume II, 1756). Having completed this, he moved back to narrate the course of events under the Tudors (1759); and finally he turned to the remotest origins of the state in the generally barbarous times before Henry VII (2 volumes, 1761). He had at first thought only of writing the history of the Stuarts. A letter to Adam Smith (24 September 1752) explains how 'the preceding Events or Causes may easily be shown in a Reflection or Review, which may be artfully inserted in the Body of the Work, & the whole, by that means, be render'd more compact and uniform'. But although he eventually filled out the narrative to what became for more than a century the standard history of England, the first two parts are in a sense an illustrative appendix to his main theme. English government in the Middle Ages was at best 'only a barbarous monarchy, not regulated by any fixed maxims, or bounded by any certain undisputed rights' (chap. XVI). The royal prerogative under the Tudors was allowed a largely uncontested predominance. As for the struggle between that prerogative and parliamentary privilege under James I and Charles I, although it prepared the ground for the modern constitution, with its just balance between authority and liberty, the fact remains that it was something new, and at the time raw and uncomely. The Stuarts may have made undue assertions of their authority; but they were, after all, reacting to a liberty which was incited by the fanaticism of religion—'a principle', Hume remarks 'the most blind, headstrong and ungovernable, by which human nature can possibly be actuated'. No historian who fails to enter into the genuine perplexity of Charles I can presume to condemn his policies—and Hume takes good care to see that his readers do indeed feel the stresses which drove Charles into the measures which eventually destroyed him.

> From the rank of a monarch, to be degraded into a slave of his insolent, ungrateful subjects, seemed of all indignities the greatest; and nothing, in his judgment, could exceed the humiliation attending such a state, but the meanness of tamely submitting to it without making some efforts to preserve the authority transmitted to him by his predecessors.   (Chap. LI)

The difficulties of the Stuarts arose, in Hume's opinion, from their reigning at a period when the older checks to the pretensions of parliament were much diminished, and the sources of

patronage available to ministers of the crown in his own day
were not yet developed. This suggestive hypothesis enables
Hume to appreciate the anxiety of the king without forgetting that the consequent royal policies could justifiably arouse
anxiety on behalf of parliamentary liberty. In rehearsing the
controversy over ship money, and Hampden's refusal to pay
it, Hume presents the arguments of Hampden's counsel with
a persuasive cogency that could hardly be equalled by the most
militant of Whigs. To allow the king's plea of necessity to justify
this species of taxation would remove all restraints on the exertion of his prerogative; 'wherever any difficulty shall occur, the
administration, instead of endeavouring to elude or overcome
it by gentle and prudent measures, will instantly represent it
as a reason for infringing all ancient laws and institutions'.
But although this chapter (LII) ends with an eloquent expression of the concern, by a great party in the nation, to resist the
continued encroachments of church and state, the next chapter
views the matter in an altogether different perspective. The
grievances suffered by the English, says Hume, scarcely deserved the name, and even ship money, considered apart from
the undesirable constitutional consequences, 'was a great and
evident advantage to the public, by the judicious use which
the king made of the money levied by that expedient'. The
transition here is indeed rather abrupt, but it admirably
illustrates one aspect of Hume's impartiality.

Another aspect of this impartiality—and one which particularly exposed him to the charge of Tory bias—was his care to
avoid as far as possible the distortion caused by judging
measures in a former period by the maxims which prevail at
present. He reminds us that in the early seventeenth century
the liberty of the press and religious toleration were generally
regarded as incompatible with all good government; and the
prosecutions for libel in the Star Chamber (for example) have
to be looked at in this context. Similarly, Laud's 'popish'
reforms of religious ceremony, although ridiculed in a lively
account of the consecration of St. Catherine's church (chap.
LII), are partly vindicated when Hume attempts a general
assessment of Laud's career (chap. LVII). In epochs of excessive
piety, such ceremonies serve to mollify the 'fierce and gloomy
spirit of devotion' by helping the worshipper's overstrained
mind to relax itself in the contemplation of works of art. Not,

indeed, that Laud regarded the matter thus. He conducted the scheme, says Hume,

> not with the enlarged sentiments and cool reflection of a legislator, but with the intemperate zeal of a sectary; and by overlooking the circumstances of the times, served rather to inflame that religious fury which he meant to repress. But this blemish is more to be regarded as a general imputation on the whole age, than any particular failing of Laud's; and it is sufficient for his vindication to observe, that his errors were the most excusable of all those which prevailed during that zealous period.

The shifts of perspective observable here, even within the compass of a few sentences, are an important element in Hume's technique as a historian. Although his point of view is firmly that of an enlightened philosopher, he can understand, in his own sceptical way, motives that are anything but enlightened: and this does much to create a genuine solidity of presentation. There is a fine instance of this in chapter LIII, when he describes the rise of the Covenant party in Scotland. All ranks of people there, he said, cherished the independence of the ecclesiastical power.

> It was commonly asked, whether Christ or the King was superior: and as the answer seemed obvious, it was inferred, that the assembly, being Christ's council, were superior, in all spiritual matters, to the parliament, who were only the King's. But as the covenanters were sensible, that this consequence, though it seemed to them irrefragable, would not be assented to by the King; it became requisite to maintain their religious tenets by military force, and not to trust intirely to supernatural assistance, of which, however, they held themselves well assured.

Hume's blandly logical tone here throws the stubborn Covenanting temper into sharp relief, especially when he describes the relationship between divine aid and military force. He goes on to remark that this 'tumultuary combination, inflamed with bigotry' showed a vigour and ability that would have done credit to a regular established commonwealth. 'The whole kingdom was, in a manner, engaged; and the men of greatest abilities soon acquired the ascendant, which their family interest enabled them to maintain.' The transition from inflamed bigotry to family interest is so smooth that it is hardly noticed;

but it quietly underlines the rooted strength of the Scottish opposition to Charles I.

Hume clarifies the issues in a complex situation, but at the same time contrives to make his readers aware of an unmanageable largeness beyond the area of clarification, of irrepressible energies that constantly threaten to overset the existing equilibrium. He is particularly stirred by occasions when a shift in the balance of power, or a movement of opinion, becomes irresistible, as at the time of the first meeting of the Long Parliament in 1640:

the near prospect of success roused all latent murmurs and pretensions which had hitherto been held in violent constraint: and the torrent of general inclination and opinion ran so strongly against the court, that the King was in no situation to refuse any reasonable demands of the popular leaders . . .   (Chap. LIV)

The same image of a violent torrent occurs at critical moments in the accounts of the overthrow of Edward II (chap. XIV) and of Richard II (chap. XVII), and something of the same effect is created by the arbitrary will of Henry VIII, aided as it was by a fawning parliament and utterly obsequious courts. Hume warms to anyone who can be shown to have held out against such daunting odds, like the Bishop of Carlisle who defended Richard II, or the amiable Archbishop Cranmer, who did not allow the turns of royal or popular favour to affect the constancy of his friendships. He is pleased, too, by instances of successful evasion of triumphant power, as in the story—too long to quote—of how Henry VIII's sixth wife, Catherine Parr, was maliciously accused of heresy—a charge made possible by her unwise love of theological discussion with her husband. She skilfully eluded the peril, and was ever after careful 'not to offend Henry's humour by any contradiction' (chap. XXXIII).

Much of the pleasure of reading Hume's *History* comes from the apparently effortless clarity of the narrative, and one appreciates this particularly if one compares it with some of his immediate sources. From Clement Walker's spirited *History of Independency* (1648) he obtained the main topics of one of Cromwell's speeches in the House of Commons, urging members to support the 'vote of non-addresses' by which Charles I was virtually deposed. Walker remarked at the end of his own account that Cromwell 'laid his hand upon his Sword at the latter end of his speech'. Hume exploits this detail by using it to heighten the effect of a twice-repeated 'beware' for which he has no warrant whatever in his source.

'Beware (and at these words he laid his hand on his sword), beware, lest despair cause them [the Army] to seek safety by some other means than by adhering to you who know not how to consult your own safety.'   (Chap. LIX)

The cumulative effect of such unobtrusive improvements is to heighten the reader's sense of Hume's mastery of his material, his ability to exhibit the workings of human nature at its most contradictory and confusing. His Oliver Cromwell may not be the whole man, but Hume gives a plausible if paradoxical portrait of a hypocrite moved by a genuinely passionate zeal which covered all his 'crooked schemes and profound artifices'. The contradictions are apparent too in that shining military genius the Marquis of Montrose, a man of wide culture:

whatever was sublime, elegant, or noble, touched his great soul. Nor was he insensible to the pleasures either of society or of love. Something, however, of the *vast and unbounded* characterised his actions and deportment; and it was merely by an heroic effort of duty that he brought his mind, impatient of superiority, and even of equality, to pay such unlimited submission to the will of his sovereign.

(Chap. LX)

Hume is following Clarendon's *History of the Rebellion* here, and to Clarendon Montrose is simply a cultivated man who was too apt to hazard himself on desperate enterprises, and who despised those who disagreed with him. Hume, inspired partly by Cardinal de Retz's account of the unhappy nobleman as a hero worthy of Plutarch, makes one feel the inadequacy of the role of a royalist general for one of his temperament and genius. Brief though the passage is, one has an immediate sense of restless internal conflict. At such moments Hume's *History* has its own special touch of the sublime.

William Robertson[1] is a less attractive writer than Hume, but his histories do not by any means merit the neglect into

---

[1] William Robertson, 1721–93, was educated at Edinburgh University, of which, after some time as a parish minister, he became Principal. He was an important figure among the 'moderates' in the Church of Scotland.

which they have fallen. It is still possible to enjoy the sheer
energy of his work, the power he displays of fusing masses of
material into a coherent exposition, the whole (as Horace
Walpole remarked of the *History of Scotland*) 'hurried on into one
uninterrupted story'. This capacity is most apparent in the
broad sweep of the 'View of the Progress of Society in Europe'
which introduces the *History of Charles V*, surveying the development of government, commerce, and manners from the downfall
of the Roman Empire to the beginning of the sixteenth century.
But it is conspicuous everywhere in his work. The masterly manner is unmistakable, as is the deliberate preoccupation with
great transactions, the effects of which are universal, or continue to be permanent. Robertson shared Bolingbroke's conviction that enlightened historians had a special responsibility to
inquire into the origins of the political system prevailing in
polished nations. The greater part of the *History of Scotland*
(1759) deals with the life and times of Mary, Queen of Scots—
a critical period in the making of the modern nation, whose
further development is rather briefly sketched at the end. The
History of Charles V (1769) narrates events at the time of the
formation of the modern European state-system, with its
balance of power. The *History of America* (1777), though concerned mainly with Spanish America, serves to illustrate the
principles and maxims upon which all European nations have
planted colonies. It is characteristic of Robertson that the revolt
of the British colonies in North America should have discouraged
him from proceeding with the history of that part of the continent. A new order of things was bound to arise there, and until
its form was clearly visible, Robertson's kind of history could
not be written. 'Inquiries and speculations [he remarked in the
preface] concerning their ancient forms of policy and laws,
which exist no longer, cannot be interesting.' The one work
which does not altogether fit this pattern is his last, the *Historical
Disquisition concerning the Knowledge which the Ancients had of India*
(1791); but even here, as he observes in the preface, his intention was to show the importance of the intercourse of Europe
with India, and 'how much that great branch of commerce has
contributed, in every age, to increase the wealth and power of
the nations which possessed it'.

Robertson was drawn to subjects which illustrated the encounter of powerful forces. 'It is one of the noblest functions of

history', he says near the beginning of Book III of the *History of America*, 'to observe and to delineate men at a juncture when their minds are most violently agitated, and all their powers and passions are called forth.' He is particularly interested in the effects of ruling passions characteristic of a particular epoch, and is so much given to speaking of 'the spirit of superstition', 'the spirit of disaffection', 'the commercial spirit', and so on, that a reader might form the impression that the principal actors in history were spirits rather than men. The effect is reinforced by unconscious transitions from the abstract use of 'spirit' to such expressions as 'the bold and aspiring spirit' of the Guise family. Individuals are merged in the spirit that informs them.

Robertson's love of vehement conflict found plenty of scope in the history of Scotland in the sixteenth century. The power of the nobility was exorbitant; that of the monarch much less, but not contemptible, particularly when one took the perpetual quarrels of the nobility into account. Robertson examines, with magisterial assurance, the motives behind the policies pursued, and displays an evident satisfaction when a concurrence of causes issues in powerful action. His account of the Reformation in Scotland (Book II) is typical. Popery, he says, was carried to its most extravagant height in the extremities of Europe. Ignorance and barbarity favoured the progress of superstition in the northern nations, and the church in Scotland was given an extraordinary share both in the national property and in the supreme council of the kingdom. The extravagance of this endowment led to a correspondingly powerful reaction when the Popish clergy became objects of contempt rather than of admiration, and the appetite for change was quickened in the Scottish nobles by the prospect of recovering the property and power alienated to the church in previous centuries.

An aversion from the established church, which flowed from so many concurring causes, which was raised by consideration of religion, heightened by motives of policy, and instigated by prospects of private advantage, spread fast through the nation, and excited a spirit, that burst out, at last, with irresistible violence.

The same commanding vigour of narrative is apparent in the account of Mary's estrangement from Darnley. Robertson lists the many causes of disgust she had conceived against him, and it is a formidable catalogue. 'Almost all the passions which operate with greatest violence on a female mind, and drive it to the most dangerous extremes, concurred in raising and fomenting this unhappy quarrel' (Book IV). Turbulent though such energies might be, however, they still formed part of a controlling system. Bothwell's aspiring mind, busy with vast projects, was forced to recognize that it was not enough to gain the queen's heart, murder the king, and be acquitted of the crime. If he was to marry the queen, the power of the nobles was such that he would have first to gain their approbation. He found means to overcome this constraint, but the victory was short-lived, and Bothwell's schemes were overthrown with the queen's own fall. 'No revolution so great', says Robertson, 'was ever effected with more ease, or by means so unequal to the end' (Book V). The accumulating hostility to Bothwell made his destruction inevitable.

The sense of great energies at work within an overruling system is even more marked in the *History of Charles V*. Charles, no less than Bothwell, was allured by vast prospects, and made considerable progress in realizing his ambitions; but Robertson makes one aware of the innumerable checks to his power. At the very outset of Charles's imperial reign, we are reminded of the distaste the Spaniards felt for the king's elevation, engendering among them 'a sullen and refractory spirit' which issued in tumult and rebellion. The pattern is constantly repeated. The Holy Junta of Castile, setting out in 1522 to establish a constitutional government that was both free and solidly based, were too emboldened by success, and impetuously proposed innovations 'which, by alarming the other members of the constitution, proved fatal to their cause'. The encroaching power of Charles was checked by the profound dissimulation and vigorous policy of Maurice of Saxony, and some of the most exhilarating pages of narrative that Robertson ever wrote occur in his account of Maurice's skilful and unscrupulous manœuvres (Book X). No less exhilarating is the passage in Book VIII which deals with Fiesco's conspiracy to overthrow the government of Genoa —an attempt which Robertson calls 'one of the boldest actions recorded in history'. Fiesco's pleasing manner masked a character of 'insatiable and restless ambition, a courage unacquainted with fear, and a mind that disdained subordination'. He planned his measures with secrecy and implemented them with superb effectiveness. But at a critical moment in the action, as he was running along a plank to the admiral's galley in the harbour, the plank overturned.

He fell into the sea, whilst he hurried forward too precipitately. Being loaded with heavy armour, he sunk to the bottom, and perished in the very moment when he must have taken full possession of every thing that his ambitious heart could desire.

The action of a vigorous spirit, and its abrupt extinction, are alike congenial to Robertson.

The *History of America*, however, gave the amplest scope to Robertson's talents. The discovery and subjugation of an immense continent is a theme which dwarfs that of his earlier histories, not least because he conceives it in part as a study of the earliest stages of human society. Book IV is a survey of the 'rude nations' of America and their environment, setting out in circumstantial detail the conditions of a way of life so unimproved that even the wretched natives of Kamchatka appear advanced in comparison. Book VII examines the independent progress of the Mexicans and the Peruvians towards some degree of civilization, illustrating phases of development (as, for instance, in approaches to the art of writing) which belong in the Old World to an age too remote for historical record. No one would now read the *History of America* for information about primitive societies, but it is still possible to enjoy the sense of discovery which Robertson so obviously feels as he adds detail after detail to his account. The narrative portions of the work, too, are informed with a controlled excitement which carries the reader on unquestioningly. Columbus's first sight of land on the far side of the Atlantic, and Balboa's crossing of the isthmus of Darien ('he beheld the South sea stretching in endless prospect before him'), are admirable set pieces; but perhaps a finer example is the account of Ponce de Leon's search for the island of Bimini with its fountain that could renew the youth of those who bathed in it. The credulity of the Spaniards, says Robertson, is astonishing; but they had come to expect the marvellous.

A new world was opened to their view. They visited islands and continents, of whose existence mankind in former ages had no conception. In those delightful countries nature seemed to assume another form; every tree and plant and animal was different from those of the ancient hemisphere. They seemed to be transported into enchanted ground; and after the wonders which they had seen, nothing, in the warmth and novelty of their admiration, appeared to them so extraordinary as to be beyond belief.   (Book III)

Robertson was much concerned with the development of the system of colonization practised by the Spaniards, and of the patterns of trade that grew up between the Old World and the New. This aspect of the *History of America* would have been much further elaborated if he had completed his design with an account of the English and French settlements in North America, but might not have added to the literary merit of the work as it stands.

His last publication was the *Historical Disquisition* on the extent of the knowledge of India possessed by the Greeks and Romans. The main body of the book is in effect a history of the commerce between Europe and India up till the beginning of the sixteenth century. It is written with Robertson's accustomed clarity, but the most striking part of the work is the long appendix which describes the manners and institutions of the people of India. It follows the method of the fourth and seventh books of the *History of America*, and indeed forms an important supplement to the general view of the history of civilization which they open up, by showing a society which was at a high state of improvement many centuries ago. Robertson is obviously indebted to Sir William Jones for his benevolent insight into Indian culture, and to the Abbé Raynal for his broad view of commercial history, but he deserves to be remembered as the first major British writer to show how history might be fully emancipated from a traditional insularity.

Edward Gibbon,[1] certainly, appears to adhere much more closely than Robertson to the central tradition of European historiography. The theme of the *History of the Decline and Fall of the Roman Empire* (1776–88) connects it with concerns that

---

[1] Edward Gibbon, 1737–94, spent some time at Westminster School and Magdalen College, Oxford, but was mainly self-educated until conversion to Roman Catholicism precipitated his exile in Lausanne, where his studies were supervised by Daniel Pavilliard, a Calvinist minister. He fell in love with Suzanne Curchod (later to become Mme Necker), but his father would not allow him to marry her. He returned to England and served in the Hampshire militia. He then travelled to Italy, reaching Rome in 1764, where he formed the project of writing his great history. He was for a time an M.P., and held a minor government post. He retired to Lausanne from 1783 to 1793, but died in London.

had preoccupied men's minds for centuries. The greatness of the Roman state so overshadowed any other form of political achievement that it must have seemed self-evident to Gibbon that its overthrow was (as he put it in the last paragraph of the *Decline and Fall*) 'the greatest, perhaps, and most awful scene in the history of mankind'. It was only towards the end of his life, when he was setting about a revision of the first volume, that he gave any indication of scepticism about the overriding importance of his subject. 'Have Asia and Africa,' he asked, 'from Japan to Morocco, any feeling or memory of the Roman Empire?' But although this afterthought is the one occasion when Gibbon can be found directly questioning the inherited framework of European history, he does not present his main narrative within a context of undifferentiated barbarism. He goes to great trouble to construct an adequate account of the nations of northern Europe and of Asia whose turbulent history led incidentally to the destruction of the Roman Empire. He is obviously disappointed when he has to admit to a 'dark interval which separates the extreme limits of the Chinese, and of the Roman, geography', preventing him from supplying every link in the chain of events that led from revolutions in Tartary to incursions into Europe by the Huns (chap. XXX). So attentive is he, indeed, to this aspect of his work—especially in the second half—that some of his contemporaries found him bewilderingly digressive. John Whitaker, the antiquarian, was one of Gibbon's more captious critics, but his diatribe against the *Decline and Fall* in the *English Review* (1788–9) heightens one's appreciation of the scale of Gibbon's achievement. For Whitaker, Gibbon's is an 'excentric genius' which delights in making 'the circuit of the globe', writing of Germans, Persians, Arabs, and so forth when our attention should be focused on Rome and Constantinople. The critic betrays an unconscious admiration for the scope of the history in the sublime images he is driven to in order to express the depths of his exasperation. Gibbon, says Whitaker, 'ranges like a great comet'. He is like an eagle, and 'the strong and violent beating of its wings' shows that it is 'anticipating a higher and a wider range'. Chapter LVI is 'like the great whirlpool of Norway, that is so terribly denominated *the navel of the sea;* and sucks into its eddy, bears, whales, ships, and every thing, that come within any possible reach of its engulphing streams.'

The range of Gibbon's interests became apparent early in life. His *Memoirs* make clear how fruitful was the voracious reading of the three years before he went, at the age of fifteen, to Oxford. The *Antient Universal History* had recently appeared in an octavo edition, and this was assiduously read, along with much else of a historical kind. He particularly remembered his discovery of the *Continuation of Eachard's Roman History*: 'I was immersed in the passage of the Goths over the Danube when the summons of the dinner-bell reluctantly dragged me from my intellectual feast.' Already his mind was drawn to the antagonists of Rome, and he soon enlarged his view by reading all that could be learned in English of Arabs, Persians, Tartars, and Turks. He guessed at the French of the *Bibliothèque orientale* of D'Herbelot and construed 'the barbarous Latin of Pocock's *Abulfaragius*'. At Oxford, in spite of the strong tradition of oriental learning established there by Edward Pocock, his tutor prudently discouraged a 'childish fancy' to study Arabic, and he turned instead to current controversy about the miracles of the primitive Church. The ensuing conversion to Roman Catholicism angered his father, who sent him away to Lausanne, where he not only recovered his Protestantism but also pursued a thorough programme of study of the authors of classical antiquity. By the time he returned to England, in fact, on the eve of his twenty-first birthday, the elements of the *Decline and Fall* had at least been surveyed; and the way in which he was to organize these materials was already beginning to be evident in his first published work, the *Essai sur l'étude de la littérature* (1761). Thus, in reading Virgil's poetry, Gibbon relates the familiar text to historical circumstances in a way which illuminates both the poetry and one's understanding of Augustan Rome. The *Georgics* do not merely express the poet's pleasure in rural pursuits. They formed part of Augustus's project for settling his soldiers on the land after the civil wars, weaning them from habits of violence. Virgil was another Orpheus, touching his lyre to tame wild beasts. Or again, Gibbon insists on the importance of a detailed understanding of the history, laws, and religion of Rome if one is to appreciate many aspects of the *Aeneid*. Virgil, he says, skilfully exploits the contrast between the earliest state of Rome, when the site of the Capitol was hidden by brambles, and the same city when it had become the centre of the civilized world. Vivid as the contrast must have been to

Virgil's contemporaries, it will not be apparent to anyone who 'brings to the reading of Virgil no other preparation than a natural taste, and some knowledge of the Latin language'. No reader of Gibbon's *Memoirs* can fail to notice the parallel between Virgil imagining the brambles of primeval Rome and Gibbon listening to the 'bare-footed fryars' singing vespers while he 'sat musing amidst the ruins of the Capitol', and conceived the first clear intimation of his great work. His imagination was caught by the concentration of centuries of historical development into a single rich impression: he appreciated Virgil's power of communicating this kind of experience, and endeavoured to do the same.

The record which Gibbon kept of his reading in the early 1760s makes clear how diligently he set about improving his acquaintance with every aspect of antiquity. He read the painstakingly detailed researches of the *Mémoires de l'Académie des Inscriptions*, acquiring thereby a distinct and particular knowledge of various arts and institutions of antiquity, and of such matters as the calendars used in different nations. He familiarized himself with erudite collections of classical topography, and studied Spanheim's great treatise on medals. His aim at this time was to compose a work of a kind which keenly interested his contemporaries: one where the past state of a region is described both through literary and medallic records, and through the observations of modern travellers. By his own travels in Italy, Gibbon hoped to produce an account of ancient Italy which would supersede its predecessors both by the comprehensiveness of its scholarship and the elegance of its presentation. Among the materials he examined with a view to extending his knowledge of the topography of the later Roman Empire were works which brought into a sharper focus the obscure course of the decay of Roman power. He learned that it was the zeal of the popes rather than the fury of the barbarians which had been principally responsible for the destruction of the actual fabric of the city of Rome. The nations which overran the Empire in the fifth century had divested themselves of much of their barbarism, indeed, and our notions of them were as false as they were unfavourable. In this context Gibbon found a special interest in the poem of Rutilius, *De Reditu*, describing the author's return (in 416) from Rome to his native Gaul. Its tone is resilient, although it belongs to a time when Alaric's power overawed the city. It records a period when a Roman citizen could still leave for a war-ravaged province confident that the Empire would rise again as it had done after such earlier disasters as the Battle of Cannae. Gibbon's discussion of the poem is generally cool, but he warms to Rutilius' bad humour about the monks he found in the island of Capraria, and sympathizes with the indignation of this 'pagan who beheld his religion sinking under the weight of years, and involving the Empire in its fall'.

Gibbon was reading Rutilius some ten months before the famous moment (15 October 1764) in the ruins of the Capitol when the idea of writing the decline and fall of the city of Rome first started to his mind. His concern with the poem illustrates not only the formation of that idea, but also the kind of materials from which the power of the finished history derives. The first impression that the *Decline and Fall* creates is one of masterly organization, forming an immense mass of events into an orderly and perspicuous narrative. But what is apt to be remembered is something rather different: a succession of sharply-realized scenes and incidents, an effect aptly compared by Professor Harold Bond to that of Roman bas-relief or frieze. The two aspects of the history can be clearly observed in the seventh chapter. On the one hand Gibbon wishes to illustrate the unequal struggle between military despotism and the enfeebled authority of the senate. The chapter is dominated by the figure of the barbarous emperor Maximin, and closes with the reign of Philip—less barbarous, indeed, but 'an Arab by birth, and consequently, in the earlier part of his life, a robber by profession'. It fell to him to celebrate the thousandth anniversary of the foundation of Rome, an opportunity which enabled him to obliterate the memory of his various crimes in the splendour of the 'secular games', and enabled Gibbon to reflect on the whole course of Roman history, and on the irony implicit in the exaltation of a Syrian, an Arab, or a Goth over the conquests and over the country of the Scipios. The reign of Maximin served also to illustrate a certain revival in the power of the senate, which, although it was unable to sustain an alternative government of its own making, became the focus of opposition to an appalling administration. In this chapter, in fact, Gibbon contrives to delineate the balance of institutions in third-century Rome, and to suggest some of the causes of this balance. But where Robertson (for example) would probably have impressed the balance itself upon the reader's mind, Gibbon is concerned with the particular emperor or senator, and the more abstract considerations arise from reflections inspired by a picturesque composition. This is evident enough from what has been said already of the 'argument' of chapter VII: nothing could provide a more picturesque contrast than that of the millennial secular games being presided over by an Arab. Gibbon's technique emerges the more clearly when one considers the details in the text which are likely to be most memorable. The best-known sentence in the chapter concerns that amiable representative of the old Roman families, the younger Gordian:

Twenty-two acknowledged concubines, and a library of sixty-two thousand volumes, attested the variety of his inclinations; and from the productions which he left behind him, it appears that the former as well as the latter were designed for use rather than for ostentation.

The verbal wit points what is still essentially a pictorial effect. Maximin, too, is probably best remembered in pictorial terms, as the 'young barbarian of gigantic stature', innocently eager to contend for the wrestling-prize, who becomes the dark, sanguinary, and suspicious tyrant, punishing supposed conspiracies by sewing his victims up in the hides of slaughtered animals.

The parallel with bas-relief needs to be supplemented, however, by one with eighteenth-century doctrines of the picturesque. The *Decline and Fall* is obviously the work of a man who appreciated the contemporary taste for 'prospects', whether in verse or landscape gardening. The reader is led from point to point, and at every turn of the path is struck by some fresh, and often startling, change of view. Thus, a passage in Claudian suggests to Gibbon a picture of idyllic calm along the Rhine frontier just before the Germanic invasion of Gaul in 407. Claudian is engaged in some rather fevered panegyric of his patron Stilichò, but there is no hint of fever in Gibbon's citation, and the sense of catastrophe is accordingly heightened:

The banks of the Rhine were crowned, like those of the Tyber, with elegant houses, and well-cultivated farms; and if a poet descended the river, he might express his doubt, on which side was situated the territory of the Romans. This scene of peace and plenty was suddenly changed into a desert; and the prospect of the smoking ruins could alone distinguish the solitude of nature from the desolation of man.   (Chap. XXX)

A similarly concise, abrupt, and well-defined juxtaposition arises from a passage in Procopius' account of Justinian's wars in North Africa. When the historian first landed there, 'he admired the populousness of the cities and country, strenuously exercised in the labours of commerce and agriculture. In less than twenty years, that busy scene was converted into a silent solitude' (chap. XLIII). The force of contrast is preserved in more elaborately-developed examples. The crossing of the Danube by the Goths in the year 376—the episode from which the young Gibbon was so reluctantly summoned to dinner—is told in some detail. The almost incomprehensible scale of the operation is underlined. The Danube at this point is over a mile wide, and had been swollen by incessant rains, so that 'many were swept away, and drowned, by the rapid violence of the current'. A census was attempted, but those employed in it 'soon desisted, with amazement and dismay, from the prosecution of the endless and impracticable task'. The episode throws into sharp relief two contrasting groups: an innumerable multitude of barbarians, 'driven by despair and hunger to solicit a settlement on the territories of a civilized nation', and an incompetent, mean-spirited, corrupt Roman administration, whose officers were more interested in making a profit out of the Goths than in serving the empire. The contrast here is part of a wider contrast developed through this chapter (XXVI) as a whole, between the 'pastoral nations' and the much degenerated but not universally unworthy Romans. It culminates in the quarrel between rival factions of Goths at the very table of the emperor Theodosius; and as such scenes of barbaric rage (Gibbon concludes) could only be kept within bounds 'by the firm and temperate character of Theodosius, the public safety seemed to depend on the life and abilities of a single man'. The fragile security suggested in this closing sentence is deliberately anti-climactic. It conspicuously fails to balance the magnificent tableau with which the chapter opens, presenting the earthquake which, in 365, shook the greater part of the Roman world—a natural disaster that was feared as the prelude to calamities yet more dreadful.

The prospects opened up before a reader of the *Decline and Fall* can span half the globe, or merely provide a glimpse of some corner of the Roman world, like the tenth-century Peloponnesus, where the worship of Venus and Neptune lingered on five centuries after it had been officially proscribed. The political and military action takes place in a landscape that is felt to be vast, the more so if one reads at the leisurely pace which Gibbon evidently intends. Long as the work is, no one should read it with more haste than is compatible with a relaxed consciousness of the notes at the foot of the page. In them Gibbon does far more than supply references to his authorities: he draws attention to points in controversy, supplements the material incorporated in the text, and in various ways—always with an admirable conciseness—makes one aware that behind the elegantly finished narrative there lies a mass of often conflicting evidence and large areas of impenetrable obscurity. Thus in the fifty-first chapter, he describes how Akbah led his Mahometan forces to the shores of the Atlantic, and there spurred his horse into the waves, exclaiming that, if it were not for this sea, he would still go on 'to the unknown kingdoms of the West, preaching the unity of thy holy name, and putting to the sword the rebellious nations who worship any other gods than thee'. A note adds that it is Otter who has given 'the strong tone of fanaticism to this exclamation'; Cardonne softens it 'to a pious wish of *preaching* the Koran. Yet they had both the same text of Novairi before their eyes.' Few readers of Gibbon will be acquainted with the three authors named, but their appearance here is no mere display of erudition. Gibbon is clarifying the status of the story in his text. He cannot resist depicting the theatrical posture attributed to Akbah, but neither can he resist indicating his uncertainty about the true interpretation of the ultimate source. His own mind obviously hesitated between two possibilities, and he conveys the hesitation with brilliant economy. Other notes provide topographical information that helps to set the scene of the action more vividly. When describing Constantine's siege of Byzantium (A.D. 323), during his second war with Licinius, Gibbon remarks that the ships of Constantine's eldest son, Crispus, were carried against the enemy by a strong south wind. A note explains the full significance of this wind: 'The current always sets out of the Hellespont; and when it is assisted by a north wind, no vessel can attempt the passage. A south wind renders the force of the current almost imperceptible.' One might well ask why this information was not included in the text. Gibbon could easily have done so without holding up the action to any appreciable extent. The fact is that, by relegating the information to a note, Gibbon gives it a peculiarly pointed emphasis. He is inviting the leisurely reader to pause and contemplate the setting before returning to the text—perhaps re-reading a sentence or two to pick up the thread. It is an oblique reminder, too, that the scene is the same to this day, and the sense of immediacy is thereby perceptibly enhanced.

Impressive as Gibbon's landscape is, the figures within it are presented in terms of a somewhat stereotyped psychology. He has little of Hume's sense of the complexity of human motivation, and even a man like Julian the Apostate, in whom he is keenly interested, remains an assemblage of characteristics viewed from the outside. A state of mind which Gibbon does, however, present with a vivid inwardness is the world of Christian bigotry. A welcome respite from the scruples of enlightened historiography is provided by the lurid landscape of prophecy, and the spurious clarity of dogma. He enters with malicious pleasure into the niceties of the Trinitarian controversy (chap. XXI), pointing out that the 'pure and distinct equality' of the Divine persons 'was tempered, on the one hand, by the internal connexion, and spiritual penetration', which united them; tempered, too, on the other hand,

by the pre-eminence of the Father, which was acknowledged as far as it is compatible with the independence of the Son. Within these limits the almost invisible and tremulous ball of orthodoxy was allowed securely to vibrate. On either side, beyond this consecrated ground, the heretics and the daemons lurked, in ambush to surprise and devour the unhappy wanderer.

Ethical questions are settled with no less lucidity. The early fathers, aspiring towards the perfection of angels, disdained 'every earthly and corporeal delight'. The senses could not be rejected altogether, but their sphere of usefulness was strictly defined. 'The first sensation of pleasure was marked as the first moment of their abuse.' It was necessary to resist, not only the 'grosser allurements' of taste and smell, but also the 'profane harmony of sounds'; Christians were taught to 'view with indifference the most finished productions of human art'. Gibbon takes an evident pleasure in this perverse and vigorous logic, and he is stirred even more deeply by the belief in an early end to the world. Civil wars, barbarian invasions, pestilence, famine, earthquakes, and the like, were all seen as forewarnings of

the great catastrophe of Rome, when the country of the Scipios and Caesars should be consumed by a flame from heaven, and the city of the seven hills, with her palaces, her temples, and her triumphal arches, should be buried in a vast lake of fire and brimstone.
(Chap. XV)

This was to be part of a general conflagration, the plausibility of which was reinforced by the nature of the country which figured as the centre of destruction, with 'its deep caverns, beds of sulphur, and numerous volcanoes'. The spectacular Christian apocalypse forms a sublime parody of the complex picture of degeneration and renewal that Gibbon's own history provides.

Entertained and scandalized as Gibbon was by the early Church, one must beware of concluding that his attitude to it can be reduced to a simple formula. It is true, for example, that he saw the difference between it and Islam in terms of the latter's power to raise men to the natural level of their capacity and courage, where Christianity tended to enervate and barbarize. But it was a Pope, Leo IV, who saved Rome from the Saracens:

the courage of the first ages of the republic glowed in his breast; and, amidst the ruins of his country, he stood erect, like one of the firm and lofty columns that rear their heads above the fragments of the Roman forum.   (Chap. LII)

Gibbon's pleasure in this noble spectacle is too great for him to wish to slight Leo on account of his superstitious practices. His martial songs of triumph may have been 'modulated to psalms and litanies', but this is not said to provoke a sneer. Gibbon is primarily struck by the element of picturesque contrast between Leo's piety and his generous but worldly nature. A similar attitude is apparent in the fifty-fourth chapter, which describes the history of the Paulician sect. It conforms at first to the familiar pattern of pitiless persecution and savage resistance. A more distant prospect, however, affords some consolation to the enlightened reader. The Paulicians proved to be the fore-runners of the Albigenses, of the Protestant Reformation, and of a 'secret reformation' more radical still, diffusing a spirit of freedom and moderation, or perhaps (for every landscape has its light and shade) a dangerous indulgence of 'the licence without the temper of philosophy'. Beside this prospect Gibbon places another, showing the stunted development of the Paulician sect within its original narrow territories in south-eastern Europe.

At the end of the last age, the sect or colony still inhabited the valleys of mount Haemus, where their ignorance and poverty were more frequently tormented by the Greek clergy than by the Turkish government. The modern Paulicians have lost all memory of their origin; and their religion is disgraced by the worship of the cross, and the practice of bloody sacrifice, which some captives have imported from the wilds of Tartary.

Gibbon evidently derived a peculiar pleasure from establishing a connection between such barbaric villagers and the enlightened peoples of modern Europe; and it is in such moments of startling juxtaposition that one comes closest to the heart of his historical method.

VIII

TRAVEL LITERATURE, MEMOIRS
AND BIOGRAPHY

THE prestige of history was closely related to the eager interest shown by eighteenth-century readers in travel narratives. Travel was slow and hazardous, but formed an indispensable element in the enlightened culture of the time. It was the age of the Grand Tour undertaken to initiate young men of fashion into the polished society and the fine art of Europe. It was also the age of travels into the remoter nations of the globe. Different though these modes of travel were, they both reflect a preoccupation with gaining the widest possible authentic experience of an immensely complex world. The climate of thought was pervasively hostile to what was called 'prejudice', at least until Burke sought to rehabilitate the word towards the end of the century. Through travel, said that enlightened churchman Dean Tucker in 1757, one can rub off local prejudices, and acquire 'that enlarged and impartial View of Men and Things, which no one single Country can afford'. An enlarged prospect of this kind made it possible to trace 'such secret, though powerful, Effects and Consequences, as are produced by the various Systems of Religion, Government, and Commerce in the World'.

It was not only the largeness of the prospect that was valued, but more particularly its fullness and immediacy. Arthur Young remarked that he never fully understood the enormity of Louis XIV's annexation of Alsace until he was actually travelling in that province.

To cross a great range of mountains; to enter a level plain, inhabited by a people totally distinct and different from France, with manners, language, ideas, prejudices, and habits all different, made an impression of the injustice and ambition of such a conduct, much more forcible than ever reading had done: so much more powerful are things than words. (19 July 1789.)

In a similar spirit, Dr. Charles Burney,[1] planning his *General History of Music*, told William Mason that mere reading would not do. He had consulted 'an incredible number of books and tracts', and was still disappointed. By travelling to Italy he could allay his thirst of knowledge at the pure source, 'which I am unable to do by such spare draughts as are to be attained from the polluted works through which it is conducted to us here' (27 May 1770). While Burney is doubtless thinking primarily of collections of written materials, there is a suggestion too of what might be learnt from musicians and connoisseurs, from the impressions that might be acquired from a wide range of musical society. Burney's 'musical tours' do something to communicate this experience, and writers of travel books generally were anxious to preserve the element of immediacy, 'to communicate', as Patrick Brydone put it in the course of his *Tour through Sicily and Malta* (1773), 'as entire as possible, the same impression I myself shall receive'. One must bear in mind here the exact weight of the word 'impression' in eighteenth-century usage. Hume uses it to convey the quality of the very act of sensation, in contrast to 'ideas', which are faint images of impressions; and while this differentiation of impression from idea is somewhat specialized, it evidently points to connotations of vivacity and power in the former term which it no longer possesses to the same extent. The alert traveller received impressions of the manners of a people, or of the landscape in which they could be seen, acquiring knowledge which had important consequences for historical inquiry.

Travel narratives placed the history of human society upon a substantial foundation. The most various kinds of polity could still be found in different parts of the world, ranging from the simplest food-gathering tribes to the most complex of modern states. A journey from one community to another could resemble a movement forwards or backwards in time. In passing from the Highlands of Scotland to the Lowlands, for example, one left a society of relatively primitive shepherds and entered a region dominated by an elaborate commercial system, trading in a world market. If one were to go further and travel on to Antwerp, one might feel—as William Beckford did—that its quiet depopulated state gave one a foretaste of what London

---

[1] Charles Burney, 1726–1814, was a pupil of Thomas Arne, and worked as an organist and conductor. He travelled widely in Europe.

would be like when the tide of commerce had passed it by. At the other end of the process of development, the various accounts of the savage Tchutzi (or Tschucktschi) of Kamchatka convinced Adam Ferguson that here was the spirit of Europe in embryo, their so-called ferocity being in fact

the spirit of national independence; that spirit which disputed its ground in the West with the victorious armies of Rome, and baffled the attempts of the Persian monarchs to comprehend the villages of Greece within the bounds of their extensive dominion.

It was the traveller's privilege to gain experience of these different phases of society, and thus acquire a more immediate sense of a past now recorded only in fragmentary monuments.

A striking illustration of this procedure is a work by the French Jesuit Lafitau, *Mœurs des sauvages amériquains*, published in 1724. Lafitau found that his residence among the Iroquois Indians helped him to understand the records of classical antiquity in a way that would have been impossible to the most diligent scholar whose experience was confined to Europe. The religion of the Iroquois had much in common with the orgies of Bacchus and the mysteries of Isis and Osiris. Their modes of campaigning, their very musical instruments, recall those attributed to the Argonauts by Apollonius Rhodius. It is true that this similarity lowered the idea Lafitau had once entertained of the glory of the early Greek heroes, and he blushed for the great princes of a later day who had felt honoured at being compared to them. The Iroquois offended against the dignity of history, and in Lafitau's time this was not easily forgiven. But as the years passed the offence seemed less grievous. In Cadwallader Colden's *History of the Five Indian Nations of Canada* (1747),[1] the American Indians are spoken of as exceeding the Romans in their love of country and contempt of death. The lofty notions of the Mohawks provide a strong instance of how rulers can make a people great by the consistent inculcation of ideas of honour and virtue. They are eloquent, and no spectator can look unmoved at their terrifying war-dances:

I have sometimes persuaded some of their young Indians to act these Dances, for our Diversion, and to shew us the Manner of them; and

[1] Cadwallader Colden, 1688–1766, studied medicine at Edinburgh University. Working in Pennsylvania and New York, he eventually became Lieutenant-Governor of the latter colony. He was a botanist of distinction.

even, on these Occasions, they have work'd themselves up to such a Pitch, that they have made all present uneasy. Is it not probable, that such Designs as these have given the first Rise to Tragedy?

Colden may have been present at the birth of tragedy, but he was outdone by Thomas Pownall,[1] who had actually viewed the Fall of Man. Recalling his dealings with the Indians while Governor of Massachusetts, Pownall perceived that the second and third chapters of Genesis could be construed as an account of the transition from the savage to a more civilized state of society. In his *Treatise on the Study of Antiquities* (1782), he suggests that the story of the Fall refers to a community of food-gatherers giving way to the 'artificial system' of agriculture, 'spoiling a good world, as the Indians of America describe the clearing it to be'. Nor was it only myths and legends that acquired solidity from being viewed in the context of the system of society that generated them. Pownall contended that most historical narratives left unexplained the social structure within which events occurred. The original writers lived 'amidst the ordinary movements, and under the constant and mechanick influence of the springs and principles, which, as things of course, operate on' the actions they were describing. Once these springs and principles become obsolete, the narrative becomes impenetrably obscure. 'We may travel in history for ages through many regions, but it will be always as in a thick fog.' Pownall was here making a plea on behalf of the antiquary as a dispeller of historical fog, but the minute particulars uncovered by antiquarian research often resemble those noted by the traveller, and it is the traveller who has the better chance of setting the particulars within an adequate context.

The reason for this is most vividly described in Herder's travel-diary of 1769. Coming for the first time to France, he was overwhelmed by the experience of hearing French spoken as a living language. It was only then that he realized how important were expletives like *eh bien* and *ma foi*, and favourite terms like the *joli*, the *amusant*, the *honnête*—all of which carry connotations for a Frenchman that do not translate readily into German. He was also impressed by the distinctive French mode of voice production: the German voice seemed to come from

---

[1] Thomas Pownall, 1722–1805, was educated at Trinity College, Cambridge. He was successively Lieutenant-Governor of New Jersey and Governor of Massachusetts. He returned to England in 1760, and later became an M.P.

lower down in the mouth and throat, the French to approximate more closely to singing. This revelation of the inadequacy of his previous understanding of French made Herder realize how defective his understanding of Greek must be—and it seemed to him more important to be proficient in Greek than in French. Homer should be heard as he was heard in Greece, understood by the rabble, sung in the streets by poets and fools. 'I wish', said Herder, 'I could find a native Greek or could get to Greece—even in its present condition—to hear this living tone of the sense, this accentuation of expressions, etc., to learn to speak like a born Greek.' Herder's ambition was being fulfilled at the very time he was formulating it, by the French traveller P. A. Guys, whose *Voyage littéraire de la Grèce* was published in 1771. Modern Greeks, he says, still retain the burning energy of their ancestors: they still dance their ancient dances, their imaginations are still powerfully superstitious, their conversation is both aggressively vivacious and sententious. The extravagant misery of bereaved mothers and widows irresistibly recalls the fury of the ancient devotees of Bacchus, or the prophesyings of the priestesses of Apollo.

A work in a similar vein had already been published by the Scottish traveller Robert Wood.[1] His *Essay on the Original Genius of Homer* (1767) described peoples around the shores of the eastern Mediterranean who retained their nomadic way of life. Their manners, accordingly, still approximated closely to those described in the *Iliad*. The modern Arab could still combine the roles of prince, shepherd, and poet, and Wood had listened to extempore compositions, crudely and hastily translated, which yet exhibited 'the wildness, irregularity, and indelicacy of [their] forefathers, with a considerable share of the same original glowing imagination'. Such an experience would clearly do much to restore the Homeric poems to their original vivacity, as did the setting of them in their own proper landscape. The *Essay* contains a finely suggestive account of the movements of Neptune and Juno around the Aegean shores, manœuvring on behalf of their favoured parties in the Trojan war, while Jupiter sits on Mount Gargara, turning away from the slaughter on the Scamandrian plain. Viewing the scene from a certain point 'clears up the action, and converts, what

[1] Robert Wood, 1717?–71, travelled widely in Europe and Asia Minor. He later became an M.P., and held minor government posts.

may otherwise appear crowded and confused, into distinct and pleasing variety'. This perspective is possible only from the Asiatic shore of the Aegean, and the legend of the war of the Titans with the gods also bears clear marks of the Ionian imagination:

When the sun goes down behind the cloud-capped mountains of Macedonia and Thessaly, there is a picturesque wildness in the appearance, under certain points of view, which naturally calls to mind the old fable of the rebel giants bidding defiance to Jupiter, and scaling the heavens, as the fanciful suggestion of this rugged perspective. And we find this striking face of Nature adapted to so bold a fiction with a fitness and propriety, which its extravagance would forbid us to expect.

Modern Italy was no less rewarding for the classical reader. Among the best illustrations is one of the earliest: the *Letter from Rome* (1729) of Conyers Middleton.[1] Middleton was preparing to write an elaborate and elegant *Life of Cicero*, to be discussed later in this chapter. He describes in his *Letter* how he had looked forward to viewing in Rome 'the *very* Place and Scene of those important Events, the Knowledge and Explication of which have ever since been the chief Employment of the learned and polite World'. The actual experience did not disappoint these expectations: rambling through the places where Cicero had spoken, he felt himself much more sensible of the force of his eloquence, 'whilst the very Impression of the Place served to raise and warm my Imagination to a Degree almost equal to that of his *old Audience*'. Middleton remarked that he had planned to concern himself with these classical objects, and to ignore the follies of modern popery. But this was a mistake, because the forms of worship were so extravagantly idolatrous, 'and made so strong an Impression on me, that I could not help considering it with a very particular regard'. He soon found himself fancying that he was wandering around the old heathen Rome. The rituals called to mind and helped to explain passages from classical authors, where the same ceremonies were described, 'in the *same Form and Manner*, and in the *same Place*, where I now saw it executed before my Eyes'. Middleton goes on to illustrate this contention in detail. He begins with

[1] Conyers Middleton, 1683–1750, was a fellow of Trinity College, Cambridge, and protobibliothecarius of the University Library. His *Free Inquiry into Miracles* put his orthodoxy in question.

the use of incense, doing so (he later explained) 'because it is *the first thing*, that strikes the senses, and surprizes a stranger, upon his entrance into their Churches'. He proceeds to the holy water, the candles, the votive gifts, the idols, and the processions characteristic of both ancient and modern Rome. While his principal purpose was evidently to score points against popery, there is no mistaking the genuineness of Middleton's concern to activate his sense of the past, or, more precisely, his sense of a common human nature acted upon by exotic circumstances. Middleton, in short, was consciously contributing to that enlarged and impartial view of men and things from which a science of human nature might be derived.

Many travel narratives of the period, making no special pretensions to literary merit, none the less serve this kind of philosophical purpose. The particular observations throw light on a larger pattern of behaviour. Thus, William Richardson,[1] in his *Anecdotes of the Russian Empire* (1784), brings to bear on the Russian national character an acuteness of analysis evident also in his various essays on Shakespeare's characters. He sees the Russians as a people deeply marked by the capricious despotism that dominates them. The peasants are degraded beyond redemption, and the state of those in a higher social position is not much better. They are victims of an ungovernable sensibility. Their feelings, too lively to be amenable to reason, reinforce their political ineffectiveness. They may work themselves up into a patriotic resentment against their government, and even talk of changes and revolutions. But then another current of feeling sets in, and hurries them on until 'they repent, confess, and from the deep sense they have of their trespass, betray their friends'. Richardson has heard Russians speaking more violently on behalf of liberty than any Brentford patriot, but this would avail them nothing.

It is scarcely probable that the Russians themselves . . . unless some dextrous, insinuating, and steady foreigner take advantage of their temporary transports, shall ever accomplish any great revolution.
(Letter XXXIV)

Richardson makes one aware of the strangeness of Russian behaviour to a true-born Briton, but it is equally apparent that

---

[1] William Richardson, 1743–1814, was educated at Glasgow University. He accompanied Lord Cathcart to Russia, 1768–72, and then returned to Glasgow, where he became Professor of Humanity.

this conduct is perfectly in accord with familiar laws of human nature. Indeed, he raises the question of whether despotism is not a more 'natural' form of government than that enjoyed by the British. British liberty, he argues, is the offspring of the feudal system, and the feudal system itself was a singular institution, a fortunate accident in the history of human improvement.

Some of the most popular works of travel were those which gave an account of man in an unimproved state—above all in those Pacific islands that were first encountered in the 1760s. John Hawkesworth's version of the journals of Byron, Wallis, Carteret, and Cook, published in 1773, was widely read, mainly (one suspects) because of the idyllic picture of indulgent sensibility and sexual liberty that Hawkesworth created out of his materials. Captain Wallis's dealings with 'Queen' Oberea of Otaheite reads like a re-creation of the story of Dido and Aeneas. When Wallis insisted that he must leave her shores, Oberea wept repeatedly and inconsolably. At the moment of final separation, Wallis made her many presents:

she silently accepted of all, but took little notice of any thing. About ten o'clock we were got without the reef, and a fresh breeze springing up, our Indian friends, and particularly the queen, once more bade us farewel, with such tenderness of affection and grief, as filled both my heart and my eyes.

When the next expedition, under Captain Cook, arrived in Otaheite, it was found that Oberea was consoling herself with a handsome young fellow called Obadée; but, as Hawkesworth is careful to explain, 'such amours gave no occasion to scandal' —in Otaheite at least. Hawkesworth took some pains to interpolate passages noting parallels between the opinions and customs among these newly-discovered peoples and those in nations long known. Even the most surprising customs are not without precedent. The Otaheitian practice of exposing the dead above ground is matched by the similar one in ancient Colchis mentioned by Aelian and Apollonius Rhodius. Rightly understood, it proves the universality of concern about the disposal of the body after death.

So strong is the association of pleasing or painful ideas with certain opinions and actions which affect us while we live, that we involuntarily act as if it was equally certain that they would affect us in the same manner when we are dead, though this is an opinion that nobody will maintain.

No force of reason, no habits of thinking, can subdue this 'happy imperfection of our nature', so valuable to the general well-being of society.

Hawkesworth's book, attractive and stimulating as it is, is less memorable than that other notable maritime journal which was published twenty-five years earlier, the *Voyage round the World* (1748) by George Anson. Here again, the literary merit of the work owes more to the editor than to the journal on which the finished text is based, and it is not clear whether the credit should go to Richard Walter (as the title-page asserts) or to Benjamin Robins. Whoever composed it, few narratives can match the account of the hazards endured by Anson's squadron after it had passed into the Pacific Ocean near Cape Horn. The story is told in a style which contrives, through its very formality, to register the extremity of distress. Cowper's poem 'The Castaway' has made familiar the passage about the seaman who was washed overboard while manning the shrouds:

we were the more grieved at his unhappy fate, since we lost sight of him struggling with the waves, and conceived from the manner in which he swam, that he might continue sensible for a considerable time longer, of the horror attending his irretrievable situation.

(Chap. VIII)

The horror is communicated, but firmly controlled. Misfortune follows misfortune, and 'our future success and safety was not to be promoted by repining, but by resolution and activity'. This note of resolution sets the tone throughout, not least when Anson's dealings with the sly, undependable Chinese are the subject. The one point in the narrative when other feelings almost subvert stoical self-command, however, is also the most striking in the book. This is at the close of Chapter VII, describing the squadron's passage of the Straits of Le Maire, near Cape Horn. There was fair weather at the time, encouraging hopes of soon possessing Chilean gold and Peruvian silver. Animated by such delusions,

we travers'd these memorable Streights, ignorant of the dreadful calamities that were then impending, and just ready to break upon us; ignorant that the time drew near, when the squadron would be separated never to unite again, and that this day of our passage was the last chearful day that the greatest part of us would ever live to enjoy.

The trials endured by travellers have always proved entertaining to readers, whether the narrative be tragical and sublime or cast in some less sombre mode. Henry Fielding's *Journal of a Voyage to Lisbon* (1755), though it will also be touched on in the general account of his work in Chapter X, deserves consideration here as a fine example of distress viewed with a carefully controlled humour. The ordeal of the almost completely incapacitated traveller is never absent from the reader's mind, but Fielding resolutely insists on examining the specimens of human nature that came to his notice with a philosophic eye, and turns his mortifications into material for hints to the legislature. The procedure serves both to distance the ordeal and add point to the speculations. There is a sharp edge to his burlesque of the antiquarian conjectures so dear to eighteenth-century travellers. In the Isle of Wight, where Fielding's party stayed while the ship was waiting for a favourable wind, their landlady proved to be a worthy successor to the least amiable ones in the novels. She was, indeed, a pure embodiment of that spirit of exploitation Fielding so often had occasion to deplore. One of the rooms in the inn was apparently constructed from the timber of a wreck, and shaped in the form of a ship's cabin. Fielding, who slept in it, thought it had probably been erected as a temple to Neptune, in thankfulness (no doubt) for gifts cast up by the sea. The building was of no great antiquity, but, as he observes, 'this island of Wight was not an early convert to Christianity; nay, there is some reason to doubt whether it was ever entirely converted'.

In his preface, Fielding claims that his voyage is narrated in a way that deviates less from truth than any other then extant, 'my Lord Anson's alone being, perhaps, excepted'. Allegations about abuses are made with the care of a conscientious magistrate; impressions are recorded exactly as they occurred. He thus achieves in his portrait of the ship's captain an effect of considerable complexity. The 'angry bashaw' is also a very good-natured man, much distressed by the falling overboard of a kitten. Unlike Anson on a comparable occasion (though the seas around the Isle of Wight are less perilous than those off Cape Horn), Fielding's captain gave the order to slacken sail, and all hands, as the phrase is, [were] employed to recover the poor animal. I was, I own, extremely surprised at all this; less, indeed, at the captain's extreme tenderness, than at his conceiving any possibility of success: for, if puss had had nine thousand, instead of nine lives, I concluded they had been all lost.

The captain's judgement was vindicated, however, to his own great joy and Fielding's wry amusement. There are obviously rich materials here for a character in a Fielding novel, but the novelist would have imposed a more conspicuous coherence on them. In the *Journal*, the author is engaged with experience that is still very close to him. He is irritated by the captain's deafness, his snores, his refusal to let any passenger dispute his authority or think that the 'pitiful thirty pounds' paid as fare confers any privileges. Fielding never quite forgave him that 'pitiful', though he was too magnanimous to allow his irritation free play.

Smollett was far less disposed than Fielding to rein in his irritations, and the *Travels through France and Italy* (1766) is notoriously deficient in urbanity. While it would be wrong to suggest that the work is one continued venting of spleen, it is at least a strikingly vivid account of impressions made on an unusually splenetic temperament. His intention, very proper in a traveller, is never to deviate from temperance and impartiality; but his indignation at the impositions he suffers from inn-keepers and the well-meant courtesies of French gentlefolk is usually too much for his ailing constitution. He is willing enough to tell a story against himself, as on the occasion when he repeatedly rebuffed the polite overtures of a *seigneur*, under the impression that he was speaking to the post-master (Letter VIII). Smollett appears genuinely mortified by the thought that his behaviour would serve to 'confirm the national reproach of bluntness, and ill-breeding, under which we lie in this country'. He is none the less pretty free with his own reproaches, his account of the French national character in Letter VII in particular being a masterpiece of sustained denigration. His temper mellowed a little under the influence of improved health, but he shows little disposition to admire the inhabitants either of ancient or of modern Italy. He expresses disgust at the filthy state of Rome, and suggests that the ancient Romans were no more cleanly than their descendants. He exploits the method of Middleton's *Letters from Rome*, giving it his own characteristic turn. Thus, he had been distressed by the custom of swaddling infants, and was astonished to find in Rome an antique statue of a child swaddled precisely in the way he had seen in a Parisian orphanage. 'The circulation of the blood', he remarks, 'must be obstructed on the whole surface of the body' —the ultimate consequence being 'the bandy legs, diminutive bodies, and large heads' too often to be seen in the south of France and Italy: presumably, therefore, in ancient Italy also. With a stern Scottish eye he notes the deplorable waste of time imposed by the numerous religious feast-days, and points out that the ancients were even more dissipated in this particular. The people of Rome must have been idle and effeminate.

I think it would be no difficult matter to prove, that there is very little difference, in point of character, between the ancient and modern inhabitants of Rome; and that the great figure which this empire made of old, was not so much owing to the intrinsic virtue of its citizens, as to the barbarism, ignorance, and imbecility, of the nations they subdued. (Letter XX)

Certainly they had nothing to boast of in their naval power, since Domitian exhibited naval engagements in an artificial lake no bigger than the lake in Hyde Park. Half a dozen English frigates, Smollett conjectures, 'would have been able to defeat both the contending fleets at the famous battle of Actium' (Letter XXXII). Smollett's assertive sense of superiority becomes increasingly hard to bear, and it is pleasant to find him occasionally in the role of stoical sufferer. In Letter XXXIV he tells how he and his wife could only avoid spending the night at a villainous inn outside the walls of Florence by walking an uncertain distance to a gate still open after sunset, assisted only by an ill-looking fellow who carried their boxes. It was dark and wet, the road slippery, dirty, ominously silent.

While I laboured under the weight of my greatcoat which made the streams of sweat flow down my face and shoulders, I was plunging in the mud, up to the mid-leg at every step; and at the same time obliged to support my wife, who wept in silence, half dead with terror and fatigue.

The ordeal cheered Smollett considerably, as it proved to him how greatly his health was improved.

Smollett, like Yorick in Sterne's *Sentimental Journey* (see pp. 446–8) places himself firmly at the centre of attention. To some extent this is true of all the major travel narratives of the period. It is important to be able to share the sensibility which is receiving the impressions recorded. This is true even with a writer like Mrs. Piozzi (formerly Mrs. Thrale)[1] in her *Observations and Reflections made in the Course of a Journey through France, Italy, and Germany* (1789). She seems bent on providing her readers with a full account of manners, the fine arts, and antiquities in the countries that she visited. But the vitality of the book consists almost entirely in the impression it conveys of a strong-willed, vivacious, and self-satisfied woman. High spirits inform her observations as insistently as ill-humour pervades Smollett's. She notes with mild exasperation the absolute impossibility of attempts to convince Italians of anything they are not disposed to believe. Argument, she observes, is not 'a style of conversation they naturally affect—as Lady Macbeth says, "*Question enrageth him*"; and the dialogues of Socrates would to them be as disgusting as the violence of Xantippe'. The account of her stay in Bologna provides a specimen of her Socratic method. She was shocked by the sight of men kneeling, 'in open defiance of the Decalogue', before a painting of a black Madonna, supposedly the work of St. Luke. Suppose it were painted by St. Luke, she said, what then?

Do you think *he*, or the still more excellent person it was done for, would approve of your worshipping any thing but God? To this no answer was made; and I thought one man looked as if he had grace enough to be ashamed of himself.

It is all too easy to imagine the effect that the lady must have made on such occasions, and passages like this provide much of the entertainment that the book affords. It is hardly conceivable that any experience could ever really subdue her. She may shriek at the sight of a scorpion in her carriage, or be indignant that she is refused access to books and manuscripts in the Vatican Library (except indeed some 'gross and indecent' love-letters of Henry VIII to Anne Boleyn). But none of this afflicts her for long. Her buoyancy carries her through even the sublime and terrible experience of arriving in Naples by night, in a

[1] Hester Lynch Piozzi, 1741–1821, was the daughter of John Salusbury, and married Henry Thrale, the London brewer. She became a close friend of Samuel Johnson, but was estranged from him after the death of Thrale when she married Gabriel Piozzi and spent three years in Italy. Thereafter she lived in England and North Wales.

violent storm, with Vesuvius vomiting fire and pouring torrents of red-hot lava down its sides. She is pleased by her French valet's exclamation that they had evidently come to Naples to see the end of the world, but she is not herself given to brooding on the Day of Judgement.

James Boswell is no less conspicuous in his own narrative than Mrs. Piozzi is in hers, but the *Journal of a Tour to Corsica* appended to his *Account of Corsica* (1768) is a notable instance of apparent egotism serving a larger purpose. He comes before us as an ardent young man, eager to visit a people fighting for liberty, a little apprehensive about their reported disposition to violence, and then joyously reassured by their unspoiled plainness and generosity. Boswell's temperament is an animating medium through which to view a spectacle which his contemporaries found in itself sufficiently animating: a people just passing from a rude, uncivilized state to one of regular authority, with a prospect of continuous improvement in manners and in the arts and sciences. This civilizing process, moreover, was taking place under the guidance of a legislator, Pasquale Paoli, worthy to stand by Solon and Lycurgus. Boswell encountered Corsicans of all kinds with an irrepressible zest, greatly enjoying his role as self-appointed ambassador from England to Corsica, and admiring his own skill in tactfully promoting Anglo-Corsican friendship. Even a failure in tact can throw this friendship into strong relief, as is shown by an experience that may have given Goldsmith a hint for *She Stoops to Conquer*:

Before I was accustomed to the Corsican hospitality, I sometimes forgot myself, and imagining I was in a publick house, called for what I wanted, with the tone which one uses in calling to the waiters at a tavern. I did so at Pino, asking for a variety of things at once; when Signora Tomasi perceiving my mistake, looked in my face and smiled, saying with much calmness and good nature, 'Una cosa dopo un' altra, Signore, One thing after another, Sir.'

Boswell makes good use of the brief snatches of Italian that he quotes from time to time. The language sounds fuller, more musical, more energetic than the English within which it is set. It gives the reader an immediate sense of the majestic simplicity of Corsican manners, and is an important element in the noble impression that Paoli himself makes on us. He emerges from Boswell's pages as the guardian of the characteristic Corsican virtues, and the inheritor of the best in classical civilization.

When he quotes a sublime sentiment from Virgil, he does so in 'the fine open Italian pronunciation' and with a dignity that made Boswell wish to have a statue of him 'taken at that moment'. It is as though he were hearing the words from the very lips of one of the heroes of Plutarch.

It was the people of Corsica that animated Boswell rather than the island's scenery. He barely notices the 'immense ridges and vast woods', although they may have contributed something to the euphoria that led him to 'enter into the ideas of the brave rude men whom I found in all quarters'. The last three decades of the eighteenth century, however, saw the publication of a number of travel narratives in which 'the picturesque' played a considerable part. The year 1768, when Boswell's *Account* was published, saw also the appearance of Arthur Young's *Six Weeks' Tour through the Southern Counties of England and Wales*.[1] Although his main concern is with agricultural improvement, Young takes note of the collections of paintings in great houses, and attempts a commentary on the various picturesque landscapes through which he travels. The vivacious impetuosity of temperament that delighted Fanny Burney found ample scope when he came to describe Valentine Morris's famous estate at Piercefield near Chepstow in Monmouthshire, with its splendid transitions from meadowland to rocks and precipices, its varied woods and immense prospects. The view from the temple erected at the highest part of the grounds moved him to ecstasy:

Imagination cannot form an idea of any thing more beautiful than what appears full to your ravished sight from this amazing point of view. You look down upon all the woody precipices, as if in another region, terminated by a wall of rocks: just above them appears the river *Severn* in so peculiar a manner, that you would swear it washed them, and that nothing parted it from you but those rocks, which are in reality four or five miles distant.

This deception, he says, was the most exquisite he had ever beheld. Here and elsewhere he implies that such compositions of landscape stimulate a range of feeling so overwhelming that no comparable effect was within the power of any human artist.

---

[1] Arthur Young, 1741–1820, was an unsuccessful farmer at Bradfield, Berkshire. He published the *Annals of Agriculture* from 1784, and became secretary to the Board of Agriculture in 1793. He made three journeys through France between 1787 and 1789.

'Would to heaven', he exclaims of another prospect (this time in the north of England), 'I could unite in one sketch the chearfulness of *Zuccarelli* with the gloomy terrors of *Pousin*, the glowing brilliancy of *Claud*, with the romantic wildness of *Salvator Rosa*.' If no painter could do justice to the scene, one might suppose that the medium of words would be judged even less adequate. This did not deter some travellers from making the attempt. The most systematic treatment is to be found in the work of William Gilpin,[1] who in various volumes of picturesque 'observations' helped the traveller to appreciate the aesthetic resources of different types of landscape, and the atmospheric conditions, physical and intellectual, in which they may be viewed. Haze, mist, and fog, he suggested, might serve to heighten the beauty of a scene by modifying and unifying its physical features; equally, an apt quotation—a potential inscription—could impress the distinctive character of a prospect on the mind. Landscape is not merely visual. The imagination is lured into the unseen. Thus, in *Observations on the Mountains and Lakes of Cumberland and Westmoreland* (1786), there is an account of the upper end of the cataract of Lodore, where two streams unite to form a larger torrent. This torrent, after

throwing itself into the thickest of the woods, which close the scene, disappears. The imagination pursues it's progress. It's roar is heard through the woods; and it is plain from the sound, that it suffers some great convulsion. But all is close; impervious rocks and thickets intervene, and totally exclude the sight.

On this occasion Gilpin had already seen the cataract from below, but 'the imagination of a stranger', he remarks, 'would be held in stimulating suspense'. The nature of such effects is explored further in the essay on picturesque travel that he published in 1792. Our immediate reaction may strike us 'beyond the power of thought', every mental operation suspended. 'In this pause of intellect; this *deliquium* of the soul, an enthusiastic sensation of pleasure overspreads it, previous to any examination by the rules of art . . .' Subsequent rumination produces a calmer species of pleasure, but one more uniform and uninterrupted, flattering us with 'the idea of a sort of creation of our own'. Writers who attempted to convey the

---

[1] William Gilpin, 1724–1804, was educated at Queen's College, Oxford. He was successively headmaster of Cheam School, and vicar of Boldre in the New Forest.

pleasures indicated here by Gilpin found a variety of means of leading the reader up to that 'pause of intellect'. Something of the range of possibilities may be indicated by three of the more striking travel narratives from this period.

One of the most exhilarating of the picturesque set pieces is to be found in Patrick Brydone's *Tour through Sicily and Malta* (1773), where he describes an ascent of Etna.[1] The region of Etna contains violent contrasts, 'every beauty and every horrour'. Black, barren rocks confront luxuriant fertility; volcanic fire coexists with immense fields of snow and ice. The view from the summit of Etna itself unites many awful and sublime objects, and affords an unbounded prospect of Sicily and the seas around it. One's sight is 'every where lost in the immensity'; only the imperfection of the eye prevents one seeing Africa and Greece. Brydone implies that he is being vouchsafed a vision as close to completeness as man's senses will allow of the operations of the universe. He was particularly impressed by the conversion of lava to fertile soil—and by the length of time that must be supposed necessary for the process to be completed: not less than 14,000 years. Contemporaries were rather scandalized by this attempt to unsettle the received Old Testament chronology, Dr. Johnson (for one) remarking that Brydone would be a good traveller if he were 'more attentive to his Bible' (17 May 1778). In the context of the account of Etna, however, it falls into place as yet another illustration of the immensity of Nature's operations—an effect reinforced by Brydone's interest in electrical phenomena. In Brydone, the picturesque becomes a vehicle for conveying an immediate sense of the illimitable powers at work around us.

Picturesque contrast serves a rather different purpose in William Coxe's *Sketches of the Natural, Civil, and Political State of Swisserland* (1779).[2] Here it is extended to include social institutions as well as 'natural objects', and the final effect created by Coxe is one of rich, irregular diversity, the product of what Gilpin called the bold, free, negligent strokes of nature. His descriptions of Alpine scenery are splendidly evocative, and his ability to suggest a sense of movement within a landscape may

[1] Patrick Brydone, 1736–1818, travelled in Europe as a tutor. Later he held the office of comptroller in the Stamp Office.

[2] William Coxe, 1747–1828, educated at Eton College and King's College, Cambridge, travelled in Europe as a tutor. He became rector of Bemerton and Archdeacon of Wiltshire.

have given a hint or two to Wordsworth, who traversed the Alps with the *Sketches* in his hand. Coxe's account of the approach to the St. Gotthard Pass, following the river Reuss, is a fair example. The road, he says,

winds continually along the steep sides of the mountains, and the Reuss sometimes appeared several hundred yards below us; here rushing a considerable way through a forest of pines, there falling in cascades, and losing itself in the valley. We crossed it several times, over bridges of a single arch, and beheld it tumbling under our feet in channels which it had forced through the solid rock; innumerable torrents roaring down the sides of the mountains; which were sometimes bare, sometimes finely wooded, with here and there some fantastic beeches hanging on the sides of the precipice, and half obscuring the river from our view.

Landscapes like this, with their sudden transitions from sublime wilderness to well-tended cultivation, form the setting for an account of the republics and dependencies which made up the confederation, an intricate political pattern superimposed on other patterns of language and religion. Coxe is much impressed by the mild government of these little states, the 'democratical' ones displaying a 'general equality and indistinction', while some at least of the aristocratic ones show that they can keep their people tranquil and contented. By the time of the second edition (*Travels in Switzerland*, 1789) political upheavals in both Switzerland and England had modified Coxe's attitude a little, and he finds in the democracy of the Grisons evidence of the bad effects that demands for reform in Britain would probably produce. Even so, the overriding mood of the book is one of satisfaction at viewing this product of an exceedingly complex historical development.

Brydone and Coxe stand apart from the phenomena they describe. William Beckford, on the other hand, seems always striving to throw himself into his landscapes, almost as literally as he did into the sea one hot day near Venice, abandoning himself utterly to the movements of the water. His *Dreams, Waking Thoughts, and Incidents* (1783) is in some respects as typical a monument of the Grand Tour as the letters from Italy of Horace Walpole and Thomas Gray; but Beckford's travels are informed with an enthusiasm that can only be called athletic. He surveys the Bay of Naples from the top of a pine tree, with nothing but a frail branch to steady him. Visiting the ducal palace in Venice when the twilight 'enlarged every portico, lengthened every colonnade, and increased the dimensions of the whole, just as imagination dictated', he stalked proudly about like an ancient Greek actor 'declaiming the first verses of Oedipus Tyrannus'. (He was thus discovered by the officers of police, who were anxious to close the gates.) He delights in the perpetually shifting movement of lights in the Venetian canals by night: 'every boat had its lantern, and the gondolas moving rapidly along were followed by tracks of light, which gleamed and played upon the waters.' Beckford is skilful at suggesting the way in which light can modify a landscape, softening irregularities and diffusing a faint aerial hue, or, in brilliant sunshine, bringing a contrasting sharpness of definition. There is a fine example of the latter effect in Letter XXVIII of the first part of the *Sketches of Spain and Portugal* (written in 1787–8), when he describes the view from a convent near Cintra. Over the 'immense expanse of sea, the vast, unlimited Atlantic' there is 'a long series of detached clouds of a dazzling whiteness, suspended low over the waves'. In pagan times, he adds, they might have appeared 'the cars of marine divinities just risen from the bosom of their element'. So far from being a routine neoclassical flourish, this last detail serves to define the sense of movement within the scene, and its luminous clarity.

As one would expect of the author of *Vathek*, Beckford is concerned with manners as well as the picturesque, and he takes a particular pleasure in exhibiting the more entertaining traits of Catholic piety. There was a memorable occasion while he was visiting the Escorial near Madrid, when he was shown a feather from the wing of the Archangel Gabriel. The surly prior who conducted him took it from a heavily perfumed cabinet, where it was displayed on a quilted silken mattress. It was

full three feet long, and of a blushing hue more soft and delicate than that of the loveliest rose. I longed to ask at what precise moment this treasure beyond price had dropped—whether from the air—on the open ground, or within the walls of the humble tenement at Nazareth; but I repressed all questions of an indiscreet tendency—the why and wherefore, the when and how, for what and to whom such a palpable manifestation of archangelic beauty and wingedness had been vouchsafed.

We all knelt in silence, and when we rose up after the holy feather had been again deposited in its perfumed lurking-place, I fancied the prior looked doubly suspicious, and uttered a sort of *humph* very doggedly; nor did his ill-humour evaporate upon my desiring to be conducted to the library.

The scepticism of the visitor, the prior's irritable awareness of that scepticism, and the atmosphere of rapt adoration which forbids any utterance of his annoyance, combined with the real beauty of the tableau conjured up before the mind's eye, unite to create a situation of considerable piquancy.

The traveller's encounter with the varieties of human manners, and the intrepid spirit needed for the enterprise, is nowhere more flamboyantly recorded than in James Bruce's *Travels to Discover the Source of the Nile* (1790).[1] He presents himself as deeply involved in the turbulence of Abyssinian affairs, risking himself in quarrels, and gaining a sickeningly vivid acquaintance with the callous ruthlessness of political life in that country. The landscape within which these adventures take place is all too appropriate, hostile even when most magnificent. A splendid description of a Nile cataract, which struck him with a kind of stupor—'a total oblivion of where I was, and of every other sublunary concern'—led him to the reflection that it seemed as if

one element had broken loose from, and become superior to, all laws of subordination; that the fountains of the great deep were again extraordinarily opened, and the destruction of a world was once more begun by the agency of water.

He enters with equal zest into the destructive effects of extreme heat. The country around Sennaar is pleasant enough at the end of August, green and well-watered, with the Nile flowing through it, 'above a mile broad, full to the very brim, but never over-flowing'. It is, he says, like the pleasantest parts of Holland;

but soon after, when the rains cease, and the sun exerts his utmost influence, the dora [millet] begins to ripen, the leaves to turn yellow and to rot, the lakes to putrefy, smell, and be full of vermin, all this beauty suddenly disappears; bare scorched Nubia returns, and all its terrors of poisonous winds and moving sands, glowing and ventilated with sultry blasts . . .

---

[1] James Bruce, 1730–94, was born at Kinnaird in Stirlingshire, and educated at Harrow and Edinburgh University. After some time in the wine trade, he became consul in Algiers, 1763, and studied antiquities in North Africa. He was in Abyssinia from 1769 to 1772.

Bruce here touches on something that goes beyond the pleasing horror of the sublime. The senses sicken at a prospect that gives no hint of the overruling operation of a mysterious providence. Equally disquieting, though in a much more sober way, is another work that displays many of the qualities honoured in eighteenth-century travel narratives: Arthur Young's *Travels in France* (1792).[1] His English travels had shown him to be, as we have seen, alert to the pleasures of the picturesque, although his main concern was with experiments in agriculture, and with 'improvement' generally. He was an accurate observer of social conditions, diligent in turning the conversation in a profitable direction, and sensitive to those 'every-day feelings that decide the colour of our lives'. This combination of qualities served to make his *Tour in Ireland* (1780) an admirable account of the state of that country. The tone is warmly philanthropic: conciliatory policies towards the Catholics, he is convinced, are the surest means to prosperity. For Young in his earlier years it was natural to assume that the whole world was moving towards 'a state of knowledge, elegance and peace', and this strain of feeling is still strongly present in the *Travels in France*. His response to the news of the taking of the Bastille was that it would be 'a great spectacle for the world to view, in this enlightened age, the representatives of twenty-five millions of people sitting on the construction of a new and better order and fabric of liberty, than Europe has yet offered'. But this mood proved to be only one element in his narrative, which is a scrupulously precise account of the experience of living through the first stages of a social cataclysm. He vividly conveys the rumours and alarms of the time, and is repeatedly struck by the absence of a soundly-based political concern among the provincial merchants and officers with whom he conversed at inns and coffee-houses. At Clermont, for example, the conversation was insignificant, inane: 'scarcely any politics, at a moment when every bosom ought to beat with none but political sensations'. He was often exasperated by the lack of newspapers: 'as to a newspaper,' he writes at one place, 'I might as well have demanded an elephant.' Intermingled with such comments are accounts of episodes where he witnessed the revolutionary spirit at uncomfortably close quarters. He watches an attack on the *hôtel de ville* in Strasbourg—placates a suspicious crowd in

[1] See further Vol. IX, p. 18.

another place by a discourse on the principles of taxation—
intrepidly defends a poor village-woman who had acted as his
guide, and was therefore being charged with aiding and abet-
ting a spy. In spite of the great upheaval that is expelling
noblemen from their estates, and raising petty lawyers to positions of authority, Young travels determinedly on, collecting
information about agricultural methods, conversing with men
of science, even contemplating the purchase of an estate. In
Provence he is delighted by his visit to the Baron d'Aigues,
whose collection of books and tracts on agriculture is nearly as
large as Young's own; but the baron's immense possessions are
now 'frittering away to nothing by the revolution'. His château,
his venerable woods ('uncommon in this naked province'), his
farms—all are now at the mercy of an armed rabble. It is a situation for which Bruce's account of September in Sennaar would
make a fine emblem: the vermin are beginning to multiply, and
there is more than a hint of the bare scorched moral landscape
of the Terror. The spirit of improvement may still perhaps
create a world where knowledge, elegance, and peace prevail;
but not yet.

It is only a short step from the travel narrative to the diarist
and the writer of memoirs. All are concerned with what Horace
Walpole called 'exact fidelity' to the impressions made on an
observer whose very faults and prejudices form part of the fabric
of narrative. The observer himself may absorb more or less of the
conscious attention of the reader, but even when the principal
interest is in the events and characters recorded, the narrator's
presence always counts for something. A fine example from the
first half of the century is Lord Hervey, in his *Memoirs* (not published until 1848). He thought of himself as resembling the chorus
in ancient drama, present throughout the action but not involved in it. He begins with the worthy intention of avoiding
such egotisms as disfigure the memoirs of Cardinal de Retz
and Bishop Burnet—'those ecclesiastical heroes of their own
romances'—but as he goes on he finds to his surprise that some
egotism cannot be avoided in a work of this kind, and indeed
the reader takes an increasing pleasure in the deferential,
caustic, good-humoured lord at the court of George II. His
presence is essential to the effect of high comedy in such episodes
as the marriage of George's eldest daughter to the Prince of

Orange: the prince's singular appearance in his brocaded night-gown, the astonished faces of the courtiers, the adoring behaviour of the bride, all are sketched with an adroit elegance which reinforces our sense of the detached objectivity of the observer. None of the political memoirs of the latter part of the century have quite the assured touch of Hervey's, but there is at least one major achievement in the genre, the *Memoirs* of Horace Walpole (not published until 1822 and 1845).

Memoirs of the Reign of King George II and *Memoirs of the Reign of King George III* are, above all, parliamentary histories. Walpole was a Member of Parliament at a time when its proceedings were still shielded by a privilege that frustrated public curiosity to an extent that he himself makes clear when considering the effect of leaving the Commons in 1768. Thereafter, he says, his account of debates must necessarily be 'mutilated and imperfect', derived from mere hearsay. Much of his enjoyment in writing—and he claims that the *Memoirs* were his favourite work—seems to come from his belief that he will be an important witness in the eyes of posterity. He takes pains to identify the main issues of debate, to convey the characters of the men who debated them, and, often, the atmosphere of a particular occasion. Thus, in a 'day of rodomontade' in a debate on the army (5 December 1755) there is a vivid summary of one of Pitt's florid declamations, drawing 'a striking and masterly picture of a French invasion reaching London, and of the horrors ensuing'. Melodrama gives way to farce: Walpole remarks, as he passes from one ridiculous speech to the next, that 'Sir Thomas Robinson played a bass to Nugent's thunder; his pompous rumbling made proper harmony with the other's vociferation'. The hints of theatre become explicit on the really striking parliamentary occasions, as when he describes Charles Townshend's splendidly inebriated speech during the debate on East India Company dividends (8 May 1767). Walpole gives only a bare indication of what Townshend actually said, but communicates the eloquent confusion, the sheer wit, abundance, and impropriety of the whole performance. His 'bacchanalian enthusiasm' exceeded the sublime Pindar's, his histrionic powers at least equalled Garrick's—'Garrick writing and acting extempore scenes of Congreve'. The very brilliance of the art evidently made it more perishable: how can an audience thus enchanted pause to record and analyse? Walpole deftly conjures up the effect upon himself, and throughout never loses sight of the utter irresponsibility of the speech, politically considered.

Perhaps the most sustained achievement of the *Memoirs* is the extended account of the trial by court martial of Admiral Byng, and the unsuccessful attempt to prevent his execution. The loss of Minorca to the French at the beginning of the Seven Years War caused a great outcry in Britain, and Byng's alleged negligence made him a convenient scapegoat. Walpole was sickened by the way a questionable military code was allowed to serve political ends, and did what he could to encourage uneasy members of the court martial to undo the effects of their own judgement. His exertions reached a climax three days before the date originally fixed for Byng's execution. Walpole was temporarily out of Parliament, having resigned one seat before taking another. His hurried, anxious quest for an M.P. to intervene for him before the House rose for the week-end—the rebuff from one member—the welcome sight of another more amenable—that member's raising the question at the moment when it was almost too late: all this might suggest melodrama of the coarsest kind. In fact it is not so. It is a moment when energetic physical action brings relief to a painfully realized deadlock between parties contending in the intractable medium of parliamentary procedure and legal argument.

Walpole's judgements of character are usually severe, but vivid and plausible. He is willing to allow contradictory feelings free expression, betraying no impulse to delete inconsistencies that reveal themselves in different parts of the text. In assessing William Pitt the Elder he responds both to the popular mood of national enthusiasm and to the astringent scepticism of his own cousin and intimate friend General Conway. In 1757 Conway had borne much of the burden of putting into effect Pitt's grandiose and unsuccessful scheme for an expedition against Rochefort, and was irritated by Pitt's cavalier inattention to detail, including the details of elementary geography. Pitt, says Walpole, 'was too sanguine to desist for a little confutation'. In spite of misgivings inspired by such traits, and his revulsion against Pitt's ruthlessness, one still detects an admiration for the Minister's spirit and energy. The cumulative effect of his references to Pitt is coherent, though it defies precise summary. Pitt's sublime vigour seems to depend on an unhealthy insulation from his fellowmen. Complexity of a different kind can be seen in Walpole's extremely hostile account of George Grenville. At one point, summing up Grenville's character with some venom, he observes that the man never blushed at his political inconsistencies 'as all his passions were expressed by one livid smile'. Four chapters later this definition of Grenville as a kind of frigid antonym of Garrick is completely subverted. Walpole met him during the riot after the burning of the *North Briton*:

> Grenville arrived in the most ridiculous and extraordinary disorder I ever saw. He could scarce articulate for passion. One would have thought the City had been taken by storm and the guards cut to pieces. Yet this was not panic. It was rage to see authority set at nought while *he* was minister.

Unexpected as this is as a sequel to the livid smile, it is, on reflection, altogether probable.

The writing of political memoirs was an art much cultivated in Walpole's time, although most were published, as his were, in the course of the following century. Even then there were perils, as Sir Nathaniel Wraxall discovered when his *Historical Memoirs* (1815) earned him a term of imprisonment for libel.[1] Wraxall himself gives a lively picture of Parliament, and the people in it, during the period after Walpole's own withdrawal from politics. He is an unreliable witness, 'better', as the historian John Ehrman charitably puts it, 'for custom and atmosphere than for specific events'. But he has an eye for details that would interest a painter, as can be seen in the fine description of Charles James Fox, whose features so readily 'relaxed into a smile, the effect of which became irresistible, because it appeared to be the Index of a benevolent and complacent disposition'. Burke, by contrast, displayed an irritability such that his friends had sometimes to hold him down in his seat, by the skirts of his coat, 'in order to prevent the ebullitions of his anger or indignation'. Wraxall, less at the centre of events than Walpole or Hervey, plays the part of the shrewd spectator upon whom nothing is lost. His *Memoirs*, incidentally, contain one of the most elaborate descriptions of the Gordon Riots of 1780.

---

[1] Sir Nathaniel William Wraxall, 1751–1831, spent some time with the East India Company in Bombay. He then became an M.P., and acted as agent for the Nabob of Arcot.

The scrupulous precision of the detail obliquely suggests a keen appreciation of this sublime spectacle. He recalls the calmness of the incendiaries in Holborn, watched by an immense crowd, many of them women, some carrying children. 'All appeared to be, like ourselves, attracted as spectators solely by curiosity.' Later, standing where the King's Bench prison could be seen enveloped in flames, Wraxall felt himself to be at a 'central point, from whence London offered on every side, before as well as behind us, the picture of a city sacked and abandoned to a ferocious enemy': thus, he adds, with a fine sense of aesthetic distance, 'presenting to the view every recollection which the classic descriptions in Virgil, or in Tacitus, have impressed on the mind in youth'.

A book like Wraxall's may be read as an assemblage of anecdotes—and to say this is not to intend any disparagement. The anecdote was a form that in the eighteenth century was diligently cultivated. Collections of brief tales and pointed sayings by the wise and good are among the oldest of literary genres, and may be found in many cultures. A specialized variety developed in seventeenth- and eighteenth-century France was the collection of sayings by men of letters, usually referred to as 'ana' from such titles as the *Menagiana* of Gilles Ménage (1613–92) and the *Huetiana* of Pierre Daniel Huet (1630–1721). Bayle, in praising the *Menagiana*, observes that it is rare to find a learned man who can effectively deploy his learning in conversation. Ménage was one such: 'his memory ranged over things ancient and modern, over court and city, over the dead languages and the living, over the serious and the facetious.' No doubt the *Menagiana* preserve only a fraction of these virtuoso performances, but the risk of such loss would diminish with the extension of the state of mind apparent in Boswell, who observed when noting down a story about Johnson in his *London Journal*, 'I like to mark every anecdote of men of so much genius and literature' (17 December 1762). The anxiety to prevent the escape of any particle of genius has a family likeness to the then current zest for inquiries into nicely discriminated passions and into the limitless variety of manners and customs. Both bear witness to a sense of infinite riches going to waste. Mrs. Thrale regrets, early in her *Thraliana*, her failure to mark resemblances between passages in different books 'as fast as they fell in my way, for one forgets again in the hurry and Tumult of

Life's Cares or Pleasures almost every thing that one does not commit to paper'. The antiquarian movement, already touched on as an aspect of historical studies (pp. 217–18), reveals a similar indiscriminate appetite. Collectors of anecdotes were doing for posterity what they wished antiquity had done more systematically for them. Those Scottish men of letters, Alexander Carlyle and Henry Mackenzie, sat down in their old age to write memoirs of the people and the events they had witnessed in a period of conspicuous 'improvement' and animated intellectual life. Such recollection, reinforced by careful inquiries, was one of the most rewarding contributions that could be made to the work of future biographers, because no matter how slight the incident or casual the remark, it might serve to add one more characteristic stroke to the portrait, and even prove to be the detail which brought the whole portrait to life. The principle was clearly stated early in the century by Roger North, in his life of his brother Francis North. He justified a concern with minute circumstances by remarking that when drawing a tree

the Leaves, and minor Branches, are very small and confused, and give the Artist more pain to describe, than the solid Trunk and greater Branches. But, if these small things were left out, it would make but a sorry Picture of a Tree.

So too thought William Oldys, a principal contributor to that great eighteenth-century enterprise the *Biographia Britannica*. As he said in the course of his *Life of Raleigh* (1736), 'a great discovery of genius may be made through a small and sudden repartee'. For Horace Walpole the genius of the Earl of Strafford appeared with a special vividness in a few words he spoke shortly before his execution. They appear in Walpole's *Catalogue of the Royal and Noble Authors of England* (1758) as a touchstone to try the authenticity of a poem supposed to be Strafford's.

When the Lieutenant of the Tower offered him a coach, lest He should be torn to pieces by the mob in passing to execution; He replied, 'I die to please the people, and I will die in their own way.' With such stern indifference to his fate, he was not likely to debase his dignity by puerile expressions of it.

The principal monument of this quest for anecdotal material was the work of John Nichols: *Literary Anecdotes of the Eighteenth Century*.[1] Although the nucleus of this immense publication was

[1] John Nichols, 1745–1826, was apprenticed as a printer to William Bowyer, and eventually took over his business.

issued in 1778, it did not appear in its final form until 1812-16. Nichols was a printer who for many years edited the *Gentleman's Magazine*, a periodical that played an important part in building up the *Literary Anecdotes* and their sequel, the *Illustrations of the Literary History of the Eighteenth Century* (1817-58). They are exceptionally untidy volumes, obviously the work of accretion rather than composition. Often the text dwindles to a line or two at the head of a closely-printed page of illustrative notes or parallel narrative. It might almost be an elaborately annotated classic, indicating the vastness of the background material needed to enter into the mind and sensibility of the author, and to understand the events of his life. Men like Malone and Steevens, both close associates of Nichols, devoted this kind of attention to the text of Shakespeare, and such preoccupations played their part in the genesis of the Waverley Novels. In Nichols the collection of anecdotes has no focus. It forms a part of his diligent activities as an antiquarian, and astonishing though the scope of his works is, they remain a quarry, almost inexhaustible, for future projects.

Other collectors of anecdotes have a certain affinity with contemporary portrait and genre painters. The affinity is suggested by Mrs. Piozzi in a passage in her *Anecdotes of the late Samuel Johnson* (1786). She concedes that her 'little memoirs of Mr. Johnson's behaviour and conversation' must appear at a great disadvantage in comparison with those written by persons better qualified, 'who having seen him in various situations, and observed his conduct in numberless cases, are able to throw stronger and more brilliant lights upon his character'. Her own book is 'a mere *candle-light* picture of his latter days'. It is not altogether apparent just how modest Mrs. Piozzi is being here. She may well have assessed the extraordinarily dramatic candle-light paintings of Joseph Wright of Derby as Richard Cumberland did when he spoke of 'bold eccentric *Wright* that hates the day'. But even if the genre is slighted as a mere curiosity, it is manifest that a candle-light can focus attention on particular elements in a face or figure, and that this is in some measure analogous to the way a striking anecdote affects the mind. Much depends on the temperament and point of view of the person recording the anecdote. Mrs. Piozzi herself is conscious of her role as a hostess in good company, for whom Johnson's bearlike behaviour was a serious problem. More trying still, her irrepressible liveliness often incurred his unpredictable displeasure. Another hostess-observer whose recollections of Johnson are coloured by such embarrassments is Frances Reynolds, Sir Joshua's sister. She was less vivacious than Mrs. Piozzi, and may have taken Johnson's indecorous outbursts more to heart. She has preserved for us an account of Johnson's speaking harshly to Mrs. Thrale, ill-treatment which she bore with great placidity. Later in the evening one of the ladies present expressed astonishment at Johnson's behaviour, to which Mrs. Piozzi only replied, 'Oh! Dear good man!' The words were duly reported to Johnson:

> He seem'd much delighted with this intelligence, and sometime after as he was lying back in his Chair, seeming to be half asleep, but more evidently musing on this pleasing incident, he repeated in a loud whisper, 'Oh! Dear good man!' This was a common habit of his, when anything very flattering, or very extraordinary ingross'd his thoughts.

Johnson is caught in a posture that might have been recorded in a painting, and the incident unites several of his idiosyncrasies with a powerful economy.

Sir John Hawkins's *Life of Samuel Johnson* (1787) is perhaps most fairly assessed as a specialized collection of anecdotes.[1] It has been censured on two main grounds: its tone is often intolerably acrimonious, and the digressions from the nominal subject exceed all reasonable limits. Bearing in mind the even greater digressive excesses of John Nichols, one may accept the shapelessness of Hawkins's work as an antiquarian's foible. Nor are the digressions altogether irrelevant, provided one takes a generous view of relevance. He does much to fill in the background of Johnson's world, and Johnson himself is seen in a fresh perspective among associates earlier than those known to most of our informants. Hawkins's long and censorious account of Samuel Dyer, one of the less edifying members of the Ivy-lane Club, is disproportionate, but the fate of the idle translator reveals snares that could have beset the lexicographer. Not even this defence can be offered for his rambling discussion of a quack doctor protected by Bubb Dodington, but the doctor's everlasting prate makes its own pleasant contribution to the noises of London: he held forth, says Hawkins, on politics and criticism in taverns and coffee-houses 'without

---

[1] Sir John Hawkins, 1719–89, was a lawyer and magistrate, knighted in 1772.

interruption, in a tone of voice that Mr. Garrick would say was like the buz of a humble-bee in a hall window'. Such attractive details are obscured by the prevailing atmosphere of harsh disapproval, but although the harshness is repulsive, it is an essential element in Hawkins's main achievement. The disparaging tone of his comments on Johnson's circle of dependants throws Johnson's philanthropic fortitude into sharper relief than any more sympathetic attitude could have done. Similarly, his stiff regularity of life heightens our sense of Johnson's convivial temper. Hawkins did not enjoy the night-long celebration of Mrs. Lennox's *Harriot Stuart*, partly because of toothache, partly because of a malaise more deep-seated. He confesses to a particularly vivid recollection of the end of the night, which in spite of its innocence somewhat resembled a debauch. 'I well remember, at the instant of my going out of the tavern door, the sensation of shame that affected me.' A brisk walk, and breakfast, restored Hawkins to his good opinion of himself. The wonder is that so 'unclubbable' a man should ever have been persuaded to act so much out of character.

The temper of the anecdotist is significant even in such a collection of 'ana' as Joseph Spence's *Observations, Anecdotes, & Characters of Books & Men*, 'Spence's Anecdotes' as it is generally called. No one could be less self-assertive than Spence: he is manifestly preoccupied with the memorable things said by others, attending to their words with scrupulous exactness. The attentiveness itself impresses one as a trait of character. His record extends for a period of more than thirty years, beginning in 1726, and although it is of special importance for the information provided about Alexander Pope, the range of speakers is wide, including men of wit and learning encountered in the course of his travels in Europe. The topics are miscellaneous too: there are hints on landscape gardening and pregnant aphorisms on literary topics, such as Christopher Pitt's answer to the question 'What is a poem?'—'Something between jest and earnest'. One has a taste of the pleasures of conversation in elegant society, and, as one reads on, it becomes apparent how surely the anecdotes reveal the character of Spence himself. The note of quietly judicious appraisal sets off the more abrasive style of a speaker like Lady Mary Wortley Montagu. Pope himself emerges from the many snatches of his conversation as a temperament close to Spence's:

discriminating, knowledgeable, complacent, kind. No single anecdote establishes this. It appears in a habitual tone that one learns to recognize.

Spence's *Anecdotes* have something in common with a diary, though they lack the interest peculiar to the latter genre of evoking a sense of the rhythm of a past life. The two most famous examples of the period—the journals of Fanny Burney and James Boswell—do this with unsurpassed zest. Fanny Burney's diary is considered elsewhere (pp. 480-2) and Boswell's journals will be discussed in connection with his *Life of Johnson*, but one difference between them may usefully be shown here. In spite of Fanny Burney's opening declaration of intent (to 'Miss Nobody') to confess '*every* thought', her journals are not among those which serve as an instrument of self-regulation and self-discovery. Boswell's journals, on the other hand, set out to record some of the most elusive elements of experience: not only the feelings of the heart, but also the whims and sallies of his 'luxuriant imagination'. He is, indeed, conscious that he is unable to paint his most exquisite sensations, but he describes, energetically and unsparingly, the contradictory impulses that left him anxious and uncertain. In the *London Journal* he likes to feel that he is 'a young fellow eagerly pushing through life'. He has a touch of the romantic highwayman Captain Macheath about him, but he is also a man of sensibility setting down the sincere sentiments of his heart—and laughing at them too, if joined by one of his unsentimental companions. At some periods he attempts to discipline himself, notably in the journal he kept in Holland in 1763-4, diligently cultivating that self-control and reserve so alien to his temperament. We see him making his choice of life, not with the deliberation of a Rasselas, but with a flamboyant restlessness that draws the reader irresistibly into the process. Such delineation of an anxiously unfixed state of mind probably accounts for the appeal of diaries like that of the sadly ineffectual Sylas Neville.[1] While Neville's diary has little of Boswell's vitality, the reader may still be enticed into sharing the diarist's attempts to formulate rules for the conduct of life, and into feeling soothed by the reassurance Neville derives from the good opinion of such people as his landlady Mrs. Willoughby, between whom

[1] Sylas Neville, 1741-1840, studied medicine with some distinction at Edinburgh, but never pursued this or any other occupation.

and himself 'a pure Platonic love' subsisted. The political journals of Bubb Dodington[1] might seem to have an even slighter literary interest, but there is more beneath the drab surface than one might at first suppose. The journals are, indeed, a minor if disagreeable work of art. Dodington's attempt to buy his way back into office by putting his parliamentary influence at the service of the Duke of Newcastle is told with much unconscious humour. A man so mercenary has no business to indulge in moral indignation, but Dodington is genuinely outraged that he should find such difficulty in regaining the king's confidence. In the account of his interview with Newcastle (21 March 1754) Dodington depicts himself holding forth with tedious insistence, exerting himself to the utmost to conjure up an idea of slighted integrity to impress the Duke and reassure himself. The exertion is too great: the Duke demurs and assents with too much deference.

He said, that what I did, was very great, that he often thought with surprise, at the ease and cheapness of the election at Weymouth. That they had nothing like it. I said I believ'd there were few that could give his Majesty 6 Members for nothing. He said he reckon'd 5, and had put down 5 to my account. I said it was so: but this attempt of Lord Egmont's made it six. He would observe I did not pretend to chuse two for Bridgewater; but by Lord Egmont's opposition, the two Members must be entirely owing to me; for if I did not exert my whole force to exclude him, he must come in, and the Court could have but one there. He thank'd me, said it was most clear, now it was explain'd, but he had not consider'd it in that light.

It comes as no surprise to learn that Dodington remained out of office, 'notwithstanding all the fine conversation of last Thursday'.

There is less art in such clerical diaries as those of James Woodforde[2] and George Ridpath,[3] but they will always appeal strongly to the reader who holds, with George Saintsbury, that

---

[1] George Bubb Dodington, 1691–1762, was M.P. for Bridgwater and then for Weymouth. He was for a time associated with the party around Frederick, Prince of Wales, the estranged son of George II. He was created Baron Melcombe near the close of his life.

[2] James Woodforde, 1740–1803, was educated at Winchester and New College, Oxford. He was rector of Weston, Norfolk.

[3] George Ridpath, 1717–72, was educated at Edinburgh University. He was minister of Stitchel, Roxburghshire.

the literature of this period offers rest and refreshment to our disturbed and feverous age. The apparently secure routine of a country clergyman lulls and reassures, although there are occasional moments of stress, as when Ridpath recalls feelings of desperation in a child's sick-room, or Woodforde finds cause to dismiss an impudent servant. Woodforde pays the servant off, noting the exact amount due: 'In all paid him 1.17.9. I threw him down a Couple of Guineas,' says Woodforde, with unusual emphasis, 'but he would not take one farthing more than the above 1.17.9.' How much is disclosed by the gratuitous repetition of the sum of money! Such a crisis of feeling was almost too much for him to bear. He was so much 'hurried', indeed, that it made him 'quite ill all Day—vomited a good deal at Night after which took a Dose of Rhubarb and was much better' (13 April 1785). Woodforde's world is one whose ills can generally be remedied by rhubarb, or something similar, and his temper is as far removed as can well be imagined from the eager sensitivity and mortifying embarrassments recorded in the diary of Fanny Burney. Ridpath's diary suggests much richer intellectual interests than Woodforde's, but the general effect of quiet equability is similar.

Woodforde and Ridpath are dominated by the routine of their parishes. John Wesley was less confined: 'I look upon all the world as my parish.' Wesley's *Journal*, which began to appear in print as early as 1739, is one long record of locomotion, an account of the triumphant progress of the gospel, setting at defiance obstacles like foul weather, false doctrine, violent mobs, ill-health, and other weaknesses of the flesh. Wesley's plain style endows the most heroic transactions with authenticity. There is no mystery about God's providence: one can see precisely how things happened as they did. Thus, when Wesley was in Falmouth in July 1745, he found himself besieged in a house by a great multitude of angry people. Only a wainscot partition stood between him and his assailants. A large looking-glass hung on it, which he thoughtfully took down, anticipating that the whole wall might fall in. His one companion, a woman, was naturally frightened.

'O sir, what must we do?' I said, 'We must pray.' Indeed at that time, to all appearance, our lives were not worth an hour's purchase. She asked, 'But, sir, is it not better for you to hide yourself? To get into the closet?' I answered, 'No. It is best for me to stand just where

I am.' Among those without were the crews of some privateers, which were lately come into the harbour. Some of these, being angry at the slowness of the rest, thrust them away, and, coming up altogether, set their shoulders to the inner door, and cried out, 'Avast, lads, avast!' Away went all the hinges at once, and the door fell back into the room. I stepped forward at once into the midst of them, and said, 'Here I am. Which of you has anything to say to me? To which of you have I done any wrong? To you? Or you? Or you?' I continued speaking till I came, bare-headed as I was (for I purposely left my hat, that they might all see my face), into the middle of the street, and then, raising my voice, said, 'Neighbours, countrymen! Do you desire to hear me speak?'

A man of indomitable faith, clearly, and an admirable tactician too. The passage conveys practical hints on how to cope with a hostile crowd: take the initiative, keep talking, isolate ring-leaders, let them see your face, arouse their curiosity. Various as the contents of the *Journal* are, this note of indefatigable competence informs every part of it, even that distressing portion first published in 1848 as the *Narrative of a Remarkable Transaction in the Early Life of John Wesley*. The story of Wesley's proposal of marriage in 1749 to Grace Murray, and the measures taken by others to thwart his intention, is told with a bare economy which heightens the sense of austere self-discipline. It is far removed from the comedy of Wesley's mild, if embarrassing, entanglement with Sophy Causton in Savannah. The depth of Wesley's passion is apparent in the unconscious eloquence of his systematic analysis of Grace Murray's suitability as a companion for an evangelist. The eloquence is kept in check elsewhere. Moments of peculiar intensity, like the decision to go to Whitehaven and not to Newcastle (where Grace Murray was), are passed over with the curtness of one used to subordinating his own comfort to the needs of his mission. A few strokes of description throw his state of mind into strong relief.

I knew this was giving up all: But I knew GOD call'd: And therefore, on Frid. 29, set out. The Storm was full in my face, and exceeding high, so that I had much difficulty to sit my Horse: Particularly as I was riding over the broad, bare backs of those enormous Mountains.

The narrative ends on a note of deep bitterness and bewilderment, and sheer pain predominates throughout, although there

is an occasional flash of the robust humour that never altogether left him. Thus, he was not much impressed by the
condemnation of his conduct by colleagues in Newcastle.

Sister Proctor would leave the House immediately. John Whitford
would preach with Mr. W. no more. Mat. Errington dream'd, the
House itself was all in flames (and most certainly it was). Another
Dreamer went a Step farther, and saw Mr. W. in hell-fire. Jane
Keith was peremptory 'John W. is a child of the Devil': Coming
pretty near J.B. himself; whose repeated word was, 'If John W. is
not damn'd, there is no GOD.'

The episode as a whole exceeded Wesley's powers of interpretation. The experience is left, as it can be in a diary, raw and
inexplicable.

In autobiography, an author may also attempt to recover
a past state of his own being in all its inexplicable vividness,
but the very act of looking back over an extended period tends
to soften the impact of particular experiences. In David Hume's
brief account of his own life, he speaks wryly of his disappointment at the unflattering reception most of his works received at
their first appearance, but does so with the ease of a man with
an assured reputation, much appreciated in Paris, a city that
abounds in 'sensible, knowing, and polite company'. His
concern, indeed, is not so much with his past as his present
state, the sceptical philosopher on the point of death, retaining
his ease and good humour, fully aware that in this way he
throws down a peculiarly provoking challenge to such orthodox
enemies as James Beattie and many other Reverend and Right
Reverend gentlemen. Hume's detachment from morbid anxiety
makes Beattie's talk in his *Essay on Truth*, of 'enemies and plagues
of mankind' seem merely maladroit. If this is the effect of the
fatal fermentation of scepticism spreading 'wider and wider
every moment, till all the mass be transformed into rottenness
and poison', then Beattie is not using the language of common
sense. Hume's stock-taking, in fact, has a deliberate and public
purpose.

A comparable, though less public, intention underlies
William Gilpin's autobiographical memoir. Gilpin is chiefly
remembered now as an exponent of the picturesque, but it is
not this that preoccupies him when he looks at what he has
achieved. He describes the regime he developed at Cheam
School—a remarkable experiment in both humane discipline

and enlightened methods of study—and then gives a similarly detailed account of his work as a clergyman in the New Forest. He writes in the third person and tries to be self-effacing, but school and parish alike are evidently monuments to his firm, kindly, cheerfully resourceful character. This effect is reinforced by the memoir's appearing as the last of a series of biographical sketches of his immediate ancestors. His great-grandfather Richard Gilpin and his descendants are presented as cultivated, moderate, prudent, ingenious people who in their various ways did much for the improvement of society. William's father, although a military man, was more typical of his family than of his profession. He had 'a variety of little innocent arts to avoid drinking', and applied similar arts to the enforcement of military discipline. It is almost as though Gilpin were attempting a kind of collective autobiography, hinting at a common Gilpin temper that forms a strong contrast to the outrageous spirit of a revolutionary age.

Another kind of stock-taking is undertaken in the eloquent autobiographical sketch that Arthur Young contributed to the *Annals of Agriculture* in 1791. Young was recovering from a serious illness when he wrote it, and he is obviously burdened by a sense of resentment and anxiety, sourly speculating on how he might have prospered if he had not been so foolish as to devote his life to the merely useful business of agricultural improvement. What preferment might not have been his if he had taken up painting, say, or music? His depression is too great to explore more than cursorily the restless activities that had ended only in a 'narrow, cramped, and anxious situation', relieved a little, indeed, by dreams of managing a fine estate in France. It is not so much an autobiography as the embryo of one, but few writings of the period pose more vividly the central autobiographical question: what have I done with my life?

In the eighteenth century, the best-established pattern of autobiography remained that of the religious confession, the narrative of God's dealings with a particular soul. A state of unregeneracy, the crisis of conversion, and later progress in faith, supply a well-marked outline for a variety of experiences. No eighteenth-century 'puritan autobiography' can be said to rival Bunyan's *Grace Abounding*, but there is much of interest in the short lives of Methodist preachers published by Wesley in the *Arminian Magazine*, many of which were collected in Thomas

Jackson's useful edition in the middle of the following century. The most famous of the Methodist autobiographies is perhaps that of the stonemason John Nelson, but his stirring account of fearless Christian militancy is not fully representative of the psychological interest of the genre. Silas Told's *Life*, for example, includes some scrupulously exact accounts of supernatural or visionary experiences. One of these, a hallucination shared by an entire ship's company, is particularly fine. While still in mid-Atlantic, they thought they had sighted land. Told recalls how the sailors made ready to anchor, clearing the decks and bending the cables.

I do not remember ever to have seen any place apparently more fertile, or better cultivated; the fields seeming to be covered with verdure, and very beautiful: and as the surf of the sea almost convinced us that it was playing on the shore, we were beyond all doubt for the space of ten hours. Our Captain, therefore, gave the man who first discovered it, ten gallons of rum and twenty pounds of sugar; but about six o'clock in the evening, as we were washing the decks, and the sun was shining clear from the westward, in less than a minute, we lost all sight of the land; nothing but the horizon, interspersed with a few pale clouds, was perceptible from the deck.

In contrast to such visionary excitements, the life of George Story provides a sober, but subtle, narrative of a long process of conversion. It is the work of a man whose wide-ranging intellectual curiosity is apparent even when he takes the 'safe though painful path' of 'staying his mind upon the Lord' and ceasing from troubled reasonings. In describing the varieties of doubt that rose up spontaneously and overturned all his consolation, it is evident that the succession of misleading arguments is still of deep interest to him. He is not thrusting his past states of mind into a limbo of repudiated errors. Others may pass through the same agonies as he has, and he is anxious to help them.

Few religious autobiographers have quite such an exotic story to tell as John Newton, in his *Authentic Narrative* (1764).[1] His time as a scapegrace sailor, his two years of servitude in West Africa, his prosperity as a slave-trader, together form an

[1] John Newton, 1725–1807, was a sailor, engaged in the slave trade. After a religious conversion, he was ordained, and held a curacy at Olney, where he befriended William Cowper. He afterwards had the parish of St. Mary Woolnoth in London, which became a centre of evangelical influence.

improbable preparation for the vocation of a minister of the gospel. The pious reflections flow perhaps too lavishly from Newton's grateful pen, but they are essential to his story, and it is idle to complain of them. The autobiography grows out of Newton's *surprise* that his life has turned out as it has. The effect would have been diminished if he had falsified the record, or not been fully committed to exploring what his life was like when it resembled that of the hero of a picaresque novel. There are reticences in his narrative, but he looks back with unashamed interest at such states of mind as possessed him in the time that followed his unsuccessful attempt to desert from the ship bound for the East Indies. He sketches a mixture of murderous and suicidal impulses, checked only by his feeling for the woman whom he later married. The temper of this analysis is not romantic in any sense of the word. There is no inclination to exalt or even set much value on this merely human affection. His feeling is presented in its barest form, but it still rings true:

> Though I neither feared God, nor regarded men, I could not bear that *she* should think meanly of me when I was dead . . . This single thought, which had not restrained me from a thousand smaller evils, proved my only and effectual barrier against the greatest and most fatal temptations. (Letter 4)

His brief references to the steps of his self-education are the more telling for the exactness with which he indicates his motives for learning. The one book he had with him in his time in Africa was a copy of Euclid, and it was evidently his main resource against total demoralization.

> It was always with me, and I used to take it to remote corners of the island by the sea-side, and draw my *diagrams* with a long stick upon the sand. Thus I often beguiled my sorrows, and almost forgot my feelings:—and thus without any other assistance, I made myself in a good measure master of the first six books of *Euclid*. (Letter 5)

His account of how he later learnt Latin creates a vivid impression of a strong will pitting itself against obstinate difficulties. There is no vanity in it, only an awareness of the part his belated accomplishments played in opening to him a sense of a deeper vocation.

Newton's is a story of triumph. The story of his friend and disciple William Cowper, on the other hand, provides one of the classic records of a morbid psychological state. Cowper's autobiographical *Memoir* of his early life, published posthumously in 1816, rehearses the circumstances which led up to his attempted suicide in 1763. He was trapped in an impossible situation created by his sense of unfitness for a post to which family influence entitled him, that of Clerk to the Journals of the House of Lords. He felt bound in honour to proceed with the application, although he knew that the family right was being contested and that he would have to endure a public examination at the bar of the House of Lords. Feeling utterly unequal to this ordeal, his hopeless preparation for it was like a protracted nightmare:

> The journal books were indeed thrown open to me; a thing which could not be refused: and from which, perhaps, a man in health and with a head turned to business, might have gained all the information he wanted; but it was not so with me. I read without perception, and was so distressed, that had every clerk in the office been my friend, it would have availed me little; for I was not in a condition to receive instruction, much less to elicit it out of manuscripts, without direction.

In such a closed labyrinth, suicide appeared the only deliberate action open to him, and the failure of his various attempts, carefully elaborated as they are, heightens the sense of oppression which informs the whole narrative. He longs for the security of dependence, a longing which is expressed first as a desire for insanity. Religious conversion, and a safe place of withdrawal, provide him with what he needs. It is not quite a happy ending. The narrative is loaded with too great a burden of anxiety to be resolved in this way. What is impressive is the steadiness with which he recalls his miserable experience.

The most famous English autobiography from this period, that of Edward Gibbon, reflects several of the preoccupations indicated here. Like Cowper, Gibbon recalls past states of his own being. Like many religious autobiographers, he tells the story of the discovery of a vocation. Like Gilpin, he sees his own achievement in the context of earlier generations of his family. These different approaches, sufficiently evident in the received text constructed by Lord Sheffield, become strikingly apparent when one reads through the half-dozen memoirs that lie behind it. The first memoir is family history, and reveals a man eager to detect anticipations of his own character and pursuits in real or supposed ancestors. Thus, he was much impressed by the seventeenth-century herald John Gibbon, who when in Virginia thought he saw in the war-paint of American Indians indications of heraldry, and concluded that heraldry was 'ingrafted naturally into the sense of human race'. Although Edward Gibbon is amused at such enthusiasm for a favourite study, there is a hint too that this earlier Gibbon had had the capacity to contribute to the evolving science of human nature. The treatise in which he created a Latin terminology for heraldic science was doubtless a misguided venture; but, says Gibbon, 'his technical language, were the object of more use and importance, might deserve as much praise as the Botanical idiom of Linnaeus'. Gibbon evidently felt that this first memoir had betrayed him into garrulity, and in his second attempt, Memoir B, he compressed the materials of the first memoir into a few pages. The emphasis now is on his formative years, explored at some length down to the eve of his crucial visit to Italy in 1764. Succeeding memoirs allot less and less space to his early life and education, until in the fifth, Memoir E, this material dwindles into a perfunctory preface to his public life. Then comes a fresh impulse. The sixth and final memoir enters into Gibbon's formative years in considerably greater detail than had been attempted even in Memoir B. Thus, taking up a slight hint in the earliest text, he traces the story of his life back to the womb, and speculates upon his existence 'floating nine months in a liquid element', then 'painfully transported into the vital air'. He needs this perspective in order to emphasize that he was not, like Milton's Adam, formed complete in all his parts, but required a long and irregular process of development.

When Lord Sheffield compiled his composite version, he skilfully preserved this sense of an unplanned evolution. A mysterious but benign providence appears to guide a chosen spirit to perform his appointed task. The wanderings of the unreclaimed sinner prove in retrospect to have been stages on the road to salvation. Gibbon takes a keen pleasure in showing how circumstances which might seem to have disqualified him for a major scholarly undertaking turned, in fact, to his advantage. He was indiscriminate and disorderly in his childhood studies, deprived by illness of regular academic education, lacking even a domestic tutor to watch the favourable moments and advance the progress of his learning. He was left instead to gratify, as he puts it, the wanderings of an unripe taste, and to devour greedily an astonishing range of miscellaneous reading, some of which pointed in the direction of his great history. The inadequate supervision of his studies at Oxford, his conversion to Roman Catholicism, and subsequent expulsion from the university, all continued the providential process. He was to profit greatly from the eager attention that he devoted to the history of the first four or five centuries of Christianity, and his knowledge and appreciation of the major authors of classical antiquity was much enhanced by the excellent tuition he received at Lausanne. A later episode, his weary service with the Hampshire militia, proved advantageous in a way he could not have foreseen at the time. 'The discipline and evolutions of a modern battalion gave me', he says, 'a clearer notion of the phalanx and the legion; and the captain of the Hampshire grenadiers (the reader may smile) has not been useless to the historian of the Roman empire.' Providence might even be seen to have watched over his affections, ensuring that his filial duty overrode his love for Suzanne Curchod. His father would not hear of this 'strange alliance', and Gibbon deferred to his authority: 'I sighed as a lover, I obeyed as a son.' He subsequently came to regard matrimony as the object of his terror rather than of his wishes, and he certainly creates the impression that his reluctant obedience in youth was rewarded by an affluence nicely calculated to foster his masterpiece. His father's estate was burdened by debt, and the ultimate inheritance was relatively modest, but he had sufficient, single as he was, to attain that first of earthly blessings, independence. It is in a tone of limitless satisfaction that he recalls the state of mind in which he began the composition of his great work: absolute master of his hours and actions, dividing the day between study and society.

Gibbon's autobiography reinforces the effect created by the *History of the Decline and Fall of the Roman Empire* of being conducted through a long series of prospects of society. The absolute mastery so highly valued by the author is intimately related to his sense of detachment from the events and passions he describes. It is appropriate that his experience of love should have been so temperate, his military service bloodless and not wholly incompatible with a continuance of study. He viewed his membership of the House of Commons in a similar spirit. He attended debates, he voted, but he did not actively intervene. 'The eight sessions that I sat in parliament', he concludes, 'were a school of civil prudence, the first and most essential virtue of an historian.' He appreciated the arts of statesmanship, but found a deep reassurance in the role of spectator. To be sure the role had its uneasy aspect before he achieved fame with the publication of his great work. In Memoir D, Gibbon speaks of his anxiety, after his return from the continent in 1765, about the way his contemporaries were advancing in their careers. 'I was left alone and immovable,' he says, 'the idle and insignificant spectator of the agitations of the state and the business of the World.' Success as a historian comfortably validated his detachment, and in retrospect he could view the pleasures of the spectator almost in terms of inebriation, as when he first came to Rome and saw for himself the theatre within which the greatest actions of Roman heroes were performed. The actions were great, but securely locked away in a past which he could contemplate with unmingled satisfaction.

After a sleepless night, I trod, with a lofty step, the ruins of the Forum; each memorable spot where Romulus *stood*, or Tully spoke, or Caesar fell, was at once present to my eye; and several days of intoxication were lost or enjoyed before I could descend to a cool and minute investigation.

The image of inebriation extends earlier images of gratified intellectual appetite. Although Gibbon insists on the systematic labour that went into the composition of his book, we are constantly reminded of the keen enjoyment that informed his diligence. If he re-reads the major Latin authors, doing so in a way that is neither hasty nor superficial, the words that come to his pen hint at the temper of a voluptuary. He *indulges* himself in his second or third reading, he studies to *imbibe* the sense and spirit most congenial to his own. Gibbon rejoices in his own well-being no less than John Newton did. Both men, looking back, view their lives with a sense of pleased astonishment. As Wordsworth was to put it a few years later, in the first book of *The Prelude*,

> How strange that all
> The terrors, pains, and early miseries,
> Regrets, vexations, lassitudes interfused

Within my mind, should e'er have borne a part,
And that a needful part, in making up
The calm existence that is mine when I
Am worthy of myself.

Admirable as Sheffield's version is, one cannot fully savour Gibbon's autobiography without reading the original text. It was natural for Sheffield to follow Memoir F when Gibbon recalled how his grandfather's absconding 'unlocked the door of a tolerable library, and I turned over many English pages of poetry and romance, of history and travels'. We may still regret the loss of the vivid words of Memoir B: 'I rioted without controul in his library, which had been hitherto locked.' It must be admitted, too, that Sheffield sometimes allowed his sense of decorum to suppress some characteristic passages, such as the description, which William Blake himself would have endorsed, of the miseries of school education.

A school is the cavern of fear and sorrow; the mobility of the captive youths is chained to a book and a desk; an inflexible master commands their attention, which every moment is impatient to escape; they labour like the soldiers of Persia under the scourge, and their education is nearly finished before they can apprehend the sense or utility of the harsh lessons which they are forced to repeat.

The omission of this passage diminishes one's appreciation of the kindness of his aunt Catherine Porten's lessons, and of the peculiar importance of the encouragement she gave to that early love of reading which he would not have exchanged, he says, for the treasures of India. Thanks to her, learned inquiries formed part of the sports of his youth: 'the Dynasties of Assyria and Egypt were my top and cricket-ball.' Other passages omitted by Sheffield heighten one's sense of Gibbon's insecurity, and make a striking contrast with the calm assurance of so much of the text. Memoir C, for example, is particularly explicit about the anxieties that oppressed him in that least satisfactory portion of his life, the years between his return from his tour of the continent and the death of his father in 1770. He was weighed down by fears that he might be left in old age without the fruits either of industry or inheritance, and if his father had not died somewhat prematurely, he would himself necessarily have been condemned to a 'hopeless life of obscurity and indigence'. Gibbon was uneasily aware of a life far less edifying than the one he was in fact able to relate, and the awareness brings his narrative closer to the more explicitly sombre elements in the autobiographies of Methodists and evangelicals.

There is another kind of autobiography which is more defensive than thankful, where the reader is conscious of critics and detractors in the background, echoing uneasiness and insecurity in the author himself. The *Memoirs* of the playwright Richard Cumberland, first published in 1806, perhaps belong in this contentious category. He is obviously conscious of the genial example of Colley Cibber's *Apology* (1739), but Cumberland's acute sensitivity to criticism, cruelly satirized by Sheridan in the character of Sir Fretful Plagiary, creates a work whose temper is quite different from Cibber's. Cibber is amused at the audacity of his own repeated attempts to suggest parallels between the stage and state affairs. Cumberland takes himself more seriously. He recalls the stressful course of his quest for academic honours as an undergraduate at Cambridge, and savours again the triumph of a public disputation where he detected his adversary's fallacy, and 'completely traced him through all the windings of his labyrinth'. Cumberland's self-esteem is strengthened when he thinks of what he might have done if he had followed the example of his ancestors and remained in his college. Instead he entered the service of Lord Halifax, and became his confidential private secretary: a career that seemed to give more scope to his ambition, but for which he had too little worldly wisdom.

> As sure as ever my history brings me to the mention of that fatal step . . . so sure am I to feel at my heart a pang, that wounds me with regret and self-reproach for having yielded to a delusion at the inexperienced age of nineteen, since which I have seen more than half a century go by, every day of which has only served to strengthen more and more the full conviction of my error.

The *Memoirs* hint at the tantalizing possibility of a Reverend Doctor Cumberland, or of a Sir Richard Cumberland, possessor of a large estate and politically influential.

The book is chiefly remembered for its theatrical anecdotes and some lively portraits, including notably amiable ones of Bubb Dodington and Dr. Johnson. The assessment of Dodington is a masterpiece of its kind. Readers of Dodington's political diary would hardly be prepared for Cumberland's account of his easy good humour, and the turn for buffoonery which found expression in readings of *Jonathan Wild* and comic scenes from Shakespeare. They might be less surprised by his taste for magnificence and display in dress and in his place of residence. Dodington's social talents, his outrageous magnificence, his mercenary manœuvring, all cohere in Cumberland's portrait because he relates them (no doubt unconsciously) to an ungainly vigour of personality. He appreciates a similar quality in Johnson. Wherever he talked, says Cumberland, there must always have been 'that splash of strong bold thought about him'.

One other autobiography deserves a place in any survey of the genre in this period: the *Memoirs* of William Hickey.[1] Like Cumberland's *Memoirs*, they were written at the beginning of the nineteenth century, but look back to a much earlier period. Hickey has a lively career to record, ranging from the life of a dissipated young man in London to that of a lawyer in Calcutta, together with the incidents of several hazardous voyages to the East and West Indies. Hickey himself was a man whom it is easy to dismiss as a nonentity. He is the ever indefatigable good fellow, delighting to be one of the crowd, constantly craving the reassurance of good fellowship. He recalls his youthful escapades uncritically, still taking pleasure in his prowess with the bottle, or at punting, or at cricket. He was a compulsive record-breaker, deeply gratified by such exploits as rowing 130 miles on the Thames in the extraordinary time of thirteen hours, or travelling from London to Portsmouth and back (with a pretty woman) in less than twenty hours, or sailing from China to England in just over four months. His need for admiration led him into uncontrollable expense, which he financed chiefly by embezzlement, using money that passed through his hands as an employee of his father's. Writing in old age, he is bewildered by his own former lack of self-mastery. The Calcutta attorney contrived to reconcile the roles of convivial fellow and man of business: in his youth the effort of reconciliation was far beyond his powers. His bewilder-

---

[1] William Hickey, 1749–1830, was a law clerk in his father's office, but his misconduct compelled him to go abroad. He became an attorney in Calcutta, and eventually held the post of clerk to the Chief Justice. He returned to England in 1808, and settled in Beaconsfield.

ment fails to prompt any sustained reflection on how the delinquent scapegrace became a successful lawyer, and to that extent Hickey is an inadequate autobiographer. In compensation, his buoyantly equable temper enables him to enjoy his own narrative of stress and storm—domestic and meteorological—and the half-acknowledged undercurrent of uneasiness serves to heighten the dramatic power of the writing. He tells a story like that of the unpleasant trip to Portsmouth with the ill-tempered Henry Mordaunt (March 1781) with a keen appreciation of Mordaunt's rage, a complacent approval of his own good temper, and an anxious awareness that Mordaunt might well have done himself or Hickey an injury. The story reaches one of its climaxes when Mordaunt, despite the remonstrances of Hickey and the landlord, insists on leaving Portsmouth in the middle of the night and over snow-bound roads. He departs with a flourish, and Hickey goes to bed.

I had not been more than ten minutes in bed when the door of my room was opened with a great bang, and in marched Mordaunt, damning and cursing all fortified towns. Enquiring what was the matter, he replied, 'The damned gate is shut and I can't get out.' To which I answered, 'It is a lucky circumstance for you; so now for God's sake go quietly to bed, and after breakfast we will set off together.'

But Hickey, although capable of giving prudent advice, was all too often indisposed to heed it himself: an indisposition that forms a considerable part of his charm.

Memoirs, autobiographies, anecdotes: all must be considered when attempting an assessment of what eighteenth-century readers expected from 'a Life'. A comprehensive view of biography would also have to take into account that encyclopedic antiquarianism which, partly inspired by Bayle's achievement in his great *Historical and Critical Dictionary*, produced several monumental works in this period. It has been justly said of Thomas Birch, who wrote over six hundred original biographies for the *General Dictionary* (1734–41), that no individual has ever contributed more to the materials of British biography than he did. William Oldys, who wrote much of the *Biographia Britannica* (1747–66), was a man of comparable energy. Gibbon gave up his project for writing a life of Sir

Walter Raleigh after looking at Oldys's biography of him, realizing that he could have nothing of substance to add. Oldys had read everything that was relevant, and had arranged his ample collections perspicuously. Not that Gibbon liked the book. It was 'tediously minute, and composed in a dull and affected style'. There was too much servile panegyric and flat apology. Oldys himself seems to have been a little daunted by his subject, and agreed that it was like 'attempting a landscape from a high hill'; the sheer multiplicity and extent of the prospects tended to distract the mind. Birch, too, in his account of Raleigh, admits to feelings of inadequacy. A life like this deserved the tribute of a Nepos or a Plutarch. Birch wished that Raleigh's merits could have been composed with the style and genius of the ancients, 'joined to that accuracy which distinguishes the moderns'. Eighteenth-century biography can best be understood in terms of this quest to unite modern accuracy with ancient genius.

To be sure, the quest was commonly unsuccessful. Birch himself is known to the general reader, if known at all, only for having prompted a lively remark of Johnson's: 'Tom Birch is as brisk as a bee in conversation; but no sooner does he take a pen in his hand than it becomes a torpedo to him, and benumbs all his faculties.' The *Biographia Britannica* hardly lived up to the hope so flamboyantly expressed in its preface that readers would be excited to emulate the virtues described in each life, regarding the work as 'a BRITISH TEMPLE OF HONOUR, sacred to the piety, learning, valour, publick-spirit, loyalty, and every other glorious virtue of our ancestors'. And yet the generalized classicism of this sentence, recalling the majestic busts and symbolic frontispieces so characteristic of the period, is more than an empty aspiration. It registers the assumption, with which Plutarch was particularly associated, that biography was essentially concerned with *illustrious* men. Equally the illustrious men had to be inspected with a stringent impartiality—stringent but magnanimous. Plutarch's eighteenth-century translators, John and William Langhorne, admired his 'peculiarly just and delicate' views on the matter of a biographer's impartiality, but even they seem to have felt that his justice was a little too delicate when it came to a man like Marcus Crassus, whom they thought contemptible. Certainly Crassus does not seem contemptible while one is under the spell of Plutarch's narrative. His doomed expedition against the Parthians is invested with a measure of dignity and even grandeur. Nevertheless all the evidence upon which the Langhornes base their judgement is present in the text. It was in this Plutarchian spirit that Johnson elevated the lamentable story of Richard Savage above the sordid atmosphere of Grub Street, while Goldsmith showed how adroitly he could profit from his own abridgement of Plutarch by composing a *Life of Richard Nash* (1762). 'Beau Nash', Master of the Ceremonies at Bath in the first half of the eighteenth century, resembled that 'monarch of *Cappadocia*, whom *Cicero* somewhere calls, *the little king of a little people*'. Nash, ruling a fashionable resort, has some of the qualities of a founding legislator. The regulations he established at Bath may seem frivolous, but, says Goldsmith,

were we to give laws to a nursery, we should make them childish laws; his statutes, tho' stupid, were addressed to fine gentlemen and ladies, and were probably received with sympathetic approbation. It is certain, they were in general religiously observed by his subjects, and executed by him with impartiality, neither rank nor fortune shielded the refractory from his resentment.

Goldsmith does not develop the parallel between presiding beau and eminent legislator with any rigorous consistency. He writes an elegant and facetious miscellany, with Nash as its focus. But the shadow of a more heroic world is never wholly absent, so that the 'torrent of insipidity' that made up so much of Nash's conversation can be seen as a great man's foible, just as his skill in raising money for charity becomes an expression of his politic genius.

Goldsmith's facetiousness is essential to the strength of the *Life of Nash*. If one wishes to compare it with a biography of graver pretensions, David Mallet's *Life of Francis Bacon* (1740) may be recommended. Although he is undistinguished as a poet and as a writer for the stage, Mallet's literary experience at least developed his ability to create a satisfying formal structure. Bacon's career is set firmly in the context of the politics of his time. Mallet produces a vivid sketch of the factions and scandals of the court of Elizabeth and James I. Everywhere one senses the hazards through which Bacon had to pick his way, and although he remains a reticent and even a remote figure, the reticence is artistically appropriate. When Mallet comes to

Bacon's part in the investigation of James's disgraced favourite Somerset, he uses some of Bacon's own correspondence to enlarge on the king's mysterious alarm over what Somerset might disclose at his trial, thus alluring the reader into scandalous conjectures about James's secret life. But conjectures they remain, heightening the impression that Bacon was a subordinate agent in matters whose bearings he did not fully understand himself. Here and elsewhere, Bacon's acceptance of the role assigned him is intelligible if not always excusable. He is unpleasantly compromised, though in a way that does not touch his lustre as a philosopher. Mallet makes an absolute separation between the aspiring courtier and the illustrious author. If, he says, we are surprised by the 'happy imagination' of Bacon's system, 'our surprize redoubles upon us when we reflect, that he invented and methodized this system, perfected so much, and sketched out so much more of it, amidst the drudgery of business and the civil tumults of a court'. One may question the abrupt contrast thus set up, but the effect is undeniably picturesque, like a calm landscape opening up behind a scene of turbulence.

In scale, Mallet's *Life of Bacon* is still close to that of the Plutarchian biography. Various influences, however, combined to encourage the writing of biographies more ambitious in scope. If truth is complex, it cannot be told concisely. As Gibbon's friend Maty observed, in his *Memoirs* of Lord Chesterfield (1777), 'it is from the number and variety of private memoirs, and the collision of opposite testimonies, that the judicious reader is able to strike out light, and find his way through that darkness and confusion, in which he is at first involved'. One biography where fullness of this kind is attempted is the *History of the Life of Marcus Tullius Cicero* (1741), by Conyers Middleton. In its way it is a literary landmark as conspicuous as Richardson's *Pamela*. Cicero's works form an authentic body of materials as ample as the documents imagined by contemporary novelists to facilitate their explorations of morality and the passions. His speeches and letters compose a story with turns of plot and ebbs and flows of feeling which, if not as various and elaborate as the fictions contrived by Richardson or Prévost, may have seemed almost as affecting. It is instructive, in this context, to read Colley Cibber's *The Character and Conduct of Cicero Considered* (1747). It is a commentary on Middleton's book, written with a vehemence which is occasionally extravagant, underlining the sublimity of the political events of Cicero's Rome:

Caesar sole Master of the World, envied! adored! assassinated! even on the Throne of Roman Glory! While *Cicero*, with a Patriot *Pleasure, saw him perish in the Capitol*!

The story that Middleton had to tell was not only sublime, but also central to the concerns and anxieties that preoccupied a generation constantly comparing itself with classical antiquity, feeling itself to be a free people whose heritage was threatened by factious and corrupt politicians. What Cicero's contemporaries had suffered, Middleton's readers could imagine themselves or their children suffering. His letters, says Middleton,

breathe the last words of expiring liberty; a great part of them having been written in the very crisis of its ruin, to rouse up all the virtue that was left in the honest and the brave, to the defence of their country.   (Section XII)

The situation is peculiarly dramatic, the more so because of Cicero's eminence as orator, moralist, and philosopher. His literary fame, says Middleton, tends to obscure his significance as a political figure: when the effort is made to realize the extent of his literary and political achievements, he can be recognized for what he is—a 'sublime specimen of perfection'. Colley Cibber may be invoked again to define the underlying intention of this species of biography. It is to Middleton, he said, that we owe an idea of Cicero 'so conspicuously intire'.

Here every common Apprehension, that had before met with only the detached Pieces, the broken Limbs, and scatter'd Remains of him, will see them now collected, all in due order replac'd, and form'd into one complete and perfect Statue of him.

This is a particularly appropriate description of the effect achieved by the long and comprehensive assessment of Cicero's work with which the *Life* ends. Middleton's intentions in the main narrative were perhaps less statuesque. Cicero wrote letters of unguarded frankness which enable the reader to enter into every shift and uncertainty of political manœuvring. To Atticus in particular he 'opened the rise and progress of each thought'. By immersing us in Cicero's writings, Middleton claims to show us a fine political intelligence in action. It must be conceded, though, that he adheres too exclusively to his

Ciceronian texts to achieve quite this end. There is not enough of Maty's 'collision of opposite testimonies' to generate the necessary detachment. What he does bring out well are the various states of Cicero's own mind, showing how political pressures caused him to swerve from pure consistency, while still leaving us with an overwhelmingly favourable impression of the hero. Thus, induced by Pompey to abandon his well-grounded hostility to Gabinius, and actually defend him in court, Cicero vindicates his own conduct by comparing himself to a prudent sailor faced with bad weather, or by claiming that while his quarrels were mortal, his friendships were immortal. But this 'flourishing style' did not express his genuine feeling. To his brother at this time he bewails the fact that he is reduced to mere drudgery in the courts, 'and neither what I love nor what I hate left free to me' (Section VI). The effect is to make Cicero seem a noble victim rather than an ignoble opportunist.

Charges of plagiarism brought against the *Life of Cicero* by Dr. Parr and others have damaged the book's reputation, to some extent justly. It is evident that Middleton relied heavily on a compilation made by the early seventeenth-century scholar William Bellenden: *De tribus luminibus Romanorum* (1633). In this work Bellenden arranges large extracts from Cicero's writings to illustrate Roman history, and does so in the form of annals, exceedingly convenient for a biographer who thus has much of his material ready sorted. Middleton was gravely at fault in not acknowledging his indebtedness, for without Bellenden there might have been less cause to admire the completeness and perfection of what Cibber called his 'Statue'. Even so, there is more to such a biography than well-sorted material. How little the elegance of the *Life of Cicero* should be taken for granted appears if one compares it with another celebrated biography of the period, John Jortin's *Life of Erasmus* (1758–60). Jortin's dependence (duly acknowledged) on material in the fifth and sixth volumes of Jean Le Clerc's *Bibliothèque choisie* (1705) is similar to Middleton's on Bellenden, but the work is disconnected and shapeless, nor is Jortin able to draw the various threads together in the splendidly assured way that Middleton does in the final part of his *Life of Cicero*.

Middleton established the kind of biography which displays its subject in a variety of perspectives and in many lights. It was a method followed with a modest success by Thomas

Davies in his *Life of Garrick* (1780). The most famous example, eclipsing all rivals, proved to be *The Life of Samuel Johnson, LL.D.* (1791), by James Boswell.[1]

Boswell leads us to suppose that it was in 1772 that he first set himself seriously to the task of making collections for a future Life of Johnson. Later he records that Johnson mentioned to him many circumstances, which he wrote down when he went home; and in the late summer of 1773, when they were in Aberdeen together, on their Scottish tour, 'I asked him', he writes, 'several particulars of his life from his early years, which he readily told me; and I wrote them down before him ... I shall collect authentick materials for THE LIFE OF SAMUEL JOHNSON, LL.D.; and, if I survive him, I shall be one who will most faithfully do honour to his memory.' He continues, in terms which show that he already knew what feature would principally distinguish his work, 'I have now a vast treasure of his conversation, at different times, since the year ... when I first obtained his acquaintance; and, by assiduous inquiry, I can make up for not knowing him sooner.'

He had no experience at that time of writing a life; but even when, as a young man of twenty-two, he first met Johnson on 16 May 1763, he had already written enough to show that he was developing a theory of biography corresponding in some respects with Johnson's own. Thus he was already keeping a diary of such amplitude as to serve for more than a mere record of daily activities. It was to be a means of discovering himself to himself, of judging with tolerable certainty what manner of man he was: a useful exercise for a young man who at that period of his life was accustomed to try out several characters, as though they were so many suits of clothes, to see which fitted him best. For this purpose the diary needed to be ample in scope; and this scope was also required for a subordinate purpose in Boswell's mind, that of laying up a store of entertainment for future years. Johnson, for his part, frequently expressed a preference for autobiography; and we may

[1] James Boswell, 1740–95, was educated at Edinburgh High School and University, and pursued legal studies in Glasgow and Utrecht. He travelled southwards from Holland through Europe, meeting Voltaire and Rousseau. He visited Corsica to meet the island's leader, Pasquale Paoli, of whose cause he became a publicist. He first met Johnson in 1763, but was not admitted to 'the Club' until 1773. He practised as an advocate in both Edinburgh and London.

say that though these purposes of Boswell's do not necessarily lead to autobiography, they are certainly not inconsistent with it. They would enable the future autobiographer to distance himself, to catch, as it were, a view of himself, or an interpretation of himself that could be presented as an independent work. Even though Boswell never came to share Johnson's preference for autobiography—or at any rate to express such a preference—it is not in the least difficult to see how such a preference could have developed. Some Boswellians would go so far as to maintain that in his diaries Boswell has written his own life, and that the skill he has shown in them make that his major work. He was indeed to publish an autobiography, but it was impersonal and brief, extending to no more than sixteen octavo pages.

An autobiography, Johnson thought, is most likely to tell the truth without concealment or modification, and the truth so told will help others to live a better life. The first point is discussed by Boswell in the second paragraph of his *London Journal*. He records there a conversation held with his friend Erskine about the dangers of too open a diary-record for fear that the manuscript should fall into the hands of his enemies. Erskine attempts to reassure him: 'I fancy you will not set down your robberies on the highway, or the murders that you commit. As to other things there can be no harm.' 'I laughed heartily at my friend's observation,' Boswell comments, 'which was so far true.' He then continues, in terms that do not sound encouraging: 'I shall be upon my guard to mention nothing that can do harm. Truth shall ever be observed, and those things (if there should be any such) that require the gloss of falsehood shall be passed by in silence.' But reticence was not a habit to which Boswell was ever much accustomed. Occasional instances of it in his diary are all the more striking, notably his refusal to reveal what was said in that famous altercation between his father and Johnson. In the event he was to find nothing that required the gloss of falsehood; and the harmless gaiety of nations has been increased thereby. So far from glossing or passing by in silence, he tells us, or seems to tell us, everything. It would take an eighteenth-century philosopher to decide whether the rest of us will accordingly live better lives, but Boswell himself, by reflecting on what he had written, was led at least to resolve upon measures for his own improvement.

A diarist of this kind will certainly be led into detail, a matter to which Johnson attached great importance in biography, provided that significant detail was chosen. From his earliest journals Boswell showed his appreciation of this. Five months before his first meeting with Johnson, he records an incident that may serve in illustration:

> I was passing by Whitehall when a little boy came and told a girl who sold gingerbread nuts that he had just given her sixpence instead of a farthing. She denied this. Upon which the poor boy cried and lamented most bitterly. I thought myself bound to interfere in the affair. The boy affirmed the charge with an open keen look of conscious innocence, while the young jade denied it with the colour of countenance and bitterness of expression that betrayed guilt. But what could be done? There was no proof. At last I put it to this test: 'Will you say, Devil take you, if you got his sixpence?' This imprecation the little gipsy roared out twice most fervently. Therefore she got off. No jury in the world could have brought her in guilty. There was now a good many people assembled about us. The boy was in very great distress. I asked him if the sixpence was his own. He said it was his mother's. I conceived the misery of his situation when he got home. 'There, Sir,' said I, 'is the sixpence to you. Go home and be easy.' (21 December 1762)

This charming miniature is admirable alike for its development, its depiction of the protagonists, and its balance of direct speech and reported speech. It promises well for the reporter of later and more notable scenes. But the important point is Boswell's reason for reporting it at all. The incident signifies something. He continues in comment:

> I then walked on much satisfied with myself. Such a little incident as this might be laughed at as trifling. But I cannot help thinking it amusing, and valuing it as a specimen of my own tenderness of disposition and willingness to relieve my fellow-creatures.

Here then is a writer with a discriminating care for the particular, in the illustration of character: here already is the man who was later to defend the narration of a trifling detail by declaring that it was 'a small characteristick trait in the Flemish picture which I give of my friend, and in which, therefore, I mark the most minute particulars'.

Perhaps there was only one opinion held firmly by Boswell that was unlikely to lead him to a theory of biography identical with Johnson's, and that was Boswell's cult of the eminent. Lion-hunting was his passion. Within a year or two of his meeting Johnson, he was to ingratiate himself with Voltaire, Rousseau, and Paoli; he was already acquainted with Hume and Robertson; and he barely restrained a powerful impulse to throw himself at the feet of Frederick the Great in a desperate effort to get to know him. Such a man might well meditate writing the lives of those distinguished for their talents—thus he was later to contemplate biographies of General Oglethorpe and Sir Joshua Reynolds—but he was unlikely to fulfil a desire often expressed by Johnson of seeing biographies written of those whose days were spent in an even tenor of life, outside the walks of fame.

These features of Boswell's mind and of his consuming interest are to be discerned in the pages of his diary from a very early date. They need never have developed into a theory of biography; but assuredly they, and other features equally manifest in the diary, determined the quality of his biographical writing once he was set upon that path. One of the most striking of these other features is his power of memory. Once the diaries were brought to light and began to be compared with the relevant passage in the *Life of Johnson*, it was no longer possible to hold what may be called the stenographical heresy. We now know better than to suppose that Boswell relied on a well-filled pocket-book always at hand for jotting down Johnson's table talk. Indeed, we ought never to have believed it, for in the pages of the *Life* Boswell frequently refers to these journals in which he has recorded so much of Johnson's conversation. He himself reflects upon the effort of memory, the mere 'stretch of mind', required to carry his harvest home to his journal. He speaks of acquiring a facility in recollecting, and then the process of recording, in substantiation of which one may note that several entries in the journal were made after an interval of as much as five or six days. Some rough notes assisted the formal entry, but the recollection of *ipsissima verba* depended upon what Boswell called 'a mind impregnated with the Johnsonian aether'. It is clear that, in speaking of Boswell's memory, we are speaking of no ordinary endowment, but of a highly specialized and cultivated faculty.

But before ever the memory came into play, other important faculties had been in use. It should not be forgotten that

Boswell was trained as a lawyer. Like Walter Scott in the next generation, he does not seem to have cared greatly for success at the bar; but like Scott, he put his legal training to the service of letters. What he did was to exercise his forensic powers upon Johnson; and he was quite well aware of what he was doing. 'I started the subject of emigration', he writes; or 'this morning I introduced the subject of the origin of evil'; and the consciousness of his procedure is indicated by the following passage:

> I also may be allowed to claim some merit in leading the conversation: I do not mean leading, as in an orchestra, by playing the first fiddle; but leading as one does in examining a witness,—starting topicks, and making him pursue them. He appears to me like a great mill, into which a subject is thrown to be ground.

As he justly reflects, 'it requires, indeed, fertile minds to furnish materials for this mill'; and for this purpose, the volatile quality of Boswell's mind was compensation for what it lacked in depth. Johnson's responsiveness to Boswell was recognized at the time. It was not everyone who could draw him. Boswell's friend Sir William Forbes admitted that he derived more benefit from the record of Johnson's discussions than he would have been able to draw from his private conversation, 'for', he explained, 'I suppose there is not a man in the world to whom he discloses his sentiments so freely as to yourself'.

We are thus confronted with a phenomenon, exceptional in biography, of a subject whose range of mind was extended by his biographer. We must not fall into the danger of overlooking the numerous topics that Johnson touches upon in the *Rambler* and other writings for the press. Nevertheless it may be claimed that he might never have formulated opinions on many subjects if it had not been for Boswell, and even that he might not have been aware of those opinions himself unless Boswell had pressed him to formulate them.

Most biographers are content, and are necessarily content, to accept their subject as he was. A limit is set to the extent of their material by the death of their subject. It remains well-defined territory to explore, a completed page to interpret. Boswell too had eventually to work within those limitations. But before he was forced to accept them, he radically enlarged his biographer's role by moulding his subject while alive, by making of him something other than he would have been if he had never met his biographer. Boswell did not merely elicit Johnson's opinions; he manhandled him, leading him into peculiar and even dangerous situations in order to see how he would behave. Boswell's father, Lord Auchinleck, resented his son's association with 'an auld dominie', a mere brute, Ursa Major; and Boswell's wife fully agreed: 'I have seen many a bear led by a man,' she is reported to have said, 'but I never before saw a man led by a bear.' But in fact the chain was around the other neck. Boswell had his bear under reasonably good control, and could make him dance too. He was a first-rate impresario. His most remarkable triumph was to draw Johnson to Scotland, remarkable partly because Johnson professed to hate the Scots and had never before been so far from home, partly because the expedition to the Western Islands in a stormy October was highly perilous, but principally because it gave rise to two classical accounts of the tour, Boswell's own and that earlier one by Johnson himself. Perhaps only *Rasselas* amongst his writings gives us a better impression of the sheer activity of Johnson's mind than the *Journey to the Western Islands of Scotland* (described above in Chapter II). There we see him responding to the historical monuments of Scotland and to Scottish scenery (though some critics of the book have unaccountably been found to deny this), but paying most attention, as was right, to life and manners. And without his biographer this book would never have been written.

One aspect of this manhandling of Johnson becomes evident to any reader of the *Tour to the Hebrides*, and that is Boswell's relish at seeing Johnson in an unusual or even in a ludicrous situation. It is a remarkable set of vignettes he offers us, and all depend on our appreciation of the contrast with Johnson's normal London habitat. Thus we see Johnson with a young lady on his knee—Boswell's epigraph for that vignette was 'The Rambler toying with a Highland beauty'—Johnson on a wild Shetland pony, led by a straw halter, through teeming rain; Johnson strutting about a room with a broadsword and target; Johnson wearing a large blue bonnet which Boswell had placed on top of his bushy grey wig, 'the image', says Boswell, 'of a venerable *Senachi*' (man of talk, reciter of tales); Johnson springing into the sea on landing at Iona and wading vigorously to shore; and best of all, Johnson crossing in an open boat to Raasay, with the boatmen singing a Gaelic song, and he

sitting 'high on the stern, like a magnificent Triton'. 'I wish,
Sir, *the club* saw you in this attitude', Boswell remarks on one of
these occasions. Johnson, indeed, must have been aware of this
manhandling, aware of the part which Boswell had cast for
him to play, the part, as Miss Mary Lascelles has suggested, of
Falstaff to Boswell's Poins.

Besides the visit to Scotland, Boswell has also to his credit
several minor successes in the same kind. On 17 April 1778 he
was present when Johnson was accosted in the Strand by a
man who had last met him as a fellow student at Oxford forty-
nine years earlier. This encounter would not have extended
beyond an exchange of greetings if Boswell had not been ready
to seize the opportunity. 'Wishing to be present', he says, 'at
more of so singular a conversation as that between two fellow-
collegians, who had lived forty years in London without ever
having chanced to meet, I whispered to Mr. Edwards that Dr.
Johnson was going home, and that he had better accompany
him now. So Edwards walked along with us, I eagerly assisting
to keep up the conversation.' Thus we are the richer for a discussion which, besides enlightening us on many of Johnson's
habits, served to illustrate his essential kindliness of heart, and
incidentally provoked from Edwards that exquisite observation, worthy of Goldsmith: 'I have tried too in my time to be
a philosopher; but I don't know how, cheerfulness was always
breaking in.'

An occasion, more skilfully contrived and brilliantly re-
created, is the dinner party on 15 May 1776 at which Johnson
found himself sitting next to Wilkes, with whom he had formerly been engaged in violent political controversy. Boswell
writes in the highest spirits as he describes each tactical move
of preparation for the party, until the moment when, with
Johnson 'fairly seated in a hackney-coach' beside him, they
drive together to their host's apartments, Boswell exulting 'as
much as a fortune-hunter who has got an heiress into a post-
chaise with him to set out for Gretna Green'. Well might
Burke exclaim of the episode that 'there was nothing to equal it
in the whole history of the Corps Diplomatique'. It is in contrived episodes of this kind that the subject of biography is
created by the biographer.

Some excellent things were said on the occasion of that
dinner party; but if we suppose that Boswell was interested

merely in the table talk, we fail to appreciate the full range of his skill. He especially relishes the situation of these two old antagonists brought together and insensibly gaining upon each other's affections. To convey this he calls upon the powers which had incidentally made of him a first-class mimic, that is to say, a shrewdness of observation and a readiness of memory to recall the significant gesture or the mannerism of speech that gives life to the whole picture.

Mr. Wilkes was very assiduous in helping him to some fine veal. 'Pray give me leave, Sir:—It is better here—A little of the brown—Some fat, Sir—A little of the stuffing—Some gravy—Let me have the pleasure of giving you some butter—Allow me to recommend a squeeze of this orange;—or the lemon, perhaps, may have more zest.'—'Sir, Sir, I am obliged to you, Sir,' cried Johnson, bowing, and turning his head to him with a look for some time of 'surly virtue', but, in a short while, of complacency.

There was no memorandum whatsoever in his journal to prompt this passage of imaginative reconstruction. We must not suppose that art of this kind came readily or unconsciously to him. Several times in his diary he confesses to the dissatisfaction he felt with his record. Sometimes it is the detail of a conversation that is at fault: 'It is impossible', he declares, 'to put down an exact transcript of conversation with all its little particulars. It is impossible to clap the mind upon paper as one does an engraved plate, and to leave the full impression.' Just as he doubts the possibility of recording the full impression of a conversation, so he doubts whether one can 'preserve in words the peculiar features of mind which distinguish individuals as certainly as the features of different countenances'. But the very doubt reveals the conscious effort and direction of his art, the struggle to discover what he once called those 'many little touches which give life to objects, [as] by how small a speck does a Painter give life to an eye'. And how he relishes the success of others in this same art!

I mentioned Dr. Douglas at the Bishop of Chester's saying, 'ONE other glass, if your Lordship pleases', with his sly glistening look. Said Sir Joshua, 'Squinting, with one eye fixed on the bottle, one on the Bishop.' Said I to Miss Hamilton, 'Sir Joshua compleats a saying. He is like a Jeweller. You bring him a diamond. He cuts it, and makes it much more brilliant. Look at it now.'

But Boswell himself knew all about cutting diamonds. Thus we find in his diary this simple record:

> Boswell. 'Sir Joshua good humoured?' Johnson. 'No.' Boswell. 'Burke?' Johnson. 'No. I look on myself as good humoured.' Beauclerk acid, Langton muddy.

After polish, this reads in the *Life* as follows:

> I mentioned four of our friends, none of whom he would allow to be good humoured. One was *acid*, another was *muddy*, and to the others he had objections which have escaped me. Then, shaking his head and stretching himself at ease in the coach, and smiling with much complacency, he turned to me and said, 'I look upon *myself* as a good humoured fellow.'   (18 April 1775)

It is interesting to note that for one word, the final word *fellow*, Boswell had no warrant in his record, though the word may nevertheless have been stamped upon his memory. Yet it is this very word that he chooses for comment in what follows: 'The epithet *fellow*, applied to the great Lexicographer, the stately Moralist, the masterly Critick, as if he had been *Sam* Johnson, a mere pleasant companion, was highly diverting; and this light notion of himself struck me with wonder.' We may observe the same sense for the illuminating gesture— whether the gesture is recollected or invented is immaterial— in the episode of Johnson's unseemly merriment over Langton's making his will. Boswell had the scene safely recorded in his journal; but in transferring it to the text of his biography, he made several .alterations, expanding his record of Johnson's words, for example, in the interest of the reader's immediate comprehension, and censoring Langton's name with his own part in the episode because Langton and he were friends. The record had begun, understandably enough, without a preliminary explanation. Johnson is discovered speaking as follows:

> Langton the TESTATOR. I dare say he thinks he has done a thing, a mighty thing. He won't stay till he gets home. He'll read his will to the Landlord of the first Inn on the road. Chambers, you helped him. Did he put in 'being of sound understanding?'

In the *Life* the reader's introduction to the scene is suitably prepared:

> I have known him at times exceedingly diverted at what seemed to others a very small sport. He now laughed immoderately, without

any reason that we could perceive, at our friend's making his will; called him the *testator*, and added, 'I dare say, he thinks he has done a mighty thing. He won't stay till he gets home to his seat in the country, to produce this wonderful deed: he'll call up the landlord of the first inn on the road; and, after a suitable preface upon mortality and the uncertainty of life, will tell him that he should not delay making his will; and here, Sir, will he say, is my will, which I have just made, with the assistance of one of the ablest lawyers in the kingdom; and he will read it to him (laughing all the time). He believes he has made this will; but he did not make it: you, Chambers, made it for him. I trust you have had more conscience than to make him say, 'being of sound understanding'.

To expand so extensively upon his record of Johnson's words was daring, though the result was no doubt justifiable to a mind 'impregnated with the Johnsonian aether'. But what makes the whole scene live is the concluding description. The record reads as follows:

Mr. Johnson could not stop his merriment. I cherished it crying, 'Langton the Testator, Langton Longshanks.' Johnson, 'I wonder to whom he'll leave his legs? Ha, ha, ha'—making all Fleetstreet resound at the silent midnight hour.

The dramatist and the censor in Boswell then get to work, and the passage is reshaped, imaginatively, as follows:

Johnson could not stop his merriment, but continued it all the way till we got without the Temple-gate. He then burst into such a fit of laughter, that he appeared to be almost in a convulsion; and, in order to support himself, laid hold of one of the posts at the side of the foot pavement, and sent forth peals so loud, that in the silence of the night his voice seemed to resound from Temple-bar to Fleet-ditch.   (9 May 1773)

These are some of the most memorable scenes from the *Life*, and perhaps it is worth observing that Boswell had accustomed himself from his youth to reconstructing such scenes in his diary. It is not therefore surprising that he should at one time have considered writing the life of Johnson 'in scenes', and that he did indeed detach one such series of scenes, the *Tour to the Hebrides*, for separate treatment, and as a specimen of the method to be employed as a whole.

It might be said with a great measure of truth that the materials Boswell found in his journal conditioned the form which his biography took. But he cannot have reached a decision on form without a good deal of deliberation. The most valuable part of his material, what was indeed unique, existed in the shape of scenes from Johnson's life; but that did not account for all of it. He had received anecdotes and *obiter dicta* from friends and correspondents; he had assembled a large collection of Johnson's letters; he had also the results of the inquiries he had conducted while Johnson was alive and after his death into Johnson's early life and into the canon of his writings.

Other people's anecdotes and *obiter dicta* could be assimilated to his own collection. The only problem they offered was the problem of authenticity. Some were immediately plausible, others not. One correspondent is thanked for his 'genuine highflavoured *Johnsoniana*'; another is dismissed with the endorsement 'Nonsense about Dr. Johnson'. When in doubt he was scrupulous in checking evidence. Anna Seward contributed a Lichfield story about what Johnson's mother said to him when he told her he intended to marry Mrs. Porter. The story appeared so strange that he thought it needed corroboration, and accordingly wrote to the Mrs. Cobb whom Miss Seward had mentioned as her source. Mrs. Cobb confirmed his misgivings, and the story was ignored.

His own researches had begun during Johnson's lifetime, and we may still admire the sense he possessed of what needed authenticating. Though we must regret that his account of the making of the *Dictionary* leaves something to be desired, we should be glad, to take one example, that he pressed Johnson for his own version of what happened when he was said to have felled Osborne the bookseller with a folio; and we may be grateful to him for obtaining from Johnson what Johnson believed to be authoritative texts of the famous letters to Chesterfield and Macpherson. Today we need not trust Johnson's memory of what he wrote to Macpherson, since Macpherson kept the original letter and it still survives; but Boswell was not to guess that Macpherson would act so improbably as to treasure such a monumental rebuke. These are but a few of many instances of Boswell's resolute search for truth, biographical, bibliographical, and textual. They were too important to be omitted, but they could not readily be accommodated into a Life of Johnson written in scenes.

Most writers are interested in the way in which their fellow writers solve their problems. Boswell had not far to look for guidance in biography, both theoretical and practical. Johnson himself had provided both, and Boswell was to begin his book with a sentence acknowledging his presumption in writing 'the Life of him who excelled all mankind in writing the lives of others'. But the guidance of Johnson's practice could only be of limited value, since apart from the *Life of Savage* and the *Life of Collins*, none is based upon intimate acquaintance; and even in those lives Johnson was not possessed of such vast and valuable material as Boswell had gathered. But in theoretical guidance Johnson was superb. How reassuring for Boswell to read in the sixtieth number of *The Rambler*:

> The business of the biographer is often to pass slightly over those performances and incidents, which produce vulgar greatness, to lead the thoughts into domestick privacies, and display the minute details of daily life, where exterior appendages are cast aside, and men excel each other only by prudence and by virtue;

or again,

> the incidents which give excellence to biography are of a volatile and evanescent kind, such as soon escape the memory;

'but not such a memory as mine', we can imagine Boswell reflecting.

In these and many other passages in Johnson's writings Boswell could find all the justification he needed; and if he wanted more precise guidance in method, he found it ready to hand, not so much in Middleton's *Cicero* as in a recent biography to which he refers at the beginning of the *Life of Johnson*: Mason's *Life of Gray*, published in 1775. Mason also had been well supplied with excellent material in the shape of a large quantity of the poet's letters. Gray had had so much to say about himself in his letters that Mason had been prompted to experiment:

> I might [he said] have written [his] life in the common form, perhaps with more reputation to myself; but, surely, not with equal information to the reader; for whose sake I have never related a single circumstance of Mr. Gray's life in my own words, when I could employ his for the purpose.

Boswell might have hit upon the same plan without the example of Mason before him, since he had already drawn upon his diary in 1768, seven years earlier, to display the character of General Paoli, the Corsican Liberator: it might be said that in the *Life of Johnson* he was applying a system tested upon Paoli to an even more congenial subject. Mason served to give him confidence in a method which would avoid the imperfections of his two principal competitors in Johnsonian biography, the sprawling life-and-times treatment of Sir John Hawkins and the table-talk treatment—the mere collection of 'ana'—of Mrs. Piozzi. Mason had succeeded with Gray; he should do even better with such very much better materials.

But even with the materials collected, a plan laid out for guidance, and the implicit approval of Johnson's theory to encourage and support him, there was still much work to be done, not merely the sheer hard work of writing. We can observe and admire the skill with which he decants anecdotes from later years, where his wealth of material lay, to adorn the relatively barren pages of the early life; and as the Yale edition of Boswell's papers progresses, we become better able to understand what the labour of organizing his material entailed. But what it is perhaps desirable to emphasize, in conclusion, is that though Boswell's methods and materials suggest a largely empirical approach to his task, he was guided in it throughout by a well-formed conception of his subject. Scene is added to scene and *obiter dictum* to *obiter dictum*, but we may rest assured that he always carried in his mind a living figure of the man, just as he always tested the record of Johnson's words by his recollection of the living voice and its characteristic rhythms. Thus he attributes to Johnson the following observation: 'You are right, Sir. We may be excused for not caring much about other people's children, for there are many who care very little about their own children' (10 April 1776). At this point in the printer's proof, the printer's reader wished to delete the second *children*, but Boswell prevented him with this comment in the margin of the proof, 'The *repetition* is the Johnsonian mode.' But over and above this vigilance in ensuring that the detail fitted into the total structure, there is evidence that all is related to a detailed analysis of Johnson's character. The *Life of Johnson* is concluded with a character sketch, following a well-established custom among biographers. Boswell was not convinced that such a sketch was needed, and indeed the sketch he wrote is not strictly a deduction from what was gone before. It was adapted from an earlier sketch that appears at the beginning of the *Tour to the Hebrides*. It had needed very little adjustment in the interval; and there is the best evidence one could wish to have for the control, the master plan, to which all this heterogeneous material is subordinated.

IX

ESSAYS, LETTERS, DIALOGUES
AND SPEECHES

ALTHOUGH the essay often appears to be one of the most characteristic and easily recognized forms of eighteenth-century literary expression, the term seems to have carried a wider and less precise significance than it does today. We now use it primarily to denote a student's written exercise upon a given theme; but we allow its applicability to short dissertations in journals intended for the edification of the learned, and we might even be prepared to extend its use to include those articles by which a newspaper columnist seeks to instruct or entertain his readers. The term carries some sense of the ephemeral, except perhaps to the learned writer who might prefer to see his essays bearing a relation to his major work such as Wordsworth had in mind when he likened his short poems to the 'little cells, oratories, and sepulchral recesses' in a Gothic church. This scholarly conception of the essay resembles Bacon's; not that the scholar aspires to write aphoristically, but that his essay, like Bacon's, represents at once knowledge in growth and a stage on his road (or just off it) where some measure of formulation is possible.

A sense of the tentative and imperfect, carried over from the French *essayer* (to test, or try, or attempt) is apparent in the early use of the term. Thus Boyle could refer to 'the green and immature essays' of those who wrote before him. Even writers who had laboured to perfect their discourse could refer to their work with a gesture of depreciation as no more than an essay. Thus Dryden interpreted the title chosen by Roscommon for his principal poem, *An Essay on Translated Verse*:

> Yet modestly he does his Work survey,
> And calls a finish'd Poem an *Essay*;

and a contemporary admirer could have proffered the same compliment upon the *Essay on Criticism* and the *Essay on Man*. Very much more striking is Locke's diffidence in naming his great work *An Essay Concerning Humane Understanding*, even though he describes it in his Epistle Dedicatory as a 'treatise'. Nothing less like an essay in the Baconian or in the modern manner, either in method or in extent, could well be imagined; yet Locke seems to have felt that an apology was needed for entering upon so formidable an inquiry, for in his 'Epistle to the Reader', he explains how

some hasty and undigested thoughts on a subject I had never before considered . . . gave the first entrance into this discourse; which having been thus begun by chance, was continued by intreaty; written by incoherent parcels; and after long intervals of neglect, resumed again, as my humour or occasions permitted.

Though an essay, in one sense of the word, had come to be regarded by 1700 as equivalent to a treatise, some of Locke's modesty continued to overtake the learned as they penned titles and wrote prefaces to their inquiries into subjects as far-reaching as the history of civil society and the nature of truth— 'my attempts in behalf of truth' wrote Beattie of his notorious attack upon Hume—or on a topic so paradoxical as the dramatic character of Sir John Falstaff.

Another common meaning of the term derived eventually from its use by Montaigne. In this sense the essay is well described by Ephraim Chambers in his *Cyclopaedia* (1728) as

a peculiar Kind of Composition; whose Character is to be free, easy, and natural; not tied to strict Order, or Method, nor work'd up and finish'd, like a formal System.

The Matter of an *Essay* is supposed to consist principally of sudden, occasional Reflexions, which are to be wrote much at the Rate, and in the Manner a Man thinks; sometimes leaving the Subject, and then returning again, as the Thoughts happen to arise in the Mind.

This is the notion of an essay that Dryden entertained when he used the term in the title of his *Essay of Dramatic Poesy* to explain and excuse the 'rude and indigested manner' of its writing; and doubtless he would have approved its use to describe his *Preface to the Fables*, for 'the nature of a preface is rambling, never wholly out of the way, nor in it. This I have learned from the practice of honest Montaigne.'

It was in this sense that the term gradually came to be applied to those short periodical articles which all eighteenth-century readers were agreed in finding at their best in the *Spectator*.[1] Steele used the term in the dedication of the first volume of the *Tatler*, and he shows his contentment with it at the end of *Spectator*, No. 442. But Addison seems to have been more hesitant. What he wrote were 'papers', or 'speculations', or 'lucubrations'. In No. 476, he attempts to distinguish between two types, some 'written with regularity and method', and others

that run out into the wildness of those compositions which go by the name of *Essays*.

In the first he has the whole scheme of the discourse in his mind before setting pen to paper; in the second,

it is sufficient that I have several thoughts on a subject, without troubling my self to range them in such order, that they may seem to grow out of one another, and be disposed under the proper heads.

In developing this distinction Addison showed his preference for the methodical discourse. He had found that thoughts arise in the process of organizing which are not apparent at the outset, and are more intelligible, and appear to better effect, when they 'follow one another in a regular series'. His claim has a touch of paradox in it: that an essay is the better for not being an essay, for not being, to quote the definition in Johnson's *Dictionary*, 'a loose sally of the mind; an irregular indigested piece'.

There was little danger of the method in Addison's best pieces being overlooked in an age when, as Blair told his Edinburgh students, the *Spectator* had become a standard book, one which as Johnson remarked in 1776 had 'for more than half a century supplied the English nation . . . with principles of speculation, and rules of practice'. The notion of what was meant by an essay changed accordingly. The time was to come again when, in the hands of Lamb, it would become once more 'a loose sally of the mind'; but for the moment it would aspire to method even when the topic was frivolous, yet would still convey a sense of what is modest and unassuming. The appeal to the superficial reader is obvious; yet, as Vicesimus Knox[2] remarked in his *Essays Moral and Literary* (1778):

[1] See Vol. VII, pp. 73–84, 102–20.
[2] Vicesimus Knox, 1752–1821, was master of Tonbridge School, and compiler of *Elegant Extracts* (c. 1781).

many subjects of morality and learning have been concisely discussed in a few pages, with a depth, solidity, and originality of thought, rarely exceeded in any formal dissertation.

An episode in Hume's career provides an excellent illustration of this. His *Treatise of Human Nature* had been misunderstood and misrepresented on its appearance in 1739; it had failed to make the expected impact on a learned audience, and Hume had begun recasting his doctrine in a form that might appeal to one more popular. He seems to have felt with Shaftesbury that 'an easier Method of treating these Subjects will make 'em more agreeable and familiar', and that the classical way of bringing philosophy out of closets and libraries, to dwell in clubs and assemblies, at tea-tables and in coffee-houses, was to begin a periodical in imitation of the *Spectator*. Second thoughts prevailed, but the *Essays Moral and Political*, published in two volumes in 1741 and 1742, show the clearest signs of Addison's influence, particularly in some of the eight essays withdrawn from subsequent editions. In an essay 'Of Essay Writing' Hume rejoices to observe signs of reconciliation between the 'learned World' and the 'conversible World', and believes that this may be carried further by 'such *Essays* as these with which I endeavour to entertain the Public'. He has therefore constituted himself

a Kind of Resident or Ambassador from the Dominions of Learning to those of Conversation; and shall think it my constant Duty to promote a good Correspondence betwixt these two States, which have so great a Dependence on each other.

It should be noticed, too, that as ambassador he addresses himself, as the *Spectator* had done, 'with particular Respect, to the Fair Sex, who are the Sovereigns of the Empire of Conversation', in pursuit of whom he wrote the essay 'Of Love and Marriage', which concludes with one of those allegories so tedious to us but calculated to appeal to the taste of the time.

This is second-rate Hume, but it will pass muster as an imitation of Addison; it serves to show with what deliberation Hume had pitched his voice in address. Even when these and the like trivialities had been weeded out, the *Essays* still met Knox's requirement that an essay should satisfy the subject, without fatiguing the attention, or overburdening the memory'.

They are distributed under three headings, moral, political, and literary. Though it was the political essays that appealed most, it is in the moral essays that Hume's skill in recasting can best be judged. 'The Sceptic', the last of four essays written 'to deliver the sentiments of sects that naturally form themselves in the world, and entertain different ideas of human life and happiness', contains the essence of that doctrine which contemporaries were to find so disturbing.

If we can depend upon any principle, which we learn from philosophy, this, I think, may be considered as certain and undoubted, that there is nothing, in itself, valuable or despicable, desirable or hateful, beautiful or deformed; but that these attributes arise from the particular constitution and fabric of human sentiment and affection. What seems the most delicious food to one animal, appears loathsome to another: What affects the feeling of one with delight, produces uneasiness in another. This is confessedly the case with regard to all the bodily senses: But, if we examine the matter more accurately, we shall find that the same observation holds even where the mind concurs with the body, and mingles its sentiment with the exterior appetite.

Desire this passionate lover to give you a character of his mistress: He will tell you, that he is at a loss for words to describe her charms, and will ask you very seriously, if ever you were acquainted with a goddess or an angel? If you answer that you never were: He will then say, that it is impossible for you to form a conception of such divine beauties as those which his charmer possesses; so complete a shape; such well-proportioned features; so engaging an air; such sweetness of disposition; such gaiety of humour. You can infer nothing, however, from all this discourse, but that the poor man is in love; and that the general appetite between the sexes, which nature has infused into all animals, is in him determined to a particular object by some qualities which give him pleasure. The same divine creature, not only to a different animal, but also to a different man, appears a mere mortal being, and is beheld with the utmost indifference . . .

We may push the same observation farther, and may conclude that, even when the mind operates alone, and feeling the sentiment of blame or approbation, pronounces one object deformed and odious, another beautiful and amiable; I say that, even in this case, those qualities are not really in the objects, but belong entirely to the sentiment of that mind which blames or praises.

There is an energy in this writing that Addison could never have commanded; yet when we compare it with the relentless argument of the *Treatise*, we are bound to recognize in Hume's *Essays* the force of the principle enunciated by Shaftesbury and Addison that the 'easier' method of treatment makes the subject more agreeable and familiar.

The success of Hume's volumes might have been used to argue that periodical publication of essays was not essential. The *Spectator* lost none of its initial prestige when the papers were collected; on the contrary, the fifty or more editions reprinted during the century served as a standard by which other essays were judged, and maintained the orthodoxy of the form for good or ill. The *Rambler* drew more respect when reprinted in volume form; and several other periodicals seem to have been undertaken with an eye to their future appearance in collected editions. In the last number of the *Adventurer* (9 March 1754), Hawkesworth relates that when the work was first planned, it was determined that whatever its success 'it should not be continued as a paper, till it became unwieldy as a book':

he knew, that the pieces of which it would consist, might be multiplied till they were thought too numerous to collect, and too costly to purchase . . . It was soon agreed, that four volumes, when they should be printed in a pocket size, would circulate better than more . . . the work, therefore, was limited to four volumes, and four volumes are now completed.

Similar considerations seem to have operated upon Edward Moore in bringing the *World*, and upon Colman and Thornton in bringing the *Connoisseur* to conclusion. Yet apart from Hume's *Essays*, it was not until 1764 that a collection first appeared in volume form without a preliminary periodical issue; this was William King's the *Dreamer*.[1] After that date, such publication was not infrequent, the best-known examples being Knox's *Essays* already mentioned and the *Observer* (1785) by Richard Cumberland. Essays continued to appear in single-sheet issues, however, throughout the century.

As the years went by, the competition which the single-sheet essay met from other types of journal grew fiercer than it had been in the days of Steele and Addison. Thus each issue of

---

[1] William King, 1685-1763, was principal of St. Mary Hall, Oxford, and a notable Jacobite, though he declared his loyalty to George III.

Fielding's *Covent Garden Journal* (1752) contained news and advertisements besides Fielding's essay; and newspapers began to carry weekly essays, of which Johnson's *Idler*, contributed to the *Universal Chronicle*, and Goldsmith's *Chinese Letters*, contributed to the *Public Ledger* (1760–1), are the most famous. In these circumstances, the principal purpose of publication in single sheets was to act, it has been suggested, as a publicity campaign for publication in volume form; as Colman and Thornton (who seem to have been the first to use the now customary term 'periodical essay') remarked in the last number of the *Connoisseur*:

> Periodical writers, who retail their sense or nonsense to the world sheet by sheet, acquire a sort of familiarity and intimacy with the public, peculiar to themselves. Had these four volumes, which have swelled by degrees to their present bulk, burst forth at once, Mr. Town must have introduced himself to the acquaintance of the public with the awkward air and distance of a stranger: but he now flatters himself, that they will look upon him as an old companion, whose conversation they are pleased with.

But it should also be borne in mind that the projector of a successful serial stood a chance of attracting a team of valued contributors who between them could vary the lucubrations of a single writer. Moore began the *World* unaided in January 1753; the following month he received the first of several contributions from Horace Walpole, Chesterfield joined them in May, and Richard Owen Cambridge, another frequent contributor, before the end of the year. Thus Moore himself, who had written thirteen essays during the first six months of his paper's existence, felt called upon to write no more than six during its last half year; in June 1753 he could already declare that his task had become 'almost a sinecure'. Colman and Thornton needed to rely more upon themselves to keep the *Connoisseur* going, but their experience is not dissimilar in kind; while Henry Mackenzie, who acknowledged in the last number of the *Mirror* (27 May 1780) a great many unsolicited contributions, revealed still another reason for periodical publication. He and some friends had formed a club to discuss manners, taste, and literature; they read papers to each other on these topics, and agreed to publish them in periodical form, the fact of publication acting as a further stimulus to production.

With physical format and the ever-present example of the *Spectator* combining to enforce uniformity of manner, it is surprising that any of these papers should have managed to assert its own individuality. But though the influence of the *Spectator* is inescapable, each is recognizably distinct. Hawkesworth[1] procured this through his taste for fiction. We have already noticed the prevalence of narrative in the *Rambler*; in the *Adventurer* half the papers consist either wholly or partly of stories and of Hawkesworth's seventy contributions as many as fifty-four are narrative, whose relation sometimes covers three successive numbers. The stories have a moral design upon the reader: this was to be expected in a writer who had enlisted Johnson in partnership, and was of course entirely in accord with *Spectatorial* principles.

But it is just here that the *World* is different. Moore indeed published early in its career a story in two parts of a wife's reclaiming an errant husband; but though he frequently had recourse to the imaginary letter in which a correspondent tells the misfortunes of his life, he never thereafter indulged his gift for writing short stories. It seems that he was influenced by the views of his eminent contributors, for Chesterfield, Whitehead, and Cambridge all wrote papers exclaiming against the extravagance and indecency of modern fiction. Nor did the *World* practise the philosophical, religious, and literary essays of the *Spectator* or the moral essays of the *Rambler*. Its aim instead was, as Cambridge remarked in No. 71, 'that gentle and good-humoured ridicule which rather indicates the wishes of paternal tenderness, than the dictates of magisterial authority':

I am not Adam Fitz-Adam [the projector's pseudonym] while the ladies wear such enormous hoops, such short petticoats, and such vast patches near the left eye; or while gentlemen ruin their fortunes and constitutions by play, or deform the face of nature by the fopperies of art.

'Mr. Town' formulates the *Connoisseur*'s policy with less grace, but to the same effect, when he declares at the beginning of his third volume (No. 71) that he has

---

[1] John Hawkesworth, 1715?–73, edited Swift's *Works* (1754–5) with a biography of the author, and the official but much criticized account of the voyages of Captain Cook and others to the South Seas (1773).

purposely avoided the worn-out practice of retailing scraps of
morality, and affecting to dogmatize on the common duties of life,
[wherein] indeed, the *Spectator* is inimitable. . . . I have therefore
contented myself with exposing vice and folly by painting mankind
in their natural colours, without assuming the rigid air of a preacher,
or the moroseness of a philosopher.

Their principal concern was with manners; and the pleasure
that they can still convey is the view they afford us upon the
modes and the accessories of living two hundred years ago. We
may see the city merchant and his wife on a Saturday packing
up for a week-end in their country 'box' near Kennington) *Connoisseur*, No. 33), and may hear complaints about traffic on the
roads on Sundays in summer (*World*, No. 21), and about the
noisiness of modern life even in a country village (*World*, No.
142). The convenience of the new turn-pikes and the success
of inoculation bring the country squire's lady more readily to
town (*World*, No. 127), where she is in danger of emptying her
husband's purse by acquiring a taste for the Chinese:

chairs, tables, chimney-pieces, frames for looking-glasses, and even
our most vulgar utensils are all reduced to this new fangled standard:
and without-doors so universally has it spread, that every gate to
a cow yard is in T's and Z's, and every hovel for the cows has bells
hanging at the corners.   (*World*, No. 12)

We are led to believe that

every gardener, that used to pride himself in an early cucumber, can
now raise a pine-apple; and one need not despair of seeing them sold
at six-a-penny in Covent-garden, and become the common treat of
tailors and hackney-coachmen.   (*World*, No. 152)

The introduction of turtle at city tables is noticed, and the
ritual of preparing and eating it is mocked (*World*, No. 123).
We learn that snuff-taking has become so tyrannous an ad-
diction that if Mr. Town drinks tea with a certain lady,

I generally perceive what escapes from her fingers swimming at the
top of my cup. . . . I never dine at a particular friend's house, but I
am sure to have as much rappee [coarse snuff] as pepper with my
turnips; nor can I drink my table-beer *out of the same mug with him*,
for fear of coughing from his snuff.   (*Connoisseur*, No. 32)

The detail we have italicized here, almost inadvertently mentioned, attracts nearly as much attention today as the behaviour
which first called for Mr. Town's censure.

The places of public resort offer the most fruitful opportunities to the social commentator. Mr. Town tells us that ladies are accompanied by their lap-dogs to church, or to the theatre, where he once

saw a tragedy monarch disturbed in his last moments, as he lay expiring on the carpet, by a discerning critic of King Charles's black breed, who jumped out of the stage-box, and fastened upon the hero's periwig, brought it off in his mouth, and lodged it in his lady's lap.   (*Connoisseur*, No. 89)

He notices the pleasure gardens being redecorated for the summer season, the artificial ruins being repaired at Vauxhall while the cascade is made to spout 'with several additional streams of block-tin'; and by recalling the experiences of an honest citizen there, he is enabled to warn his readers of the exorbitant charges they may expect (No. 68).

It is inevitable that two critics of the manners of the mid-fifties should cover some of the same ground. Both the *World* and the *Connoisseur* comment on the fashion for exposing more and more of the female body; both attack betting and gaming, and laugh at the absurd claims of quack doctors; and both are more seriously alarmed at the spread of duelling and the rise in the rate of suicide. Yet though their policies are so similar, there is little difficulty in distinguishing them in detail and in tone. Adam Fitz-Adam keeps returning to the absurdities of *chinoiserie* both in the house and in the garden, and doubtless he called upon his powers of invention when suitable illustrations eluded his memory. But Mr. Town has a better eye for an interior, whether it be of a theatre, a coffee-house, or a tavern; and it is to him we owe the pleasing and bibliographically interesting detail of his contemplating 'my numbers in the public coffee-houses strung upon a file, and swelling gradually into a little volume' (No. 29). The *Connoisseur*, too, is fundamentally more serious in tone. With one or two rare exceptions, such as the meditation on the Lisbon earthquake (No. 162), the *World* turns all to jest; thus when departing so far from the recognized policy of avoiding literary criticism as to write two papers of intended compliment on the imminent publication of Johnson's *Dictionary* (Nos. 100, 101), Chesterfield must needs give a gloss of triviality to the serious topic of lexicographical authority, and play one more variation, admittedly witty, on the traditional theme of a dictionary's being principally useful to women who, as women, cannot of course spell; and the *World* was a more appropriate repository than the *Connoisseur* for some sniggering obscenities of Horace Walpole (Nos. 28, 160). The *Connoisseur* interprets the censure of manners sufficiently broadly to permit 'exposing the absurd tenets of our modern free-thinkers and enthusiasts', and its readers are given no opportunity of underestimating the importance of suppressing the 'frolics' of those gangs of irresponsible adolescents from which we too suffer today (No. 54). In short, there is a warmth of admonition about the observations of the *Connoisseur* that gives a tone by which to distinguish it from the mere witticism of the *World*. It was the nicety of judgement in determining its tone that Goldsmith commended in his notice of the *Connoisseur* in the *Monthly Review* (1757, xvi. 443):

> He is the first writer since Bickerstaff, who has been perfectly satirical yet perfectly good-natured; and who never, for the sake of declamation, represents simple folly as absolutely criminal.

Goldsmith, too, and his somewhat grudging admirer Boswell, offer still further examples of individuality within a firmly prescribed tradition. Each conducted for several months what today we should call a column in a newspaper. Taking advantage of the contemporary rage for Chinese, or rather pseudo-Chinese, decoration, Goldsmith imagined a visit to London by a Chinese traveller whose experiences are retailed by letter to a friend at home. These letters appeared in the *Public Ledger* in 1760–1. Many of his readers would have recalled how successfully the device had been used by Montesquieu in his *Lettres persanes* (1721), and few would have forgotten the famous *Spectator* (No. 50), in which Addison translated for his readers' benefit some observations on London society supposed to have been written by one of the four Iroquois chieftains who had visited Queen Anne in 1710. Still more recently Lord Lyttelton had produced an imitation of Montesquieu (1735), and Horace Walpole had invented a philosophical Chinaman Xo Ho, to meditate upon Admiral Byng's execution and attempt an explanation of the episode for his friend Lien Chi at Peking (1757). The well-worn device provided Goldsmith with a courteous, tolerant, guileless, rather gullible sage as commentator on the contemporary scene. By means of Lien Chi Altangi

he could make a fresh approach to such favourite topics of
the periodical essayist as the London theatre (21) and quack
doctors (24), and could describe the incredulity and boredom
of English listeners when told what far eastern taste in literature and decoration is really like (14, 33). The device is less
valuable in presenting descriptions of clubs, a topic as old as
the *Tatler*; and a character sketch, such as that admirable
account of the Man in Black (27) who so diligently attempts
to disguise his charities, neither needs nor indeed obtains any
colour from an observer for his display. But though Goldsmith
sometimes conveniently forgets that his observer is Chinese and
a sage, the disguise even at its thinnest permits him to indulge
a taste for generalization upon national characteristics that
his own wanderings had doubtless encouraged. This taste is
apparent in *The Traveller*; in *The Citizen of the World* (for that is
the title which Goldsmith chose for his 'Chinese' Letters when
he collected them) it offers him topics which normally lay
outside the range of the periodical essayist, such as the Englishman's parrot-cries about his liberty (4, 50), his humanity
towards prisoners of war (23), his respect for law contrasted
with the Frenchman's (38), the influence of climate upon
temper (91), the evil tendency of increasing penal legislation
(80), and the supposed civility of the French analysed (78).
The wisdom manifest in these essays is not beyond Johnson's
reach. He too had condemned the severity of penal legislation
(*Rambler*, No. 114) and had noticed the growing humanitarianism of the age (*Idler*, No. 4). But it is wisdom not readily found
elsewhere in the periodical essay; and it might be claimed that
the stance of foreign observer that Goldsmith adopted and the
frequent drollery of his illustrations serve to attract the attention of those for whom the gravity of the *Rambler* has a lesser
appeal.

Boswell's policy was quite different. In the essays which for
nearly six years he contributed to the *London Magazine* under
the title of *The Hypochondriack* (1777–83) he took no more
notice of the meteors of fashion than the *Rambler* had done; nor
did he resort to such habitual modes of the periodical essayist
as the character, the club, the short story, the vision, the
allegory, the imaginary letter. In his first paper he regards
himself as belonging to the tradition initiated by 'the constella-
tion of wits in Queen Anne's reign'; but he belongs to it solely

by virtue of offering 'papers of instruction and entertainment'. He discusses literary questions from time to time; but his custom is to reflect upon the common issues of social life: marriage, education, disputation, flattery, swearing, these are some of his topics. It was a convention of each periodical that the work was directed by a projector—Isaac Bickerstaff, the 'Spectator', Adam Fitz-Adam, Mr. Town—whose imaginary personality was adopted by each contributor. So Boswell's essays were written by The Hypochondriack, and perhaps his readers once more accepted the convention without questioning it. But those who know much about Boswell from other sources soon recognize that, far from inventing a personality, he trusted simply to the secret of a pseudonym to conceal his own. He is the Hypochondriack in a sense in which neither Steele nor Addison was ever the Spectator; he wrote from a fund of experience in living without attempting to raise it to the pitch of generalization, as Johnson had done in the *Rambler*. He does not indulge his idiosyncrasies, as Lamb was to do; but he recognizes his weaknesses, acknowledges them, and even attempts to explore them:

> I do fairly acknowledge that I love Drinking; that I have a constitutional inclination to indulge in fermented liquors, and that if it were not for the restraints of reason and religion I am afraid I should be as constant a votary of Bacchus as any man. To be sensible of this is a continual cause of fear, the uneasiness of which greatly counterbalances both the pleasure of occasional gratification and the pride of frequent successful resistance, and therefore it is certainly a misfortune to have such a constitution.   (No. 30)

> His distempered fancy darts sudden livid glaring views athwart time and space. He cannot fix his attention upon any one thing, but has transient ideas of a thousand things; as one sees objects in the short intervals when the wind blows aside flame and smoke.
>   (No. 39, on hypochondria)

Though the prose has no resemblance to De Quincey's, it is possible nevertheless to discern a closer kinship between the Opium Eater and the Hypochondriack than either could claim with the Spectator.

But the *Spectator*'s influence was not yet exhausted. Mackenzie and his colleagues knew that, when writing their papers for the *Mirror* (1779–80) and its sequel the *Lounger* (1785–7), they must be judged by the standards of Steele and Addison. They knew that 'a periodical paper, though it may sometimes lift its voice against a neglect of the greater moralities, yet has for its peculiar province the correction and reform of any breach of the lesser' (*Lounger*, No. 2). Their range both of topic and of mode more closely approximates to the *Spectator*'s than any periodical discussed in this chapter, for apart from satirizing fashions and reflecting upon the common issues of social life in character sketches, imaginary letters, and short stories, they allow more space than their predecessors had afforded to essays in literary criticism, of which Mackenzie's review of Burns (*Lounger*, No. 97) is the best known, but his numerous papers on the novel are the most distinguished. Yet there is no doubt about the individuality of these periodicals, an individuality that is owing in great part to accidents of place and time. Mackenzie felt that a paper conducted in Edinburgh began under a disadvantage, since local characters and temporary follies were neither various nor important enough for their purpose, and that even in the very place-names of London there was a classic privilege that did not extend to the Canongate and Blackfriars Wynd. Yet it is in delineating Scottish types that part of their success lies. The *Mirror* and the *Lounger* were also periodicals for their times; and contributors were fully aware of recent changes in the climate of opinion. The man of feeling seemed to offer, especially to Mackenzie, a rich area for exploration, both in representation of behaviour and in analysis. The most successful of Mackenzie's short stories, the story of La Roche (*Mirror*, Nos. 42–4) and the story of Father Nicholas (*Lounger*, Nos. 82–4), are of this kind; the one is told to show how religion 'as a feeling, not a system . . . [may appeal] to the sentiments of the heart, not to the disquisitions of the head', and the other illustrates 'the power of corrupt society and false shame over the natural feelings of virtue'. It can be argued, therefore, that though each story may claim a measure of independence, it falls within the declared policy of the *Mirror*:

to discover the springs and motives of action which are sometimes hid from the actors themselves . . . to mark those approaches to error into which unsuspecting innocence and integrity are too apt to be led; and, in general, to investigate those passions and affections of the mind which have the chief influence on the happiness of individuals or of society.

This care for the integration of the parts is no less apparent in the numerous papers chronicling the affairs of the Homespun family, and in a single paper such as the *Mirror*, No. 27, where the silent expression of sorrow is conveyed by describing the behaviour of Mr. Wentworth after the early death of his beloved wife, or the *Lounger*, No. 77, prompted by the character of Mr. Woodfort whose eye kindles at the recital of a benevolent or a generous deed, 'yet, in real life . . . Woodfort's feeling and generosity unaccountably forsake him'.

The theme serves to illustrate the adaptability of the *Spectator* tradition to different times and circumstances. Periodical essays continued to appear in the periods covered by the next two volumes of this History (see, for example, volume X, p. 271), though Hazlitt in the fifth of his *Lectures on the English Comic Writers* (1819; on the Periodical Essayists) gives the impression of discussing a form which by that time was defunct. Yet in 1839 when Dickens came to write the preface to *Nicholas Nickleby*, he chose to call himself a 'periodical essayist', and took leave of his readers by quoting from the last number of the *Lounger*; and when later that year he outlined to Forster the project of his next work, *Master Humphrey's Clock*, a magazine that was eventually to contain only *The Old Curiosity Shop* and *Barnaby Rudge*, he said that he proposed

to start, as *The Spectator* does, with some pleasant fiction relative to the origin of the publication; to introduce a little club or knot of characters and to carry through their personal histories and proceedings through the work; to introduce fresh characters constantly . . . to write amusing essays on the various foibles of the day as they arise; to take advantage of all passing events; and to vary the form of the papers by throwing them into sketches, essays, tales, adventures, letters from imaginary correspondents and so forth, so as to diversify the contents as much as possible.

It is some testimony to the opportunities which the form still seemed to offer that not only should Dickens discuss such a project but that Forster, his adviser, and Chapman and Hall, his publishers, should receive it without demur.

The eighteenth-century 'letter' displays so much variety in manner, structure, and theme as scarcely to constitute a distinct literary kind, yet no short prose composition is more character-

istic of the period. Many, or perhaps most, of them are not
genuine letters, in the sense that they were not transmitted
through the post from one correspondent to another. Such are
the imaginary letters contributed to periodical essays; such too
are Melmoth's *Letters of Sir Thomas Fitzosborne on several subjects*
(1742–9), Bolingbroke's *Letters on the Spirit of Patriotism* (1749),
Hurd's *Letters on Chivalry and Romance* (1762), Watson's *An
Apology for Christianity, in a series of letters, addressed to Edward
Gibbon, Esq.* (1776), and many another book where the term
is used in the title to convey a tone of familiarity in treatment, perhaps even some limitation of numbers in the assumed
audience.

Melmoth's *Letters* and Hurd's *Letters* are essentially essays
on the topics they choose to treat, but they are essays in a more
familiar dress than those discussed in the previous section.
Melmoth[1] makes pretence of writing to a named individual
whose identity one can attempt to believe in; Hurd does not
trouble to offer even this concession; but each uses forms of
personal address that are foreign even to so familiar a form as
the essay of the time: 'if you require a comparison, I can tell
you where it is to be made, with much ease, and to great
advantage . . . . This circumstance, you know, has given offence
to the austerer and more mechanical critics. . . . Judge of the
Fairy Queen by the classic models, and you are shocked with its
disorder: consider it with an eye to its *Gothic* original, and you
find it regular. . . . Would you desire a better reason for his
choice? Yes, you will say, a poet's method is not that of his
subject. I grant you . . .' These passages are all taken from
Hurd's *Letters*, an ingenious work in which he sought to justify
the chivalric romance by an extension of the classical doctrine
of decorum. The imaginary letter provided him with a form
suitable for discussing a paradoxical topic where the rhetoric
of persuasion was needed, a form which allowed the maximum
familiarity of address consistent with elegance.

The letter is also especially well adapted to controversy,
whether it be the courteous kind practised by Richard Watson,[2]

---

[1] William Melmoth, 1710–99, was educated at Emmanuel College, Cam-
bridge, and spent a long period of scholarly seclusion near Shrewsbury, translating
Cicero and Pliny. Later he became a commissioner of bankrupts, and settled in
Bath.

[2] Richard Watson, 1737–1816, enjoyed one of the most remarkable careers of
his day. Beginning as a mathematician, he was appointed (1764) to the Chair of

whom Gibbon called 'the most candid of my adversaries', or the jets of venom which 'Junius' directed at the Duke of Grafton with such precision and elegance, or 'the lash of the merciless Porson'[1] in his *Letters to Mr. Archdeacon Travis, in answer to his defence of the three heavenly witnesses* (1790), 'the most acute and accurate piece of criticism', in Gibbon's view, 'which has appeared since the days of Bentley'. None of these writers forgets for a moment that he is ostensibly addressing himself to the private ear of his adversary ('I proceed to take notice of another difficulty in your fifteenth chapter'—Watson, p. 159; 'It is not that your indolence and your activity have been equally misapplied; but that the first uniform principle, or if I may so call it, the genius of your life, should have carried you through every possible change and contradiction of conduct, without the momentary imputation or colour of a virtue'— Junius, 30 May 1769; 'I should indeed have almost distrusted the evidence of my own senses, when I saw you commit above twenty gross and palpable errors in less than half a dozen pages, if I had not been acquainted with the source from which they flowed'—Porson, p. 171). Thus the impression of familiarity and briskness of discourse is maintained. But each is aware that he is overheard, that the private controversy is open to the public; and to that public he may appeal. Porson provides a lively example in a passage immediately preceding that already quoted. Leaving Travis, whom he has been addressing directly in these words, 'when you have read a little more concerning this subject than you have already, that is, when you have read at all, you will find, that Beza does actually mention four of these six examples', he turns aside to a wider audience:

There is one advantage in telling enormous rather than moderate falsehoods. Mankind are in general so lazy and credulous, that when once they are prejudiced in favour of any person's veracity, they will regard another as a calumniator who endeavours to convince

Chemistry at Cambridge, a subject of which he had never read a syllable. Though equally unqualified in divinity, he was appointed to the Regius Chair (1771), to several livings in the church, and eventually (1782) to the see of Llandaff. He went to live on the banks of Lake Windermere (1789), published his chemical lectures, occupied himself in political, economic, and religious questions, and visited his diocese once in three years.

[1] Richard Porson, 1759–1808, was a Fellow of Trinity College, Cambridge, 1782; Regius Professor of Greek, 1792; librarian of the London Institution, 1806. His principal scholarly work was on the Greek metres and the text of Euripides.

them that they have bestowed their approbation upon an unworthy object. They will argue, as I have already observed, from the enormity of an offence, and the easiness of detection, against the probability of its ever being committed.

But if I shall be fortunate enough to have one reader of learning and probity, I request him, I exhort him, to peruse this letter, and the other passages where I pawn my own word, with particular attention. He will then find that I have stated the facts simply as they are, and that however astonishing the instances of Mr. Travis's assurance may seem, I have spoken of them without distortion or exaggeration.

As for genuine letters, that is to say, letters written to correspondents as private communications, it was unusual for authors to decide on publication, except in such special circumstances as those of a traveller making use of his letters to reinforce a sense of authenticity. Johnson did not in fact publish the unusually long letters he wrote to Mrs. Thrale from Scotland; but he seems to have designed them, in part at least, as a record of his tour, and to have had recourse to them when writing the *Journey to the Western Islands*. Samuel Sharp,[1] whose *Letters from Italy, describing the Customs and Manners of that Country* (1766) were commended by Johnson, declared that the letters were indeed those actually dispatched; they 'were not originally intended for the press', but the friends who kept them 'have persuaded me to believe they may possibly amuse the World'. Accordingly he sent them to the printer 'a little altered and curtailed' and apologized to his readers for his superficiality, since 'had I foreseen this Publication, I might, with very little Trouble, have been circumstantial in many particulars'.

Lady Mary Wortley Montagu[2] proceeded in different fashion when she came to record her experiences in travelling to Constantinople and back with her husband, who had been appointed Ambassador to the Court of Turkey. For this purpose, according to Professor Halsband, she kept a journal, which

[1] Samuel Sharp, c. 1700–78, was one of the best surgeons of his day. It was after discontinuing practice that he paid the visit to Italy (1765) recorded in his *Letters*.

[2] Lady Mary Wortley Montagu, 1689–1762, was the daughter of the fifth Earl of Kingston. On their return from Constantinople (1718), the Wortley Montagus went to live in Covent Garden and Twickenham, where Lady Mary enhanced her reputation as a wit, a poet, and a political journalist. Growing estranged from her husband, she left England in 1739 and spent all but the last months of her life in Italy and France. See further, Vol. VII, pp. 353–6.

no longer exists: 'The journal served her as a literary storehouse from which she drew material for letters to her friends (only a few of these survive) and for a series of fifty-two letters, compiled within a few years after her return to England.' We cannot be certain how many of these letters are genuine, in the sense of being copies made by Lady Mary before dispatch of the originals. If we knew, we could define precisely what is fictitious in her project. But even assuming that all are later compilations—we may reasonably suspect those which she has dated inaccurately—we could commend her decision to produce a lasting record of her travels in a form capable of responding to variety of observation and experience. She makes a suitable choice of correspondent for what she has to convey. Thus her female friends will be interested in details of the dress of Turkish ladies, of what they eat, of the degree of freedom they enjoy, and of their whole domestic economy; it is possible, too, to detect that Lady Rich was felt to be a more appropriate recipient of what is frivolous than Lady Bristol to whom observations on Turkish women's way of life are addressed. The Abbé Conti, an Italian savant, receives letters on more solid topics, the country, architecture, and political and religious behaviour; while it is to Pope she writes when she detects the survival of Homeric manners:

> I can assure you that the princesses and great ladies pass their time at their looms, embroidering veils and robes, surrounded by their maids, which are always very numerous, in the same manner as we find Andromache and Helen described. . . . The snowy veil that Helen throws over her face, is still fashionable; and I never see (as I do very often), half a dozen old bashaws with their reverend beards, sitting basking in the sun, but I recollect good King Priam and his counsellors.

The Embassy letters were designed for posthumous publication. When they appeared in 1763, less than a year after Lady Mary's death, they enjoyed a success their freshness and clarity of description and witty observation undoubtedly deserved; they convey vividly the intrepidity of Lady Mary's character, her readiness to face unusual experiences, and her power of sympathizing with the people whose countries she visited. Those who are made uneasy by her consciousness of performing in public may prefer the letters written to her daughter, when she regarded herself as that 'uncommon kind of creature . . . an old woman without superstition, peevishness, or censoriousness', letters in which she is content to 'tattle on' about herself, and her acquaintances past and present, and the books she has been reading:

I have long thought myself useless to the world. I have seen one generation pass away; and it is gone; for I think there are very few of those left that flourished in my youth. You will perhaps call these melancholy reflections: they are not so. There is a quiet after the abandoning of pursuits, something like the rest that follows a laborious day. I tell you this for your comfort. It was formerly a terrifying view to me, that I should one day be an old woman. I now find that Nature has provided pleasures for every state. Those are only unhappy who will not be contented with what she gives, but strive to break through her laws, by affecting a perpetuity of youth, which appears to me as little desirable at present as the babies do to you, that were the delight of your infancy. I am at the end of my paper, which shortens the sermon.

Certainly these letters were not intended for the public eye, and in fact they were not published until the following century. But they were written with no less consciousness of a literary performance than the Embassy letters. In the interval she had changed her views about how letters should be written. She had read the letters of Madame de Sévigné in 1726, and allowed them her grudging admiration. She felt that she herself could do as well, or better; but Madame de Sévigné served at least as a standard by which an older tradition could be tested and found wanting:

Well-turned periods or smooth lines, are not the perfection either of prose or verse; they may serve to adorn, but can never stand in the place of good sense. Copiousness of words, however ranged, is always false eloquence, though it will ever impose on some sort of understandings. How many readers and admirers has Madame de Sévigné, who only gives us, in a lively manner, and fashionable phrases, mean sentiments, vulgar prejudices, and endless repetitions? Sometimes the tittle-tattle of a fine lady, sometimes that of an old nurse, always tittle-tattle; yet so well gilt over by airy expressions, and a flowing style, she will always please the same people to whom Lord Bolingbroke will shine as a first-rate author.

We know less than we should like to know about the composition of Gilbert White's[1] *Natural History of Selborne* (1789); but

[1] See further, Vol. IX, pp. 40–1.

it seems that White's procedure in preparing his private letters for publication bore some resemblance to Lady Mary's. He too kept a journal, a naturalist's journal or calendar invented by his friend Daines Barrington, and this with other personal records supplied him with material for the letters to Pennant, the zoologist, and Barrington, on which the *Natural History* was based. But it was in converting his records into letters that White's achievement lay. This was not simply a matter of shaping rough notes into acceptable prose, but involved meditation, inference, the erecting of scientific hypothesis, and generalization, in which White, though since surpassed by Darwin and others, was unparalleled amongst the naturalists of his day. For his was the day of the great systematizer, Linnaeus. White, on the other hand, was less interested in forms than in behaviour and the reasons for behaviour; he was indeed unduly contemptuous of systematics:

Faunists, as you observe, are too apt to acquiesce in bare descriptions, and a few synonyms: the reason is plain; because all that may be done at home in a man's study, but the investigation of the life and conversation of animals is a concern of much more trouble and difficulty, and is not to be attained but by the active and inquisitive, and by those that reside much in the country.

(Letter X, to Barrington)

His bent of mind is to inquire why, for example, of two Selborne owls, one should hoot in A flat and the other in B flat ('do these different notes proceed from different species, or only from various individuals?'); or why cuckoos do not hatch their own eggs. Can it be that there is some 'internal structure of their parts, which incapacitates them for incubation?' White proceeds to investigate by dissecting a cuckoo, and finds that the crop being placed 'just upon the bowels must, especially when full, be in a very uneasy situation during the business of incubation'. But he saw, quite rightly, that the conclusion needed testing, and for this purpose he chose the fern-owl, a bird known to sit on its eggs, which when dissected was found to resemble the cuckoo in the disposition of its intestines. The hypothesis must therefore be discarded, 'and we are still at a loss for the cause of that strange and singular peculiarity in the instance of the *cuculus canorus*'.

It is characteristic of White's mind that he was not content with observing that year after year eight pairs of swifts haunted the church at Selborne, 'and play and rendezvous round it'. He is led from this into speculations which were to occupy the mind of Malthus at the beginning of the next century and were to mature in the great Victorian hypotheses of Natural Selection and the Survival of the Fittest:

> Now as these eight pairs, allowance being made for accidents, breed yearly eight pairs more, what becomes annually of this increase; and what determines every spring which pairs shall visit us, and reoccupy their ancient haunts?
>
> Ever since I have attended to the subject of ornithology, I have always supposed that that sudden reverse of affection, that strange αντιστοργη, which immediately succeeds in the feathered kind to the most passionate fondness, is the occasion of an equal dispersion of birds over the face of the earth. Without this provision one favourite district would be crowded with inhabitants, while others would be destitute and forsaken. But the parent birds seem to maintain a jealous superiority, and to oblige the young to seek for new abodes; and the rivalry of the males, in many kinds, prevents their crowding the one on the other.   (Letter XXXIX, to Barrington)

White was encouraged by his two correspondents to publish, and presumably they returned him his letters for this purpose. Though private and personal, the letters could contain nothing to embarrass him when printed; but they needed some additions before they could qualify as a contribution towards writing local history, which as noted earlier (p. 217) is a characteristic aspect of late eighteenth-century civilization in this country. It seems likely that the first letters in the book, some nine or so, describing Selborne and the district round about, were written at this time and for this purpose. Possibly some others were added for the sake of completeness. White must have been aware that the nature of his correspondence with Pennant differed a little from the letters he wrote to Barrington. Pennant he addressed as an equal, confident that scraps of information sent to him could be profitably used and that Pennant would at once recognize what must be regarded as knowledge in growth. Barrington, however, was White's inferior in understanding and experience. This had its effect upon the form of the letters, those sent to Barrington being hardly distinguishable from familiar essays of instruction on stated topics. These seem to have lent themselves more readily to additions on still further topics within the same series. But in maintaining the letter form, whether the more precisely shaped letters to Barrington or the more haphazardly constructed letters to Pennant, many of which consist of answers to specific inquiries, White preserved a tone of modesty and deference at once appealing to a modern reader and well suited to a scientist cautiously assembling and generalizing from a lifetime's observations.

But most of the great collections of the century were posthumously gathered, and were not intended by their authors for publication. When Mrs. Eugenia Stanhope decided to publish the letters her dead husband had received from his father, the Earl of Chesterfield,[1] she was actuated in large part by her disappointment at the size of her legacy. She recognized that in these letters she possessed documents of unusual value that would be eagerly read by the public, not for any scandalous content, because that was negligible, nor for any light they might throw on the Earl's character—that was abundant indeed for those who cared to take notice; but it was incidental, and seems not to have entered into her calculations—but because they constituted a peculiar kind of courtesy book.

If Chesterfield himself had prepared these letters for the press—and there is no reason to suppose that he ever contemplated it, or ever saw them again when once they had left his hand—he must necessarily have prevented certain misconceptions about their nature. For nearly twenty years he had addressed these short lessons in conduct to his son. They were intended for the edification of a particular young man, whose disposition, merits, and shortcomings were well known to his father, and whose career had been determined. This accounts for many features of the letters which have often been misunderstood. Chesterfield keeps emphasizing the importance of the social graces, not because he believed that religious and moral principles were less necessary, but because his son was defective in the graces, and because no one who aimed at a diplomatic career could expect to get very far without them. Chesterfield writes:

> I never mention to you the two much greater points of Religion and Morality, because I cannot suspect you as to either of them . . .

[1] Philip Dormer Stanhope, fourth Earl of Chesterfield. 1694–1773, was ambassador to The Hague, 1728–32. Spoke against the Stage Licensing Bill, 1737. Lord Lieutenant of Ireland, 1745–6. Secretary of State, 1746–8. Proposed and carried the reformation of the calendar, 1751.

but remember, that manners must adorn knowledge, and smooth its way through the world. Like a great rough diamond, it may do very well in a closet by way of curiosity, and also for its intrinsic value; but it will never be worn, nor shine, if it is not polished. It is upon this article, I confess, that I suspect you the most, which makes me recur to it so often.   (1 July 1748)

The society of eighteenth-century courts where young Philip's destiny lay was glaringly public: women exerted great influence, hence the importance of learning how to conduct one's commerce with the sex; and since all eyes were turned upon the newcomer, a young man could never afford to forget that he was acting a part:

if he is attentive to his part, instead of staring negligently about; and if, upon the whole, he seems ambitious to please, they willingly pass over little awkwardnesses and inaccuracies, which they ascribe to a commendable modesty in a young and inexperienced actor.

(30 December 1748)

Let us entertain for a moment, if we can, the notion of Chesterfield preparing these letters for the press, or what is more easily imaginable, for a series of contributions to the *World*, in which the scope of an essay was similar to the scope of a letter. It seems reasonable to assume that he would have modified what was intended for the eye of an individual reader so as to suit a wider audience; that in doing so, he might well have acted like Gilbert White and written some letters on topics neglected in the private series, and that he might have felt the need of adapting the rhetoric of persuasion. Mrs. Stanhope noticed the deliberate repetitiveness of the advice, and rightly felt that she was not at liberty to curtail it; but Chesterfield himself in directing his mind to the general reader would certainly have made some cuts. Presumably he would have retained some passages like the following, in which a precept of behaviour is reinforced by the sketch of a character in action; for this is almost appropriate, bating some vulgarity of detail, to the manner of the *World*:

Awkwardness can proceed but from two causes; either from not having kept good company, or from not having attended to it. . . . When an awkward fellow first comes into a room, it is highly probable that his sword gets between his legs, and makes him stumble, at least. . . . At dinner, his awkwardness distinguishes itself particularly, as he has more to do; there he holds his knife, fork, and spoon differently from other people, eats with his knife, to the great danger of his mouth, picks his teeth with his fork, and puts his spoon, which has been in his throat twenty times, into the dishes again.

(25 July 1741)

But it seems all too probable that he would have thought he should expand his maxims, so suited in their crispness to a young man's digestion, into the more rounded and ironical manner to which readers of the *World* were accustomed. Such is the closeness of relationship between the essay and the letter, that these small distinctions of manner in dealing with identical topics can actually be observed in Chesterfield's work.

If people had no vices but their own, few would have so many as they have. For my own part, I would sooner wear other people's clothes than their vices; and they would sit upon me just as well.

(15 May 1749)

Even some people's vices are not their own, but affected and adopted (though at the same time unenjoyed) in hopes of shining in those fashionable societies, where the reputation of certain vices gives lustre. In these cases the execution is commonly as awkward, as the design is absurd; and the ridicule equals the guilt.

(*World*, No. 120)

The thought in both passages is the same; but no one, surely, could fail to distinguish the father writing to his son from Adam (Chesterfield) Fitz-Adam addressing the readers of the *World*.

The first collections of the letters of Gray and Cowper were posthumous also; they were published by their biographers in illustration and support of their narratives. The tasks of Mason and Hayley were similar. The subject of each biographer was a close though not an intimate friend, a man of distinction whose life had been outwardly uneventful but inwardly perplexing and problematical—an obvious victim, had he lived in recent years, for any biographer with a taste for psycho-analytical inquiry. Each subject also possessed in marked degree a capacity for self-examination that he was willing to indulge in letters to chosen friends. These letters were made available in abundance to both biographers, who garbled the text as they thought fit. Except for stylistic falsifications, Hayley may be excused for what he did in that he had to work under the apprehensive surveillance of Cowper's friends and relations. Mason's wantonness in manipulation, however, deserves the severity of chastisement his work has received; yet it is to his credit that he recognized the value of his material, and that he clearly enunciated a new biographical principle in claiming that 'Mr. Gray will become his own biographer'.

Though Gray and Cowper were both reserved in disposition, each was able on occasion to use the letter for exploring his own state of mind. Gray confesses to 'a white Melancholy, or rather Leucocholy' as well as to

> another sort, black indeed, which I have now and then felt, that has somewhat in it like Tertullian's rule of faith, Credo quia impossible est; for it believes, nay, is sure of every thing that is unlikely, so it be but frightful . . . (27 May 1742)

This was written to West, an intimate friend of his schooldays and a fellow-sufferer, who could be helped both by being roused and told 'what a sin it is to have the vapours, and the dismals', and by such a self-conscious act of sharing an experience as Gray performs in this letter. But we are less affected by this youthful exercise in self-examination than by the admissions extorted from an elderly recluse at separation from a newly found and mercurial young companion:

> Alas! how do I every moment feel the truth of what I have somewhere read: *Ce n'est pas le voir, que de s'en souvenir*, and yet that remembrance is the only satisfaction I have left. My life now is but a perpetual conversation with your shadow. The known sound of your voice still rings in my ears. There, on the corner of the fender you are standing, or tinkling on the Pianoforte, or stretch'd at length on the sofa. Do you reflect, my dearest Friend, that it is a week or eight days, before I can receive a letter from you, and as much more before you can have my answer, that all that time (with more than Herculean toil) I am employ'd in pushing the tedious hours along, and wishing to annihilate them; the more I strive, the heavier they move and the longer they grow.
>
> (To Bonstetten, 19 April 1770)

> Your letter has made me happy; as happy as so gloomy, so solitary a Being as I am is capable of being. I know and have too often felt the disadvantages I lay myself under, how much I hurt the little interest I have in you, by this air of sadness so contrary to your nature and present enjoyments: but sure you will forgive, tho' you can not sympathize with me. It is impossible with me to dissemble with you.

Such as I am, I expose my heart to your view, nor wish to conceal a single thought from your penetrating eyes. All that you say to me, especially on the subject of Switzerland, is infinitely acceptable. It feels too pleasing ever to be fulfill'd, and as often as I read over your truly kind letter, written long since from London, I stop at these words: *La mort qui peut glacer nos bras avant qu'ils soient entrelacés.*

(To Bonstetten, 9 May 1770)

The low spirits were real enough, and so was their accompanying lassitude. But they are only a part of the pattern. Mason was right in recognizing that plentiful quotation from Gray's letters was needed to represent the richness and variety of his interests and personality. His letters show, as Mason said, that 'excepting pure mathematics, and the studies dependent on that science, there was hardly any part of human-learning, in which he had not acquired a competent skill'. Their range is to be seen in a casual admission here ('I have been exercising my eyes at Peterborough, Crowland, Thorney, Ely, &c: and am grown a great Fen-Antiquary'), and in a detail there that will entertain a particular correspondent '(Observe from this Calendar it appears, that there is a wonderful difference between the earlier Phaenomena of the Spring in Sweden and in England, no less than 78 days in the flow'ring of the Snow-Drop . . . yet the Summer-flowers nearly keep time alike in both climates'), and by the tone of authority in which he gives his views on literary questions, on operatic singing, and landscape gardening, to offer but a few examples. Similarly we take note of the owl Gray kept in his garden at Pembroke College 'as like me, as it can stare', and relish the tone of a half-serious rebuke addressed to Mason in his prebendal stall at York Minster:

no sooner do people feel their income increase than they want amusement! why what need have you of any other, than to sit like a Japanese Divinity with your hands folded on your fat belly wrap'd and (as it were) annihilated in the contemplation of your own *corpses*[1] and revenues?   (17 March 1762)

We notice his embarrassment at Walpole's proposal to include his portrait as a frontispiece to an edition of his poems ('I conjure you immediately to put a stop to any such design. . . . To appear in proper Person at the head of my works . . . would be worse than the Pillory'). We chuckle over the whimsical

---

[1] The technical term for the endowment of a prebend.

obituary he forecasts for himself in 'some Corner of a London Evening Post':

yesterday, died the Revnd Mr John Grey, Senior-Fellow of Clare-Hall, a facetious Companion, and well-respected by all that knew him. His death is supposed to have been occasion'd by a Fit of an Apoplexy, being found fall'n out of Bed with his Head in the Chamber-Pot.   (25 April 1749)

It is while we are assembling these and a score of other passages that the seriousness, and gaiety, and fussiness, and responsiveness of Gray's personality begins to be displayed in all its complexity.

Gray's letters, then, were originally published to help us in understanding his life and character: we learn about his life by means of the almost continuous narrative they afford; we come to know him as he attempts to describe and account for his own disposition, but we see him much more clearly in those less self-conscious letters where he responds to the personality of a friend and to the great diversity of his own activities. The first collection of Cowper's letters, in Hayley's biography, was intended to serve the same purpose. They too survive in sufficient numbers to afford an almost continuous narrative, and their nature is such as to provide an insight into Cowper's character. He led an even more secluded life than Gray, and was even shyer in disposition. His range of interests was narrower: he was less intellectual, less scholarly and bookish; but a poet who knew how to grow cucumbers and to till his garden, and who made tables and bird-cages, and trap-doors for his pet hares, could lay claim to some domestic versatility. His range of activities affords less opportunity for the unconscious display of personality; yet no reader of the letters could complain that opportunities were missed. The escape of a pet hare and its recovery, the visit of a parliamentary candidate for a vote—famous episodes in these letters—are described with the zest and humour that we relish in *The History of John Gilpin*. The command of mock-heroic in describing the commonplace that has already been noticed in *The Task* sets an affectionate tone for a letter to a friend in London, seated in his box at the coffee-house:

No doubt the waiter, as ingenious and adroit as his predecessors were before him, raises the teapot to the ceiling with his right hand,

while in his left the teacup descending almost to the floor, receives
a limpid stream; limpid in its descent, but no sooner has it reached
its destination, than frothing and foaming to the view, it becomes
a roaring syllabub;

and this serves to introduce a contrast in evening entertainments, wherein the poet reveals his contentment and his inherent mildness of demeanour, rejoicing in

a domestic fireside, in a retreat as silent as retirement can make it;
where no noise is made but what we make for our own amusement.
. . . One of the ladies has been playing on the harpsichord, while
I, with the other, have been playing at battledore and shuttlecock.
A little dog, in the meantime, howling under the chair of the former,
performed, in the vocal way, to admiration.   (7 December 1782)

Such an 'interior' is as characteristic of Cowper's letters as the
'conversation piece' is of the paintings of Zoffany, his exact
contemporary; but Cowper's are warmer and altogether more
personal, and occasionally they glow with excitement and
affection, as when he anticipates a visit from his cousin, Lady
Hesketh:

I shall see you again. I shall hear your voice. We shall take walks
together. I will show you my prospects, the hovel, the alcove, the
Ouse, and its banks, everything that I have described. . . . My dear,
I will not let you come till the end of May or beginning of June,
because before that time my greenhouse will not be ready to receive
us, and it is the only pleasant room belonging to us. When the
plants go out we go in. I line it with mats, and spread the floor with
mats; and there you shall sit with a bed of mignonette at your side,
and a hedge of honey-suckles, roses, and jasmine; and I will make
you a bouquet of myrtle every day.   (9 February 1786)

Let it not then be said that a narrow and sequestered life prevented the display of the sweetness, and what Izaak Walton
might have called the 'primitive simplicity', of Cowper's
character.

   Cowper was less versatile than Gray, and more self-conscious.
His self-consciousness, if not religious in origin, is expressed in
religious terminology highly coloured by Calvinistic awareness
of possessing a soul predestined to an eternity of salvation or
(more probably) damnation. Though exceedingly shy, he had
friends in whom he could confide his fears and with whom he
could explore the recesses of his soul. These confessional letters

make painful reading. His pleasures, however simple, were always intense and consequently fatiguing, and from exhaustion he could all too readily succumb to gloom. This he recognized and could describe; but for all that, he could wonder nevertheless

that a sportive thought should ever knock at the door of my intellects, and still more that it should gain admittance. It is as if harlequin should intrude himself into the gloomy chamber where a corpse is deposited in state.   (To Newton, 12 July 1780)

It will be observed that the poet in him stands ready there, as in 'The Castaway', to handle his sufferings; and in this he may seem to foreshadow the poetic achievements of Coleridge in 'Dejection' and 'The Pains of Sleep', and of other poets of the next generation, as they too capitalize their miseries. Cowper can see his situation yielding to an almost Odyssean treatment:

I could draw the picture of Despair at any time; I could delineate the country through which he travels, and describe his progress, could trace him from melancholy to rage, from rage to obduracy, and from obduracy to indifference about the event; and this I could do in prose or verse with the greatest facility.   .
(To Newton, 8 March 1784)

The paradox of his situation, too, seems conducive to poetical treatment, for he is

both free and a prisoner at the same time. The world is before me; I am not shut up in the Bastille; there are no moats about my castle, no locks upon my gates, of which I have not the key; but an invisible, uncontrollable agency, a local attachment, an inclination more forcible than I ever felt, even to the place of my birth, serves me for prison-walls, and for bounds which I cannot pass.
(To Newton, 27 July 1783)

and his predicament is apt to appear in such imaginative terms as might have occurred to his distant relative, John Donne:

I know the ground before I tread upon it; it is hollow, it is agitated, it suffers shocks in every direction; it is like the soil of Calabria, all whirlpool and undulation; but I must reel through it,—at least if I be not swallowed up by the way.   `

Some passages in Cowper's letters were subsequently turned into the other harmony of verse, 'The Dog and the Water-

Lily', for example. But difficult as it is to believe that so shy a man could have gone so far in public self-revelation as to write 'The Shrubbery'—'The Castaway' was posthumously published —it is yet more difficult to imagine him writing the still greater poetry that these passages so tantalizingly promise, and quite inconceivable that he should ever have contemplated their publication as letters. They remain, like Gray's, completely private, and are so constructed as to bear no resemblance to the essay in form. They are also to a very large degree unpremeditated; he may sometimes write himself in by elaborating a jest, but he is to be believed when he says that a letter is written as a conversation is maintained, by resolving not to stop before the end (6 August 1780). His theory lies at the nether and negative end of the art, and disclaims all models and all rules, except the counsel of patience and freedom of movement.

With Gray it had been rather different. He too showed no signs of contemplating publication, but he evidently cultivated a taste for other people's letters. Shenstone's afforded the most meagre interest; Lady Mary's he thought would surely appeal; Madame de Sévigné's he approved, to judge from his quotations; while Pope's he justly commended for 'the Humanity and Goodness of Heart, ay, and Greatness of Mind' that runs through them. It would not be surprising if he had felt some sense of emulation, and was determined for his own pleasure and that of a few friends to perform as well as he could, that is to say, with freedom, elegance, and flow of soul, for the letter of witty compliment, of which Voiture was the master, had gone out of fashion while Pope was still a young man. Several of his letters, though not comparable as works of art with some of Pope's, are worthy and self-conscious performances. Some of them are to be found amongst travel letters, which he might have edited for publication without much trouble or embarrassment.

Two of the earliest describe visits to the Grande Chartreuse. They are exercises in the sublime with almost all detail carefully subordinated to a few grand strokes. A passage from a letter to his mother seems to have been modelled with special care:

It is six miles to the top; the road runs winding up it, commonly not six feet broad; on one hand is the rock, with woods of pine-trees hanging over head; on the other, a monstrous precipice, almost perpendicular, at the bottom of which rolls a torrent, that sometimes tumbling among the fragments of stone that have fallen from on high, and sometimes precipitating itself down vast descents with a noise like thunder, which is still made greater by the echo from the mountains on each side, concurs to form one of the most solemn, the most romantic, and the most astonishing scenes I ever beheld: Add to this the strange views made by the craggs and cliffs on the other hand; the cascades that in many places throw themselves from the very summit down into the vale, and the river below; and many other particulars impossible to describe; you will conclude we had no occasion to repent our pains.   (13 October 1739)

This was perhaps as much as he could expect his mother to appreciate; it is only in describing the scene in a letter to the sensitive West, written a month later, that he incorporates some exclamations of romantic response:

> Not a precipice, not a torrent, not a cliff, but is pregnant with religion and poetry. . . . One need not have a very fantastic imagination to see spirits there at noon-day.   (16 November 1739)

By comparison, the letter to Wharton of 30 September 1765 describing his visit to the Highlands, is cool in tone. His principal interests lay in details of farming in that remote part of the country, and in estimating the opportunities for a landscape gardener afforded by the Earl of Strathmore's 'policies'. But the pass of Killiecrankie appealed to the historian in him, and as a man of letters he permitted himself to discern in some grotesque masses of rock near by 'the sullen countenances of Fingal and all his family frowning on the little mortals of modern days'. The most accomplished of his travel letters is the series about the Lake District transcribed from his diary for the benefit of Wharton, who had been prevented from accompanying him. Thomas Wharton (not to be confused with Thomas Warton the poet) was a physician by profession, a naturalist and well versed in books; though he lived far off in County Durham, he was Gray's most intimate friend. The nature of his correspondent and the character of the countryside bring out the best in Gray's descriptive powers. There is no lack of close and detailed observation, yet it is subordinated to a contrast between the Sublime and the Beautiful that Borrowdale and the Vale of Keswick might seem to have been designed to offer. Gray's description illustrates and justifies the exclamation of Charles Avison, the Newcastle musician, on his first visit to Derwentwater some years earlier: 'Here is beauty indeed—Beauty lying in the lap of Horrour!':

Behind you are the magnificent heights of *Walla*-crag; opposite lie the thick hanging woods of Lord Egremont, and *Newland*-valley with green and smiling fields embosom'd in the dark cliffs; to the left the jaws of *Borodale*, with that turbulent Chaos of mountain behind mountain roll'd in confusion; beneath you, and stretching far away to the right, the shining purity of the *Lake*, just ruffled by the breeze enough to shew it is alive, reflecting rocks, woods, fields, and inverted tops of mountains, with the white buildings of *Keswick, Crosthwait*-church, and Skiddaw for a back-ground at distance.

It is Gray's habit to summarize with a quotation the mood conveyed by emotive words in this and other passages. He liked to use the spectacles of books to clarify his view of the scene before him. Thus the threatening chaos at Gowder Crag of rocks 'hanging loose and nodding forwards' extorts the tribute of a shudder, and reminds him of

those passes in the Alps, where the Guides tell you to move on with speed, and say nothing, lest the agitation of the air should loosen the snows above, and bring down a mass that would overwhelm a caravan. I took their counsel here and hasten'd on in silence.

Non ragioniam di lor; ma guarda, e passa.[1]

Similarly the stupendous Gordale Scar, visited nine days later on his way home through Yorkshire and described with as much 'sublime' emotion as James Ward conveys on his huge canvas of the same scene (in the Tate Gallery), reminds him of a passage from *King Lear*; while the calm beauties of Derwentwater at sunset seem to demand a note of pathos and melancholy that the opening of *Samson Agonistes* is called upon to provide. He saw the solemn colouring of night draw on:

the last gleam of sunshine fading away on the hill-tops, the deep serene of the waters, and the long shadows of the mountains thrown across them, till they nearly touch'd the hithermost shore. At distance heard the murmur of many waterfalls not audible in the day-time. Wish'd for the Moon, but she was *dark to me and silent, hid in her vacant interlunar cave.*

---

[1] 'Let us not speak of them; but look, and pass on.' Dante, *Inferno*, iii. 51.

Gray might have prepared these travel records for the press. Had he done so, it would have been he rather than William Gilpin who would have been credited with 'a new species of writing, unknown before in this Country' (W. J. Temple, *Diary*, 18 November 1790). In doing so, he might well have subdued what is personal in favour of the more pedagogical manner adopted by Gilpin, who visited the same district three years later, and wrote up his notes (*Observations, relative chiefly to Picturesque Beauty . . . on several Parts of England; particularly the Mountains, and Lakes of Cumberland, and Westmoreland*, 1786) as a manual of instruction on the Sublime, the Beautiful, and the Picturesque, where readers are taught how to recognize and appreciate these features in the scenes before them. Gilpin appealed to the aesthetic theory and sensibility of the day, and readers paid him the compliment of requiring several editions of his numerous 'picturesque tours';[1] but we may rest quite satisfied with Gray's tours as he left them. In choosing to address his accounts to a sympathetic friend, he made a record of his experiences so personal and intimate in kind as only a private letter (in prose) can give.

Horace Walpole[2] more than any other writer of the age regarded letter-writing as his vocation. He was quite clear about his aims, he knew how closely he had achieved them, and he recognized the lasting value of what he had written. He chose his correspondents with even greater care than Lady Mary had exercised, and took more pains than she had done to ensure that his letters were preserved.

He told his friends from time to time what he thought a letter should be and how it should be written. Neither Aristotle nor Bossu had delivered rules, and so a man was left free to say 'whatever comes uppermost'. St. Paul, he continues,

is my model . . . who being a man of fashion, and very unaffected, never studies for what he shall say, but in one paragraph takes care of Timothy's soul, and in the next of his own cloak.

(To Lady Ossory, 8 October 1777)

---

[1] See further, Chapter VIII, pp. 259–60, and Vol. IX, pp. 57–8.

[2] Horace Walpole, 1717–97, was a younger son of Sir Robert Walpole. He was educated at Eton and King's College, Cambridge, and travelled through France and Italy with Thomas Gray. Between 1741 and 1767 he was an M.P., closely associated with his cousin Henry Seymour Conway. At his 'Gothic' residence at Strawberry Hill near Twickenham he kept a printing press, where he published a number of his own works. In 1791 he became fourth Earl of Orford.

We need not take the critical judgement seriously so long as we attend to the ideal of informality expressed. Voiture, the idol of Pope's youth, disgusted him. He sends Lord Lincoln a parody of his manner: 'Monseigneur,' he writes,

> though you have employed the finest words in the world in the letter you did me the honour to write me, yet there was something in it, that I was more intent upon than those happy expressions. The five lines that you blotted out, gave me more pain, than the two most eloquent sides that ever were wrote, gave me pleasure. Certes 'tis the only way your pen can give pain, when it effaces what it has wrote itself.

Then after a few more lines about his efforts to decipher the blot, he breaks off, exclaiming

> My dear Lord, I can't go on with this affected stuff, which makes me as sick to write as it will you to read; yet these civil periods and unreal turns were the admiration of the age an hundred years ago . . . I have no patience with people that don't write just as they would talk.   (5 September 1744)

An 'extempore conversation upon paper' was his aim, an aim which women reached more easily than men, he thought, since

> our sex is too jealous of the reputation of good sense, to condescend to hazard a thousand trifles and negligences, which give grace, ease, and familiarity to correspondence.
>   (To Lord Strafford, 11 December 1783)

These were the qualities he found to perfection in the letters of Madame de Sévigné.

An effect of ease and familiarity could only be assured by an easy and familiar relationship with a correspondent. It is difficult to determine how consciously and deliberately Walpole made his choice. He knew that Cole would be interested in his antiquarian pursuits, that Bentley and Chute would be responsive on matters of taste, that Montagu buried in the country would appreciate society gossip, and that Mann in ambassadorial exile at the court of Florence would welcome a regular packet of news from London. Walpole's letters to these and other friends were provoked and supported by theirs; and when any of them failed him, he needed to look elsewhere; thus Lady Ossory profited from Montagu's laziness in reply. But though any one of these correspondences is homogeneous in tone, it is not chemically 'pure': Mann may be told what is happening at Strawberry Hill and teased for his ignorance in his supposing that 'my garden is to be Gothic too'; while it is to his gossip Lady Ossory rather than to Mann that he writes about the sinking of the *Royal George*, a disaster as affecting to him as to Cowper, who commemorated it in 'Toll for the Brave!':

Admiral Kempenfelt is a loss indeed; but I confess I feel more for the hundreds of poor babes who have lost their parents! If one grows ever so indifferent, some new calamity calls one back to this deplorable war!

The vast correspondence with Mann does not display Walpole's most attractive qualities as a writer. There is certainly more gaiety in the letters to men and women with whom he was more closely associated. It was to Conway that he sent his charming first impressions of Strawberry Hill, 'set in enamelled meadows, with filigree hedges', where 'barges as solemn as Barons of the Exchequer move under my window . . . Dowagers as plenty as flounders inhabit all round, and Pope's ghost is just now skimming under my window by a most poetical moonlight'; and it was Montagu who received the brilliant accounts of George II's funeral and George III's coronation, in the first of which Walpole does equal justice to the opening pomp and the concluding farce, with the Duke of Newcastle standing on the Duke of Cumberland's train to avoid the chill of the marble. More characteristic of his correspondence with Montagu and Chute are those letters where his wit takes charge in the absence of anything important to communicate, as for example, a letter to Montagu of 15 June 1768 where a dozen variations are played in the manner of Addison upon the seemingly barren theme of a cold, wet summer: we put too much trust in poets who learnt their trade from the Romans, and taught us to expect shady groves and cooling breezes instead of sore throats and agues; our Zephyr comes from the northeast, makes Damon button up to the chin and pinches Chloe's nose; our best sun is made of Newcastle coal; the only warmth is generated by politics.

All this is well enough, but it is less substantial in kind than the letters to Mann, and Walpole himself seems to have recognized this. He secured the return of his letters from other correspondents, and annotated some of them, but his letters to

Mann he transcribed and lightly revised, and he prefaced them with an introduction intended for the eye of posterity. On re-reading these letters he had

found some facts, characters and news, which, though below the dignity of history, might prove entertaining to many other people: and knowing how much pleasure, not only himself, but many other persons have often found in a series of private and familiar letters, he thought it worth his while to preserve these, as they contain something of the customs, fashions, politics, diversions and private history of several years; which, if worthy of any existence, can be properly transmitted to posterity, only in this manner.

Such pre-eminently are the letters recording the progress and decline of the second Jacobite rebellion, assisted as they now are in the Yale edition by the preliminary warnings and apprehensive comments of Mann. It is true that as time went by without ever refreshing their friendship with another meeting, they recognized that they were forced, as Walpole said, 'to write . . . of such events only as one would write to posterity'. Thus some of the intimacy of other correspondences was lost. Yet Mann remained, as it were, a representative of posterity who could be addressed in person and relied upon to reply. Gazetteers they had become; but, as Walpole so truly remarked in a letter to Dalrymple (30 November 1761): 'Nothing gives so just an idea of an age as genuine letters; nay, history waits for its last seal from them.'

Behind the essays and letters we have been considering stands an ideal of friendly intercourse, of informal argument, which is of particular importance when one turns to the composition of dialogue: dialogue, that is, in the sense of an argument or controversy presented by way of an artfully constructed conversation. Among several discussions of the genre in the eighteenth century, William Melmoth's (in one of his *Letters of Sir Thomas Fitzosborne*) may be recommended as an elegant summary of the conventional view. Conversation, he says, corrects the bias which naturally develops in solitude, and 'discovers those latent flaws which would probably have lain concealed in the gloom of unagitated abstraction'. It follows that the temper of impartial debate can be caught by a writer of dialogue only if he sets himself to ensure that one disputant is not 'tamely silenced' by another, but that each should support his sentiments 'with all the strength and spirit of a well-bred opposition'. This last phrase is the crucial one: the contest, if it is to engage our interest, must be keen, but with a keenness tempered by the rules of good society. As we shall see, some of the best dialogues of the period make one aware that good breeding and vigorous argument are not easily reconciled; but few people would have disagreed with the view which Shaftesbury expressed at the beginning of the century, that 'we shall grow better *Reasoners*, by reasoning pleasantly, and at our ease'. This mode of discussion, he said, 'gives the fairest hold, and suffers an Antagonist to use his full Strength hand to hand, upon even ground'. It is true that Shaftesbury thought his own contemporaries too inclined to adopt dogmatic attitudes to achieve success in this kind, and even when one takes into account the dialogues of Berkeley and Hume, it is clear that the genre never became a major one in the sense that it was in classical antiquity, or even to the extent that it became so in France. There is nothing in English to match the mercurial inventiveness of Fontenelle, or the remorseless animus of Pascal as he exposes the extremes of Jesuit pliability in the dialogues of the earlier *Lettres provinciales*. It was none the less a form that attracted more interest than might at first appear. The formal discussion of a topic in dialogue, for instance, evidently appealed more strongly to eighteenth-century novel-readers than it does to their modern counterparts, who are apt to find them an irritating interruption of the main business of the work. Or again, the most famous single work of the period could be described as a large collection of conversations, although Boswell's recollections of Johnson's talk belong to the genre of anecdote rather than of dialogue: the emphasis being on the one leading speaker, and on the climax rather than on the unfolding of an argument. Johnson, too, is a figure who has pleased his admirers partly on account of his very refusal to allow his roughness to be polished by what Shaftesbury called the 'amicable collision' of good company. After an evening in which he had played the gladiator with even more vigour than usual, he remarked to Boswell that they had had good talk. 'Yes, Sir,' said Boswell, 'you tossed and gored several persons.' But in spite of such moments, and notoriously they are very numerous, *The Life of Johnson* is still a characteristic monument of an age which placed a high value on affability. Its most elaborately contrived incident is the famous meeting between those great opposites in morality and politics, Johnson himself and John Wilkes. The result of Boswell's superb stroke of diplomacy was not, indeed, as a writer of dialogue would have made it, a regular discussion of the principles on which the two men differed. Such openness is not in practice quickly achieved, and Boswell noted as an instance of remarkable good humour on this occasion the fact that when Wilkes spoke lightly of being prosecuted for libel in the *North Briton* case, Johnson 'said not a word'. He could easily have been furiously angry. Mere silence was an outstanding achievement.

If one can at all isolate a quality specially characteristic of the best dialogues of the eighteenth century, it is this capacity for suggesting controversial heat held in check. It is as though the sharp confrontations of *The Pilgrim's Progress* were presented with the good manners of *An Essay of Dramatic Poesy*. Some writers, indeed, took delight in exploring the heat of controversy rather than its constraint. While Voltaire's *Le dîner du Comte de Boulainvilliers* is not altogether incredible as dinner-table conversation, one suspects that the Abbé Couet, the hapless apologist for Catholicism, must have had an attack of indigestion afterwards. Among English writers, Fielding takes the keenest pleasure in subjecting urbanity to severe trials, often pushing polite conversation beyond the point of breakdown. The poet and the player in *Joseph Andrews* pass from elaborate mutual compliments to angry recrimination at the end of a skilfully articulated argument about the decay of acting and of poetry, while Parson Adams's discussion with Peter Pounce about the nature of charity finds its appropriate outcome in Adams's indignant descent from Peter's coach. In *Amelia*, Dr. Harrison's spirited attack on duelling puts Colonel Bath's respect for the cloth to a formidable test:

'Drink about, doctor,' cried the colonel; 'and let us call a new cause; for I perceive we shall never agree on this. You are a churchman, and I don't expect you to speak your mind.'

'We are both of the same church, I hope,' cries the doctor.

'I am of the church of England, sir,' answered the colonel, 'and will fight for it to the last drop of my blood.'

'It is very generous in you, colonel,' cried the doctor, 'to fight so zealously for a religion by which you are to be damned.'

Fortunately Booth is present to turn the conversation, or at least to give it some semblance of that 'sceptical inconclusive air', as Bishop Hurd called it, 'which the decorum of polite dialogue necessarily demands'.

Pugnacity is far less inimical to that decorum, however, than is the temper of a pedagogue addressing a pupil, and this effect was one that enlightened writers of dialogue in the eighteenth century went to some trouble to avoid. There were exceptions— James Harris's vehement dialogue *Concerning Happiness* springs to mind—but they were apt to incur ridicule, and Boswell, for one, wished that Harris had cast his work into the form of an essay. Even Bishop Berkeley, who was as anxious as a man could well be to inculcate a system, makes a show in his exceedingly polemical *Alciphron: or. the Minute Philosopher* of recording an argument between intellectual equals; while the *Three Dialogues* between Hylas and Philonous represent a genuine effort to enter into the difficulties which immaterialism encountered in the minds of readers who had not yet lost their prejudices in favour of 'material substance'. 'There is indeed something in what you say,' concedes the bewildered Hylas in the course of the second dialogue; 'but I am afraid you do not thoroughly comprehend my meaning.' In a world where it was increasingly obvious that men of sense could hold to fundamentally opposed systems of belief, the cultivated reader was well aware how readily one man might fail to comprehend another's meaning. Equally, every man's mind was capable of reflecting some measure of light, as the lawyer Edward Wynne noted in an essay prefixed to his *Eunomus: or, Dialogues concerning the Law and Constitution of England* (1774); and (he added)

one would rather wish the ray of light that comes from the reason of one man to have its own proper refraction, as it passes through the medium of another's understanding; than to be like a ray falling on a polished surface, and reflected back again exactly as it falls.

Dialogues which are not otherwise of any great literary merit may yet successfully convey an idea of the irreducible complexity of truth. One example of this is the series of *Dialogues concerning Education* by David Fordyce.[1] They are stilted, too

---

[1] David Fordyce, 1711–51, was Professor of Moral Philosophy at Marischal College, Aberdeen. He was drowned at sea while returning from his travels in Europe.

formal, too crowded with speakers whose characters are imperfectly differentiated. But Fordyce is sometimes surprisingly
successful in depicting the shifting perspectives of an eagerly
contested discussion. Thus, in his sixth dialogue he considers
the issue of how far the natural genius of the pupil may be
allowed free scope: should he be allowed to imitate the wandering and yet industrious bee?—or should there not rather be
strict control of the impressions that are allowed to inscribe
themselves on the blank sheet of paper that is the infant mind?
But then, does the infant mind indeed resemble a blank sheet of
paper? Is it not rather a seed 'which contains all the Stamina
of the future Plant'? If so, then how is one to foster good habits
without enervating the vigour of the mind by inculcating undue dependence on authority? These contradictory metaphors,
each suggestive in its own way, are taken up and explored, and
while Fordyce's grasp of the more formal aspects of dialogue is
weak, he shows himself to be possessed of the quality which
Shaftesbury held to be indispensable for success in this kind, a
freedom from that lazy effeminacy which is unable to bear
being kept in suspense. Men who fancy themselves drowning
whenever they dare trust to the current of reason cannot, he
said, write good dialogue. They seem to themselves to be 'hurrying away, they know not whither; and are ready to catch at the
first Twig'.

It must be admitted that the most popular dialogues of this
period—Lord Lyttelton's *Dialogues of the Dead*[1]—exhibit no
such alarming tendency to hurry their readers away. They owe
their success partly to the advantage of conforming to a pattern
established by that most entertaining of the ancients, Lucian,
and adapted to modern purposes by Fontenelle and Fénelon.
The conversation of carefully contrasted ghosts in the underworld gives obvious scope for satire and edification, because
death strips off the many disguises that men and women assume
to help them through the stresses of life. As Fontenelle remarked, the dead may be supposed to be people of deep reflection, reasoning better than they did in life because they may
look at events with more impartiality. Fontenelle uses this
vantage-point to sketch a sceptical, disenchanted, and yet

---

[1] George Lyttelton, Baron Lyttelton, 1709-73, was a prominent politician
associated with the patriotic opposition to Walpole, and later with Pitt and the
Grenvilles. He was a generous patron.

paradoxically animating view of life, throwing out ideas which in one form or another were deeply influential in the eighteenth century. His Artemisia and Raymond Lully discuss the value of a quest for an impossible achievement, mentioning the philosopher's stone and conjugal fidelity as examples. In doing so they anticipate Adam Smith's insight into the absurd confidence that men have in their own good fortune. People, it is argued, would never put themselves on the road if they expected to arrive only where they actually do arrive; 'they must have in view an imaginary Stage to animate 'em.' Or again, Fontenelle's Herostratus gives one a hint of Hume's doctrine that reason is, and ought to be, the slave of the passions. Herostratus is presented conversing with the disconsolate Demetrius of Phalerum whose 360 statues were all destroyed by his successor in the government of Athens. He reminds him that there would be 'nothing done upon Earth, if Reason govern'd all'. There is little or nothing of this kind of intellectual stimulus to be found in Lyttelton's *Dialogues of the Dead*, which are closer to the model provided by Fénelon, exploiting encounters which give scope for a more traditional kind of moral commentary. Lyttelton, indeed, is apt to turn the impartiality of the dead into something close to triteness. Controversy is so mitigated by the 'mild air of the Elysian Fields' that it becomes insipid. No one would take that redoubtable warrior of the fifteenth century, the Earl of Douglas, to be a likely convert to the idea of a Union between England and Scotland; but Lyttelton sees to it that he is brought round by the principal architect of the Act of Union, John, Duke of Argyll and Greenwich. Lucian, again, has evidently become a much tamer character since his death. Lyttelton makes him regret that he and Rabelais did not make a better use of their agreeable talents, employing their ridicule only to 'strip the foolish faces of Superstition, Fanaticism, and Dogmatical Pride of the serious and solemn masks with which they are covered', combating at the same time the flippancy of mockers of religion and virtue. Lucian and Rabelais are admittedly writers whom one would not expect Lyttelton to enjoy in an unexpurgated text, but one might have hoped for more from the encounter of those sharply contrasted colonizers, Cortez and William Penn. Lyttelton's sense of irony is not sufficiently acute to exploit the possibilities, however, and he simply makes each the mouthpiece of the ordinary reasonable man when it is his turn to expose the crimes or the follies of the other, and the dialogue never catches fire. One must allow that the dialogues are neatly turned and sometimes ingenious. It was a pleasant idea to fight the quarrel of the ancients and moderns over again in terms of luxury at the table, as Lyttelton does in the dialogue between Apicius and Dartineuf. But his dialogues are most interesting when the speakers deal with an issue where his own sympathies are divided, as they are to some extent in the conversation between Scipio and Caesar, and even more so in that between Atticus and Brutus. The latter dialogue is in effect a discussion of the respective merits of uncompromising tenacity and prudent trimming. Brutus' final eloquent assertion of the value of the noble feelings of the heart, overriding all other considerations, perhaps seizes Lyttelton's imagination more powerfully, but the good sense of Atticus is too carefully argued to be easily dismissed, and the reader is left at the end in a state of real perplexity.

Even here, Lyttelton presents the issue in terms too bare to avoid some resemblance to a school exercise. Far more elaborate and with a greater subtlety of presentation, are the *Moral and Political Dialogues* of Richard Hurd.[1] He wrote what is probably the most illuminating of contemporary theoretical discussions of the genre, and the dialogues themselves show a considerable variety of structure, suggesting that he was consciously exploring the various kinds available, the impartial and the partisan, the dialogue concerned with manners, and the dialogue concerned with the exposition of ideas. In examining the genre in the preface to the edition of 1762, Hurd lays much emphasis on the inexpediency of the modern practice of using fictitious persons as the speakers (he has Shaftesbury and Berkeley in mind), because although character is important in an effective dialogue, it is necessarily secondary to the unfolding of the argument. The use of historical figures, as was customary among the ancients, not only lends authority to what is said, but also facilitates characterization by slight and careless strokes which would be ineffective if the persons were not previously known. Hurd's first dialogue, between Edmund

---

[1] Richard Hurd, 1720–1808, was educated at Emmanuel College, Cambridge. He was a close associate of William Warburton. In 1774 he became Bishop of Lichfield and Coventry, and in 1781, Bishop of Worcester.

Waller and Dr. Henry More, illustrates his deft exploitation of commonly known historical circumstances. The conversation represents an encounter between the claims of personal honour or sincerity on the one hand, and the demands of worldly prudence on the other, the time-serving poet-politician attempting to vindicate himself before the other-worldly piety of the Cambridge Platonist. Where Lyttelton keeps an even balance between Atticus and Brutus, Hurd leaves one in no doubt about his antipathy to Waller. But he redresses the balance by the sheer ingenuity of the poet's defence of his betrayal of his accomplices in the royalist plot of 1643. His sophistries are so plausible, and expressed with so much verve, that the reader is almost persuaded, and it is only when Waller pushes his case a little too far that one is reminded how abject his position is. Dr. More asks him, for example, whether the symptoms of a disturbed mind, which he displayed after the discovery of the plot, were entirely counterfeit:

> As certainly as those of the Roman BRUTUS [says Waller], who, to tell you the truth, was my example on that occasion. It was the business of both of us to elude the malice of our enemies, and reserve ourselves for the future service of our respective countries.

The comparison, so smoothly made and so violently incongruous, between the pliant Waller and the stern antagonist of Tarquin the Proud, is characteristic of Hurd's method throughout the dialogue. One reviewer complained that Hurd might mislead the young into supposing that he was actually commending Waller's conduct. This view, though evidently absurd, bears witness to Hurd's ironical weighting of the argument in Waller's favour. So taken aback is More by the sheer impudence of Waller's apparent candour that he makes only the briefest interjections, which are borne down by the irresistible flow of Waller's eloquence. Hurd was himself a reserved man, perhaps not very competent in the art of holding his own in conversation. In the encounter of Waller and More, one can see him making himself some amends for his deficiency.

Another dialogue, between Abraham Cowley and his biographer Thomas Sprat, follows a similar strategy. The conversation is related by Sprat, who is trying to reason the poet out of his unprofitable retirement. Although the whole narrative is apparently biased in Sprat's direction, the weighty arguments are all Cowley's. Hurd admirably catches the tone of the earnest sensibility of the poet, protesting against the falsities and tedium of court life—not, he insists, courteously deferring to Sprat's profession, that he intends any reflection on the clergy who surround the king. When one considers how offensive to them the slavish manners and libertinism of the court must be, their zeal is all the more impressive, seeing that they 'continue to discharge their office so painfully, and yet so punctually, in that situation'.

The remaining dialogues are in a different vein, more concerned with ideas than with manners. The two dialogues on the Age of Queen Elizabeth show Hurd deliberately aiming at a sceptical conclusion. He supposes a conversation between Addison, Dr. Arbuthnot, and William Digby. Arbuthnot's Tory sympathies dispose him to vindicate the values of the age of chivalry, including its last efflorescence in the reign of Elizabeth. The *Letters on Chivalry and Romance* which form an appendix to these dialogues show that Hurd was keenly alive to the attractions of this point of view; but the part that Addison plays in the argument suggests that he was unwilling to endorse it without qualification. It is true that the main weight of his censure is directed against the personal character of the Queen, but this reinforces some more sweeping condemnations made at the beginning of the talk. As Hurd explains, in a footnote found only in the first edition, Addison's acrimony against those who indulged the humour of magnifying Elizabeth's character showed that he must have 'foreseen, by a kind of political divination, the factious use that was one day to be made of this argument'. The despotic Tudors provided all too attractive a model for those who wished to disparage the true genius of the British constitution, and Hurd had no wish to countenance such views. But his Arbuthnot is certainly no man of straw. The reader is left, like Mr. Digby, perplexed rather than convinced, though with the satisfaction of seeing a major controversy brought into a commendably clear focus.

In the remaining dialogues, Hurd is plainly committed to one particular point of view. Those on the constitution of the English government are a sober exposition of the Whig interpretation of history; those on the uses of foreign travel show Shaftesbury defending and Locke more cogently questioning the value of the 'Grand Tour' for young gentlemen. Hurd shows his usual skill in presenting arguments in a way appropriate to the particular speaker, and the tone of polished controversy is invariably maintained, but these dialogues do not provide the best conditions for Hurd's remarkable gift for expressing a controlled passion: unless, indeed, one excepts the prophetic strains in which he makes Locke foretell a radical improvement in the English universities, with the appointed lecturers of our youth becoming 'the first to explode slavish doctrines and narrow principles', and setting 'the noble and ingenuous youth entrusted to their care, the brightest examples of diligence, sobriety, and virtue'.

At first sight, David Hume's dialogues might seem to form a strong contrast to Hurd's. Hume's interest in the dialogue appears to have arisen from its potential for insinuating views that he judged would otherwise meet substantial resistance. The two dialogues which are included in the *Enquiries* show considerable skill in disarming the reader of his prejudices. That between 'Palamedes' and Hume (appended to the *Enquiry concerning the Principles of Morals*) is cast in the form of a debate on whether the only foundation of moral judgements is custom, or whether there are indeed universally valid moral principles. The argument is won, as is very proper, by the upholder of universal principles, but on terms which imply an urbane tolerance of the most extreme varieties of human behaviour. Neither this dialogue, however, nor the one in section XI of the *Enquiry concerning the Human Understanding*, show the subtlety or the dramatic power that mark the *Dialogues concerning Natural Religion*. Here Hume's dialectical skill is married to a vehemence that Hurd himself might have envied. Few dialogues ever written convey as vividly the variable pace of discussion, the occasional sharp exchanges and interruptions, and the headlong eloquence of a speaker who feels he is making his point effectively. He went to some trouble to ensure fair play for the arguments of Cleanthes, champion of 'the hypothesis of design in the universe', and sought assistance from Gilbert Elliot to achieve this. The effect of genuine argument is reinforced by the nicely-differentiated characterization. The orthodox Christian, Demea, is distinguished by an anxious rigidity of mind which makes him an easy dupe of the sceptical Philo's disingenuous attempts at reassurance. The anxiety is neatly suggested by his scolding of Philo and Cleanthes for

conceding that proofs of a deity fall short of perfect evidence—
and worse still making this concession in the hearing of a young
person (Pamphilus, the narrator of the dialogues). Cleanthes'
temperament is altogether different. His massive equanimity
is not to be disturbed by any man's displays of dialectical
finesse. When his partners in debate combine to overwhelm
him with the languors and vexations of human existence, he
observes coolly that he has indeed noticed symptoms of this
perennial dissatisfaction in some people, 'but I confess I feel
little or nothing of it in myself, and hope that it is not so common as you represent it'. As for Philo, his dominant trait is an
animated proposing of objections and difficulties, somewhere between jest and earnest. He is equally apt to enter into Demea's
feelings about the miseries of life, and to develop, in apparently effortless flights of imagination, plausible alternatives to
the arguments for theism based upon an appearance of design
in the universe. The world, he says, more resembles an animal
or a vegetable than it does a watch or a knitting-loom. This
great vegetable, the world, produces within itself certain seeds,
which, being scattered into the surrounding chaos, vegetate
into new worlds. A comet, for instance, is the seed of a world;
and after it has been fully ripened, by passing from sun to sun,
and star to star, it is at last tossed into the unformed elements,
which everywhere surround this universe, and immediately
sprouts up into a new system. For the sake of variety, the comet
could be seen as an egg, laid in the same manner as an ostrich's,
which without further care is hatched and produces a new
animal. Demea indignantly rejects the idea of drawing inferences from such slight, imaginary resemblances. 'Objects,
which are in general so widely different; ought they to be a
standard for each other?'—'Right!' Philo exclaims; 'This is
the topic on which I have all along insisted.' Philo's triumphant
intervention here marks a critical point in the unfolding of the
argument, and it is a proof of Hume's dramatic skill that it can
be made with such disconcerting abruptness.

The apparent alliance between Demea and Philo, sustained
uneasily until the last dialogue but one, is a continual source
of demure amusement to Hume. But the most piquant jest is
reserved for the last dialogue, after Demea has been scandalized
into leaving the discussion. Philo appears to perform an obliging
volte-face, and accept the substance of Cleanthes' position:

'A purpose, an intention, a design strikes everywhere the most careless, the most stupid thinker.' Having laboured to convince Cleanthes that our experience of design is only applicable to our narrow corner of the world; having slighted thought as a 'little agitation of the brain' which is quite unworthy to serve as a model of the universe; having ridiculed the idea that nature must incessantly copy herself—a presumption so gross that a peasant, 'who makes his domestic œconomy the rule for the government of kingdoms', is pardonable in comparison: having done all this, Philo asserts his conviction that the works of nature bear a great resemblance to the productions of art. Knowing Philo, one is on the alert for the argument that will make this concession meaningless, and sure enough he proceeds to show that the controversy between theists and atheists is merely verbal: the theist will allow that the divine intelligence is very different from human reason; the atheist, that the various operations of nature bear some remote inconceivable analogy to each other, including 'the œconomy of human mind and thought'. The difference between them is one of degree, and disputes of this kind are impossible to resolve, although (he adds) 'the works of Nature have a much greater analogy to the effects of *our* art and contrivance, than to those of *our* benevolence and justice'. The severity of this last qualification can only be appreciated by those who come fresh from Philo's earlier denunciations of the unnecessary miseries of human life.

It would be a mistake to suppose that Hume identifies himself with Philo to the extent of denying Cleanthes any serious significance. If Cleanthes often reminds one of Shaftesbury in his more enthusiastic frame of mind, he also resembles the Hume of *The Natural History of Religion*, whose admiration for the superb construction of the human body anticipates Cleanthes' feeling that the structure and contrivance of the eye made the idea of a contriver flow in upon one 'with a force like that of sensation'. The status of such a feeling might be open to question, but if Cleanthes was mistaken, his was an understandable mistake. If Philo dominates the dialogues—and he does so increasingly as they proceed—this does not exclude the possibility that he might be in error, error engendered by his too luxuriant powers of thought, which smothered his natural good sense in 'a profusion of unnecessary scruples and objections'. Few modern readers are likely to doubt that Philo does in fact get the best of the argument, but it is a measure of Hume's literary skill that he is able to make the controversy alive for us again. Philo, Cleanthes, and Demea are perennial types of controversialist, and it is possible to derive a pleasure independent of the particular subject of the *Dialogues* from their encounter. Philo's eventual predominance, indeed, forms part of the pleasure which the dialogue gives. The opposition, is not, in Melmoth's words, tamely silenced, but no reader can fail to be stirred (whether with alarm or exultation) by Philo's cry of victory: 'Here, CLEANTHES, I find myself at ease in my argument. Here I triumph.' The satisfaction which readers of Boswell's *Johnson* derive from the triumphs of the Great Cham of literature is more easily achieved than this; but its essence is not altogether different. Even the most cautiously impartial mind takes some pleasure in the buoyancy of a man who feels he is gaining the upper hand.

The public address was more formal than either the essay or the letter, and writers of the two principal kinds, the sermon and the speech, were conscious of certain rules governing their composition. But in that they were also necessarily more conscious than historians and writers of treatises of addressing a particular audience of limited size, and presumably responding to the requirements of that audience, we may appropriately consider their work in a chapter concerned mainly with essayists and letter-writers.

The sermon, as Dr. Johnson reminded Wilkes, still made a considerable branch of English literature. No doubt there were many clergymen like Fielding's Parson Adams who nourished the hopeless ambition of seeing their sermons published in three volumes, and many like the Revd. Jonathan Dustwich in Smollett's *Humphry Clinker* who, when they approached a London bookseller for that purpose, were told 'You need not take the trouble to bring up your sermons on my account— No body reads sermons but Methodists and Dissenters.' Yet a glance at the lists of monthly publications in the *Gentleman's Magazine* will serve to substantiate Johnson's opinion.

The style of preaching advocated by Wilkins and South in the middle of the seventeenth century was still in vogue a hundred years later. The best exponent was often considered to

be Archbishop Tillotson (1630–94). Johnson had some reserva-
tions about his style; and Warburton preferred Jeremy Taylor
and Barrow, though allowing that Tillotson preached 'fine
moral discourses . . . simple, elegant, candid, clear, and
rational'; but the esteem in which he was still held was such
that his sermons were re-delivered from eighteenth-century pul-
pits, and were taken as models both in doctrine and in method
by many preachers of the time. We discover them following
Tillotson in beginning with a short paraphrase of the text,
dividing it into two or at most three parts suitable for exposition, and concluding with a practical application of the doctrine.
They followed him also in making little or no use of the
exemplum—the pertinent anecdote, whose homeliness brightens
the sermons of Latimer in the sixteenth century—or of the
tropes and figures of Taylor, the linguistic analysis of Andrewes
and the imaginative excursions of Donne. Their ideal was less
exciting, less richly idiosyncratic, less imaginative, but also
less pedantic, more practical, and more consistently edifying.
John Wesley was not the only preacher who could have claimed
in the preface to his published sermons:

> Nothing here appears in an elaborate, elegant, or oratorical dress.
> . . . I design plain truth for plain people: therefore, of set purpose,
> I abstain from all nice and philosophical speculations; from all per-
> plexed and intricate reasonings; and, as far as possible, from even
> the show of learning.
>
> (Preface to *Sermons on Several Occasions*, 1746)

An exception was rightly made in sermons addressed to learned
audiences; but it was only a young divine fresh from the
university who needed the *Connoisseur*'s warning against
'shewing the world, that they have been reading the Fathers'
(No. 27). As to the images and figures that a preacher might
use, even those of the Bible had come to appear extravagant:
we find Archbishop Secker, in an Ash Wednesday sermon on
'They that are Christ's have crucified the flesh', acknowledging
'the surprising warmth and boldness of figure . . . a phrase far
out of the road of our daily conversation', but defending it as
denoting 'a reasonable, a necessary duty' which it describes
'not only in a strong, but elegant manner'. So plain has the
language of the pulpit become that we experience a shock of
surprise when Sterne, speaking of the believer who continues
to sin in spite of his pastor's warning, concludes:

These notices of things, however terrible and true, pass through his understanding as an eagle through the air, that leaves no path behind.

(*Sermons*, vol. vi, No. XII, on External Advantages of Religion)

Warburton commended Tillotson's 'fine moral discourses', and the complaint is sometimes made that eighteenth-century preachers were content to offer nothing else. The most famous in this kind, the sermons delivered by Bishop Butler at the Rolls Chapel (1726), lie outside our period. Though, unlike Butler, he attempts no contribution to ethical theory, Sterne chose to preach sermons of moral persuasion with little appeal to religious support or religious sanctions; a pleasing example is Sermon VII, a 'Vindication of Human Nature', in which Men of Feeling, one of whose greatest pleasures is 'the mutual communications of kind offices', are praised with zeal and affection becoming the author of *A Sentimental Journey*. But it is notable how often in a sermon of morals religious support is invoked. Thus Bishop Wilson, a favourite of Matthew Arnold, drawing to the conclusion of a Whitsuntide sermon, and warning his congregation of growing 'conceited of their own wisdom and ability to govern themselves', concludes:

And now, good Christians, you see the necessity of Christian baptism, by which we have the Spirit given unto us; without which Spirit it is impossible for any man to work out his salvation. . . . You see what little use it is to be convinced of the truth of the Christian religion, if we do not seriously apply to the Spirit for grace to live as becomes the gospel of Christ. Lastly, you see the danger of neglecting the means of grace which the providence of God affords us: it is the ready way to be forsaken of God, and left to ourselves.

Sterne too has another type of sermon, in which he expounds a Biblical story and applies its lesson. Some of the happiest are Sermon IV on the Good Samaritan, Sermon V on Elijah and the Widow of Zarephath, and Sermon V of his third volume on the Prodigal Son. The close attention which Sterne had paid to painting and theories of art, abundantly shown in *Tristram Shandy*, served him in good stead as he endeavoured to re-create scenes in the eyes of his congregation: Elijah, 'the holy man approaching with the child in his arms—full of honest triumph in his looks, but sweetened with all the kind sympathy which a gentle nature could overflow with upon so happy an event'; or the broader canvas of the Prodigal Son leaving home:

I see the picture of his departure:—the camels and asses loaden with his substance, detached on one side of the piece, and already on their way:—the prodigal son standing on the fore ground, with a forced sedateness, struggling against the fluttering movement of joy, upon his deliverance from restraint:—the elder brother holding his hand, as if unwilling to let it go:—the father,—sad moment! with a firm look, covering a prophetic sentiment 'that all would not go well with his child,'—approaching to embrace him, and bid him adieu.

No less characteristic of Sterne are his comments: on the father's joy at the prodigal's return, 'When the affections so kindly break loose, Joy is another name for Religion'; and the 'application' for his listeners of the widow's reception of Elijah, 'True charity is always unwilling to find excuses . . . in generous spirits, compassion is sometimes more than a balance for self-preservation.'

George Whitefield[1] was also highly skilled in the exposition and application of Biblical story, an accomplishment that will serve to show how alike, and yet how very different the revivalist preachers were when compared with their traditionalist brethren. Whitefield preached on the Prodigal Son at Glasgow in 1741, and his most famous sermon in this kind was on Abraham and Isaac (1756). Like Sterne he calls upon the congregation to 'see', but not so much to admire as connoisseurs as to participate in drama, to behold Abraham as he wonders what Sarah will say ('How can I ever return to her again, after I have imbued my hands in my child's blood'?), as he walks 'with his dear Child in his hand, and now and then looking upon him, loving him, and then turning aside to weep', till the great moment of the interruption of the sacrifice. Like Sterne, Whitefield makes his application, interjecting it after each episode of the story; but unlike Sterne's application, it is less moral than religious:

I see your Hearts affected, I see your Eyes weep (and indeed who can refrain weeping at the Relation of such a Story?) But, behold,

---

[1] George Whitefield, evangelist, 1714–70, was educated at Pembroke College, Oxford, where he came to know the Wesleys. He was ordained in 1736, and preached the first of some eighteen thousand sermons. He began open-air preaching in 1739, visiting many parts of the British Isles. The first of several visits to the American colonies, where he died, was made in 1738.

I shew you a Mystery, hid under the Sacrifice of Abraham's only Son, which, unless your Hearts are hardned, must cause you to weep Tears of Love, and that plenteously too. I would willingly hope you even prevent me here, and are ready to say: It is the Love of God, in giving Jesus Christ to die for our Sins. Yes, that is it.

The directness of address is characteristic. Whitefield sometimes admonishes a section of the congregation—the young apprentices, for example, that he sees before him in the Castle Yeard at Glasgow in 1753. He tells them a story, and adjures them to be warned by his example ('Dear young men, do not be angry with me, I am sure you will not be angry with me in another world'); and he concludes with a final exhortation: 'I am a poor Stranger, I came many Miles to preach to you, do not let me go without some of you coming to Jesus Christ.'

Wesley,[1] too, rejects the comfortable corporateness of the first person plural in favour of the disturbingly forceful 'you' and 'I'. His sermons are organized with a Tillotsonian strictness of which Sterne was quite innocent, for regularity was not to be expected of the author of *Tristram Shandy*. Wesley is accustomed to paraphrase his text, divide it into two or three topics, expound them and reason upon them in as disciplined a manner as any traditionalist could desire. In all this he is at one with the custom of his age. It is only in the application that he sets himself apart from the rest, and individualizes his address:

Whosoever thou art, who desirest to be forgiven and reconciled to the favour of God, do not say in thy heart, 'I must *first do this*; I must *first* conquer every sin. . . . Alas, my brother! thou art clean gone out of the way, thou art still 'ignorant of the righteousness of God' and art 'seeking to establish thy own righteousness' as the ground of thy reconciliation. . . . Do not say, 'But I am not *contrite enough*: I am not *sensible enough* of my sins.' I know it. I would to God thou wert *more sensible* of them, more *contrite* a thousand fold than thou art. But do not stay for this. It may be, God will make thee so, not before thou believest, but by believing. It may be, thou wilt not weep much, till thou lovest much because thou hast had much forgiven. In the meantime look unto Jesus. Behold, how he loved thee!   (*Sermons*, 1746, No. VI, on Justification by Faith.)

[1] John Wesley, 1703–91, was a Fellow of Lincoln College, Oxford, 1726–51, where with his brother Charles, the hymn-writer, he formed a group for religious study and strict observance, nicknamed 'Methodists'. Went on a mission to Georgia, 1735–8. Began (1739) itinerant preaching in the open air, and the organization of Methodist societies.

The sternness of Wesley's admonishment contrasts with the unc-
tuousness of Whitefield's appeal; yet the directness of address
to the congregation, not as a body but as individuals, distinguishes them both from other preachers of the day. We shall
return to this briefly in the concluding chapter.

Another kind of public address, the academic lecture, was
becoming more and more frequently printed. There are some
notable English examples, namely Bentley's lectures in the
Boyle foundation, *A Confutation of Atheism* (1692), Lowth's
lectures on Hebrew poetry (1753) delivered from the recently
founded Chair of Poetry at Oxford—in Latin, as the custom
was from that chair until Matthew Arnold changed it in the
mid-nineteenth century—and Blackstone's *Commentaries on the
Laws of England* (1765–9), also delivered at Oxford. But considering the state of the English universities at this time, it is
surprising that lectures were published at all when, as Adam
Smith affirmed and Gibbon agreed, 'the greater part of the
public professors have for these many years given up altogether
even the pretence of teaching'. Smith spoke from experience of
Oxford, but at Cambridge the situation was no different. Thus
the phenomenon of lecturing and publishing lectures was
largely Scottish, for the Scottish universities, more particularly
those of Glasgow and Edinburgh, were manned by scholars of
great activity and renown. It is often said that Francis Hutcheson,[1] who was appointed to the Chair of Moral Philosophy at
Glasgow in 1729, was the first to lecture in English. Certainly
he was one of the first philosophy professors to publish his
lectures. Adam Smith, Hutcheson's pupil, used the material of
his lectures on ethics for his *Theory of Moral Sentiments* (1759).
Having published this book, he was enabled to spend more
time on other aspects of his course—particularly on juris-
prudence and political economy: such was the breadth of
academic philosophy in Scotland—and from this he drew the
materials for another book, *The Wealth of Nations*, published in
1776. Thomas Reid,[2] Smith's successor in the Glasgow chair,
is quite specific about the relationship between his *Essays*

---

[1] See Vol. VII, pp. 271–4, 331–4.
[2] Thomas Reid, 1710–96, was Librarian of Marischal College, Aberdeen, 1733–6,
Professor of Philosophy, King's College, Aberdeen, 1751–64, and Professor of
Moral Philosophy, Glasgow University, 1764.

on the Intellectual Powers of Man (1785) and his professorial lectures:

the substance of these Essays [he writes] was delivered annually, for more than twenty years, in Lectures to a large body of the more advanced students in this University. . . . Those who heard me with attention . . . will recognize the doctrine which they heard . . . delivered to them more diffusely, and with the repetitions and illustrations proper for such audiences.

The survival of students' notes sometimes permits us to discover what the nature of the revision was, and sometimes these notes remain the only record of what was said. A famous course of lectures on rhetoric and belles-lettres delivered by Adam Smith, first in Edinburgh and subsequently enlarged for his Glasgow students, has survived only in this form. One of his auditors was Hugh Blair,[1] soon to become (1762) the first Regius Professor at Edinburgh (or indeed at any university) of a subject which we are now agreed to call English Literature. Blair acknowledged his indebtedness to Smith for much of a course which, when published in 1783, was to become a standard textbook for many years. Students' notes of his lectures preserved in Edinburgh University Library and the National Library of Scotland show that for publication he softened his judgements upon Johnson's prose style, inserted some modern examples (for Blair was ready to survey the whole of literature from Homer to his own contemporaries), removed his addresses to his class and his comments on the written work they presented to him, but retained essentially unaltered the balance of the course between the art of speech, the art of writing, and the study of literature by kinds.

But unquestionably the most important set of lectures to be published in approximately the same words as were spoken are the fifteen *Discourses* on art delivered by Sir Joshua Reynolds[2] before the Royal Academy in his capacity as its first president (1769–91). These lectures form the last authoritative statement of principles and precepts formed during years of meditation

---

[1] Hugh Blair, 1718–1800, was minister of the high church of St. Giles, Edinburgh, 1758, a charge which he held with his university chair until his death.

[2] Sir Joshua Reynolds, 1723–91, was apprenticed to Thomas Hudson, portrait painter, 1740–4. Studied in Italy, 1750–2. Rapidly established his pre-eminence as a portrait painter. Appointed president of the newly formed Royal Academy, and knighted 1769.

and discussion with such friends as Burke, Goldsmith, and Johnson. Johnson in particular, who 'qualified my mind to think justly', brought him to recognize those 'many precepts and rules established in our art, which did not seem to me altogether reconcileable with each other', and prompted him to 'clear away those difficulties' in a series of addresses to students, and to establish 'the rules and principles of our Art on a more firm and lasting foundation'.

In some respects Reynolds's achievement is like Pope's in the *Essay on Criticism*, for that also is a compendious statement of the neoclassical theory of art. Each writer might justly claim, in Reynolds's words, that to 'reconcile those contrary opinions, it became necessary to distinguish the greater truth, as it may be called, from the lesser truth'; that he had not lent his 'assistance to foster *newly-hatched unfledged* opinions' (such, perhaps, as the 'waving-line, or line of beauty', to which Hogarth referred so many triumphs of art), and that in establishing the rules and principles of his Art, he made no pretence to new discovery. For both Reynolds and Pope Nature was 'at once the *Source*, and *End*, and *Test* of *Art*', for 'Nature is and must be the fountain which alone is inexhaustible, and from which all excellencies must originally flow' (*Discourse* VI). Reynolds would not have disputed that Nature is a reflection in the visible creation of the order, rule, and harmony existing in the mind of God, the meaning of the term prevalent in Pope's day and earlier. He readily admits that 'beauty or truth . . . is formed on the uniform, eternal and immutable laws of nature, and . . . of necessity can be but *one*' (*Discourse* VII); this is the Nature that Pope pronounced to be *'unerring . . . one clear, unchang'd, and Universal* Light'. But Reynolds habitually recurred to another meaning of the term, one which had been current since the time of Plato, and depended on the conception of an ideal more perfect than any individual in the visible creation can supply; the painter is to 'overlook the accidental discriminations of nature', and 'to exhibit distinctly, and with precision, the general forms of things' (*Discourse* III).

Although the climate of critical opinion was changing, it was still widely agreed that the imitation of Nature was the purpose of every artist in whatever medium he worked, and to the elucidation of this purpose Reynolds addressed himself. It is altogether appropriate that the friend and (in a broad sense) the

pupil of Johnson should detest jargon, should practise discrimination in the use of terms, and should brush the cobwebs from
the minds of his pupils. What then is 'imitation'? Assuredly it
is not such copying as aims at deceiving the spectator. It is not
the painter's business 'to exhibit the minute discriminations,
which distinguish one object of the same species from another'
(*Discourse* III); instead he will behave like the philosopher,
'consider nature in the abstract, and represent in every one of
his figures the character of its species':

> If deceiving the eye were the only business of the art, there is no
> doubt, indeed, but the minute painter would be more apt to succeed:
> but it is not the eye, it is the mind, which the painter of genius
> desires to address; nor will he waste a moment upon those smaller
> objects, which only serve to catch the sense, to divide the attention,
> and to counteract his great design of speaking to the heart.
>
> (*Discourse* III)

To imitate is to select with judgement. The artist must reduce
the variety of nature to the abstract idea; and by accustoming
his eye to contemplation, he will learn to recognize blemishes
and to 'correct nature by herself, her imperfect state by her
more perfect'.

In this the artist should recognize that he inherits the achievements of the great masters. He has their experience to guide
him. His condition is like 'young Maro's' in the *Essay on
Criticism*, who

> when t'examine ev'ry Part he came,
> *Nature* and *Homer* were, he found, the *same*:
> Convinc'd, amaz'd, he checks the bold Design,
> And Rules as strict his labour'd Work confine,
> As if the *Stagyrite*[1] o'erlook'd each Line.

Pope's conclusion is

> Learn hence for Ancient *Rules* a just Esteem;
> To copy *Nature* is to copy *Them*.

The imitation of the Ancients and the validity of the Rules
were both topics that had been extensively discussed since
Pope's day, and Reynolds took note of the discussions when
pronouncing his own formulations.

---

[1] Aristotle.

When may imitation be censured as plagiarism? Johnson sets himself to answer the question in the *Rambler* No. 143. His conclusion (that plagiarism may be suspected where 'there is a concurrence of more resemblance than can be imagined to have happened by chance') is of less interest than his opening reminder of the inevitability of some resemblances when 'a common stock of images, a settled mode of arrangement, and a beaten track of transition' is available to all. The argument was ably developed at greater length by Hurd in his 'Discourse concerning Poetical Imitation' (1751). The glory of poetry, Hurd claimed, consists in the operations of the mind upon that common stock: 'after all the praises that are deservedly given to the novelty of a *subject*, or the beauty of *design*, the supreme merit of poetry, and that which more especially immortalizes the writers of it, lies in the *execution*.' Joseph Warton would not have agreed. His *Essay on the Genius and Writings of Pope* (volume I, 1756; volume II, 1782), the work of a garrulous scholar, was undertaken as a revaluation of Pope by the highest standards; and these, in his opinion, were not the merits of poetical execution, in which he allowed Pope to excel, but the imaginative force, in which he considered him deficient—'not that the author of the *Rape of the Lock*, and *Eloisa* can be thought to want *imagination*', but this was not Pope's predominant talent. This mode of argument would have appealed to Goldsmith; at least we may suppose so when we find him, in the *Bee* (1759; no. IV) and *An Enquiry into the Present State of Polite Learning in Europe* (1759), urging writers to strike out afresh and abandon the cautious role of the imitator. Warton must have recognized that the argument would appeal to Young, for he confidently addressed his *Essay* to him, in the knowledge, perhaps, that Young was already meditating his *Conjectures on Original Composition* (1759). This famous essay, like *Night-Thoughts*, is the work of a writer at the mercy of an undisciplined fancy. As a piece of argument it cannot be commended; but it may be allowed to have earned its place in literary history by the alluring vigour of its over-simplification. There are two kinds of imitation, one of nature (i.e. 'original'), the other of authors:

the pen of an *original* writer, like *Armida*'s wand, out of a barren waste calls a blooming spring: Out of that blooming spring an *Imitator* is a transplanter of laurels, which sometimes die on removal, always languish in a foreign soil.

The same year Johnson took the opportunity afforded by *Rasselas* of reverting to this topic. He had written a favourable review of Warton's first volume and had perceptibly modified the position he had adopted in the *Rambler* No. 143. Imlac had begun by reading and memorizing all the poets of Persia and Arabia, but he had 'soon found that no man was ever great by imitation'. Accordingly he transferred his studies to 'all the appearances of nature' and 'all the modes of life', but he recognized that, if his style was to be worthy of his thoughts, he 'must, by incessant practice, familiarize to himself every delicacy of speech and grace of harmony' (ch. X).

Reynolds must have been familiar with this recent debate, since except for Hurd all the participants mentioned were his close acquaintances. His position is nearer to Hurd's than any other's, but he shows that he has given a good deal more thought to the question. In *Discourse* VI he states the case for imitation, and begins by encouraging the unhappy student who has perhaps been reading Young:

> To derive all from native power, to owe nothing to another, is the praise which men, who do not much think on what they are saying, bestow sometimes upon others, and sometimes on themselves; and their imaginary dignity is naturally heightened by a supercilious censure of the low, the barren, the groveling, the servile imitator. It would be no wonder if a student, frightened by these terrifick and disgraceful epithets, with which the poor imitators are so often loaded, should let fall his pencil in mere despair; (conscious as he must be, how much he has been indebted to the labours of others, how little, how very little of his art was born with him;) and, consider it as hopeless, to set about acquiring by the imitation of any human master, what he is taught to suppose is matter of inspiration from heaven.

But the student is bidden to take heart and turn from 'the gaiety of rhetorick' to sobriety and reason. Of course, there was never a painter who did not begin by studying the work of other painters. Furthermore, he may continue to study them throughout his life without 'enfeebling the mind, or preventing [himself] from giving that original air which every work undoubtedly ought always to have'. The study of other men's judgement helps to sharpen one's own, to catch excellences while avoiding mere peculiarities, and to discern the opportunity of new combinations. But Reynolds was too honest not to recognize another side to the argument. In *Discourse* XII he warns the student against 'an entire dependence upon former masters' and discusses what he calls '*The art of seeing Nature*'. Boucher is censured for drawing figures from memory instead of refreshing his mind with living models, for

> he who recurs to nature, at every recurrence renews his strength. . . . Nature is refined, subtle, and infinitely various, beyond the power and retention of memory; it is necessary, therefore, to have continual recourse to her. In this intercourse, there is no end of his improvement; the longer he lives, the nearer he approaches to the true and perfect idea of Art.

It was not difficult for Hazlitt, in *Table Talk* (1821), to show Reynolds's inconsistencies. They arose not from thinking too little, but from recognizing that truth is many-sided and that statements need qualifying.

This indecisiveness is apparent, too, in what Reynolds has to say about the Rules. Indeed no one who honestly and coolly discusses the topic can avoid indecisiveness. The reckless arrogance of Rymer in the late seventeenth century demanded an exact observance of the dramatic unities; a hundred years later Johnson was to discard them with other rules in 'the gaiety of rhetorick'; but apart from impatient asides uttered by Congreve and Vanbrugh, the majority of intervening critics allowed them some limited validity. The escape-clause was the doctrine of *je ne sais quoi*, the recognition (to quote the *Essay on Criticism*) of

> *nameless Graces* which no Methods teach,
> And which a *Master-Hand* alone can reach;

they lie, in short, 'beyond the Reach of Art'. The doctrine can be traced back to classical times, but had been revived in Pope's day with the renewed interest in the criticism of Longinus. Even Dennis, who taught that poets who did not please by rule could only please by chance, allowed that 'a less Law may be violated to avoid the infringement of a greater', and that 'seeming Irregularities' are permissible when 'indispensably necessary to the admirable Conduct of a great and a just Design'.

By Reynolds's time the doctrine of the rules had been treated to a good deal of ridicule. Johnson had despised them in the preface to his edition of Shakespeare (1765), and so had Maurice Morgann in a short treatise seemingly little read by his contemporaries, *An Essay on the Dramatic Character of Sir John Falstaff* (1777). There Morgann invokes the ghost of Aristotle to rebuke his modern disciples:

I see that a more compendious *nature* may be obtained; a nature of *effects* only, to which neither the relations of place, or continuity of time, are always essential. Nature, condescending to the faculties and apprehensions of man, has drawn through human life a regular chain of visible causes and effects: But Poetry delights in surprise, conceals her steps, seizes at once upon the heart, and obtains the Sublime of things without betraying the rounds of her ascent: True Poesy is *magic*, not *nature*; an effect from causes hidden or unknown.

This was to appeal once more to a *je ne sais quoi*. But this doctrine too had already been impugned by the empiricist Hogarth, who could find nothing magical in nature, and Burke had agreed with him.

To watch Reynolds working in this climate of opinion is to admire once more the patience and moderation of his thought. He recognized, as Dennis had done at the beginning of the century, that the rules are not penal nor prescriptive, that their purpose is simply to present the practice of great masters in easily digestible form, and that their authority is neither that of the codifier, nor even that of the master, but that of educated taste, for their appeal is to the mind and the emotions; 'what has pleased and continues to please, is likely to please again: hence are derived the rules of art, and on this immoveable foundation they must ever stand' (*Discourse* VII). So far does Reynolds trust the rules that he can find little use for the *je ne sais quoi*. There is nothing mysterious in the operations of genius, for genius works—and he comes near to anticipating Carlyle—by an infinite capacity for taking pains, for 'nothing is denied to well directed labour' (*Discourse* II). Furthermore, the inventions of genius are themselves subject to rule, that is to say, to an orderly system in the mind of man, but they will in turn extend the area of rule in that they will exist for the guidance of future practitioners. Much must depend, however, on the intelligence of the student and on his capacity for intellectual development. To succeed—this is the subject of *Discourse* VIII—he must advance from precepts to be found in books, and even from precepts drawn from the practice of his predecessors, to 'precepts in the mind', to the 'operations of intellectual nature'. That is to say, he must bring his judgement to bear upon the rules, to understand when and why they may be disregarded, and even in the moment of disregard to understand their purpose. After examining several instances, Reynolds concludes by emphasizing once more the need of

an intimate acquaintance with passions and affections of the mind, from which all rules arise, and to which they are all referable. Art effects its purpose by their means; an accurate knowledge therefore of those passions and dispositions of the mind is necessary to him who desires to affect them upon sure and solid principles.

It may be safely said that though this was the last to be heard of the rules, their validity had never before been so carefully examined and so clearly expounded. Neoclassical criticism is most liberal and persuasive at the end.

Although the political speech, like the sermon and the lecture, was (and still is) a form of public address, it differed in important respects from the forms discussed in the last two sections. The preacher, the lecturer, and the statesman prepared their discourses with a specific audience in view, and the audience remains more or less apparent in the printed record that survives; but there can be no question that the statesman lost most heavily when his words were submitted to print. Smith, Reid, and Blair carefully adapted their spoken words to the altered situation of a single reader in his study. We today may momentarily regret that we can no longer hear the asides they addressed to their classes, but we rest assured that we have lost nothing of the substance of their discourses, and we may even assume that the substance is set before us in a shape better suited to our solitary consideration. To regret that we can never enter an eighteenth-century classroom is largely sentimental; but never to have heard Wesley and Whitefield preach is to be cut off from understanding the full power of their evangelism, and from appreciating how far they responded to the emotions they generated in their congregations. Yet the printed words that carry their message remain; it was the message that was important. And it was by virtue of their doctrine that other Anglican preachers hoped to edify. No doubt all would have agreed with Blair that 'the great end for which a Preacher mounts the pulpit [is] to infuse good dispositions into his hearers, to persuade them to serve God, and to become better men' (Lecture XXIX). But not all would necessarily have agreed with his deduction that the arts of persuasion must therefore be sedulously cultivated, particularly 'the chief characteristics of the Eloquence suited to the Pulpit', namely Gravity and Warmth. Blair allowed that the preacher has great advantages:

> He is secure from all interruption. He is obliged to no replies, or extemporaneous efforts. He chuses his theme at leisure; and comes to the Public with all the assistance which the most accurate premeditation can give him. (Lecture XXIX)

It might be true, as Blair claimed, that 'no discourse, which is designed to be persuasive, can have the same force when read [by a preacher] as when spoken'; but if 'the most accurate premeditation' was essential, it was tempting to follow in the custom of reading sermons aloud, or at least to commit a prepared discourse to memory as Blair recommended, rather than to preach impromptu.

Thus the printed lecture and the printed sermon share certain marmoreal qualities: even though they originated in discourses prepared for specific occasions and still retain some evidence of having once been delivered to an audience, they may be said to reach beyond the original audience and appear in a shape of such permanence as time and changes in taste permit. But the conditions in which the statesman worked were markedly different. He was subject to interruption, and necessarily more responsive to the flickering mood of his audience than a preacher needed to be. Though his words might affect the nation's policy for years to come, his energies were bent to the immediate occasion of influencing a vote, and to the immediate occasion of that debate only. The occasion of a great debate has obvious affinities with drama. The words printed on the page help to reconstruct the occasion of each, but reconstruction is difficult without some measure of imaginative effort brought by the reader, and some supplementary description and comment such as Shaw supplied in generous measure but Burke and Shakespeare scarcely provided at all.

There is a temptation, therefore, to be content with all we certainly have, namely the printed text, and to discuss a play in terms suited to a novel and a speech in terms suited to a tract. Moreover, the distance of time which separates us from the original performance of a play of Shakespeare or from an eighteenth-century parliamentary debate is so long as to baffle the imagination, more especially since the records of each are so imperfect.

The imperfection with which most eighteenth-century speeches have been recorded has had equivocal results. We allow the last half of the eighteenth century to be a great age of what the rhetoricians called deliberative oratory, and we justify this preference partly on the evidence of a few celebrated speeches more or less reliably reported (such as Lord Chatham's during the American War of Independence), and partly on the evidence of those best placed to judge. The opinions of men who had access to parliamentary debates survive in the memoirs of the day, and are more voluminous, detailed, and enthusiastic than those surviving from earlier periods. Thus the judgement of posterity is based almost as much on what the casual 'parliamentary correspondent' said as upon the parliamentary reporter's evidence. In fact the reputation of some speakers rests entirely on hearsay; for nothing survives of the oratory of Charles Townshend, whom Burke called 'the delight and ornament of this house', and Walpole characterized as 'Garrick writing and acting extemporary scenes of Congreve'. What influence was exerted at the time by the opinion of those who attended sessions of Parliament is difficult to estimate. Hume was persuaded that the age was witnessing a necessary decline in eloquence; even amongst the best parliamentary speakers, he thought that none

have attained much beyond a mediocrity in their art, and that the species of eloquence, which they aspire to, gives no exercise to the sublimer faculties of the mind, but may be reached by ordinary talents and a slight application.

Hume's essay 'Of Eloquence' was published in 1741, frequently reprinted, but never revised. The opinion there expressed was shared by Adam Smith, as is evident from lectures on oratory he delivered in 1763, and by Blair, who though commendably up-to-date in his reading, as befits a Professor of English Litera-

ture, and always ready to draw the attention of his students
to the eminence of modern practitioners, could find no examples
of British oratory to praise. Perhaps none of these critics had
had access to a parliamentary debate or had discussed modern
eloquence with those who had listened to Bolingbroke and
Pitt.

But if an orator's fame was restricted by the inadequacy of
contemporary reporting, it might be claimed that he profited
by a sense of the privacy of debate. He could direct his attention simply to the business before the House, without having
to reflect that his words would be submitted to a different kind
of scrutiny the next morning. Unlike a modern statesman, he
had for the moment only one audience, and to influence that
he could apply his undistracted talents.

The records, such as they are, leave us in no doubt of the
elder Pitt's eminence, the command he exerted over each
House, the sense of urgency he conveyed, the downrightness
of assertion—as when he declared in the House of Lords (18
November 1777) that 'if I were an American, as I am an
Englishman, while a foreign troop was landed in my country,
I never would lay down my arms—never—never—never'—
the vehemence of his extempore, as when at the end of the
same speech he rounded on the Earl of Suffolk, who had ventured to defend the employment of Indians in the American
war. We can still readily respond to the report of the old man
rising in the House, wrapped in flannels and supported on
crutches, declaring

you may ravage—you can not conquer; it is impossible; you can
not conquer the Americans. You talk, my Lords, of your numerous
friends among them to annihilate the Congress, and of your powerful
forces to disperse their army. I might as well talk of driving them
before me with this crutch!

Assuredly these were great scenes in the history of Parliament,
but they yield little material for the literary critic to work
upon. The speeches of Charles James Fox, no less than those
of Chatham (or of the younger Pitt, for that matter), help the
imagination to re-enact some great occasions, for clearly Fox
was a consummate debater, alive to all the important issues
raised and ready to turn them to his purpose. His fame as an
orator is perhaps more substantially based than Chatham's:

it depends less upon reporters' anecdotes; but he too has left little for the literary critic.

With Burke[1] it is different. He was a man of letters before he entered the House of Commons; as a statesman his literary skill was at the service of his party; and in the last stage of his career, which lies outside the time-limits of this volume,[2] he found some compensation in appealing from the deafness of the Commons to a wider audience of readers, in his *Reflections on the Revolution in France* (1790), *An Appeal from the New to the Old Whigs* (1791), and his *Letters . . . on the Proposals for Peace, with the Regicide Directory of France* (1796). Though there are records of very many speeches delivered by him in Parliament, there are few that were published with his approval and under his supervision. Of these the most important lying within our period are two on American affairs, *on American Taxation, April 19, 1774*, and *on . . . Conciliation with the Colonies, March 22, 1775*; one *on . . . The Retrenchment of Public Expenses 15 December 1779*; and two on Indian affairs, *on Mr. Fox's East India Bill*, and *on . . . the Nabob of Arcot's Debts*, delivered on 1 December 1783 and 28 February 1785 respectively.

In one of his journals Boswell records a description of 'Cavendish taking down while Burke foamed like Niagara'. Sir Henry Cavendish, who was member for Lostwithiel from 1768 to 1774, was accustomed to take verbatim notes in shorthand of parliamentary debates, in the course of which he recorded no fewer than 250 of Burke's speeches, though only one of those mentioned above. While Cavendish remained a member of the House, Burke could rely on his reports when he chose to prepare a speech for print; thus the anonymous editor of the *Speech . . . on American Taxation* (perhaps Burke himself), in the course of explaining the occasion of its publication and the reasons for some months' delay, remarked that 'the means of gratifying the public curiosity were obligingly furnished from the notes of some Gentlemen, Members of the last Parliament'.

[1] Edmund Burke, 1729–97, was educated at Trinity College, Dublin, and trained in the law. He became associated with the Marquis of Rockingham, and entered Parliament, representing first Wendover, then Bristol, and then Malton. He was dedicated to a variety of causes: 'economical reform', conciliation with the Americans, fair trade between England and Ireland, Catholic emancipation, good government in India. The last years of his life were dominated by his leading role in the impeachment of Warren Hastings and in the campaign against supporters of the French Revolution.

[2] See Vol. IX, pp. 18–23.

It seems not to have been Burke's custom to prepare a full draft of a speech before delivery, nor does he seem to have spoken from notes. But his surviving papers suggest that, whenever time permitted, he drafted and redrafted the most crucial passages. These fragmentary drafts were kept, and by their means and by his memory of the occasion, as well as by the imperfect records kept by others, he could prepare a text for the press. The printed version might therefore vary in detail from the actual speech more frequently than could happen today; it might even have been subjected to literary polish; but it was evidently close enough to the spoken word to merit the testimonial of verisimilitude—it could be no more than that— which Gibbon paid in his *Autobiography* to 'the correctness of Mr. Burke's printed speeches, which I have heard and read'. It should be recognized that the limits within which the printed version might deviate from the spoken were defined by the structure of the classical oration, with its exordium or introduction, narration, proposition, division, confirmation, and peroration. (The conduct of a discourse as expounded by a professional rhetorician of the time may be studied in Blair's thirty-first and thirty-second lectures.) Not all Burke's speeches illustrate so well as the speech on Fox's East-India Bill his adherence to this form; but just as the order of the sections would serve to guide him in delivery, so they would also serve to prompt him at the later stage of reconstruction for the printer.

The preface to *American Taxation* points to its being 'much the subject of conversation', to its value as a refutation of certain charges made against the Rockingham party, and to the important matters of information it contained. This seems to imply that contemporary readers could be trusted to replace much of the context from which the speech had been extracted. Yet for them, as for us, it survives as a great operatic aria sung on a concert platform.

Like the aria 'Come scoglio' in *Così fan tutte*, the speech contributed to the drama of the occasion and has lost something by being removed from its context, but can manage to stand alone in its own right. *American Taxation* may be thought to have lost more than Burke's later aria in the grand opera of American Independence, *Conciliation with the Colonies*. The two speeches are differently designed. The earlier is very largely devoted to a discussion of recent events; first, the narrower topic of taxing commodities, and then the broader issues of colonial policy. Though a modern reader needs to refresh his mind to an extent which contemporary readers and listeners did not require if he is to make a full response, he can appreciate even without refreshment the consummate grasp of detail that Burke exhibits, and still more the 'weighty instruction' necessarily derived from Burke's lesson in the history of colonial administration. It was a 'delicate subject' to trace 'the innumerable checks and counter-checks . . . that infinite variety of paper chains by which you bind together this complicated system of the Colonies'. The system was operated under the guidance of statesmen, and it is Burke's concern to show how individuals had contributed to changes in the direction of policy. A great part of the enduring appeal of *American Taxation* is contained in its character studies of statesmen in power during the recent past; and for these studies Burke was already prepared by virtue of his early literary apprenticeship. His first contributions to the *Annual Register* had numbered many characters written in a tradition handed down from the seventeenth century; and the Notebook published in 1957, which he and his kinsman William Burke kept in the early 1750s, contains several more. Seventeenth-century writers had studied the traits common to types of men as well as the characters of their great contemporaries. Burke too was practised in both kinds of study, the one content with an analytical presentation, the other though based on analysis of individual behaviour proceeding thence to synthesis. Each demands shrewdness of observation, and seventeenth-century Theophrastan writers were agreed in feeling that what they observed was best set off by wittiness of conceit. But it is remarkable that as a young man Burke never succumbed to this temptation. Though he was in possession of a mind teeming with imagery, he seems to have recognized that the nervous energy of his style needed no such ostentatious decoration. This was the literary experience that lay behind him when his essay in historical retrospect called him in this speech to show how 'great men are the guideposts and land-marks in the state', and how 'the credit of such men at court, or in the nation, is the sole cause of all the publick measures'. In presenting his characters of Grenville, Conway, and Townshend, Burke was no doubt aware that he was following in the steps of Clarendon, though each had his own method, suited to the ends he had in view, of integrating character-studies in the body of his discourse. Thus Burke presents the Revenue Act of 1767, a fine-spun scheme designed to placate all parties however irreconcilable, as emerging from the mind of a Chancellor of the Exchequer, Charles Townshend, whose ruling passion was to please, more especially his fellow members of the House of Commons; one who 'adapted himself to your disposition, and adjusted himself before it, as at a looking-glass', one 'to whom, a single whiff of incense withheld gave much greater pain, than he received delight, in the clouds of it, which daily rose about him from the prodigal superstition of innumerable admirers'. It is by means of these character-sketches, as varied in manner as the individuals who prompted them, that Burke steers us from point to point in his historical retrospect. We are allowed to see Conway, fresh from his triumph on moving the repeal of the Stamp Act in February 1766, with representatives of the trading interests, jumping 'upon him like children on a long absent father', clinging 'about him as captives about their redeemer', and he not insensible

to the best of all earthly rewards, the love and admiration of his fellow-citizens. *Hope elevated and joy brightened his crest.* I stood near him; and his face, to use the expression of the Scripture of the first martyr, 'his face was as if it had been the face of an angel'.

It is some measure of Burke's range that he can pass from such elevated picturesque to that celebrated exhibition of his wit at its most florid, employed at the expense of Chatham's new government of August 1766:

He made an administration, so checkered and speckled; he put together a piece of joinery, so crossly indented and whimsically dovetailed; a cabinet so variously inlaid; such a piece of diversified Mosaic; such a tesselated pavement without cement; here a bit of black stone, and there a bit of white; patriots and courtiers, king's friends and republicans; whigs and tories; treacherous friends and open enemies: that it was indeed a very curious show; but utterly unsafe to touch, and unsure to stand on. The colleagues whom he had assorted at the same boards, stared at each other, and were obliged to ask, 'Sir, your name?—Sir, you have the advantage of me—Mr. Such a one—I beg a thousand pardons—' I venture to say, it did so happen, that persons had a single office divided between them, who had never spoke to each other in their lives; until they found themselves, they knew not how, pigging together, heads and points, in the same truckle-bed.

Matthew Arnold might have complained, as he did of other passages in Burke, that this is *Asiatic*, 'barbarously rich and overloaded'. But it should be borne in mind that what in prose might be deemed overwrought could serve to catch and to hold the attention of an audience.

For the short remainder of *American Taxation* Burke proceeded to offer advice on suitable action and to make a brief statement of those principles which should govern the relations of a mother country with her colonies. There is much of his characteristic thinking and mode of expression—'I am not here going into the distinctions of rights, nor attempting to mark their boundaries. I do not enter into these metaphysical distinctions; I hate the very sound of them' (a sentiment that Swift would have applauded)—but it is better studied in the companion speech, *Conciliation with the Colonies*. Brilliantly as *American Taxation* exhibits Burke's powers, it makes greater demands upon a modern reader than *Conciliation with the Colonies*, where less depends upon close acquaintance with details of trade and recent parliamentary history. In *Conciliation with the Colonies* Burke is more concerned with broader considerations of policy, more particularly with that conception of Empire touched upon in his earlier speech and now embodied in some constitutional proposals.

If we note, as indeed we should, that the supreme moments in this speech are achieved in aphorisms, such as 'the thing you fought for is not the thing which you recover; but depreciated, sunk, wasted, and consumed in the contest', or the more famous 'I do not know the method of drawing up an indictment against a whole people', we need to reflect that the skill is a literary skill, as much as the skill shown in character-drawing, and like that can be traced back to the literary exercises of the early Notebook. The young man who kept that Notebook was already manifesting a Baconian taste, and an almost Baconian skill, in aphorism, very suitable to a period of life when knowledge is still in growth. But as Bacon said of aphorisms, those of the Notebook are based on some quantity of observation, particularly on the behaviour of man in society; and in some of the best of them, the aphorisms are already being organized into method, a process whose culmination appears in the speeches. Furthermore, like Bacon, the young Burke was learning to use figures of speech in the formulation of his aphorisms:

Knowledge is the Culture of the mind; and he who rested there, would be just as wise as he who should plough his field without any intention of sowing or reaping.

Great subtelties and Refinements of reasoning are like Spirits drawn from Liquors; which disorder the Brain, and are much less useful than the ordinary Liquors, tho of a grosser Nature. . . . I never would have our reasoning too much dephlegmatic, much less would I have its pernicious activity exerted on the forms and ceremonies that are used in some of the material Businesses and more remarkable changes of Life.

There can be little doubt that this early rehearsal accustomed Burke to give ready and well-shaped expression in *Conciliation with the Colonies* and elsewhere to the effusions of a mind peculiarly addicted to analogical thinking. Thus in defending the words of the resolution he was about to move, he says he has adopted them from ancient Acts of Parliament:

It is the genuine produce of the ancient, rustick, manly, home-bred sense of this country.—I did not dare to rub off a particle of the venerable rust that rather adorns and preserves, than destroys the metal. It would be a profanation to touch with a tool the stones which construct the sacred altar of peace. I would not violate with modern polish the ingenuous and noble roughness of these truly constitutional materials. Above all things, I was resolved not to be guilty of tampering, the odious vice of restless and unstable minds. I put my foot in the tracks of our forefathers; where I can neither wander nor stumble.

As he contemplates this favourite topic, the respect that we owe to the wisdom of our ancestors, the images rise up ready to be shaped into maxims for our guidance. But if Burke could have spared a moment in the torrent of debate, he might have cautioned us to reflect that these maxims are real only in so far as they emerge from the argument. When in fact the debate was over and *Conciliation with the Colonies* published, he wrote to his friend O'Hara (26 July 1775) pointing out that it was never his custom to

ask what Government may do in *Theory* except *Theory* be the *object*; When one talks of *Practice* they must act according to circumstances.

If you think it worth while to read that Speech over again you will find that principle to be the Key of it.

His habits in this respect were like those of his friend Dr. Johnson, who frequently states a critical principle in the course of discussing a poet's work. His critical utterances have been articulated in our day, and the same service has been performed for Burke's political thought; but in spite of the philosophical bent of their minds, they were too pragmatical to write a treatise on politics or on criticism. A specific political situation (or a specific poem) called for attention, and then 'the situation of man is the preceptor of his duty' (*Speech on Mr. Fox's East-India Bill*).

A man must do the best he can in his situation, but that best is likely to be more or less adequate according to whether he has succeeded in accustoming his mind to think morally. This seems to have been Burke's belief and to account for his resort to imaginatively shaped axioms of political conduct in his speeches. A remarkable passage in the early Notebook both prepares us for his later practice, and anticipates the views expressed by Shelley in the preface to *Prometheus Unbound* and elsewhere on the preceptive function of poetry. Burke writes:

> The great powers of Eloquence and poetry, and the great Benefits that result from them, are not in giving precepts but creating habits. . . . The mind when it is entertained with high fancies, elegant and polite sentiments, beautiful language, and harmonious sounds, is modelled insensibly into a disposition to elegance and humanity. For it is the bias the mind takes that gives direction to our lives.

Perhaps therefore he reckoned that the imagery of his speeches would insensibly lead his hearers into correct attitudes of mind. Certainly he seems to have been aware that his imagery was functional, for his papers show him expanding upon an image through several drafts until it becomes the organizing principle of a passage. Analogies drawn from the world of nature rose readily before him. In November 1772 he urges the Duke of Richmond to consider that persons in his station of life ought to look beyond the immediate future; for while Burke and his kind

> by the Rapidity of our growth and of the fruit we bear, flatter ourselves that while we creep on the Ground we belly into melons that

are exquisite for size and flavour, yet still we are but annual plants that perish with our Season and leave no sort of Traces behind us. You if you are what you ought to be are the great Oaks that shade a Country and perpetuate your benefits from Generation to Generation.

This was written in a private letter several months before the earliest of the great published speeches. At the end of his career, some twenty-four years later, he was to use the same image, in an open *Letter* to another *Noble Lord*, to convey his sense of desolation on the death of his son:

The storm has gone over me; and I lie like one of these old oaks which the late hurricane has scattered about me. I am stripped of all my honours; I am torn up by the roots, and lie prostrate on the earth! . . . I live in an inverted order. They who ought to have succeeded me are gone before me. They who should have been to me as posterity are in the place of ancestors.

In the speeches that intervene—and the limits of this volume confine us to those already mentioned—images of the fruitfulness of nature are used to persuade the Commons to act as is right and fitting, and images of an 'inverted order', of hurricane, pestilence, indiscipline, and decay, condemn the results of misconceived policy, or are used to pelt his political opponents. Thus, in concluding his speech on *Conciliation with the Colonies*, he claims that

it is the spirit of the English constitution, which, infused through the mighty mass, pervades, feeds, unites, invigorates, vivifies, every part of the empire, even down to the minutest member;

while the proposal to refuse crown grants of land to the expanding population overseas must necessarily be wrong, since it attempts 'to forbid as a crime, and to suppress as an evil, the command and blessing of Providence, "increase and multiply"';
and in *American Taxation* mischievous court reporters are compared to vermin, who 'when they are forced into day upon one point, are sure to burrow in another'; but after their falsehoods have been proclaimed:

thus perish the miserable inventions of the wretched runners for a wretched cause, which they have fly-blown into every weak and rotten part of the country, in vain hopes that when their maggots had taken wing, their importunate buzzing might sound something like the public vote!

The state of India under the administration of the East India Company roused Burke's passions to a more marked degree. His two published speeches show a control of detail that is even more impressive having regard to the greatness and complexity of the issues involved and the remoteness of Indian civilization from contemporary Western experience. It was evidently a matter of prime importance to raise in the minds of his hearers an idea of the immensity of India, of the age and respectability of its institutions, and of the reverence its civilization should inspire. This was matter suited to the opening of his speech on *The East-India Bill*, which he and Fox vainly hoped would prove to be 'the *magna charta* of Hindostan', a country whose people had been 'cultivated by all the arts of polished life, whilst we were yet in the woods', whose merchants and bankers 'have once vied in capital with the bank of England', a country which could still boast 'millions of ingenious manufacturers and mechanicks', but had been so rudely handled of late that one of its great potentates, the Grand Mogul, 'the descendant of Tamerlane, now stands in need of the common necessaries of life'. The East-India Bill was to restore sound administration and root out corruption by substituting for the old private Company a public Board, appointed by the Crown and protected from day-to-day interference by politicians. Such a system, Burke believed, would permit the forces of nature to reassert themselves after the terrible attacks to which they had been subjected. Though he was possessed with the idea of a civilization in which ancestral wisdom had provided for modern needs—the eleven hundred reservoirs of the Carnatic, for example, those 'monuments of real kings, who were the fathers of their people', built 'to extend the dominion of their bounty beyond the limits of nature'—nevertheless it was indignation at the havoc wrought that principally urged him on. Consequently the great imaginative passages in these speeches represent 'inverted order'— images of 'inexpugnable tape-worms which devour the nutriment, and eat up the bowels of India', of abuses 'full of their own wild native vigour' that flourish under neglect; and

instead of what was but just now the delight and boast of creation, there will be cast out in the face of the sun, a bloated, putrid, noisome carcass, full of stench and poison, an offence, a horrour, a lesson to the world.

These passages are to be found in the speech on *The Nabob of Arcot's Debts*, a speech which also contains perhaps his most memorable vision of 'inverted order', the devastation created in the Carnatic by the invasion of Hyder Ali. Just as so much of Burke's rhetorical art can be traced in the theory and practice of the early Notebook, so his treatment of the desolation left by Hyder Ali seems to depend on his early study of the Sublime. Descriptions of fire and slaughter contribute to the ideas of terror, privation, and power which combine to create what as a young theorist he had called Astonishment, and defined as 'that state of the soul, in which all its motions are suspended, with some degree of horrour'. But when it came to the plague of hunger, Burke found himself unable to proceed:

these details are of a species of horrour so nauseous and disgusting; they are so degrading to the sufferers and to the hearers; they are so humiliating to human nature itself that, on better thoughts, I find it more adviseable to throw a pall over this hideous object, and to leave it to your general conceptions.

Behind this climax of the mature orator lies the young theorist's recognition that what is 'wrapt up in the shades of its own incomprehensible darkness, [is] more awful, more striking, more terrible, than the liveliest description . . . could possibly represent it'.

It is beyond the scope of this chapter to examine the full range of Burke's oratory; but in so far as it is based on philosophical principles, and exhibited in maxim, character, and image, it can thus be seen to lie embedded in the young man's studies. Burke was a conscious artist well prepared for the work of his maturity by the literary labours of his youth.

X

FOUR MAJOR NOVELISTS

To say that the English novel began in the 1740s with the work of Richardson and Fielding is to invite qualification, if not contradiction. The Elizabethans had plenty of novels to read, by Nashe, Greene, Lodge, and Deloney; in the latter half of the seventeenth century there were numerous translations and imitations of the French romance; and Mrs. Behn, Defoe, and Mrs. Manley have all some claims upon the historian of the novel. Yet there is something in the broad contention which Richardson and Fielding, for all their differences, would have approved. Recalling the circumstances of his writing *Pamela* (1740) Richardson claimed, in a letter to a friend, that he had hit upon 'a new species of writing', and Fielding was equally confident that *Joseph Andrews* (1742) was a 'kind of writing, which I do not remember to have seen hitherto attempted in our language'. At least some of their readers were prepared to acknowledge the claim. Dr. Johnson, writing in 1750, when *Clarissa*, *Tom Jones*, and Smollett's *Roderick Random* had also been published, was able to distinguish one important difference between the new style of fiction and the old. In the *Rambler* No. 4, he remarks that

The works of fiction, with which the present generation seems more particularly delighted, are such as exhibit life in its true state, diversified only by accidents that daily happen in the world, and influenced by passions and qualities which are really to be found in conversing with mankind. . . . Its province is to bring about natural events by easy means, and to keep up curiosity without the help of wonder: it is therefore precluded from the machines and expedients of the heroick romance, and can neither employ giants to snatch away a lady from the nuptial rites, nor knights to bring her back from captivity; it can neither bewilder its personages in deserts, nor lodge them in imaginary castles.

Such, Johnson would have us believe, were the themes and incidents of the older style of fiction. All the writer had to do was to 'let loose his invention, and heat his mind with incredibilities; a book was thus produced without fear of criticism, without the toil of study, without knowledge of nature, or acquaintance with life'. Very different, in Johnson's opinion, was the equipment of the modern novelist. Besides 'learning which is to be gained from books', he must have 'experience which . . . must arise from general converse and accurate observation of the living world'; his books will then be not merely 'just copies of human manners', but they will also serve as 'lectures of conduct, and introductions into life'.

Perhaps Johnson was not altogether fair to the older style of fiction. Many novelists from the time of Sidney onwards had been interested in providing 'lectures of conduct'; and many besides Defoe (whom Johnson seems to have overlooked) were acquainted with life. But one of the principal differences between the old and the new he has made very clear in his emphasis upon 'accidents that daily happen in the world': the men and women in the novels of Richardson and Fielding act 'in such scenes of the universal drama as may be the lot of any other man' or woman. That is true of neither Sidney nor Defoe. A young man might imagine himself feeling like Sidney's Musidorus or acting like Robinson Crusoe; but he could never expect to share their experiences, as he might expect to share the experiences of Tom Jones. A young woman might well believe all that Moll Flanders reports had happened to her; but she could scarcely say of Moll, as she could say of Amelia or even of Clarissa, 'there but for the grace of God go I'.

But when Richardson, Fielding, and Johnson insisted that such accidents as 'daily happen in the world' must be the staple of the new style of fiction, they were writing not at the beginning but towards the end of a critical tradition. The marvellous had long been losing esteem, and writers of romances in the previous century had been accustomed to discuss in their prefaces to what use historical incidents might be put. Thus Sir George Mackenzie, in the preface to his *Aretina* (1660), had censured those who have 'stuffed their Books with things impracticable, which because they were above the reach of man's power, they should never have fallen within the circle of his observation'; and Robert Boyle took credit for having chosen an episode from history for his *Theodora* (1687), since

True Examples do arm and fortify the mind far more efficaciously, than Imaginary or Fictitious ones can do; and the fabulous labours of *Hercules*, and Exploits of *Arthur* of *Britain*, will never make men aspire to Heroick Vertue half so powerfully, as the real Examples of Courage and Gallantry afforded by *Jonathan*, *Cæsar*, or the *Black Prince*.

These novelists were following in the steps of de Scudéry, the most famous of the French romance writers, whose *Ibrahim* (1641) had been translated into English in 1652. In the preface to that work de Scudéry claimed that he had observed

the Manners, Customs, Religions, and Inclinations of People: and to give a more true resemblance to things, I have made the foundations of my work Historical, my principal Personages such as are marked out in the true History for illustrious persons.

Even though the practice of these writers did not always accord with their theory, it is easy to see how in time the desire for 'a more true resemblance to things' could lead the author of *Robinson Crusoe* to declare that 'the Editor believes the thing to be a just History of Fact; neither is there any Appearance of Fiction in it'. The innocent deception of passing off fiction as history or biography is perpetrated in several title-pages. Thus the reader is offered *The Life and Strange Surprising Adventures of Robinson Crusoe, of York, Mariner. Written by Himself*, or *The Fortunes and Misfortunes of the Famous Moll Flanders. Who was Born in Newgate, was Twelve Year a Thief, Eight Year a Transported Felon in Virginia. Written from her own Memorandums.* Twenty years later, novelists were less concerned for the success of their deceptions. *Pamela, or Virtue Rewarded* is merely *A narrative which has its foundations in Truth and Nature*; but the tradition of offering 'a more true resemblance to things' is maintained in such titles as *The History of the Adventures of Joseph Andrews and of his friend Mr. Abraham Adams*; *Clarissa. Or, the History of a Young Lady*; *The History of Tom Jones, a Foundling*.

Richardson and Fielding were both men of letters deflected accidentally into this 'new species of writing'. Richardson[1] had figured much less conspicuously in the public eye. He had provided a new edition of Defoe's *Tour thro'* . . . *Great Britain* (1738) with 'very great Additions, Improvements, and Correc-

---

[1] Samuel Richardson, 1689–1761, was the son of a joiner, and became a leading London printer, associated with many important publishing ventures. He was printer to the House of Commons and Master of the Stationers' Company.

tions', and had written a preface and 'Instructive Morals and Reflections' for a version of Aesop's *Fables* (1740); he had also supplied a dedication, preface, and index for *The Negotiations of Sir Thomas Roe, in his Embassy to the Ottoman Porte, from the Year 1621 to 1628 Inclusive* (1740): useful but humble tasks, within the scope of a not illiterate master printer, though scarcely indicative of his latent powers. Nor perhaps might more have been expected of the Complete Letter-Writer which two friendly booksellers invited him to compile. This work, however, ensured that his imagination was engaged upon the petty emergencies of everyday life. The tradesman to whose family the book was directed is taught how to write a letter consoling a friend in prison for debt, or offering excuses to a person who wants to borrow money, or excusing delay in the payment of his rent, and his wife is told how to recommend a wet-nurse or a chambermaid. But guidance was more frequently required through the perplexities of family relationships. How should 'a tender Father' most effectively expostulate with 'an ungracious Son', or a young lady be best advised 'not to change her Guardians, nor to encourage any clandestine Address'? Above all, how should a young lady acquaint her father with a proposal of marriage made to her, and how should the father reply? The situation required placing. Polly is found to be staying in Nottingham with her Cousin Morgan, who receives 'some overtures, in the way of courtship to me' from 'a gentleman of this town, by name Derham, and by business a linen-draper'. Her father replies from Northampton approving, and alternatively disapproving, the young man's addresses. He in turn apprises the father of his affection for his daughter; the cousins send their commendations; and after the daughter's return to Northampton the young Gentleman writes 'to his Mistress, on her Arrival at her father's' a letter which 'puts the matter into such a train, as may render more writing unnecessary'.

A situation has developed through a series of seven letters, into an episode, commonplace enough, but one which calls not merely for some elementary skill in letter-writing but for a modicum of that 'nature, propriety of character, and plain sense' which the preface declares to have been 'the chief objects of the author's intention'. The letters, in fact, were to serve for 'rules to think and act by' in the more common predicaments

of life, as well as 'forms to write after'. We may well suppose
that it was the rules of conduct which Richardson had in mind,
rather than the forms of expression, when he composed two
letters, one from 'A Father to a Daughter in Service, on hearing
of her Master's attempting her Virtue', the second from the
daughter in reply. The 'grieved and indulgent Father' reminds
his child that her reputation is all she has to trust to: 'and if you
have not already, which God forbid! yielded to him, leave it not
to the hazard of another temptation; but come away directly
(as you ought to have done on your own motion).' The daughter admits that she should not have stayed a moment after her
master's 'vile attempt';

> But he was so full of his promises of never offering the like again,
> that I hoped I might believe him; nor have I yet seen any thing
> to the contrary: But am so convinced, that I ought to have done as
> you say, that I have this day left the house; and hope to be with
> you soon after you will have receiv'd the letter.

(Letter CXXXIX)

It seems to have been at this point that Richardson pushed
aside his uncompleted manuscript—later to be resumed and
published with the title, *Letters Written To and For Particular
Friends, On the most Important Occasions* (1741)—in favour of a
different and fuller treatment of this theme. The young woman
of the *Letters* was made to behave with obedience and propriety;
but Richardson recalled—or rather, he later said that he recalled—a story of a virtuous young woman who had repelled
her master's attempts but had survived to marry him. Essentially the story is of a young woman's marriage outside her
station in life, and its widespread appeal is witnessed by the
stories of King Cophetua and the beggar maid, Ruth and
Boaz, Cinderella, Jane Eyre, and many a more recent example.
The final triumph is won at the expense of social conventions,
and is frequently accompanied by a presumption that the
association would normally have been illegitimate. 'Why, what
is all this, my dear,' said Sir Simon Darnford, one of Richardson's characters, to his wife, 'but that our neighbour has a
mind to his mother's waiting maid! And if he takes care she
wants for nothing, I don't see any great injury will be done her.
He hurts no *family* by this.' And Parson Williams reports the
opinion of Parson Peters that this was 'too common and fashionable a case to be withstood by a private clergyman or two'.

What made this particular case uncommon was that Pamela resists her would-be seducer, yet cannot help loving him in spite of his ill-treatment; and that while Mr. B. expects to be able to seduce Pamela, and circumstances favour his designs, he is won by her behaviour and against the opinion of the world to offer her marriage.

Thus Pamela's Virtue is Rewarded. But though Richardson emphasizes that aspect of his story in his sub-title, there is much more to the novel. Had that been all, we might have expected that her virtue would be rewarded by marriage in the last chapter. But the ceremony takes place two-thirds of the way through; and yet we read on, since it is not merely Pamela's chastity but the integrity of her personality which is tested.

Her chastity is indeed the *sine qua non*. It is that for which she is called upon to suffer a persecution which provides for the excited, unsophisticated reader an escape into the world of romance. She is as forlorn in Mr. B's Lincolnshire mansion as any damsel in an imaginary castle, and Mr. B. employs in Mrs. Jewkes a housekeeper as ruthless and ugly as any guardian ogre, while the aid of Parson Williams is as effectively baffled as that of any knight errant. The setting is realistic, but the romantic impression of virtue in distress is powerfully presented —and of virtue in the well-established form of a hapless, unprotected damsel, relentlessly pursued and encircled by evil. But by a sudden transformation, not unparalleled in romance, Mr. B. is discovered to possess knightly virtues, and an honourable marriage is staged. And yet we read on. What follows in the remainder of *Pamela*, and in the sequel *Pamela II* which spurious continuations provoked Richardson to add, is neither so romantic nor so exciting, nor be it admitted so salacious; but it belongs to a world more immediately recognizable in spite of its contemporary detail. The testing is continued, not so violently, but more searchingly, and with a wider audience of characters watching the result. Pamela must be shown preserving in her new station her humility, her thankfulness, her piety, and her intelligence. Hers is, throughout both parts, a most difficult task. She is required to loathe Mr. B.'s behaviour, and yet to love him; to be content with her lowly position, yet to aspire to Mr. B.'s hand; to be humble, yet to reprobate aristocratic vice; to be meek, yet outspoken; to be simple, yet quickwitted; to be innocent, yet wide-awake and on her guard. Latterly she must win the reluctant admiration of Mr. B.'s sister and his uncle; she must retain the affection and gain the respect of her fellow servants—teaching her aristocratic neighbours, as they admitted, 'a way they never could have found out, to descend to the company of servants, and yet to secure, and even augment, the respect and veneration of inferiors at the same time' (II, Letter XXXII). She must also express sound though untutored opinions on suckling infants, educating children, presenting to church livings, and managing a household. She must know precisely how to win back Mr. B. from backsliding (with a Countess Dowager), how to express a proper feeling ('a strange grief and pleasure mingled at once in my breast') on being introduced to Mr. B.'s bastard by a former mistress, and how to deal with a lady's maid in her own service, who showed some signs of following, though less discreetly, in her mistress's path ('it behoved me, on many accounts, to examine this matter narrowly; because if Mr. H. should marry her, it would have been laid upon Mr. B.'s example.—And if Polly were ruined, it would be a sad thing, and people would have said, "Aye, she could take care enough of herself, but none at all of her servant" '—II, Letter XXXVII). ' "Why this," ' as the Countess of C. exclaims on one occasion (II, Letter XXXII), ' "must be *born* dignity—*born* discretion— Education cannot give it." '

It would seem almost impossible that Richardson should succeed in steering so intricate a path. The experience gained in compiling his *Letters on Important Occasions* was not without value. The variety of situations in that book had shown him how to project himself into the parts assumed; and it should be recognized that they are not more numerous in *Pamela* than in the *Letters*, for besides the indulgent fathers, dutiful daughters, and hopeful suitors, there is an abandoned lover, a resentful coquette, a facetious young lady, a humorous bottle-companion, and a prudent young woman who describes to her aunt her two admirers, 'a gay, fluttering Military Coxcomb' and 'a Man of Sense and Honour'. None is required to be sustained for so long as even Mrs. Jewkes, Mrs. Jervis, or Lady Davers, and certainly none exhibits so many traits as Pamela; but already in the *Letters* it is possible to watch Richardson using restricted opportunities to recall the spirit of a scene. Conversations are recalled in every detail, with stage directions to assist the reader's imagination ('*Thank you, madam!* said he: *What's sport to you, is death to me*—And so he sigh'd, and took a turn or two about the room.—I was standing all this time.'— Letter CLXIII); replies are used to direct the reader's response; a letter is even abruptly broken off as a visitor enters the room. The wider canvas of the novels permitted him to develop this technique, encouraged him to recognize how the fluttering of the heart can be rendered by 'writing to the moment', as he called it:

So good-night. May-be I shall send this in the morning; but may-be not; so won't conclude, though I can't say too often, that I am (though with great apprehension) *your most dutiful daughter*.

* * * * *

O let me take up my complaint, and say 'Never was poor creature so unhappy, and so barbarously used as poor Pamela.' Indeed, my dear father and mother, my heart's just broke! I can neither write as I should, nor let it alone: to whom but you can I vent my griefs, and keep my poor heart from bursting? Wicked, wicked man! —I have no patience when I think of him!—But yet, don't be frighted, for I hope I am honest!—If my head and my hand will let me, you shall hear all. Is there no constable or head-borough, to take me out of his house? I am sure I can safely swear the peace against him: but, alas! he is greater than any constable: he is a justice: from such a justice deliver me!   (Letters XXIV–XXV)

It is a long step from the *Letters*, vividly as they sometimes succeed in depicting a scene, to the dramatic change and the momentary anguish of such a passage as this; but the step is imaginable, perhaps even a logical one to take, just as it was logical to develop the simple integration into narrative of several units in the *Letters* to the continuity of the correspondence and diary-entries of *Pamela*.

Even more important to notice is the independent attitude of the author to his work, defined in the *Letters* and maintained with varying degrees of success in each of the novels. He is merely the editor of a number of documents, which he hopes may yield amusement and edification, when suitably arranged, annotated, and indexed. There is a certain clumsiness of contrivance in the first part of *Pamela*. Between Letters XXXI and XXXII a long editorial interpolation is required 'to make the sequel better understood'; and Letter XXXII, which occupies the greater part of the book, consists of a diary written by Pamela 'to amuse and employ her time in hopes some opportunity might offer to send it to her friends'. The journal ends with the arrival of Pamela and her husband at her parents' house; and the reader is asked to indulge the editor, in the last few pages, with 'a few brief observations, which naturally result from the story and characters; and which will serve as so many applications of its most material incidents to the minds of the YOUTH OF BOTH SEXES'. But the journal itself has had exciting adventures: parts of it have been conveyed to Parson Williams, have been hidden under a rosebush, sewn in Pamela's under-coat about her hips, stolen by Mrs. Jewkes, and read by Mr. B. In fact Mr. B.'s perusal of the journal does much to bring him to a more virtuous frame of mind. Thus the earlier part of the novel becomes a document which exerts an effect upon a principal character described in it: it is as though a character in the novel is reading the novel alongside of us.

The two-way correspondence of the first pages of *Pamela* is resumed in *Pamela II* and continued both in *Clarissa* and in *Sir Charles Grandison*. In *Clarissa* it is largely conducted, as the 'editor' himself explains, 'in a Series of Letters, written principally in a double, yet separate correspondence between two young ladies of virtue and honour, bearing an inviolable friendship for each other . . . and between two gentlemen of free lives, one of them glorying in his talents for stratagem and invention, and communicating to the other, in confidence, all the secret purposes of an intriguing head and resolute heart'. One reason for abandoning the method of continuous journal employed in *Pamela* is there made evident. Richardson felt the need of confidants for his principal characters, though the danger of admitting confidants must have been immediately obvious. The isolation of Pamela is suitably conveyed by her having recourse to a journal: she is so strictly guarded in Lincolnshire that she is prevented from conducting a correspondence. Clarissa's isolation is no less hapless and complete, and from time to time her correspondence with Miss Howe is interrupted under the stress of circumstances. But though it is conducted at best by desperate and extraordinary stratagems, it is never interrupted for long; and yet the sense of isolation is never impaired. This is some measure of Richardson's art; but it also shows how urgent was the need of confidence. Miss Howe represents the world of normal domestic relationships from which Clarissa has been excluded, and she provides the comment of that world upon Clarissa's story, at its least generous when she reports her mother's views, at its most generous when she gives expression to her own.

But there is more to it than that. A journal account such as Pamela gives of her own sufferings would not have fully answered Richardson's purpose. 'To this hour', writes Clarissa, towards the end of the novel, 'I know not by what means several of his machinations to ruin me were brought about; so that some material parts of my sad story must be defective, if I were to sit down to write it' (volume vii, letter X). Her plan is to make use of the other side of the 'double, yet separate correspondence', between Lovelace and Belford. That 'such a gay, lively, young fellow as this, who rides, hunts, travels, frequents the public entertainments, and has *means* to pursue his pleasures, should be able to set himself down to write for hours together' is, as Miss Howe remarks, a 'strange thing' (volume i, letter XII). But that we must accept as best we can. The whole of Lovelace's correspondence with Belford is not presented, since much of it would have been, as Richardson admits in an editorial note, 'pretty much to the same effect with the lady's', and therefore only as much of his is given as 'will serve to embellish hers; to open his views; or to display the humorous talent he was noted for' (volume iii, letter VII). His views when ·opened serve principally to underline the irony of the situation; they show how wide of the mark are even the shrewdest of Clarissa's or Miss Howe's interpretations of his behaviour. They are, of course, reprobated by Belford, who acts as the mouthpiece of the reader's response, and is himself converted by them from his own evil ways. But—a master stroke of irony upon irony—they are eventually used by Clarissa as her own justification:

it will be an honour to my memory, with all those who shall know, that I was so well satisfied of my innocence, that having not time to write my own story, I could intrust it to the relation which the destroyer of my fame and fortunes has given of it.

(Vol. vii, letter XX)

This skilful and intelligent use of the letter as a medium of narrative may be thought to compensate for the desperate shifts and some patent absurdities in which Richardson is involved, the letters exchanged between persons living in the same house, the copies made, the exactness of memory for details of conversation, and, above all, the time occupied by his characters at their writing-tables. But to keep his readers fully aware of the documentary evidence is Richardson's consistent purpose. The reader is invited to make his own story out of evidence which Sir Leslie Stephen aptly likens to 'a blue-book full of some prolix diplomatic correspondence', while Richardson stands at his elbow ready with convenient cross-references ('see his reasons for proposing Windsor, p. 130, 131'; 'the reader will see how Miss Howe accounts for this in p. 188').

In *Grandison* the reader is made even more conscious of the record. There for the first time Richardson has to narrate, at a later stage in the story, a long account of what happened before the novel opened; and there for the first time he conducts the reader overseas to witness events of great importance to the happiness of Harriet Byron, who has been left apprehensively behind in England. In each case the documentary nature of the record is impressed upon us. Before leaving upon his second visit to Italy, Sir Charles acquainted Harriet with the most material particulars of the state of his relationship with the Lady Clementina; but he left the Reverend Dr. Bartlett to fill in the detail by transcripts from his letters. With the help of his nephew, the indefatigable Doctor transcribes thirteen substantial extracts. These, extending over one-half of the third volume, are sent to Harriet, who forwards them with her comments to her cousin Lucy (who is desired to forward them in turn to her cousin Reeves). Sir Charles sends Dr. Bartlett accounts of his experiences in Italy, and these letters are in turn communicated by him to Sir Charles's sister Lady G., who sends them to Harriet and exchanges comments with her upon them. If this should appear a little involved as a method of narrative, the reader should reflect that it has important advantages. Sir Charles must work out his destiny in Italy far away from the apprehensive Harriet; but though she cannot be present, she must not be lost sight of. It is difficult to see what better scheme Richardson could have devised than to permit us, as it were, to read Sir Charles's letters over Harriet's shoulder, and then to share her reflections with Lady G.

In this way we are kept up to date. The freshness of response
is preserved:

Thou'lt observe, Belford [says Lovelace], that though this was
written afterwards, yet (as in other places) I write it as it was spoken
and happened, as if I had retired to put down every sentence as
spoken. I know thou likest this lively *present-tense* manner, as it is
one of my peculiars. (Vol. v, letter XXXI)

But it is not his 'peculiar'; he shares the characteristic with all
the principal correspondents in each novel. Various and individual as their manners are—and Lovelace can even parody
Clarissa's (volume vi, letter LXXIII)—they all write 'to the
moment'. So Pamela and Clarissa convey their anguish and
Harriet her fears ('O my dear Lady G.! I am undone! Emily is
undone! We are all undone!—I am afraid so!—My intolerable
carelessness!—I will run away from him!—I cannot look him
in the face!'—volume vi, letter XXV); and so the vivacious
Lady G., who loves to write to the moment ('a knack I had
from you and my brother . . . no *pathetic* without it'), whimsically conveys the greetings of her sister in the form of dictation
like the Letter Duet in *The Marriage of Figaro* (volume vi,
letter IX). This is the occasion of Richardson's prolixity, and
the sufficient excuse he makes for it in the preface to *Grandison*:

The nature of familiar letters, written, as it were, to the *moment*,
while the heart is agitated by hopes and fears, on events undecided,
must plead an excuse for the bulk of a collection of this kind. Mere
facts and characters might be comprised in a much smaller compass;
but, would they be equally interesting?

The theme of *Clarissa* is not essentially different from that of
Pamela. This also is the story of a young woman whose lover
comes from a different station in life. The Harlowes are indeed
country gentry, but they seem to have recently emerged from
the city; whereas Lovelace is heir to a nobleman. This is a
difference in station which would not preclude marriage, but
it is enough to make the Harlowes suspicious of Lovelace, and
Lovelace contemptuous of them, enough in fact to have produced the star-crossing which might have blighted lovers in a
different type of story. Destiny in *Clarissa* works in another way.
Lovelace is the descendant of the intriguing rakes of Restoration Comedy, as dashing, gallant, and immoral as they were,

as ingenious in making his intellect serve the purpose of his passions, but more subtle, more consistent, and infinitely more dangerous. Whereas the typical rake, like Mr. B., was eventually persuaded, in the spirit of comedy, into an honest marriage, Lovelace is determined that Clarissa shall first be his mistress. There is no question, as in *Pamela*, of *droit de seigneur*: this is instead a complicated matter of revenge and self-satisfaction, and a kind of devilish gratification represented by such a remark as:

> I love, when I dig a pit, to have my prey tumble in with secure feet and open eyes: then a man can look down upon her, with an, *O-ho, charmer! how came you there?*   (Vol. iii, letter XXXI)

but it is essentially a repetition of pitiless male determination matched against a captured, helpless, and isolated female. And as in *Pamela*, it is the female who wins.

Lovelace is a masterly schemer who derives almost as much satisfaction from his plotting as from the object of his plots. With the help of agents in the Harlowe household, he contrives that Clarissa is reduced to the desperate alternatives of marrying the hateful Solmes, her father's choice, or of seeking Lovelace's protection. Her flight with Lovelace takes place before the end of the second volume, and the impasse to which she had been reduced is evident before the end of the first; but it is of the essence of Richardson's purpose that we should not be permitted to hurry to this first climax. There is much to be done. The principal characters are to be delineated; Lovelace's schemes are to be viewed from each side of the double correspondence; but much more important is the motivation of the Harlowe family in insisting upon her marriage with Solmes and of Clarissa in resisting their wishes. Parents were to be cautioned by these scenes and their sequel against 'the undue exercise of their natural authority over their children in the great article of marriage'; but another way of looking at them is to recognize that an individual has been brought into conflict with the social code. The code admits of no relaxation—at any rate, as it is interpreted by the Harlowes—but the individual cannot sacrifice her principles either: she cannot 'cajole, fawn upon, and play the hypocrite with a man to whom I have an aversion' (volume ii, letter XII). The case is argued in great detail on either side; and it is not merely the more unpleasant of the Harlowes who are seen trying to make Clarissa conform; her mother and her beloved Mrs. Norton add their pleas as well. This protracted casuistry can itself exercise a powerful fascination on the reader, but it subserves the more important purpose of testing Clarissa's integrity. 'I cannot help conjuring you, my dear,' she writes to Miss Howe (volume i, letter XL), 'to pray *with* me, to pray *for* me, that I may not be pushed upon such indiscreet measures as will render me inexcusable to myself: for that is the test, after all.'

So early in the novel is Clarissa's integrity tested, and the remainder of the novel may be considered an extended test thereof, in which every move is subjected to this same casuistical scrutiny. 'After Clarissa finds herself, against her will and intention, in the power of her lover,' writes Mrs. Barbauld (*Correspondence of S.R.*, i. lxxxvii), 'the story becomes, for a while, a game at chess, in which both parties exert great skill and presence of mind, and quick observation of each other's motions.' It is well said. The appeals of Lovelace to Clarissa have at times an almost Satanic subtlety, which reminds the reader of *Paradise Regained*. He has promised Clarissa that she shall have a visit from his aunt Lady Betty, who will take her into her protection and will appeal to her on Lovelace's behalf; but rather than submit to Lady Betty's appeals, would it not be more generous to forgive of her own accord an erring man for whom she once nourished some affection?

How much more agreeable to *yourself* . . . must it be, as well as *obliging to me*, that your first personal knowledge of my relations, and theirs of you, (for they will not be denied attending you) should not be begun in recriminations, in appeals! As Lady Betty will be here so soon, it will not perhaps be possible for you to receive her visit with a brow absolutely serene. But dearest, dearest creature, I beseech you, let the misunderstanding pass as a slight one—as a misunderstanding cleared up. Appeals give pride and superiority to the persons appealed to, and are apt to lessen the appellant, not only in their eye, but in her own. Exalt not into judges those who are prepared to take lessons and instructions from you. The individuals of my family are as proud as I am said to be. But they will cheerfully resign to your superiority—you will be the first woman of the family in every one's eyes.   (Volume v, letter XX)

A nicely contrived appeal to proper pride and generosity, which (as Lovelace says) 'might have done with any other woman'.

But just as the Jesus of *Paradise Regained* shows his mettle in rejecting the most tempting of Satan's compliments, so Clarissa disclaims this:

> Yes, indeed!—and there she stopt a moment, her sweet bosom heaving with a noble disdain—Cheated out of myself from the very first!—A fugitive from my own family! Renounced by my relations! Insulted by you!—Laying humble claim to the protection of yours! —Is not this the light in which I must appear not only to the ladies of your family, but to all the world?—Think you, sir, that in these circumstances, or even had I been in the *happiest*, that I could be affected by this plea of undeserved superiority?—You are a stranger to the mind of Clarissa Harlowe, if you think her capable of so poor and so *undue* a pride!

The reader, while admiring the contestants' skill, is never permitted to overlook what is at stake. It is Clarissa's virginity, the prime symbol of her integrity, as in the previous novel it had been Pamela's. Though the odds are against them, we feel sure that they will never willingly yield. Pamela's virginity is preserved by romantic intervention: Clarissa loses hers under the influence of a drug; but the triumph which Lovelace enjoys is as dusty as the triumph of Satan in *Paradise Lost*, and his failure to recognize the virtue of his adversary is as blind as Satan's when in *Paradise Regained* he bids Jesus stand upon the topmost pinnacle of the Temple. Milton's Jesus confounded Satan by achieving what he had supposed impossible. So Lovelace, about to commit his crime, builds upon a plausible but false assumption:

> Is she not a woman?—What redress lies for a perpetrated evil?— Must she not *live*?—Her piety will secure her life.—And will not *time* be my friend?—What, in a word, will be her behaviour afterwards?—She cannot fly me!—She must forgive me—and, as I have often said, *once forgiven, will be for ever forgiven.*
>
> (Vol. v, letter XXXI)

But she does not live. Her violation is the climax of the tragedy, and evokes (as Fielding himself admitted in a generous letter to Richardson) terror and pity in a high degree, terror on account of the ruthlessness of Lovelace and his brutal instruments, pity for the distress of a heroic character. For Clarissa is unmistakably heroic in fighting so long single-handed against

overwhelming odds. That she has brought her ruin upon herself
is strictly true, and she admits it:

> My crime was, the corresponding with him at first, when pro-
> hibited so to do by those who had a right to my obedience; made
> still more inexcusable, by giving him a clandestine meeting, which
> put me into the power of his arts.   (Vol. vi, letter XXXVIII)

But the error is generous—she wishes to prevent a quarrel
between unruly spirits—and, as in other tragedies, it is quite
out of proportion to her punishment. The words of Butcher are
applicable here as to Greek drama:

> The tragic irony sometimes lies precisely herein, that owing to
> some inherent frailty or flaw—it may be human short-sightedness, it
> may be some error of blood or judgment—the very virtues of a man
> hurry him forward to his ruin.

But (to quote A. C. Bradley, discussing the death of Cordelia
in *King Lear*) 'the heroic being, though in one sense and outwardly he has failed, is yet in another sense superior to the
world in which he appears'. Clarissa's defeat is more apparent
than real; her integrity is inviolate, and virtue is shown triumphant in an adversity depicted with Hogarthian realism. It is
this, rather than Virtue's eventual Reward in Heaven, which
provides the catharsis of the tragedy, as Richardson himself
points out in a long Postscript justifying the course of the action:

> who that are in earnest in their profession of Christianity, but will
> rather envy than regret the triumphant death of CLARISSA?

Lovelace appealed to contemporary readers almost as strongly
as Clarissa, and even in our more sophisticated age the presentation of the intellectual rake may be allowed to have
merit. But the subtlety of Lovelace's casuistry and his ability
to analyse his own motives were perhaps less attractive than
his mixture of good and evil qualities. He had to be endowed
with some merits in order to qualify him for Clarissa's regard.
He is therefore shown, as often as occasion permits, to be brave,
generous, courteous, appreciative of Clarissa's virtues, and even
sensitive to the pain he causes and the false hopes he raises in her:

> so *very* much affected, I never was—for, trying to check my sensibility,
> it was too strong for me, and I even sobbed—yes, by my soul, I

audibly sobbed, and was forced to turn from her before she had well finished her affecting speech.   (Vol. iv, letter L)

Surely such a man might eventually be forgiven, might even be worth reclaiming. But though Richardson was adamant to the appeals of his female friends, he yielded to the argument that he had been partial to their sex and unkind to his own. 'I am teazed by a dozen ladies of note and of virtue, to give them a good man', he wrote to a correspondent in January 1751. The original request seems to have come from his friend Lady Bradshaigh more than a year earlier, and it is interesting to observe that it arose from their discussion of *Tom Jones* and the inadequacies of Fielding's 'good man'. Richardson was conscious of the difficulties from the beginning, and enlisted the advice of his friends. He received it in abundance, and turned 'that kind of flower-garden of ladies' in which he lived into a court of love to pronounce upon the predicaments of the characters in his new story as they arose fresh from his pen. It would scarcely be an exaggeration to say that *Sir Charles Grandison* was written in committee.

One piece of advice he rejected. A Mrs. Donnellan wrote to him with the following suggestion:

Suppose the woman he likes engaged in her affections before she knew him, to one of a more modern cast, could we not make our hero shew virtue and honour, and at last to the credit of my sex, triumph over the man of mode?

Perhaps Richardson felt that such a theme would imply a reversion to *Clarissa*, with the 'good man' rescuing the heroine from the clutches of Lovelace; but even if the man of mode and the good man had been presented as an open choice to the heroine, the interest must have rested upon her because the choice, and therefore the testing, was hers. If he weighed this suggestion carefully, it would seem that he rejected it for some such reason, since he decided for his central episode on a situation which placed the burden upon the good man's decision and not upon the heroine's. Sir Charles Grandison's affections are engaged by two ladies of apparently equal merit, and he must make his choice between them.

Thus the way is cleared for Richardson's favourite theme, the test of integrity. But if a test implies a severe conflict in the mind with at least the possibility that a flaw will be detected, then it is Harriet and Clementina who are tested and not Sir Charles. Clementina's choice lies between her religion and the man she loves; the difficulty, and finally the impossibility, of bringing herself to marry a Protestant produces a strain acute enough to affect her reason. She is one of Richardson's most ambitious creations, a woman whose mind manifests its greatness even when reason is unbalanced and when only the bosom can 'heave with the grandeur of her sentiments'. One of Richardson's correspondents felt that she had 'annihilated' Harriet, and certainly her plight is pathetic. But Harriet too suffers for her love, in body if not in mind, and has ample opportunity to show how magnanimous she can be when it seems probable that Sir Charles must marry Clementina. Here is testing enough, and Harriet is even allowed to give occasional vent to petulance in the stress of circumstances. But Sir Charles cannot suffer as the girls do, except vicariously for the sufferings of Clementina. He is impervious to the grosser temptations and is not subjected to any that are more subtle. He frequently confesses to anger and pride, but both vices are so well controlled that we should not be aware of them without his admission. 'This man, of sentiments the most delicate, of life and manners the most unblamable' (as an Italian admirer characterizes him) is a model of social discretion, and it is here that Richardson exhibits most skill in holding our attention. The issue will not be in doubt; Sir Charles will emerge with honour; but we shall still be interested to learn how he avoids a challenge to a duel, how he deals with a passionate Italian lady who attacks him with a poniard, how he answers Clementina's haughty relations, or how, when Clementina would assent to marry him on the impossible condition of his accepting the Catholic faith, he can decently decline.

The social adroitness demanded of Sir Charles is one of many things which might well have been decided in committee. In this novel, which is more loosely constructed than *Clarissa*, more widely ranging in scene, and more densely populated with characters, Richardson was in effect returning to the problems of *Pamela II* and his *Letters*. He was once more concerning himself with questions of conduct, even of social finesse. The strong interest in casuistry evident in *Clarissa* is apparent here too, but it is exercised with few (if any) tragic implications. 'Many things', he wrote to Lady Echlin (*Correspondence*, v. 34), 'are thrown out in the several characters, on purpose to provoke friendly debate; and perhaps as trials of the reader's judgment, manners, taste, and capacity.' Sir Charles's role as lover, though his most prominent, is by no means his only one. He is exhibited for our admiration as a brother, a nephew, a guardian, a son, a husband, and a landlord; even as a grandson-in-law. Only Sir Charles as a father is lacking. In each of these relations he has a course to take on which someone less adroit might have stumbled. The eventual meeting of Clementina with Harriet, now Lady Grandison, might have occasioned some embarrassment, but 'the *tender friend* in her, the *beloved wife*, were, with the nicest propriety, distinguished by him'. On an earlier occasion, Harriet saw fit to commiserate with him on the pain he must feel to be 'once more present to the woes of the inimitable Clementina'. How should Sir Charles reply?

Had he praised me highly for this my address to him, it would have looked, such was the situation on both sides, as if he had thought this disinterested behaviour in me, an extraordinary piece of magnanimity and self-denial; and, of consequence, as if he had supposed I had views upon him, which he wondered I could give up. His is the most delicate of human minds! (Vol. iv, letter VII)

Questions of social finesse such as these were debated in Richardson's literary court. They are the most enduring parts of the novel, and may perhaps justify the claim that it was written in committee. He had achieved nothing more delicate in his earlier books, and though today we may find the robustness of *Pamela* and the tragic intensity of *Clarissa* more appealing, it was *Sir Charles Grandison* which revealed the possibilities of the novel of domestic manners. It was *Sir Charles Grandison* which was Jane Austen's favourite.

Like Richardson, Fielding[1] was accidentally deflected into this 'new species of writing', but he was well prepared for it by his experience of men and books, and by his previous career as a writer. He came of a family of small landowners in the West Country related to the Earls of Denbigh: amongst his immediate

---

[1] Henry Fielding, 1707–54, was educated at Eton and Leyden. He wrote for the stage, but became obnoxious to Walpole's administration, and was silenced by the Licensing Act of 1737. He took up journalism and practised as a barrister. He became justice of the peace for Westminster, and his zeal in this office makes him an important figure in the history of the police system.

forebears we find men who had risen to positions of some distinction in the learned professions. It might be suspected that the novelist derived his inclination towards the law from his mother's father, who was a Justice of the Queen's Bench, and that to his paternal grandfather, an archdeacon of Salisbury, he owed both his love of learning and the strong bent towards Christian moral teaching which characterize his novels.

At the early age of twenty-one, he wrote his first play, *Love in Several Masques*, a comedy of manners. Partly no doubt owing to the patronage of his cousin, Lady Mary Wortley Montagu, the play was performed at Drury Lane Theatre (1728), and ran for four nights. But though he was to lead a busy life as a dramatist and theatre-manager between 1730 and 1737, Fielding now decided not to pursue his modest success but to enrol as a student in the Faculty of Letters at the University of Leyden under the redoubtable critic Peter Burman. In later years he was to mock Burman's editorial manner in the notes to his burlesque tragedy *Tom Thumb*; but it is probable that he now received his first instructions in critical theory, and began to obtain his extensive knowledge of classical literature. Certainly he was later to own a remarkable library of classical and modern texts, and his novels show that he possessed what Johnson considered the primary equipment of the modern novelist, 'learning which is to be gained from books'.

At the age of thirty-five when he began to write *Joseph Andrews*, he had had sufficient opportunity to acquire the second item in Johnson's equipment, 'experience which . . . must arise from general converse and accurate observation of the living world'. If we did not know this from *Joseph Andrews* itself, we should know it from the plays written during the seven years following his return from Leyden in 1730 and from his journalistic essays. These serve to show something of the range of that experience as well as indicate how the experience might be used by the future novelist.

Writing for the stage had taught him how to manipulate dialogue and to devise speech rhythms for distinguishing a country squire from a man about town or a modish lady from a young miss. It had taught him to contrive a concatenation of incidents by which the principal characters are brought together in the final scene of play or novel for the denouement.

It seems also to have accustomed him to imagine some of his scenes in terms of a drawing-room set on a stage of limited dimensions, and to offer in the novel scenes which experience told him would be effective in the theatre. His plays abound in scenes where characters are interrupted by an unexpected entry which disturbs and perplexes their existing relationships. Thus in Act III of *The Temple Beau* (1730), an early play, young Wilding is pretending to make love to Lady Lucy Pedant and has just taken her in his arms when they are interrupted by the entry first of her husband ('Hoity-toity? Hey-day! What's here to do? Have I caught you, gentlefolks?' . . .) and, immediately after, of Wilding's father, who has lately discovered his son's deceptions. This use of the unexpected entry is more skilfully developed in *Tom Jones* (XV. 5), in a scene where Lord Fellamar's unwanted attentions to Sophia in Lady Bellaston's house are interrupted by the entry of Squire Western, who has at last discovered where Sophia has taken refuge. Western is followed by Lady Bellaston, who joins him in representing to Sophia the advantages of agreeing to a proposal of marriage. Lord Fellamar, being assured that he was meant by Lady Bellaston and assuming that he must also be meant by Western, decides to take advantage of the new turn in the situation:

Coming up therefore, to the squire, he said, 'Though I have not the honour, sir, of being personally known to you; yet, as I find I have the happiness to have my proposals accepted, let me intercede, sir, in behalf of the young lady, that she may not be more solicited at this time.'

'You intercede, sir!' said the squire; 'why, who the devil are you?'

'Sir, I am Lord Fellamar,' answered he, 'and am the happy man, whom I hope you have done the honour of accepting for a son-in-law.'

'You are the son of a b——,' replied the squire, 'for all your laced coat. You my son-in-law, and be d——n'd to you!'

'I shall take more from you, sir, than from any man,' answered the Lord; 'but I must inform you, that I am not used to hear such language without resentment.'

'Resent my a——,' quoth the squire. 'Don't think I am afraid of such a fellow as thee art! because hast got a spit there dangling at thy side. Lay by your spit, and I'll give thee enough of meddling with what doth not belong to thee.—I'll teach you to father-in-law me. I'll lick thy jacket.'

'It's very well, sir,' said my lord, 'I shall make no disturbance

before the ladies. I am very well satisfied. Your humble servant,
sir; Lady Bellaston, your most obedient.'

There can be little doubt that in this episode Fielding has made
use of his theatrical experience, as he has also done in scenes
involving the use of stage properties, even though the number
of these is meagre. The most notable example in his plays is
perhaps to be found in Act III of *The Letter Writers* (1731),
where Mrs. Wisdom and her gallant Rakel are disturbed by
the arrival of Mrs. Softly, and Rakel, tender of Mrs. Wisdom's
reputation, hides under the table. Mrs. Softly is followed by
Mr. Wisdom and a nephew, who in a drunken fit overturns
the table, and discovers Rakel. This is the prototype of more
memorable discoveries, of Lady Bellaston discovering Mrs.
Honour in hiding behind the bed in Jones's room (XV. 7), and
of Jones discovering the philosopher Square behind a rug in
Molly Seagrim's bedchamber (V. 5). It is surprising that after
his early experiment in *The Letter Writers* Fielding should not
have improved upon the device in a subsequent play. The hint
was to be taken by Sheridan, however, who shows, in the scene
of Lady Teazle's discovery behind a screen in Joseph Surface's
room, that he had learned something from each of the episodes
in *Tom Jones*, for he there combined both the embarrassment
of Square's discovery and the reversal of fortune which sprang
from Mrs. Honour's.

During his career as a dramatist Fielding had attempted a
considerable number of forms. He had written witty comedies
of intrigue in the Restoration manner, farces, ballad operas
with political implications, burlesques, comedies reflecting upon
modern manners, and satirical comedies on the pattern of Buckingham's *Rehearsal* in which an absurd play is rehearsed with
comments from the author, a critical acquaintance, and the
players. Two of the last of these, *Pasquin* (1736) and *The Historical Register* (1737), were amongst the most successful of his
plays, and the device which he there employs of accompanying
the action with critical comment from the wings may perhaps
have suggested to him the 'prolegomenous' chapters of *Tom
Jones* which, on a more serious level, serve the same purpose.
Equally significant is his early experience of burlesque in *Tom
Thumb* (1730) and *The Covent-Garden Tragedy* (1731), where by
burlesquing an old-fashioned 'kind', he produced a new 'kind',
as it were, by mutation. Though the burlesque of epic is not so

prominent in *Joseph Andrews* and its successors as the burlesque of tragedy in *Tom Thumb*, it is by a similar process of 'mutation' that the novels arose.

Fielding's experience as a journalist was scarcely less useful to his future career than his experience in the theatre. From 1739 to 1741 he was the leader of a group of writers responsible for conducting an Opposition newspaper called the *Champion*. To this journal Fielding contributed a number of essays modelled on the *Spectator*. Just as Addison had invented a Spectator Club and had defined the *persona* of one member of the club who should write his lucubrations, aided and abetted by his fellow members, so Fielding assumed the *persona* of Captain Hercules Vinegar, whose business it was to write about the issues of the day, aided by his wife Joan and their two sons. Like Addison too he varies the form of his articles, now character sketches, now lay sermons, or letters from imaginary correspondents, visions, critical papers, essays in instalments, and Saturday papers on religious matters. These essays reveal a more serious-minded Fielding than we might have supposed judging from the plays alone. Here he is to be seen formulating his views on the moral problems which form the staple of his three novels, and illustrating those problems by anecdotes and character sketches. He was also unwittingly practising himself in what was regarded as an important part of the novelist's duty. The novelist was expected to provide, in Johnson's phrase, 'lectures of conduct'. He was not merely to edify by the story he told, but to make sure that his lesson was understood. Hence the pithy, and summary, comment upon manners, common alike to the novelist and the essayist.

For much of his future work Fielding was well prepared both in theory and in practice. It is not surprising, therefore, that from the beginning his command was assured, even though his approach was haphazard, even accidental. If it had not been for *Pamela*, he might never have become a novelist. In that novel Richardson had attempted to exact an unhesitating belief in Pamela's word and in the truth of appearances. Such are his powers and so implicit his belief that he almost persuades us to believe too. Almost, but not quite. Many contemporaries were persuaded; but others saw that a different interpretation was possible, and amongst these was Fielding.

To convey this alternative interpretation, Fielding called

upon his experience in burlesque and produced (1741), pseud-onymously, *An Apology for the Life of Mrs. Shamela Andrews. In which, the many notorious Falshoods and Misrepresentations of a Book called Pamela, are Exposed and refuted; and all the matchless Arts of that young Politician, set in a true and just Light. Together with A full Account of all that passed between her and Parson Arthur Williams; whose Character is represented in a manner something different from what he bears in Pamela. The whole being exact Copies of authentick Papers delivered to the Editor.* It is a riotous travesty, in which Pamela is shown as a shameless and designing hussy, yet ready to talk for 'a full Hour and a half, about my Vartue' or 'of honourable Designs till Supper-time', and Mr. B.'s full name is discovered to be Booby. And just as the rehearsed plays in *Pasquin* and *The Historical Register* had been enclosed within a framework of commentary from the supposed author and his friend, so these authentic letters are sent to Parson Tickletext, who had taken *Pamela* at Richardson's valuation, by Parson Oliver who knew the facts.

If any moral is to be drawn, it is that the distinction between being and seeming must be recognized. No exponent of the comedy of manners could fail to draw such a distinction, and Fielding's plays are especially rich in characters who are not what they seem, from Lady Gravely, the affected prude of *The Temple Beau*, to the false and grasping Valences of *The Fathers*. But Fielding had more than a professional dramatist's interest in unmasking appearances. He returned to the subject in an essay on the Pursuit of Reputation, published in the *Champion*, 4 March 1740, where he showed that folly and vice 'are continually industrious to disguise themselves', and wear the habits of virtue and wisdom; 'which the world, always judging by the outside, easily suffers them to accomplish'; and the irony of *The Life of Mr Jonathan Wild the Great* (1743) is sustained—tediously, it must be admitted—to prove that the Great Man, properly considered, is a bully and a thief. Even in *A Journey from this World to the Next*—also published in 1743—while the satire is far more miscellaneous, and the successive reincarnations of Julian the Apostate as a slave, a Jew, a courtier, a statesman, an alderman, and so on, give scope for forays in all imaginable directions, the preoccupation with overreaching and self-deception is unmistakable.

The distinction between being and seeming is the guiding

principle of *Joseph Andrews*. In the preface to his novel Fielding explains that the Ridiculous is his province, that the only source of the true Ridiculous is Affectation, and that Affectation 'proceeds from one of these two causes, Vanity or Hypocrisy'. To display the Ridiculous he has devised this new kind of writing, the comic epic poem in prose, observing the best epic practice in such matters as fable and characters; but whereas the epic fable is customarily grave and solemn, his will be light and ridiculous, and whereas epic characters are of the highest, his will mostly be of inferior rank and manners. The difficulty is to see how Fielding interprets the representation of the fable in action. Fortunately he is more explicit in the preface he wrote for his sister's novel, *David Simple* (1744). There, after referring to his preface to *Joseph Andrews*, he mentions the two great originals of all epic writing, the *Iliad* and the *Odyssey*, which

differ principally in the action, which in the *Iliad* is entire and uniform; in the *Odyssey*, is rather a series of actions, all tending to produce one great end.

The followers of Homer have all observed this principal difference, whether their imitations were serious or comic; and so we see that just as Pope in *The Dunciad* fixed on one action, Butler and Cervantes fixed on a series. Sarah Fielding's work belongs to the latter category;

the fable consists of a series of separate adventures, detached from and independent on each other, yet all tending to one great end.

The same may also be seen in *Joseph Andrews*. That also is an Odyssean epic, 'consisting of a series of separate adventures, detached from and independent on each other, yet all tending to one great end'; and it may be observed that just as the *Odyssey* relates the adventures of Odysseus in finding his way home and the hardships which befell him after incurring the wrath of Poseidon, so Fielding relates the adventures of Joseph Andrews and Parson Adams in finding their way home and the hardships which befell them after Joseph had incurred the wrath of Lady Booby. Perhaps contemporary readers might have noticed an even closer application of the burlesque. The critic Ramsay had pointed out that in Fénelon's *Aventures de Télémaque* it is the hatred of Venus rather than the wrath of Poseidon that supplies the cause of the action, and that 'the Hatred of *Venus* against a young Prince, that despises Pleasure for the Sake of Virtue, and subdues his Passions by the Assistance of Wisdom, is a Fable drawn from Nature, and at the same Time includes the sublimest Morality'. No reader could fail to relish the notion of the lascivious Lady Booby in the role of Venus, whose desire for her handsome footman Joseph Andrews is turned to hatred when that young Prince despises Pleasure for the sake of Virtue, and subdues his passions by the assistance of his sister Pamela's wisdom.

But what is the great end to which all the separate adventures are tending? Why, surely, the display of the Ridiculous, ef those affectations which arise from vanity and hypocrisy. This is the characteristic common to Lady Booby, Mrs. Slipslop, and Mrs. Grave-airs, all of them women who pretend to more modesty, more learning, or more gentility than they possess. And this is the characteristic of the innkeepers and their wives who can make a show of human kindness once they are satisfied of the standing of their guests, of the soldiers who pretend to valour, of the justices who pretend to a knowledge of the law, and of the parsons who pretend to Godliness. Even Parson Trulliber can make a show of Methodism, when he is satisfied that Adams has not come to buy his pigs: 'Get out of my doors,' he cries, when Adams tells him that, in addition to faith, he must perform the good works of giving to the needy; 'Fellow, dost thou speak against faith in my house? I will no longer remain under the same roof with a wretch who speaks wantonly of faith and the Scriptures.'

The two interpolated stories fall into place in this pattern. The Unfortunate Jilt is a story of pretence to affection, and the story of Mr. Wilson is a tale of the pretences practised in London life. Vanity of vanities is Mr. Wilson's theme as he recalls his experiences of life in the Temple amongst smart fellows who drank with lords they did not know and intrigued with women they never saw; and of town coquettes animated solely by vanity who sometimes have a whim to affect wisdom, wit, good-nature, politeness, and health, but are also affected to put on ugliness, folly, nonsense, ill-nature, ill-breeding, and sickness in their turns.

Such are Mr. Wilson's reflections. Far from being an idle digression, they are highly appropriate to Fielding's scheme and purpose; for his action, by confining him to the high road and the inn, precludes him from commenting upon London life, and it is a sample of London society which Mr. Wilson's story exposes.

But these at worst are transient characters, and at best they are minor. What of Parson Adams himself? He too has his vanities, innocent vanities indeed, of his learning and his power as a preacher. His role, however, is that of a modern Don Quixote; a man of good sense, good parts, and good nature, as Fielding declares, but 'as entirely ignorant of the ways of this world as an infant just entered into it could possibly be'. His book-reading did not, like his illustrious prototype's, lead him to mistake windmills for giants or inns for castles; it led him instead to expect on every hand an honest, undesigning, Christian behaviour. He is therefore constantly the victim of deceit. But he never loses our affection, partly because his expectations are noble, and partly because (like Don Quixote again) he hurls himself upon the oppressor thinking only of the blows his two fists or his crabstick will deliver, and nothing of those he will receive. It is not merely in such episodes as the fight at the inn which interrupts the story of The Unfortunate Jilt, or the 'roasting' of Adams by the fox-hunting squire (which recalls the treatment of Don Quixote at the hands of the Duke and Duchess), or the midnight tussle with Mrs. Slipslop where Adams believes himself bewitched, that the reader recognizes the justice of the assertion on the title-page of *Joseph Andrews*, that it is 'Written in Imitation of the Manner of Cervantes'.

But there are two sides to the relationship of being and seeming. While most of the men and women we meet in *Joseph Andrews* are worse than they seem, others are better. And though the bedraggled appearance of the worthy Adams is the most prominent example, Fielding asks us to notice that the man who pays the stranded travellers' bill is not the wealthy Parson Trulliber but 'a fellow who had been formerly a drummer in an Irish regiment, and now travelled the country as a pedlar'; that when Joseph lies sick at the Tow-wouses' inn, it is not the surgeon, or the parson, or the innkeeper, who looks after him, but Betty the chambermaid, whose morals are no better than they should be; and when Joseph has been found wounded and naked in a ditch, it is not any of the fine ladies in a passing coach who take pity on him, but the postilion, (a lad who hath been since transported for robbing a hen-roost), [who] voluntarily stript off a greatcoat, his only garment, at the same time swearing a great oath (for which he was rebuked by the passengers), 'that he would rather ride in his shirt all his life than suffer a fellow-creature to lie in so miserable a condition.'

To some extent, this anatomy of the ridiculous is a counter-blast to *Pamela*, and by recalling certain incidents in that novel and introducing one or two of its characters Fielding made sure that we should keep *Pamela* in view. Richardson had placed an implicit trust in the truth of appearances. But that way lies self-deception: it is only by the most careful scrutiny that we can see beneath appearances and find the true springs of human action.

Yet appearances are important too. 'It is not enough', Fielding writes, 'that your designs, nay that your actions, are intrinsically good; you must take care that they shall appear so'; for 'prudence and circumspection are necessary even to the best of men'. The passage occurs in one of those chapters of *Tom Jones* (III. 7) 'in which the author himself makes his appearance on the stage', and it is close to the heart of the novel. The theme is in fact announced in similar terms in the Dedication:

> I have endeavoured strongly to inculcate, that virtue and inno-
> cence can scarce ever be injured but by indiscretion; and . . . it is this
> alone which often betrays them into the snares which deceit and
> villany spread for them.

To illustrate this Fielding chose a hero as typical of his order of society as the epic hero was of his. We are asked to recognize that Tom, in spite of lapses from prudence and circumspection, and in spite of some contraventions of the moral code, is essentially a good man. It might be said of Tom as Ramsay had said of Fénelon's Telemachus:

> Our Poet does not lift *Telemachus* above Humanity; he makes him
> fall into such Weaknesses, as are compatible with a sincere Love of
> Virtue.

Young Mr. Blifil, on the other hand, with whom Tom is brought up in Mr. Allworthy's household, has more than enough of prudence and circumspection, but his love of virtue is on a par with the affectations which Fielding exposed in

Joseph Andrews. The distinction is one which Sheridan was to familiarize when, as we have already noted (pp. 186–7, above) he contrasted the brothers Charles and Joseph Surface in *The School for Scandal*.

The best critical theory of the day was agreed that an epic should have a beginning, a middle, and an end, that the beginning should deal with the causes of the action, and that in the causes might be observed two opposite 'designs', the hero's and the design of those who opposed him. In adopting these sensible precepts, Fielding provided an introductory section of six books in which numerous incidents open Tom's character and reveal the designs of Blifil and his two tutors, Thwackum and Square, who sought to blacken Tom in the eyes of Mr. Allworthy and to prevent him from marrying Sophia and inheriting Squire Western's estate. Tom is shown (IV. 6) to have 'somewhat about him, which, though I think writers are not thoroughly agreed in its name' (Shaftesbury had called it the 'moral sense')

doth certainly inhabit some human breasts; whose use is not so properly to distinguish right from wrong, as to prompt and incite them to the former, and to restrain and withhold them from the latter. . . . Though he did not always act rightly, yet he never did otherwise without feeling and suffering for it.

Thus the boy is incited to sell the little horse which Mr. Allworthy had given him so as to prevent the family of a dismissed servant from starving, and he is prompted to risk his neck in recovering Sophia's pet bird which Blifil had maliciously allowed to escape. And if as a young man he is also prompted to fornication with the gamekeeper's daughter, he is prepared to deal honourably with her until he discovers that he was not the first to seduce her; and if he was drunk and disorderly in Mr. Allworthy's house, it was because he had already been thrown into an 'immoderate excess of rapture' on hearing that Mr. Allworthy was recovering from his dangerous illness. Allworthy summarizes (V. 7) what Fielding wishes us to think of Tom, when he says to him on his sickbed:

I am convinced, my child, that you have much goodness, generosity, and honour, in your temper: if you will add prudence and religion to these, you must be happy.

But in spite of his conviction, Allworthy allows his mind to be poisoned by the malicious insinuatious of Blifil, and turns Tom away from his house into a series of adventures on the high road, corresponding to those of Joseph Andrews and Parson Adams. They fill the second six books of the novel and correspond, in epic terms, to 'the Shipping off of *Æneas*, his Voyages, his Battels, and all the Obstacles he met with', which (in the words of Le Bossu) 'compose a just Middle; [for] they are a Consequence of the Destruction of Troy . . . and these same Incidents require an End'.

The high road leads to London, and on it are not only Tom (and Partridge, his Sancho Panza) but Sophia, who has fled from her father's house to escape being forced into marriage with Blifil. As in *Joseph Andrews* the high road and the inn provide a suitable scene for the testing of character, the recognition of bad nature masquerading as good, and of good nature concealed or tainted by imprudence. Tom has something to learn even from the Man of the Hill who, like Mr. Wilson and like many a character in epic, is permitted to interrupt the narrative with his story. The Man of the Hill provides further instances of imprudence, in particular of incautiousness in placing his affections, and as a result he had become a misanthrope and a hermit. But, as Tom permits himself to comment (VIII. 15), 'What better could be expected in love derived from the stews, or in friendship first produced and nourished at the gaming table?' One must not think evil of the rest of mankind on that account, for, as Tom continues, enunciating Fielding's doctrines of the Good-Natured Man and the deceptiveness of appearances,

If there was, indeed, much more wickedness in the world than there is, it would not prove such general assertions against human nature, since much of this arrives by mere accident, and many a man who commits evil is not totally bad and corrupt in his heart.

Sophia too is learning as much as Tom, directly in such scenes as that at the inn at Upton, and by proxy as she listens to Mrs. Fitzpatrick's cautionary tale of her imprudent marriage, interrupted as it is by appeals to Sophia to declare how she would have acted in like circumstances.

The lovers reach London independently and the final section of six further books begins. Tom's good nature is as clear as ever, notably in his generous treatment of the highwayman who was driven by penury to attack him, and in his chivalrous championship of Mrs. Miller's daughter; but alas, his imprudence is clearer still in 'the ignominious circumstance of being kept' by Lady Bellaston. Fielding never asks his readers to overlook Tom's misdemeanours. His worst offence is most severely punished, for his relations with Lady Bellaston cannot be forgiven by Sophia; and we see him at the end of the Sixteenth Book at the nadir of his fortunes, rejected by Sophia, dismissed from Allworthy's favour, and imprisoned on a charge of murdering his opponent in a duel. 'Such', Fielding muses (XVII. 1), 'are the calamities in which he is at present involved, owing to his imprudence... that we almost despair of bringing him to any good; and if our reader delights in seeing executions, I think he ought not to lose any time in taking a first row at Tyburn.' Readers of the epic will recognize that the time is ripe for a Discovery or a Reversal of Fortune, perhaps even for both, and they will recall that it was not unusual for the author to invoke divine aid for rescuing a hero in distress. Fielding has prepared both for his Discovery—that was allowed for in making Tom a foundling—and for his Reversal of Fortune; but he disdains to employ the marvellous. It is true that luck is on Tom's side when his victim in the duel recovers from his wound, and when the facts of his parentage (concealed by Blifil) are discovered; but in other respects the reader is asked to recognize that Tom has worked his passage. He has cast his bread upon the waters in acts of abundant good nature, and by the assistance of Mrs. Miller's representations to Mr. Allworthy he finds it after many days. His Virtue is Rewarded by restoration into the favour of Allworthy and the good graces of Sophia. Since he is now discovered to be Allworthy's nephew and heir, Squire Western has no further objection to bestowing his daughter upon him; they marry, and 'preserve the purest and tenderest affection for each other, an affection daily increased and confirmed by mutual endearments, and mutual esteem'.

This is a pious hope which the reader may find it difficult to share, for it rests upon the large assumption that Tom had ceased to be indiscreet. Furthermore he was at best a good-natured man; and though endowed with a well-developed Moral Sense, he required on Allworthy's evidence to add religion as well as prudence to his good nature. Even if we allow that he had become prudent, there is nothing to show that he had become religious. Some such reflections seem to have occurred to Fielding, for his next novel *Amelia* (1752) begins where *Tom Jones* leaves off. Captain and Mrs. Booth also entertained the purest and tenderest affection for each other and confirmed it by mutual endearments and mutual esteem, yet various accidents befell them owing partly to Booth's character, and it is with these accidents and with their effect upon this worthy couple that the novel is concerned.

The decision to deal with the accidents of domestic life set Fielding some new problems in structure. The high road and the inn could have no place here since married folk are not usually nomadic, and consequently we miss the Odyssean-Quixotic episodes which provided him in the earlier novels with so many shining opportunities for unmasking affectation and testing character. He had also to decide how to relate the earlier history of his couple, a problem he had not been required to face before. But the comic adaptation of epic conventions was ready to hand here as it had been at the beginning of *Joseph Andrews*. Just as Aeneas was stranded on the coasts of Carthage, was succoured there by Dido, related to her his story, and consummated his furtive love in a cave, so Captain Booth was stranded in Newgate Prison, was succoured there by Miss Matthews, a high-class courtesan, related to her his story, and consummated his furtive love in a superior kind of cell. Nor is this merely an ingenious piece of burlesque. Booth's misdemeanour with Miss Matthews, which he is ashamed to confess to Amelia, dogs him throughout the novel; while the sombreness of the opening scenes in Newgate Prison set the tone of the book. Fielding takes care to show us the squalor and oppression which is the lot of the penniless prisoner, and on the other hand the relative comfort which is to be had at the price of a bribe; and he describes the coarse and depraved ruffians, male and female, the tricksters and sharpers, who molest and prey upon the weak, the unfortunate, and even the innocent who have come there through a miscarriage of justice. This is the scene in which we first discover Booth, whose previous history shows him to be imprudent, liable to deception, with 'very slight and uncertain' notions of religion, yet essentially good-natured. He will not return to Newgate, but he will always be in danger of return.

And when he escapes, the reader recognizes that Newgate was only a somewhat more lurid epitome of society outside, where merit counts for nothing, where civil and military places go by influence exerted for a bribe, where those in high place have rogues, pimps, and bawds in their pay, and where gallantry is a cover for fornication and adultery. Fielding had said as much long ago in his play *The Modern Husband* (1731), and had repeated it in *Jonathan Wild*; and if *Joseph Andrews* and *Tom Jones* appear lighter in tone than *Amelia*, it is only because the scene is laid more frequently in the country. London is the breeding-place for such creatures as Lord Fellamar and Lady Bellaston, and Mr. Wilson anticipates Booth in finding that in London 'poverty and distress, with their horrid trains of duns, attorneys, bailiffs, haunted me day and night. My clothes grew shabby, my credit bad, my friends and acquaintance of all kinds cold.'

The scene is in fact so sombre that a tragic conclusion seems inevitable. Even a stronger and a better man than Booth could scarcely escape that fate. In considering the conclusion to which he was leading his 'worthy couple', Fielding is likely to have paid attention to the best critical teaching available. The consensus of opinion amongst commentators upon the epic pointed to a conclusion favourable to the hero. Le Bossu indeed could discover no reason why that should be so; he concludes:

yet if any heed be given to Authority, I do not know any one Instance of a Poet, who finishes his Piece with the Misfortunes of his Heroe. . . . The *Epick Poem*'s Action is of a larger Extent than that of the Theatre; [and] it would perhaps be less satisfactory to the Reader, if, after so much Pains and so long Troubles with which this kind of Poem is always fill'd, it should at last bring them to a doleful and unhappy End.

The easiest way of bringing the Booths to a happy end might well have been to repeat the formula of *Tom Jones* and show the eventual reward of the hero's virtuous actions. But Fielding seems to have been no longer content with such teaching. It was Booth's mistake to believe that as men 'act entirely from their passions, their actions can have neither merit nor demerit'. If a man's ruling passion happened to be benevolence, he would relieve the distress of others; but if it were avarice, ambition, or pride, other men's miseries would have no effect upon him. Booth is eventually to be corrected of an error, which to Amelia seemed little better than atheism, by reading a volume of Barrow's sermons while detained in the bailiff's house; but in the meanwhile Fielding allows him little opportunity for charity. The reader notices instead how his imprudence in the use of what little money he has reduces Amelia to penury, and how his ill-placed trust and his single act of fornication endanger her chastity. She, however, shows herself to be on all occasions a model of wifely prudence, constancy, obedience, forgiveness, and love.

'To retrieve the ill consequences of a foolish conduct, and by struggling manfully with distress to subdue it, is one of the noblest efforts of wisdom and virtue': that is all that Fielding asks of his worthy couple; and having displayed their struggles, he is not averse to rescuing them by an epic Discovery (that Amelia is an heiress) and an epic Reversal of Fortune, which enables a now prudent and Christian Booth to retire to a country estate.

In *Amelia*, as in *Tom Jones*, Fielding implies that at the end of the book the hero is in some respects an altered man without persuading us of the fact. Dickens was the first novelist to succeed in such persuasion and George Eliot the first to specialize in showing the modifying effect of incident upon character. These Victorian successes have made demands which the modern reader is inclined to impose both upon earlier novelists and upon earlier dramatists without perhaps reflecting whether changes in character are altogether necessary or always important. *Amelia*, like *Tom Jones*, deals with wider issues than the modification of character. It has to do not merely with Booth and his wife, but with miseries and distresses typical of mid-eighteenth-century London life. No other novel provides such a wide panorama of London society or better conveys an impression of London life in the 1750s.

In a paper which he wrote for the last of his periodicals, the *Covent Garden Journal* (28 January 1752) Fielding declared that he would not trouble the world with any more novels. He had not been entirely committed to the profession of letters since the abrupt termination of his dramatic career. The severity of his attack upon Walpole's government in *Pasquin* had led directly to the Licensing Act of 1737 and to the closure of all theatres but Drury Lane and Covent Garden. Fielding's Little

Theatre in the Haymarket was the principal victim, and his chief source of income was thus removed. He thereupon began a serious study of the law, was called to the Bar in 1740, and practised for some time on the Western Circuit. Shortly after completing *Tom Jones* in 1748, and before its publication, he had been appointed a police-court magistrate at Bow Street, and his jurisdiction was soon extended to the whole of the County of Middlesex. As a magistrate he was exceptionally industrious, and did much to break up the gangs of thieves which infested London. His *Enquiry Into the Causes of the late Increase of Robbers* (1751), dedicated to Lord Chancellor Hardwicke, shows both an extensive knowledge of the law, and an intimate acquaintance with the evil and its origin. His energies might have been directed more and more to clearing up the criminal underworld if his health had not broken down. In the summer of 1754 he undertook a sea trip to Lisbon with his wife and daughter in a desperate search for health, and whiled away his time in keeping a diary. This he revised, and the manuscript was posthumously published as *A Journal of a Voyage to Lisbon*. Not the least of its merits is the picture it gives us of the man himself, affectionately considerate to his family, patiently suffering from an incurable disease, yet observing with undiminished zest the oddities of human behaviour, and seizing such opportunities as incidents offered for social or political comment. The book is prefaced by a disquisition on travel literature comparable in kind to the disquisition on the comic epic poem in prose which prefaces *Joseph Andrews*. Once again Fielding declared that he was laying down the rules for a kind of writing which had not been properly undertaken before (except by Lord Anson in the account of his circumnavigation: see above, pp. 252–4); for travellers seem to have fallen either into the fault of 'filling their pages with monsters which nobody hath ever seen, and with adventures which never have, nor could possibly have happened to them', or on the other hand they

waste their time and paper with recording things and facts of so common a kind, that they challenge no other right of being remembered than as they had the honour of having happened to the author.

This opportunity of reforming travel literature was as haphazard as the chance he took of reforming the novel; but even if he had lived longer, it was not likely that he would have had occasion to write more in this kind. It is easy, however, to see that his theories might have been profitably applied to biography, and that he was well equipped by imagination, a reverence for truth, judgement, and a sense of proportion to succeed in that kindred form.

But this is idle speculation. Even though he may have felt that he had outgrown the novel, it is there that his achievement lies; and it is an achievement typical of an age which relished the mock-epics of Pope and the ballad operas of Gay. Fielding brought literary experience gained in other writing and a wealth of critical learning to bear upon the production of a new form, but a form which constantly recalls older, well-tried forms and adapts them to the spirit and use of his own times; and he used this form to display 'just copies of human manners' and to offer 'lectures of conduct, and introductions into life'.

Smollett,[1] like Fielding, reached the novel after trying other forms, though his attempts at tragedy and at verse-satire were neither instructive to him nor significant to us. *The Adventures of Roderick Random* (1748) was the work of eight months' interrupted writing in the summer and autumn of 1747. It was hastily written; but the preface shows that Smollett had given some thought to the question of form. He recognized that distinction between the novel and the romance which Johnson was to draw so clearly in the *Rambler* (see pp. 384–5), and he seems to have believed that the novel as an anti-romance had not yet been attempted in English. *Pamela* he might justly regard as something different in kind, a quite unsuitable model for his purpose. *Joseph Andrews* would have served him better; but it is not surprising that this solitary example of an English anti-romance did not make so powerful an impression upon him as Lesage's *Gil Blas*, that massive work of the greatest living French novelist. His purpose would have been served equally well by either model, for each provides a suitable opportunity of representing 'familiar scenes in an uncommon and amusing point of view'; in each the reader is permitted to 'gratify his curiosity in pursuing the adventures of a person in whose favour he is

[1] Tobias George Smollett, 1721–71, was educated at Glasgow University, and became a surgeon. In 1741 he took part in the ill-fated expedition to Cartagena (in what is now Colombia) during the war against Spain. Returning to London, he practised surgery and became a professional author. As editor of the *Critical Review* he was imprisoned for libel, 1759. He died in Italy, near Leghorn.

prepossessed; [to] espouse his cause, [and to] sympathise with him in distress'; and in each, 'the vicissitudes of life appear in their peculiar circumstances, opening an ample field for wit and humour': these are Smollett's stated intentions. But whereas the pattern of *Joseph Andrews* would have confined him to a single journey along an English highway, the looser pattern of *Gil Blas* gave the perhaps illusory freedom of a whole lifetime's adventures.

But though Lesage had shown how the knavery and foibles of life might be described 'with infinite humour and sagacity', the extravagance of some of the situations and the ludicrous disgraces to which Gil Blas is subjected prevent 'that generous indignation which ought to animate the reader against the sordid and vicious disposition of the world'. Smollett, in short, had no use for the *picaro*, the rogue whose exploits keep him moving from place to place; but he would retain the scenes of the *picaro*'s adventures, since his reader will

find entertainment in viewing those parts of life, where the humours and passions are undisguised by affectation, ceremony, or education; and the whimsical peculiarities of disposition appear as nature has implanted them.

The centre of his stage is occupied, not by the *picaro*, but by a young man of good birth and sound education exposed, as an inexperienced orphan, to the 'selfishness, envy, malice, and base indifference of mankind'. He has come from a remote region (Scotland), where manners are simple, to make his way in a society where men and women, of both high and low degree, are marked by affectation and deceit. He is an innocent whose character will be toughened by experience of the world. The time was yet to come when a novelist could make a child of virginal innocence the hero of his adventures, as Dickens was to do in *Oliver Twist* and *The Old Curiosity Shop*, and as Kafka was to do in *Amerika*, imagining that child holding his solitary way 'among a crowd of wild grotesque companions, the only pure youthful object in the throng'. The opportunities latent in this situation were doubtless beyond Smollett's power to seize— opportunities not merely for pathos, but for enlisting the reader's generous sympathies on behalf of the defenceless, beset by evil, yet remaining uncontaminated. His aim was essentially similar; but he seems to have thought that our sympathies will be most readily enlisted for the ordinary sensual man, sanguine in temperament and of 'an amorous complexion', quick to defend himself with his fists, or to revenge an insult, or to dally with a wench who takes his fancy; but loyal to his friends, generous with his purse whenever it is full, and practical in relieving distress. This blend of inexperience and impulsiveness serves to motivate a wide diversity of adventures. Such a man is likely to be often down on his luck, but his resilience will ensure that he takes the momentary advantage in any turn of the wheel of fortune; and this permits Smollett's observation to take an extensive view of mankind, if not as widely as from China to Peru, at least from Jamaica to Bath, and from the battlefield of Dettingen to the quarter-deck of a man-of-war in a sea-fight.

In his observation of mankind Smollett was not concerned to make subtle discriminations. He introduces us once more to the well-established types inherited from Latin comedy, the bully, the braggart, the old miser, the proud coquette, and the honest whore; and he assists our recognition in the traditional manner by dubbing them with allegoric names, Banter, Chatter, Bragwell, and Cringer. He also takes a hint from Shakespeare's *Henry V*, and brings together in a ship's cabin typical representatives from England, Scotland, Ireland, and Wales; and perhaps it was Ben in Congreve's *Love for Love* who revealed to him the humorous possibilities of the sailor on shore. The hint once taken, he could supply from his own experience as a ship's doctor material for his imagination to shape into Lieutenant Bowling in *Roderick Random* and Commodore Trunnion and his associates in *Peregrine Pickle*.

But though he worked in an inherited tradition of types, he made them, or many of them at least, his own. He possessed the eye of a caricaturist, which by grossly exaggerating a feature or two converts the human form into a gargoyle. One of Roderick's employers, a French apothecary, was a little old withered man, 'with a forehead about an inch high, a nose turned up at the end, large cheek-bones that helped to form a pit for his little grey eyes, [and] a great bag of loose skin hanging down on each side in wrinkles like the alforjas of a baboon'; and the body of his former master Mr. Launcelot Crab, a surgeon, was no less distorted in an opposite direction:

This member of the faculty was aged fifty, about five feet high, and ten round the belly; his face was capacious as a full moon, and much the complexion of a mulberry; his nose, resembling a powder-horn, was swelled to an enormous size, and studded all over with car-buncles; and his little grey eyes reflected the rays in such an oblique manner, that, while he looked a person full in the face, one would have imagined he was admiring the buckle of his shoe. (Ch. vii)

It is doubtful whether any reader could retain the impression of such a figure throughout the episodes in which the character appears. Nor need he try. It is enough if he responds to the description with delighted astonishment, and is conditioned to expect extravagant manners from such extravagant deformity.

For it was manners rather than men that exercised Smollett's attention. The vicissitudes of his inexperienced hero provide the opportunity of extending the polite reader's experience by showing him aspects of life which he knows to exist, but with which he is probably not acquainted at first hand. He has passed stage-wagons on the road, but he does not know what it is like to travel that way; Smollett tells him. He has heard of the press-gang, he may have seen a gang at work; Smollett tells him of the victim's fate. He has read about recent battles at sea; Smollett tells him how the sailor lives, and describes how, when he is ill on board, he must lie suspended in his hammock with fifty other wretches,

so huddled one upon another, that not more than fourteen inches' space was allotted for each with his bed and bedding; and deprived of the light of day, as well as of fresh air; breathing nothing but a noisome atmosphere of the morbid steams exhaling from their own excrements and diseased bodies, devoured with vermin hatched in the filth that surrounded them, and destitute of every convenience necessary for people in that helpless condition. (Ch. xxv)

Or the reader may have wondered how the down-and-out feed; Smollett takes him to a cellar, and shows him:

descending very successfully, [I] found myself in the middle of a cook's shop, almost suffocated with the steams of boiled beef, and surrounded by a company of hackney coachmen, chairmen, draymen, and a few footmen out of place, or on board wages, who sat eating shin of beef, tripe, cowheel, or sausages, at separate boards, covered with cloths which turned my stomach. (Ch. xiii)

The sense of physical repulsion in such passages as these is forcibly conveyed. The vividness of the reporting might almost seem to be its own justification: it might seem almost enough that Roderick Random, endowed with his creator's nervously irritable sensibility, should pass from one scene to another and record what he observes. But Smollett was not content with a 'documentary', however vivid; he must devise some means of deploying his characters. Thus as Roderick surveys the scene in the cook's shop, he is followed by his man Strap, who misses his footing on one of the steps, tumbles headlong into the room and overturns the cook, as she carries a porringer of soup; the hot soup scalds the legs of a customer, who roars with the pain, and the cook strips off the customer's stocking to empty the contents of a salt-cellar on the wound. This misadventure, like Roderick's subsequent misadventure in the ship's sick-bay, is of a sort which today we associate with comic strips designed for children. The episodes are mostly short and violent: they are more or less ingenious variations on the booby-trap by which inexperience is startled, or dignity is humiliated, or arrogance and conceit are revenged; but a few, such as the barbarous 'roasting' of Dr. Wagtail and Roderick's vengeance upon the Lavements by a design expounded by Chaucer's Reeve, extend to a complete chapter. *The Reeve's Tale* exists both in its own right and as part of a larger pattern of story-telling; but no such co-ordinating design can be discerned in the jests and tales which make up *Roderick Random*, except in so far as all are part of Roderick's manifold adventures. We might be reminded of the Merry Tales of an Elizabethan Jest Book, if it were not for the inclusion of narrative material of a different kind. Thus the history of Miss Williams, the reluctant and repentant prostitute (chapters xxii and xxiii), belongs to a recognizable literary type; and many of the episodes on board ship are as old as the Greek romances; while the account of Roderick's shipwreck off the coast of Sussex (chapter xxxvii) is modelled directly upon the wreck of the *Wager* as described in Anson's *Voyages*. Other episodes are more or less strictly autobiographical, notably the account of the Cartagena expedition, and the experience of Melopoyn the dramatist with patrons and actor-managers. The reader's attention is not kept by watching the unfolding of a plot, but he is bustled along by the author's gusto towards a conventional ending, Roderick's happy discovery of a long-lost father and his eventual reunion with the colourless Narcissa.

In *The Adventures of Peregrine Pickle* (1751) the change of scene is no less frequent and little less diversified; the merry tales, in

still greater profusion, are more carefully staged; the character-
types are even more numerous, and so, alas, are the booby-traps.
Peregrine himself is engineer-in-chief, and he exercises his barbarous powers of invention at the expense of his uncle, his tutor,
his travelling companions, the physicians of Bath, and ladies
in high society. 'The wild and ferocious Pickle', as Walter Scott
described him, 'who,—besides his gross and base brutality
towards Emilia, besides his ingratitude to his uncle, and the
savage propensity which he shows, in the pleasure he takes to
torment others by practical jokes resembling those of a fiend in
glee—exhibits a low and ungentleman-like tone of thinking,
only one degree higher than that of Roderick Random.' Scott's
castigation is morally justifiable, but it overlooks a difference
in function between the two heroes, which points to a difference
in purpose and structure between the novels, similar as they
appear to be in their dependence upon picaresque adventure.
Roderick's responses are violent, but they do not affect his
role as a victim of a cruel society; and though his new-found
father at the end of the novel blessed God for his son's adver-
sities

which, he said, enlarged the understanding, improved the heart,
steeled the constitution, and qualified a young man for all the duties
and enjoyments of life, much better than any education which
affluence could bestow, (ch. lxvi)

the reader is not permitted to observe this improvement, since
his attention is directed entirely to Roderick's misfortunes.
Peregrine, however, received the best education 'which affluence could bestow'; but it clearly and totally failed to qualify
him 'for all the duties and enjoyments of life'. He is represented
as a young man remarkable for his wit and high spirits, with
a fund of good nature and generosity in his composition, and
liberal to profusion; but so vain of his parts, so passionate, and
so ungovernable, that neither Winchester, Oxford, nor a private
tutor could restrain his irregularities. Though his foreign tour
was less futile than the young rake's in *The Dunciad*—for he was
not deficient in spirit and sense—it yielded ample opportunities for display of folly and obstinacy, which were to land him
in the Bastille and to require the British Ambassador's skill
to extricate him. His behaviour on his return to England is
directed by no higher principle than self-conceit. His conduct

to his Emilia, which Scott so sternly censured, is not excused by Smollett, who invites the reader to witness

this degeneracy in the sentiments of our imperious youth, who was now in the heyday of his blood, flushed with the consciousness of his own qualifications, vain of his fortune, and elated on the wings of imaginary expectation. Though he was deeply enamoured of Miss Gauntlet, he was far from proposing her heart as the ultimate aim of his gallantry, which, he did not doubt, would triumph over the most illustrious females of the land, and at once regale his appetite and ambition. (Ch. lxvi)

As to the fortune of thirty thousand pounds, inherited from his uncle, this

did not at all contribute to the humiliation of his spirit, but inspired him with new ideas of grandeur and magnificence, and elevated his hope to the highest pinnacle of expectation. (Ch. lxxiii)

These warning notes may sound a little muted amidst the *brio* of Smollett's horse-play; but it should be clear enough that Peregrine is riding for a fall. He loses his mistress, his fortune is dissipated in imprudent political adventures, and his attempt to revenge himself in political journalism brings him to the Fleet prison, where he languishes, relieving so far as he is able the distresses of others, and metamorphosed from a sprightly, gay, and elevated youth into 'a wan, dejected, meagre, squalid spectre; the hollow-eyed representative of distemper, indigence, and despair' (ch. ci). Peregrine has learnt his lesson, and it is time for Smollett to effect his rescue and to possess him both of Emilia and of 'a fortune more ample than his first inheritance, with a stock of experience which would steer him clear of all those quicksands among which he had been formerly wrecked' (ch. civ).

Thus *Peregrine Pickle* can be seen to conform with a theory of the novel which Smollett was to formulate in the preface to *Ferdinand Count Fathom* (1753):

A novel is a large diffused picture, comprehending the characters of life, disposed in different groups, and exhibited in various attitudes for the purposes of an uniform plan, and general occurrence, to which every individual figure is subservient. But this plan cannot be executed with propriety, probability, or success, without a principal personage to attract the attention, unite the incidents, unwind the clue of the labyrinth, and at last close the scene, by virtue of his own importance.

Yet as he, or an associate of his, admitted in an article in the *Critical Review* in January 1763, 'a romance writer may slacken the reins of his genius occasionally, without fear of offence, and sport with his subject in a careless manner'. All need not be pointed to the primary issue; and we are not required to search for the bearing upon Peregrine's career of such an elaborately staged episode as the feast in the manner of the ancients (chapter xliv), or the baffling of the bailiffs (chapter xcvii), still less in the Memoirs of a Lady of Quality (chapter lxxxi) inserted in the novel to oblige Lady Vane. Smollett cannot resist a good story: he can even turn aside in the penultimate chapter, when Peregrine is hurrying to a reconciliation with Emilia, for a jest at the expense of a country squire who was so incensed at Vandyke's portraits of his ancestors 'with a parcel of loose hair hanging about their eyes, like zo many colts', that he employed 'a painter vellow from Lundon to clap decent periwigs upon their skulls, at the rate of vive shillings a head'.

With the reins held loosely in his hand, Smollett always has time to indulge us with such titbits. But there are two dangers: the reader loses sight of the main issue, and the author impoverishes his estate. Dickens had begun to write with the same generous expenditure of his resources, and we are told by his biographer John Forster that by the time he reached the end of *Nicholas Nickleby* he was already beginning to feel the strain upon his fancy. The course he took to relieve the strain was to adopt a more economical mode of writing. It seems probable that Smollett felt the strain too. In the early 1750s he had begun to turn to those works of translation, compilation, and synthesis which were to occupy so much of his time, and which were eventually to ruin his health. He began work on his version of *Don Quixote* in 1748; he signed an agreement in 1753 for a new collection of voyages and travels to be completed in seven volumes; from 1756 till 1762 he owned and edited the *Critical Review*, though this, as he explained to an inquiring friend, was but 'a small branch of an extensive Plan which I last year projected for a sort of academy of the belles lettres'; and throughout this decade he was engaged upon his *Complete History of England*, the first four volumes of which he finished late in

1757. With these prodigious enterprises on his hands, not much could be expected of the two novels which belong to this period of his career, *The Adventures of Ferdinand Count Fathom* (1753) and *The Adventures of Sir Launcelot Greaves*, published serially in the *British Magazine* in 1760 and 1761. In fact he failed to escape from the problems posed by his conception of the novel. His 'large diffused picture' of life involved him in stories of multifarious adventures, but his stock was depleted. In purposely choosing the principal character of *Ferdinand Count Fathom* 'from the purlieus of treachery and fraud', he was turning his back upon the resolutions which had guided him in *Roderick Random* and attempting the true picaresque. This certainly enabled him to widen his range. The reader is accordingly introduced to the arts of the card-sharper, the quack-doctor, and the quack-connoisseur, aspects of life which the scope of *Roderick Random* and of *Peregrine Pickle* had not given him sufficient opportunity to describe. But scenes like these, and the rogue stories which arise from them, were not enough to cover Smollett's generous canvas, and he was led, almost instinctively compelled, into that world of romance which he had rejected in the preface to *Roderick Random*. Important tracts of the novel deal with adventures in a kind of fairyland, where knights-errant attempt to rescue ladies imprisoned in castles; or where desperate deeds of banditry are committed on lonely heaths in midnight thunderstorms; or where an owl may be heard to screech from the ruined battlement of a church, as the door is opened by a sexton

who, by the light of a glimmering taper, conducted the despairing lover to a dreary aisle, and stamped upon the ground with his foot, saying, 'Here the young lady lies interred.' (Ch. lxii)

The first type of episode looks back into the seventeenth century and beyond, the other two look forward into a world of 'gothic' adventures which was to be more resolutely and frequently explored in the next few decades.

The flirtation with romance was temporary. In *Sir Launcelot Greaves* we are back in familiar scenes: the reader witnesses a parliamentary election, he is shown a country magistrate at work, and is conducted to the King's Bench Prison and a madhouse, where he is allowed an appreciative glimpse (chapter xxiii) of the eminent psychiatrist, Dr. William Battie. Smollett's model was no longer *Gil Blas* but *Don Quixote*, and *Don Quixote* imitated at that in the most mechanical way. Whereas Parson Adams inherited the characteristics of his Spanish prototype, Sir Launcelot Greaves inherited his armour too. In the second chapter he enters a village house cap-à-pie and explains to the assembled company that his intention is 'to combat vice in all her forms, redress injuries, chastise oppression, protect the help-less and forlorn, relieve the indigent'. He does; and the plan may be admitted to lend coherence to another of Smollett's 'large, diffused pictures'. But it is a mere piece of copying, unworthy of Smollett's powers of invention. The reader is tempted to adopt the words of the morose Ferret, as he com-ments on Sir Launcelot's proposal:

'What! you set up for a modern Don Quixote? The scheme is rather too stale and extravagant. What was a humorous romance and well-timed satire in Spain near two hundred years ago, will make but a sorry jest, and appear equally insipid and absurd when really acted from affectation, at this time of day, in a country like England.'

The search for a suitable manner of representing 'familiar scenes in an uncommon and amusing point of view' was con-tinued after an interval of ten years in Smollett's last novel, *The Expedition of Humphry Clinker* (1771). As in *Roderick Random*, the principal character (Matthew Bramble, not Humphry Clinker) has come from a remote region where manners are simple to observe the ways of a life in a reputedly civilized community. This time the remote region is not Scotland but Wales, for Scottish manners will be needed for further contrast with English manners in the latter part of the book; and the protagonist, though unused to the ways of the world he visits, is neither a raw young man, nor a vain young man, neither a picaro nor a Quixote, but an elderly country squire, peevish but benevolent, ailing in body, but still in full possession of his senses, and endowed with an even fuller measure of that nervously irritable sensibility already remarked in Roderick Random.

With an elderly valetudinarian at the centre of the novel, Smollett's choice of form was restricted. One might claim that it was fortunately restricted. The picaresque of *Fathom* was ruled out by his character; the quixotry of *Greaves* and the redemptive process in *Pickle* were alike ruled out by his age. So too was the lifetime's span of *Random*. It would seem as though Smollett were forced back by his protagonist on that fruitful and well-tried form, the journey.

And other considerations seem to have combined to affect his choice. The success of his recent *Travels through France and Italy* (1766) had shown how suitably the record of a journey could take account of the character and customs of a country; and the form of letters to imaginary correspondents, in which the *Travels* were presented, encouraged a familiar manner of writing, in which the jaundiced exasperation of the traveller himself is disclosed. It also permitted an occasional anecdote, now more sparingly used than in *Roderick Random* and *Peregrine Pickle*, and more economically and pointedly related; and it allowed for different subjects to be discussed with different correspondents: thus Letter VII to a lady describes women's fashions in France, and Letter XI to a doctor describes a consultation with a French physician. The point of view of the writer is slightly shifted as he turns from one correspondent to another.

It is not surprising that Smollett should have decided to profit by this experience when he returned once more, in *Humphry Clinker*, to his large diffused picture of life. Taking a hint from Anstey's *New Bath Guide* (1766), he increased the number of his letter-writers, and thus provided himself with a simpler means of shifting his topic and his point of view. Bramble is the principal letter-writer; but we are also allowed to read the letters of his fellow travellers, his nephew and niece, Jery and Lydia Melford, his sister, Tabitha Bramble, and their servant, Winifred Jenkins. Each has a character to sustain and acquaintances to describe. Many of them we have already met in classical comedy. But Smollett also has a touch of nature at his command to individualize his types—Bramble is something more than the testy old gentleman, Lismahago something more than the soldier of fortune. He has shown that he can 'catch the manners living as they rise': the Duke of Newcastle is drawn from life at one of his levees, and (a much greater achievement) in Micklewhimmen he has drawn the first of a type of Scots lawyer in whom Scott was later to specialize. Better still are his more distant views of humanity in the mass: the caddies' banquet at Edinburgh; the mixture of social classes in the Pump Room at Bath, where we see

a broken-winded Wapping landlady squeeze through a circle of peers, to salute her brandy merchant, who stood by the window, propped upon crutches; and a paralytic attorney of Shoe Lane, in shuffling up to the bar, kicked the shins of the Chancellor of England, while his lordship, in a cut bob, drank a glass of water at the pump;

or the Rowlandsonian vision of the clergy off duty:

Not a soul is seen in this place, but a few broken-winded parsons, waddling like so many crows along the North Parade. There is always a great show of the clergy at Bath; none of your thin, puny, yellow, hectic figures, exhausted with abstinence and hard study, labouring under the *morbi eruditorum*; but great overgrown dignitaries and rectors, with rubicund noses and gouty ankles, or broad bloated faces, dragging along great swag bellies, the emblems of sloth and indigestion.

Scenes such as these point to a shift of interest, perhaps even to a different intention. Smollett has not yet exhausted his merry tales, and he still retains his enjoyment of the booby-trap; but his principal characters are now deployed to see more often than to act. It is true that his criticism of the Methodists is achieved by showing how the women of the party were affected. Thus Winifred Jenkins recounts to her friend Mary Jones the delights of Sadler's Wells, but remembers in time to add

But, thank God! I'm now vaned from all such vanities; for what are all those rarities and vagaries to the glory that shall be revealed hereafter? O Molly! let not your poor heart be puffed up with vanity.

She then proceeds:

I had almost forgot to tell you, that I have had my hair cut and pippered, and singed, and bolstered, and buckled in the newest fashion, by a French freezer. *Parley vow Francey—Vee Madmansell.* I now carries my head higher than arrow private gentlewoman of Vales. Last night, coming huom from the meeting, I was taken by lamp-light for an imminent poulterer's daughter, a great beauty. But, as I was saying, this is all vanity and vexation of spirit. The pleasures of London are no better than sower whey and stale cyder, when compared to the joys of the New Gerusalem.

It is also true that a plot of sorts is provided: Lydia languishes in love for a strolling player, who is later discovered to be the son of an old friend of her uncle, and Tabitha Bramble's search for a husband is at last rewarded by Lismahago; but this scarcely serves to distract the characters from their principal duty of observing and recording what are often divergent opinions on what they see. To Lydia the pleasure gardens of Vauxhall are

> part laid out in delightful walks; bounded with high hedges and trees, and paved with gravel; part exhibiting a wonderful assemblage of the most picturesque and striking objects, pavilions, lodges, groves, grottoes, lawns, temples, and cascades; porticoes, colonnades, and rotundas; adorned with pillars, statues, and painting; the whole illuminated with an infinite number of lamps disposed in different figures of suns, stars, and constellations; the place crowded with the gayest company, ranging through those blissful shades, or supping in different lodges on cold collations, enlivened with mirth, freedom, and good-humour, and animated by an excellent band of music.

But to Matthew Bramble's jaundiced eye the same scene presents

> a composition of baubles, overcharged with paultry ornaments, ill conceived, and poorly executed, without any unity of design, or propriety of disposition;

and as for the company, the 'crowds of noisy people', he sees them

> sitting on covered benches, exposed to the eyes of the mob, and, which is worse, to the cold, raw, night air, devouring sliced beef, and swilling port, and punch, and cider.

And it is Bramble, of course, with the keen recollection of the Welsh farm he has left behind him, who draws attention to the Londoners' food, their bread 'a deleterious paste, mixed up with chalk, alum, and bone-ashes', their sophisticated wine, their adulterated milk, 'the tallowy rancid mass called butter, manufactured with candle grease and kitchen stuff'; and as for the fruit,

> it was but yesterday that I saw a dirty barrow-bunter in the street, cleaning her dusty fruit with her own spittle; and who knows but some fine lady of St. James's parish might admit into her delicate mouth those very cherries, which had been rolled and moistened between the filthy, and perhaps ulcerated chops of a St. Giles's huckster.

The social historian who might consider using this passage would do well to reflect that it is not pure reporting. It is an account as seen through the eyes of a character of a peculiar disposition, and it is part of a view of society set out to prepare for one more favourable when this party from Wales has reached Scotland. It is a view based on fact, used for the purposes of fiction. The form itself helps to place the reporting on the borderland of fiction and fact. 'There have been so many letters upon travels lately published,' writes the imaginary bookseller, in the second letter of the novel; 'What between Smollett's, Sharp's, Derrick's, Thickness's, Baltimore's, and Baretti's, together with Shandy's Sentimental Travels, the public seems to be cloyed with that kind of entertainment.' Here was a pretence of another in the same kind, another 'mutation' of form such as the writers of this century delighted to produce; and in this variant Smollett found the happiest answer to the problem, which had engaged him from the first, of representing 'familiar scenes in an uncommon and amusing point of view'.

In some obvious respects, Laurence Sterne[1] stands apart from the novelists who have so far been considered. The mutation of epic travesty, letter-book, travel-book, or picaresque story into the new genre of the novel is a process that appears readily intelligible, at least in retrospect. *Tristram Shandy* is a mutation too, but of a genre more remote from the novel as readers in the nineteenth century came to understand it. Rabelais's *Gargantua and Pantagruel* and Swift's *Tale of a Tub* represent a fiction subordinated to the extravagant display of learned wit, in 'flim-flam stories, and pleasant fooleries', as Urquhart puts it. The vivacity of spirit that Pantagruel displayed amidst his books— 'like a great fire amongst dry wood, so active it was, vigorous and indefatigable'—is an essential element in Swift's genius, and the same quality is admirably caught by Sterne. The virtuoso exploitation of Lockian psychology in *Tristram Shandy*, the adroit conjuring with recondite terms and names, the exuberant rhetoric and keen, indiscriminate appetite for projects of all kinds, mark it as an accomplished performance in the same tradition. The nature of Sterne's mutation is partly identified

[1] Laurence Sterne, 1713–68, was the son of a junior army officer. He was born at Clonmel in Ireland, but educated in Halifax and at Jesus College, Cambridge. He was ordained, and spent some twenty years in the parish of Sutton-in-the-Forest, near York. In 1760 he moved to the parish of Coxwold, also in Yorkshire, but spent considerable periods in France on account of ill health. He died in London.

by Leigh Hunt in his remark that the novelist was Rabelais reborn 'at a riper period of the world, and gifted with sentiment'. The facetious Yorkshire parson preached sermons which displayed a sober awareness of the uncertain and perplexed state of human nature, and a tender concern to strengthen the social affections of his flock. He grows indignant at the world's censoriousness, and the disguises which malice assumes. A common slanderer, he says in his sermon on evil speaking, needs such a complication of badness that one might suppose this character to be 'as rare and difficult a production in nature as that of a great genius, which seldom happens above once in an age'. But in these latter days the art of slander has been carried to high perfection: 'a proper management of light and shade' creates such a convincing effect that 'no one but a discerning artist is able to discover the labours that join in finishing the picture'. Sterne is a discerning artist with benevolent intentions.

He is not, however, simply a Rabelaisian entertainer endowed with a warm sensibility. Contemporary philosophy had sharpened his perception that man lives among mysteries and riddles. As he remarks in his sermon on Felix and Paul, 'almost every thing which comes in our way, in one light or other, may be said to baffle our understandings'. This is no mere speculative observation, but points to an understanding that deeply affects the very texture of his fiction. A hint of his method as a novelist is already apparent in one of his earliest-known compositions, the fragment brought to light by Paul Stapfer, and first published by him in 1870. This fragment tells how the author, having meditated on the infinite relativity of time and space, fell asleep and dreamt that he had become (although he did not know it) one of the minute inhabitants of a plum on a tree in his orchard. He was, indeed, exceptional in this unfamiliar world inasmuch as his life greatly exceeded the normal span of years, enabling him to advance scientific studies by slow degrees. After some ages, a vast streak of light appeared in the heavens. He recollected an ancient tradition that there had once been a golden age when the heavens and earth were decked with a sevenfold radiance, and, bearing in mind his painfully acquired knowledge of the slow revolution of the heavens, he inferred the return of the golden god who had then governed the world. Then came a huge noise and fragor in the skys, as if all nature was approaching to her dissolution. The stars seem'd to be torn from their orbits, and to wander at random thro' the heavens. . . . All was consternation, horrour, and amaze; no less was expected than an universal wreck of nature.

This proved to be the brisk gale of wind which is common at about sunrise. The philosopher found himself in his own bed, and, on rushing out into the orchard found that several plums had fallen from the tree.

O ye mountains, rivers, rocks and plains, which ages had familiariz'd to my view! with you I seem'd at home; here I am like a banish'd man; everything appears strange, wild and savage! O the projects I had form'd! the designs I had set on foot, the friendships I had cultivated! How has one blast of wind dash'd you to pieces! . . . But thus it is: *Plumbs* fall, and *Planets* shall perish.

Sterne quotes Pope's line

> And now a Bubble burst, and now a World,

but the effect of the fragment and that of the *Essay on Man* are strikingly different. Pope is playing with ideas over which he has full control. He views the creation with a godlike eye. Sterne's eye is emphatically that of a creature. He uses the speculations of Pascal and Fontenelle to form the outline of a fictitious autobiography, the autobiography of one who suffered persecution from bigots and infidels in his plum-world, and who was himself fully conditioned by the limitations of his environment. Brief as the fragment is, it shows with how much particularity Sterne was able to entertain the idea that 'two nations on each side a Fibre of a green leaf may meet and perform actions as truly great as any we read of in the history of Alexander'. When Rabelais introduces us to the world inside Gargantua's mouth, we never lose sight of the fact that the whole episode is a hyperbolical joke. Swift's Gulliver always remains in firm contact with the scale of things in our own world. Sterne, for his part, effortlessly loses himself in the abyss of relativity that opens before him.

It is thus in perfect keeping with this early fragment that *The Life and Opinions of Tristram Shandy, Gentleman* should begin with an account of the hero's being in its most rudimentary form. It is only to the eye of folly and prejudice, says Tristram, that the minute *homunculus*, newly conceived, appears unworthy of attention.

> To the eye of reason in scientifick research, he stands confess'd—a BEING guarded and circumscribed with rights:—The minutest philosophers, who, by the bye, have the most enlarged understandings, (their souls being inversely as their enquiries) shew us incontestably, That the HOMUNCULUS is created by the same hand,—engender'd in the same course of nature, endowed with the same loco-motive powers and faculties with us:—That he consists, as we do, of skin, hair, fat, flesh, veins, arteries, ligaments, nerves, cartilages, bones, marrow, brains, glands, genitals, humours, and articulations;—is a Being of as much activity,—and, in all senses of the word, as much and as truly our fellow-creature as my Lord Chancellor of England. (I. 2)

This is evidently the stuff of which satire on pedantry is made, and yet the effect is too disturbingly circumstantial to be just that. Every embryo is endowed with the same consequence as the most dignified English custodian of those wider rights and claims which govern humanity in the mass. One is hardly surprised, a few chapters later, to find Tristram invoking the workings of the solar system to explain his mode of conducting a narrative. The violent shifts in perspective and changes in direction deny readers the reassurance of expectations which are gradually fulfilled; and yet, as the narrative proceeds, a peculiarly satisfying coherence begins to emerge.

Early in *Tristram Shandy* we are introduced to the 'world' of an English village—a circle of four miles in diameter—seen initially in terms of the local midwife and of her patron the local parson, Yorick. The village manifests itself less as a physical locality than as a churlish public opinion, the medium in which Yorick's actions are constantly twisted and refracted from their true directions. This view is supported in the account of Mrs. Shandy's vexatious journey home from London after the false alarm of a pregnancy, when Walter Shandy conjures up the foolish figure he and she are likely to make at church the first Sunday after their return (I. 16). An altogether different perspective appears in the legal pedantry of the marriage settlement that doomed Tristram to be born in the country. The solidity with which the husband's duty to his wife in the event of a pregnancy is set out underlines the contention made in Sterne's sermon 'Vindication of Human Nature' that the life of man is 'beset and hemmed in with obligations'. Unlike Yorick, however, who is eventually borne down by the society which hems him in, Walter Shandy asserts himself indomitably. He imagines himself as an absolute prince, an Asiatic monarch, putting the health of the nation to rights, entering eagerly into new projects of reform. Throughout the novel the reader can hardly avoid responding appreciatively to his imperial intellect. His mind may be a distorting medium, but it distorts with an engaging vigour, particularly on behalf of the welfare of his son, the hero of the novel, for whom nothing will serve but the utmost care and attention from the moment of birth, nay, of conception. This, at least, is the theory. The practice is quite another matter. The hero's conception stands in ironic contrast to that of Hercules as described by Rabelais near the beginning of *Gargantua and Pantagruel*: '*Jupiter* made the night, wherein he lay with *Alcmena*, last fourty eight houres, a shorter time not being sufficient for the forging of *Hercules*, who cleansed the world of the Monstres and Tyrants, wherewith it was supprest.' Walter, reserving such business for due attention on the first Sunday in the month, is fatally distracted at the critical moment by his wife's ungovernable association of ideas. His project for having his son delivered, after the manner of certain towering geniuses, by Caesarean section, might have been some compensation—but Mrs. Shandy turned pale as ashes at the very idea. His remaining hopes for his son, a substantial nose and a worthy Christian name, came to nothing. Walter's very eloquence is frustrated of its effect. It exploits every resource of rhetorical theory, but his principal audience consists of persons exceptionally ill-qualified to appreciate it—his wife and Uncle Toby. For all that, however, Walter does not live in our minds as a victim. As Tristram is at pains to point out (V. 3), a misfortune could be at least no disadvantage to him if it let loose his tongue with a good grace: 'where the pleasure of the harangue was as *ten*, and the pain of the misfortune but as *five*—my father gained half in half, and consequently was as well again off, as if it never had befallen him.' Few characters in fiction better illustrate that quality of eloquence which Emerson called 'great volumes of animal heat'. The effect is the more exhilarating because he takes such care to keep out of the common highway of thinking. The imagination is satisfied in despite of common sense when Walter argues that 'to come at the exact weight of things in the scientific steelyard, the fulcrum . . . should be almost invisible, to avoid all friction from popular tenets' (II. 19). What a fine chain of reasoning supports his objections to the received mode of birth, head downwards through the mother's uterus! Few readers, while actually under the spell of the text, can fail to share Walter's horror at the notion of 470 pounds avoirdupois acting perpendicularly upon the apex of the head where 'all the minute nerves from all the organs of the seven senses concentred'. Almost as persuasive is Walter's 'North-west passage to the intellectual world' by way of the auxiliary verbs, setting the soul 'a-going by herself upon the materials as they are brought her', opening new tracks of inquiry, making every idea engender millions (V. 42). Even the slow progress of literary composition is seen in terms of the utmost exertion of intellectual energy. John de la Casse, Archbishop of Benevento, contended that a writer's first thoughts are always temptations of the evil one:

from the very moment he took pen in hand—all the devils in hell broke out of their holes to cajole him.—'Twas Term time with them, —every thought, first and last, was captious—how specious and good soever,—'twas all one;—in whatever form or colour it presented itself to the imagination, 'twas still a stroke of one or other of 'em levelled at him, and was to be fenced off.—So that the life of a writer, whatever he might fancy to the contrary, was not so much a state of *composition*, as a state of *warfare*; and his probation in it, precisely that of any other man militant upon earth,—both depending alike, not half so much upon the degrees of his WIT—as his RESISTANCE. (V. 16)

'My father', says Tristram, 'was hugely pleased with this theory.' For him the devil is that multitude of prejudices we imbibe with our education: no man of spirit should submit tamely to what they obtrude upon his mind.

Walter Shandy is a champion of that liberation from prejudice which makes possible a reverence for the genius within: a gospel memorably preached by Edward Young in his *Conjectures upon Original Composition*, published the year before the two first volumes of *Tristram Shandy*. It is a cast of mind that opens up before mankind unlimited possibilities of improvement. This is sufficiently obvious from Young's essay, but the animating prospect is sketched with particular distinctness in a little book possibly known to Sterne, *A Dissertation upon Genius* (1755). The author was William Sharpe, Curate of Leaden Roding in Essex;

if it had been anonymous, it would have been tempting to attribute it to the pen of Walter Shandy himself. He attacks the notion of inherited characteristics with an environmentalism so extreme that it must have staggered even those most amenable to what he calls 'the present reigning passion for enquiry'. There are, he claims, no intrinsic differences between children. If there seem to be so, it is the effect of influences that operate so early that we cannot account for it by experiment or observation. He does not quite say that a propitious environment would create a population composed entirely of geniuses, but he does think that Shakespeare was essentially the product of a specially favourable education: not a regular one, it is true, but the fruit of conversation, company, books, observation, and experience. Walter Shandy, for his part, believed like Sharpe that there was no original difference in the texture of the 'thinking substance' of the most acute and the most obtuse understandings. But he invokes a much wider range of environmental influences than Sharpe does to account for the differences in capacity that do in fact develop, including (as we have seen) the havoc and destruction wrought on the tender texture of the *cerebellum* in the course of the normal mode of birth.

Sterne must be counted among the satirists of such theories, but his deflation of them actually heightens their attractiveness. Walter Shandy's inexhaustible vigour is the more keenly enjoyed because it coexists with something approaching paralysis in the affairs of the world (the parlour door-hinge is never likely to be mended). The invigorating effects of 'true Shandeism', opening the heart and lungs, and forcing the vital fluids to run freely through their channels, is quite independent of solid achievement. The great Curse of Ernulphus, in which the powers of heaven, catalogued in copious detail, curse the excommunicated one in all his parts and doings, is a splendidly comprehensive utterance, and its employment to relieve Dr. Slop's exasperated feelings about Obadiah's unmanageable knots, and the consequent injury to his thumb, is a nice stroke of mock-heroic extravagance. But the truly Shandean touch is Walter's conjecture that the text supplied to Dr. Slop is an 'institute of swearing', produced at a time when anathematizing was falling into decay with a view to saving its laws from oblivion, much as the Institutes of Justinian were compiled in the decline of the Roman Empire. The curse is a systematically virtuoso display, the effect of which is profoundly reassuring. No devils break loose from hell, no God in heaven frowns, but Walter's fancy is delighted, and Dr. Slop's anger assuaged. In *Tristram Shandy* the most vehement emotions are expressed in accordance with laws propounded after what has evidently been careful analysis. Walter 'prostrate across his bed in the wildest disorder imaginable', after hearing of Tristram's broken nose, is a figure composed with the eye of a diligent painter. The rubbing of Trim's injured knee, by which the fair Beguine won her way to his heart, is described with great anatomical precision. When we read *Tristram Shandy*, we inhabit a world which, in spite of its complexity and bewildering shapelessness, can be scientifically dissected and manipulated.

Sterne emphasizes the pleasures of manipulation in his characteristic treatment of time. Every reader of *Tristram Shandy* will have been struck by the flamboyant transitions from one period to another in the course of the novel. The effect of these transitions is complex, and not to be explained briefly, but one point can be made in a sentence: they heighten our sense of the constant and insistent presence of the narrator. In the twenty-first chapter of the first volume, Tristram is about to relate what Uncle Toby thinks about the noise above-stairs, when he breaks off:

But to enter rightly into my uncle *Toby*'s sentiments upon this matter, you must be made to enter first a little into his character, the outlines of which I shall just give you, and then the dialogue between him and my father will go on as well again.

Tristram arrests the action much as Sheridan's Mr. Puff in *The Critic* arrests the performance of *The Spanish Armada* in order to explain some necessary circumstance. An actor is caught in mid-sentence, and left there while the presenter takes the centre of the stage. The remaining five chapters of this volume, and the first five of the second, are given over to an elaborate account of Toby's character and his hobby-horse. Then the dialogue resumes. We learn what Toby thinks. 'I think, replied he,—it would not be amiss, brother, if we rung the bell.' The anti-climax, the cheating of the reader's expectations, itself underlines the arbitrary power of the narrator.

Sterne's anti-climaxes, however, are no mere exercises in the mock-heroic. One of the most striking characteristics of the work, and one that eluded Sterne's many imitators, is its spaciousness. When Trim is about to tell the story of the King of Bohemia and his seven castles, Toby bids him assign it to any date he chooses; and only Sterne could have done justice to Trim's response—the bow which acknowledges his employer's courtesy in subjecting 'this vast empire of time and all its abysses at his feet' (VIII. 19). Then again, Bobby's death, although it can have drawn few tears from even the most lachrymose eighteenth-century reader, is invested by Walter with an eloquence so sublime that it temporarily obliterates Bobby from his mind altogether. He moves so naturally among his classical authorities that Uncle Toby and Mrs. Shandy are quite unable to distinguish between quotation and personal confession. Indeed, as Tristram remarks to the reader, 'when the provocation ran high, and grief touched his lips with more than ordinary powers,—sir, you scarce could have distinguished him from *Socrates* himself' (V. 13). Some of Walter's effects are broad and obvious, as when he adopts the famous letter of Servius Sulpicius to Cicero, consoling him for the loss of his daughter. Others are more oblique. An allusion to Josephus' history of the Jewish War provides the context for a particularly fine Shandean display. It is Josephus who reports the speech of Eleazer to the beleaguered Jews at Masada, urging them to kill their wives, their children, and themselves, rather than submit to the Romans, invoking the contempt of death among the people of India as an argument why they should not be much attached to life. Since Walter was one who contended on occasion that the life of a family was as nothing in comparison to a hypothesis, he would doubtless have found the speech congenial enough, But the special appeal of the sentiment quoted in the text— *that we and our children were born to die—but neither of us born to be slaves—* resides for Tristram in its allegedly Indian origin. It opens up a prospect of the trade routes of the ancient world: that taken overland by the armies of Alexander the Great, and the sea route across the Indian Ocean, up the Red Sea, across to the Nile, and then downstream to Alexandria

where the SENTIMENT would be landed at the very foot of the great staircase of the Alexandrian library;—and from that storehouse it would be fetched.—Bless me! what a trade was driven by the learned in those days! (V. 12)

This large scholarly perspective on Bobby's death soon narrows abruptly to an eavesdropping Mrs. Shandy behind the door (she has been left listening with all her powers some eight chapters earlier, but now bursts into the action again).

Such characteristic transitions from the wide world to the Shandy household form a major ingredient in one of Sterne's most famous creations, Uncle Toby's hobby-horse. The steady zeal with which Toby and Trim re-enact military exploits in the idyllic setting of the bowling-green or in Walter's parlour derives much of its piquancy from the implied contrast between this amiàble pair and the harsh face of war. Toby himself is a pointed departure from the traditional character of a soldier. He conforms to convention, indeed, in being open-hearted, frank, plain-dealing; but he lacks the *iracundus, inexorabilis,* military qualities insisted on by those who prized the authority of Horace. For Othello, the plumed troop and the big wars made ambition virtue; for Toby, war was 'the getting together of quiet and harmless people, with their swords in their hands, to keep the ambitious and the turbulent within bounds' (VI. 32). For Bardolph in *Henry IV,* as for Toby, a soldier was 'better accommodated than with a wife', but how different are their reasons! The chastity of Toby's mind is as unconventional for a soldier as his benign inability to take offence. Admittedly Uncle Toby forms part of a distinct and striking change in popular ideas of what a soldier should be. Smollett, for example, in summing up the character of General Wolfe—mortally wounded at the taking of Quebec in September 1759—makes him into something of a hero of sensibility, 'generous, gentle, complacent, and humane'; while Horace Walpole (perhaps unconsciously influenced on this occasion by a recent reading of *Tristram Shandy*) told Sir David Dalrymple that Admiral Wager, 'one of the bravest and best men I ever knew' never killed a fly willingly (20 June 1760). Toby, we are constantly reassured, is a man of matchless courage, and would have marched up the glacis at Namur with the same warmth he displayed when, momentarily imagining himself in battle, he enthusiastically rose up, pushed his crutch like a pike, and set his foot upon a stool (IV. 18). Toby is really brave, just as Walter is really eloquent: they are alike in having only a diminutive theatre to act in.

The quiet and seclusion of Toby's theatre of war would have hit the fancy of Sterne's first readers the more particularly because the first half-dozen books appeared while the Seven Years War was still being fought. It was a war distinguished by the unprecedented distances across which the armed forces operated. Admittedly Sterne takes some trouble to place the action of *Tristram Shandy* in exact chronological relation to historical events from the end of the seventeenth century until the early Hanoverian years, and in doing so invests the whole narrative with a certain nostalgia. But although the campaigns of Marlborough did not range as far afield as those directed by the towering and eloquent genius of the elder Pitt, there were some points of similarity between the two wars, even in detail. The demolition of the fortifications of Dunkirk, which so exercised Toby and Trim, figured as conspicuously in the negotiations leading to the Treaty of Paris as in those leading to the Treaty of Utrecht. Vauban may have been dead for over half a century, but his system of fortification, with its apparatus of ravelins, bastions, curtains, and hornworks, was much in the public mind in 1761 during the expedition to Belle Île. He had constructed the defences there, and they were reckoned almost impregnable. It was against this background that Toby indulged himself in the enjoyment of his war-game, on a rood and a half of ground sheltered from the house by a tall yew-hedge, and 'covered on the other three sides from mortal sight, by rough holly and thick-set flowering shrubs' (II. 5). The very gunfire is produced by tobacco smoke.

Toby's one hobby-horse is matched by a whole stable of Walter's. The reader enters with keen sympathy into the enjoyment of both, not least when their incompatible preoccupations collide. A later generation was to speak of 'the collision of intellect' as a great agency of intellectual improvement. In *Tristram Shandy* there is much collision but no improvement. Walter does his utmost to explain to Toby the various accounts given by learned men of the causes of short and long noses, but Toby's unreceptive brain was not assisted by Walter's use of Slawkenbergius' treatise on noses. The Latin had to be translated for Toby, and as Walter himself was no great master of that language his translation was not, says Tristram, of the purest,

and generally least so where 'twas most wanted,—this naturally open'd a door to a second misfortune;—that in the warmer paroxisms of his zeal to open my uncle *Toby*'s eyes, my father's ideas run on, as much faster than the translation, as the translation out-moved my uncle *Toby*'s;—neither the one or the other added much to the perspicuity of my father's lecture. (III. 39)

With a few deft touches, Sterne has sketched a tutor's nightmare, the ultimate in student perplexity. The one lesson in teaching technique that Walter has learned is that he must avoid words that will set Toby astride his hobby-horse at an inopportune moment. At one point in his oration upon Bobby's death he lets slip the word 'evolutions'.

> Brother *Shandy*, said my uncle *Toby*, laying down his pipe at the word *evolutions*—Revolutions, I meant, quoth my father,—by heaven! I meant revolutions, brother *Toby*—evolutions is nonsense.—'Tis not nonsense—said my uncle *Toby*.—But is it not nonsense to break the thread of such a discourse upon such an occasion? cried my father. (V. 3)

Walter's dilemma is absolute, for these thread-breaking words are the only ones that can secure Toby's attention. The word 'siege', Tristram tells us, 'like a talismanic power, in my father's metaphor, wafting back my uncle *Toby*'s fancy, quick as a note could follow the touch,—he open'd his ears' (III. 41). The effect of this awakening is one of Walter's more splendid explosions: nothing, Tristram explains, could 'make his passions go off so like gunpowder, as the unexpected strokes his science met with from the quaint simplicity of my uncle *Toby*'s questions'.

The frustration which Toby occasions his brother, however, serves only to heighten the compensating effect of his fraternal affection. After one of these 'unexpected strokes', Walter took off his wig to rub his head with a handkerchief while he argued the point with Toby. He took off his wig with his right hand, and with his left sought the handkerchief in his right coat pocket. It was never an easy matter, Tristram points out, 'to have forced your hand diagonally, quite across your whole body, so as to gain the bottom of your opposite coat-pocket'. The fashion in 1718, when coat pockets were cut very low down in the 'skirt', made it extremely difficult. Walter's face reddened—

> six whole tints and a half, if not a full octave above his natural colour;—any man, madam, but my uncle *Toby*, who had observed this,—together with the violent knitting of my father's brows, and the extravagant contortion of his body during the whole affair,— would have concluded my father in a rage; and, taking that for granted,—had he been a lover of such kind of concord as arises from two such instruments being put into exact tune,—he would instantly have skrew'd up his, to the same pitch;—and then the devil and all

had broke loose—the whole piece, madam, must have been played off like the sixth of *Avison*'s Scarlatti—*con furia*—like mad. (III. 5)

Not uncle Toby, however. He waits patiently for Walter to find his handkerchief, looking on with inexpressible goodwill.

Walter and Toby are intimately related, as flint is to tinder. When they are together something fresh is struck out of their mutual respect and their comic misunderstanding, which enlightens us about both of them. Here is a subtler revelation of character than previous novelists had reached. In Fielding and Smollett the characters are independently conceived; often they embody moral considerations or types of affectation in Fielding's work, and in Smollett they are often caricatures of professional types. They rub up against similar characters without deeply affecting them. Richardson had achieved a more satisfactory interlocking of characters, for Clarissa's fate depends upon Lovelace, as much as Lovelace's depends upon her. But it was left for Sterne to convince us that Uncle Toby, Walter Shandy, Mrs. Shandy, and Corporal Trim were born for each other, and devised to elicit each other's quintessence.

Toby's benign affections unite with Walter's indomitable energy to set the tone of the book. In spite of the misfortunes that dog his conception, birth, and childhood, Tristram is still the heir to the Shandean virtues. His father's intellectual vehemence becomes in him a more consciously aesthetic pleasure in subtleties and complexities. While he can participate in Dr. Slop's baffled rage at being unable to untie Obadiah's accursed knots, Tristram believes that knots are made to be untied, not cut. He delights in his father's comparison (borrowed from Locke) of the succession of one's ideas to the images in the inside of a lanthorn turned round and round by the heat of the candle. He delights equally in his uncle's rejoinder: *his* ideas, he says, are more like a smoke-jack. Tristram laments that the conversation went no further, his father being then

in one of his best explanatory moods,—in eager pursuit of a metaphysic point into the very regions where clouds and thick darkness would soon have encompassed it about;—my uncle *Toby* in one of the finest dispositions for it in the world;—his head like a smoak-jack;—the funnel unswept, and the ideas whirling round and round about in it, all obfuscated and darkened over with fuliginous matter!

(III. 19)

Even in a state of the utmost confusion, a Shandy mind works in terms of vividly-perceived, well-defined images; and, as Locke remarked in the 'Epistle to the Reader' prefixed to his *Essay concerning Human Understanding*, 'It is not every one, nor perhaps any one, who is so careful of his language as to use no word till he views in his mind the precise determined idea which he resolves to make it the sign of.' Toby approaches as nearly to this ideal as the nature of things will perhaps admit. His trains are always trains of artillery; he never willingly bewilders himself with a train of ideas.

Walter, however, can never leave him alone. An element of pleasing bewilderment is an essential part of the appreciation of *Tristram Shandy*. It is the effect obviously aimed at in Tristram's fast-talking showman's patter, explaining the workings of that strange machine the Shandy family. At another level the novel is reassuringly predictable. No reader has ever failed to notice what censorious critics call Sterne's prurience, or 'nasty trifling'. It is typical of *Tristram Shandy* that it should open with its hero's conception—and equally typical that this event should be presented with such a disingenuous display of discretion. A similar display is elaborated in the last book, when Sterne relates the widow Wadman's mistake about Toby's offer to show her the very place where he was wounded. A demure concern to observe the proprieties is professed, while the reader's mind is allured into titillating reflections. Sterne amuses himself with proving to the reader that, where sexual innuendo is in question, the mind is embarrassingly adept at making inferences. The chapter upon whiskers (V. 1) is an extreme case of the reader's being given no specific information at all about the indecent use that is being referred to, but the uninitiated mind is nudged and coaxed and teased into working out what Sterne would be at. He is determined that, so far as his novel is concerned, even the least attentive are not going to miss 'the subtle hints and sly communications of science'—words which serve to introduce that curious consultation of the doctors of the Sorbonne on the possibility of baptism before birth by means of 'une petite Canulle', or squirt. This digression is itself a fine illustration of the novel's method: the smooth gravity and scientific detachment of the theologians' elegant analysis of the question (effects heightened for the English ear by the apparent ease and fluency of the French text) are there to set off a pious kind of indecent assault.

Prurience as entertaining as Sterne's needs no apology; but it may not be improper to remark its interest from the point of view of a disciple of Locke. Sexual organs are acutely sensitive, a fact of which Sterne frequently reminds us, with physiological exactness. Among the most famous incidents in *Tristram Shandy* are three which associate the male member with agonizing pain: Toby's wound, Phutatorius's accident with the hot chestnut, and Tristram's involuntary circumcision. These are nicely calculated to engender determinate ideas in the mind, more determinate (to judge from Cleland's *Fanny Hill*) than ideas of sexual pleasure could ever be. The eye may have a quicker commerce with the soul than words can ever contrive, but Sterne has a virtuoso's ambition to show how much can be done with an imperfect medium.

The virtuoso achieved his most perfect performance in *A Sentimental Journey through France and Italy* (1768). He quits the persona of the gaily unfortunate Tristram for that of the mercurial Parson Yorick, keenly alert to the slightest nuances of feeling. It is this which enables him to rise above the insular prejudices of such travellers as Smollett, and to do justice to that imperturbable good humour and flawless courtesy that distinguish the French national character. The licentiousness continually hinted at serves mainly to create situations where, with effortless grace, the parties may display their repertory of good manners. A momentary flirtation with a shopkeeper's wife in Paris is consummated in a way which is both sensual and delicate:

If it is the same blood which comes from the heart [says Yorick] which descends to the extremes (touching her wrist), I am sure you must have one of the best pulses of any woman in the world—Feel it, said she, holding out her arm. So laying down my hat, I took hold of her fingers in one hand, and applied the two fore-fingers of my other to the artery. . . . I had counted twenty pulsations, and was going on fast towards the fortieth, when her husband coming unexpected from a back parlour into the shop, put me a little out of my reckoning—'Twas nobody but her husband, she said—so I began a fresh score—Monsieur is so good, quoth she, as he pass'd by us, as to give himself the trouble of feeling my pulse—The husband took off his hat, and making me a bow, said, I did him too much honour—and having said that, he put on his hat and walk'd out.

The social ritual embodied in the management of the hat stands in elegant contrast to the pulsation of the artery against two naked fingers. It is fitting that the episode should close with the purchase (at an enhanced price) of two pairs of gloves.

Yorick is so bent on discerning goodness of heart through differences of custom, climate, and religion, that he omits to mention, until more than half-way through his narrative, that Britain and France are at war. This little circumstance requires him to be in possession of a passport, and, having no such document, he is alarmed by the possibility of incarceration in the Bastille. In the event he suffers nothing worse than a courteous interview with the Count de B—— at Versailles, ending with an examination by Yorick of the French character. The English have a greater variety and originality, the French are more polished—so far he moves safely within the world of received commonplace. If the French lack the variety of the English, he continues, they

have so many excellencies, they can the better spare this—they are a loyal, a gallant, a generous, an ingenious, and good-temper'd people as is under heaven—if they have a fault—they are too *serious*.

Mon Dieu! cried the Count, rising out of his chair.

Mais vous plaisantez, said he correcting his exclamation.—I laid my hand upon my breast, and with earnest gravity assured him it was my most settled opinion.

Sterne enjoys creating surprise by his bland flouting of patriotic prejudice, venturing (for example) to defend that which Smollett found peculiarly offensive: the French lack of reticence in matters where English custom peremptorily demands it. Madame de Rambouliet, Yorick assures us, was of all women the most correct, virtuous and pure of heart. While travelling with him she asked him to stop the coach. 'I asked her if she wanted any thing—*Rien que pisser*, said Madame de Rambouliet.' Yorick had been long enough in France to find this inconsequent and perfectly innocent. He handed her out of the coach, 'and had I been the priest of the chaste CASTALIA, I could not have served at her fountain with a more respectful decorum'. It was at such moments as these that Saintsbury could hear a distasteful snigger, but Sterne's amusement is rather a smug enjoyment of his own skill at adapting himself to a new set of social conventions. Sometimes, indeed, he must concede that his sensations are not wholly innocent. But then, 'if Nature has so wove her web of kindness that some threads of love and desire are entangled with the piece, must the whole web be rent in drawing them out?' The question is one that underlies a great part of Sterne's work. He was not alone in asking it.

XI

OTHER PROSE FICTION

MUCH of the fiction written in the latter half of the eighteenth century is preoccupied with tracing what Henry Fielding called 'the Mazes, Windings and Labyrinths, which perplex the Heart of Man'. Fielding wrote these words in the preface to his sister's *David Simple* (1744), the forerunner of a long line of novels dedicated to the exploration of sensibility and suffering. In Sarah Fielding's[1] work, too, there are labyrinths more external, and it is obvious that a major impulse behind many novels of the time is the concern to depict the mazes and windings of the social scene, the manners and modes, the follies and vices of mankind. In others, again, the doctrinal purpose may be so strong as to raise a doubt whether one can usefully discuss them as works of fiction. Both Henry Brooke, for example, in *The Fool of Quality*, and Thomas Day, in *Sandford and Merton*, are mainly interested in expounding their views on the education of the young. There is, however, a crucial difference between them: Brooke allows his stories to run away with him, and Day does not, so that the former provides incomparably richer materials for our consideration. An uncertainty of this kind has been expressed about Sarah Fielding herself by her most recent editor, who argues that 'she is not really a novelist at all': that is, her interest is not primarily in manners and mannerisms, in rendering the substance of life dramatically. One may concede this and yet insist that she had learned, to an extent then achieved by few English writers—and perhaps only by Richardson himself—to delineate emotional states with the fineness to which Marivaux for one had accustomed his own countrymen, especially in the successive instalments of *La Vie de Marianne* (1731–42). It comes as no surprise to learn that in France *David Simple* was among the most widely read English works of

---

[1] Sarah Fielding, 1710–68, Henry Fielding's sister, came to live in Hammersmith, near London, where she became acquainted with Samuel Richardson and his circle. Later she lived near Bath.

fiction. If it is misleading to call it a novel, it is at least an admirable 'Moral Romance', to use her own term. She can probe nature with unflinching sensitivity—too unflinching sometimes to be quite comfortable. There is little she does not know about the unscrupulous deviousness with which people try to preserve their self-esteem. But the results of her probing are often set out with the directness of a moralist writing a periodical essay. Fiction for her originates in the *exemplum*, the case that will illustrate her analysis. It colours and makes vivid the introspective examination of states of mind and the abstract discussion of moral issues. When reading the fiction of the period one should never forget that this order of priorities may obtain. Johnson's famous advice on how to read Richardson deserves to be given more weight than it has been, and applied more widely: 'You must read him for the sentiment, and consider the story as only giving occasion to the sentiment.' Richardson's own admiration for Sarah Fielding has been considered excessive, but it is not indiscriminate. His praise is specifically for her knowle˙ge of the human heart, incomparably better (he tells her) than her brother's: 'His was but as the knowledge of the outside of a clock-work machine, while yours was that of all the finer springs and movements of the inside.' Richardson ascribed this view to 'a critical judge of writing', probably Johnson, and years afterwards Boswell heard Johnson apply the same image to Fielding and Richardson himself. In some ways it has more point in its original context. In reading the work of both the Fieldings, it is the systematically analytical intelligence that is impressive. They are alike in the assurance with which they anatomize human behaviour. The difference is one of range. Sarah Fielding's world is more restricted than her brother's, and the voices heard in it are less richly varied; but in *David Simple*, certainly in the sequel published in 1753, she ventures into disturbing levels of experience inaccessible to his more vigorous genius.

Henry Fielding himself, as we have seen, praised the skill with which Sarah had made every episode in *David Simple* bear 'a manifest Impression of the principal Design', to display friendship in all its varieties, genuine and spurious. The book can be considered as an informal anatomy of friendship, a melancholy *De Amicitia* for the eighteenth century, drawing upon the incidental observations of the poets, and keeping in mind the set discussions of the theme to be found in the periodical essayists of the time. The form of the earlier part of the novel is closely related to the short narratives characteristic of the *Spectator* and its imitators, and the unity achieved is that of the quest defined in the full title: *The Adventures of David Simple; containing an Account of his Travels through the Cities of London and Westminster in the Search of a Real Friend.* David is defrauded of his inheritance by his scheming younger brother, who finds no difficulty in enlisting two servants as his accomplices. In defiance of the conventions of romance, which would reserve to the end of the story the restoration of the true heir, the fraud is perpetrated in the second chapter and unmasked in the third. The incident is only there to give David his first shocking lesson that a specious appearance cannot be relied on, and thus initiated he embarks on his quest. What he finds is a world dominated by the mercenary, the self-regarding, and the self-deceiving. Guided by the penetrating intelligence of Mr. Orgueil he learns, among other things, why it is possible for people to express the greatest aversion for vices to which they are particularly prone. Not that he can confide in Mr. Orgueil, whose own shortcomings are soon exposed by Mr. Spatter. Spatter is in turn dissected by Mr. Varnish, and David himself contrives to see through Varnish. By this time David has come to doubt whether he would ever meet anyone he could esteem for more than a week, but he does now encounter the three people who prove to be true friends: Cynthia, Camilla, and Valentine. Their merits are defined for us in a context of victimization; they have all suffered from the effects of gross misrepresentation by those who have had the means to exert power over them. In Sarah Fielding's world, it is rare enough to merit the good opinion of an impartial spectator, and those who do merit it are rewarded by an enhanced vulnerability to attack. The partnership of the just with which the novel originally ended is a precarious league against barbarous insensibility.

It should not be supposed, however, that the pattern is simply that of an antithesis between the elect and the damned. The obstacles to a good understanding are all-pervasive, and some of Sarah Fielding's subtlest observations are of the failure of *rapport* between her amiable characters. Thus, when David finds himself in a state of tortured anxiety about Camilla's affections towards him, his feelings take a strange turn:

> For an Instant, he felt a Passion which he had before never conceived for her, nor indeed for any other; and which I should not scruple to call Hatred, had it not been one of those abortive Thoughts which are the first Sallies of our Passions, and which immediately vanish on Reflection. (IV. 6)

In the long and melodramatic narrative told by the amiable Isabelle in another part of *David Simple*, the situation created by the tragic passion of Dorimene for Dumont is rich in possibilities for a bewildering conflict of obligations, and Dumont in particular finds himself 'involved in such a perplexing Labyrinth, that whichever way he turned his Thoughts he met with fresh Difficulties and new Torments' (IV. 2). Isabelle sees her brother, her sister, and her lover apparently involved in one common madness, and she has no one to whom she can disclose her anxiety. Here, as often in Sarah Fielding, the labyrinth is also a trap. She is particularly skilful in creating the sense of entrapment, nowhere more so than in 'Volume the Last', added to *David Simple* in 1753. Its story is one of financial loss and the way the two couples respond to it. The distinctive painfulness of the situation grows out of the part played by so-called friends, who lead them into greater difficulties, wound them with censure, and inflict (always by indirect means) actual physical harm. The mortality, indeed, is frightful, and would do credit to a Jacobean tragedy: only Cynthia and one of David's children survive. But the firmly analytical manner is never abandoned, even at the most comfortless moments, and controls the paralysing hopelessness that constantly threatens to dominate the story. This control is reinforced by one's indignation against such malign powers of the earth as Mrs. Orgueil. Her envious hatred of Cynthia is remorselessly dissected, her tone of voice deftly hinted at. One example will illustrate the mordant economy of the presentation. She is deeply angered by a landlady's tactlessness in calling little Cynthia 'Miss', thus implying equality with Mrs. Orgueil's own Henrietta. There is a difficulty about finding her somewhere to sleep (Henrietta will not have her in *her* bed), except in

one little spare Bed, up in the Garret, in which the Child might lie, after this one Night; but, as it had been washed that very Morning, she was afraid Miss would take cold. On this Mrs. *Orgueil* mustered her whole Stock of Insolence into her Countenance, repeated the Word MISS half a dozen Times; and then desired MISS to go to bed, without any Whims or Airs. The Child, fatigued with her tiresome Journey, with a pale and wan Countenance, obeyed, wondering what was the matter. (VI. 2)

The uncomprehending bewilderment of landlady and child forcibly underlines the pathological extent of Mrs. Orgueil's inner insecurity.

In no other of her writings does Sarah Fielding attain the intensity of 'Volume the Last', although her powers always seem to be enhanced when she treats the theme of her friend Jane Collier's once-celebrated *Essay on the Art of Ingeniously Tormenting* (1753). She wrote one book in collaboration with Jane Collier, *The Cry: a New Dramatic Fable* (1754). It is a somewhat stylized dialogue between virtuous integrity (solo) and ungenerous prejudice (chorus), exploring the kind of emotional situation that Richardson concerned himself with when narrating Clarissa Harlowe's relationship with her family, but in a more formal and abstract way. The heroine, Portia, tells her story before an audience whose turbulent uncharitableness would reduce many heroines to tears and speechless rage long before the end of the first scene. The effect of uncomprehending antagonism is softened a little by the magnanimous Una who presides over the assembly, and later also by the erring but sympathetic character called Cylinda. But Portia needs all her strength of mind to survive the ordeal—all her proud awareness that 'the Cry's' hostility springs from fear, the fear they experience as 'they felt the image of their own wisdom sliding by degrees from their minds'. To read this book is emotionally exhausting. It leaves one with frayed nerves, and a sense that one's temper has been much tried. Authors have complained of the malice and stupidity of their critics from time immemorial, but Sarah Fielding and Jane Collier must be the first to have given quite so much prominence in the very structure of a sustained work of fiction to the reactions of the malicious and the stupid.

The introduction to *The Cry* formulates a suggestive connection between old romance and new fiction. The modern heroine may not have to traverse gloomy forests and fall in the way of giants and savage beasts, but she still meets deadly enemies and has much need of a faithful knight:

the puzzling mazes into which we shall throw our heroine, are the perverse interpretations made upon her words; the lions, tigers, and giants, from which we endeavour to rescue her, are the spiteful and malicious tongues of her enemies. In short, the design of the following work is to strip, as much as possible, *Duessa* or Falshood, of all her shifts and evasions; to hunt her like a fox through all her doublings and windings.

These last words might well preface *The Lives of Cleopatra and Octavia* (1757), extended dramatic monologues in which the evil manipulator Cleopatra is contrasted with the candid friend Octavia—an operation which Sarah Fielding undertakes with a cold, deliberate zest. They also provide a clue to the dominant interest of her two later novels, *The History of the Countess of Dellwyn* (1759) and *The History of Ophelia* (1760). The Countess's career illustrates, with acute psychological insight, the old comic theme of the difficulties of a marriage between January and May—an elderly husband and a young wife. The development of the relationship between Lord Dellwyn and his lady is perhaps set out too plainly for anyone whose taste has been affected by the idea of the novel formed by nineteenth- and twentieth-century practice. There is something almost diagrammatic about the Countess's progression from a period of terrifying self-constraint, when she had to inspect every thought before venturing to give it utterance in case her aversion should peep out, to a time of greater confidence when husband and wife learned to talk *at* each other: a form of discourse nicely adapted to the venting of spleen. The process continued from 'the Language Contradictory', or a state of mutual defiance upon all topics of conversation, to an anger that could not be content with words when both became diligent in vexing and teasing each other. One might almost be summarizing a paper from the *Spectator* or the *Rambler*, but Sarah Fielding is not simply composing an expanded version of a periodical essay. Her peculiar art appears clearly in the concurrent, self-justifying internal soliloquies of Lord and Lady Dellwyn (I. 14). They are couched in similar terms, and end in identical accusations of base ingratitude. The exactness of the parallel produces an effect of farcical caricature, but it is an essential part of the author's insight into the situation that both parties do genuinely experience an identical sense of grievance. In making this apparent, she stimulates her readers to cut through obscuring circumstances in their own experience to achieve a similar diagnosis of their own underlying motives. The effect is striking, but very uncomfortable. As Sarah Fielding herself remarked,

> Whenever this kind of Conversation happens between Man and Wife, all those Persons present, who are endued with Modesty and Good-nature, are confounded, and ready to blush for the Folly of those who have not Decency enough to blush for themselves.
>
> (I. 14)

The second half of the novel, with its narrative of downright infidelity, divorce, and consequences, suffers from diffuseness and some uncertainty of direction, but it is always impressive in its insight into motivation. The closing prospect of the Countess's future life—one of continual mortifications and incurable dissatisfaction—is chilling.

Ophelia is altogether more light-hearted. The heroine is something of a noble savage, an ingenuous observer who constantly stumbles over the curious arrangements that society takes for granted: that doctors, for example, should require payment for their services, or that ladies of fashion should leave a public room in order of precedence. Ophelia once made the mistake of going out in front of a young lady who was determined to assert her prerogative, and in fact asserted it so forcibly that she threw her downstairs, thereby (says Ophelia) 'impressing my want of good-breeding strongly on my mind'. The comedy of *Ophelia* sometimes passes into farce, but the farce is the overflow of high spirits in an observer who remains exceptionally alert and perceptive. A fine example is the portrait of the dependent cousin whose servility to the Marchioness of Trente has deprived her of all liberty of thought:

> She entirely forgot the method of pronouncing the word No: her language was composed of nothing but expressions of assent and affirmatives; and she would contradict her own senses as often as her violent and capricious cousin happened to err. So accustomed to obey, she scarcely could find out terms that would express her refusal of the liberty she dared not grant me.   (II. 1)

Even when Sarah Fielding is engaged in presenting a panoramic view of contemporary manners, it is the inwardness of the presentation that is impressive. Other writers with similar intentions rely far more on what are essentially dramatic techniques, though set in a framework very different from the careful structuring of stage action. Characteristic dialogue and strong scenes are put together not so much in a plot as in a series of tableaux, creating a sense of the amplitude, variety, and labyrinthine complexity of the social scene. The reader identifies with a more or less alien observer who might, following the example of Marana and Montesquieu, impersonate a foreigner, or might, like Mrs. Haywood, say, be invisible. The presiding genius of this species of panoramic fiction was the Asmodeus of Lesage's *Diable boiteux* (1708), by diabolical power heaving up the roofs of houses to reveal whatever was underneath. In England Asmodeus's most accomplished disciple occupied a humble station in the chain of being, that of a lap-dog. Francis Coventry's[1] *History of Pompey the Little* (1751) does not make more than a perfunctory attempt to enter into the mind and sensibility of a canine observer, but the little dog's bewildering succession of masters and mistresses conveys, obliquely but emphatically, the instability of mortal life. Not that there is the least hint of pathos in the account: the author's detachment is sustained throughout, and he displays particular skill in catching the authentic note of matrimonial discord. If he does warm to one character more than any other, it is to his lawyer in Lincoln's Inn, so competently soothing his client at the same time as he opens up in his own mind a large prospect of fees. 'Now tho' a dog be of a *following nature*,' he explains to the lady who has had Pompey snatched from her by Lady Tempest,

and may be sometimes tempted, and seduced, and inveigled away in such a manner, as makes it difficult— do you observe me—makes it difficult, I say, madam, to fix a theft on the person seducing; yet, wherever property is discovered and claimed, if the possessor refuses to restore it on demand,—on demand, I say, because demand must be made—refuses to restore it on demand, to the proper, lawful owner, there an action lies, and, under this predicament, we shall recover our lap-dog. (II. 14)

Pompey emerges from the convolutions of legal rhetoric with the suddenness of an experienced conjuror's rabbit.

[1] Francis Coventry, d. 1759?, was educated at Magdalene College, Cambridge, and became vicar of Edgware, near London. He was acquainted with Thomas Gray.

The technical adroitness of Coventry's book is exceptional. The most popular of the works in the same genre, Charles Johnstone's[1] *Chrysal, or the Adventures of a Guinea* (1760–5) seems clumsy in comparison, although it has some memorable episodes. The story of the clergyman's wife whose guile secured her husband a fat living gives full scope to Johnstone's rather sour comic talent, especially when the ambitious but somewhat pedantic bishop launches into a long discourse on the interpretation of dreams. The discourse is inspired by a dream of himself as archbishop, but Johnstone sustains the note of clerical unction without faltering:

And though the heathens were guilty of great superstitions in this particular of dreams, it was not in the credit they gave them, but in the methods which they used to procure them,—such as offering sacrifices, and sleeping in the skins of the victims, and many others; whereas the dream that comes from Heaven, comes unsought and unexpected, and should be received with reverence; and if this is such, and I own it has much of the appearance, thy will be done, O Lord! Thy servant submits, as it is his duty. (II. 15)

His wife and the clergyman's wife can hardly refrain from laughing in his face, but their suppressed laughter is not of the same kind, and the outmanœuvring of the bishop's wife by her friend suggests the movements of rival predators. Well constructed though this episode is, it illustrates how slight the connection is between the substance of the fiction and the device used to secure a formal unity: the coin that passes from hand to hand. There is little difference between the shape of a book like *Chrysal* and one like John Shebbeare's[2] *Lydia* (1755), where the detached and observant alien (an American Indian) might have been expected to unify the miscellaneous materials of the novel. But for much of the time Cannassatego—the noble savage—is forgotten, and such interest as the book has comes from the individual episodes. The interest is not altogether negligible: like Fielding and Smollett, Shebbeare keenly appreciated a hot disputation. The political argument between Mr. Goodfellow and Mr. Mathematick certainly deserves to

---

[1] Charles Johnstone, ?1719–?1800, was educated at Trinity College, Dublin, and practised law, although handicapped by deafness. In 1782 he went to Calcutta, where he became a journalist and eventually a newspaper proprietor.

[2] John Shebbeare, 1709–88, was a surgeon and political pamphleteer. He was twice imprisoned for libel.

be remembered, if only as a warning to any unpatriotic sceptics who might be tempted to follow Mr. Mathematick's example and doubt the possibility of marching from the Ohio River to Hanover in two days (chapter 85).

The work of Shebbeare and Johnstone shows fiction at the point where it becomes almost indistinguishable from a panoramic miscellany. Little or nothing of the writer's energy was invested in the consciousness of his observers. Such novelists may display, as Eliza Haywood notably did, a titillating awareness of each phase of the process of seduction, or of what it feels like to be arrested, unexpectedly, for a debt of £2,575 incurred secretly by one's wife. But even *The History of Miss Betsy Thoughtless* (1751), where some critics have discerned faint anticipations of the art of Fanny Burney, remains a rather perfunctory succession of episodes. The narrator holds herself too firmly apart from the action, and is too comprehensively aware of what is happening, to suggest the texture of immediate experience. Mrs. Haywood is hardly touched by contemporary philosophical perplexities about the nature of perception. Such perplexities were increasingly reflected in the use of narrators whose sensibility and point of view were carefully individualized. Richardson explored the possibilities of this strategy with greater fullness and subtlety than any of his contemporaries, but others had their own special competence too. One remarkable *tour de force* is John Cleland's[1] *Memoirs of a Woman of Pleasure* (1748-9), more generally known as *Fanny Hill*. Although it is probably one of the most popular of eighteenth-century novels, it has not until recently received much attention from literary historians, perhaps because its merits are most apparent precisely when it violates the traditional decencies most shamelessly. Cleland shows great skill in rendering the avid curiosity of a young person about the mysteries of sexual intercourse. The loosely-structured, headlong sentences are an admirable vehicle for the breathless eagerness of the narrator, and partly distract the reader's attention from the book's systematic organization, which passes under review the major varieties of the sexual act. It is easy to mock at the rather stilted turns of expression to which Cleland often resorts, but the arch periphrases are an integral part of an attempt,

[1] John Cleland, 1709-89, was educated at Westminster School, and held posts in Smyrna and Bombay. He eventually became a professional writer in London.

displaying considerable ingenuity, to describe sexual experience with physiological exactness, carefully setting down 'the minute detail of things'. He is not content to communicate a notion of sexual climax through rapturous generalities. He is carefully attentive to the muscular reflexes in the female parts, and notes the kind of stimulus they receive from

the stream of a warm liquid that is itself the highest of all titillations, and which they thirstily express and draw in like the hot-natured leech, which to cool itself, tenaciously attracts all the moisture within its sphere of exsuction.

No such exsuctions, alas, are recorded in *The Memoirs of a Coxcomb* (1751), and without them Cleland is a novelist of no great distinction.

Fanny Hill is an animating presence, but her character is developed only in a narrowly specialized way. A more variously elaborated narrative personality was achieved, apparently unawares, by that eccentric author Thomas Amory.[1] If we can trust his own account (and, making due allowance for artistic exaggeration, there is nothing intrinsically implausible about it) he was engaged for many years on a work of vast scope called *The Ancient and Present State of Great Britain*. For this he travelled extensively through the British Isles, and drafted and re-drafted his findings. His manuscript, he says, was then accidentally burnt. Instead of submitting to the dauntingly long labour of reconstructing it according to the original plan, he set about using the material in a free effusion of his natural genius, uniting fragments of autobiography with elaborate and obvious fabrications. As occasion offered, he expounded his Unitarian religious beliefs and enlarged on his favourite mathematical and scientific subjects. The first instalment of this miscellany appeared as the initial volume of a series of *Memoirs of Several Ladies of Great Britain* (1755), the one lady treated of being a Mrs. Marinda Benlow. But even this volume, the only one published under the title, strays widely from its first apparent intention. Much of it is devoted to a curious tour of the Hebrides, reaching a climax in the account of an elegant society of recluse ladies living on the Green Island, some ten or

[1] Thomas Amory, ?1691–1788, was educated at Trinity College, Dublin, and had some medical training. He was acquainted with Swift. He subsequently passed a life of gentlemanly leisure, mainly in Dublin and London.

more leagues (he supposed) to the west of St. Kilda. The ladies would clearly have felt at home with the most talented of the Blue Stockings—with Mrs. Carter, with Mrs. Chapone, or with Mrs. Montagu herself. And the vegetation of this remote place is as rich as the intellectual life there. In grounds laid out in imitation of the Elysian Fields, there are clumps of cocoa and other trees perpetually green, 'and the whole in form of an amphitheatre, is surrounded with woods on rising grounds'. This splendid piece of exotic landscaping is further embellished with statues of numerous worthies, ancient and modern, including life-size representations of the foundress of the community and her eleven immediate disciples. And so it goes on. The reader is bound to wonder why Amory should have felt impelled to place the eighteenth-century dream of a recluse academy in a setting quite so improbable. The answer emerges in the two subsequent volumes (published in 1756 and 1766) which created the figure with which Amory has become identified: *The Life and Opinions of John Buncle, Esquire.* Buncle roams through the wilder parts of north-west England, traversing frightful hills, muddy bottoms, treacherous quagmires, and labyrinthine caves. His descriptions of this scenery, overdrawn though they may be, create a vigorous impression of the untamed majesty of nature, perilous but exhilarating. Thus, he tells of a great torrent rushing down through a cave which he was tempted to explore, though he was afraid to ascend more than forty yards,

not only on account of the terrors common to the place, from the fall of so much water with a strange kind of roar, and the height of the arch which covers the torrent all the way: but because, as I went up, there was of a sudden, an increase of noise so very terrible, that my heart failed me, and a trembling almost disabled me. The rock moved under me, as the frightful sounds encreased, and as quick as it was possible for me, I came into day again. It was well I did; for I had not been many minutes out, before the water overflowed its channel, and filled the whole opening in rushing to the lake.

In spite of such alarms, Buncle is evidently at home in this landscape, constantly led on by his foolhardy curiosity, and sustained by his extraordinary stamina. The small oases of intellectual culture that flower in sheltered spots are as much a part of the scene as the terrors and the wonders of nature.

The charm of these oases is heightened by their association with Buncle's career as a frequent widower. He is constantly encountering learned and beautiful women in lonely places. To marry one, and then (the hand of death assisting) to take up with another, reinforces the fantasy of being one to whom all ways are open. The greater part of the book, to be sure, is concerned neither with Buncle's wooing nor even his travels. It is rather a record of discourse and speculation, vehement and dogmatic. Buncle would be an opinionated bore if it were not for the sheer verve with which his opinions are uttered. He resembles his fair Azora: 'without the least appearance of labour, her ideas seemed to flow from a vast fountain'. He inhabits an enchanted world of eloquence and energy, in which he moves with all the assurance of Bottom the Weaver in *A Midsummer Night's Dream*.

The euphoric extravagance one finds in John Buncle resembles qualities that readers at the time associated with Don Quixote: though deluded, even crazed, he was endowed with an enviable vitality. He was no passive recipient of external pressures, but confronted society with an exhilaratingly alien system of values. There is a trace of Quixotism in the recurrent vision of nurture in virtuous isolation, such as that enjoyed by the Abbé Prévost's Cleveland, in a remote cave and under the eye of a careful mother:

> The solitude he was brought up in; the excellent moral authors which his fond parent put into his hands; and the judicious comments she made upon them, gave a peculiar bent to Mr. Cleveland's mind; so that when he came to enter upon the stage of the world, which he did with the utmost reluctance, it appear'd to him in a quite different light, from what it does to the rest of men.

The reluctance marks the hero of sensibility, not the Quixote; but the 'peculiar bent' is precisely what defines the Quixotic heroes of the time: Parson Adams, for example, or Sir Launcelot Greaves. There was a rich vein of Quixotism in the early Methodist preachers, and it was exploited with relish by Richard Graves[1] in *The Spiritual Quixote* (1773). His hero, Geoffrey Wildgoose, is not quite a representative Methodist,

---

[1] Richard Graves, 1715–1804, was educated at Pembroke College, Oxford, and became a fellow of All Souls. He moved to the parish of Claverton, in Somerset, where he was rector. He was a friend of William Shenstone.

being a young man of property who has frivolously taken exception to the vicar of his parish, and embarked on a course of
irregular and solitary study of books of sectarian theology dating from Cromwell's time. Although he develops an engagingly
picturesque style of preaching, his fanaticism is of a relatively
tepid and gentlemanly sort. Like the hero of Graves's one other
successful novel, *Columella*, (1779) Wildgoose is a man who
deserts the duty to which his position in society calls him. His
preaching tour with honest Jeremiah Tugwell is a 'summer's
ramble', the narration of which provides a fresh and convincing
picture of roads and inns and conventicles. The secular and
the sacred are on startlingly intimate terms in this portrait of
Methodism: the very brothel-keeper makes her 'poor Lambs
read the Bible every Sunday, and go to church in their turn'.
Graves knows how to capture the idiom of popular speech,
and has a keen eye for vividly pictorial effects, such as that
when Wildgoose harangues in Bristol, 'with the pretty Mrs.
Cullpepper (like the Angel usually painted at the back of
St. Matthew) leering over his shoulder' (VII. 4).

Wildgoose's religious Quixotism is not rigorously sustained,
however, and the novel is a less distinctive example of the type
than *The Female Quixote* (1752), by Charlotte Lennox.[1] This
was indeed by far the most systematic attempt in English to
create a modern version of Cervantes' work. Her Arabella's
world is conjured up from the French romances of the previous
century, and thus conditioned she transforms the familiar
community around her into something far more satisfying to
her imagination and her self-esteem. Suitors importune her and
ravishers threaten. Reality, of course, is constantly breaking
in, but she can never quite believe that she was not abducted,
while in a swoon, by the foppish Mr. Tinsel, in spite of the
unwelcome assurances of her maid:

> Indeed, Madam, replied *Lucy*, I have given your Ladyship a
> faithful Relation of all I can remember.
> When, resum'd *Arabella* surpriz'd?
> This Moment, Madam, said *Lucy*.
> Why, sure thou dream'st Wench, replied she, Hast thou told me
> how I was seiz'd and carry'd off? How I was rescu'd again? And—

---

[1] Charlotte Lennox, 1729?–1804, passed her childhood in New York, but came
to England and worked as an actress before settling into the life of a professional
writer.

No, indeed, Madam, interrupted *Lucy*, I don't dream; I never told your Ladyship that you was carry'd off.

Well, said *Arabella*, and why dost thou not satisfy my Curiosity? Is it not fit I should be acquainted with such a momentous Part of my History?

I can't, indeed, and please your Ladyship, said *Lucy*.

What can'st thou not, said *Arabella*, enrag'd at her Stupidity.

Why, Madam, said *Lucy* sobbing, I can't make a History of nothing.

Of nothing, Wench, resum'd *Arabella*, in a greater Rage than before . . .   (VII. 14)

To the heroine the attitudes she strikes are sublime, but to everyone else they look absurd and often extremely indelicate or discourteous. At the approach of one supposed ravisher, she acutely embarrasses her cousin Mr. Glanville by the way she makes clear that the stranger is the subject of their conversation: 'If you please, Madam,' he says in vexation, 'we will endeavour to join our Company.' She does not take the hint, but proceeds to a further, and enormous, breach of propriety. Glanville had exasperatedly asked her who was going to molest her. ' "He whom you see there," replied Arabella, pointing to him with her Finger' (IV. 4).

Charlotte Lennox skilfully manipulates the opportunities for misunderstanding provided by the conventions of polite conversation, and exploits her heroine's credulous acceptance of such smooth humbugs as Sir George Bellmour. 'Humbugging' in the sense of hoaxing was a fashionable word in the early 1750s, a fact which may be an index of a new susceptibility to the pleasures of the imagination. The then unsated appetite for humbug will sufficiently account for one defect which has almost invariably dismayed later readers of this novel—the fact that the jest is protracted so laboriously. Indeed, it sometimes has the appearance of a study in morbid psychology, although this was evidently not quite the author's intention. She goes to some trouble to emphasize that Arabella was intelligent, benevolent, and not without good sense, in contrast to her cousin Miss Granville, who although perfectly sane is shallow and can be spiteful. An appearance of lunacy, it seems, may well coexist with the most estimable virtues, and even engender them. It then requires only tact (or a little kindly humbug) to set the amiable heroine on the way to a full recovery of common sense. Not that the moral is as simple as that: one detects a hankering after the world of fine fabling that Arabella inhabited and Sir George Bellmour affected to inhabit, where a country gentleman can be the heir to the ancient kingdom of Kent, and a young lady can still follow the magnanimous examples of Thalestris, Queen of the Amazons, and the virtuous though much-maligned Cleopatra.

Charlotte Lennox's first novel, *Harriot Stuart* (1750), had exhibited a heroine as much exposed to undesired suitors and alarming ravishers as Arabella's imagination could possibly have devised. The author had then identified herself with her Harriot completely, even to the extent of crediting her with the composition of some of her earlier published poems. The Quixotic Arabella may be viewed as an attempt to present Harriot in rigorously objective terms, perhaps as the result of improving conversations between Charlotte Lennox and her admiring friend Samuel Johnson. By the time she was writing her other successful novel, *Henrietta* (1758), the female Quixote has dwindled, in the person of Miss Woodby, to a mere object of satire. She is much given to forming (and dissolving) 'violent friendships', and would feel no concern if a hundred men died of love for her—which they are not likely to do, she being extremely ugly. Miss Woodby, however, is only a marginal figure in *Henrietta*, just one of the characters observed by a heroine whose powers of discernment are heightened by varieties of dependence, whether on the wealthy aunt who wants her to embrace Romanism and an elderly husband, or when she offers her services as a maid to uncongenial employers. The novel could almost be classified with the social panoramas discussed earlier, but the reader is always aware of the heroine's presence. We wince with her as the obtuse Miss Cordwain discusses her with a friend, saying that there is no objection to her lack of experience in domestic service.

'For, to say the truth,' said she, addressing herself to her companion, 'those sort of poor gentlewomen, when they are reduced, as they call it, to wait upon us, who could buy their whole generation, often know their distance better, and are more humble, than such as have been bred to service.'

'Oh!' said the other lady, with an applauding smile, 'ever while you live, Madam, chuse a gentlewoman for your maid.'   (III. 5)

The scene would have done well in a play, but on stage the

words would tend to lose the sharpness they acquire when perceived through Henrietta's mind as she submits to her ordeal of voluntary servitude. Charlotte Lennox has obviously learned from Richardson in this matter, as she has too from Fielding's insight into the varieties of self-deception. Above all she has profited from exploring the mind of her female Quixote, learning how differently the same words may sound to different people.

When *Henrietta* was published, readers on both sides of the Channel had had over twenty years to grow familiar with the niceties of psychological insight explored by Marivaux. In their different ways, Richardson and Sarah Fielding had developed this vein, and a vocabulary of sensibility, a method of examining the more elusive passions, was becoming widely understood. The female Quixote herself showed an easy mastery of the routine: the narrative of her life, she told Lucy, must include not only all her words and actions, but also all her thoughts, 'however instantaneous'. Her poor maid must

relate exactly every Change of my Countenance; number all my Smiles, Half-smiles, Blushes, Turnings pale, Glances, Pauses, Full-stops, Interruptions; the Rise and Falling of my Voice; every Motion of my Eyes; and every Gesture which I have used for these Ten Years past; nor omit the smallest Circumstance that relates to me.   (III. 5)

Sensitivity to such slight indications of feeling was an index of the qualities indispensable to the improvement of man and of society. Deference to wealth and rank was an odious distraction from the qualities of character which really did honour to the species, and it was part of the mission of sentimental authors to help their readers not to be thus distracted. Hence the importance for them of tenderness and, in particular, of tears. David Hume's discussion of goodness and benevolence in the third book (published in 1740) of his *Treatise of Human Nature* provides as clear an account as may be found anywhere of the rational basis of the cult of sensibility. 'A propensity to the tender passions', he says, 'makes a man agreeable and useful in all the parts of life, and gives a just direction to all his other qualities, which otherwise may become prejudicial to society.' Not that tenderness is valued only because it makes one a good citizen. Man being what he is, love is immediately agreeable to him. Tears naturally start in the eyes at the conception of a tender sentiment, 'nor can we forbear giving a loose to the same tenderness towards the person who exerts it'. We are particularly touched by any instance of extraordinary delicacy in love or friendship, and such delicacy gives a value to the most apparently trifling matters—the more minute, the more engaging, and 'a proof of the highest merit in any one who is capable of them'. Even the weaknesses of benevolence are virtuous: 'a person, whose grief upon the loss of a friend were excessive, would be esteemed upon that account. His tenderness bestows a merit, as it does a pleasure, on his melancholy.'

Hume's analysis forms a particularly appropriate introduction to the work of Frances Brooke.[1] In 1760 she published *Letters from Juliet Lady Catesby*, a translation from the French of Mme Riccoboni. This work exhibits considerable virtuosity in charting the currents and eddies of feeling in a sensitive soul, and uses all the resources of typography to convey the unutterable emotions that emerge between broken sentences. Thus, Lady Catesby finds her emotions towards Lord Ossory changing as she reads a letter from him over again.

> It appears to me in a new Light: Those very Expressions that excited my Anger, now move my tenderest Compassion: How affecting is that Passage where he speaks of my Letters! *He pressed them to his Lips, they were his only Consolation*—but what were then his Sorrows? *His Exile!*—If he had loved me—Ah! how could he have wedded another, if his Heart—I can comprehend nothing.

When Frances Brooke comes to attempt an original fiction, in *Lady Julia Mandeville* (1763), she exploits similar techniques but relates her sensitive souls to a social context and a framework of political ideology. Harry Mandeville and Lady Julia Mandeville are typically ingenuous protagonists: Julia describes herself as 'artless as the village maid, every sentiment of my soul is in my eyes: I have not learnt, I will never learn to disguise their expressive language'. Harry's love for her develops in a landscape benignly dominated by her father, the great landowner Lord Belmont. Like Walter Shandy, Lord Belmont

---

[1] Frances Brooke, 1724–89, spent some years in Canada with her husband, while he was chaplain of the Quebec garrison, but for much of her life she was a professional writer in London.

believes that gentlemen should avoid the smoking furnace of London and live on their estates, bringing prosperity and stability to the countryside. He is contrasted with another landowner, Lord T——, whose method of estate management leads to the kind of general depopulation that Goldsmith was to deplore some seven years later in 'The Deserted Village':

a dreary silence reigns over their deserted fields; the farm houses, once the seat of cheerful smiling industry, now useless, are falling in ruins around him; his tenants are merchants and ingrossers, proud, lazy, luxurious, insolent, and spurning the hand which feeds them.

Lord Belmont intends that Harry shall succeed him as enlightened ruler over his estates (though Harry himself has been kept in ignorance of this), and clearly the young man is as well qualified for this station as sensibility can make him. But all this prospect of good is conjured up to be annihilated: the most memorable element in the novel is its miserable catastrophe. The misunderstanding that leads to Harry's death, and Julia's, may perhaps be interpreted as part of the discipline of misfortune that softens the heart and so strengthens the virtuous in their virtue. The unhappy parents 'indulge in all the voluptuousness of sorrow', and their indulgence makes them more alert to their social responsibilities. Even so, there is a disturbing force in the exclamation of one of the characters: 'The worthless live and prosper: the virtuous sink untimely to the grave!' Frances Brooke is responding to an impulse that now becomes increasingly conspicuous in the literary scene—the yearning for a distress which found a perverse pleasure in its own intensity, and hinted at an ultimate emptiness and despair. Such moods were already familiar to English readers from the more sombre pages of the novels of the Abbé Prévost, and had recently been elaborately explored by Frances Sheridan in the agonies of Sidney Bidulph. Frances Brooke herself, however, did not descend further into the depths. *The History of Emily Montague* (1769) is a study in delicate sensibility against the exotic background of the Province of Quebec. The exotic remains in the background, however: Sir George Clayton could have been the 'lifeless composition of earth and water' that he is on either side of the Atlantic, and the same is true of Emily's trembling excess of passion and Edward Rivers's eloquent countenance. The extreme cold of a Canadian winter provides material for a lively description by the lively Arabella —'the largest wood fire, in a wide chimney, does not throw out its heat a quarter of a yard'—but the sensation of frozen faculties is not exploited, or even communicated.

Her one remaining novel takes a different direction. When Lord Chesterfield's *Letters to his Son* were published posthumously in 1774, they offended many readers by their insistence on good-breeding, manners, and 'address', to the exclusion of weightier considerations. S. J. Pratt ('Courtney Melmoth') is a fair representative of those who were offended. He created a vigorously calculating seducer for his *Pupil of Pleasure* (1777) who was inspired by the Chesterfield system:

whatever fancy, passion, whim, or wickedness, suggest, only command your countenance, check your temper, and throw before your heart and bosom the shield of Dissimulation, and snatch it—seize it —enjoy it.

In *The Excursion* (also published in 1777), Frances Brooke attempted something more complex than Pratt's compound of Iago, Lovelace, and Chesterfield. She delineates a young man, Lord Melvile, who has received a Chesterfieldian education from his father, but who has not reacted entirely as planned. His 'system of conduct' followed his father's injunctions, but his heart was apt to revolt against the system. 'His principles were narrow and selfish, his feelings generous and humane.' There is much scope for the imagination of a novelist here, and even though the author does little to take advantage of the possibilities, she deserves credit for having glimpsed the interest of the situation. The main achievement of the novel, however, is the pleasantly ingenuous Maria Villiers, whose course of fashionable expenditure was backed by a considerable sum in her portmanteau, represented by her epic poem, her novel, and her play: 'she estimated her epic poem at £100, her novel at £200, and her play, including the copy, at £500: on the whole £800.' The sincere, rash, credulous Maria is by far the most engaging of Frances Brooke's heroines. On occasion one is reminded, distantly, of Jane Austen.

Frances Sheridan's[1] work has much in common with

---

[1] Frances Sheridan, 1724–66, was the wife of Thomas Sheridan and mother of Richard Brinsley Sheridan. When in London she became acquainted with Samuel Richardson, who encouraged her to write. She spent her last two years in France, at Blois.

Frances Brooke's, but the author of the *Memoirs of Miss Sidney Bidulph* (1761) was an artist of greater stamina than the creator of Lady Julia Mandeville. Even at the age of fifteen she was able to write a remarkably competent and attractive novel, *Eugenia and Adelaide*. Its ingenious plot is worked out with rather too much youthful facility, and some of it is absurd, but already she displays a talent for presenting scenes of acute embarrassment. This work was not published, however, until long after her death, and her reputation was founded on the distresses of Sidney Bidulph: distresses that were felt to exceed all precedent. Dr. Johnson wondered whether she had a moral right to make her readers suffer so much, and certainly the sheer scale and careful contrivance of the plot suggest a massive concentration of misfortunes that would have crushed a much more resilient spirit than that of this heroine, who felt that she had never known what it was to have a will of her own. The novel is obviously indebted to Richardson, with skilful exploitation of the heroine's anxieties, uncertainties, and imperfect information. The hero, the chivalrous Orlando Faulkland, is given an original turn by being made as resourceful, as ruthless, and as entertaining as Lovelace himself; but his vitality, thwarted by events as it is, serves only to heighten the sense of helplessness engendered by the story as it unfolds. Much of the plot turns on Sidney Bidulph's mistaken scruples about the Miss Burchell whom she thinks to have a prior claim on Faulkland. Although every reader must be exasperated by her persistence in these scruples, the persistence is genuinely convincing. The novel is in effect a study of a rigidly conventional conscience whose rigidity is subjected to ever-increasing strain from uneasiness about Miss Burchell, Sidney passing from remorseful sympathy with her to half-conscious jealousy, and then to outright detestation. The process is presented through an accumulation of details not easy to illustrate briefly, but a couple of sentences may throw some light on it. They describe Miss Burchell's behaviour after Faulkland has agreed to marry her. She comes in (says Sidney) with pleasure dancing in her eyes. Sidney advises her to restrain her joy in case Sidney's mother should be upset by it.

She smiled; and, thanking me for the hint, immediately composed her features to such a decorum, (I will not call it demureness) that it was impossible to discover she was agitated by any extraordinary emotion. I own, I was amazed at the command she so suddenly assumed over her countenance.

The jealous feeling that obtrudes beneath the resolute effort to be fair is deftly touched, and shows a kind of penetration into the subtleties of human motive that was highly valued by mid-century critics. What must have been even more striking, however, was the novel's conclusion, with its evocation of indescribable abysses of misery opening up beyond the last fragmentary document that had come to the hand of the 'editor'. The effect, unhappily, was impaired when Frances Sheridan yielded to the temptation of writing a sequel. In this *Continuation of the Memoirs* (1767) Sidney reappears in not uncomfortable circumstances, and although she suffers again, and dies, one feels cheated of one's original misery. This annoyance apart, the sequel proceeds briskly enough, with a villainously dissembling brother and sister intriguing together to erect a 'vast fabric of iniquity' whose weight eventually crushes all beneath it.

Frances Sheridan found no difficulty in creating her 'vast fabric'. Henry Brooke,[1] another novelist who delighted in moments of warm, tearful sensibility, preferred the less exacting convention, reinforced by the success of Sterne, that permitted an author to assemble scenes, inset narratives, and disquisitions into a loosely-structured fiction. Not that Brooke's principal work, *The Fool of Quality* (1766–72), is altogether shapeless. It develops a large contrast between the Earl of Moreland and his brother Mr. Clinton (or Fenton as he is called through much of the narrative): a contrast between the values of a decadent polite society and those of a vigorous and humane merchant class. Against this background Brooke works out his central theme, the education of the Earl's second son, Harry Clinton, on wiser and more generous principles than were then customary. The story is set in a perfunctorily suggested historical past—the latter half of the seventeenth century, that heroic age of the British constitution. William III is represented as contemplating the adoption of young Harry as heir to the throne, an honour that Henry (or rather his admirable mentor Mr.

---

[1] Henry Brooke, *c.* 1703–83, was educated at Trinity College, Dublin, and was a student at the Temple, spending some time in England. He returned to Dublin in 1740, where he became barrack-master in about 1745. He advocated some relaxation of penal laws against Irish Catholics. He was often short of money, and in his last years suffered from an incapacitating depressive illness.

Fenton) was far too discerning, far too well grounded in constitutional principles, to wish for. The educational theme was
no doubt suggested by the success of Rousseau's *Émile*, which
had won immediate fame upon its publication in 1762, but
Émile's success was itself evidence of a widespread preoccupation (satirized in *Tristram Shandy*) with the possibility of making,
in Mr. Fenton's words, 'a new nation of infants, and consequently of men'. It is perhaps too much of a compliment to
Brooke to say that his novel expounds a theory of education,
though it is clear that he had read Locke's *Thoughts* on the
subject, and entered with gusto into the philosopher's commendation of 'confident Communication' between parent and
child. Brooke displays the unreserved mutual affection of Mr.
Fenton and his nephew with almost embarrassing exuberance,
and uncritically endorses the young boy's sense of power, or
mischief. The tone is apparent in the first episode, when little
Harry, fresh from his humble foster-home, sets a decorous
assembly of gentlefolk in an uproar by playing ducks and drakes
with a hat among the wine-glasses, and performing other inconvenient feats of strength and dexterity. In the same vein, the
flogging pedant Mr. Vindex is humiliated by the inventive
genius of Harry's schoolfellow Ned, who devises one piece of
intricate machinery to pierce his backside by remote control,
and another to manipulate his door-knocker. Such ingenious
horse-play alternates with lavish displays of bounteous generosity
to the unfortunate distressed. The temper of Brooke's world,
and especially its note of hectic euphoria, is aptly summed up
in a sentence from his later novel *Juliet Grenville* (1774), where
the heroine recalls a time when her life 'passed and glided
away, in a paradisiacal delirium of infantine deliciousness'.

Mr. Clinton (or Fenton) is a good deal more than an
idealized representative of the mercantile interest. He seems to
wield a greater power than that of kings or princes, and there
is even a hint of divinity in his attributes. His bounty emulates
that of an all-loving father-god. The passage in which Mr.
Meekly recalls his encounter with Mr. Clinton and his Louisa
in Holland many years previously associates them with the
unfallen Adam and Eve, with Abraham and Sarah, and then
with a greater than these:

'Why, pray, [said Meekly to the innkeeper] is he a lord?—A lord?
quotha; not so little as that comes to neither. No, sir; he is a prince—

the very prince of our merchants, and our merchants are princes above all lords.—And, pray, how do they style or call him?—He has many names and titles. When our traders speak of him, they call him Mynheer Van Glunthnog; but others style him my lord of merchants, and others my lord the brother-man, and my lord the friend of the poor.

Brooke contrives to blend the mercantile interest with New Testament associations, and suffuses the whole with fevered nostalgia peculiar to himself. He even sees the promotion of canals as a means to bring in the millennium.

Brooke's euphoria is often displaced by distress of the most unsettling kind. He is fascinated by the moment when one's last sixpence is spent, and nothing, nothing whatever, stands between oneself and starvation. This sixpence is not just a rhetorical flourish. Like Defoe, Brooke has the knack of alluring his readers into calculating how far a character's resources will go, sometimes with an exhilarating effect which makes deprivation all the more overwhelming when it comes. The 'History of a Man of Letters'—a long inset narrative in the earlier half of the novel—can still disturb a sympathetic reader with its sickening reversals of fortune, which end only when the unhappy Hammel Clement and his family crawl into the protection of Mr. Fenton and Harry. Such destitution has an irresistible tendency to inspire a doubt in providence, a doubt that is memorably expressed in some words of Hammel Clement: 'I saw nothing', he says, 'but the labyrinth within my own soul; and from thence I could perceive neither outlet nor escape.' Brooke's temperament compels him to ensure that relief comes to his characters, and the godlike Mr. Clinton is the principal agency of relief. The shadow of ultimate destitution is reserved for subordinate characters, for people set at a little distance from the reader. The fool of quality is under divine protection: he is at least relatively invulnerable.

Brooke's feverishly energetic attempt to reconcile contrary states—the sense of providence with the sense of abject helplessness in a hostile world—made him attractive to a section at least of the religious public of his day, and anticipated elements of the 'muscular Christianity' of the following century. Both John Wesley and Charles Kingsley thought him worth reprinting. But *The Fool of Quality* has never quite established itself as even a minor classic. Its unwieldy shape seems to have no discernible artistic function, and the self-indulgent emotional turbulence has not worn well. It forms a strong contrast in these respects with a work, also first published in 1766, which one is tempted to describe as the most assured minor classic ever written, *The Vicar of Wakefield*. Oliver Goldsmith had already shown his deft mastery of the kind of story-telling that is little more than an anecdote, the tale that has to be confined within the limits of a periodical essay. It would be difficult to imagine anything more elegantly turned than the sad story of Choang and his faithless wife Hansi in Letter 18 of the *Citizen of the World*. The sense of elegance is not merely the effect of an absurdly ingenious symmetry, but also of a half-awareness that the situation could be far more emotionally charged than the actual narrative allows it to appear. The tone, the symmetry, the very conciseness of the telling, all conspire to exclude passion; but the possibility of its presence remains as a latent pressure on our consciousness. There is something demurely impudent about narrating such a story in this way at all. *The Vicar of Wakefield* does not have the same flawless elegance, but sustains, in its larger dimensions, an easy grace to which structural symmetry and a dispassionate temper both contribute. The use of the Vicar, Dr. Primrose, as narrator ensures that any unduly disturbing emotions will not be registered, although the materials of a deeply affecting tragedy of sensibility are obviously present, and were exploited by W. G. Wills in his Victorian stage adaptation *Olivia* (1878). The change of title indicates Wills's strategy, creating a role for the young Ellen Terry that she performed with a gaiety and tender grace remembered poignantly by a whole generation of playgoers. From Wills's point of view, Goldsmith's tale must have been a series of missed opportunities. Few of its readers can have shed tears over it, even though the situation of the Vicar and his family in the second half of the narrative must have invited that exploration of the heights and depths of passion to which the cult of sensibility was so dedicated. The degradation of a daughter, the loss of almost all worldly goods, imprisonment in the county gaol; all these are calamities which Frances Sheridan would have savoured at length, and Henry Brooke narrated with uncontrolled vehemence. The Vicar records events briefly, even briskly, without being fundamentally unsettled by any of them. He expresses appropriate passions, but is not disposed to elaborate on states of feeling. What he does elaborate is intellectual argument. He shows how the sufferings of the poor are compensated for in the hereafter, and develops his Cartesian theory of political power in an austerely mathematical idiom. He never long loses sight of his role of law-giver to a little republic: the family, the parish, the prison. If he seems not always in command, it is because he is no tyrant but a constitutional monarch—constitutional to a fault. He may venture on a peremptory assertion of his paternal authority, but has to expect 'sullen looks and short answers the whole day ensuing' (chapter IX). He is, indeed, apparently helpless to control the social ambitions of his womenfolk, but he still contrives to avoid a sense of undue subjection to the inferior sex. The first half of the story records a game of skill played between wife and husband, with points scored on both sides. If his wife insists on riding to church instead of walking, all his objections may be overruled; but the horses prove refractory, and the family never gets to church at all. 'I own', says the Vicar smoothly, 'their present mortification did not much displease me, as it would give me many opportunities of future triumph, and teach my daughters more humility' (chapter X). He could adopt more active measures, as when he frustrated his daughters' cosmetic preparations for a visit from the wicked squire by surreptitiously overturning the pan in which the face-wash was being heated (chapter VI). He could be defeated and then ignominiously participate in the course he had formerly resisted:

notwithstanding all I could say—and I said much—it was resolved that we should have our pictures done too. Having, therefore, engaged the limner (for what could I do?) our next deliberation was to show the superiority of our taste in the attitudes. . . . My wife desired to be represented as Venus, and the painter was requested not to be too frugal of his diamonds in her stomacher and hair. Her two little ones were to be as Cupids by her side; while I, in my gown and band, was to present her with my books on the Whistonian controversy (chap. XVI).

The Vicar's diplomatic flexibility shows to better advantage in his nicely-calculated sermon to his fellow prisoners (chapter XXVI), followed as it is by a striking reformation in a place of apparently hopeless depravity. The order and decency that he produces in this unpromising environment is an achievement comparable (it is implied) to that of the great legislators of antiquity, bringing their peoples 'from their native ferocity into friendship and obedience' (chapter XXVII). Dr. Primrose's talents, however, though they might have sufficed to make him a Solon or a Lycurgus, are inadequate when matched with modern villainy.

The portrait of the Vicar is a coherent but not a simple one which constantly resists any tendency on the reader's part to identify too readily with him. He is an amiable humorist and a pathetic victim, intended to inspire laughter, pity, and esteem. Goldsmith's sympathetic detachment finds expression in the deliberate symmetry of the structure, emphasizing as it does a stylized quality far removed from the free-ranging spontaneity cultivated by other writers we have examined. When one remarks that the first half of the story is a comedy, the second half a pathetic narrative, the halving is no mere approximation. There are thirty-two chapters in all, and they fall precisely into two sets of sixteen. Each set of sixteen falls further into two sets of eight chapters, chapter IX marking the point where the assault on the virtue of the Vicar's daughters is first seriously prosecuted, and chapter XXV the point where the Vicar goes to prison and meets the rogue Jenkinson again: not this time to be cheated by him, but assisted. It happens that the three poems incorporated in the text are placed close to each of the three turning-points of the action, a coincidence which serves to underline the symmetrical effect. One could carry this analysis further, but enough has been said to indicate the lengths to which Goldsmith could go to suggest the creation of an artefact.

The playful rigour of form in which Goldsmith delighted is far removed from the method—equally deliberate—of that most notorious of sentimental novels, *The Man of Feeling* (1771). Henry Mackenzie[1] here produces an ingenious variation on the convention by which a novel is constructed from a mass of supposed documents selected and set in order by an 'editor'. The manuscript account of Harley's life, we learn, has been partly destroyed by a sporting clergyman, who uses its pages to make wadding for his gun. Thus we are provided with an object-lesson in how sensibility is slighted by coarse natures.

---

[1] Henry Mackenzie, 1745–1831, was educated at Edinburgh High School and Edinburgh University. He was a practising lawyer, and in 1799 was made comptroller of taxes for Scotland.

At the same time, the excisions produce an effect of concentration: nothing need be left in except what illustrates the nature of a fine sensibility. The machinery of a plot is irrelevant to the effect in which Mackenzie is interested, and the curate's depredations enable him to disregard it. The calculatedly fragmentary text shows a man whose warm sympathies and delicacy of feeling make him even more incapable of contending with a deceitful world than is the Vicar of Wakefield. Like Goldsmith's Vicar he succumbs to the trickery of practised rogues, but unlike the Vicar he does not succumb because his self-esteem has been flattered. On the contrary, Harley is at first all too willing to pay tribute to admirable traits that he thinks he discerns in others. An apparently benevolent countenance serves as an impenetrable mask for any card-sharper lucky enough to have Harley to deal with. But Harley's good-will is not always misdirected: the prostituted Miss Atkins proves to be indeed worthy of his interest and support. Harley's worldly-wise friends, however, make no distinction between the sharper and the prostitute. His credulity is a mere symptom of folly, or worse:

'Gentlemen', said the lawyer . . . 'here's a very pretty fellow for you: to have heard him talk some nights ago, as I did, you might have sworn he was a saint; yet now he games with sharpers, and loses his money; and is bubbled by a fine story invented by a whore, and pawns his watch; here are sanctified doings with a witness!'

(Chap. XXVII)

For Mackenzie, Harley's willingness to expose himself in compromising situations, to endure shame in an uncomfortably literal way, is the supreme test of his virtue. It is part of the same pattern that he should lack the ability to achieve worldly success. He finds his chief pleasure in assisting those who have been unjustly treated by the successful. He does not even presume to seek the hand in marriage of the lady he loves, though his confession of love to Miss Walton on his death-bed is a splendid example of the language of feeling as it had been cultivated by the disciples of Mme Riccoboni. The temper of the book demands that the broken, indirect expressions should convey their meaning—reinforced by tears flowing without control—only at the moment of death. Love is more strongly felt when yearning for consummation than when consummated,

and that which is never consummated is therefore most powerful of all. Again, the most powerful feelings are precisely those
which cannot be uttered. A few asterisks, a paragraph left
incomplete, indicate where the reader must look into his own
breast to catch the meaning of what is not said. When Miss
Walton gives some pretty clothes to the orphaned grand-
children of the much-suffering Edwards, Edwards himself is
almost overcome.

'I cannot speak, young lady,' said he, 'to thank you.' Neither
could Harley. There were a thousand sentiments; but they gushed so
impetuously on his heart, that he could not utter a syllable. ****
('A Fragment', following chap. XXXVI)

In its emphasis on benevolent, quietly melancholy refinement
The Man of Feeling was in tune with much that had preceded
it: anyone who responded sympathetically to David Simple
would be well prepared to appreciate Harley. Even so, there
are hints of a new kind of interest in such moral audacities as
the juxtaposition in one of the chapter-headings, 'The Man of
Feeling in a Brothel'. Harley is far removed from the passionate
bewilderment of the Chevalier des Grieux after he has fallen
under the spell of Manon Lescaut, but some of Mackenzie's
subsequent works discreetly skirt their way round these waste
places of the spirit. *The Man of the World* (1773) derives such
interest as it has, not from the tepidly-imagined villain-hero Sir
Thomas Sindall, but from the presentation of the sufferings of
his victims. The last few chapters of the first part can be recommended to any reader who wishes to study a calculated climax
of agony. Each stage in the process deepens the sense of hopeless
despondency: the enforced and miserable elopement of the
pregnant Harriet from her aged father's house—his death in
total ignorance of her circumstances—her discovery that she has
been handed over to some low-bred creature of her seducer's—
the ensuing premature childbirth, and Harriet's death after the
double shock of hearing first a report of her father's death
and then of her baby's. Mackenzie visibly labours to heighten
the distress to the limit, but having done so he imitates the
unfortunate example of Frances Sheridan and writes a sequel.
The second part gives one the satisfaction of knowing that
Harriet's baby had not died after all, restores Harriet's exiled
brother (another of Sindall's victims), and suitably punishes

Sindall himself. Much space is devoted to an account of the brother's life with the Cherokee Indians, and Mackenzie seems to have intended the happy ending to show the purification of our corrupt society by the representative of one more primitive. The effect is rather too glib.

In *Julia de Roubigné* (1777), Mackenzie's last extended work of fiction, he allows the tragic story to proceed unchecked. The epistolary convention is skilfully used to bring out the remoteness from each other of an impeccably virtuous husband and wife. Montauban and Julia are a kind of modern Othello and Desdemona, but no Iago intervenes to vulgarize the story with the taint of evil. The emotional intensity to which Mackenzie aspires is the effect of passionate regret that Julia ever allowed the sentiment of gratitude to lead her into marriage with an ageing man for whom she felt no warm affection. The return of her former lover Savillon merely precipitates a crisis that was latent before. As a study in intricate and contradictory motives the novel still has some interest, but most readers are probably carried along by sympathies resembling those with which they enter into Harley's feelings about Miss Walton. The beauty of the love of Savillon and Julia is precisely that they can never marry. All their passion is concentrated into a single, sinless meeting, followed immediately by her death. The remorse of the husband who has murdered her supplies the reader with an additional luxury of distress.

In later pieces of short fiction, Mackenzie showed that he was still haunted by the nightmare of irremediable remorse, or at · least by milder emotions of compunction and regret. In the *Lounger* (Nos. 82–4) there is the story of Father Nicholas, which explores the state of mind of a man who abandoned his wife and baby son because he could not bear to tell her that gambling debts had left him penniless. Her consequent delirium and death are reported to him when he is far from them, and he spends the remainder of his life mortifying his body in a monastery and torturing his mind by meditating on a picture of his wife and child. We approach this story through a visual impression of the ascetic Benedictine monk kneeling at a distance from the altar and near a Gothic window,

through the painted panes of which a gleamy light touched his forehead, and threw a dark Rembrandt shade on the hollow of a large, black, melancholy eye. It was impossible not to take notice of

him. He looked up, involuntarily no doubt, to a picture of our
Saviour bearing his cross; the similarity of the attitude, and the
quiet resignation of the two countenances, formed a resemblance that
could not but strike every one.

The story provides a mournfully ironic background to this
figure, but the final effect is a tranquil one, comparable to that
created by the story of the old pastor La Roche (in the *Mirror*,
Nos. 42–4), who buries his only daughter, and preaches the
funeral sermon on this distressing occasion. Again the scene is
dimly lighted, except for the central figure:

La Roche sat, his figure bending gently forward, his eyes half-
closed, lifted up in silent devotion. A lamp placed near him threw
its light strong on his head, and marked the shadowy lines of age
across the paleness of his brow, thinly covered with gray hairs.

The age of the sufferer emphasizes both the accumulated burden
of his experience and his present quiet resignation. The surrounding darkness is a reminder of how easily he could himself
be lost in it; but in that darkness too there are sympathetic if
powerless observers, including the agnostic philosopher who
had been half in love with the daughter, and whom the scene
has almost touched into a state of religious belief.

Mackenzie enjoyed a high reputation in his own time, partly
because of the real excellence of his literary craftsmanship, even
more, perhaps, because of the skill he displayed in reconciling
intractably disturbing emotions with the claims of reason and
morality. A controlled sensibility was increasingly in demand
towards the end of the century, a fact that accounts for such
novels as Richard Cumberland's *Henry* (1794), a quite remarkable emasculation of *Tom Jones* in the interests of a highly
moral 'enthusiasm of feeling'. It finds crisp expression in
Dinarbas (1790), the sequel to Johnson's *Rasselas* written by
Ellis Cornelia Knight.[1] She found Johnson's tale morbidly
sombre, and her Rasselas is more self-critical than Johnson's.
'To my own restless disposition', he is made to remark, 'I owe
the humiliation of fruitless inquiry.' Her continuation attempts
to prove that in spite of poignant grief and maddening disappointment, the virtuous and sensitive are rewarded by

[1] Ellis Cornelia Knight, 1757–1837, was acquainted with Sir Joshua Reynolds
and Samuel Johnson in London. Later she lived in Italy, and came to know Sir
William and Lady Hamilton. For a time she held appointments at court, but was
dismissed in 1814. After 1816 she lived mainly abroad, and died in Paris.

precious moments of ecstasy and consolatory reflection. She contrives to make some acute criticisms of Johnsonian pessimism, notably her defence of the surliness of shepherds (chapter VIII). But the work as a whole is too facile to bear comparison with *Rasselas*, and by general consent it has slipped into oblivion.

Controlled sensibility is an important element in the work of Fanny Burney.[1] Her heroines are in a direct line of descent from the Marianne of Marivaux, but the perplexities which beset Marianne in her uneasy state of dependence are milder than the succession of exquisitely poignant mental torments that the Burney heroines endure. Even so, the torments are an ordeal from which they emerge wiser and stronger. Fanny Burney's world is one in which the worthless live and prosper, certainly, but the virtuous do not sink untimely to the grave, or not quite. The novels are informed with all the anxiety of a young woman unaccustomed to the way of the world, a world that is full of perilous traps and perplexing rules, where she is expected to display modesty, reserve, submission, and at the same time to possess the active qualities plainly necessary for survival. This essential material of her fiction is to be found in plenty in her diary. She is continually drawn into dangerous situations that she would rather run away from. Good manners always hold her to her duty, a rare exception being the time she met the mad King George III in Kew Gardens: 'Heavens, how I ran! I do not think I should have felt the hot lava from Vesuvius—at least not the hot cinders—had I so run during its eruption' (2 February 1789). Even then she was forced to go through with the encounter, reckoning it 'the greatest effort of personal courage I have ever made'. But she would have needed every scrap of this palpitating moral courage for such occasions as the dinner when Dr. Johnson made a gratuitous attack on William Waller Pepys for venturing to be offended by Johnson's *Life* of Lord Lyttelton. Her intense anxiety about the dispute, or rather about Johnson's vehemence and bitterness, throws the contest into the sharpest possible relief. She is aware of Johnson's irritation about 'the *sneaking* complaints and murmurs of

---

[1] Frances Burney, 1752–1840, was the daughter of Dr. Charles Burney, and like him associated with the Johnson circle in London. She was given an appointment at court, which adversely affected her health. She married General d'Arblay, a French refugee, in 1793, and lived in France from 1802 till 1812. She spent the last years of her life in England.

the Lytteltonians' and has some sympathy with it; but she sympathizes also with the temperate, good-humoured Pepys, uttering 'all that belonged merely to himself with modesty, and all that immediately related to Lord Lyttelton with spirit'. She is torn apart. The only relief comes from the philistine absurdities of a Mr. Cator, evidently a model for several low-bred characters in her fiction. When the conflict is finally stopped by an indignant Mrs. Thrale, Fanny Burney finds a new anxiety in the ill-success of her efforts to suppress her own amusement at the irrepressible Cator.

> I found it impossible to keep my countenance, and was once, when most unfortunately he addressed himself to me, surprised by him on the full grin. To soften it off as well as I could, I pretended unusual complacency, and instead of recovering my gravity, I continued a most ineffable smile for the whole time he talked, which was indeed no difficult task. Poor Mr. Seward was as much off his guard as myself, having his mouth distended to its full extent every other minute.   (June 1781)

Only the most intrepid good manners were a match for muscular reflexes subjected to this kind of strain. The stresses were even more severe when Fanny Burney was given a place at court, holding the office of Assistant Keeper of the Queen's Robes. It is perhaps enough to refer the reader to her 'Directions for coughing, sneezing, or moving, before the King and Queen' (17 December 1785). Etiquette, of course, did not permit one to cough, or sneeze, or move:

> if your nose membranes feel a great irritation, you must hold your breath; if a sneeze still insists upon making its way, you must oppose it, by keeping your teeth grinding together; if the violence of the repulse breaks some blood-vessel, you must break the blood-vessel— but not sneeze.

The caricature hardly exceeded the reality. Only the most accomplished performing animals in the circus could be said to come into competition with Lady Charlotte Bertie, who once had to withdraw from the King's presence when suffering from a sprained ankle. It was painful for her to walk at all, but etiquette demanded that she should walk backwards, and back she went some twenty yards, 'perfectly upright, without one stumble, without ever looking once behind to see what she might encounter; and with as graceful a motion, and as easy an air, as I ever saw' (12 August 1786). Fanny Burney's experience of such conflict between social role and personal feeling was invaluable to her as a novelist, but she was never able to suppress her feelings in the way that an accomplished courtier should. When she attended the first day of the trial of Warren Hastings (13 February 1788), she found herself constrained by friendship and good manners to talk to William Windham, one of the chief promoters of the prosecution, and therefore peculiarly odious to her royal employers. To be seen by the Queen, as she was, engaged in close and eager conversation with such a man, was acutely embarrassing, but as she wanted to put in a word for the defendant, she heroically brazened it out.

Fanny Burney imagined for her heroines situations no less embarrassing. *Evelina* (1778) presents a range of society comparable in extent to that of the panoramic novels of mid-century, but the unifying presence is not a guinea or a lap-dog or even a young man of great health and spirits like Tom Jones who, as Henry James aptly remarked, was as finely bewildered as anyone could be who hadn't a grain of imagination. Evelina, tremblingly anxious to do the proper thing, to be well thought of by those who enjoy a secure position in the best society, finds that sound moral principles and a 'confused idea' of social etiquette are a painfully inadequate basis for this undertaking. While she has access to fashionable society, she is burdened also by cousins in the City, who involve her in gross discourtesy to her admired Lord Orville. The sequence of events in Letter 54, when the Branghtons and Madame Duval exploit Evelina's name in order to request the use of Lord Orville's coach, forms a climax of distress which is more relentless than the most laboured efforts of Henry Mackenzie. The crucial element in the situation, the source of its effect of nightmare, is Evelina's powerlessness. She sees to the full the frightful impropriety of making any such request, the more so because Lord Orville's benevolence would not allow him to refuse. But Madame Duval is impenetrable to persuasion; the Branghtons are in talkative high spirits throughout a ride which mortifies Evelina into a tearful silence; young Branghton uses her name to solicit business for himself from Lord Orville—after occasioning serious damage to his carriage. Evelina is afflicted by a sense of responsibility for actions which she opposed with all her might. A similar effect is achieved by the earlier episode (Letter 21) in which she is manœuvred into an unwanted *tête-à-tête* with Sir Clement Willoughby in his carriage. Her eager attention to the way she is being driven is an attempt to compensate for the frustration of her desire to escape, but the attempt is useless: she is quite unacquainted with the right way anyhow. Here and elsewhere she is almost helpless in a labyrinth, but exerts such pressures as she can with a fierce determination that carries her (aided indeed by such benign powers as Lord Orville and the sharp-tongued Mrs. Selwyn) to ultimate felicity.

The art of *Evelina* appears particularly in the way we are made to forget that the distress is occasioned by causes relatively insignificant. The agony experienced by Evelina in Sir Clement's carriage is far more intimately felt than that of many previously abducted heroines, but there is evidently no likelihood of any tragical outcome. In this respect, Fanny Burney's next novel, *Cecilia* (1782), is not so ingenious, though no less impressively imagined. The heroine's situation is one that might make anyone quail, helpless as she is not simply to prevent mortifying impertinence but the squandering of her fortune. The pressures to which she is subjected by her heedlessly extravagant guardian Harrel when he wants to get money from her are intolerable, and we feel that she has no choice but to give in. Having lost a considerable part of her inheritance, she then finds that this in itself will be judged blameworthy. Mrs. Delvile, that austere mother-figure, mortifies Cecilia exceedingly by ill-timed praise of her 'uncommon prudence and sagacity' which must surely have saved her from being drawn into Harrel's difficulties. Since it is inconceivable that prudence and sagacity could have done any such thing, Cecilia feels as rebellious as it is possible to be when one is nicely brought up and has nobody to confide in:

> Yet something she could not but murmur, that an action so detrimental to her own interest, and which, at the time, appeared indispensable to her benevolence, should now be considered as a mark of such folly and imprudence that she did not dare own it.
>
> (V. 8)

She is troubled by intractable bewilderments of this kind through much of the story, and has little guidance upon which she can rely. Few novelists can ever have given a heroine such an astonishing array of father-figures, ranging from the inadequate to the execrable. Her distresses reach a climax in a carriage journey more tormented than Evelina's, one in which she goes in quest of her husband, whom she thinks to be engaged in a duel. It is a hackney-coach, the driver somewhat drunk, and her only companion is an amiable but stupid tradesman, Mr. Simkins. His one concern is to make sure that the coachman does not cheat her, a concern that eventually immobilizes them. He begins a tedious calculation of the fare, the coachman becomes more outrageous, a mob collects, a strange gentleman too gallantly offers his assistance. Then follows Cecilia's collapse. In spite of the melodramatic circumstances, the author has her eye unflinchingly focused on the development of a state of mind.

Cecilia, breathless with vehemence and terror, was encircled, yet struggled in vain to break away; and the stranger gentleman, protesting, with sundry compliments, he would himself take care of her, very freely seized her hand.

This moment, for the unhappy Cecilia, teemed with calamity; she was wholly overpowered; terror for Delvile, horror for herself, hurry, confusion, heat, and fatigue, all assailing her at once, while all means of repelling them were denied her, the attack was too strong for her fears, feelings, and faculties, and her reason suddenly, yet totally failing her, she madly called out. (X. 7)

The egregious Mr. Simkins is only one of several admirably grotesque characters in *Cecilia*, and it should be noted that we are generally made to view them through the heroine's anxiety or embarrassment. Thus, Cecilia's dash to London in the seventh book is maddeningly slowed by an unwelcome encounter with some of the more strongly caricatured figures in the novel. In the party in Vauxhall Gardens which culminates in Harrel's suicide, Harrel's gaiety expresses itself in bringing together, in a state of uneasy hostility, representatives of the trading and fashionable worlds. His noisy, riotous singing dominates the microcosm of society that he has created, and then, at the very moment when his wife and Cecilia find their mortification so insupportable that we feel the party must break up, he leaps out of sight into the garden and shoots himself. *Cecilia* is a novel that contains glimpses of a society in many respects sickeningly unstable. No other English writer of the period achieved anything quite so disturbing.

Camilla (1796) repeats the theme of the young lady entering society, and enduring experiences of shame and exposure in

consequence. This time the emphasis is on involuntarily incurred debts. Fanny Burney displays what appears to be personal knowledge of how inexperience and lack of self-confidence
can betray one into unmanageable expense. Inability to handle
the repertory of social behaviour is registered by the mounting
burden of debt. As in the earlier novels, the more grotesque
characters are particularly effective when seen through the
medium of inflamed anxiety in the heroine's mind. The low
Mr. Dubster, the mercenary Mrs. Mittin, acquire their very
considerable power through the distress they occasion Camilla.
A mere grotesque like the scholarly Dr. Orkborne is too laboured
to carry conviction.

The main line of the narrative is perhaps rather slight to
carry the weight of feeling with which it is charged. The mutual
love of Camilla and Edgar is hampered by distractions not
solidly enough based to catch the imagination. Edgar's scruples
are too negative. The length of the novel hardly justifies itself
either, except in so far as it provides the conditions for Camilla's
accumulating debts, and gives ample scope for the anxieties
which come to a head in the final disclosure, when her father is
imprisoned for debt in Winchester gaol. When the shameful
news is brought to her, her feelings are described with all the
exactness one has come to expect of Fanny Burney at such
moments: Camilla's distraction makes the letter wholly unintelligible, yet she 'could not read it a second time; her eyes
became dim, her faculties confused, and she rather felt deprived
of the power of thinking, than filled with any new and dreadful
subjects for rumination' (X. 4). At this stage of the narrative,
the reader will be too overwrought to notice the fine economy
with which these new and dreadful subjects are made to loom
just below the threshold of the heroine's consciousness; but he
will be affected by it just the same. Such relentless exploration
of states of shame is offset, in some measure, by the cheerful
shamelessness of one of Fanny Burney's most engaging characters,
Camilla's brother Lionel. Although the author firmly indicates
the evils of which he is the cause, she enters with evident relish
into his exhilarating freedom from scruple of any kind. He has
a scheme for extorting money from his uncle Relvil by means
of threatening letters. The money came,

'and we thought it all secure, and agreed to get the same sum
annually'.

'Annually!' repeated Camilla, with uplifted hands.

'Yes, my dear. You have no conception how convenient it would have been for our extra expenses. But, unluckily, uncle grew worse, and went abroad, and then consulted with some crab of a friend, and that friend with some demagogue of a magistrate, and so all is blown!'   (III. 8)

It is impossible not to admire the easy air of aristocratic assurance implied in that 'demagogue'—a word of terror to men of property and propriety in the aftermath of the French Revolution.

Fanny Burney's last novel, *The Wanderer*, was not published until 1814, and although it is a less attractive work than its predecessors, it manifests a vigorous concern to find fresh and trenchant ways of exploring the perplexities of those who have to make their own way in an unstable world. The heroine, Juliet Granville, only discloses her identity to the reader by tortuously gradual steps. She appears at first as an unknown figure taken up into a boat carrying refugees from Robespierre's reign of terror in France. For much of the first volume of this five-volume novel she is referred to simply as 'the Incognita', but in chapter IX one of the characters sees a packet addressed to her with the initials 'L.S.'. This is interpreted as 'Ellis', and she is 'Miss Ellis' until the beginning of the third volume, when we learn (chapter XLI) that she is 'Juliet'. In the next volume (chapter LXIX) her surname is revealed, as also the reasons for her being in France in the first place, and her kinship to other characters in the story. It is not until the final volume that we learn why she has been so anxious to conceal her identity and in particular who the mysterious pursuer is from whom she has been flying. At the very moment when this pursuer, a repulsive Frenchman, intercepts her, we learn the full story. He claims to be her husband, having forced her into marriage by a cruel exercise of his authority as an agent of Robespierre. It is difficult to convey how tantalizingly the heroine is kept at a distance from the reader. The point of view from which the story is told is in a sense that of the heroine herself, but the reluctance of the author to inform us about her circumstances imposes a severe limitation on our ability to identify ourselves with her. The reader is in a position similar to that of the various sympathetic but baffled observers who endeavour to help Juliet through her difficulties. Fanny Burney forces us to share in the restless

conjectures of those who watched Juliet act the part of Lady
Townley in a production of Colley Cibber's *The Provoked Husband*, and were struck by the air of inquietude evident beneath
the gaiety of her exertions. Many of those she encounters
are, of course, far from sympathetic: the novel depicts a splendid
variety of reprehensible responses to Juliet's predicament, from
the hideous tyranny of Mrs. Ireton to the frivolous insensibility
of Miss Arbe. The characters, though sharply observed, are
sometimes over-laboriously developed, and it is hard not to
grow weary of Sir Jaspar Herrington, with his remorsely sustained whimsies about little fairy elves and goblins, imps and
devils, and other machinery of enchantment. As in *Camilla*,
the plot hardly justifies the great length of the narrative. And
yet it is far from unreadable. Indeed, it is often impressive,
particularly when Fanny Burney enters into the misgivings of
those driven to earn a living by means to which they are
unaccustomed. One shares Juliet's sick hopelessness when she
finds that her supposed resource of becoming a needlewoman
does not exist: she would need to provide a premium, and there
is a waiting-list of eight or nine young ladies already (chapter
XXIX). There is a fine account (chapter LXVII) of the
difficulties a novice experiences when running a shop. Juliet's
friend Gabrielle was unfamiliar with the art of keeping a large
stock to maintain her circle of customers. She was new to

the usage of rating at an imaginary value whatever is in vogue, in
order to repair the losses incurred from the failure of obtaining the
intrinsic worth of what is old-fashioned or faulty;—new to all this,
the wary shopkeeper's code, she was perpetually mistaken, or duped.

The analysis might have formed part of a periodical essay, but,
placed as it is, it intensifies the sense of diffuse anxiety that over-
shadows these refugees from the Terror. The novel reminds us
that the French Terror did not lack counterparts in England:
less gross, indeed, but hardly less despicable. At least, we are left
in some doubt about how much worse Juliet's French 'husband'
is than Mrs. Ireton.

The menace of some terror, not usually as well-defined as it
is in *The Wanderer*, is a conspicuous element in all the Burney
novels, though never a dominant one. It is in the so-called
Gothic novels that terror comes to be deliberately fostered for

its own sake. This genre attained its fullest development in the period after that covered by the present volume. In the last decade of the century there was a profusion of tales of mystery and terror, set amid castles, towers, caverns, or forests, and peopled by ghosts, banditti, or wicked monks. Similar ingredients are common enough at an earlier period (for example, in some of the novels of Prévost), and it was only a short step from the moral labyrinths through which Sarah Fielding and her successors wandered, to their embodiment in the endless galleries and dark corridors of the Gothic castles of fiction. Sarah Fielding and Jane Collier had seen the modern heroine as one who still had to contend with threatening giants and treacherous dames, even though they appeared in a new and subtler guise than formerly. In a 'Gothic' environment, shaped out of solid details supplied by architecture, heraldry, painting, and archaic piety, perceived through a gloom which gave full scope to the heated fancy, it was easier to set aside the constraints of naturalism. 'I gave rein to my imagination,' said Horace Walpole to Mme du Deffand; 'visions and passions choked me.' He was describing the writing of *The Castle of Otranto* (1765), generally allowed to be the first regular Gothic novel, and much of the pleasure of reading it comes from the sheer cheerfulness with which the author indulges in a wanton extravagance of invention. This is surely the spirit in which we are meant to take such famous incidents as the descent of Manfred's grandfather from his portrait. The same spirit finds expression in the magnificent fury of the usurper Manfred's passions, and in the vigorous life of those with whom he strives. Isabella fleeing from Manfred through dark cloisters has her lamp extinguished and is left in total darkness, a situation whose horror is no doubt, as the narrator alleges, beyond the reach of words.

Alone in so dismal a place, her mind imprinted with all the terrible events of the day, hopeless of escaping, expecting every moment the arrival of Manfred, and far from tranquil on knowing she was within reach of somebody, she knew not whom, who for some cause seemed concealed thereabouts, all these thoughts crowded on her distracted mind, and she was ready to sink under her apprehensions.

(Chap. I)

But the tension is essentially that of a chase: the anxious,

debilitating insecurity explored by several of Walpole's contemporaries is simply not present. 'The fleshless jaws and empty
sockets of a skeleton, wrapt in a hermit's cowl' may dismay the
vacillating Frederic, but we enjoy the act of creating a shudder
rather than experience any such dismay as Fanny Burney can
effortlessly induce when she has manœuvred her heroine into
a sufficiently compromising situation. The sensation of conscious
enjoyment is heightened by the skilful use of Shakespearian
echoes and by such elaborately stylized confrontations as that
between Manfred and the deputation of silent knights in
armour. Above all, it was in its conception a flamboyant humbug. It was not just an attempt, like Macpherson's Ossian and
the medieval forgeries of Chatterton, to reconstruct a fragment
of a past state of society. Walpole's purposes are more devious
than that. The original preface enters, with much display of
scholarly caution, into various conjectures about the possible
date of composition. Walpole suggests that it might have been
fraudulently written at the time of the Reformation by an
'artful priest' to 'confirm the populace in their ancient errors
and superstitions'. No mention is made of the fact, but there
had once been a notable Manfred who would have been
anathema to such an artful priest. He was a thirteenth-century
king of Sicily, enemy to a succession of Popes, much admired by
the esteemed and enlightened historian Giannone—and, incidentally, conqueror of Otranto. Giannone reports a declaration by one of the Popes who complained that the Holy See
had suffered for half a century from the injuries inflicted by
Frederick, Conrad, and Manfred: it was therefore necessary to
'extirpate that impious and cursed Race'. To Giannone, however, Manfred was a gallant hero, fit to be compared to 'the most
famous Captains among the Ancients'. He promoted piety,
justice, and learning, and was a deep philosopher and expert
mathematician. There would be a nice irony in Walpole's
fabricating, in the papal interest, a defamatory legend about
a prince of this name, for all the world as if he were another
Shakespeare writing a propagandist play against the last of the
Plantagenets. He certainly showed how skilfully he could perform the operation in reverse when, three or four years later, in
his *Historic Doubts* on Richard III (1768), he attempted to
rescue that monarch from the calumnies of a succession of
apologists for the Tudor dynasty.

Walpole's tale did not immediately prompt imitators. It was in 1777 that Clara Reeve[1] published *The Champion of Virtue* (later revised as *The Old English Baron*), and her acknowledged debt to *The Castle of Otranto* is qualified by criticism which shows how remote Walpole was from the prevailing temper of readers of fiction. His 'machinery' of the marvellous, says Clara Reeve, 'is so violent, that it destroys the effect it is intended to excite'. Her machinery, modest as it is, serves only to reinforce her presentation of the manners of an earlier age. Even a hero, if he lived in superstitious times, might well be supposed capable of hearing a dismal hollow groan from the concealed body of a murdered father. Such local colour is an intrinsic part of a simplified moral world where the virtuous outsider Edmund finds that he was the true heir after all. The story is briskly told, and the tension in some of the incidents is heightened with unobtrusive skill. This is true not only of such manifestly dramatic scenes as those in the haunted rooms, but in an episode such as the interview with Margery Twyford which reveals Edmund's true parentage. The interest of a probing cross-examination is intensified by being conducted under the stress of fear that Margery's husband might come home too soon and interrupt the revelation. The novel reaches a climax in a day of retribution, 'of triumph to the innocent, of shame and confusion to the wicked'. One could not adopt quite this resonant tone in writing of contemporary life and manners, although Clara Reeve did her best in her other novels. They have not been remembered.

Flight into an imagined English or European past was not the only way to give scope to fine fabling. It was equally possible to travel for the purpose to regions more remote, although the accelerating progress of maritime discovery had diminished those blank areas on the map which were so convenient to Swift's Gulliver. A late specimen of the imaginary voyage into lands unknown is that buoyant work *The Life and Adventures of Peter Wilkins* (1751), by Robert Paltock.[2] Paltock not only creates a language and institutions appropriate to his flying Indians, but conveys some impression of an unfamiliar physiology. The account of Peter's long journey by air to the

---

[1] Clara Reeve, 1729–1807, was born at Ipswich and died there after an uneventful life.

[2] Robert Paltock, 1697–1767, was an attorney at Clement's Inn.

king's court illustrates Paltock's ingenuity in suggesting the
sensation of flight. The Indians who carry Peter do not fly in
a direct, horizontal course, but first climb to an immense
height and then descend.

In the highest of our flight, you could not distinguish the globe of
the earth but by a sort of a mist, for every way looked alike to me;
then sometimes on a cue given, from an inexpressible height my
bearers would dart as it were sloping like a shooting star, for an
incredible distance, almost to the very surface of the sea, still keeping
me as upright as a Spaniard on my seat.   (Chap. XXXVIII)

As a mode of flight, this combination of climbing and gliding is
peculiarly exhilarating, partly no doubt because the movements
bear some resemblance to those possible to a human body,
though under less restraint. Peter's role in the suppression of a
rebellion indulges a gratifying sense of power, and the tender
Youwarkee is everything that a wife should be. It is a piece of
wish-fulfilment almost as audacious as *John Buncle*, and was in
consequence much admired by Leigh Hunt and his friends.

It was the so-called 'oriental tale', however, that seems to
have been most congenial to those who yearned for affections
more idyllic, passions more unrestrained, and wisdom more
absolute than any that modern Europe could afford. From the
beginning of the century, the French translation of the *Arabian
Nights* had provided a model for entertainingly extravagant
story-telling, while a developing interest in the culture and
institutions of the countries between Turkey and India helped
to legitimize exotic canons of art. Sedate and stylized though
many of the English oriental tales are, they depict a world in
which strange, surprising adventures are commonplace, where
the supernatural needs no apology, tyrants are outrageously
arbitrary and heroes outrageously intrepid. Hawkesworth's
wicked Almoran can change himself into any shape he finds
convenient (*Almoran and Hamet*, 1761), while John Langhorne's
Solyman and Almena (1762) describes an impious tyrant who is
utterly impervious to all moral or tender feeling. Fortunately
for the beautiful Almena, when he has secured her within his
loathed embraces, her cries pierce the cell where her beloved
Solyman is imprisoned:

With the united strength of rage and terror, he burst the door of
his prison; and, running through the apartments of the castle with

a dagger in his hand, which he had fortunately snatched up in the
way, he flew to the garden.   (Chap. XXI)

The dagger, of course, is plunged into the tyrant's heart.
Charles Johnstone's oriental tale, *The History of Arsaces, Prince
of Betlis* (1774), shows similar characteristics. He derives intense pleasure from the moments when the guilt of eminent
wrongdoers is revealed and summarily punished. The author
of *Chrysal* might well have wished to smite off the heads of
several persons he pillories there. In the setting of *Arsaces* he
can do so. Much of the story is a slightly-disguised comment on
the struggle between Britain and her American colonies. His
sympathies are with the Americans, and he has no difficulty,
in the simplistic world of the oriental tale, in showing the
consequence of an unjust war: the Byrsan (that is, the British)
state is annihilated. Perhaps the most admired of these moralizing oriental tales was Frances Sheridan's *History of Nourjahad*
(1767). The inventive skill she displays in her other novels
is equally apparent here. Indeed, the story is almost cruelly
ingenious. A benevolent sultan allows his friend to learn the
folly of indulging his desires by giving him apparently unlimited
scope for indulgence, including a life prolonged to eternity. It is
all a hoax: the tale of grandiose wish-fulfilment turns out to be
one of humiliating manipulation. The idea is skilfully elaborated,
particularly in the use made of the prolonged sleeps to which
Nourjahad is supposedly subject and from which he awakes like
Rip Van Winkle.

The explicit moral concern of the oriental tales so far mentioned keeps their extravagances well within the bounds of
decorum. Actual or apparent translators from the oriental
languages had more freedom. James Ridley allows himself an
occasional sadistic vehemence in his *Tales of the Genii* (1764)
that would have come less readily in an avowedly original composition. Alexander Dow's translation of the *Tales of Inatulla*
(1768) reproduces with zest both the florid expressions of his
author and his ribaldry. The ludicrous 'Story of the Fourth
Companion' recalls the spirit of Chaucer's *Miller's Tale*, and
forms a striking contrast to the coy innuendo of Sterne or Byron.

The uninhibited energies which one glimpses in Ridley and
Dow find triumphant expression in William Beckford's[1] *Vathek*

---

[1] William Beckford, 1759–1844, was the son of a prominent London merchant
and politician of the same name. He travelled widely in Europe. He acquired a

(1784). From the very first paragraph, when we learn of the dreadful power to stun and kill possessed by one of the Caliph Vathek's eyes, the story proceeds with an unremitted vigour. The hideous Indian merchant, impudent and voracious, embodies a vitality greater even than Vathek's, and the episode where the population of Samarah is irresistibly impelled to kick the Indian out of the city into a deep chasm at the foot of the mountains is told with relish almost ecstatic. There can be few people so phlegmatic as to read it without a sympathetic itching in the toe.

> Every foot was up and aimed at the Indian, and no sooner had any one given him a kick, than he felt himself constrained to reiterate the stroke.
>
> The stranger afforded them no small entertainment; for, being both short and plump, he collected himself into a ball, and rolled on all sides at the blows of his assailants, who pressed after him, wherever he turned, with an eagerness beyond conception, whilst their numbers were every moment increasing.

In every phase of the story, as Vathek hastens impiously to his damnation, the author betrays a prurient excitement. His mouth waters over the 'small plates of abominations' with which Vathek supplies a feast, to the great scandal of the faithful. If reverend mullahs return from Mecca with a sacred besom, then Vathek must receive them in the privy, and use the besom for dusting cobwebs. These incidents, like the flamboyantly entertaining one of Bababalouk's involuntary session on the harem swing, display a quality which is perceptible throughout, a keen enjoyment of the humiliation of others. The conclusion with Vathek and his companions in the palace of Eblis awaiting the moment when their everlasting torments are to begin, is unexpectedly sombre, but the note of restless excitement persists. It was a fine stroke to present the tortures of the damned as agony experienced by a heart enveloped in flames, the rest of the body surviving intact to endure the pain to its fullest extent, but with an external appearance dreary rather than horrifying.

somewhat scandalous reputation in sexual matters, but in spite of this spent a number of years as an M.P. His mansion at Fonthill, which he transformed into Fonthill Abbey, is a famous example of Gothic extravagance. The main tower collapsed only seventeen years after it had been completed.

They went wandering on, from chamber to chamber, hall to hall, and gallery to gallery; all without bounds or limit; all distinguishable by the same lowering gloom; all adorned with the same awful grandeur; all traversed by persons in search of repose and consolation, but who sought them in vain; for every one carried within him a heart tormented in flames.

Vathek was composed in French, and translated, under Beckford's supervision, by Samuel Henley. It was in his translation that the book first appeared. He also added copious notes, reinforcing the impression that the text itself creates of a mind thoroughly at home in an exotic world where every odoriferous plant breathes a richer fragrance than is known to our more humid climates, where passions are flaunted more vehemently and punished more arbitrarily. Such materials served to anaesthetize any sense of guilt that Beckford's audacity might have engendered, and *Vathek* is the most wholehearted expression, among English works published in the 1780s, of that sheer iconoclastic exhilaration that shortly afterwards found definitive utterance in Blake's *Marriage of Heaven and Hell*. Vathek might still find himself trapped in a labyrinth, but he did not suffer the dismal perplexities of sensitive souls in the novels of Sarah Fielding and Fanny Burney. In the wilderness he is compelled to dine upon roast wolf, stewed vultures, and some other delicacies to 'ulcerate the throat and parch up the tongue'; the whole washed down with a few phials of abominable brandy. The Caliph, we are told, notwithstanding 'eat with tolerable appetite'. His appetite failed him at the end, no doubt; but a despair so grandly operatic might well seem alluring in comparison with sufferings more domestic and banal.

XII

CONCLUSION: THE QUEST FOR ENERGY

A WORK like *Vathek* assumes the existence of a reading
public that sets a high value on strong sensations and
will respond to them uninhibitedly. The sensations in that
tale of damnation are admittedly extreme, but no writer was
altogether unaffected by the prevailing interest in vivid impressions, with the actual texture of experience in all its elusive
complexity. The wide prospects beloved of Augustan poets had
become less well defined. There were depths of melancholy to
be explored with an enhanced sensibility. It was a generation
elevated by original genius, enchanted by fancy, stunned by
the sublime, and it was these qualities that occupied the centre
of critical attention, giving a new shape to what writers thought
they were trying to achieve. The doctrines associated with the
traditional literary kinds slipped into the background. For a
critic like Hugh Blair, in his *Lectures on Rhetoric and Belles Lettres*
(1784), it was a matter of course that the sublime in writing
should occupy a position of special prominence at the very
outset. No writer could be temperamentally more disposed to
see excellence in terms of mastery of the techniques appropriate to particular forms, but he feels bound to admit that
sublimity, if it comes at all, comes unsought—comes when the
writer is struck by some great and awful object in nature, or
a magnanimous and exalted affection of the human mind:
'thence, if you can catch the impression strongly, and exhibit
it warm and glowing, you may draw the sublime.' His examples
of the sublime come from a variety of literary kinds: the poetry
of the Old Testament, the epic verse of Homer and Milton, the
oratory of Demosthenes, and the philosophical dialogue of
Plato. It is important to understand the nature and resources of
each kind, but even more important, it would seem, to catch impressions strongly, and exhibit them warm and glowing. Hence
Blair's admiration for Macpherson's Ossian. As he explained in
his influential *Critical Dissertation on the Poems of Ossian* (1763),

On all occasions he is frugal of his words; and never gives you more of an image, or a description, than is just sufficient to place it before you in one clear point of view. It is a blaze of lightning, which flashes and vanishes.

It would have been evident to any reader of Burke's *Philosophical Inquiry into the Origin of our Ideas of the Sublime and Beautiful* (1757) that lightning was a peculiarly appropriate emblem of the sublime: it is associated with terror, with loud noise, with an uncertain and yet brilliant light that serves both to reveal an extensive landscape and to intensify darkness. It was also associated with the very recent discovery, by Benjamin Franklin, that electricity could be drawn from thunderclouds. Franklin's researches helped to establish the idea of electricity as a vast natural force, still mysterious, but gradually coming to be understood. As Beccaria put it, his daring genius disarmed the thunder of its terrors and taught the fire of heaven to obey him. For Joseph Priestley,[1] writing his *History and Present State of Electricity* (1767), such progress and improvement of knowledge, extending into an indefinite future, revealed 'a prospect really boundless and sublime'. A variety of such prospects opens up before the reader of Priestley's multifarious works, in the natural sciences, in the study of man, and in theology. Although literature plays a humble role in Priestley's scheme of things, one sees how readily the nature of taste, the operations of genius, and the communication of feeling might be assimilated to the collective inquiry undertaken by the enlightened philosophers of the time into the potential capacities of the human race. The electric shocks generated by Ossian were as much part of the phenomena to be investigated and analysed as was the more routine association of ideas, or the complex pattern of human sympathies.

Priestley himself thought of 'belles-lettres' as comparatively no more than the amusements of childhood, requiring none of that vigorous exertion of the mind essential to the natural and moral sciences. But even he was prepared to allow that history

[1] Joseph Priestley, 1733–1804, was educated for the presbyterian ministry at Daventry Academy, but became a Unitarian. He was minister at Nantwich, and later a tutor at Warrington Academy, where he conducted many of his scientific inquiries. Then he moved to Birmingham, 1780. He was an associate of the Earl of Shelburne. In 1791 his house was attacked by a loyalist mob, and in 1794 he emigrated to Pennsylvania.

could be approached with a scientific purpose. Fictions, he said in his *Lectures on History and General Policy* (1788), amuse the imagination and give play to the passions; and so does history. But 'true history, being an exhibition of the conduct of Divine Providence, in which every thing has, perhaps, infinite relations and uses, is an inexhaustible mine of the most valuable knowledge'. If fiction is a kind of globe or orrery, history is an air pump or electrical machine by which the actual operations of nature are exhibited. What Priestley does not take into account here is the status of fiction masquerading as history, an issue which is also raised by a distinction he attempts to establish in the twelfth of his *Lectures on Oratory and Criticism* (1777). There he suggests that fictions are always apt to fall short in the particulars that give a sense of reality, '*whereas a redundancy of particulars . . . will croud into a relation of real facts*'. Priestley's argument helps one to appreciate just why so many eighteenth-century novelists were anxious to blur the distinction between fact and fiction by various kinds of redundant particularity. To render experience with precision it was necessary to create a sense of the inexhaustible detail of nature. It may, as Imlac is made to argue in the tenth chapter of *Rasselas*, be bad tactics to number the streaks of the tulip; but then the reader also needs a reminder that there are streaks to be numbered. Whatever procedure the writer adopts, his art must grow out of a wealth of impressions, impressions that may be extremely elusive. In some unpublished additions to his *Essay on the Dramatic Character of Sir John Falstaff* (1777), Maurice Morgann invoked *latent impressions*, which strike the sensibility but escape the understanding, to account for his response to Shakespeare's plays. We shall never appreciate Falstaff, he suggests, if we attend only to what our reasoning faculty tells us. Reason is a 'dignified Miss', a 'drawn up Madam', who 'idly weaves general propositions': it is our sensations and appetites and passions which do all the real work, and these a great artist will exploit.

Imlac's contention is subverted in a different way by Robert Lowth,[1] in his *Lectures on the Sacred Poetry of the Hebrews*, first delivered in Oxford in the 1740s. Lowth insists on the

---

[1] Robert Lowth, 1710–87, was educated at Winchester and New College, Oxford. He was Professor of Poetry at Oxford, 1741–50. He became bishop successively of Oxford and of London.

importance of understanding the original social context of the
Old Testament, much as Johnson had insisted on the importance
of neglected sixteenth-century materials in interpreting Shakespeare. An acquaintance with obsolete customs and forgotten
circumstances can restore perspicuity to what might otherwise
have seemed hopelessly obscure. The poetic force of a passage
may be apparent only to someone with a knowledge of the
climate and countryside of Palestine. Imagery, says Lowth,
derives from natural objects,

and since these images are formed in the mind of each writer, and
expressed conformably to what occurs to his senses, it cannot otherwise happen, but that, through diversity of situation, some will be
more familiar, some almost peculiar to certain nations; and even
those which seem most general, will always have some latent connexion with their immediate origin, and with their native soil.

(Lecture VI)

Scholars like Lowth and Thomas Harmer (author of *Observations on Divers Passages of Scripture*, 1764) do much to explore this
latent connection, and in so doing restore to scriptural texts
something of their original energy. But even where it is not
possible to do this, even where it is only possible to remark that
vehement emotions are being uttered, distracting the mind
and dividing its attention, it is still apparent that the expression
is sublime and deeply affecting, its 'scattered rays' breaking
with difficulty through the thick clouds that surround it. The
metre of ancient Hebrew poetry is irrecoverably lost, but there
are marks and vestiges of verse, and when it is translated literally into the prose of another language it will retain 'much of its
native dignity, and a faint appearance of versification'. In his
twenty-fifth lecture Lowth deplores our ignorance of the sacred
music of the Hebrews:

we at present possess only some ruins as it were of that magnificent
fabric, deprived of every ornament, except that splendour and
elegance, which, notwithstanding the obscurity that antiquity has
cast over them, still shine forth in the sentiments and language.

This is a theme to which Lowth often returns. But although
he may regret the inevitable consequences of linguistic change
—'the vital grace is wanting, the native sweetness is gone, the
colour of primeval beauty is faded and decayed'—the effect
of his analysis is curiously buoyant. The original texture of
Hebrew poetry may be so involved in obscurity that it is hope-

less to attempt useful conjectures about it, but this ungrudging admission throws into sharper relief the admirable qualities that are still apparent. The fabric, magnificent in its ruined state, suggests possibilities of beauty exceeding anything that actually exists. Lowth takes a keen pleasure in the sheer activity of mind demanded by such inferences, stimulating the reader to conjure up a state of being no longer sensibly present. When he speaks of the 'latent connexion' between general images and their native soil, one has a hint of the rich variety of perceptions exerting an invisible pressure on the apparently generalized expression. The particulars may remain stubbornly imperceptible, but they are certainly present in some way. It may seem a fanciful analogy, but it is at least remarkable that in the 1760s the Edinburgh chemist Joseph Black was explaining in his lectures the notion of latent heat, heat that does not affect the thermometer, but becomes energy, converting ice into water or water into vapour. The imaginative leap needed to suppose that heat could be present, and not make its presence felt in the obvious way, is audacious. Lowth's notion of a latent particularity in general images is less so, but one can see how speculations of this sort could prepare the mind for the apparent paradox involved in Black's theory. The connection between the two lines of thought is the more evident when one recalls that Black believed in the materiality of heat. Particles float around freely in the eighteenth-century imagination: any given bit of heat might be latent, and so might any particular image. *Merely* general images, one may infer, would be deficient in energy.

Lowth's view of the Bible as a kind of splendid ruin serves as a reminder that the fascination exercised in this period by the ruinous and fragmentary was not merely a symptom of nostalgia. Ruins are the vestiges of former energies, which an alert imagination can enter into and exploit. They are like those 'admirable remains' of Greek and Roman statuary which, as William Duff observed in his *Essay on Original Genius* (1767), acted with such vigour on the Italian painters of the time of Leo the Tenth, 'heightening their idea of excellence . . . and kindling their ambition'. Nor is this effect found only in the arts. In the third of Richard Hurd's *Dialogues Moral and Political* (1759), where he supposes a conversation between Addison and Arbuthnot in the ruins of Kenilworth Castle, the antique towers of that place falling into rubbish and the 'shattered remnants' of the hall and tiltyard recall the pride, despotism, valour, hospitality, generosity, and genius of the age of Elizabeth. As has been suggested in Chapter IX (p. 353), the dialogue holds a rather perplexing balance between two points of view. But although Arbuthnot's Elizabethan enthusiasm must be taken with some reserve, his views are unquestionably fortified by the setting. A beautiful landscape incorporates the 'shapeless ruins' of a splendid past. The day is clear, the light not glaring. The effect is tranquil, congenial, reassuring: a mood to which even the evidence of destruction is subdued. The lake on which the shows and pageants of Leicester's entertainments were displayed has become a meadow, in which the naval glory of Elizabeth's England, once proclaimed there by nereids, tritons, and Neptune himself, is still present to be evoked by the fine spell of Arbuthnot's words. Although the vision is private, even whimsical, one forms the impression that this is how the virtues of a golden age may be transmitted in an age of baser metal, under the just, moderate, richly uninteresting rule of the Hanoverian monarchs.

Hurd develops the theme in his *Letters on Chivalry and Romance* (1762). He explores the golden age of fine fabling that manifests itself in 'Gothic' romance and its aftermath in the poetry of the sixteenth and seventeenth centuries. Such romantic poetry is, he claims, a monument to a political constitution and a system of manners which 'never did subsist but once, and are never likely to subsist again'. If a Homer had lived at the time, he would have been furnished with finer materials than any he could have derived from the barbarity of the Greeks. 'As it is, we may take a guess of what the subject was capable of affording to real genius from the rude sketches we have of it, in the old Romances.' These 'rude sketches' display the gentler and more humane affections as well as courage and enterprise. There is a dignity, a magnificence, a variety, which Homeric manners lack. There is also a greater energy in the ideas of the supernatural, lavishly nourishing the sources of the terrible sublime in Shakespeare and Milton. 'We are upon enchanted ground,' Hurd observes at the end of Letter VI, 'and you are to think yourself well used that I detain you no longer in this fearful circle. The glympse, you have had of it, will help your imagination to conceive the rest.'

At times one might suppose that Hurd, like Addison (*Spectator* 419), was commending 'the faery way of writing' to modern poets. He insists that those who address the imagination rather than the affections can claim a privilege of imposing on the reader's credulity. The divine dream, the delirious fancy, are among the noblest of such a writer's prerogatives. But this is not a line of argument that he sustains. He advises against any attempt to revive faery tales in a modern epic. 'Some ages', he remarks, 'are not so fit to write epic poems in, as others.' Gothic fictions no longer have any footing in popular belief, and it is common prudence for writers to confine themselves to what they 'at least observe in others a facility of believing'. He obviously regrets that fine fabling should no longer be possible, that Fancy, having 'wantoned it so long in the world of fiction', should now be constrained to form an alliance with strict truth in order to 'gain admittance into reasonable company' (Letter XII). The submission is reluctant. It is also complete. There is no convincing model for the *marvellous* in modern poetry, and one can hardly avoid the conclusion that the highest poetic achievements are no longer possible. Here as elsewhere, Hurd is reinforcing an undertone of despondency insistently audible in the period, a depressing sense that—as Blake was to put it in his early poem 'To the Muses'—

> The languid strings do scarcely move!
> The sound is forc'd, the notes are few.

The temptation was certainly great to imagine for oneself more favourable circumstances, to inhabit, as Chatterton did, a little world of one's own creating in which heroic impulse and magnificent display were customary and familiar. Hurd resisted the temptation. His prescription may be studied in the elaborate and perceptive 'Discourse on Poetical Imitation' (1751), where he urged writers not to be distracted from a competent performance by 'anxious dread of imitation'; or again in 'The Idea of Universal Poetry' (1766), where he emphasizes the importance of appropriate technique. For example, verse heightens one's pleasure in language, and a competent prose-writer will keep this in mind, even though pleasure is not his first object, tuning his sentences to some agreement with song. He 'transfers into his coolest narrative, or gravest instruction, something of that music with which his ear vibrates from poetic impressions'.

Novels strike him as radically misconceived: 'hasty, imperfect, and abortive poems'. It is not here that he recognizes the revived wantonings of fancy, though the phrase seems applicable enough to *Tristram Shandy*.

Thus, although Hurd made an important contribution to the development of new critical attitudes, his influence was on the whole conservative. The 'Discourse on Poetical Imitation', indeed, seems to have provoked the outstanding manifesto on behalf of the wantonings of genius, Edward Young's *Conjectures on Original Composition* (1759). For Young, imitation is a thwarting of the design of Nature. At birth, everyone is an original: 'no two faces, no two minds, are just alike . . . Born originals, how comes it to pass that we die copies?' Young's impassioned question anticipates the starting-point of Rousseau's *Du contrat social* (1762): man is born free, and everywhere he is in chains. To those who were weary of constraint, weary of wretched unanimity with the throng, Young's message is emphatic: *Know thyself; Reverence thyself.*

> Dive deep into thy bosom; learn the depth, extent, bias, and full fort of thy mind; contract full intimacy with the stranger within thee; excite and cherish every spark of intellectual light and heat, however smothered under former negligence, or scattered through the dull dark mass of common thoughts; and collecting them into a body, let thy genius rise (if a genius thou hast) as the sun from chaos.

The enthusiasm which Young communicates must make every reader feel that he or she too is an original genius. After Hurd's 'Discourse' the effect is almost intoxicating. Genius, we read, is not as uncommon as one might suppose, and it is chiefly necessary to allow it to develop uninhibitedly. It is of a vegetable nature—it rises spontaneously—it grows, it is not made. It has no connection with what scholars call education: if Shakespeare had read more, he might have thought less. Young does not develop these and similar ideas in the *Conjectures* in any great detail, but other writers were prepared to continue his work and investigate the operations of genius more systematically. Alexander Gerard's *Essay on Genius* (1774) is the most diligently comprehensive of these studies, but the temper of the *Conjectures* is more convincingly sustained in William Duff's[1] *Essay on Original Genius* (1767). One genuinely feels the subject growing under his hand, 'new prospects

---

[1] William Duff, 1732–1815, was minister in various parishes in Aberdeenshire.

opening themselves to the imagination, in proportion to the progress he had made'. He celebrates the native energy of genius, delighting to expand its faculties in any appropriate sphere of exertion, whether philosophy, poetry, painting, oratory, music, or architecture. In terms which anticipate Coleridge's distinction between imagination and fancy, he differentiates between the copious, plastic powers of genius, with its vivid conceptions and extensive combinations of ideas, and the mere quickness or readiness of wit and fancy. He also examines some of the burdens endured by genius. First, he insists, as Young had insisted, on the uneasy relationship between the genius and his more pedestrian fellows. His enthusiastic flights expose him to ridicule; his bold irregularities will be checked by rules of criticism, if he is so unwise as to pay attention to them. It is best for poetical genius to remove itself from the din and tumult of an advanced society. 'It spreads forth all its luxuriance in the peaceful vale of rural tranquility.' The flower is well advised to blush unseen, and waste its fragrance on the desert air. Duff may have picked up this idea from sources more robust than Gray's 'Elegy'. Simon Pelloutier's celebrated *Histoire des Celtes* (1750) had emphasized the refusal of the Celts to constrain their children, allowing them to follow their own inclinations. They were like forest trees that were not cut back, and thus grew tall and strong. This was a notion that was to appeal to Keats, and his 'grand democracy of Forest Trees' suggests a solution to the problem of alienated genius that is perhaps hinted at by Duff himself. But there is another problem more intractable, which remains even when we disregard the cavilling of unsympathetic readers. Almost all the productions of genius are necessarily flawed and incomplete. In Duff's view, 'words are too weak to convey the ardor of his sentiments'. He is apt to sink 'under the immensity of his own conceptions'. His successes, when they come, will be fitful and irregular. But a reader of taste will know how to appreciate the exuberance apparent in spite of these inequalities.

The appropriate method had been admirably sketched nearly a century before the publication of Duff's book, in the preface to the original edition of Pascal's *Pensées* (1670). On the one hand the fragmentary thoughts were negligently expressed, being written by Pascal for himself alone. But—on the other hand—any attempt to expand and regularize their expression 'would only have rendered them faint and languishing'. Every reader takes more pleasure in 'opening' the thought for himself than in having it done for him. At the time, the preface must have seemed a piece of special pleading for a manifestly faulty work. But in the course of the eighteenth century, readers became more prepared to accept an argument along these lines, to allow, as Blair said of Ossian, that a work might need to be often re-read before beauties would 'open' even to someone with the necessary sensibility. Such elusive beauties could be finer than any that were more immediately accessible. As Burke observed, in his *Philosophical Inquiry*, unfinished sketches in drawing often pleased him more than the best finishing 'because the imagination is entertained with the promise of something more, and does not acquiesce in the present object of sense' (II. xi). In his *Salon* for 1767, Diderot took for granted that a fine sketch could please more effectively than a finished painting: it had more life, more warmth, more evidence of genius. The viewer felt his imagination called into play. It was like the word or phrase that could awaken a great thought. In the vehemence of passion, disconnected, incomplete, inarticulate expression could still make itself perfectly understood. It was a sketch in words: passion makes nothing but sketches. Diderot's view is closely related to Sterne's virtuoso exploitation of the immense power exerted by things that are not said. There was something of a fashion for expressive reticence, oblique hints, aposiopesis, a fashion that manifested itself in many forms. One may detect it in Gilbert White's *Natural History of Selborne* (letter to Barrington, 9 September 1778), where he speaks of the language of birds—'very ancient, and, like other ancient modes of speech, very elliptical; little is said, but much is meant and understood.' The Earl of Cork reveals a similar preoccupation. In an essay on the silence of Dido when Aeneas meets her in the underworld, he regards it as the silence 'of a distracted and uneasy mind, whose horrible sensations dread to give themselves utterance' (*The Old Maid*, 3 January 1756). Sheridan gave a definitive utterance to the idea in *The Critic* when he displayed Lord Burleigh shaking his head without saying a word. Mr. Puff explains the full implications of the pregnant gesture, and Sneer objects: 'The devil! did he mean all that by shaking his head?'—'Every word of it,' says Puff, 'if he shook his head as I taught him.'

If silence could be eloquent, words carried with them resources of meaning that were virtually inexhaustible. The extent
to which significance could be extracted from a single word (at
least when the word was placed in context by Shakespeare)
was sufficiently proved by the French translator of Martin
Sherlock's *Advice to a Young Poet* (1779). Sherlock had drawn
attention to the potency of Coriolanus' final words of defiance—

> like an eagle in a dovecote, I
> Flutter'd your Volscians in Corioli.

The French language, said the translator, is unable to convey in
a single word

all the ideas that are included in that emphatical expression Flut-
ter'd. This word not only marks the disorder and alarm; it also
paints the tumult of a flock of birds, whom a sudden affright occasions to take wing all at once, the trembling, the sound, and, as it
were, the vibration of their wings, when they begin to take flight.
Then see how striking is this contrast! An eagle among doves, an
eagle, the strongest and most forcible bird, and doves, effeminate
birds, if I may so express myself, who are always considered as a
symbol of gentleness, and consequently of fear.

Thus the descent of an eagle into a dovecote

is the highest degree of terror. Heaped one upon another, shut up as
in a prison, which keeps them in the presence of a tyrant, pressing,
crowding each other on every side, endeavouring in vain to escape
through passages that are too narrow, their perplexity, their misery,
is at the height.

No audience in a theatre could ever consciously tease out all
these overtones, whatever a closet-reader might do, but the
actor might well convey the whole at an unconscious level.
Such, at least, seems to be the view implicit in some of Garrick's
remarks on his art. He told one correspondent that actors
should not know all that they are going to do in advance,
because then

the Heart has none of those instantaneous feelings, that Life blood,
that keen Sensibility, that bursts at once from Genius, and like
Electrical fire shoots through the Veins, Marrow, Bones and all, of
every Spectator . . . The greatest strokes of Genius, have been unknown to the Actor himself, 'till Circumstances, and the warmth of
the Scene has sprung the Mine as it were, as much to his own Surprize, as that of the Audience.   (3 January 1769)

There is ample testimony to the efficacy of Garrick's 'electrical fire', and the aesthetic theories we have been considering do perhaps find their most convincing application in the context of theatre and oratory rather than in that of the written word. Readers of Pascal and Ossian might or might not have the sense or the sensibility to 'open' these texts for themselves. Listening to Wesley or Whitefield was apt to be a more uncontrollably agitating experience. When Burke spoke, on the fifth day of the trial of Warren Hastings, about the atrocities committed in Dinajpur, only Mrs. Sheridan fainted away altogether, but many must have been similarly affected. Even though the orator's performance is locked up in the past, this does not make it totally irrecoverable. An impression of the performance is still communicated by the text, and it is impressions of this kind that Kames considers in his discussion of what, in the *Elements of Criticism* (1762), he calls an 'ideal presence', when 'lively and distinct images' throw the reader

into a kind of reverie; in which state, losing the consciousness of self, and of reading . . . he conceives every incident as passing in his presence, precisely as if he were an eye-witness.   (II, i)

Kames remarks, justly enough, that this function of the mind had not previously attracted the attention of critics. His own interest in the matter reflects a new disposition in both writers and the reading public to appreciate the role of the audience in the process of interaction with the performer. An adequate estimate of much that was written at this time must take into account such conscious dependence on the willingly co-operative imagination of the reader.

A preoccupation such as we have described with the latent, the fragmentary, the irregular, the apparently delirious, obviously exposes its advocates to charges of extravagance and self-deception. As Johnson said of Macpherson's Ossian, 'a man might write such stuff for ever, if he would abandon his mind to it'. One is bound to ask how debilitating was the effect of the intensely-felt need to count for something, to be the hero of one's own romance, if necessary in a world of one's own devising. It is possible, of course, to expound the system of sensibility in a rational and unimpassioned way. John Ogilvie's[1]

---

[1] John Ogilvie, 1733–1813, was educated at Aberdeen University and became minister of Midmar, in Aberdeenshire.

Observations on Composition (1774) is a laboriously-argued work, worth reading to see just how prosaic a description can be attempted of energies discernible only by readers endowed with delicate internal perceptions. Ogilvie, grave presbyterian that he is, convinces one that he can indeed enter into a 'train of *concealed ideas*' establishing 'a connection *not less real*, because it may be at first imperceptible'. But Ogilvie's ponderous deliberation is hardly representative. Percival Stockdale[1] expresses himself in a tone of lofty enthusiasm that is far more prevalent. Stockdale, a vehement champion of the genius of Chatterton, was the author of an *Inquiry into the Nature, and Genuine Laws of Poetry* (1778). This was an attack on the first volume of Joseph Warton's *Essay on the Writings and Genius of Pope* (1756), usually considered a manifesto on behalf of 'creative and glowing IMAGINATION'. But Warton does not glow consistently enough for Stockdale. There is in him, he claims, something of the frigidity and barrenness of a mathematician, alien to the poetic temper.

The mind of the poet is ardent, and luxuriant; it pervades, with a rapid flight, the fertile and exhaustless regions of fancy; the images which it forms with emotion, with enthusiasm, inspire those who can adopt them with a flame congenial with its own.

There is a hectic undertone in such utterances which betrays their insecurity. Stockdale is painfully aware that genius, like sensibility, is often unappreciated. The feeling was widespread. His generation was haunted by the cruel situation of imagined sufferers like Sidney Bidulph or real ones like Chatterton. The life of the painter James Barry prompted his first biographer to formulate the maxim, 'The more eminent their genius, the less happy their condition.' It was in this spirit that Gilbert Stuart undertook his fervently partisan *History of Scotland* (1782), vindicating Mary Queen of Scots against all her enemies, particularly Queen Elizabeth. 'No insolence of tyranny,' we learn,

no refinement of anger, and no pang of woe could conquer or destroy her greatness and her fortitude. Her mind, which grew in its powers

---

[1] Percival Stockdale, 1736–1811, was educated at grammar schools in Alnwick and Berwick. He spent nearly two years in the army, and was with Byng's unsuccessful expedition to Minorca, 1756. He was ordained deacon, and combined various clerical employments with an active career as a writer.

under struggles and calamity, seemed even to take a strain of vigour from the atrocious passions of her rival.

Inward strength and outward weakness are intimately related in this portrayal. The unfriendly environment, though defied, is not overborne. Something of this feverish quality informs the writings of that early master of political journalism, the well-disguised 'Junius'. His letters entice the mind into a world where it can take pleasure in its own potency, the potency of an implacable and impenetrably anonymous avenger. The anonymity is peculiarly important, contributing as it does to the quasi-godlike role the author assumes. But although it is still possible to enjoy the calculated glitter of his style, Junius's innuendo and sarcasm often seem merely shrill. A set piece like the 'Address to the King' (19 December 1769) has a brittle eloquence, particularly evident in the references to the Wilkes case.

The rays of Royal indignation, collected upon him, served only to illuminate, and could not consume . . . Hardly serious at first, he is now an enthusiast. The coldest bodies warm with opposition, the hardest sparkle in collision.

The note of exultation here is as hectic as the enthusiasm of Percival Stockdale.

A far greater political author than Junius, Edmund Burke, resembles him at least in the somewhat melodramatic temper of his imagination. Like Stockdale's poet, his mind pervades fertile and inexhaustible regions of fancy. His view of Warren Hastings's India has been called a hallucination; Paine speaks of his 'theatrical exaggerations' about the initial stages of the revolution in France. Theatrical or hallucinatory his eloquence may be, but here at least the private hallucinations cast their spell so effectively that they become public property. One seems to hear his voice conjuring up a world of vigorous energies shaping richly realized materials, whether it be the exotic legal systems of Asia which explode Warren Hastings's notions of arbitrary power, or those eleven hundred reservoirs of the Carnatic (referred to in Chapter IX, p. 382) which Burke invoked during his speech on the Nabob of Arcot's debts. The reservoirs are reconstituted in our minds with the intricate particularity suggested by the map of the region that Burke laid before the House of Commons while he was speaking. Their authenticity is reinforced by our sense of the 'mounds of earth and stones, with sluices of solid masonry', of which they are constructed; their magnificence enhanced by 'the reachings and graspings' of the vivacious minds capable of conceiving such a project. In Burke, the prospects opening up before us create an irresistible impression of reality, and yet we are always conscious of the informing personality of the orator, ardent and luxuriant, crushing opposition.

The ardent and luxuriant mind could manifest itself in a more sober idiom. William Paley[1] has never figured conspicuously in discussions of imaginative literature, although Sir Leslie Stephen, for one, praised the attractive clarity of his writing. It is not just the clarity which is attractive. An irrepressible sense of enjoyment suffuses page after page of his work, indicating what friends had in mind when testifying to the 'peculiar naïveté' of his manner. It is best illustrated in his last book, *Natural Theology* (1802), which, although its publication falls outside the limits of the present volume, deserves a place here as a spirited response to the scepticism of Hume's *Dialogues concerning Natural Religion*. Paley's attempt to find evidences of divine design throughout the natural kingdom can carry little conviction in a post-Darwinian world, but the wealth of illustration that he brings in support of his argument, presented as it is with a disarming benignity, can still give great pleasure to the sympathetic reader. Paley shows how the very refractoriness of our environment contributes to our happiness, and rejoices in the presence on our planet of the gnats that animate the forests of North America, and the mice that crowd the otherwise desolate plains of Siberia. His joy admittedly often depends on the distance of the prospect. There is a characteristic passage in the book where he relates the experience of seeing what looks like a dark cloud or thick mist rising half a yard or so along the edge of the sea-shore. The scene he sets is a pleasant one, a calm evening, an ebbing tide, the cloud

stretching along the coast as far as the eye could reach, and always retiring with the water. When this cloud came to be examined, it

---

[1] William Paley, 1743–1805, was educated at Christ's College, Cambridge, and spent some years as a college lecturer there. He moved to the north of England, and eventually became Archdeacon of Carlisle, 1782. Thereafter he wrote the theological works on which his reputation rests.

proved to be nothing else than so much space, filled with young *shrimps*, in the act of bounding into the air from the shallow margin of the water, or from the wet sand. If any motion of a mute animal could express delight, it was this: if they had meant to make signs of their happiness, they could not have done it more intelligibly. Suppose then, what I have no doubt of, each individual of this number to be in a state of positive enjoyment; what a sum, collectively, of gratification and pleasure have we here before our view.

(Chap. XXVI)

The description begins with a cloud, and ends with a curiously abstract 'sum'. The shrimps come into focus only in order to make more vivid a generalized spirit of delight. Paley rejoices in the sense of well-being that flows through him and through the whole creation. In any such prospect there will be a bright spot, and his eye rests upon that. He is aware of the miseries of the world, but for him they are so closely interwoven with the benevolent designs of the deity that they hardly provide even an element of picturesque contrast.

The prospects sketched by Goldsmith or by Gibbon have more light and shade, but resemble Paley's in assuming a secure observer. They share the detachment displayed by Lord Monboddo, who, being very deaf, did not stir from his seat in the court of King's Bench when the roof was supposed to be falling in. He took for granted that the panic rush of judges, lawyers, and others was an annual ceremony, an interesting remnant of antiquity for a visitor to witness. This sense of the world as a fine spectacle is distinctive of much that was written at the time, but increasingly people felt that the roof really might fall in. The appetite for overpowering sensation was bound to prove destructive of the observer's tranquillity. Later writers, notably the great romantic poets, can be seen absorbing, at some cost to their emotional stability, astonishingly disruptive sensations into their prospects of nature and society. But in the 1780s at least, the energies at work in the creation still tend to be viewed within a well-structured landscape. John Playfair relates how the geologist James Hutton visited Siccar Point on the Berwickshire coast in the summer of 1788, and pointed out to his companions how the rock formations there testified to vast and remote upheavals in the earth's surface.

We felt ourselves necessarily carried back to the time when the schistus on which we stood was yet at the bottom of the sea, and when the sandstone before us was only beginning to be deposited, in the shape of sand or mud, from the waters of a superincumbent ocean. An epocha still more remote presented itself, when even the most ancient of these rocks, instead of standing upright in vertical beds, lay in horizontal planes at the bottom of the sea, and was not yet disturbed by that immeasurable force which has burst asunder the solid pavement of the globe. Revolutions still more remote appeared in the distance of this extraordinary perspective. The mind seemed to grow giddy by looking so far into the abyss of time.

Dizzy the prospect may be, but still the setting is reassuring, the voice of the philosopher imperturbable.

In spite of the calm tone, one suspects that this experience would have been beyond Wordsworth's powers of digestion. One catches a glimpse of the intellectual world of Charles Darwin's time. In the late eighteenth century, the most aesthetically satisfying expressions of creation's bewildering complexity are conceived on a more limited scale. Perhaps the finest example is a poem by Thomas Warton, his 'Verses on Sir Joshua Reynolds's Painted Window at New College, Oxford' (1782). The poem affects to be a renunciation of the Gothic taste that Warton himself did so much to foster, a willing acceptance of that disenchantment that Hurd submits to so grudgingly in the *Letters on Chivalry*. But in fact the Gothic mode is so solidly realized that it is unaffected even by the disenchanted view of brawny prophets, frowning virgins, and other unsophisticated figures with which Warton enforces his recantation of former beliefs. The disenchantment adds a new perspective to a scene already vividly presented. We perceive Gothic art the better in contrast with that of Reynolds. Most satisfyingly of all, since the modern work is in glass, the very process of its creation suggests the fusion of varied materials into an enduring and brilliant unity.

> The mighty Master spreads his mimic toil
> More wide, nor only blends the breathing oil;
> But calls the lineaments of life compleat
> From genial alchymy's creative heat;
> Obedient forms to the bright fusion gives,
> While in the warm enamel Nature lives.

Warton's poem achieves an unusual equilibrium. The inclusiveness is commonly untidier, notably so in that influential poem by James Beattie, *The Minstrel* (1771–4). Edwin the minstrel, the early progress of whose genius the poem describes, is a youth of sensibility, a 'lone enthusiast', an original, strange, wayward:

> Some deem'd him wondrous wise, and some believ'd him mad.

His powers are fostered by ballads and by the beauties of nature. He learns from the sage who instructs him to transcend the world of Fancy and enter that of Reason and Philosophy. As in Warton's poem, there is less a sense of repudiation than of greater inclusiveness. It was the exclusiveness, the narrow focus, of the modern metaphysicians that formed a leading theme of Beattie's *Essay on Truth* (1770). Such philosophers were like 'a short-sighted landscape-painter':

> they might possibly delineate some of the largest and roughest figures with tolerable exactness: but of the minuter objects, some would wholly escape their notice, and others appear blotted and distorted, on which nature had bestowed the utmost delicacy of colour, and harmony of proportion.

Rising above such limitations, the minstrel is fit to become the legislator (acknowledged or otherwise) of mankind:

> When tyrants scourge, or demagogues embroil
> A land, or when the rabble's headlong rage
> Order transforms to anarchy and spoil,
> Deep-vers'd in man the philosophic sage
> Prepares with lenient hand their frenzy to assuage.

Taking a hint from Percy's 'Essay on Ancient Minstrels', with its account of the exalted status formerly enjoyed by bards, Edwin embodies the hope that men of letters could recover their lost inheritance.

There was no resisting this alluring mixture: lone enthusiasm with aspirations after power—nostalgia for a pastoral simplicity developing into a broad appreciation of what polished society had achieved. The poem proved popular, and for many early nineteenth-century readers it was the definitive account of what a poet ought to be. If William Wordsworth was a wayward youth, it was natural for his sister to excuse him by invoking the example of Beattie's Edwin. *The Minstrel* was, after all, *The Prelude* in embryo. It furnished hints, too, for Byron's *Childe Harold* and delighted Keats—until he came to 'see through' poets like Beattie and Mrs. Tighe. It also helped to form the self-image entertained by some rather more improbable contemporaries. James Stanier Clarke, the Prince Regent's librarian, evidently saw himself mirrored in Edwin, and half-confessed as much to Jane Austen, wishing her

to delineate in some future work the habits of life, and character, and enthusiasm of a clergyman, who should pass his time between the metropolis and the country, who should be something like Beattie's Minstrel—

> Silent when glad, affectionate tho' shy,
>   And in his looks was most demurely sad;
> And now he laughed aloud, yet none knew why.

(16 November 1815)

Miss Austen was not greatly impressed; and indeed, when lone enthusiasm and wide-ranging prospects had become so comfortably accommodated in Carlton House, it was more than time to subject them to her astringent scrutiny. The quest for energy had become something of a routine.

CHRONOLOGICAL TABLE
1740–1789

Date	Public Events	Literary History	Verse
1740	Anson embarks on circumnavigation of the world. War of Austrian Succession begins; Frederick II invades Silesia.	Boswell b. Woodforde the diarist b. Tickell d.	Dyer, *Ruins of Rome*.
1741	Highway Act. Unsuccessful British naval expedition to the Caribbean (Cartagena).	Sylas Neville b. Hester L. Salusbury (later Thrale, Piozzi) b. Arthur Young b.	
1742	Walpole resigns; Carteret ministry.	G. Stuart b. R. Bentley d. W. Somerville d.	Collins, *Persian Eclogues*. Pope, *New Dunciad* (i.e. *Dunciad* IV). Shenstone, *Schoolmistress* (revised). E. Young, *The Complaint, or Night-Thoughts* (concluded 1746).
1743	George II present at French defeat at Dettingen.	Paley b. H. Carey d. Savage d.	R. Blair, *The Grave*. Collins, *Verses to Sir Thomas Hanmer*. P. Francis, trans. *Odes* etc. of Horace. Pope, *Dunciad* (final version).
1744	Pelham ministry. French declare war on Britain: invasion alarm. Clive arrives in Madras.	Pope d. L. Theobald d.	Akenside, *The Pleasures of Imagination*. Armstrong, *Art of Preserving Health*. J. Warton, *The Enthusiast*.
1745	Charles Edward (the Young Pretender) wins battle of Prestonpans.	Hayley b. Holcroft b. Mackenzie b. J. Nichols b. Pye b. Swift d.	Akenside, *Odes on Several Subjects*. J. Brown, *Essay on Satire*.
1746	Charles Edward defeated at Culloden; subjugation of Scottish highlands.	(Sir) William Jones b. R. Blair d. F. Hutcheson d. T. Southerne d.	Blacklock, *Poems*. Collins, *Odes*. P. Francis, trs. *Satires* etc. of Horace. J. Warton, *Odes on Various Subjects*.

Prose	*Drama (date of acting)*
Cibber, *Apology for his Life.* Hume, *Treatise of Human Nature* ii (vol. i 1739). Richardson, *Pamela* (concluded 1741). Whitefield, *Short Account of God's Dealings with George Whitefield.*	Thomson and Mallet, *Alfred.*
Arbuthnot *et al.*, *Memoirs of Scriblerus.* Fielding, *Shamela.* Hume, *Essays Moral and Political* (concluded 1742). Johnson, 'Debates in the Senate of Lilliput' (to 1744). Middleton, *Life of Cicero.* Richardson, *Familiar Letters.* Warburton, *Divine Legation of Moses* ii (vol. i 1738).	Garrick, *The Lying Valet.*
Fielding, *Joseph Andrews.*	
Fielding, *Miscellanies.*	Fielding, *The Wedding Day.*
Berkeley, *Philosophical Reflections concerning Tar-Water.* Sarah Fielding, *David Simple.* Johnson, *Life of Savage.*	
Fordyce, *Dialogues concerning Education* (concluded 1748). Johnson, *Observations on Macbeth.* Swift, *Directions to Servants.*	Thomson, *Tancred and Sigismunda.*
James Hervey, *Meditations and Contemplations.*	

Date	Public Events	Literary History	Verse
1747	British naval victories off Atlantic coast of France; David Hume present at raid on L'Orient.	Anna Seward b. Voltaire, *Zadig*.	Gray, *Ode on Eton College*. Lyttelton, *Monody*. Mason, *Musaeus*. T. Warton, *Pleasures of Melancholy*.
1748	Peace of Aix-la-Chapelle.	Bentham b. Thomas Day b. Thomson d. Watts d. Montesquieu, *Esprit des Lois*.	Akenside, *Ode to the Earl of Huntingdon*. Dodsley, *Collection of Poems* i–iii, inc. Gray, 'Ode to Spring', 'On Death of a Favourite Cat'. Hamilton of Bangour, *Poems on Several Occasions*. Thomson, *Castle of Indolence*.
1749	Interest on government stock lowered to reduce national debt.	Hickey b. Charlotte Smith b. Buffon, *Histoire naturelle*.	Collins, *On the Death of Thomson*. Johnson, *Vanity of Human Wishes*. T. Warton, *Triumphs of Isis*. West, trs. *Odes* Pindar. Collins, *The Passions*.
1750	Two minor earthquakes shake London.	Fergusson b. Martin Sherlock b. Aaron Hill d. Conyers Middleton d.	Smart, *Eternity of Supreme Being*. Thomson, *Poems on Several Occasions*.
1751	Frederick Lewis, Prince of Wales, dies. Clive takes Arcot. Gin Act.	R. B. Sheridan b. Wraxall b. Henry St. John, Viscount Bolingbroke, d. Fordyce d. Voltaire, *Siècle de Louis XIV*.	Cambridge, *Scribleriad*. Gray, *Elegy wrote in a Country Churchyard*. West, *Education*.
1752	Clive takes Trichinopoly. Reform of calendar in Britain	Frances Burney b. Chatterton b. Vicesimus Knox b. Joseph Butler d.	Smart, *Poems on Several Occasions*.
1753	Hardwicke's Marriage Act.	Elizabeth Inchbald b. Berkeley d.	Gray, *Hymn to Adversity*. Smart, *Hilliad*. Wilkie, *Epigoniad*.

Prose	Drama (date of acting)
Kippis *et al.*, *Biographia Britannica* (1st edn. concluded 1766). Richardson, *Clarissa* (concluded 1748). Sterne, *The Case of Elijah*.	Garrick, *Miss in her Teens*. Hoadly, *The Suspicious Husband*.
Cleland, *Memoirs of a Woman of Pleasure* (concluded 1749). Gilpin, *Dialogue upon the Gardens at Stow*. Hume, *Philosophical Essays concerning Human Understanding*. Melmoth, *Letters by Sir Thomas Fitzosborne*. Smollett, *Roderick Random*.	E. Moore, *The Foundling*.
Bolingbroke, *On the Spirit of Patriotism*; *Idea of a Patriot King*. Fielding, *Tom Jones*. Hartley, *Observations on Man*. *Monthly Review* (to 1845).	
Dodsley?, *Œconomy of Human Life*. Johnson, *The Rambler* (to 1752). Lennox, *Harriot Stuart*. Warburton, *Julian*.	H. Brooke, *The Earl of Essex*. W. Whitehead, *The Roman Father*.
Coventry, *Pompey the Little*. Fielding, *Amelia*; *Late Increase of Robbers*. J. Harris, *Hermes*. Haywood, *Betsy Thoughtless*. Hume, *Enquiry concerning Principles of Morals*. Kames, *Principles of Morality and Natural Religion*. Paltock, *Peter Wilkins*. Smollett, *Peregrine Pickle*.	
Bolingbroke, *Letters on the Study and Use of History*. Hume, *Political Discourses*. Lennox, *Female Quixote*.	
Jane Collier, *Essay on the Art of Ingeniously Tormenting*. Sarah Fielding, 'Volume the Last' of *David Simple*. Hogarth, *Analysis of Beauty*. Lennox, *Shakespear Illustrated*. Lowth, *Praelectiones de sacra poesi Hebraeorum*. Richardson, *Sir Charles Grandison* (concluded 1754). Smollett, *Ferdinand Count Fathom*. Also *The Adventurer* (to 1754). *The World* (to 1757).	Glover, *Boadicea*. E. Moore, *The Gamester*. E. Young, *The Brothers*.

Date	Public Events	Literary History	Verse
1754	Pelham dies; Newcastle ministry. Anglo-French war begins in North America.	Crabbe b. Coventry d. Fielding d. Hamilton of Bangour d.	
1755	Lisbon earthquake. Paoli's Corsicans rise against Genoa.	Voltaire, *Orpheline de la Chine*. Rousseau, *Discours sur l'Inégalité*.	Dodsley, *Collection of Poems* iv. Grainger, *Ode on Solitude*.
1756	Outbreak of Seven Years War: invasion alarm. French take Minorca. Pitt enters ministry. 'Black hole' of Calcutta.	Gifford b. Godwin b. Eliza Haywood d. G. West d. Voltaire, *Le Désastre de Lisbonne*.	Mason, *Odes*. E. Moore, *Poems*, etc.
1757	Admiral Byng shot. Coalition of Pitt and Newcastle.	Blake b. Cibber d. Hoadly d. E. Moore d. Whitehead Poet Laureate.	Dyer, *The Fleece*. Gray, *Odes* ('Progress of Poesy', 'The Bard') Wilkie, *The Epigoniad*.
1758	Canal from Liverpool to Leeds begun.	E. C. Knight b. Dyer d. James Hervey d. Allan Ramsay d.	Dodsley, *Collection of Poems* v–vi.
1759	Invasion alarm. Battles of Minden and Quebec. Naval battles at Lagos and Quiberon Bay. British Museum opens.	Burns b. Mary Wollstonecraft b. Collins d.	
1760	George II dies. Wedgwood opens pottery works at Etruria, Staffordshire.	Beckford b. Diderot, *La Religieuse*.	Lloyd, *The Actor*. Macpherson, *Fragments of Ancient Poetry*.
1761	Pitt resigns.	Cawthorn d. William Law d. Oldys d. Richardson d.	Churchill, *Rosciad*.

Prose

Drama (date of acting)

Hume, *History of Great Britain* (concluded 1763). T. Warton, *Observations on the Faerie Queene*. E. Young, *The Centaur not Fabulous*. Also, *The Connoisseur* (to 1756).

F. Brooke, *Virginia*. W. Whitehead, *Creusa, Queen of Athens*.

Amory, *Memoirs of Several Ladies of Great Britain*. Fielding, *Voyage to Lisbon*. Johnson, *Dictionary*. Shebbeare, *Lydia*. Smollett, trs. *Don Quixote* of Cervantes.

J. Brown, *Barbarossa*.

Amory, *John Buncle*. Burke, *Vindication of Natural Society*; J. Warton, *Essay on the Writings and Genius of Pope*. Also, *Critical Review* (to 1817).

J. Brown, *Athelstan*. Foote, *Englishman Returned from Paris*.

J. Brown, *Estimate of the Manners and Principles of the Times*. Burke, *Philosophical Enquiry into the Sublime and Beautiful*. Hume, *Four Dissertations*. Smollett, *History of England* (to 1765).

Home, *Douglas*.

E. Carter, trs. Epictetus. Gibbon, *Essai sur l'étude de la littérature*. Johnson, *The Idler* (to 1760). Kames, *Historical Law Tracts*. Lennox, *Henrietta*. Walpole, *Catalogue of Royal and Noble Authors*.

Dodsley, *Cleone*.

Sarah Fielding, *Countess of Dellwyn*. Gerard, *Essay on Taste*. Goldsmith, *Present State of Polite Learning*; *The Bee*. Hurd, *Moral and Political Dialogues*. Johnson, *Rasselas*. Robertson, *History of Scotland*. Adam Smith, *Theory of Moral Sentiments*. E. Young, *Conjectures on Original Composition*. Also *Modern Universal History* (concluded 1766).

Macklin, *Love à la Mode*.

Sarah Fielding, *Ophelia*. Goldsmith, *The Chinese Letters* (to 1761). Johnstone, *Chrysal*. Lyttelton, *Dialogues of the Dead*. Shebbeare, *History of the Sumatrans*. Sterne, *Tristram Shandy* i–ii (to 1767). Smollett, *Sir Launcelot Greaves* (concluded 1761).

Colman, *Polly Honeycombe*. Foote, *The Minor*. Murphy, *The Way to Keep Him*.

Hawkesworth, *Almoran and Hamet*. F. Sheridan, *Sidney Bidulph*.

Murphy, *All in the Wrong*.

Date	Public Events	Literary History	Verse
1762	Bute ministry.	Bowles b. Cobbett b. Joanna Baillie b. Bubb Dodington d. Lady Mary Wortley Montagu d. Johnson granted pension. Rousseau, *Contrat Social*; *Émile*. Diderot, *Neveu de Rameau*.	Churchill, *Night; The Ghost* i–iii. Macpherson, *Fingal*.
1763	Peace of Paris. Grenville succeeds Bute. Wilkes publishes No. 45 of the *North Briton*; arrested on general warrant.	Rogers b. Shenstone d.	Churchill, *Prophecy of Famine*. Macpherson, *Temora*. Mason, *Elegies*. Smart, *Song to David*. Thornton's burlesque *Ode on St. Caecilia's Day*.
1764	Wilkes expelled from Commons. Hargreaves invents spinning-jenny. Black measures latent heat.	Ann Radcliffe b. Churchill d. Dodsley d. Hogarth d. R. Lloyd d. Voltaire, *Dictionnaire philosophique*.	Churchill, *The Candidate*. E. Evans, *Specimens of the Ancient Welsh Bards*. Goldsmith, *The Traveller*. Grainger, *Sugar-Cane*.
1765	Stamp Act (to tax American colonies). Rockingham's ministry. Watt invents condenser.	(Sir) James Mackintosh b. Mallet d. Ridley d. E. Young d.	Beattie, *Judgment of Paris*. Percy, *Reliques of Ancient English Poetry*.
1766	Stamp Act repealed. Grafton–Pitt (Chatham) ministry. British occupy Falkland Islands.	J. Brown d. Grainger d. F. Sheridan d. Rousseau in England. Lessing, *Laokoon*.	Anstey, *New Bath Guide*.
1767	Townshend introduces taxes on tea and other goods in American colonies. Grafton forms ministry.	Maria Edgeworth b. Paltock d.	Jago, *Edge-Hill*. W. J. Mickle, *The Concubine*.
1768	Wilkes sentenced for libel. Corsica ceded to French. Royal Academy founded.	Sarah Fielding d. Spence d. Sterne d. Thornton d.	Gray, *Poems*.

Prose	*Drama (date of acting)*
G. Campbell, *Dissertation on Miracles.* Goldsmith, *Life of Nash.* Hurd, *Letters on Chivalry and Romance.* Kames, *Elements of Criticism.* Walpole, *Anecdotes of Painting* (concluded 1771). Warburton, *Doctrine of Grace.*	W. Whitehead, *The School for Lovers.* Foote, *The Lyar.*
Blair, *Critical Dissertation on Ossian.* F. Brooke, *Lady Julia Mandeville.* J. Brown *Dissertation on Poetry and Music.* Johnson, 'On Life and Writings of Collins'.	G. Colman, sen., *The Deuce is in him.* Foote, *The Mayor of Garret.* Murphy, *The Citizen.* F. Sheridan, *The Discovery.*
H. Brooke, *The Fool of Quality* (concluded 1770). Goldsmith, *History of England, in a Series of Letters.* J. Newton, *Authentic Narrative.* Reid, *Enquiry into the Human Mind.* Ridley, *Tales of the Genii.*	Foote, *The Patron.* Macklin, *The Trueborn Scotsman* (*The Man of the World*, 1781). Murphy, *What we must all come to* (*Three Weeks after Marriage*, 1776).
Blackstone, *Commentaries on the Laws of England* (concluded 1769). Johnson, edition of Shakespeare. Walpole, *Castle of Otranto.*	
Goldsmith, *Vicar of Wakefield.* Smollett, *Travels through France and Italy.*	Colman, sen., and Garrick, *The Clandestine Marriage.*
Duff, *Essay on Original Genius.* Farmer, *Essay on the Learning of Shakespeare.* Ferguson, *Essay on the History of Civil Society.* Lyttelton, *History of Henry II.* Priestley, *History and present State of Electricity.* F. Sheridan, *History of Nourjahad.* Wood, *Essay on the Original Genius of Homer.*	Garrick, *Peep behind the Curtain.* Murphy, *The School for Guardians.*
Boswell, *Account of Corsica.* A. Dow, *Tales from the Persian of Inatulla.* Capell, edition of Shakespeare. Sterne, *Sentimental Journey.* G. Stuart, *Historical Dissertation concerning the Antiquity of the*	Foote, *Devil upon Two Sticks.* Goldsmith, *The Good Natur'd Man.* Kelly. *False Delicacy.* Murphy, *Zenobia.*

Date	Public Events	Literary History	Verse
1769	Wilkes expelled from Commons; thrice re-elected. French defeat Paoli in Corsica.	Shakespeare Jubilee at Stratford-on-Avon	Chatterton, 'Elinoure and Juga'. Herd, *Ancient and Modern Scots Songs.*
1770	North ministry. Printers and publishers of 'Junius' tried for seditious libel.	James Hogg b. Wordsworth b. Akenside d. Chatterton d. Guthrie d. Jortin d. Whitefield d.	Goldsmith, *The Deserted Village.* Sir David Dalrymple, Lord Hailes, *Ancient Scottish Poems* (Bannatyne MS.).
1771	Spain cedes Falkland Islands to Britain. Arkwright's first spinning mill.	Walter Scott b. Gray d. Smart d. Smollett d. Wood d.	Beattie, *The Minstrel.* i. Percy, *The Hermit of Warkworth.*
1772	Boston Assembly's threat of secession. Warren Hastings governor of Bengal.	Coleridge b. Ridpath d. Wilkie d. Lessing, *Emilia Galotti*	Chatterton, *Execution of Sir Charles Bawdin.* W. Jones, *Poems . . . Translations from the Asiatick Languages.* Mason, *English Garden* (concluded 1781).
1773	Boston 'tea party'.	Jeffrey b. James Mill b. Hawkesworth d. Lyttelton d. P. D. Stanhope, Earl of Chesterfield d. Goethe, *Götz von Berlichingen.*	Fergusson, *Poems.* Mason, *An Heroic Epistle to Sir William Chambers.*
1774	First Congress of American colonies. Accession of Louis XVI of France.	Southey b. Fergusson d. Goldsmith d. Goethe, *Werther.*	Goldsmith, *Retaliation.* J. Langhorne, *The Country Justice.*

Prose	Drama (date of acting)
English Constitution. Wilkes, *English Liberty* (concluded 1770). A. Young, *Six Weeks' Tour through the Southern Counties.*	
F. Brooke, *Emily Montague.* Goldsmith, *Roman History.* 'Junius' letters (to 1772). Reynolds, *Discourses to the Royal Academy* (to 1790). Robertson, *History of Charles V.* Smollett, *Adventures of an Atom.* A. Young, *Six Months' Tour through the North of England.*	Cumberland, *The Brothers.* Home, *The Fatal Discovery.*
Beattie, *Essay on Truth.* Burke, *Thoughts on the Present Discontents.* Ferguson, *Institutes of Moral Philosophy.* Goldsmith, *Life of Parnell.* Johnson, *False Alarm.*	Foote, *The Tame Lover.* Kelly, *A Word to the Wise.*
C. Burney, *Present State of Music in France and Italy.* J. Dalrymple, Memoirs *of Great Britain.* Goldsmith, *History of England.* Johnson, *Thoughts on Falkland's Islands.* Mackenzie, *Man of Feeling.* Millar, *Observations concerning the Distinction of Ranks.* Pennant, *Tour in Scotland.* Smollett, *Humphry Clinker.* Walpole, *Modern Gardening.*	Cumberland, *The West Indian.* Foote, *The Maid of Bath.*
	Cumberland, *The Fashionable Lover.* Murphy, *The Grecian Daughter.*
Brydone, *Tour through Sicily and Malta.* C. Burney, *Present State of Music in Germany.* Chapone, *Letters on the Improvement of the Mind.* Graves, *Spiritual Quixote.* Hawkesworth, *Account of the Voyages undertaken in the Southern Hemisphere.* Mackenzie, *Man of the World.* Monboddo, *Origin and Progress of Language* (concluded 1792).	Goldsmith, *She Stoops to Conquer.* Mackenzie, *The Prince of Tunis.*
H. Brooke, *Juliet Grenville.* Burke *Speech on American Taxation.* Chesterfield, *Letters to his Son.* Goldsmith, *Grecian History*; *History of the Earth and*	Kelly, *The School for Wives.*

Date	Public Events	Literary History	Verse
1775	Battles of Lexington, Concord, and Bunker Hill. Watt's steam engine perfected.	Jane Austen b. Lamb b. Landor b. M. G. Lewis b. J. Hill d. Beaumarchais, *Le Barbier de Séville*.	Crabbe, *Inebriety*.
1776	American Declaration of Independence. Necker finance minister in France.	Hume d. Goethe, *Stella*.	Mickle, trs. *Lusiad* of Camoens. J. Scott, *Amwell*. Skinner, *Tullochgorum*.
1777	Burgoyne capitulates at Saratoga.	T. Campbell b. Foote d. Kelly d.	Chatterton, *Poems . . . by Rowley*, ed. T. Tyrwhitt. T. Warton *Poems*.
1778	Pitt (Earl of Chatham) dies. Franco-American alliance formed; Britain declares war on France.	Hazlitt b. Rousseau d. Voltaire d. Herder, *Volkslieder*.	
1779	War with Spain; siege of Gibraltar. Crompton invents spinning mule.	Thomas Moore b. Galt b. Armstrong d. Garrick d. J. Langhorne d. Warburton d. Lessing, *Nathan der Weise*.	Cowper and Newton, *Olney Hymns*.
1780	Yorkshire petition for parliamentary reform. Gordon riots. British take Charleston.	Blackstone d. James Harris d. Wieland, *Oberon*.	Crabbe, *The Candidate*.

Prose

Drama (date of acting)

Animated Nature. Johnson, *The Patriot.*
Kames, *Sketches of the History of Man.*
W. Richardson, *Philosophical Analysis
of some of Shakespeare's Remarkable
Characters.* T. Warton, *History of
English Poetry* (concluded 1781).

Burke, *Speech on Conciliation with the
Colonies.* Johnson, *Journey to the Western
Islands of Scotland; Taxation no Tyranny.*
Mason, edition of Gray, with Life.
Pratt, *Liberal Opinions* (concluded
1777).

Garrick, *Bon Ton.* R. B. Sheridan, *The
Rivals; St. Patrick's Day; The Duenna.*

Beattie, *Essays.* Bentham, *Fragment on
Government.* C. Burney, *History of Music*
i (concluded 1789). G. Campbell,
Philosophy of Rhetoric. Sir D. Dalrymple,
Annals of Scotland i (concluded 1779).
Gibbon, *Decline and Fall of the Roman
Empire* i (concluded 1788). Sir J. Haw-
kins, *History of Music.* Adam Smith,
Wealth of Nations. R. Watson, *Apology
for Christianity.*

Boswell, *The Hypochondriack* (to 1783).
Hume, *Life, Written by Himself; Two
Essays* (on suicide and on immortality).
Mackenzie, *Julia de Roubigné.* Morgann,
*Essay on the Dramatic Character of Sir
John Falstaff.* Reeve, *The Champion of
Virtue (The Old English Baron,* 1778).
Robertson, *History of America.*

Hannah More, *Percy.* Murphy, *Know
your own Mind.* R. B. Sheridan, *A Trip
to Scarborough.*

F. Burney, *Evelina.* Knox, *Essays,
Moral and Literary.* Stockdale, *Inquiry
into the Laws of Poetry.* G. Stuart, *View
of Society in Europe.*

Cumberland, *The Battle of Hastings.*
Foote, *The Nabob.*

Coxe, *Sketches of Swisserland.* Gibbon,
*Vindication of some Passages in the Decline
and Fall.* Graves, *Columella.* Hume,
Dialogues concerning Natural Religion.
Johnson, *Prefaces, Biographical and Critical, to the Works of the English Poets.*
Monboddo, *Antient Metaphysics* (concluded 1799). Also, *The Mirror* (to
1780).

R. B. Sheridan, *The Critic.*

Davies, *Memoirs of Garrick.* J. Nichols,
Anecdotes of Mr. Hogarth. A. Young,
Tour in Ireland.

Date	Public Events	Literary History	Verse
1781	Cornwallis capitulates at Yorktown.	Jago d. Lessing d. Kant, *Kritik der reinen Vernunft.* Rousseau, *Confessions.* Schiller, *Die Räuber.*	Crabbe, *The Library.*
1782	North succeeded by Rockingham and then by Shelburne. Burke's 'economical reform'. Ireland granted legislative independence. Rodney defeats French fleet at battle of The Saints.	S. Ferrier b. Henry Home, Lord Kames d. Laclos, *Les Liaisons dangereuses.*	Cowper, *Poems* ('Table Talk', 'The Progress of Error', etc.); *John Gilpin.* T. Warton, *Verses on Reynold's Painted Window.* Wolcot, *Lyric Odes to the Royal Academicians.*
1783	Fox–North coalition, followed by Pitt the Younger's first ministry. Peace of Versailles.	H. Brooke d. J. Scott d.	Blake, *Poetical Sketches.* Crabbe, *The Village.*
1784	Pitt's India Act	Leigh Hunt b. Johnson d. Alexander Ross d. Diderot d. Beaumarchais, *Le Mariage de Figaro.* Herder, *Ideen zur Philosophie der Menschheit.* Schiller, *Kabale und Liebe.*	
1785	Warren Hastings returns from India. Cartwright invents power-loom.	T. L. Peacock b. De Quincey b. H. Kirke White b. John Wilson b. W. Whitehead d. T. Warton becomes Poet Laureate.	Cowper, *The Task.* Crabbe, *The Newspaper.* Wolcot, *The Lousiad* i.
1786	Coal-gas first used for lighting.	G. Stuart d.	Burns, *Poems, Chiefly in the Scottish Dialect.* Wolcot, *Bozzy and Piozzi.*

Prose	*Drama (date of acting)*
Bage, *Mount Henneth.* Knox, *Liberal Education.* R. Watson, *Chemical Essays* (concluded 1787).	Pratt, *The Fair Circassian.*

F. Burney, *Cecilia.* Gilpin, *Observations on the River Wye.* Priestley, *History of the Corruptions of Christianity.* G. Stuart, *History of Scotland.* J. Warton, *Essay on the Genius and Writings of Pope* ii.

Beattie, *Dissertations Moral and Critical.* Beckford, *Dreams, Waking Thoughts, and Incidents.* H. Blair, *Lectures on Rhetoric and Belles Lettres.* Day, *Sandford and Merton* (concluded 1789). Ferguson, *History of the Roman Republic.* Reeve, *The Two Mentors.*

Bage, *Barham Downs.* Burke, *Speech on Fox's India Bill.* Bubb Dodington, *Diary.* W. Richardson, *Anecdotes of the Russian Empire; Essays on Shakespeare's Dramatic Characters.*

Boswell, *Tour to the Hebrides.* Burke, *Speech on the Nabob of Arcot's Debts.* Johnson, *Prayers and Meditations.* Paley, *Principles of Moral and Political Philosophy.* Reeve, *The Progress of Romance.* Reid, *Essay on the Intellectual Powers of Man.* J. Scott, *Critical Essays.* Walpole, *Hieroglyphic Tales.* Also, *The Lounger* (to 1787).

Beckford, *Vathek.* Gilpin, *Observations on the Mountains and Lakes of Cumberland and Westmoreland.* J. Moore, *Zeluco.* Piozzi, *Anecdotes of Johnson.* Charlotte Smith, *Romance of Real Life.* Tooke, *Diversions of Purley* (concluded 1805).

Date	Public Events	Literary History	Verse
1787	Impeachment of Warren Hastings initiated. Association for Abolition of Slave Trade begun. U.S. Constitution signed.	Lowth d. B. de Saint-Pierre, *Paul et Virginie*.	Wolcot, *Instructions to a Celebrated Laureat*.
1788	Trial of Warren Hastings begins. French States-General summoned. George III's first attack of 'madness'.	Byron b. Amory d. Mickle d. Shebbeare d. T. Sheridan d. Charles Wesley d.	Collins, *Ode on the Popular Superstitions of the Highlands*.
1789	George III recovers. Bastille falls; Declaration of the Rights of man.	Frances Brooke d. Cleland d. Sit J. Hawkins d.	Blake, *Songs of Innocence*. W. L. Bowles, *Sonnets*. E. Darwin, *The Loves of the Plants*.

Prose	*Drama (date of acting)*
Bage, *The Fair Syrian.* Sir J. Hawkins, *Life of Johnson.* Millar, *Historical View of the English Government.* Wollstonecraft, *Thoughts on the Education of Daughters.*	Colman, jun., *Inkle and Yarico.*

Bage, *James Wallace.* Graves, *Recollection of the Life of Shenstone.* Knox, *Winter Evenings.* Hannah More, *Thoughts on the Importance of the Manners of the Great.* Reid, *Essay on the Active Powers of Man.* Charlotte Smith, *Emmeline.*

Bentham, *Principles of Morals and Legislation.* Gilpin, *Observations on the Highlands of Scotland.* Sir W. Jones, trs. *Sacontala* of Kalidasa. Piozzi, *Observations in a Journey through France, Italy and Germany.* Ann Radcliffe, *Castles of Athlin and Dunbayne.* W. Richardson, *Essays on Shakespeare's Dramatic Character of Falstaff, and his Imitation of Female Characters.* White, *Natural History of Selborne.*

BIBLIOGRAPHY

This bibliography is selective, providing only an outline of each author's work, and in particular giving only the slightest indication of the wealth of material to be found in scholarly periodicals. An attempt has been made, however, to help readers find appropriate sources of more detailed information.

CONTENTS:

ABBREVIATIONS

ARS	*Augustan Reprint Society*
DNB	*Dictionary of National Biography*
E&S	*Essays and Studies by Members of the English Association*
EC	*Essays in Criticism*
ECS	*Eighteenth-Century Studies*
EL	*Everyman's Library*
ELH	*English Literary History*
ES	*English Studies*
HLB	*Harvard Library Bulletin*
HLQ	*Huntington Library Quarterly*
JEGP	*Journal of English and Germanic Philology*
JHI	*Journal of the History of Ideas*
MLN	*Modern Language Notes*
MLQ	*Modern Language Quarterly*
MLR	*Modern Language Review*
MP	*Modern Philology*
NCBEL	*New Cambridge Bibliography of English Literature*

PMLA *Publications of the Modern Language Association of America*
PQ *Philological Quarterly*
RES *Review of English Studies*
SEL *Studies in English Literature 1500–1900*
SP *Studies in Philology*
TSLL *Texas Studies in Literature and Language*
WC *World's Classics*

Other abbreviations used are:

Anderson *The Works of the British Poets*, ed. R. Anderson, 13 vols., Edinburgh, 1792–5; vol. xiv, 1807.

Chalmers *The Works of the English Poets*, ed. A. Chalmers, 21 vols., 1810.

The following collections of essays are referred to by short titles:

J. L. Clifford Festschrift, 1971 *English Writers of the Eighteenth Century. Essays in Honor of James Lowry Clifford Presented by his Students,* ed. J. H. Middendorf, New York, 1971.

L. A. Landa Festschrift, 1970 *The Augustan Milieu: Essays Presented to Louis A. Landa,* ed. H. K. Miller, E. Rothstein, and G. S. Rousseau, Oxford, 1970.

A. D. McKillop Festschrift, 1963 *Restoration and Eighteenth-Century Literature: Essays in Honor of Alan Dugald McKillop,* ed. C. Camden, Chicago, 1963.

S. H. Monk Festschrift, 1967 *Studies in Criticism and Aesthetics, 1660–1800: Essays in Honor of Samuel Holt Monk,* ed. H. Anderson and J. S. Shea, Minneapolis, 1967.

F. A. Pottle Festschrift, 1965 *From Sensibility to Romanticism: Essays Presented to Frederick A. Pottle,* ed. F. W. Hilles and H. Bloom, New York, 1965.

L. F. Powell Festschrift, 1965 *Johnson, Boswell and their Circle: Essays Presented to Lawrence Fitzroy Powell in Honour of his Eighty-Fourth Birthday,* ed. M. Lascelles *et al.*, Oxford, 1965.

D. Nichol Smith Festschrift, 1945 *Essays on the Eighteenth Century Presented to David Nichol Smith in Honour of his Seventieth Birthday,* Oxford, 1945.

C. B. Tinker Festschrift, 1949 *The Age of Johnson: Essays Presented to Chauncey Brewster Tinker,* ed. W. S. Lewis, New Haven, 1949.

I. GENERAL BIBLIOGRAPHIES AND WORKS OF REFERENCE

The second volume of *NCBEL*, covering the period 1660–1800, is indispensable. Among the annual bibliographies, the most important for this period is 'English Literature 1660–1800', published in *PQ* since 1926, and reprinted in 6 vols. covering the years 1926–70, Princeton, 1950–72. This has brief critical assessments of the more important items. The major annual bibliographies which contain sections on English literature of this period include the *Annual Bibliography of English Language and Literature, The Year's Work in English Studies*, and the bibliography produced by the Modern Language Association of America, appearing in *PMLA* from 1922 to 1968, and now issued as a separate annual volume. *MLA Abstracts of Articles in Scholarly Journals* have appeared in an annual volume since 1970. There is a very selective annual survey of recent studies in the Restoration and eighteenth century published in *SEL*. The *Subject Guide to Books in Print*, New York, published annually since 1957, can be helpful. For Scottish literature see *Annual Bibliography of Scottish Literature*, 1969– , published as a supplement to *The Bibliotheck*.

Among older works of reference, R. Watt's *Bibliotheca Britannica*, 4 vols., 1824, has never been superseded as a subject index for this period. S. A. Allibone, *A Critical Dictionary of English Literature, and British and American Authors*, 3 vols., Philadelphia, 1859–71, and W. T. Lowndes, *Bibliographer's Manual of English Literature*, rev. ed. H. G. Bohn, 6 vols., 1869, are useful supplements to the British Museum's *General Catalogue of Printed Books* and the American *National Union Catalog. Pre-1956 Imprints*.

There are a number of general bibliographies on a smaller scale (for example, F. W. Bateson, *Guide to English Literature*, 2nd edn., 1967), but three which have special relevance to this period are J. E. Tobin, *Eighteenth-Century Literature and its Cultural Background*, New York, 1939; H. V. D. Dyson and J. Butt, *Augustans and Romantics*, 3rd edn., 1961; and D. F. Bond, *The Eighteenth Century*, Northbrook, Ill., 1975.

In addition to *DNB*, biographical information is helpfully summarized in S. J. Kunitz and H. Haycraft, *British Authors before 1800*, New York, 1952. Much detailed information is still most conveniently available in the *Biographia Britannica* (by Andrew Kippis and others), 6 vols. (in 7 parts), 1747–66, and 6 vols., corrected and enlarged, 1778–93; and J. Nichols, *Literary Anecdotes of the Eighteenth Century*, 9 vols., 1812–15 and *Illustrations of the Literary History of the Eighteenth Century*, 8 vols., 1817–58.

II. LITERARY HISTORY AND CRITICISM

GENERAL SURVEYS

In the *Cambridge History of English Literature*, ed. A. W. Ward and A. R. Waller, vol. x, *The Age of Johnson*, Cambridge, 1913, covers the period in considerable detail. G. Saintsbury's *The Peace of the Augustans: a Survey of Eighteenth Century Literature as a Place of Rest and Refreshment*, 1916, provides an animated and idiosyncratic commentary. O. Elton's *Survey of English Literature, 1730–1780*, 2 vols., 1928, is wide-ranging and thorough. Two later surveys deserve particular mention: A. D. McKillop's *English Literature from Dryden to Burns*, New York, 1948; and G. Sherburn's *The Restoration and Eighteenth Century (1660–1789)*, forming vol. iii of *A Literary History of England*, ed. A. C. Baugh, New York, 1948. The latter has been revised by D. F. Bond, New York, 1967. There is much of value in the *Pelican Guide to English Literature*, ed. B. Ford: vol. iv, *From Dryden to Johnson*, 1957. Another excellent co-operative work is vol. iv of the *Sphere History of Literature in the English Language*, *Dryden to Johnson*, ed. R. Lonsdale, 1971. For Scottish literature, see K. Wittig, *The Scottish Tradition in Literature*, 1958; and D. Craig, *Scottish Literature and the Scottish People 1680–1830*, 1961.

Among the many general studies that might be mentioned, three provide particularly helpful approaches to the period: A. R. Humphreys, *The Augustan World*, 1954; M. Price, *To the Palace of Wisdom: Studies in Order and Energy from Dryden to Blake*, Garden City, N.Y., 1964; and P. Fussell, *The Rhetorical World of Augustan Humanism: Ethics and Imagery from Swift to Burke*, Oxford, 1965.

1. POETRY

The great collections of the British poets, beginning with Hugh Blair's in 1773, continuing with Johnson's, 1779–81, and

achieving their fullest development in the monumental editions
of R. Anderson, 1792–5, and A. Chalmers, 1810, are indispensable for the serious student of eighteenth-century poetry. The
most satisfactory general anthology is still D. Nichol Smith's
Oxford Book of Eighteenth-Century Verse, 1926, but in *Minor British
Poetry 1680–1800*, Metuchen, N.J., 1973, J. E. Barlough picks
up some poets not to be found in other collections, and *The
Penguin Book of English Pastoral Verse*, ed. J. Barrell and J. Bull,
1974, is helpful for our period.

Dodsley's *Collection of Poems by Several Hands* is studied by
R. W. Chapman in *Oxford Bibliographical Society: Proceedings and
Papers* iii, pt. iii, 1933. For contents and contributors, see W. P.
Courtney's study, 1910, and the index compiled by D. D. Eddy,
Publications of the Bibliographical Society of America lx, 1966.

As a general introduction, J. Sutherland's *Preface to Eighteenth-
Century Poetry*, Oxford, 1948, is helpful, but see also the essay by
D. J. Greene, ' "Logical Structure" in Eighteenth-Century
Poetry', *PQ* xxxi, 1952. R. Trickett, *The Honest Muse: a Study in
Augustan Verse*, Oxford, 1967, has a good chapter on Johnson,
and M. H. Nicolson's *Newton Demands the Muse. Newton's
'Opticks' and the Eighteenth Century Poets*, Princeton, 1946, is a
suggestive study of mid-century poetry. There is an important
study by J. Miles, *Eras and Modes in English Poetry*, Berkeley,
1957, and a particularly helpful essay by R. Cohen, 'The Augustan Mode in English Poetry', *ECS* i, 1967, reprinted in *Studies in
the Eighteenth Century*, ed. R. F. Brissenden, Canberra, 1968. See
also E. Miner, 'From "Narrative" to "Description" and "Sense"
in Eighteenth-Century Poetry', *SEL* ix, 1969. On metre, the
best study is by P. Fussell, Jr., *Theory of Prosody in Eighteenth-
Century England*, New London, Conn., 1954. There are several
studies which focus on the heroic couplet: a general history by
W. B. Piper, Cleveland, 1969, an essay by E. R. Wasserman on
the return to the 'enjambed couplet', *ELH* vii, 1940, and W. C.
Brown's book *The Triumph of Form: a Study of the Later Masters
of the Heroic Couplet*, Chapel Hill, 1948. P. W. K. Stone, in *The
Art of Poetry 1750–1820*, 1967, emphasizes the contrast between
'neo-classical' and 'romantic'.

On poetic diction, see the fine essay by G. Tillotson in *E&S*
xxv, 1940, enlarged in his *Essays in Criticism and Research*, Cambridge, 1942, and in his *Augustan Studies*, 1961. D. Davie's *Purity
of Diction in English Verse*, 1952, has interesting studies of late

eighteenth-century poetry. E. R. Wasserman has a useful study of personification, *PMLA* lxv, 1950, and see also C. F. Chapin, *Personification in Eighteenth-Century English Poetry*, New York, 1955. Topographical poetry is thoroughly surveyed in R. A. Aubin's study, New York, 1936, although Aubin's method is criticized by J. W. Foster in his 'A Redefinition of Topographical Poetry', *JEGP* lxix, 1970. C. V. Deane's study of nature poetry, Oxford, 1935, is still useful. See also J. Arthos, *The Language of Natural Description in Eighteenth-Century Poetry*, Ann Arbor, 1949. The 'georgic' has been surveyed by D. L. Durling, New York, 1935, and J. Chalker, 1969. Virgilian influences are also considered in M. L. Røstvig's *The Happy Man*, vol. 2. Oslo, 1958.

R. D. Havens's *The Influence of Milton on English Poetry*, Cambridge, Mass., 1922, is exhaustively detailed. So are the relevant volumes of H. N. Fairchild's survey, *Religious Trends in English Poetry*: vol. ii, *1740–80, Religious Sentimentalism in the Age of Johnson*, New York, 1942; and vol. iii, *1780–1830, Romantic Faith*, New York, 1949. There is also a shorter study by D. B. Morris, *The Religious Sublime: Christian Poetry and Critical Tradition in Eighteenth-Century Poetry*, Lexington, 1972. Havens's book on Milton includes a survey of the sonnet in our period. See also the edition of Thomas Edwards's sonnets by D. G. Donovan, Los Angeles, 1974, *ARS*.

There are two excellent studies by P. M. Spacks: *The Insistence of Horror*, Cambridge, Mass., 1962, dealing with aspects of the supernatural; and *The Poetry of Vision*, Cambridge, Mass., 1967. W. J. Bate considers another aspect of poetry in the period in his book *The Burden of the Past and the English Poet*, Cambridge, Mass., 1970, London, 1971. Yet another perspective is provided by I. Kovacevich, 'The Mechanical Muse: the Impact of Technical Inventions on Eighteenth-Century Neo-Classical Poetry', *HLQ* xxviii, 1965.

On satire, I. Jack's *Augustan Satire*, Oxford, 1952, is mainly concerned with the period before 1740, although he discusses Johnson. K. Hopkins, in *Portraits in Satire*, 1958, examines Churchill and others from our period. H. D. Weinbrot develops an interesting thesis in *The Formal Strain: Studies in Augustan Imitation and Satire*, Chicago, 1969. P. K. Elkin's *The Augustan Defence of Satire*, Oxford, 1973, considers the changing attitudes to satire in the latter half of the century. In 'Satire, Sublimity, and Sentiment: Theory and Practice in Post-Augustan Satire',

PMLA lxxxv, 1970, W. B. Carnochan considers Juvenal's displacement of Horace as a model.

On ballads and similar genres there is a good study by A. B. Friedman, *The Ballad Revival: Studies in the Influence of Popular on Sophisticated Poetry*, Chicago, 1961. See also the essay by K. Stewart, 'The Ballad and the *Genres* in the Eighteenth Century', *ELH* xxiv, 1957. J. E. Congleton has a study of theories of pastoral poetry, Gainesville, 1952, and J. Sambrook considers some 'poets of the poor' in *Studies on Burke and his Time* xi, 1970.

On Scottish poetry, see the surveys and criticism listed under Robert Burns and Robert Fergusson below, pp. 577–8 and 590. D. Daiches considers eighteenth-century vernacular poetry in *Scottish Poetry: a Critical Survey*, ed. J. Kinsley, 1955, and T. Crawford has a useful essay on Scottish popular ballads and lyrics, *Studies in Scottish Literature* i, 1963. The selection from eighteenth-century writers in *The Oxford Book of Scottish Verse*, ed. J. MacQueen and T. Scott, Oxford, 1966, is useful, but T. Scott's *Penguin Book of Scottish Verse*, 1970, has a somewhat wider range.

2. Drama

The main collections of plays are *Bell's British Theatre*, 21 vols., 1776–81, 36 vols., 1791–1802, and Mrs. Inchbald's *British Theatre*, 25 vols., 1808, 20 vols., 1824. There are supplements to both collections containing farces and entertainments: Bell, 4 vols., 1784, and Inchbald, 7 vols., 1809, W. H. Rubsamen has edited a collection of 171 musical plays in 28 vols., under the title *The Ballad Opera*, New York, 1974. Two useful modern anthologies are *Burlesque Plays of the Eighteenth Century*, ed. S. Trussler, 1969, and *Eighteenth-Century Drama: Afterpieces*, ed. R. W. Bevis, 1970.

Among the standard surveys of drama in this period Allardyce Nicoll's *History of Early Eighteenth Century Drama*, 1925, and *History of Late Eighteenth Century Drama*, 1927, are outstanding. They have been revised and reprinted as vols. ii and iii of his *History of English Drama*, 1952–9. This work includes lists of plays, with dates of performance. Only one relevant volume of the projected *Revels History of Drama in English* has so far been published, vol. vi, by M. R. Booth *et al.*, 1975, covering the period 1750–1880. It takes account of recent research on theatres, actors, and plays, and has a full and helpful bibliography.

Among the shorter recent general studies, that by C. Price, *Theatre in the Age of Garrick*, Oxford, 1973, is admirable, concisely covering many aspects of the subject.

Earlier sources that may be usefully consulted include the *Biographia Dramatica*, a revision (1782) by Isaac Read of D. E. Baker's *Companion to the Playhouse*, 2 vols., 1764. A further revision by Stephen Jones appeared (3 vols.) in 1812. Another major work is by John Genest, *Some Account of the English Stage, 1660–1830*, 10 vols., Bath, 1832. Modern works of reference include R. Lowe, *A Bibliographical Account of English Theatrical Literature*, 1888, revised by J. F. Arnott and J. W. Robinson in 1970 under the title *English Theatrical Literature 1559–1900*. For subsequent studies, see C. J. Stratman, D. G. Spencer, and M. E. Devine, *Restoration and Eighteenth-Century Theatre Research: a Bibliographical Guide, 1900–1968*, Carbondale, Southern Illinois University Press, 1971.

There are two other major reference works from the same publisher. One is already complete: *The London Stage, 1660–1800. A Calendar of Plays, Entertainments & Afterpieces, together with Casts, Box-Receipts and Contemporary Comment, compiled from the Playbills, Newspapers and Theatrical Diaries of the Period*, 11 vols., Carbondale, 1960–8. Parts 3 to 5 cover our period: 1729–47, ed. A. H. Scouten, 2 vols., 1961; 1747–76, ed. G. W. Stone, 3 vols., 1962; and 1776–1800, ed. C. B. Hogan, 3 vols., 1968. The extensive and valuable 'critical introductions' to the various parts have also been issued separately. The other reference work is in progress: a twelve-volume *Biographical Dictionary of Actors, Actresses, Musicians, Dancers, Managers, and other Stage Personnel in London, 1660–1800* by P. H. Highfill, Jr., K. A. Burnim, and E. A. Langhans, Carbondale, 1973– . Among earlier compilations, those of Dougald MacMillan are still worth consulting: *Drury Lane Calendar 1747–1776*, Oxford, 1938, and *Catalogue of the Larpent Plays in the Huntington Library*, San Marino, Calif., 1939.

Various aspects of the theatre are illustrated by J. J. Lynch, *Box, Pit, and Gallery: Stage and Society in Johnson's London*, Berkeley, 1953; D. F. Smith, *The Critics in the Audience of the London Theaters, from Buckingham to Sheridan*, Albuquerque, 1953; H. W. Pedicord, *The Theatrical Public in the Time of Garrick*, New York, 1954; and L. Hughes, *The Drama's Patrons*, Austin, 1971. J. A. Kelly, *German Visitors to English Theaters in the Eighteenth Century*, Princeton, 1936, may also be consulted.

Several studies deal with the drama outside the main theatres: two by S. Rosenfeld, *Strolling Players and Drama in the Provinces, 1660–1765*, Cambridge, 1939, and *The Theatre of the London Fairs in the Eighteenth Century*, Cambridge, 1960; C. Price, *The English Theatre in Wales*, Cardiff, 1948; A. Hare, *The Georgian Theatre in Wessex*, 1958; W. S. Clark, *The Irish Stage in the County Towns, 1720–1800*, Oxford, 1965; and E. Sheldon, *Thomas Sheridan of Smock-Alley*, Princeton, 1967.

For actors and acting, see, in addition to the entry for David Garrick below (pp. 594–5), the lives of J. P. Kemble by H. Baker, 1942, of Mrs. Siddons by Yvonne Ffrench, rev. 1954, and R. B. Manvell, 1970, and Mrs. Jordan by B. Fothergill, 1965. A. S. Downer discusses styles of acting in 'Nature to Advantage Dressed', *PMLA* lviii, 1943. See also E. R. Wasserman, 'The Sympathetic Imagination in Eighteenth-Century Theories of Acting', *JEGP* xlvi, 1947, and G. Taylor, 'The Just Delineation of the Passions', in *Essays on the Eighteenth-Century English Stage*, ed. K. Richards and P. Thomson, 1972.

Much information about the physical appearance of theatres and theatrical decor may be found in the more general studies of the theatre, notably R. Leacroft, *The Development of the English Playhouse*, 1973; R. Southern, *Changeable Scenery*, 1952; S. Rosenfeld, *A Short History of Scene Design in Great Britain*, 1973; and vol. xxxv of the Greater London Council's *Survey of London* (general editor F. H. W. Sheppard): *The Theatre Royal, Drury Lane, and the Royal Opera House, Covent Garden*, 1970. See also two publications called *The Georgian Playhouse*, one a study by R. Southern, 1948, the other the detailed catalogue by I. Mackintosh and G. Ashton of a major Arts Council exhibition in London in 1975. There is an interesting essay by R. Thomas, 'Contemporary Taste in the Stage Decorations of London Theaters, 1770–1800', *MP* xlii, 1944.

J. Loftis, in *The Politics of Drama in Augustan England*, Oxford, 1963, deals with the period before 1740. Related topics are dealt with by J. B. Kern, *Dramatic Satire in the Age of Walpole 1720–1750*, Arnes, Iowa, 1976, and L. W. Conolly, *The Censorship of English Drama 1737–1824*, San Marino, Calif., 1976. F. W. Bateson, *English Comic Drama, 1700–1750*, Oxford, 1929, and L. Hughes, *A Century of English Farce*, Princeton, 1956, are useful surveys in their fields. More material on comedy will be found in the entries for R. B. Sheridan and Oliver Goldsmith below (pp. 641–2 and 600). On sentimental drama, the classic study is that of E. Bernbaum, *The Drama of Sensibility, 1696–1780*, Boston, 1915; but his work has been superseded to some extent by A. Sherbo, *English Sentimental Drama*, East Lansing, Mich., 1957. An interesting article, by R. D. Hume (in *Studies in Change and Revolution*, ed. P. J. Korshin, Menston, Yorks., 1972), questions the supposed anti-sentimental revolution achieved by Goldsmith and Sheridan. See also the entries for Richard Cumberland and Hugh Kelly below (pp. 586 and 619–20). Studies of tragic drama tend to be more concerned with critical theory than with the theatre, as in E. Hnatko's essay, 'The Failure of Eighteenth-Century Tragedy', *SEL* xi, 1971. Gothic plays from Horace Walpole onwards, are surveyed by B. Evans in *Gothic Drama*, Berkeley, 1947. Though J. W. Donohue's *Dramatic Character in the English Romantic Age*, Princeton, 1970, is mainly concerned with a later period than ours, several sections are illuminating on play-writing and acting in the mid-eighteenth century and it has a very useful bibliography.

An important theatrical institution of the period is discussed in M. E. Knapp, *Prologues and Epilogues of the Eighteenth Century*, New Haven, 1961. P. Kaufman considers the reading of plays in an article in the *Bulletin of the New York Public Library* lxxiii, 1969.

Much of the discussion about the place of Shakespeare in the mid-century theatre is naturally related to Garrick, but among more general studies G. C. D. Odell, *Shakespeare from Betterton to Irving*, 2 vols., New York, 1920, and G. C. Branam, *Eighteenth-Century Adaptations of Shakespearean Tragedy*, Berkeley, 1956, are both helpful. See also A. C. Sprague, *Shakespeare and the Actors*, Cambridge, Mass., 1944, B. Joseph, *The Tragic Actor*, 1959, and D. Bartholomeusz, *Macbeth and the Players*, Cambridge, 1969. C. B. Hogan has compiled *Shakespeare in the Theatre 1701–1800: A Record of Performances in London*, 2 vols., Oxford, 1952–7. On this there is an acute comment by A. H. Scouten, 'The Increase in Popularity of Shakespeare's Plays in the Eighteenth Century: a Caveat for Interpreters of Stage History', *Shakespeare Quarterly* vii, 1956. J. R. Sutherland discusses Shakespeare's imitators at this time, *MLR* xxviii, 1933. Critical attitudes are helpfully illustrated in a study by R. G. Noyes, *The Thespian Mirror. Shakespeare in the Eighteenth-Century Novel*, Providence, 1953. See also Noyes's further study on Restoration and eighteenth-century tragedy, *The Neglected Muse*, Providence, 1958.

English theatre music in the eighteenth century is discussed at length in a book of that title by R. Fiske, 1973; but see also chapters ii and iii of E. W. White, *The Rise of English Opera*, 1951; D. Nalbach, *The King's Theatre, 1704–1867: London's First Italian Opera House*, 1972; and T. J. Walsh, *Opera in Dublin, 1705–1797*, Dublin 1973. There is a survey of ballad opera by E. M. Gagey, New York, 1937, and the achievement of the greatest composer to set English texts in our period is anatomized by W. Dean in *Handel's Dramatic Oratorios and Masques*, 1959.

3. HISTORY

The best general study is still J. B. Black's *The Art of History*, 1926, but L. Braudy's *Narrative Form in History and Fiction*, Princeton, 1970, raises more interesting theoretical issues. T. P. Peardon, *The Transition in English Historical Writing 1760–1830*, New York, 1933, provides a competent survey, though it does not compare with a work like F. Meinecke's *Die Entstehung des Historismus*, 2 vols., Munich, 1936, in which chaps. v and vi are devoted to English and Scottish writers. The background of the Scottish historians is well treated by R. L. Meek in *Social Science and the Ignoble Savage*, Cambridge, 1976, but see also G. Bryson's *Man and Society: the Scottish Inquiry of the Eighteenth Century*, Princeton, 1945, and the essay by P. Stein on law and society in eighteenth-century Scottish thought, in *Scotland in the Age of Improvement*, ed. N. T. Phillipson and R. Mitchison, Edinburgh, 1970. A. L. Owen draws on some of the minor historical writers in *The Famous Druids*, Oxford, 1962. J. W. Johnson's study, *The Formation of English Neo-Classical Thought*, Princeton, 1967, contains much that is relevant to the development of historiography. Three further essays should be mentioned: K. Stewart, 'Ancient Poetry as History in the Eighteenth Century', *JHI* xix, 1958; H. Trevor-Roper, 'The Historical Philosophy of the Enlightenment', *Studies on Voltaire and the Eighteenth Century* xxvii, 1963; and T. R. Preston, 'Historiography as Art in Eighteenth-Century England', *TSLL* xi, 1969. For literary history, see R. Wellek, *The Rise of English Literary History*, Chapel Hill, 1941, and L. Lipking, *The Ordering of the Arts in Eighteenth-Century England*, Princeton, 1970.

4. TRAVEL AND BIOGRAPHY

As a guide to the very numerous texts available, E. G. Cox's *Reference Guide to the Literature of Travel*, 3 vols., Seattle, 1935–49, is indispensable. On the Grand Tour, see W. E. Mead, *The Grand Tour in the Eighteenth Century*, Boston, 1914, P. F. Kirby, *The Grand Tour in Italy*, New York, 1952, and particularly L. Schudt, *Italienreisen im 17. und 18. Jahrhundert*, Vienna, 1959. See also the essay by J. Burke, 'The Grand Tour and the Rule of Taste', *Studies in the Eighteenth Century*, ed. R. F. Brissenden, Canberra, 1968. Ideas on the significance of travel in this period are developed by P. Fussell in *The Rhetorical World of Augustan Humanism*, Oxford, 1965, by D. Greene in *Samuel Johnson*, New York, 1970, and by C. McIntosh, in *The Choice of Life*, New Haven, 1973.

Biographical writing is surveyed by M. Longaker, in *English Biography in the Eighteenth Century*, Philadelphia, 1931, and by D. A. Stauffer in *The Art of Biography in Eighteenth-Century England*, 2 vols., Princeton, 1941. More selective surveys may be found in E. Johnson, *One Mighty Torrent: the Drama of Biography*, New York, 1937, and in R. D. Altick, *Lives and Letters: a History of Literary Biography in England and America*, New York, 1965. The volume edited by P. B. Daghlian, *Essays in Eighteenth-Century Biography*, Bloomington, 1968, provides some incisive analysis, and an excellent bibliography (by R. D. Kelley). There is a useful essay by F. Brady, 'The Strategies of Biography and some Eighteenth-Century Examples', in *Literary Theory and Structure*, ed. F. Brady, J. Palmer, and M. Price, New Haven, 1973.

On autobiography, the study by J. N. Morris, *Versions of the Self*, New York, 1966, is helpful, and there is a good account of eighteenth-century material in R. A. Fothergill, *Private Chronicles: a Study of English Diaries*, 1974. Anecdotes are discussed, briefly, by F. P. Wilson, in 'Table Talk', *HLQ* iv, 1941, by R. Folkenflik, 'Johnson's Art of Anecdote', and P. J. Korshin, '*Ana*-Books and Intellectual Biography in the Eighteenth Century', both in *Studies in Eighteenth Century Culture* iii, 1973.

J. L. Clifford has edited some important materials in his *Biography as an Art*, New York, 1962. He considers his own experience as a biographer in *From Puzzles to Portraits*, Chapel Hill, 1970. W. Matthews has compiled annotated bibliographies of *British Diaries*, Berkeley, 1950, and of *British Autobiographies*, Berkeley, 1955.

Of the Methodist autobiographies mentioned in the text, John Nelson's *Journal* was first published in Bristol, 1767, and later included in T. Jackson's *Lives of the Early Methodist Preachers*, 3rd edn., 1865–6, vol. i; *An Account of the Life and Dealings of God with Silas Told* first appeared in 1786, and was last reprinted in 1954; George Story's *Life* is included in T. Jackson's *Lives*, vol. iii in the 1st edn., 1837–8, vol. v in the 3rd edn., 1865–6.

5. Essays, Letters, Dialogues, and Speeches

Periodical Essays: The essays discussed in Chap. IX (except for the *Hypochondriack*) are most readily obtained in the early nineteenth-century collections of *British Essayists*, notably those of A. Chalmers (45 vols., 1817), L. T. Berguer (45 vols., 1823), and R. Lynam (30 vols., 1827). There is an excellent range of material in James Harrison's *British Classics*, 8 vols., 1796–7. For editions of the *Rambler*, the *Idler*, and *The Citizen of the World*, see under Johnson and Goldsmith. The *Hypochondriack* has been edited by M. Bailey, 2 vols., Stanford, 1928, reissued 1951.

There are historical surveys of the periodical essay from the *Rambler* onwards in H. Walker, *The English Essay and Essayists*, 1915, G. S. Marr, *The Periodical Essayists of the Eighteenth Century*, 1923, and W. Graham, *English Literary Periodicals*, New York, 1930. More generally instructive, in spite of the limitation of approach dictated by his thesis, is the excellent book by R. D. Mayo, *The English Novel in the Magazines 1740–1815*, Evanston, 1962. There is a detailed study of the *Mirror* and the *Lounger* by H. W. Drescher, *Themen und Formen des periodischen Essays im späten 18. Jahrhundert*, Frankfurt, 1971.

Useful studies of specialized aspects of the subject include M. R. Watson's *Magazine Serials and the Essay Tradition 1746–1820*, Baton Rouge, 1956, and 'The Printing History of *The World*', by G. P. Winship, Jr., in *Studies in the Early English Periodical*, Chapel Hill, 1957: a volume that also contains an essay on the development of the periodical press from 1700 to 1760 by the editor, R. P. Bond. Reviewing is discussed by E. A. Bloom in 'Labors of the Learned: Neoclassic Book Reviewing Aims and Techniques', *SP* liv, 1957. The political aspect is illustrated by R. D. Spector in *English Literary Periodicals and the*

Climate of Opinion during the Seven Years' War, The Hague, 1966. C. L. Carlson has written a history of the *Gentleman's Magazine*, Providence, 1938, and B. C. Nangle has compiled an index of contributors and articles in the *Monthly Review*, First Series, 1749–89, Oxford, 1934.

Letters: There are two major studies: W. H. Irving, *The Providence of Wit in the English Letter Writers*, Durham, N.C., 1955; and the collection of essays edited by H. Anderson, P. B. Daghlian, and I. Ehrenpreis, *The Familiar Letter in the Eighteenth Century*, Lawrence, Kansas, 1966.

Dialogues: Although there is a survey by E. Merrill, *The Dialogue in English Literature*, New York, 1911, it is rather slight. Far more helpful is the discussion of Fielding's use of dialogue in H. K. Miller, *Essays on Fielding's Miscellanies: a Commentary on Volume One*, Princeton, 1961. There is a stimulating essay also in D. Davie's 'Berkeley and the Style of Dialogue', in *The English Mind*, ed. H. S. Davies and G. Watson, Cambridge, 1964. Modern readers can still profit from Richard Hurd's classic discussion of the genre, 'Preface on the Manner of Writing Dialogues', in *Moral and Political Dialogues*, vol. i, 1765 and subsequent editions. On the 'dialogue of the dead', there is a good modern survey by F. M. Keener, New York, 1973. See also J. S. Egilsrud, *Le 'Dialogue des Morts' dans les littératures française, allemande et anglaise (1644–1789)*, Paris, 1934.

Sermons: There are two general studies: J. Downey's *The Eighteenth-Century Pulpit*, Oxford, 1969, and R. P. Lessenich's *Elements of Pulpit Oratory in Eighteenth-Century England (1660–1800)*, Cologne, 1972. See also N. Sykes, *Church and State in England in the Eighteenth Century*, 1934, in which chap. iv is devoted to a discussion of the parson's performance of his duties.

Other Speeches: In the absence of any general study of the elements of political oratory in the period, the student may derive some hints from U. Schindel's study *Demosthenes im 18. Jahrhundert*, Munich, 1963, and from J. T. Boulton, *The Language of Politics in the Age of Wilkes and Burke*, 1963.

6. THE NOVEL

The standard collections of the novel are *The Novelist's Magazine*, 23 vols., 1780–8, and *Ballantyne's Novelist's Library*,

10 vols., 1821–4, to which Sir Walter Scott wrote introductions later collected as *Lives of the Novelists*.

The fullest history of the English novel is the survey by E. A. Baker: vol. iii, 1929, vol. iv, 1930, and vol. v, 1934, relate to this period. J. M. S. Tompkins, *The Popular Novel in England 1770–1800*, 1932, provides a spirited supplement, and is admirably organized. Perhaps the most influential study of the novel in recent years is I. Watt's *The Rise of the Novel*, 1957. Two other important studies are those by A. D. McKillop, *The Early Masters of English Fiction*, Lawrence, Kansas, 1956, and R. Paulson, *Satire and the Novel in Eighteenth-Century England*, New Haven, 1967. R. D. Mayo, in *The English Novel in the Magazines 1740–1815*, Evanston, 1962, illuminates many aspects of fiction in this period, and his book is most impressively documented. F. W. Bradbrook's *Jane Austen and her Predecessors*, Cambridge, 1966, and H. R. Steeves's *Before Jane Austen: the Shaping of the English Novel in the Eighteenth Century*, 1966, are both helpful surveys, and some interesting points are made on occasion in F. R. Karl's *The Adversary Literature*, New York, 1974, published in London, 1975, as *A Reader's Guide to the Development of the English Novel in the Eighteenth Century*. W. C. Booth's study, *The Rhetoric of Fiction*, Chicago, 1961, contains extensive discussions of eighteenth-century novels. See also his important essay, 'The Self-Conscious Narrator in Comic Fiction before *Tristram Shandy*', *PMLA* lxvii, 1952. Another aspect of the structure of fiction in the period is considered by D. Brooks in *Number and Pattern in the Eighteenth-Century Novel*, 1973.

French fiction is closely related to English fiction in this period, and studies of the French novel can be helpful. See especially G. May, *Le Dilemme du roman au XVIIIᵉ siècle*, Paris, 1963, P. R. Stewart, *Imitation and Illusion in the French Memoir-Novel, 1700–1750: the Art of Make-Believe*, New Haven, 1969, and E. Showalter, Jr., *The Evolution of the French Novel 1641–1782*, Princeton, 1972. A useful essay in this field is J. R. Foster's 'The Abbé Prévost and the English Novel', *PMLA* xlii, 1927.

The epistolary convention is surveyed in studies by G. F. Singer, Philadelphia, 1933; by C. E. Kany, who considers its beginnings in France, Italy, and Spain, Berkeley, 1937; by F. G. Black, *The Epistolary Novel in the Late Eighteenth Century*, Eugene, Oregon, 1940; and by R. A. Day, *Told in Letters: Epistolary Fiction before Richardson*, Ann Arbor, 1966. For the novel of sensibility, see W. F. Wright, *Sensibility in English Prose Fiction 1760–1814*, Urbana 1937, and the wide-ranging study by R. F. Brissenden, *Virtue in Distress: Studies in the Novel of Sentiment from Richardson to Sade*, 1974. There is an essay by E. Birkhead, 'Sentiment and Sensibility in the Eighteenth-Century Novel', *E&S* xi, 1925. See also J. R. Foster's survey, *A History of the Pre-Romantic Novel in England*, New York, 1949. The Gothic novel has been considered by E. Birkhead, *The Tale of Terror*, 1921, by E. Railo, *The Haunted Castle*, 1927, by M. Summers, *The Gothic Quest*, 1938, and by D. Varma, *The Gothic Flame*, 1957. D. J. McNutt has compiled a bibliography of criticism, *The Eighteenth-Century Gothic Novel*, Folkestone, 1975. See also the relevant parts of M. Summers's *A Gothic Bibliography*, 1941. On the picaresque, see the books by R. Alter, *Rogue's Progress*, Cambridge, Mass., 1964, and A. A. Parker, *Literature and the Delinquent. The Picaresque Novel in Spain and Europe 1599–1753*, Edinburgh, 1967. On the fable, there is a study by T. Noel, *Theories of the Fable in the Eighteenth Century*, New York, 1975. Studies on the relationship between author and reader include J. Preston's book, *The Created Self: the Reader's Role in Eighteenth-Century Fiction*, 1970, and W. Iser, *The Implied Reader*, Baltimore, 1974.

7. CRITICISM

Although G. Saintsbury's *History of Criticism*, 3 vols., Edinburgh, 1900–4, still has its points of interest for connoisseurs, it has been superseded so far as our period is concerned by the first volume of R. Wellek's *History of Modern Criticism, 1750–1950*, 1955. It is detailed and well annotated. In *Literary Criticism: a Short History*, New York, 1957, W. K. Wimsatt, Jr., and C. Brooks offer a helpful guide to the period too. Neither A. Bosker, in *Literary Criticism in the Age of Johnson*, Groningen, 1930, rev. 1953, nor J. W. H. Atkins, in *English Literary Criticism: 17th and 18th centuries*, 1951, is so satisfactory. The latter work prompted an important essay by R. S. Crane, 'On Writing the History of English Criticism, 1650–1800', *University of Toronto Quarterly* xxii, 1953. See also Crane's essay on neoclassical criticism in *Critics and Criticism*, Chicago, 1952. G. Watson's study, *The Literary Critics*, 1962, is concerned mainly in this period with Johnson and Fielding. S. K. Sen's *English Literary Criticism in the Second Half of the Eighteenth Century*,

Calcutta, 1965, is very detailed and sketches some interesting ideas.

As a guide to primary sources, J. W. Draper's *Eighteenth Century English Aesthetics: a Bibliography*, Heidelberg, 1931, is still of value. Supplementary material is provided by R. D. Havens, *MLN* xlvii, 1932, and W. D. Templeman, *MP* xxx, 1933. The best anthology of the eighteenth-century critics, with full and helpful annotations, is that by S. Elledge, *Eighteenth-Century Critical Essays*, 2 vols., Ithaca, 1961. There are smaller collections by G. W. Chapman, *Literary Criticism in England, 1660–1800*, New York, 1966, and O. Sigworth, *Criticism and Aesthetics, 1600–1800*, New York, 1971. The *WC* collection of *English Critical Essays* from the sixteenth to the eighteenth centuries, ed. E. D. Jones, includes some of the most important texts.

Studies specially concerned with the shift of taste within the period include W. J. Bate's *From Classic to Romantic: Premises of Taste in Eighteenth-Century England*, Cambridge, Mass., 1946; M. H. Abrams's *The Mirror and the Lamp: Romantic Theory and the Critical Tradition*, New York, 1953; and L. Lipking's *The Ordering of the Arts in Eighteenth-Century England*, Princeton, 1970. W. Folkierski, *Entre le classicisme et le romantisme*, Cracow, 1925, has a helpful analysis of Diderot. R. Cohen surveys a wide range of critical discussion in his fine study, *The Art of Discrimination: Thomson's 'The Seasons' and the Language of Criticism*, 1964.

Other important issues are considered by S. Elledge, 'The Background and Development in English Criticism of the Theories of Generality and Particularity', *PMLA* lxii, 1947, and by W. Jackson, *Immediacy: the Development of a Critical Concept from Addison to Coleridge*, Amsterdam, 1973. The psychological criticism of our period is surveyed by G. McKenzie, *Critical Responsiveness: a Study of the Psychological Current in Later Eighteenth-Century Criticism*, Berkeley, 1949, and by M. Kallich, *The Association of Ideas and Critical Theory in Eighteenth-Century England*, The Hague, 1970.

Any attempt to define an 'Age of Sensibility' (see N. Frye's famous essay on the subject, *ELH* xxiii, 1956, reprinted in his *Fables of Identity*, New York, 1963) entails study of a number of crucial concepts. R. S. Crane makes 'Suggestions toward a Genealogy of the "Man of Feeling"', *ELH* i, 1934, reprinted in his *The Idea of the Humanities*, Chicago, 1967, vol. i. A. R.

Humphreys discusses 'the Friend of Mankind', *RES* xxiv, 1949, and E. Erämetsä has a useful *Study of the Word 'Sentimental'*, Helsinki, 1951. The latter should be read along with S. I. Tucker's book on that 'dark ambiguous word' *Enthusiasm: a Study in Semantic Change*, Cambridge, 1972. S. M. Tave, in *The Amiable Humorist*, Chicago, 1960, provides a fresh perspective on the man of feeling, a topic also surveyed by T. R. Preston in his book *Not in Timon's Manner: Feeling, Misanthropy, and Satire in Eighteenth-Century England*, University, Ala., 1975. L. I. Bredvold sets the phenomenon in a less favourable light in *The Natural History of Sensibility*, Detroit, 1962. On genius there is a suggestive essay by H. Dieckmann, 'Diderot's Conception of Genius', *JHI* ii, 1941, and there are a number of studies of melancholy: J. W. Draper, *The Funeral Elegy and the Rise of English Romanticism*, New York, 1929, and E. M. Sickels, *The Gloomy Egoist*, New York, 1932, for example. J. F. Sena has compiled *A Bibliography of Melancholy, 1660–1800*, 1970. On the sublime, the standard work is by S. H. Monk, New York, 1935, but see also M. Nicolson, *Mountain Gloom and Mountain Glory: the Development of the Aesthetics of the Infinite*, Ithaca, 1959, and T. E. B. Wood, *The Word 'Sublime' and its Context 1650–1760*, The Hague, 1972. On the displacement of beauty in favour of sublimity, see J. Stolnitz, ' "Beauty": Some Stages in the History of an Idea', *JHI* xx, 1961, On the idea of the picturesque, see the section on the Arts, below, p. 562; and add the essay by M. Price, 'The Picturesque Moment', in *F. A. Pottle Festschrift*, 1965.

Other aspects of criticism are considered by P. W. K. Stone, *The Art of Poetry, 1750–1820: Theories of Composition and Style*, 1967, and by H. T. Swedenberg, *The Theory of Epic in England, 1650–1800*, Berkeley, 1944. D. M. Foerster illustrates the historical approach in the eighteenth century in his study, *Homer in English Criticism*, New Haven, 1947. See also the fine survey by E. R. Wasserman, *Elizabethan Poetry in the Eighteenth Century*, Urbana, 1947, and A. Johnston, *Enchanted Ground: The Study of Medieval Romance in the Eighteenth Century*, 1964. On the particular position of Shakespeare, two older studies are still of value: R. W. Babcock, *The Genesis of Shakespeare Idolatry, 1766–1799*, Chapel Hill, 1931, and H. S. Robinson, *English Shakespearian Criticism in the Eighteenth Century*, New York, 1932.

On reviewers, see E. N. Hooker, 'The Reviewers and the New Criticism, 1754–70', *PQ* xiii, 1934, and 'The Reviewers and the

New Trends in Poetry, 1754–70', *MLN* li, 1936. C. E. Jones has two articles on the *Critical Review*: *MLQ* ix, 1948 (poetry), and *MLQ* xx, 1959 (dramatic criticism).

8. CLASSICAL AND FOREIGN RELATIONS

Many titles that might be included under this heading appear in other sections, and in general these are not repeated here.

For classical scholarship, see M. L. Clarke, *Greek Studies in England 1700–1830*, Cambridge, 1945, and the second volume of R. Pfeiffer, *History of Classical Scholarship*, Oxford, 1976. There is a useful series of books by J. A. K. Thomson: *The Classical Background of English Literature*, 1948, *Classical Influences on English Poetry*, 1951, and *Classical Influences on English Prose*, 1956. Some attitudes to the Bible are examined by M. Roston in his *Prophet and Poet: the Bible and the Growth of Romanticism*, Evanston, 1965.

J. W. Johnson's study, *The Formation of English Neoclassical Thought*, Princeton, 1967, has a bearing on the intercourse between England and several European countries. So has P. Van Tieghem, *Le Préromantisme: études d'histoire littéraire européenne*, 3 vols., Paris, 1924–7.

The relations between France and Britain were very close, and a book like R. G. Saisselin's *The Rule of Reason and the Ruses of the Heart*, Cleveland, 1970, although described as 'a philosophical dictionary of classical French criticism, critics, and aesthetic issues', is readily applied to conditions on the English side of the Channel. F. C. Green's fine study, *Minuet: a Critical Survey of French and English Literary Ideas in the Eighteenth Century*, 1935, has sections on the drama, on poetry, and on the novel. See also the bibliographical catalogues compiled by J. A. R. Seguin of French works in English translation, 1731–90, 6 vols., Jersey City, 1965–8.

Voltaire is a figure of outstanding importance, and the student should consult the large series of *Studies on Voltaire and the Eighteenth Century*, ed. T. Besterman, 1955– . See also the useful study by B. N. Schilling: *Conservative England and the Case against Voltaire*, New York, 1950. C. Dédéyan has written a useful set of guides to major French authors in relation to Britain: *Voltaire et la pensée anglaise*, Paris, 1956; *Montesquieu et l'Angleterre*, Paris, 1958; and *Rousseau et la sensibilité littéraire à la fin du XVIIIᵉ siècle*,

Paris, 1967. H. Roddier's large study, *J.-J. Rousseau en Angleterre au XVIIIᵉ siécle*, Paris, 1950, is indispensable. See also J. H. Warner's articles on Rousseau in England, *PMLA* xlviii, 1933, lii, 1937, lix, 1944; also *MLN* lv, 1940. Finally, it can be instructive to read the fiercely partisan book by L. Reynaud, *Le Romantisme*, Paris, 1926, describing the corrupting effect of English and German literature upon the French in this period.

On German influences, there are useful suggestions in books by W. D. Robson-Scott, *German Travellers in England 1400–1800*, Oxford, 1953, and *The Literary Background of the Gothic Revival*, Oxford, 1965. On Scandinavia, there is the study by S. B. Hustvedt, *Ballad Criticism in Scandinavia and Great Britain during the Eighteenth Century*, New York, 1916. The influence of *Don Quixote* is examined by S. Staves in an essay in *Comparative Literature* xxiv, 1972. R. D. S. Jack has a useful chapter on the eighteenth century in his study, *The Italian Influence on Scottish Literature*, Edinburgh, 1972. There is a good survey by R. Marshall, *Italy in English Literature 1755–1815*, New York, 1934, and another by B. H. Stern, *The Rise of Romantic Hellenism in English Literature 1732–1786*, Menasha, 1940. T. J. B. Spencer covers some of the same ground in his *Fair Greece, Sad Relic: Literary Philhellenism from Shakespeare to Byron*, 1954.

Further afield, there is an account by R. Schwab of the beginnings of oriental studies in Europe, *La Renaissance orientale*, Paris, 1950. P. J. Marshall has edited a useful set of documents in *The British Discovery of Hinduism in the Eighteenth Century*, Cambridge, 1970. It contains essays by Alexander Dow, Warren Hastings, Sir William Jones, and others. On China, see W. W. Appleton, *A Cycle of Cathay. The Chinese Vogue in England*, New York, 1951.

Transatlantic relations have been considered by A. Hook, *Scotland and America: a study of Cultural Relations, 1750–1835*, Glasgow, 1975.

9. LANGUAGE

The most convenient bibliography is R. W. Bailey and D. M. Burton, *English Stylistics: a Bibliography*, Cambridge, Mass., 1968: there is a section on neoclassicism to 1800. Contemporary material is listed in R. C. Alston's *Bibliography of the English Language from the Invention of Printing to the Year 1800*, 10 vols.,

Leeds, 1965–72; rev., Ilkley, 1974. Many of the titles listed here have been reprinted, Menston, 1967–   .

There are a number of good surveys of the history of the English language. A recent one is that by B. M. H. Strang, *A History of English*, 1970. An excellent short introduction to our period is A. S. Collins's 'Language 1660–1784', in *From Dryden to Johnson*, 1957, part of the *Pelican Guide to English Literature*, ed. B. Ford. More specialized studies of interest to students of literature include I. Michael, *English Grammatical Categories and the Tradition to 1800*, Cambridge, 1970, and R. S. Sugg, Jr., 'The Mood of Eighteenth-Century English Grammar', *PQ* xliii, 1964. R. Quirk supplies 'A Glimpse of Eighteenth-Century Prescriptivism' in *The Linguist and the English Language*, 1974. H. Aarsleff, *The Study of Language in England, 1780–1860*, Princeton, 1967, has a good chapter on Sir William Jones.

Samuel Johnson's *Dictionary of the English Language*, 2 vols., 1755, is a major linguistic landmark in the period, and it is admirably assessed in J. H. Sledd and G. J. Kolb, *Dr. Johnson's Dictionary: Essays in the Biography of a Book*, Chicago, 1955. See also G. E. Noyes, 'The Critical Reception of Johnson's *Dictionary* in the Latter Eighteenth Century', *MP* lii, 1955. Its predecessors are considered by De Witt T. Starnes and G. E. Noyes in *The English Dictionary from Cawdrey to Johnson, 1604–1755*, Chapel Hill, 1946. An important aspect of the function of dictionaries is examined by N. E. Osselton in *Branded Words in English Dictionaries before Johnson*, Groningen, 1958. Although the author restricts his study of proscription to the period 1658–1749, he has some interesting pages on George Campbell's *Philosophy of Rhetoric* (1776).

Much has been written on 'correctness' in this period. S. Leonard's *The Doctrine of Correctness in English Usage 1700–1800*, Madison, 1929, has been described as 'a book full of interesting data and false conclusions'. It should be supplemented by S. Elledge's admirable study, 'The Naked Science of Language, 1747–1786', *S. H. Monk Festschrift*, 1967. J. H. Neumann has an article on 'Chesterfield and the Standard of Usage in English', *MLQ* vii, 1946, and there are three interesting studies by W. Matthews, 'Some Eighteenth-Century Phonetic Spellings', *RES* xii, 1936; 'Polite Speech in the Eighteenth Century', *English* i, 1937; and 'Some Eighteenth-Century Vulgarisms', *RES* xiii, 1937. See also K. G. Hornbeak, *The Complete Letter-Writer in*

English 1568–1800, Northampton, Mass., 1934, and N. E. Osselton, 'Formal and Informal Spelling in the Eighteenth Century', *English Studies* xliv, 1963. E. K. Sheldon examines Boswell's English in the 'London Journal', *PMLA* lxxi, 1956. On pronunciation, see B. Holmberg, *On the Concept of Standard English and the History of Modern English Pronunciation*, Lund, 1964.

There are a number of studies of prose style, and a useful introduction is provided by B. Wackwitz, *Die Theorie des Prosastils im England des 18. Jahrhunderts*, Hamburg, 1962. W. K. Wimsatt has written two standard works on Johnson, *The Prose Style of Samuel Johnson*, New Haven, 1941, and *Philosophic Words: a Study of Style and Meaning in the 'Rambler' and 'Dictionary' of Samuel Johnson*, New Haven, 1948. See also the two articles by W. V. Reynolds in *RES*, 'Johnson's Opinions on Prose Style', ix, 1933, and 'The Reception of Johnson's Prose Style', xi, 1935. William Kenney examines the 'energetick' style in relation to Addison and Johnson, *Studia Neophilologica* xxxiii, 1961. D. J. Greene and F. Brady contribute a pair of articles on 'Tory' and 'Whig' prose styles to the *Bulletin of the New York Public Library* lxvi, 1962. More generally, useful points are made in J. R. Sutherland's essay, 'Some Aspects of Eighteenth-Century Prose', *D. Nichol Smith Festschrift*, 1945, and I. A. Gordon's book, *The Movement of English Prose*, 1966.

Two books by S. I. Tucker are of special interest to students of the period: *Protean Shape: a Study in Eighteenth-Century Vocabulary and Usage*, London, 1967; and *Enthusiasm: a Study in Semantic Change*, Cambridge, 1972. J. Copley has produced a cautionary list of words whose meaning has changed since the eighteenth century: *Shift of Meaning*, 1961.

10. THE BOOK TRADE

For the student of literature, R. W. Chapman's essay, 'Authors and Booksellers', in vol. ii of *Johnson's England*, ed. A. S. Turberville, 1933, is an excellent introduction to the subject, as is J. A. Cochrane's biography of William Strahan, *Dr. Johnson's Printer*, 1964. A. S. Collins, *Authorship in the Days of Johnson*, 1928, is helpful on copyright, but for a more recent examination of this issue see G. Walters, 'The Booksellers in 1759 and 1774: the Battle for Literary Property', *Library* 5th ser. xxix, 1974.

A. Birrell's *Seven Lectures on the Law and History of Copyright in Books*, 1899, is still a standard work, but should be supplemented by A. W. Pollard's article, 'Some Notes on the History of Copyright in England, 1662–1774', *Library*, 4th ser. iii, 1922. On the payment of writers, see J. D. Fleeman, 'The Revenue of a Writer: Samuel Johnson's Literary Earnings', in *Studies in the Book Trade in Honour of Graham Pollard*, Oxford Bibliographical Society, *Publications*, N.S. xviii, 1975. See also P. J. Korshin, 'Types of Eighteenth-Century Literary Patronage', *ECS* vii, 1974.

The section on book production and distribution in *NCBEL* by T. Belanger and H. G. Pollard is comprehensive. Two other standard works of reference should be noted: A. Growoll and W. Eames, *Three Centuries of English Booktrade Bibliography*, New York, 1903, and H. R. Plomer *et al.*, *A Dictionary of Printers and Booksellers 1726–1775*, Oxford, 1932, reissued 1968. See also R. W. Chapman, 'Eighteenth-Century Booksellers', *Book-Collector's Quarterly* ix, 1933. R. H. Carnie and R. P. Doig supplement Plomer's Scottish entries, *Studies in Bibliography*, xii, xiv, xv, 1959, 1961–2; and R. H. Carnie has a study of source-material, 'Scottish Printers and Booksellers 1668–1775', *Bibliotheck*, iv, 1966. For Ireland, see A. R. Eager, *A Guide to Irish Bibliographical Material*, 1964.

The standard surveys of the book trade are F. A. Mumby's *The Romance of Bookselling*, 1910, revised as *Publishing and Bookselling*, 1930, and last revised 1974 (by I. Norrie in part ii). See also M. Plant, *The English Book Trade: an Economic History*, 1939, rev. 1965. Among the histories of particular publishers, H. Carter's *a History of the Oxford University Press*, vol. i (to the year 1780), Oxford, 1975, is outstanding in its fullness. C. J. Longman and J. E. Chandler have provided a register of books published by one firm, in *The House of Longman, 1724–1800, a Bibliographical History*, 1936. Much useful material is presented in E. E. Kent's study, *Goldsmith and his Booksellers*, Ithaca, 1933, and this may be supplemented by L. M. Knapp's article, 'Ralph Griffiths, Author and Publisher, 1746–50', *Library*, 4th ser. xx, 1939. An important witness in the period itself is James Lackington, whose *Memoirs* were first published in 1791.

R. M. Wiles, *Serial Publication in England before 1750*, Cambridge 1957, has considerable relevance to the period after 1750 also. On printing, much information is conveniently accessible in

W. T. Berry and H. E. Poole, *Annals of Printing*, 1966. Aesthetic aspects are admirably discussed in B. H. Bronson's pamphlet, *Printing as an Index of Taste in Eighteenth-Century England*, New York, 1958, rev. 1963. Two studies of famous printers are recommended: William Bennett, *John Baskerville, the Birmingham Printer*, 2 vols., 1937–9; and Johnson Ball, *William Caslon, 1693–1766*, Kineton, 1973.

See also under Robert Dodsley and Samuel Richardson below (pp. 587 and 635–7).

III. BACKGROUND

1. POLITICAL HISTORY

In *The New Cambridge Modern History*, vols. vii and viii relate to this period: *The Old Regime 1713–1763*, ed. J. O. Lindsay, Cambridge, 1957; and *The American and French Revolutions 1763–1793*, ed. A. Goodwin, Cambridge, 1965. Associated with this work is *A Bibliography of Modern History*, ed. J. Roach, 1968, which is helpful for many aspects of the period. See also the two relevant volumes of the *Oxford History of England*: B. Williams, *The Whig Supremacy, 1714–1760*, Oxford, 1939, rev. 1962, and J. S. Watson, *The Reign of George III, 1760–1815*, Oxford, 1960. For a concise narrative, J. H. Plumb's *England in the Eighteenth Century*, Harmondsworth, 1950, rev. 1963, may be consulted. J. B. Owen's *The Eighteenth Century 1714–1815*, 1974, reflects the views of the school of Sir Lewis Namier, and even the non-specialist needs to pay attention to Namier's work, in particular *The Structure of Politics at the Accession of George III*, 2 vols., 1929, *England in the Age of the American Revolution*, 1930, and *Personalities and Powers*, 1955. See also the attractively written books by H. Butterfield, *George III, Lord North, and the People, 1779–1780*, and *King George III and the Politicians*, Oxford, 1953. Two other books which are helpful in creating a sense of the political climate are K. G. Feiling's *The Second Tory Party, 1714–1832*, Oxford, 1938, and A. S. Foord's *His Majesty's Opposition, 1714–1830*, Oxford, 1964. More radical political activity is analysed by I. R. Christie in *Wilkes, Wyvill and Reform: the Parliamentary Reform Movement in British Politics 1760–1785*, 1962. See also S. Maccoby, *English Radicalism 1762–1785*, 1955, and G. Rudé,

Wilkes and Liberty, Oxford, 1962. E. Halévy's *The Growth of Philosophic Radicalism*, Paris, 1901–4, English translation by M. Morris, 1928, is helpful for its approach to Bentham, the subject of the first part. C. Robbins, in *The Eighteenth-Century Commonwealthsman*, Cambridge, Mass., 1959, emphasizes continuities with the seventeenth century.

R. A. Smith's *Eighteenth-Century English Politics: Patrons and Place-Hunters*, New York, 1973, is a useful guide to recent studies. Anthologies of eighteenth-century political texts are provided by J. Hart, *Political Writers of Eighteenth-Century England*, New York, 1964, and by H. T. Dickinson, *Politics and Literature in the Eighteenth Century*, 1974.

One literary study deserves particular mention here: J. T. Boulton's *Arbitrary Power: an Eighteenth-Century Obsession*, Nottingham, 1967, reprinted in *Studies in Burke and his Time* ix, 1968.

The political aspect of newspapers is surveyed by R. R. Rea, *The English Press in Politics 1760–1774*, and by L. Werkmeister, *The London Daily Press 1772–1792*, both published in Lincoln, Nebr., 1963. There are helpful bibliographical essays in each. R. L. Haig's study of one daily newspaper, *The Gazetteer, 1735–1797*, Carbondale, 1960, forms an indispensable introduction to the whole field. A. Aspinall, *Politics and the Press* c. *1780–1850*, 1949, should also be consulted.

2. SOCIAL HISTORY

Every aspect of social life in the period is considered in *Johnson's England: an Account of the Life and Manners of his Age*, ed. A. S. Turberville, 2 vols., Oxford, 1933. Another collection of essays, *Aristocratic Government and Society in Eighteenth-Century England*, ed. D. A. Baugh, New York, 1975, provides through its useful bibliography a guide to more recent studies.

Among the surveys available, M. D. George's *London Life in the Eighteenth Century*, 1925, and *England in Transition: Life and Work in the Eighteenth Century*, 1953, are of basic importance, but a more recent approach is illustrated by G. Rudé, *Hanoverian London, 1714–1808*, 1971. A. Parreaux makes good use of literary evidence in his *Daily Life in England in the Reign of George III*, 1969 (originally published in French, 1966). Two popular studies by C. Hibbert are well documented: *The Road to Tyburn*, 1957, and *King Mob*, 1958 (on the Gordon Riots, 1780). For society outside London, see E. Hughes, *North Country Life in the Eighteenth Century*, 2 vols., 1952–65, and G. E. Mingay, *English Landed Society in the Eighteenth Century*, 1963. Another social class is well surveyed by J. J. Hecht, *The Domestic Servant Class in Eighteenth-Century England*, 1956.

Ireland may be approached through two books by C. Maxwell: *Dublin under the Georges, 1714–1830*, 1936, rev. 1956, and *Country and Town in Ireland under the Georges*, 1940. There is an attractive sketch by M. Craig, *Dublin 1660–1860*, 1952, rev. Dublin, 1969. Scottish society is admirably surveyed by T. C. Smout in *A History of the Scottish People, 1560–1830*, 1969, with which may be read the suggestive short study by D. Daiches, *The Paradox of Scottish Culture: the Eighteenth-Century Experience*, 1964. See also the essays collected by N. T. Phillipson and R. Mitchison, *Scotland in the Age of Improvement*, Edinburgh, 1970. An important work of reference in this context is D. D. McElroy's *Scotland's Age of Improvement. A Survey of Eighteenth-Century Literary Clubs and Societies*, Washington, 1969.

Other aspects of social life are considered in R. W. Malcolmson's *Popular Recreations in English Society, 1700–1850*, Cambridge, 1973, and in essays by A. W. Coats, 'Changing Attitudes to Labour in the Mid-Eighteenth Century', *Economic History Review*, 2nd ser. xi, 1958; E. P. Thompson, 'Time, Work-Discipline, and Industrial Capitalism', *Past and Present* xxxviii, 1967; J. Viner, 'Man's Economic Status', in *Man versus Society in Eighteenth-Century Britain*, ed. J. L. Clifford, Cambridge, 1968; and J. M. Beattie, 'The Pattern of Crime in England, 1600–1800', *Past and Present* lxii, 1974. The essays by Coats and Thompson are reprinted in *Essays in Social History*, ed. M. W. Flinn and T. C. Smout, Oxford, 1974.

References to costume in eighteenth-century writings can sometimes puzzle the uninitiated reader, who should consult C. W. Cunnington and P. Cunnington, *Handbook of English Costume in the Eighteenth Century*, 1957, rev. 1972. See also I. Brooke, *Dress and Undress: the Restoration and Eighteenth Century*, 1958.

References to London's pleasure gardens, and to the various institutions at Bath, can best be elucidated by, respectively, W. Wroth and A. E. Wroth, *The London Pleasure Gardens of the Eighteenth Century*, 1896, and A. Barbeau, *Life and Letters at Bath in the Eighteenth Century*, 1904. The latter includes a good bibliography of earlier material.

3. Education

The relevant parts of H. G. Armytage's survey, *Four Hundred Years of English Education*, Cambridge, 1964, rev. 1970, and of J. Lawson and H. Silver, *A Social History of Education in England*, 1973, should be consulted. Special aspects are considered by M. G. Jones, *The Charity School Movement*, Cambridge, 1938, and by R. S. Tompson, *Classics or Charity? The Dilemma of the 18th Century Grammar School*, Manchester, 1971. The role of the dissenters is examined by N. Hans, *New Trends in Education in the Eighteenth Century*, 1951, and by J. W. Ashley Smith, *The Birth of Modern Education: the Contribution of the Dissenting Academies 1660–1800*, 1954. Rousseau's contribution to education is best surveyed by H. Roddier, *Rousseau en Angleterre*, Paris, 1950. See also William Gilpin, below (p. 598).

Attitudes to children are admirably surveyed by J. H. Plumb, 'The New World of Children in Eighteenth-Century England', *Past and Present* lxvii, 1975. The standard survey of publishing for children is by F. J. Harvey Darton, *Children's Books in England*, Cambridge, 1932, rev. 1958. In view of the special position of John Newbery in this field, the reader should consult the book on him by C. Welsh, *A Bookseller in the Last Century*, 1885 (inadequate, but still indispensable), and the bibliography by W. Noblett, Wormley, Herts., 1973.

C. Wordsworth's two books on the universities are informative: *Social Life at the English Universities in the Eighteenth Century*, Cambridge, 1874, was abridged by R. B. Johnson as *The Undergraduate*, 1928; *Scholae Academicae*, Cambridge, 1877, gives an account of university studies. There are several works on particular institutions, notably C. E. Mallet's *History of the University of Oxford*, vol. iii, Oxford, 1927 (see also A. D. Godley's *Oxford in the Eighteenth Century*, 1908); D. A. Winstanley's *Unreformed Cambridge*, Cambridge, 1935; C. Maxwell's *History of Trinity College Dublin*, Dublin, 1946; D. B. Horn's *Short History of the University of Edinburgh 1556–1889*, Edinburgh, 1967; J. D. Mackie's history of the University of Glasgow, Glasgow, 1954; and J. M. Bulloch's history of the University of Aberdeen, 1895. An interesting recent study is the lecture by L. S. Sutherland, *The University of Oxford in the Eighteenth Century. A Reconsideration*, Oxford, 1973.

4. Religion

N. Sykes, *Church and State in England in the Eighteenth Century*, Cambridge, 1934, is a standard survey. For Methodism there is a comparable survey edited by R. Davies and G. Rupp, *A History of the Methodist Church of Great Britain*, vol. i, 1965. See also under John and Charles Wesley, below, pp. 653–5, but add the studies by T. B. Shepherd, *Methodism and the Literature of the Eighteenth Century*, 1940; and R. F. Wearmouth, *Methodism and the Common People of the Eighteenth Century*, 1945; also A. M. Lyles's *Methodism Mocked: the Satiric Reaction to Methodism in the Eighteenth Century*, 1960. R. N. Stromberg's *Religious Liberalism in Eighteenth-Century England*, 1954, should be consulted, as should A. Lincoln's *Some Political and Social Ideas of English Dissent, 1763–1800*, Cambridge, 1938. For Scotland, see A. L. Drummond and J. Bulloch, *The Scottish Church 1688–1843. The Age of the Moderates*, Edinburgh, 1973.

D. H. M. Davies, *Worship and Theology in England from Watts and Wesley to Maurice, 1690–1850*, Princeton, 1961, surveys its subject well. See also R. A. Knox's *Enthusiasm. A Chapter in the History of Religion with Special Reference to the XVIIth and XVIIIth Centuries*, Oxford, 1950.

For preaching, see the section on sermons, above, p. 545. In *The Polished Shaft: Studies in the Purpose and Influence of the Christian Writer in the Eighteenth Century*, 1950, W. E. M. Brown does not quite fulfil the promise of his splendid title, but provides a helpful approach to several writers, including James Hervey of the *Meditations among the Tombs*, 1746–7.

5. Philosophy and Science

Although some of its judgements are no longer acceptable, Sir Leslie Stephen's *English Thought in the Eighteenth Century*, 2 vols., 1876, is an indispensable survey, taking into account a wide range of writers interesting to the student of literature. His *English Literature and Society in the Eighteenth Century*, 1907, is also still worth consulting. B. Willey's *Eighteenth Century Background*, 1940, is on a much smaller scale, but is an attractive introduction to the field. It should be read along with a book with a rather different approach, G. R. Cragg's *Reason and Authority in the Eighteenth Century*, Cambridge, 1964.

The paramount influence of John Locke is of particular importance for the study of literature, and K. MacLean's survey, *John Locke and English Literature of the Eighteenth Century*, New Haven, 1936, is helpful.

On the influential movement of thought known as the Enlightenment, the basic study is E. Cassirer's *The Philosophy of the Enlightenment*, originally published in 1932, and translated by F. C. A. Koelln and J. P. Pettegrove, Princeton, 1951. There is a lively and elaborate study by P. Gay, *The Enlightenment: an Interpretation*, 2 vols., New York, 1966–9. The long bibliographical essays at the end of each volume provide an admirable introduction to the literature of the subject. The compact survey by N. Hampson, *The Enlightenment*, Harmondsworth, 1968, is useful, as is the study by A. C. Chitnis, *The Scottish Enlightenment: a Social History*, 1976.

A more literary approach is adopted by C. Becker's *The Heavenly City of the Eighteenth-Century Philosophers*, New Haven, 1932, and by L. I. Bredvold in his somewhat partisan study, *The Brave New World of the Enlightenment*, Ann Arbor, 1961. The related topic of primitivism is surveyed, entertainingly, by C. B. Tinker in his *Nature's Simple Plan*, Princeton, 1922, and by L. Whitney in *Primitivism and the Idea of Progress in English Popular Literature of the Eighteenth Century*, Baltimore, 1934. See also the essays on Scottish primitivists by R. H. Pearce, *ELH* xii, 1945, and D. M. Foerster, *PQ* xxix, 1950. Another aspect is well treated by C. Vereker, *Eighteenth Century Optimism*, Liverpool, 1967.

On science, there is a good survey by R. E. Schofield, *Mechanism and Materialism. British Natural Philosophy in an Age of Reason*, Princeton, 1970. Schofield has also written a study of the Lunar Society of Birmingham, Oxford, 1963. See also A. Wolf, *A History of Science, Technology and Philosophy in the Eighteenth Century*, 1938, rev. 1952. Joseph Black's chemical researches figure prominently in A. L. Donovan's interesting book, *Philosophical Chemistry in the Scottish Enlightenment*, Edinburgh, 1975. On James Hutton, see the study by E. B. Bailey, *James Hutton, the Founder of Modern Geology*, Amsterdam, 1967. There is a convenient selection from Hutton's writings, together with John Playfair's memoir, in *Contributions to the History of Geology*, ed. G. W. White, vol. v, Darien, Conn., 1970.

6. THE ARTS

English Art 1714–1800, by J. Burke, Oxford, 1976 (vol. ix of *The Oxford History of English Art*), is an excellent survey, with much to interest the student of literature. See also the relevant parts of three volumes of *The Pelican History of Art*: E. K. Waterhouse, *Painting in Britain 1530 to 1790*, 1953; J. Summerson, *Architecture in Britain 1530 to 1830*, 1953; and M. Whinney, *Sculpture in Britain 1530 to 1830*, 1964.

Movements of taste are surveyed in B. Sprague Allen, *Tides in English Taste 1619–1800*, 2 vols., Cambridge, Mass., 1937. On a smaller scale, J. Steegman, *The Rule of Taste from George I to George IV*, 1936, is helpful, and E. F. Carritt, *A Calendar of English Taste from 1600 to 1800*, 1949, collects a wide range of material. See also an essay by O. F. Sigworth, 'The Four Styles of a Decade (1740–1750)', *Bulletin of the New York Public Library* lxiv, 1960. E. K. Waterhouse's short book, *Three Decades of British Art 1740–1770*, Philadelphia, 1965, offers a suggestive thesis. R. Rosenblum, *Transformations in Late Eighteenth-Century Art*, Princeton, 1967, is an important commentary on a variety of aspects of the period. F. Klingender, *Art and the Industrial Revolution*, 1947, rev. and ed. A. Elton, 1968, contains valuable comment on the sublime and the picturesque, and on the painter Joseph Wright of Derby. (The study of Wright by B. Nicolson, 2 vols., 1968, should also be consulted.)

On the Gothic taste, see Kenneth Clark, *The Gothic Revival*, 1928, rev. 1950, and J. Macaulay, *The Gothic Revival 1745–1845*, 1975. The neoclassical movement is admirably treated by R. Rosenblum (above), but see also D. Irwin, *English Neoclassical Art: Studies in Imagination and Taste*, 1966, and H. Honour, *Neoclassicism*, Harmondsworth, 1968.

On caricature, see two works by M. D. George: *English Political Caricature*, 2 vols., Oxford, 1959, and *Hogarth to Cruikshank: Social Change in Graphic Satire*, 1967.

Relationships between literature and other arts are considered in a number of studies. The most influential is that by J. H. Hagstrum, *The Sister Arts: the Tradition of Literary Pictorialism and English Poetry from Dryden to Gray*, Chicago, 1958. There is a more recent study by J. S. Malek, *The Arts Compared: an Aspect of Eighteenth-Century British Aesthetics*, Detroit, 1974. C. B. Tinker's *Painter and Poet*, Cambridge, Mass., 1938, includes chapters on Hogarth, Reynolds, Gainsborough, and Richard Wilson. R. Paulson, in *Emblem and Expression. Meaning in English Art of the Eighteenth Century*, 1975, relates mid-century art to the tradition established by Hogarth, analogous to the work of the great novelists and of poets like Cowper. L. Lipking, *The Ordering of the Arts in Eighteenth-Century England*, Princeton, 1970, is an excellent study of such enterprises as the histories of music by Hawkins and Burney, and Warton's *History of English Poetry*. The various arts are also related in M. C. Battestin, *The Providence of Wit: Aspects of Form in Augustan Literature and the Arts*, Oxford, 1974. A more specialized study, but one with a bearing on many aspects of the art and literature of the period, is B. Smith's *European Vision and the South Pacific 1768–1850*, Oxford, 1960.

For landscape and the idea of the picturesque, three books are of basic importance: E. W. Manwaring, *Italian Landscape in Eighteenth Century England*, 1925; C. Hussey, *The Picturesque: Studies in a Point of View*, 1927; and W. J. Hipple, *The Beautiful, the Sublime, and the Picturesque in Eighteenth-Century British Aesthetic Theory*, Carbondale, 1957. C. Hussey has also written *English Gardens and Landscapes 1700–1750*, 1967, and there is a useful study by E. G. Malins, *English Landscaping and Literature, 1660–1840*, 1966. See also William Gilpin (below, pp. 597–8).

Landscape gardening has been surveyed by H. F. Clark, *The English Landscape Garden*, 1948; and there are useful books on particular gardens and gardeners, notably M. Jourdain's on William Kent, 1948, D. Stroud's on 'Capability' Brown, 1950, and K. Woodbridge's on the garden at Stourhead, 1970. There is an excellent guide by B. Jones to follies and grottoes, 1953, rev. 1974. See also William Mason and Horace Walpole (below, pp. 624–5 and 650–1). There is a good anthology of documents in the history of landscape gardening, *The Genius of the Place*, ed. J. D. Hunt, and P. Willis, 1975. Chinese influence has been examined by O. Sirén, *China and Gardens of Europe of the Eighteenth Century*, 1950.

For music, P. M. Young, *History of British Music*, 1967 (especially ch. x), provides a good survey. See also E. D. Mackerness, *A Social History of English Music*, 1964, and R. Fiske, *English Theatre Music in the Eighteenth Century*, 1973. In *Invitation to Ranelagh, 1742–1803*, 1946, M. Sands uses Ranelagh Gardens as a 'vantage point to survey the English musical world' of that period. There is an interesting special study by R. McGuinness, *English Court Odes, 1660-1820*, Oxford, 1971. See also Charles Burney and Sir John Hawkins (below, pp. 575 and 603–4). For Scottish music, see the admirable survey by H. G. Farmer, *A History of Music in Scotland*, 1947. The section on the eighteenth century is particularly helpful. The vocal music of lowland Scotland is among the topics treated in F. Collinson, *The Traditional and National Music of Scotland*, 1966.

Josiah Wedgwood's work provides an important insight into some aspects of late eighteenth-century art. See the study by W. Mankovitz, 1953, and the selection from his letters, ed. A. Finer and G. Savage, 1965.

Among the architects of the period, Robert Adam deserves special attention. Although written before the discovery of the correspondence of Robert and James Adam from Italy, *The Age of Adam* by J. Lees-Milne, 1947, is still a good general introduction, with admirable illustrations. It should be supplemented by J. Fleming's *Robert Adam and his Circle in Edinburgh and Rome*, 1962, and D. Yarwood's *Robert Adam*, 1970. *The Works in Architecture of Robert and James Adam*, originally published in 3 vols., 1773–1822, has been edited by R. Oresko, 1975. Another important architect, Sir William Chambers, is the subject of a good study by J. Harris, 1970.

IV. INDIVIDUAL AUTHORS

AKENSIDE, MARK, 1721–70

The Pleasures of Imagination. A Poem. In Three Books was published in 1744. A revised and expanded version, now entitled *The Pleasures of the Imagination*, with the beginning of a fourth book appeared posthumously in *Poems*, 1772, an edition which also contained odes additional to those already published, viz. *Odes on Several Subjects*, 1745; *An Ode to the Right Honourable The Earl of Huntingdon*, 1748; *An Ode to the Country Gentlemen of England*, 1758; *An Ode to the Late Thomas Edwards, Esq.*, 1766. His two political satires are *A British Philippic*, 1738, and *An Epistle to Curio*, 1744. 'The Virtuoso; in Imitation of Spencer's Style and Stanza' appeared anonymously in the *Gentleman's Magazine*, vii (April, 1737).

There are lives of Akenside by Johnson in *The Lives of the Poets*, by Alexander Dyce in his 'Aldine' edition of the poems, 1835, and by C. T. Houpt (Philadelphia, 1944), and there is a bibliography and appreciation by I. A. Williams in his *Seven XVIIIth Century Bibliographies*, 1924.

Mrs. Barbauld's sympathetic exposition of *The Pleasures of Imagination*, prefixed to her edition of the poem, 1794, is still one of the best critical studies of Akenside. His place in the history of ideas has received attention from M. H. Nicolson in *Newton Demands the Muse*, Princeton 1948, and from R. L. Brett in *The Third Earl of Shaftesbury*, 1951, as well as several articles: G. R. Potter, 'Mark Akenside, Prophet of Evolution', *MP* xxiv, 1926; A. O. Aldridge, 'Eclecticism of Mark Akenside's *The Pleasures of Imagination*', *JHI* v, 1944, 'Akenside and Imagination', *SP* xlii, 1945, 'Akenside and the Hierarchy of Beauty', *MLQ* viii, 1947; M. Kallich, 'The Association of Ideas and Akenside's *Pleasures of Imagination*', *MLN* lxii, 1947 (later included in Kallich's *The Association of Ideas and Critical Theory in Eighteenth-Century England*, The Hague, 1970); R. Marsh, 'Akenside and Addison: the Problem of Ideational Debt', *MP* lix, 1961 (see also Marsh's *Four Dialectical Theories of Poetry*, Chicago, 1965). The revised version of *The Pleasures of Imagination* is discussed by J. Hart in *PMLA* lxxiv, 1959.

AMORY, THOMAS, 1691?–1788

Memoirs: containing the Lives of Several Ladies of Great Britain was published in 1755, and its sequel, the far more celebrated *Life and Opinions of John Buncle, Esq.*, appeared in two parts, in 1756 and 1766.

Hazlitt devoted one of his *Round Table* essays to *John Buncle*, and Leigh Hunt includes an appreciation of the book in vol. i of *A Book for a Corner*, 1849. There is an edition of *John Buncle* by E. A. Baker, 1904. K. A. Esdaile contributed a biographical essay to *E&S* xxvi, 1940. See also G. L. Jones, 'Lessing and Amory', *German Life and Letters* xx, 1967.

ANSTEY, CHRISTOPHER, 1724–1805

Anstey's *New Bath Guide: or, Memoirs of the B——t——d Family. In a Series of Poetical Epistles*, was first published in 1766. Later, less celebrated, poems include *The Patriot*, Cambridge,

1767; *An Election Ball*, 1776; *Envy*, 1778; and *Speculation: or a Defence of Mankind*, 1780.

Anstey's poems were collected by his son, and published, with a biographical introduction, in 1808. The edition of his poems produced by J. Britton, 1830, includes useful background material. There is an edition by P. Sainsbury, 1927.

The fullest study is by W. C. Powell, *Christopher Anstey: Bath Laureate*, Philadelphia, 1944.

ARMSTRONG, JOHN, 1709–79

The Art of Preserving Health, Armstrong's most considerable poem, was published in 1744. It was preceded by *The Oeconomy of Love*, 1735, and succeeded by *Of Benevolence: an Epistle to Enmenius*, 1751; *Taste: an Epistle to a Young Critic*, 1753 (reprinted in *ARS* xxx, 1951, with prose essays on Taste); and *A Day: an Epistle to John Wilkes of Aylesbury, Esq.*, 1761. A collected edition, omitting *The Oeconomy of Love*, but embodying his prose *Sketches*, 1758, was published in 2 volumes in 1771, with the title *Miscellanies*. He published his *Medical Essays* in 1773.

The best account of Armstrong is by Lewis M. Knapp in *PMLA* lix, 1944. There is a bibliography and appreciation in I. A. Williams's *Seven XVIIIth Century Bibliographies*, 1924.

BARRY, JAMES, 1741–1806

An Inquiry into the Real and Imaginary Obstructions to the Acquisition of the Arts in England was published in 1775, and his *Letter to the Dilettanti Society respecting the Obtention of Certain Matters Essentially Necessary for the Improvement of Public Taste* in 1798.

The Works of James Barry, 2 vols., including his lectures on painting and a biographical introduction, was published in 1809. The lectures on painting (together with those of Opie and Fuseli) were edited by R. J. Wornum, 1848.

BEATTIE, JAMES, 1735–1803

Besides his principal poem, *The Minstrel*, first published in two parts, *Book the First*, 1771, and *Book the Second*, 1774, Beattie published *Original Poems and Translations*, 1760; *The Judgment of Paris*, 1765; *Poems on Several Subjects*, 1766; *Poems on Several Occasions*, 1776. No collected edition has been published since Dyce's Aldine edition was last reprinted in 1891.

An Essay on the Nature and Immutability of Truth was published in 1770, and passed through numerous editions. Associated with it is a short allegory, *The Castle of Scepticism*, first published in 1948, ed. E. C. Mossner, *Texas Studies in English*, xxvii. Beattie also published collections of *Essays*, 1776, and *Dissertations Moral and Critical*, 1783, as well as a short dictionary of *Scoticisms*, 1779; *Evidences of the Christian Religion*, 2 vols., 1786; and *Elements of Moral Science*, 2 vols., 1790–3.

Beattie's life was well written by Sir William Forbes, 2 vols., 1806, and again in more detail by M. Forbes, *Beattie and his Friends*, 1904. There is a judicious estimate of his work by R. S. Walker in the preface to *James Beattie's London Diary 1773*, Aberdeen, 1946, a scrupulous record of daily life in Georgian London. Walker has also published *James Beattie's day-book*, 1773–98, Aberdeen, Third Spalding Club, 1949.

V. M. Bevilacqua considers Beattie's theory of rhetoric in *Speech Monographs* xxxiv, 1967, J. S. Malek assesses his indebtedness to empirical psychology in *Enlightenment Essays* i, 1970, and S. K. Land considers his views on language, *PQ* li, 1972. There is a study of Beattie as critic by K. Kloth, *James Beatties ästhetische Theorien*, Munich, 1973.

BECKFORD, WILLIAM, 1760–1844

In 1777 Beckford wrote *The Long Story*, but it was not published until 1930 (as *The Vision*, ed. G. Chapman).

His first published work, *Biographical Memoirs of Extraordinary Painters*, appeared in 1780. His travel diaries of 1780–1 were published in 1783 as *Dreams, Waking Thoughts, and Incidents*, but this version was suppressed by the author. A radically revised version was issued in 1834 as *Italy: with Sketches of Spain and Portugal. Recollections of an Excursion to the Monasteries of Alcobaca and Batalha* appeared in 1835. G. Chapman includes the 1783 text in *The Travel Diaries*, 2 vols., 1928, and there is an edition of it by R. J. Gemmett, Cranbury, N.J., 1971.

Vathek was first published in the original French in 1786 (in Lausanne), and an English translation appeared in the same year. There have been many reprints, including one in the Everyman *Shorter Novels of the Eighteenth Century*. The best modern edition is by R. Lonsdale, 1970. The supplementary *Episodes of Vathek* first appeared in *The English Review* in 1909–10, and were translated by Sir F. T. Marzials, 1912. *Vathek* and the *Episodes* were edited by G. Chapman, 1929, and the original French text of both has been edited by E. Giddey, Lausanne, 1962. The relationship between the French and the English texts is discussed by K. W. Graham in an excellent article in *Studies in Bibliography* xxviii, 1975.

Two other minor satires published during his life were *Modern Novel Writing, or the Elegant Enthusiast*, 1796, and *Azemia: a Descriptive and Sentimental Novel*, 1797.

B. Alexander has edited *The Journal of William Beckford in Portugal and Spain, 1787–1788*, 1954, the 1794 *Journal* (included in *William Beckford of Fonthill*, New Haven, 1960), and some of Beckford's correspondence in *Life at Fonthill, 1807–1822*, 1957. See also 'Lewis Melville', *The Life and Letters of William Beckford*, 1910.

There are biographies by J. W. Oliver, 1932; G. Chapman, 1937, rev. 1952; B. Alexander, 1962; and J. Lees-Milne, Tisbury, 1976 (a particularly well-illustrated volume). H. A. N. Brockman, *The Caliph of Fonthill*, 1956, is specially concerned with Beckford's architectural interests. A. Parreaux, *William Beckford, auteur de Vathek*, Paris, 1960, is the most comprehensive study.

There is a good collection of critical essays, ed. F. M. Mahmoud, *William Beckford of Fonthill*, Cairo, 1960. Three articles in *Criticism* are of interest: J. H. Rieger, '*Au Pied de la Lettre*: Stylistic Uncertainty in *Vathek*', iv, 1962; J. K. Folsom, 'Beckford, *Vathek* and the Tradition of Oriental Satire', vi, 1964; and K. W. Graham, 'Beckford's *Vathek*: a Study in Ironic Dissonance', xiv, 1972. The chapter on *Vathek* in R. Kiely, *The Romantic Novel in England*, Cambridge, Mass., 1972, is perceptive.

There is a characteristic essay by Sacheverell Sitwell, *Beckford and Beckfordism*, 1930.

BIRCH, THOMAS, 1705–66

Birch edited and was a major contributor to the *General Dictionary*, 10 vols., 1734–41. See J. M. Osborn, 'Thomas Birch and the "General Dictionary" ', *MP* xxxvi, 1938. He also contributed to the *Biographia Britannica*, vols. i–v, 1747–60.

His work as an editor can only be touched on here: he edited the *Historical, Political, and Miscellaneous Works of John Milton* (with a biography), 2 vols., 1738; the works of Francis Bacon,

4 vols., 1740 (with a later volume of letters, speeches, etc., 1763); Spenser's *Faerie Queene* (with a biography), 3 vols., 1751; and the works of Sir Walter Raleigh (with a biography), 2 vols., 1751. His most important historical work was an edition of the state papers of John Thurloe (with a biography of Thurloe), 7 vols., 1742.

Birch's life of Dryden in the *General Dictionary* is discussed by J. M. Osborn in *John Dryden: some Biographical Facts and Problems*, New York, 1940. There is an interesting biographical article by E. L. Ruhe, 'Birch, Johnson, and Elizabeth Carter', *PMLA* lxxiii, 1958.

BLACKSTONE, SIR WILLIAM, 1723–80

The *Commentaries on the Laws of England*, 4 vols., Oxford 1765–9, have often been reissued and abridged. Jeremy Bentham's famous critique, *A Fragment on Government*, appeared in 1776.

The best modern biography is by D. A. Lockmiller (1938), and there is an excellent study by D. Boorstin: *The Mysterious Science of the Law*, Boston, 1941. There is a useful approach to Blackstone in H. G. Hanbury's study, *The Vinerian Chair and Legal Education*, Oxford, 1958.

BLAIR, HUGH, 1718–1800

The *Critical Dissertation on the Poems of Ossian* was first published in 1763, and appeared in an expanded version in 1765.

Lectures on Rhetoric and Belles Lettres, 2 vols., 1783, has often been reprinted. There is a modern edition by H. F. Harding, 2 vols., Carbondale, 1965. Blair also edited Shakespeare, 8 vols., Edinburgh, 1753, and a major collection of British poets, 44 vols., Edinburgh, 1773. His sermons were popular and often reprinted. The first collection appeared in 1777, and 5 vols. in all were published, the last, posthumously, in 1801.

The best of the early biographies is by John Hill, Edinburgh, 1807. There is an admirable study by R. M. Schmitz, New York, 1948. Among more recent studies, V. M. Bevilacqua, 'Philosophical Assumptions underlying Hugh Blair's Lectures', *Western Speech* xxxi, 1967, is of special interest.

BLAIR, ROBERT, 1700–46

Besides *The Grave*, 1743, Blair has been credited with *A Poem dedicated to the Memory of William Law*, 1728, and certain shorter pieces first printed in *The Edinburgh Miscellany*, 1720. He has his place in the collections of Anderson viii and Chalmers xv, and was edited by G. Gilfillan, Edinburgh, 1854 (with James Beattie and William Falconer). J. Means has edited *The Grave* for *ARS*, 1973, and examines the composition of that poem in *Studies in Scottish Literature* x, 1972.

The Grave was illustrated by William Blake, 1805, and the illustrations have been arranged 'as Blake directed', with a commentary by S. Foster Damon, Providence, 1963.

BOSWELL, JAMES, 1740–95

Boswell was the author of numerous pamphlets and broadsides details of which may be found in F. A. Pottle's study, *The Literary Career of James Boswell, Esq.*, Oxford, 1929, supplemented by the same author's bibliography in *NCBEL*. Two of these minor works have been reprinted in the present century, *Dorando: a Spanish Tale*, 1767, reprinted 1930, and *Critical Strictures on the New Tragedy of Elvira written by Mr. David Malloch* (written in collaboration with A. Erskine and G. Dempster), ed. F. A. Pottle, Los Angeles, 1952 (*ARS*).

His first major work was *An Account of Corsica; the Journal of a Tour to that Island, and Memoirs of Pascal Paoli*, Glasgow, 1768. There is an edition of the *Tour* by S. C. Roberts, Cambridge, 1923, and it is included in *Boswell on the Grand Tour: Italy, Corsica and France*, ed. F. Brady and F. A. Pottle, 1955. He contributed a series of 70 essays, *The Hypochondriack*, to the *London Magazine*, 1777–83. These have been edited by M. Bailey, 2 vols., Stanford, 1928, reprinted 1951 (as *Boswell's Column*). *The Journal of a Tour to the Hebrides with Samuel Johnson LL.D.* followed in 1785. This has been edited as part of the *Life of Johnson*, ed. G. B. Hill, vol. v, Oxford, 1887, rev. by L. F. Powell, Oxford, 1950, and by R. W. Chapman with Johnson's *Journey to the Western Islands of Scotland*, Oxford, 1924. There is an edition based on the manuscript ed. F. A. Pottle and C. H. Bennett, 1936.

The Life of Samuel Johnson LL.D. appeared in 2 vols., 1791. The standard edition is by G. B. Hill, 6 vols., Oxford, 1887 (with *Tour*), rev. by L. F. Powell, Oxford, 1934–50. It has also been edited by S. C. Roberts, 2 vols., 1949 (*EL*) and by R. W. Chapman, Oxford, 1953.

After the discovery of Boswell's private papers at Malahide Castle, a preliminary publication in a limited edition was undertaken by G. Scott and F. A. Pottle, and appeared in 18 vols., 1928–34. An index was published in 1937. Further papers were found at Fettercairn House: see the catalogue by C. C. Abbott, Oxford, 1936. Ten vols. of the 'trade edition' of the papers have appeared: *Boswell's London Journal 1762–1763*, ed. F. A. Pottle, 1950; *Boswell in Holland 1763–1764*, ed. F. A. Pottle, 1952; *Portraits by Sir Joshua Reynolds*, ed. F. W. Hilles, 1952; *Boswell on the Grand Tour: Germany and Switzerland 1764*, ed. F. A. Pottle, 1953; *Boswell on the Grand Tour: Italy, Corsica and France 1765–1766*, ed. F. Brady and F. A. Pottle, 1955; *Boswell in Search of a Wife 1766–1769*, ed. F. Brady and F. A. Pottle, New York, 1956; *Boswell for the Defence 1769–1774*, ed. W. K. Wimsatt, Jr., and F. A. Pottle, New York, 1959; *Boswell's Journal of a Tour to the Hebrides with Samuel Johnson LL.D. 1773*, ed. F. A. Pottle and C. H. Bennett, New York, 1961; *Boswell: the Ominous Years 1774–1776*, ed. C. Ryskamp and F. A. Pottle, 1963; *Boswell in Extremes 1776–1778*, ed. C. McC. Weis and F. A. Pottle, 1970. The research edition now includes the correspondence with John Johnston of Grange, ed. R. S. Walker, 1966, and correspondence relating to the making of the *Life of Johnson*, ed. M. Waingrow, 1969.

The correspondence available before the discoveries at Malahide and Fettercairn was edited by C. B. Tinker, 2 vols., Oxford, 1924. C. B. Tinker also wrote a biography, *Young Boswell*, Boston, 1922, now largely superseded by F. A. Pottle, *James Boswell: the Earlier Years, 1740–1769*, 1966. There is a good study of his political career by F. Brady, New Haven, 1965. His relations with Mrs. Thrale (afterwards Piozzi) are examined by M. M. C. Hyde in *The Impossible Friendship*, Cambridge, Mass., 1972. There is a recent general study by A. R. Brooks, 1971.

Three book-length studies of the *Life of Johnson* have appeared. G. Scott's admirable work, *The Making of the Life of Johnson*, appears as vol. vi of the *Private Papers*, 1929. More recently D. L. Passler has written *Time, Form, and Style in Boswell's 'Life of Johnson'*, New Haven, 1971, and W. R. Siebenschuh *Form and Purpose in Boswell's Biographical Works*, Berkeley, 1972. There are many essays on various aspects of Boswell's biographical art, including two excellent studies by F. A. Pottle: 'The Power

IV. AUTHORS: BOSWELL–BROOKE

of Memory in Boswell and Scott', *D. Nichol Smith Festschrift*, 1945, and 'Boswell Revalued', *Literary Views: Critical and Historical Essays*, ed. C. Camden, Chicago, 1964. Other helpful essays are those by L. Baldwin, 'The Conversation in Boswell's *Life of Johnson*', *JEGP* li, 1952; S. E. Molin, 'Boswell's Account of the Johnson–Wilkes Meeting', *SEL* iii, 1963; R. W. Rader, 'Literary Form in Factual Narrative: the Example of Boswell's *Johnson*', *Essays in Eighteenth-Century Biography*, ed. P. B. Daghlian Bloomington, 1968; P. K. Alkon, 'Boswell's Control of Aesthetic Distance', *University of Toronto Quarterly* xxxviii, 1969; C. Tracy, 'Boswell; The Cautious Empiricist', *The Triumph of Culture. Eighteenth-Century Perspectives*, ed. P. Fritz and D. Williams, Toronto, 1972; and I. S. Lustig on Boswell's 'animadversions' on Mrs. Piozzi, *MLR* lxvii, 1972. F. R. Hart considers Boswell's influence on nineteenth-century biographical theory, *ELH* xxvii, 1960, and I. Jack compares Lockhart and Boswell as biographers, *L. F. Powell Festschrift*, 1965. There is much useful material in *Twentieth-Century Interpretations of Boswell's 'Life of Johnson'*, ed. J. L. Clifford, Englewood Cliffs, 1970. Studies on other Boswellian works include one by L. F. Powell on the two versions of the *Tour*, *E&S* xxiii, 1938, and another by D. Day, 'Boswell, Corsica, and Paoli', *ES* xlv, 1964. A comprehensive listing of these and other studies may be found in the bibliography by A. E. Brown, Hamden, Conn., 1972.

The story of the discovery of the Boswell papers is well told by D. Buchanan, *The Treasure of Auchinleck*, 1975.

BROOKE, FRANCES, 1724–89

As 'Mary Singleton, Spinster' she conducted *The Old Maid*, 1755–6. Her translation of Marie-Jeanne Riccoboni's *Letters from Lady Julia Catesby* appeared in 1760, and was followed by *The History of Lady Julia Mandeville* in 1763. Her Canadian novel, *The History of Emily Montague*, was published in 1769, and *The Excursion* in 1777. She wrote two tragedies, *Virginia*, 1756, and *The Siege of Sinope*, 1781, and two comic operas, *Rosina*, 1783, and *Marian*, 1788.

Lady Julia Mandeville was edited by E. Phillips Poole, 1930, and *Emily Montague* by C. F. Clinck, Toronto, 1961.

See also W. H. New, 'Frances Brooke's Chequered Gardens', *Canadian Literature* lii, 1972.

BROOKE, HENRY,? 1703–83

Brooke's poetry and plays are listed in the bibliography to Vol. VII.

The Fool of Quality; or, The History of Henry Earl of Moreland appeared in 5 vols., 1764–70. John Wesley's abridgement, 2 vols., 1781, and Charles Kingsley's edition, 2 vols., 1859, are interesting documents in the history of Christian taste. Brooke's last work, *Juliet Grenville; or, The History of the Human Heart*, appeared in 3 vols., 1774.

There are studies by H. M. Scurr, Minneapolis, 1927, and by H. Högl (on *The Fool of Quality*), Erlangen, 1930. See also the chapter on Brooke in M. Gassenmeier, *Der Typus des Man of Feeling*, Tübingen, 1972. *The Fool of Quality* is discussed in the standard surveys of the novel, but has otherwise had little critical attention.

BROWN, JOHN, 1715–66

Brown's earliest publications were poems: *Honour*, 1743; *An Essay on Satire*, 1745 (prefixed by Warburton to his edition of Pope, 1751); and *On Liberty*, 1749. His poetry is included in Anderson x. His *Essays on the Characteristics of the Earl of Shaftesbury* were published in 1751: there is a modern edition by D. D. Eddy, New York, 1969. The celebrated *Estimate of the Manners and Principles of the Times*, 1757, was followed by *An Explanatory Defence of the Estimate*, 1758. *A Dissertation on the Rise, Union and Power, the Progressions, Separations and Corruptions, of Poetry and Music*, 1763, was somewhat shortened in another version, *The History of the Rise and Progress of Poetry, through its Several Species*, Newcastle, 1764. There is a useful study of this work by H. M. Flasdieck, *John Brown . . . und seine Dissertation On Poetry and Music*, Halle, 1924.

His tragedies, *Barbarossa* and *Athelstan*, were published in 1755 and 1756 respectively, and *Barbarossa* was often reprinted, appearing (for example) in Mrs. Inchbald's *British Theatre* xv, 1808.

The often reprinted *Description of the Lake of Keswick*, written in 1753, and first published in 1771, is an early example of admiration for the scenery of the Lake District.

There is a bibliography by D. D. Eddy, New York, 1971. The life by Andrew Kippis in the second edition of the *Biographia Britannica*, vol. ii, 1780, is full and interesting.

BRYDONE, PATRICK, 1736–1818

A Tour through Sicily and Malta was published in 2 vols., 1773. There is a study by P. Fussell, Jr., 'Patrick Brydone: the Eighteenth-Century Traveller as Representative Man', *Bulletin of the New York Public Library* lxvi, 1962.

Apart from the *Tour*, Brydone was the author of papers in the *Philosophical Transactions of the Royal Society*, on various electrical phenomena.

BURKE, EDMUND, 1729–97

For the text of many of Burke's writings and speeches one has still to depend on the edition of his works in 16 vols. completed between 1803 and 1827, or subsequent reprints based on this. There is an excellent edition of his correspondence, under the general editorship of T. W. Copeland, 9 vols., Cambridge, 1958–70. There are bibliographies by W. B. Todd, 1964, and P. J. Stanlis, 1972. The latter covers Burke studies to 1968.

The separately published works of special concern to literary students are *A Vindication of Natural Society*, 1756; *A Philosophical Enquiry into the Origin of our Ideas of the Sublime and Beautiful*, 1757 (with an 'Introduction on Taste' added in 1759); *Thoughts on the Cause of the Present Discontents*, 1770; *The Speech on Moving his Resolution for Conciliation with the Colonies*, 1775; *Speech on the Motion made for Papers relative to the Nabob of Arcot's Debts*, 1785; *Reflections on the Revolution in France*, 1790; *An Appeal from the New to the Old Whigs*, 1791; *A Letter to a Noble Lord*, 1796; *Thoughts on the Prospects of a Regicide Peace*, 1796.

The *Philosophical Enquiry* has been admirably edited, with a comprehensive introduction, by J. T. Boulton, 1958, There are useful editions of *Conciliation with the Colonies* by J. Hart, Chicago, 1964, and of the *Reflections* by W. B. Todd, New York, 1959. C. C. O'Brien's introduction to the Pelican edition of the *Reflections*, 1969, presents an interesting reassessment of Burke's political attitudes. Burke's early notebook has been edited by H. V. F. Somerset, Cambridge, 1957.

There are several volumes of selections, notably *Burke's Politics. Selected Writings and Speeches . . . on Reform, Revolution, and War*, ed. R. J. S. Hoffman and P. Levack, New York, 1949; *The Philosophy of Edmund Burke*, ed. L. I. Bredvold and R. G. Ross,

Ann Arbor, 1960; and *Selected Writings and Speeches*, ed. P. J. Stanlis, Garden City, 1963. The selection by W. J. Bate (New York, 1960) has a particularly helpful introduction.

Sir J. Prior's life of Burke appeared in 1824. Additional information is to be found in T. Macknight, *Life and Times of Edmund Burke*, 3 vols., 1858–60, and A. P. I. Samuels, *Early Life, Correspondence, and Writings of Edmund Burke*, Cambridge, 1923. There are good biographical studies by R. H. Murray, Oxford, 1931, and Sir P. Magnus, 1939, but C. B. Cone, *Burke and the Nature of Politics*, 2 vols., Lexington, 1957–65, gives a more detailed account than either. There is a study of Burke and his literary friends by D. C. Bryant, St. Louis, 1939.

Two aspects of Burke's political career have been authoritatively treated by T. H. D. Mahony, *Edmund Burke and Ireland*, Cambridge, Mass., 1960, and by P. J. Marshall, *The Impeachment of Warren Hastings*, Oxford, 1965. Burke as a political philosopher has been studied by a number of scholars, notably by P. Stanlis in *Edmund Burke and the Natural Law*, Ann Arbor, 1958. See also the studies by C. Parkin, *The Moral Basis of Burke's Political Thought*, Cambridge, 1956, F. Canavan, *The Political Reason of Edmund Burke*, Durham, N.C., 1960, and B. T. Wilkins, *The Problem of Burke's Political Philosophy*, Oxford, 1967. G. Chapman's *Edmund Burke. The Practical Imagination*, Cambridge, Mass., 1967, is one of the few studies to give an adequate place to Burke's attitudes to India. An approach different from those adopted in the studies mentioned so far is outlined by J. G. A. Pocock in 'Burke and the Ancient Constitution', *Historical Journal* iii, 1960. See also the books by C. P. Courtney, *Montesquieu and Burke*, Oxford, 1963, and F. O'Gorman, *Edmund Burke: his Political Philosophy*, 1973.

The aesthetic theories underlying the *Enquiry* have been studied by S. H. Monk, *The Sublime*, New York, 1935, and W. J. Hipple, *The Beautiful, the Sublime, and the Picturesque in Eighteenth-Century British Aesthetic Theory*, Carbondale, 1957. See also two articles in *Studies in Burke and his Time* xii, 1970–1: J. E. Faulkner, 'Burke's Early Conception of Poetry and Rhetoric', and B. C. Oliver, 'Burke's *Enquiry* and the Baroque Theory of the Passions'. Studies that consider Burke's political writing in an aesthetic perspective include N. Wood's 'The Aesthetic Dimension of Burke's Political Thought', *Journal of British Studies* iv, 1964, and an article by N. R. Joy on *Conciliation with the Colonies* as epic prophecy and satire, *Studies in Burke and his Time* ix, 1967.

For those aspects of Burke's work discussed in this volume (Chap. IX) reference should be made to the following articles by D. C. Bryant: 'The Contemporary Reception of Edmund Burke's Speaking', *Studies in Honor of F. W. Shipley*, St. Louis, 1942, since amplified in *Historical Studies of Rhetoric and Rhetoricians*, ed. R. F. Howes, Ithaca, 1961; 'The Frustrated Opposition: Burke, Barré, and their Audiences', *Studies in Memory of F. M. Webster*, St. Louis, 1951; to J. L. Mahoney, 'Edmund Burke and the East India Bill: the Classical Oration in the service of Eighteenth-Century Politics', *Burke Newsletter* iv, 1963; to W. D. Love, 'Burke's Transition from a Literary to a Political Career', ibid. vi, 1965; and to the books by T. W. Copeland, *Our Eminent Friend, Edmund Burke: Six Essays*, New Haven, 1949, and J. T. Boulton, *The Language of Politics in the Age of Wilkes and Burke*, 1963.

Any reader interested in Burke will be well advised to consult the *Burke Newsletter*, 1959–67 (since 1967 *Studies in Burke and his Time*). The articles from it mentioned in this brief bibliography are only a sample of the useful material available there.

BURNEY, CHARLES, 1726–1814

The Present State of Music in France and Italy was published in 1771. This was based on a manuscript travel journal, ed. H. E. Poole, 1969. Two modern editions of the 1771 text have made use of the manuscript, C. H. Glover's, 1927, and P. A. Scholes's, 1959.

The Present State of Music in Germany, the Netherlands, and the United Provinces, 2 vols., 1773, has also been edited, with additions from Burney's manuscript journal, by C. H. Glover, 1927, P. A. Scholes, 1959.

A General History of Music, from the Earliest Ages to the Present Period was published in 4 vols., 1776. There is an edition by F. Mercer, 2 vols., 1935.

There are two major studies of Burney's work: P. A. Scholes, *The Great Doctor Burney*, 2 vols., 1948; and R. Lonsdale, *Dr. Charles Burney: a Literary Biography*, Oxford, 1965. The latter makes use of the collections of Burney family papers which became available after the publication of Dr. Scholes's work.

BURNEY, FRANCES, later D'ARBLAY, 1752–1840

Evelina, or, A Young Lady's Entrance into the World, appeared in 3 vols., 1778. There is a good modern edition by E. A. Bloom, 1968. Her other publications include: *Cecilia, or Memoirs of an Heiress*, 5 vols., 1782; *Camilla: or, A Picture of Youth*, 5 vols., 1796 (ed. E. A. Bloom and L. D. Bloom, 1973); *The Wanderer, or, Female Difficulties*, 5 vols., 1814; and an unsatisfactory life of her father, *Memoirs of Dr. Burney*, 3 vols., 1832.

She also wrote eight plays, including *Edwy and Elgiva*, performed in 1795, ed. M. J. Benkovitz, Hamden, 1957. Her dramatic works are discussed by J. Hemlow, *University of Toronto Quarterly* xix, 1950.

The *Diary and Letters of Madame D'Arblay*, ed. C. Barrett, appeared in 7 vols., 1842–6; *The Early Diary of Frances Burney, 1768–1778*, ed. A. R. Ellis, in 2 vols., 1889. There are various volumes of selections, including one by L. Gibbs (*EL*) and another by J. Wain, 1961. C. B. Tinker collected the passages relating to Samuel Johnson in *Dr. Johnson and Fanny Burney*, 1912. J. Hemlow is the general editor of the definitive edition of the *Journals and Letters*, 10 vols., Oxford, 1972–   .

Biographical information will also be found in *The Queeney Letters*, ed. the Marquis of Lansdowne, 1934; in J. L. Clifford, *Hester Lynch Piozzi (Mrs. Thrale)*, Oxford, 1941; and *Thraliana, the Diary of Mrs. Hester Lynch Thrale (later Mrs. Piozzi), 1776–1809*, ed. K. C. Balderston, 2 vols., 1942.

The standard biography is by J. Hemlow: *The History of Fanny Burney*, Oxford, 1958. Her study, 'Fanny Burney and the Courtesy Books', *PMLA* lxv, 1950, is important. There are good essays on *Evelina* by E. Montague and L. L. Martz, *Tinker Festschrift*, New Haven, 1949, and by K. Malone, *Papers on English Language and Literature* i, 1965. A. Bugnot undertakes a rehabilitation of *The Wanderer*, *Études Anglaises* xv, 1962. E. White has attempted a critical estimate of Burney's work as a whole in *Fanny Burney, Novelist*, Hamden, 1960.

BURNS, ROBERT, 1759–96

Editions of Burns's poems were published during his lifetime at Kilmarnock, 1786, and at Edinburgh, 1787, 1793, 1794. His songs appeared principally in James Johnson's *The Scots Musical*

Museum, 6 vols., 1787–1803 and, sometimes in garbled form, in George Thomson's *A Select Collection of Original Scottish Airs for the Voice*, 5 vols., 1793–1818.

An unsatisfactory collected edition of the works, with an unsatisfactory life, was undertaken by J. Currie in 4 vols., Liverpool, 1800, and was often republished. (The fair-minded will wish to read R. D. Thornton's study of Currie, Edinburgh, 1963, before passing a final judgement on him.) The standard modern edition of the poems and songs is by J. Kinsley, 3 vols., Oxford, 1968. Burns as writer and collector of bawdry may be studied in *The Merry Muses of Caledonia*, ed. G. Legman, New Hyde Park, 1965. There is an excellent selection of the poems, ed. W. Beattie and H. W. Meikle, Harmondsworth, 1946, and often reprinted.

The standard edition of the letters is by J. De Lancey Ferguson, 2 vols., Oxford, 1931. There is a selection by the same editor, 1953 (*WC*). A new edition of the letters is being prepared by G. Ross Roy. *Robert Burns's Commonplace Book 1783–1785*, ed. J. C. Ewing and D. Cook, was published in Glasgow, 1938.

Of the older biographies, J. G. Lockhart's, 1828, is the best. There are good modern biographies by C. Carswell, 1930, F. B. Snyder, 1932, H. Hecht, 1936, J. De Lancey Ferguson, 1939, and R. T. Fitzhugh, 1970.

Of the older studies A. Angellier, *Robert Burns, la vie, les œuvres*, 2 vols., Paris, 1893, may be mentioned. Of modern studies, D. Daiches, *Robert Burns*, 1952, C. Keith, *The Russet Coat*, 1953, and T. Crawford, *Burns: a Study of the Poems and Songs*, Edinburgh, 1960, are particularly recommended. D. Daiches has also written a helpful study for the general reader, *Robert Burns and his World*, 1971. There are a few excellent paragraphs by D. Nichol Smith in *Some Observations on Eighteenth-Century Poetry*, Toronto, 1937. R. Bentman contributes an important essay on Burns's use of Scottish dialect to the *F. A. Pottle Festschrift*, 1965, and in 'Burns's Declining Fame', *Studies in Romanticism* xi, 1972, makes a vigorous plea for more study of a poet who is 'one of the great innovators'. J. C. Weston assesses Burns's use of the verse-epistle form, *PQ* xlix, 1970. Another aspect of the poetry is examined by F. L. Beaty, 'Burns's Comedy of Romantic Love', *PMLA* lxxxiii, 1968. The best modern study of the songs is contained in the last section of J. Kinsley's 'The Music of the Heart', *University of Nottingham Renaissance and*

Modern Studies viii, 1964, reprinted in *Critical Essays on Robert Burns*, ed. D. A. Low, 1975.

Burns is discussed in many surveys of English and Scottish poetry, but three of these deserve particular mention: J. Speirs, *The Scots Literary Tradition*, 1940, enlarged 1962; K. Wittig, *The Scottish Tradition in Literature*, 1958; and D. Craig, *Scottish Literature and the Scottish People 1680–1830*, 1961.

There is a bibliography by J. W. Egerer, Edinburgh, 1964. D. A. Low has edited the Burns volume in the *Critical Heritage* series, 1974. M. Lindsay, *The Burns Encyclopaedia*, 1959, rev. 1970, is a convenient reference-book.

CAMPBELL, GEORGE, 1719–96

Campbell's critique of Hume, *A Dissertation on Miracles*, appeared in 1762, and *The Philosophy of Rhetoric*, 2 vols., in 1776. There is a modern edition of both these works by L. F. Bitzer, Carbondale, 1963. His *Lectures on Ecclesiastical History* were published posthumously, 2 vols., 1800, with a life by G. S. Keith. *Lectures on Systematic Theology and Pulpit Eloquence* followed in 1807.

There is a full discussion of Campbell's rhetoric in W. S. Howell's excellent study, *Eighteenth-Century British Logic and Rhetoric*, Princeton, 1971 (chap. vi, sect. 5). See also the essay on *The Philosophy of Rhetoric* by V. M. Bevilacqua in *Speech Monographs* xxxii, 1965.

CAMBRIDGE, RICHARD OWEN, 1717–1802

The Scribleriad was published in 1751. Cambridge was one of the contributors to the *World* (1753–6). His works in prose and verse were published with a life by his son in 1803. There is a study of his work by R. D. Altick: *Richard Owen Cambridge: Belated Augustan*, Philadelphia, 1941.

CARTER, ELIZABETH, 1717–1806

Mrs. Carter was chiefly celebrated for her translation of Epictetus, 1758. She published two collections of poems, 1738 and 1762, and contributed to the *Rambler* (Nos. 44 and 100). Her correspondence was edited by M. Pennington, 4 vols., 1809 (to Catherine Talbot and Mrs. Vesey), and 3 vols., 1817 (to Elizabeth Montagu). M. Pennington also wrote *Memoirs of the Life of Mrs. Elizabeth Carter*, 1807, with her poems and some essays. Information on Mrs. Carter's personal life is provided by E. Ruhe, 'Birch, Johnson, and Elizabeth Carter: an Episode of 1738-9', *PMLA* lxxiii, 1958.

CAWTHORN, JAMES, 1719-61

His *Poems* were published in a collected edition in 1771, and he is included in Anderson x, and Chalmers xiv. *Abelard and Heloise* was first published in 1747.

CHAPONE, HESTER MULSO, 1727-1801

Letters on the Improvement of the Mind, addressed to a Young Lady were published in 2 vols., 1773, and often reprinted. Mrs. Chapone contributed to the *Rambler* (No. 10) and the *Adventurer* (77-9, 'The Story of Fidelia'). Her *Posthumous Works*, 2 vols., 1807-8, contain her correspondence with Richardson and Mrs. Carter.

CHATTERTON, THOMAS, 1752-70

A collected edition of Chatterton's poems was published by Robert Southey and Joseph Cottle, 3 vols., 1803. Subsequent editions are those of W. W. Skeat, 2 vols., 1871; H. D. Roberts, 2 vols., 1906; and S. Lee, 2 vols., 1906-9; but these have been superseded by the *Collected Works*, ed. D. S. Taylor with B. B. Hoover, 2 vols., Oxford, 1971. The Rowley poems alone were first collected and edited by Thomas Tyrwhitt, 1777, whose third edition, 1778, is the basis of M. H. Hare's edition, Oxford, 1911. Of the Rowley poems, 'Elinoure and Juga' had appeared in the *Town and Country Magazine*, May 1769, and *Bristowe Tragedy* in 1772.

The best biography is by E. H. W. Meyerstein, 1930. See also Meyerstein's essay on Chatterton in *Essays by Divers Hands* (*Transactions of the Royal Society of Literature*) xvi, 1937. L. Kelly, *The Marvellous Boy: the Life and Myth of Thomas Chatterton*, 1971, does not add substantially to previous work.

Doubts about the authenticity of the Rowley poems were raised by Thomas Warton in the second volume of his *History of English Poetry*, 1778. Though Warton reached the right conclusion, it remained for Skeat (see above) to prove unquestionably that the poems are spurious. For various aspects of the Rowley controversy, see L. F. Powell, 'Thomas Tyrwhitt and the Rowley Poems', *RES* vii, 1931; A. Watkins Jones, 'Bishop Percy, Thomas

Warton, and Chatterton's Rowley Poems (1773–1790)', *PMLA* l, 1935. Apart from the criticism in Meyerstein's *Life*, the most valuable appreciations are those of Walter Scott in his review of the Southey–Cottle edition, *Edinburgh Review* iv, 1804; F. S. Miller, 'The Historic Sense of Thomas Chatterton', *ELH* xi, 1944; B. H. Bronson, 'Thomas Chatterton', *C. B. Tinker Festschrift*, 1949. Bronson has also demonstrated, in 'Chattertoniana', *MLQ* xi, 1950, the use Chatterton made of Elizabeth Cooper's chronologically arranged specimens of early English poetry, *The Muses Library*, 1737.

CHESTERFIELD, PHILIP DORMER STANHOPE, 4th EARL OF, 1694–1773

The *Letters to his Son* were first published in 1774. These have often been reprinted, and are included in the comprehensive edition by B. Dobrée, 6 vols., 1932. This edition includes, in the first volume, an excellent general study of Chesterfield's life and work. Additions to the correspondence have been made by S. L. Gulick, *Some Unpublished Letters of Lord Chesterfield*, Berkeley, 1937.

Chesterfield's essays in the *World*, his 'characters', his speeches, and some of his correspondence are collected in his *Miscellaneous Works*, 2 vols., 1777, edited with a memoir by M. Maty. There is a bibliography by S. L. Gulick, *Publications of the Bibliographical Society of America* xxix, 1935.

There are biographies by S. Shellabarger, 1935, and W. Connely, 1939. See also two studies that concentrate on Chesterfield as a notable Francophile: R. A. Barrell, *Chesterfield et la France*, Paris, 1968, and A. Mellor, *Lord Chesterfield et son temps*, Paris, 1970.

J. E. Mason provides invaluable background for an understanding of the *Letters to his Son* in *Gentlefolk in the Making. Studies in the History of English Courtesy Literature and Related Topics*, Philadelphia, 1935. The reader should also consult the following: V. G. Heltzel, 'Chesterfield and the Anti-Laughter Tradition', *MP* xxvi, 1928; the chapter on Chesterfield in B. Willey, *The English Moralists*, 1964; C. Pullen, 'The Chesterfield Myth and Eighteenth-Century Ethics', *Dalhousie Review* xlvii, 1967, and 'Lord Chesterfield and Eighteenth-Century Appearance and Reality', *SEL* viii, 1968. In 'Gentlemen and Dancing-Masters', *ECS* i, 1967, C. J. Rawson explores the strong contrast between the moral worlds of Chesterfield and Fielding. This perceptive essay is reprinted in *Henry Fielding and the Augustan Ideal under Stress*, 1972. Chesterfield's reputation is analysed in a useful study by R. Coxon, *Chesterfield and his Critics*, 1925. Probably the best brief assessment of the *Letters* is the essay contributed by C. Price to *The Familiar Letter in the Eighteenth Century*, ed. H. Anderson, P. B. Daghlian, and I. Ehrenpreis, Lawrence, 1966.

CHURCHILL, CHARLES, 1732–64

Churchill published the following poems: *The Rosciad*, 1761; *The Apology. Addressed to the Critical Reviewers*, 1761; *Night, An Epistle to Robert Lloyd*, 1761; *The Ghost* in four books, 1762. *The Prophecy of Famine. A Scots Pastoral*, 1763; *An Epistle to William Hogarth*, 1763; *The Conference*, 1763; *The Author*, 1763; *The Duellist* in three books, 1764; *Gotham* in three books, 1764; *The Candidate*, 1764; *The Farewell*, 1764; *The Times*, 1764; *Independence*, 1764. Some shorter pieces appeared in magazines; the 'Dedication to Warburton', prefixed to his *Sermons*, was published posthumously in 1765. Collected editions were published in 1763 and subsequent years. The standard edition is by D. Grant, Oxford, 1956. The correspondence of Churchill with John Wilkes has been edited by E. H. Weatherley, New York, 1954.

The most reliable account of Churchill's life is by W. C. Brown, Lawrence, 1953. Brown has also examined the structure of Churchill's verse in *The Triumph of Form*, Chapel Hill, 1948. The most discriminating evaluations of Churchill's poetry (which arrive at markedly different conclusions) are by I. Simon, 'An Eighteenth-Century Satirist, Charles Churchill', *Revue belge de philologie et d'histoire* xxxvii, 1959, and Y. Winters, who has expanded a few pages of *In Defense of Reason*, 1947, to form two articles in *Poetry* xcviii, 1961, reprinted in *Forms of Discovery*, Chicago, 1967.

Other articles recommended include two by E. H. Weatherley, 'Churchill's Literary Indebtedness to Pope', *SP* xliii, 1946, and 'Churchill: Neo-Classic Master', *University of Kansas Review* xx, 1954. M. Golden has examined Churchill's literary influence on Cowper, *JEGP* lviii, 1959, and contributed an interesting general assessment, 'Sterility and Eminence in the Poetry of Charles Churchill', *JEGP* lxvi, 1967. See also W. F.

Cunningham, 'Charles Churchill and the Satiric Portrait', in *Essays and Studies in Language and Literature*, ed. H. H. Petit, Pittsburgh, 1964, and the chapter on Churchill in W. B. Piper, *The Heroic Couplet*, Cleveland, 1969.

There is a bibliography and appreciation in I. A. Williams, *Seven XVIIIth Century Bibliographies*, 1924.

CLELAND, JOHN, 1709–89

Memoirs of a Woman of Pleasure was published in 2 vols., 1748–9, rev. 1750. It has been edited by P. Quennell, 1963. There is an abridged edition in French, with illustrative documents and a bibliographical introduction, by G. Apollinaire, 1914. *Memoirs of a Coxcomb: or the History of Sir William Delamere* followed in 1751, and *The Surprises of Love* in 1764. Cleland also wrote a tragedy, adapted from Metastasio, *Titus Vespasian*, 1755, and other dramatic pieces. He wrote three philological studies with a view to recovering the lost 'universal elementary language of Europe': *The Way to Things by Words*, 1766; *Specimen of an Etimological Vocabulary*, 1768; and *Additional Articles to the Specimens*, 1769.

There is a general study by W. H. Epstein, *John Cleland: Images of a Life*, New York, 1974. Critical essays on the *Memoirs of a Woman of Pleasure* include a fine one by M. Bradbury, 'Fanny Hill and the Comic Novel', *Critical Quarterly* xiii, 1971, reprinted as chap. iii of *Possibilities: Essays on the State of the Novel*, 1973. E. W. Copeland compares Richardson's *Clarissa* with *Fanny Hill* as 'sisters in distress', *Studies in the Novel* iv, 1972, and L. Braudy considers *Fanny Hill* and materialism, *ECS* iv, 1972.

COLLIER, JANE, ?1710–?55

An Essay on the Art of Ingeniously Tormenting appeared in 1753. *The Cry*, which she wrote in collaboration with Sarah Fielding, followed in 1754. The *Essay* was several times reprinted in the early nineteenth century. She was among Samuel Richardson's correspondents.

COLLINS, WILLIAM, 1721–59

Persian Eclogues. Written Originally for the Entertainment of the Ladies of Tauris was published in 1742. His *Verses, Humbly*

Address'd to Sir Thomas Hanmer. On his Edition of Shakespeare, followed in 1743, and a second, revised, edition in 1744. The *Odes on Several Descriptive and Allegoric Subjects*, 1747, were followed by the *Ode occasion'd by the Death of Mr. Thomson*, 1749, and *The Passions. An Ode*, 1750. The *Ode on the Popular Superstitions of the Highlands of Scotland* was published posthumously in 1788. The manuscript of this last poem was rediscovered in 1967, and has been described by C. Lamont in *RES* N.S. xix, 1968. Other drafts and fragments of poems were edited by J. S. Cunningham, Oxford, 1956.

The first collected edition was undertaken by John Langhorne in 1765, together with a memoir and appreciation. The best modern edition is by R. Lonsdale, 1969 (with Gray and Goldsmith). There is a good selection by A. Johnstone, 1967.

The standard biography is by P. L. Carver, 1967. There is a bibliography and appreciation in I. A. Williams, *Seven XVIIIth Century Bibliographies*, 1924. Other critical essays from this period include J. M. Murry's, in *Countries of the Mind*, 1st ser., 1922, A. D. McKillop's, *SP* xx, 1923, J. W. Mackail's, *Studies of English Poets*, 1926, H. W. Garrod's, Oxford, 1928, and E. Blunden's, prefixed to his edition of the *Poems*, 1929.

Among the general surveys available, those by O. Doughty, 1964, and O. F. Sigworth, New York, 1965, may be mentioned, and there is an interesting lecture by A. Johnstone, 'The Poetry of William Collins', *Proceedings of the British Academy* lix, 1973, which clarifies Collins's ideas about the role of the poet in society. Among other essays, there are two by A. S. P. Woodhouse, 'Collins and the Creative Imagination: a Study in the Critical Background of his Odes', *Studies in English by Members of University College, Toronto*, Toronto, 1931; and 'The Poetry of Collins Reconsidered', *F. A. Pottle Festschrift*, 1965. Also recommended are two essays on the 'Ode to Evening', one by A. D. McKillop, *TSLL* v, 1960, the other by M. E. Brown, *EC* xi, 1961. J. R. Crider has a study of Collins's 'progress poems', *SP* lx, 1963, and E. R. Wasserman considers the 'Ode on the Poetical Character', *ELH* xxxiv, 1967.

COLMAN, GEORGE, the Elder, 1732–94

Colman conducted the *Connoisseur* (with Bonnell Thornton) 1754–6, collected in 4 vols., 1757. He collaborated with Robert Lloyd in writing parodies of Gray, the *Two Odes* (to Obscurity, to Oblivion), 1760. He wrote many plays, including *Polly Honeycombe*, 1760, *The Jealous Wife*, 1761, *The Deuce is in him*, 1763, and *The Clandestine Marriage*, 1766 (with Garrick). He translated the comedies of Terence, 1765. Some of his miscellaneous writings are collected in *Prose on several Occasions, accompanied with some Pieces of Verse*, 3 vols., 1787; vol. iii includes the translation of Horace's *Ars Poetica* (first published 1783).

Colman's life was written by R. B. Peake (*Memoirs of the Colman Family*, 2 vols., 1841). There is a modern study by E. R. Page, New York, 1935. The collaboration between Colman and Garrick is studied in F. L. Bergmann, 'Garrick and *The Clandestine Marriage*', *PMLA* LXVII, 1952. R. D. Spector examines the functions of a persona in relation to the *Connoisseur*, *J. L. Clifford Festschrift*, 1971.

COVENTRY, FRANCIS, 1725–54

The History of Pompey the Little was published in 1751. There was an edition by A. del Re, 1926. The standard edition is that by R. A. Day, 1974.

He also wrote *An Essay on the New Species of Writing founded by Mr. Fielding*, 1751, ed. A. D. McKillop, 1962 (*ARS*).

Coventry's work is examined by T. A. Olshin, '*Pompey the Little*: a Study in Fielding's Influence', *Revue des langues vivantes* xxxvi, 1970.

COWPER, WILLIAM, 1731–1800

Cowper's principal publications were *Olney Hymns* (in collaboration with John Newton), 1779; *Anti-Thelyphthora; a tale in verse*, 1781; *Poems*, 2 vols. (containing the satires and some shorter poems), 1782; *The History of John Gilpin* (in the *Public Advertiser*), 1782; *The Task*, 1785; a translation of Homer, 1791; *Poems* (containing 'On the receipt of my Mother's Picture' and 'The dog and the Waterlily'), 1798. His translation of Milton's Latin and Italian poems appeared posthumously in 1808. The standard edition is edited by H. S. Milford, 1905; revised N. H. Russell, 1967.

The first biography of Cowper, *Life and Posthumous Writings* by William Hayley, 1803–4, contained many of his letters in truncated or sophisticated texts. Cowper's cousin, John Johnson, published editions of his correspondence in 1817, 1820, and 1824. The standard edition is still that of T. Wright, 1904, but a new edition is in preparation by C. Ryskamp. There are several selections. Cowper's autobiographical narrative of the period 1763–5 was written at Huntingdon about 1766 and published in two editions of differing texts in 1816. This *Memoir*, ed. M. J. Quinlan, is reprinted in *Proceedings of the American Philosophical Society* xcvii, 1953. There is a good selection of Cowper's poetry and prose, ed. B. Spiller, 1968 (Reynard Library).

Since Hayley, Cowper's principal biographers have been Southey, 1835; Wright, 1892 (revised 1921); H. I'A. Fausset, 1928; Lord David Cecil, *The Stricken Deer*, 1929; G. Thomas, *William Cowper and the Eighteenth Century*, 1935; and M. Quinlan, 1953. C. Ryskamp's *William Cowper of the Inner Temple, Esquire*, 1959, is a carefully documented study of life and works up to 1768. There is a general survey by W. N. Free, New York, 1970. Cowper's evangelicalism is expounded by H. N. Fairchild in *Religious Trends in English Poetry*, ii, 1942. The most satisfactory study of his poetry is by N. Nicholson in *William Cowper*, 1951, but there are perceptive observations in M. Golden, *In Search of Stability: the Poetry of William Cowper*, New York, 1960.

A bibliography to 1837 has been compiled by N. H. Russell, Oxford, 1963. Later studies have been listed in an annotated bibliography by L. Hartley, *William Cowper: the Continuing Revaluation*, Chapel Hill, 1960. Hartley has also indicated the range of Cowper's social interests in *William Cowper, Humanitarian*, Chapel Hill, 1938.

More specialized essays include two by H. P. Kroitor, 'Cowper, Deism, and the Divinization of Nature', *JHI* xxi, 1960, and 'The Influence of Popular Science on William Cowper', *MP* lxi, 1964. D. Davie considers Cowper's critical principles in the *Cambridge Journal* vii, 1953, and has valuable comments in *Purity of Diction in English Verse*, 1952, rev. 1967. R. W. Desai discusses Cowper in relation to the visual arts, *Bulletin of the New York Public Library* lxxii, 1968. The *Memoir* has been examined by B. J. Mandel, *TSLL* xii, 1970.

COXE, WILLIAM, 1747–1828

Sketches of the Natural, Civil, and Political State of Swisserland appeared in 1779; subsequent editions (3 vols., 1789, 2 vols.,

1794, 3 vols., 1801) progressively enlarged the work. Coxe also wrote *Travels into Poland, Russia, Sweden, and Denmark*, 3 vols., 1784. He was the author of several historical compilations, notably *Memoirs of the Life and Administration of Sir Robert Walpole*, 3 vols., 1798, and *Memoirs of Horatio, Lord Walpole*, 1802.

P. Fritz argues that Coxe should be seen as the first of the 'modern' English political biographers: see his essay in *The Triumph of Culture: Eighteenth-Century Perspectives*, ed. P. Fritz and D. Williams, Toronto, 1972.

CUMBERLAND, RICHARD, 1732–1811

Cumberland's sentimental comedies include *The Brothers*, 1769, *The West Indian*, 1771, and *The Fashionable Lover*, 1772. His tragedy *The Battle of Hastings*, 1778, was ridiculed by Sheridan in *The Critic*.

Anecdotes of Eminent Painters in Spain appeared in 2 vols., 1782, and he published a volume of essays called *The Observer* in 1785. His novels, *Arundel, Henry*, and *John de Lancaster*, were published in 1789, 1795, and 1809 respectively. He wrote a number of poems, including *Calvary; or the Death of Christ*, 1792. His *Memoirs* appeared in 2 vols., 1806–7.

The standard study of Cumberland is by S. T. Williams, New Haven, 1917. There is a useful essay by R. J. Detisch, 'The Synthesis of Laughing and Sentimental Comedy in *The West Indian*', *Educational Theatre Journal* xxii, 1970. E. M. Yearling compares Cumberland with Goldsmith and Sheridan in an article on good-natured heroes, *MLR* lxvii, 1972.

DALRYMPLE, SIR DAVID, LORD HAILES, 1726–92

Dalrymple edited a number of verse collections, notably *Ancient Scottish Poems published from the MS. of George Bannatyne*, Edinburgh, 1770. The most important of his historical works was *Annals of Scotland*, 2 vols., Edinburgh, 1776–9 (from the accession of Malcolm III to the accession of the House of Stewart). He also wrote a reply to Gibbon, *An Inquiry into the Secondary Causes which Mr. Gibbon has assigned for the Rapid Growth of Christianity*, 1786. His correspondence with Thomas Percy appears in *The Percy Letters*, vol. iii, ed. A. F. Falconer, Baton Rouge, 1954. Horace Walpole's correspondence with Dalrymple is collected in vol. xv of the Yale Edition, ed. W. S. Lewis *et al.*, New Haven, 1952.

Dalrymple's work on ballads is discussed by A. Watkins Jones, 'Bishop Percy and the Scottish Ballads', *E&S* xviii, 1932, and by J. J. Campbell, *PQ* xxix, 1950. R. H. Carnie considers Dalrymple and Macpherson's *Fragments of Ancient Poetry*, *ES* xli, 1960.

DALRYMPLE, SIR JOHN, 1726–1810

Vol. i of *Memoirs of Great Britain and Ireland* appeared in 1771, vol. ii, consisting mainly of letters illustrating the narrative, in 1773. The narrative continued in vol. iii, Edinburgh 1788. The *Memoirs* cover the period 1681–1702.

DAVIES, THOMAS, ?1712–85

Davies wrote a life of John Henderson ('the Bath Roscius'), 1777, a life of Garrick, 2 vols., 1780, and *Dramatic Miscellanies*, 3 vols., 1783–4. Some of his letters appear in James Granger's *Letters*, ed. J. P. Malcolm, 1805.

DAY, THOMAS, 1748–99

The History of Sandford and Merton: a Work intended for the Use of Children appeared in 3 vols., 1783–9. Day also wrote a number of poems, including some against slavery. They are collected in vol. lviii of *The British Poets*, Chiswick, 1822.

There are two books about Day: G. W. Gignilliat, *The Author of Sandford and Merton*, New York, 1932; and S. H. Scott, *The Exemplary Mr. Day*, 1935. An abridged version of *Sandford and Merton* is included in *Three Sentimental Novels*, ed. A. J. Kuhn, New York, 1970.

DODINGTON, GEORGE BUBB, 1691–1762

Dodington's *Diary* was first published, with a controversial preface, by H. Penruddock Wyndham, 1784. There is an excellent modern edition by J. Carswell and L. A. Dralle, Oxford, 1965. His best-known poem,

> Love thy Country, wish it well,
> Not with too intense a care,

was first published in the Singer edition of Spence's *Anecdotes*, 1820. There is a study of his career by L. Sanders, *Patron and Place-Hunter*, 1919.

DODSLEY, ROBERT, 1703-64

The standard account of Dodsley's Life and work is by R. Straus, *Robert Dodsley. Poet, Publisher and Playwright*, 1910. It includes a bibliography of his own works and of books published by him. While his chief importance was as a bookseller and publisher, he began his career as the author of *Servitude: a Poem*, 1729, and *A Man in Livery: or the Footman's Miscellany*, 1732. He was probably the author of *The Oeconomy of Human Life*, 1750.

He published the important *Select Collection of Old Plays* in 12 vols., 1744-5, and *A Collection of Poems. By Several Hands*, 3 vols., 1748, vol. iv, 1755, vols. v-vi, 1758. On the latter, see R. D. Havens, 'Changing Taste in the Eighteenth Century: a Study of Dryden's and Dodsley's Miscellanies', *PMLA* xliv, 1929.

DOW, ALEXANDER, ?-1779

The *Tales translated from the Persian of Inatulla of Delhi* appeared in 1768, and *The History of Hindustan, translated from the Persian of Ferishta*, in the same year. He also wrote two plays, *Zingis*, 1769, and *Sethona*, 1774. The *Tales of Inatulla* are included in *Tales of the East*, ed. H. Weber, vol. 2, Edinburgh, 1812.

DUFF, WILLIAM, 1732-1815

The *Essay on Original Genius* first appeared in 1767, and was supplemented by *Critical Observations on the Writings of the Most Celebrated Geniuses in Poetry*, 1770. The latter includes a section which is in effect an addition to the argument of the *Essay*, 'Of the Effects of Genius on the Temper and Character, and of the Advantages and Disadvantages attending the Possession of it'. Duff also wrote *The History of Rhedi, the Hermit of Mount Ararat*, 1773, and *Letters on the Intellectual and Moral Character of Women*, Aberdeen, 1807.

The 1767 *Essay* has been reprinted with an introduction by J. L. Mahoney, Gainesville, 1964.

DUNBAR, JAMES, ?-1798

Dunbar's *Essays on the History of Mankind in Rude and Cultivated Ages* appeared in 1780. He also wrote *Caledonia: a Poem*, 1778.

EVANS, EVAN, 1731–89

Some Specimens of the Poetry of the Ancient Welsh Bards appeared in 1764. His correspondence with Thomas Percy is in *The Percy Letters*, vol. v, ed. A. Lewis, Baton Rouge, 1957. There is an account of Evans in S. Lewis, *A School of Welsh Augustans*, Wrexham, 1924.

FARMER, RICHARD, 1735–97

An Essay on the Learning of Shakespeare was published in Cambridge, 1767, and was often reprinted. His correspondence with Thomas Percy is in *The Percy Letters*, vol. ii, ed. C. Brooks, Baton Rouge, 1946. D. Nichol Smith includes the *Essay* in *Eighteenth-Century Essays on Shakespeare*, Glasgow, 1903.

FERGUSON, ADAM, 1723–1816

The *Essay on the History of Civil Society* was published in Edinburgh, 1767. *Institutes of Moral Philosophy* followed in 1769. *The History of the Progress and Termination of the Roman Republic* appeared in 3 vols., 1783, and *Principles of Moral and Political Science* in 2 vols., 1792. Ferguson's 'Dialogue on a Highland Jaunt' was first published (ed. E. C. Mossner) in the *A. D. McKillop Festschrift*, 1963.

There are three major studies of Ferguson's work: W. C. Lehmann, *Ferguson and the Beginnings of Modern Sociology*, New York, 1930; H. H. Jogland, *Ursprünge und Grundlagen der Soziologie bei Ferguson*, Berlin, 1959; and D. Kettler, *The Social and Political Thought of Adam Ferguson*, Columbus, Ohio, 1965. See also Kettler's article, 'The Political Vision of Adam Ferguson', *Studies in Burke and his Time* ix, 1967.

FERGUSSON, ROBERT, 1750–74

Sixty-five of Fergusson's 107 poems first appeared in the pages of Walter Ruddiman's *Weekly Mazazine, or Edinburgh Amusement*, most of them between February 1771 and December 1773. A collected edition was published in 1773 and reissued with a second part in 1779. Additional poems appeared in the edition of 1782. The standard edition is by M. P. McDiarmid, 2 vols., Edinburgh, 1954–6 (Scottish Text Society). It contains a good biography and critical study. There is a selection from his poetry (together with poems by Allan Ramsay) ed. A. M. Kinghorn and A. Law, Edinburgh, 1974.

Robert Fergusson 1750-1774: Essays by Various Hands, Edinburgh, 1952, contains interesting contributions by S. G. Smith, the editor of the volume, J. W. Oliver (on Fergusson and *Ruddiman's Magazine*), A. D. Mackie (on Fergusson's language), W. Montgomerie (on the Scottish folk-song tradition in Ramsay, Fergusson, and Burns), and others.

There is a general study by A. H. MacLaine, New York, 1965.

FIELDING, HENRY, 1707-54

Fielding's first publication was a poem, *The Masquerade*, 1728. There followed a long series of plays, of which the most notable are *The Author's Farce*, 1730; *Tom Thumb, a Tragedy*, 1730 (revised as *The Tragedy of Tragedies; or the Life and Death of Tom Thumb the Great*, 1731); *Rape upon Rape; or, the Justice Caught in his own Trap, a Comedy*, 1730; *The Welsh Opera: or, the Grey Mare the Better Horse*, 1731 (revised in the same year as *The Genuine Grub-Street Opera*); *Don Quixote in England: a Comedy*, 1734; *Pasquin. A Dramatick Satire on the Times*, 1736; and *The Historical Register for the Year 1736*, 1737.

He published *The Champion, or the British Mercury*, 1739-41, contributing about 70 essays to it. In 1741 *An Apology for the Life of Mrs. Shamela Andrews, by Mr. Conny Keyber* appeared: Fielding's authorship has been demonstrated by C. B. Woods, *PQ* xxv, 1946. It was followed by *The History of the Adventures of Joseph Andrews and of his Friend Mr. Abraham Adams, written in Imitation of the Manner of Cervantes*, 2 vols., 1742.

In 1743 Fielding published 3 vols. of *Miscellanies*. Vol. i contains poems, essays, dialogues and other satirical pieces; vol. ii, *A Journey from This World to the Next* and two plays, *Eurydice* (a farce performed in 1737) and *The Wedding Day* (performed in 1743); vol. iii, *The Life of Mr. Jonathan Wild the Great*. *Jonathan Wild* was revised and enlarged, if not improved, in 1754.

One of Fielding's most important critical essays appeared in 1744: the preface to the second edition of Sarah Fielding's *Adventures of David Simple*. He also contributed the preface and letters 40-44 of *Familiar Letters between the Principal Characters in David Simple and Some Others*, 1747. The 1745 rebellion drew several political publications from him, including *A Serious*

Address to the People of Great Britain. He contributed to the *True Patriot*, 1745–6, and the *Jacobite's Journal*, 1747–8. Miscellaneous works from this period include his account of the scandalous case of Mrs. Mary Hamilton, *The Female Husband*, 1746, and *Ovid's Art of Love Paraphrased and Adapted to the Present Time*, 1747.

The History of Tom Jones, a Foundling, appeared in 6 vols., 1749. In 1751 Fielding published his pamphlet *An Enquiry into the Causes of the Late Increase of Robbers. Amelia* followed, 4 vols., 1752, revised in Murphy's edition of Fielding's works, 1762. Among his last publications were the *Covent-Garden Journal*, which appeared through eleven months of 1752, and *A Proposal for Making an Effectual Provision for the Poor*, 1753. The *Journal of a Voyage to Lisbon* was published posthumously, in 1755.

The first collection of Fielding's works was Arthur Murphy's, 4 vols., 1762. The most complete edition at present is that by W. E. Henley, 16 vols., 1903, reissued New York, 1967. The definitive 'Wesleyan Edition' is in course of publication: *Joseph Andrews*, ed. M. C. Battestin, Oxford, 1967; *Miscellanies, Volume One*, ed. H. K. Miller, Oxford, 1972; *Tom Jones*, ed. M. C. Battestin and F. Bowers, 2 vols., Oxford, 1974; and *The Jacobite's Journal and Related Writings*, ed. W. B. Coley, Oxford, 1974. There have been many reprints not only of the major novels but of the minor works. The best listing of these is in M. C. Battestin's contribution to *The English Novel. Select Bibliographical Guides*, ed. A. E. Dyson, 1974. Fielding's critical writings were collected by I. Williams, 1970. C. J. Rawson illustrates several aspects of Fielding's art in his volume in the *Profiles in Literature* series, 1965.

M. C. Battestin contributed the section on Fielding to *NCBEL*, but there is a fuller bibliographical description of Fielding's own works in W. L. Cross's biography, 3 vols., New Haven, 1918. This is still the standard life, in spite of the much later work by F. H. Dudden, 2 vols., Oxford, 1952. B. M. Jones's short biography, *Henry Fielding, Novelist and Magistrate*, 1933, is useful.

F. T. Blanchard's *Fielding the Novelist. A Study in Historical Criticism*, New Haven, 1926, surveys earlier attitudes, and *Henry Fielding: the Critical Heritage*, ed. R. Paulson and T. Lockwood, 1969, supplies many of the texts on which Blanchard's study is based. There are a number of useful critical anthologies: *Fielding: a Collection of Critical Essays*, ed. R. Paulson, Englewood Cliffs, 1962; *Twentieth Century Interpretations of 'Tom Jones'*, ed. M. C. Battestin, Englewood Cliffs, 1968; *Henry Fielding und der englische Roman des 18. Jahrhunderts*, ed. W. Iser, Darmstadt, 1972; and the Fielding volume, ed. C. J. Rawson, in the series of *Penguin Critical Anthologies*, 1973.

Recent work on Fielding has been considerably indebted to M. C. Battestin's *The Moral Basis of Fielding's Art. A Study of 'Joseph Andrews'*, Middletown, 1959. See also M. Golden, *Fielding's Moral Psychology*, Amherst, 1966. There has been much discussion of Fielding's comic method, for example by A. R. Humphreys, *RES* xviii, 1942, by A. E. Dyson, *MLQ* xviii, 1957, by A. Wright, *Henry Fielding: Mask and Feast*, 1965, by G. R. Levine, *Henry Fielding and the Dry Mock: a Study of the Techniques of Irony in his Early Works*, and—notably—by G. W. Hatfield, *Henry Fielding and the Language of Irony*, Chicago, 1968. Another useful general study is by R. Alter: *Fielding and the Nature of the Novel*, Cambridge, Mass., 1968. C. J. Rawson's *Henry Fielding and the Augustan Ideal under Stress*, 1972, is a suggestive and wide-ranging book which pays particular attention to *Jonathan Wild* and *Amelia*; H. K. Miller's fine study of the first volume of *Miscellanies*, Princeton, 1961, is indispensable for any adequate understanding of Fielding's art.

Other books on aspects of Fielding include E. M. Thornbury's study of his theory of the comic prose epic. Madison, 1931; W. R. Irwin, *The Making of 'Jonathan Wild'*, New York, 1941; B. Kreissman, *Pamela-Shamela: a Study of the Criticisms, Burlesques, Parodies, and Adaptations of Richardson's 'Pamela'*, Lincoln, Nebr., 1960; M. R. Zirker, Jr., *Fielding's Social Pamphlets*, Berkeley, 1966; and H. Goldberg, *The Art of 'Joseph Andrews'*, Chicago, 1969. Among the many articles that might be mentioned, three are of special importance: R. S. Crane on the plot of *Tom Jones*, first published in the *Journal of General Education* iv, 1950, and revised in his *Critics and Criticism Ancient and Modern*, Chicago, 1952; W. Empson on *Tom Jones*, *Kenyon Review* xx, 1958; and G. Sherburn on *Amelia*, *ELH* iii, 1936. Among recent essays, that by M.-S. Røstrig, '*Tom Jones* and the Choice of Hercules', in *Fair Forms*, ed. M.-S. Røstvig, Cambridge 1975, is particularly helpful.

There are good sections on Fielding in A. D. McKillop's

Early Masters of English Fiction, Lawrence, 1956, in I. Watt, *The Rise of the Novel*, 1957, in R. Paulson, *Satire and the Novel in Eighteenth-Century England*, 1967, in J. Preston, *The Created Self: the Reader's Role in Eighteenth-Century Fiction*, 1970, and in W. Iser, *The Implied Reader*, Baltimore, 1974. There are sections on Fielding's plays in F. W. Bateson, *English Comic Drama 1700–1750*, 1929, in J. Loftis, *Comedy and Society from Congreve to Fielding*, 1959, and in I. Donaldson, *The World Upside-Down. Comedy from Jonson to Fielding*, Oxford, 1970.

FIELDING, SARAH, 1710–68

Sarah Fielding's first publication was *The Adventures of David Simple*, of which there were two editions in 1744. There followed, in 1747, *Familiar Letters between the Principal Characters in David Simple*. Her brother Henry Fielding wrote a preface both to the second edition of the *Adventures* and to the *Familiar Letters*. In 1749 she published *The Governess, or, The Little Female Academy*, and in 1753 a continuation of *David Simple*, 'Volume the Last'. *The Cry: a New Dramatic Fable*, written with Jane Collier, appeared in 1754, *The Lives of Cleopatra and Octavia* in 1757, *The History of the Countess of Dellwyn* in 1759, and *The History of Ophelia* in 1760.

Like Jane Collier, Sarah Fielding was one of Richardson's correspondents, and she may have written the anonymous *Remarks on Clarissa, Addressed to the Author*, 1749.

There is an excellent edition of *David Simple* by M. Kelsall, 1969.

FOOTE, SAMUEL, 1720–77

Foote's best play, *The Minor*, appeared in 1760. Other plays include *The Lyar*, 1762, though not printed till 1764; *The Mayor of Garret*, 1763; *The Patron*, 1764; *The Lame Lover*, 1770; and *The Maid of Bath*, 1771. His works were collected in 4 vols., 1770–86.

There are studies by P. H. Fitzgerald, 1910, M. M. Belden, New Haven, 1929, G. Sinko, Wroclaw, 1950, and S. Trefman, New York, 1971.

FORDYCE, DAVID, 1711–51

Fordyce's *Dialogues concerning Education* were published in 2 vols., 1745–8. *Theodorus, a Dialogue concerning the Art of Preaching* appeared posthumously in 1752, and *The Elements of Moral Philosophy* in 1754. Akenside was acquainted with Fordyce, and three letters of his to Fordyce throw some light on the composition of the *Dialogues concerning Education*. See C. T. Houpt, *Mark Akenside*, Philadelphia, 1944.

GARRICK, DAVID, 1717–79

Garrick's first farce, *The Lying Valet*, was performed in 1741, and thereafter he wrote or adapted or had a hand in over 40 pieces for the stage. Among the more important are *Miss in her Teens: or the Medley of Lovers*, 1747; *A Peep Behind the Curtain: or the New Rehearsal*, 1767; *The Jubilee*, 1769; *Bon Ton: or High Life Above Stairs*, 1775. He collaborated with George Colman in *The Clandestine Marriage*, 1766. Among his versions of Shakespeare, six are available in facsimile, two of *A Midsummer Night's Dream* (1755 and 1763), 1969; *Catherine and Petruchio* (1756), 1969; *Florizel and Perdita* (1758), 1969; *Romeo and Juliet* (1750), 1969; and *King Henry VIII* (1762), 1970.

Garrick's dramatic works were first collected in 3 vols., 1768, but the edition of 1798, also in 3 vols., is fuller. *Three Farces*, ed. L. B. Osborn, New Haven, 1925, contains *The Lying Valet, a Peep Behind the Curtain*, and *Bon Ton*; *Three Plays*, ed. E. P. Stein, New York, 1926, contains *Harlequin's Invasion, The Jubilee*, and *The Meeting of the Company; or, Bayes's Art of Acting*—first printed here.

His poems were collected in 2 vols., 1785. His letters have been edited by D. M. Little and G. M. Kahrl, 3 vols., Cambridge, Mass., 1963. A diary of 1751 (in Paris) has been edited by R. C. Alexander, New York, 1928, and another of 1763 (in France and Italy) edited by G. W. Stone, Jr., New York, 1939. M. E. Knapp has compiled a checklist of Garrick's verse, Charlottesville, 1955, and G. M. Berkowitz an annotated bibliography, in *Restoration and Eighteenth-Century Theatre Research* xi, 1972.

The early biographies by Thomas Davies (2 vols., 1780) and Arthur Murphy (2 vols., 1801) are still worth consulting on points of detail. There is useful material in the biography by P. H. Fitzgerald, 2 vols., 1868, rev. 1899, and in *Garrick and his Circle* by F. Parsons, 1906.

Among modern studies of Garrick, there is an excellent book by K. A. Burnim, *David Garrick, Director*, Pittsburgh, 1961. E. P.

Stein has written of Garrick as a dramatist, New York, 1938, and there are biographies by M. Barton, 1948, and C. Oman, 1958. J. M. Stochholm has considered the Shakespeare Jubilee of 1769 in *Garrick's Folly*, 1964, as has M. W. England, New York, 1962, rev. Columbus, 1964. G. W. Stone, Jr., has written a number of articles on various aspects of Garrick and Shakespeare: see *PMLA* xlix, 1934, *RES* xiii, 1937, and xv, 1939, *PMLA* liv, 1939, *SP* xxxviii, 1941, and xlv, 1948, *PMLA* lxv, 1950, *Shakespeare Quarterly* xv, 1964, *PQ* xlv, 1966, and in *On Stage and Off: Eight Essays in English Literature*, ed. J. W. Ehrstine *et al.*, Pullman, Wash., 1968. His essay on Garrick's theory of acting and dramatic composition is in *J. Q. Adams Memorial Studies*, Washington, 1948. D. MacMillan has two useful articles, on Garrick as critic, *SP* xxxi, 1934, and as manager, *SP* xlv, 1948.

GEDDES, ALEXANDER, 1737–1802

Although his chief importance is as a Biblical critic—his *Critical Remarks on the Hebrew Scriptures*, 1800, were too rationalistic to please his fellow Catholics—Geddes translated Horace's *Satires*, 1779, and wrote the 'Dissertation on the Scoto-Saxon Dialect' which appeared in *Transactions of the Society of Antiquaries of Scotland*, 1792.

GERARD, ALEXANDER, 1728–95

An Essay on Taste appeared in 1759, revised 1764. There is a modern reprint, ed. W. J. Hipple, Jr., Gainesville, 1963. *An Essay on Genius*, 1774, has been edited by B. Fabian, Munich, 1966. Gerard also published a number of theological works.

Gerard is discussed in most surveys of criticism, and particular attention is paid to him in an essay by M. Grene, *MP* xli, 1943, and in R. Cohen's 'Association of Ideas and Poetic Unity', *PQ* xxxvi, 1957.

GIBBON, EDWARD, 1737–94

The *Essai sur l'étude de la littérature* appeared in 1761, and *Mémoires littéraires de la Grande Bretagne* in 2 vols., 1767–8 (with G. Deyverdun). *Critical Observations on the Sixth Book of the Aeneid* followed in 1770 (in reply to part of Warburton's *Divine Legation of Moses*). The first volume of *The History of the Decline and Fall of the Roman Empire* appeared in 1776, with vols. ii and iii following in 1781, and iv, v, and vi in 1788. He replied to some of his critics in *A Vindication of Some Passages in the XVth and XVIth Chapters of the History of the Decline and Fall of the Roman Empire*, 1779. The *Miscellaneous Works* published by Lord Sheffield in 2 vols., 1796, included 'Memoirs of his Life and Writings composed by himself'. This is a version of the auto-biography put together by Sheffield; Gibbon's original six drafts were not published until 1896, ed. J. Murray, and have not been edited in this form since, although G. A. Bonnard, 1966, uses much of the material excluded by Sheffield. An expanded edition of the *Miscellaneous Works* was published in 5 vols., 1814. There is a definitive modern edition (excluding the autobiography) by P. B. Craddock, Oxford, 1972.

The diaries have been published as follows: *Gibbon's Journal*, ed. D. M. Low, 1929; *Le Journal de Gibbon à Lausanne*, ed. G. A. Bonnard, Lausanne, 1945; *Miscellanea Gibboniana*, ed. G. A. Bonnard, G. R. de Beer, and L. Junod, Lausanne, 1952; and *Gibbon's Journey from Geneva to Rome*, ed. G. A. Bonnard, 1961. The letters have been edited by J. E. Norton, 3 vols., New York, 1956.

There is a bibliography by J. E. Norton, Oxford, 1940, and F. Cordasco has compiled a handlist of critical studies, New York, 1950. The catalogue of the books in Gibbon's library, ed. G. L. Keynes, 1940, is an important aid to Gibbon studies.

The best edition of the *Decline and Fall* is that of J. B. Bury, 7 vols., 1896–1900, revised 1909–14 and 1926–9. The best edition of the Sheffield text of the autobiography is also by J. B. Bury, 1907.

Most of the early critics of Gibbon were concerned with his views on the early church, for example Richard Watson in his *Apology for Christianity*, Cambridge, 1776, Sir David Dalrymple, Lord Hailes, in his *Inquiry into the Secondary Causes which Mr. Gibbon has assigned for the Rapid Growth of Christianity*, 1786, and Joseph Priestley in his *History of the Corruptions of Christianity*, Birmingham, 1782. Two exceptions are William Hayley, *An Essay on History*, 1780, and John Whitaker, *Gibbon's History Reviewed*, 1791 (reprinted from the *English Review* xii–xiii, 1788–9).

Among modern studies, Gibbon's art is dealt with most satisfactorily by H. L. Bond, *The Literary Art of Edward Gibbon*, Oxford, 1960, L. Braudy, *Narrative Form in History and Fiction*:

Hume, Fielding, and Gibbon, Princeton, 1970, and D. P. Jordan, *Gibbon and his Roman Empire*, Urbana, 1971. See also J. B. Black, *The Art of History*, 1926, and two essays by D. M. Oliver: 'The Character of an Historian', *ELH* xxxviii, 1971, and 'Gibbon's Use of Architecture as a Symbol', *TSLL* xiv, 1972. Gibbon's revisions of his own work are considered by P. B. Craddock, *Studies in Bibliography* xxi, 1968.

The political significance of the *Decline and Fall* is examined by L. P. Curtis, 'Gibbon's *Paradise Lost*', in *C. B. Tinker Festschrift*, 1949. Studies which assess his status as a historian include C. Dawson, 'Edward Gibbon and the Fall of Rome', in *The Dynamics of World History*, ed. J. J. Mulloy, New York, 1956; A. Momigliano, 'Ancient History and the Antiquarian', and 'Gibbon's Contribution to Historical Method', both in his *Studies in Historiography*, 1966; and H. R. Trevor-Roper, 'The Historical Philosophy of the Enlightenment', *Studies on Voltaire and the Eighteenth Century* xxvii, 1963. There is a wide-ranging study by G. Giarrizzo, *Edward Gibbon e la cultura europea del settecento*, Naples, 1954; and J. W. Johnson, in *The Formation of English Neo-Classical Thought*, Princeton, 1967, views Gibbon as the central figure of English neoclassicism. P. Gay has an acute chapter on Gibbon in his *Style in History*, 1975. Gibbon's religious views, and the attacks on them, are examined by S. T. McCloy in *Gibbon's Antagonism to Christianity*, Chapel Hill, 1933.

The standard biography is by D. M. Low, 1937, and there are helpful general studies by G. M. Young, 1932, M. Joyce, 1953, C. V. Wedgwood, 1955, and R. N. Parkinson, New York, 1973.

Among recent studies of the autobiography, R. J. Porter's essay, 'Filling up the Silent Vacancy', *ECS* viii, 1974, is particularly helpful. See also B. J. Mandell's study of the six drafts, 'The Problems of Narration in Edward Gibbon's *Autobiography*', *SP* lxvii, 1970; and the essays by D. M. Oliver, 'The Character of an Historian: Edward Gibbon', *ELH* xxxviii, 1971, and R. Folkenflik, 'Child and Adult: Historical Perspective in Gibbon's Memoirs', *Studies in Burke and his Time* xv, 1973.

H. Trowbridge considers Gibbon as a literary critic, *ECS* iv, 1971.

GILPIN, WILLIAM, 1724–1804

A Dialogue upon the Gardens of the Right Honourable the Lord Viscount Cobham at Stow in Buckinghamshire appeared in 1748. It was published anonymously, as was *An Essay upon Prints*, 1768. *Observations on the River Wye, and several parts of South Wales, etc., relative chiefly to Picturesque Beauty* appeared in 1782; *Observations on . . . the Mountains and Lakes of Cumberland and Westmoreland*, in 2 vols., 1786; *Observations on . . . the Highlands of Scotland*, in 2 vols., 1789; *Remarks on Forest Scenery*, in 2 vols., 1791; *Observations on the Western Parts of England*, in 1798; *Observations on . . . Cambridge, Norfolk, Suffolk, and Essex*, in 1809. Gilpin's principles are concisely set out in his *Three Essays: On Picturesque Beauty; On Picturesque Travel; and On Sketching Landscape*, 1792.

Gilpin wrote numerous biographies, notably of Bernard Gilpin, 1752, of Bishop Latimer, 1755, of Wiclif and other reformers, 1765, and of Cranmer, 1784. His most remarkable biographical work was published posthumously: *Memoirs of Dr. Richard Gilpin . . . and of his Posterity in the two succeeding Generations . . . together with an Account of the Author, by himself; and a Pedigree of the Gilpin Family*, ed. W. Jackson, Carlisle, 1879.

His *Dialogues on Various Subjects* appeared in 1807, with a prefatory essay 'On Dialogue Writing'.

W. D. Templeman's study, *The Life and Work of William Gilpin*, Urbana, 1939, is comprehensive, and has a good bibliography, but should be supplemented by C. P. Barbier, *William Gilpin: his Drawings, Teaching, and Theory of the Picturesque*, Oxford, 1963. Barbier also wrote *Samuel Rogers and William Gilpin: their Friendship and Correspondence*, 1959. Gilpin's letters to Samuel Henley are edited by F. Neiman, *HLQ* xxxv, 1972. J. Macaulay discusses Gilpin in chap. x of *The Gothic Revival 1745–1845*, 1975. His regime at Cheam School is considered in chap. i of W. A. C. Stewart and W. P. McCann's survey, *The Educational Innovators 1750–1880*, 1967.

GOLDSMITH, OLIVER, ?1730–74

Goldsmith began his literary career by reviewing for the *Monthly Review*, 1757. In 1759 he started to write for the *Critical Review* and other journals. In the same year he published *An Enquiry into the Present State of Polite Learning in Europe* and *The Bee*. *The Chinese Letters* appeared in the *Public Ledger*, 1760–1, and were reprinted as *The Citizen of the World*, 2 vols., 1762. He abridged Plutarch's *Lives*, 7 vols., 1762, and compiled *The Life of Richard Nash of Bath, Esq.* in the same year. *An History of England, in a Series of Letters from a Nobleman to his Son* followed in

2 vols., 1764, and was often reprinted. *The Traveller, or a Prospect of Society* was published at the end of the same year. *The Vicar of Wakefield: a Tale* appeared in 2 vols., 1766, and has been reprinted in many editions, the best now available being by A. Friedman, 1974. Goldsmith's remaining major publications were as follows: *The Good Natur'd man: a Comedy*, 1768; *The Roman History*, 2 vols., 1769; *The Deserted Village*, 1770; *The History of England, from the Earliest Times to the Death of George II*, 4 vols., 1771; *She Stoops to Conquer: or, the Mistakes of a Night. A Comedy*, 1773; *Retaliation: a Poem*, 1774; *The Grecian History*, 2 vols., 1774; *An History of the Earth and Animated Nature*, 8 vols., 1774.

A bibliography of Goldsmith's writings appears in I. A. Williams, *Seven XVIIIth Century Bibliographies*, 1924, but the fullest listing of his work (and of writings on him) is by A. Friedman, in *NCBEL*. A. Friedman is also the editor of the *Collected Works of Oliver Goldsmith*, 5 vols., Oxford, 1966. For his letters, see the edition by K. C. Balderston, Cambridge, 1928. The best edition of the poems is by R. Lonsdale (with Gray and Collins), 1969. Among the many collections of Goldsmith's major writings, that by R. Garnett, 1950, is particularly recommended.

Among the earlier lives, the memoir in the *Miscellaneous Works*, 1801, is important because written with the authority of Thomas Percy: see the study by K. C. Balderston, Cambridge, 1926. Other lives that are still worth consulting are those by J. Prior, 1837, J. Forster, 1848, and A. Dobson, 1888. A. L. Sells, whose *Les Sources françaises de Goldsmith*, Paris, 1924, is a valuable specialized study, is also the author of a good general survey, 1974. R. M. Wardle's biography, Lawrence, Kansas, 1957, is excellent. See also the introductory studies by R. Quintana, New York, 1967, and C. M. Kirk, New York, 1967.

The earlier critics of Goldsmith are assembled by G. S. Rousseau in a volume in the Critical Heritage series, 1974. The introduction is a stimulating survey of attitudes to Goldsmith's work, past and present. Three other general essays on Goldsmith may be mentioned here: M. Golden, 'The Family-Wanderer Theme in Goldsmith', *ELH* xxv, 1958; J. A. Dussinger, 'Oliver Goldsmith, Citizen of the World', *Studies on Voltaire and the Eighteenth Century* lv, 1967; and R. Helgerson, 'The Two Worlds of Oliver Goldsmith', *SEL* xiii, 1973—an essay which considers the opposition of rural and urban settings in Goldsmith's work, and incidentally moderates some wayward views of R. H. Hopkins, *The True Genius of Oliver Goldsmith*, 1969. On *The Citizen of the World*, the study by H. J. Smith, New Haven, 1926, is still useful, but see also the essay by M. D. Patrick, 'Oliver Goldsmith's *Citizen of the World*: a Rational Accommodation of Human Existence', *Enlightenment Essays* ii, 1971.

On the poems, R. J. Jaarsma has two useful essays, 'Satire, Theme, and Structure in *The Traveller*', *Tennessee Studies in Literature* xvi, 1971, and 'Ethics in the Wasteland: Image and Structure in Goldsmith's *The Deserted Village*', *TSLL* xiii, 1971. E. Miner considers 'The Making of *The Deserted Village*', *HLQ* xxii, 1959, and L. F. Storm analyses literary convention in the same poem, *HLQ* xxxiii, 1970. D. Davie has an essay on *The Deserted Village*, 'Poem as Virtual History', *Twentieth Century* clvi, 1954.

On *The Vicar of Wakefield* there are perceptive essays by D. W. Jefferson, *Cambridge Journal* iii, 1950, and MacD. Emslie, *Goldsmith: 'The Vicar of Wakefield'*, 1963. There is a detailed study by S. Bäckman, *This Singular Tale*, Lund, 1971.

On the plays, A. N. Jeffares provides *A Critical Commentary on Goldsmith's 'She Stoops to Conquer'*, 1966. There is an important essay by R. D. Hume, 'Goldsmith and Sheridan and the Supposed Revolution of "Laughing" against "Sentimental" Comedy', in *Studies in Change and Revolution*, ed. P. J. Korshin, York, 1972. Another helpful study is by J. H. Smith, 'Tony Lumpkin and the Country Booby Type in Antecedent English Comedy', *PMLA* lviii, 1943.

GRAINGER, JAMES, ?1721–66

Grainger contributed his 'Ode on Solitude' to Dodsley's *Collection of Poems*, vol. iv, 1755. In his *Poetical Translation of the Elegies of Tibullus; and of the Poems of Sulpicia*, 2 vols., 1759, he was assisted by Thomas Percy, who translated the first elegy. 'Bryan and Pereene: a West-Indian Ballad' was published by Percy in his *Reliques of Ancient English Poetry*, vol. i, 1765, where he describes it as 'founded on a real fact'. *The Sugar-Cane: a Poem. In Four Books. With Notes* was finished in 1762 and published in 1764.

The standard edition of his poems is by R. Anderson (2 vols., Edinburgh, 1836), who was encouraged and assisted by Percy:

see J. Nichols's *Illustrations of the Literary History of the Eighteenth Century*, vol. vii, where the correspondence of Percy and Grainger is published. Grainger also published several medical works, and reviewed for the *Monthly Review*.

R. A. Knox discusses the poet facetiously in chap. vii of *Literary Distractions*, 1958. He is treated with more respect by J. Chalker in *The English Georgic*, 1969.

GRAVES, RICHARD, 1715–1804

Graves's first publication was *The Festoon: a Collection of Epigrams, Ancient and Modern, with an Essay on that Species of Composition*, 1766. *The Spiritual Quixote, or the Summer's Ramble of Mr. Geoffry Wildgoose: a Comic Romance*, followed in 3 vols., 1773. *Columella, or the Distressed Anchoret: a Colloquial Tale*, appeared in 2 vols., 1779, *Eugenius: or Anecdotes of the Golden Vale, an Embellished Narrative of Real Facts*, 2 vols., 1785; *Recollections of some Particulars in the Life of the late William Shenstone, Esq.*, 1788. He also published some verse, and some miscellanies, including *Euphrosyne, or Amusements on the Road of Life*, 2 vols., 1776–80, *The Reveries of Solitude*, 1793, and *Senilities*, 1801.

The Spiritual Quixote has been edited by C. Whibley, 1926, and C. Tracy, 1967. There is a study of Graves's literary career by C. J. Hill, Northampton, Mass., 1934. C. J. Hill considers his relations with Shenstone in an essay in *PMLA* xlix, 1934.

GRAY, THOMAS, 1716–71

Ode on a Distant Prospect of Eton College was published in 1747, and appeared in Dodsley's *Collection of Poems*, vol. ii, 1748, with the 'Ode on Spring' and the 'Ode on the Death of a Favourite Cat'. *An Elegy wrote in a Country Church Yard* appeared in 1751; *The Progress of Poesy* and *The Bard* in 1757 (at Strawberry Hill). Gray collected his poems in 1768. The poem 'On Lord Holland's Seat near Margate, Kent', was published anonymously in *The New Foundling Hospital for Wit*, iii, 1769.

The standard edition of the poems is by H. W. Starr and J. R. Hendrickson, Oxford, 1966. There is an admirably annotated edition by R. Lonsdale, 1969 (with Collins and Goldsmith). The letters have been edited by P. Toynbee and L. Whibley, 3 vols., Oxford, 1935, revised 1971. There are two bibliographies: C. S. Northup's, New Haven, 1917, and the continuation by H. W. Starr, Philadelphia, 1953.

The best biography is that by R. W. Ketton-Cremer, Cambridge, 1955, and there is an admirable study by W. P. Jones, *Thomas Gray, Scholar*, Cambridge, Mass., 1937. R. Martin's *Essai sur Thomas Gray*, Paris, 1934, is still worth consulting, and there is a useful survey by M. Golden, New York, 1964. There is a fine chapter on Gray in J. H. Hagstrum's *The Sister Arts*, Chicago, 1958. See also C. F. Bell, 'Thomas Gray and the Fine Arts', *E&S* xxx, 1945. Recent approaches to Gray's work are well illustrated in *Fearful Joy: Papers from the Thomas Gray Bicentenary Conference*, Montreal, 1974.

On the *Elegy*, see A. L. Read, *The Background of Gray's Elegy*, 1924; C. Brooks, 'Gray's Storied Urn', in *The Well-Wrought Urn*, New York, 1947; F. H. Ellis, 'Gray's *Elegy*: the Biographical Problem in Literary Criticism', *PMLA* lxvi, 1951; A. E. Dyson, 'The Ambivalence of Gray's *Elegy*', *EC* vii, 1957; and the essays by F. Brady, B. H. Bronson, and I. Jack in the *F. A. Pottle Festschrift*, 1965. H. W. Starr has edited *Twentieth-Century Interpretations of Gray's Elegy*, Englewood Cliffs, 1968.

On the Odes, see W. P. Jones, 'The Contemporary Reception of Gray's *Odes*', *MP* xxviii, 1930, and A. Johnstone, *Thomas Gray and 'The Bard'*, Cardiff, 1966. Other essays on Gray's poetry include Lord David Cecil's Warton Lecture, *Proceedings of the British Academy* xxxi, 1945, reprinted in *Poets and Story-Tellers*, 1949, P. M. Spacks, 'Statement and Artifice in Thomas Gray', *SEL* v, 1965, and D. C. Mell, 'Form as Meaning in Augustan Elegy', *Papers on Language and Literature* iv, 1968 (with special reference to the Sonnet on West).

GUTHRIE, WILLIAM, 1708-70

Guthrie wrote *A General History of England, from the Invasion of Julius Caesar to the Revolution in 1688*, 4 vols., 1744-51; and *A General History of Scotland, from the Earliest Accounts to the Present Time*, 10 vols., 1767-8. He also organized and contributed to *A General History of the World*, 12 vols. and index, 1764-7. In another vein, he wrote *The Friends: a Sentimental History describing Love as a Virtue as well as a Passion*, 1754. He was an important contributor to the *Critical Review*.

There is some discussion of Guthrie in D. Forbes, *Hume's Philosophical Politics*, Cambridge, 1975, chap. viii.

HAMILTON, WILLIAM, of BANGOUR, 1704–54

Hamilton's first publication was an ode, *The Faithful Few*, Edinburgh, 1734. *The Eighteenth Epistle of the Second Book of Horace Imitated* followed in 1737, *Three Odes* in 1739, and *Contemplation, or the Triumph of Love* in 1747. His *Poems on Several Occasions* appeared in Glasgow, 1748. His poems were collected in Anderson ix and Chalmers xv. *Poems and Songs*, with a life by J. Paterson was published in Edinburgh, 1850. There is a study by N. S. Bushnell, Aberdeen, 1957 (with bibliography).

HARRIS, JAMES, 1709–80

Harris's *Three Treatises*, 1744, include the dialogue on happiness. He was chiefly celebrated for his *Hermes, or a Philosophical Inquiry concerning Universal Grammar*, 1751. *Philological Inquiries* appeared in 2 vols., 1780–1. His work is considered by R. Marsh in his *Four Dialectical Theories of Poetry: an Aspect of English Neoclassical Criticism*, Chicago, 1965.

HAWKESWORTH, JOHN, 1715–73

Hawkesworth edited the *Adventurer*, 1752–4, and contributed some 70 essays to it. He edited Swift, 12 vols., 1754–5, with the letters, 3 vols., 1766. *Almoran and Hamet, an Oriental Tale*, appeared in 2 vols., 1761. He compiled the *Account of the Voyages Undertaken in the Southern Hemisphere*, 3 vols., 1773. His contributions to the *Gentleman's Magazine* have been considered by D. D. Eddy, *PQ* xliii, 1964.

HAWKINS, SIR JOHN, 1719–89

A General History of the Science and Practice of Music appeared in 5 vols. in 1776, and *The Life of Samuel Johnson* in 1787. The *Life* occupies vol. i of his edition of Johnson's works, 1787–9. B. H. Davis has published an abridgement, 1961.

There is much interesting material about Hawkins in the *Anecdotes, Biographical Sketches and Memoirs* of his daughter, L.-M. Hawkins, 2 vols., 1822. There are two general studies of Hawkins, one by P. A. Scholes, Oxford, 1953, and the other by B. H. Davis, *A Proof of Eminence*, Bloomington, 1973. B. H. Davis has also written a study of the biography of Johnson: *Johnson before Boswell*, Bloomington, 1960. L. Lipking's fine book, *The Ordering of the Arts in Eighteenth-Century England*, Princeton, 1970, includes a sympathetic analysis of Hawkins's intentions and method in *The History of Music*.

HAYWOOD, ELIZA, 1693–1756

See vol. vii, but note also the useful short essay by J. P. Erickson, '*Evelina* and *Betsy Thoughtless*', *TSLL* vi, 1964–5.

HERD, DAVID, 1732–1810

Ancient and Modern Scots Songs was published in 1769, and enlarged, Edinburgh, 2 vols., 1776. An edition of songs from Herd's manuscripts was published by H. Hecht, Edinburgh, 1904. This contains an account of Herd, and extracts from George Paton's correspondence with Thomas Percy. See also vol. vi of the *Percy Letters*, ed. A. F. Falconer, New Haven, 1961, and M. L. MacKenzie's essay, 'The Great Ballad Collectors: Percy, Herd, Ritson', *Studies in Scottish Literature* ii, 1965.

HICKEY, WILLIAM, 1749–1830

His *Memoirs*, ed. A. Spencer, first appeared in 4 vols., 1913–25. There is an abridgement by P. Quennell, 1960, enlarged 1975.

HILL, JOHN, ?1716–75

While his main importance is as a botanist (his *Vegetable System*, 26 vols., 1759–75, is an early example of the use of the Linnaean classification), Hill was a prolific miscellaneous writer. He edited the *British Magazine*, 1746–50, and contributed to the *London Advertiser*, 1751–3, as 'The Inspector'. He was involved in many controversies, and was attacked by Christopher Smart in *The Hilliad*, 1753.

Hypochondriasis: a Practical Treatise, 1766, has been edited by G. S. Rousseau, 1969 (*ARS*). Rousseau has a biography in preparation: see his article 'The Much-Maligned Doctor', *Journal of the American Medical Association* ccxii, 1970.

HOADLY, BENJAMIN, 1706–57

The Suspicious Husband was performed and published in 1747. Samuel Foote wrote a pamphlet on it: *The Roman and English Comedy Consider'd and Compar'd. With Remarks on the Suspicious Husband*, 1747.

HOGARTH, WILLIAM, 1697–1764

The Analysis of Beauty appeared in 1753. The edition by J. Burke, Oxford, 1955, includes Hogarth's 'autobiographical notes'. Further Hogarth MSS. were published by M. Kitson, 'Hogarth's "Apology for Painters", *The Walpole Society* xli, 1968. These materials were first published by J. Ireland in *A Supplement to Hogarth Illustrated*, but the text is unreliable.

John Nichols wrote *Anecdotes of Mr. Hogarth*, 1780, enlarged in 1781, and forming the nucleus of *The Genuine Works of William Hogarth*, 3 vols., 1808–17. George Steevens contributed a commentary on the plates. *Hogarth's Graphic Works*, ed. R. Paulson, 2 vols., New Haven, 1965, rev. 1970, includes an authoritative commentary, supplemented in the same author's *The Art of Hogarth*, 1975. The latter has an excellent short bibliography. Paulson's biography is also essential: *Hogarth: his Life, Art and Times*, 2 vols., New Haven, 1971. Other important studies are by F. Antal, *Hogarth and his Place in European Art*, 1962, and R. E. Moore, *Hogarth's Literary Relationships*, Minneapolis, 1948, the latter being mainly concerned with Fielding and Smollett. Although now out of date, A. Dobson's *William Hogarth*, 1891, remains an attractive introduction.

Two essays deserve particular mention: one by R. Paulson, 'Hogarth and the English Garden: Visual and Verbal Structures', in *Encounters: Essays on Literature and the Visual Arts*, ed. J. D. Hunt, 1971; the other by R. R. Wark, 'Hogarth's Narrative Method in Practice and Theory', in *England in the Restoration and Early Eighteenth Century*, ed. H. T. Swedenberg, Berkeley, 1972.

Contemporary reactions to Hogarth are illustrated by the commentaries on his engravings written by G. C. Lichtenberg for the *Göttinger Taschenkalender*, 1784–96. These have been translated into English by I. and G. Herdan, 1966, and more satisfactorily by A. S. Wensinger and W. B. Coley, in *Hogarth on High Life*, Middletown, 1970.

HOME, JOHN, 1722–1808

Home published his three tragedies, *Agis* (written 1747, performed 1758), *Douglas* (1756 performed 1757), and *The Siege of Aquileia* (1760) together in 1760. *The Fatal Discovery* (1769), *Alonzo* (1773), and *Alfred* (1778) appeared with the earlier plays in his *Dramatic Works*, 2 vols., 1798. Home also wrote *The History of the Rebellion of 1745*, 1802.

A collected edition of Home's *Works*, with a life by Henry Mackenzie, was published in 3 vols. in 1822, and reviewed by Walter Scott in the *Quarterly Review* xxxvi, 1827. *Douglas* has been edited by H. J. Tunnay, Lawrence, 1924, and by G. D. Parker, Edinburgh, 1972. The reception of *Douglas* and the controversy raised by its performance are described in Alexander Carlyle's *Autobiography*, 1860.

There is a useful study of Home by A. E. Gipson, Caldwell, Idaho, 1917, and a chapter on his relations with David Hume in E. C. Mossner's *The Forgotten Hume*, New York, 1943. J. S. Malek attempts a revaluation of *The Siege of Aquileia* in *Studies in Scottish Literature* x, 1973, and considers the role of providence in *Douglas* in The *New Rambler* xv, 1974.

HUME, DAVID, 1711–76

A Treatise of Human Nature appeared in 2 vols., 1739–40; *Essays, Moral and Political*, followed in 2 vols, Edinburgh, 1741–2. *Philosophical Essays concerning Human Understanding* were published in 1748, and reissued in 1758 as *An Enquiry concerning Human Understanding*. *An Enquiry concerning the Principles of Morals* appeared in 1751, and *Political Discourses* in Edinburgh, 1752. The first volume of *The History of Great Britain*, covering the reigns of James I and Charles I, was published in 1754; the second volume, covering the Commonwealth, and the reigns of Charles II and James II, followed in 1757. In the same year Hume published a volume of *Four Dissertations* (including *The Natural History of Religion*). The *History of England under the House of Tudor* was published in 2 vols., 1759, and the last 2 vols. (from Julius Caesar to the accession of Henry VII) in 1763. Hume's last publication during his lifetime was a pamphlet explaining the quarrel with Rousseau: *Exposé succinct de la contestation qui s'est élevée entre M. Hume at M. Rousseau*, Paris, 1766. In 1777 was published *The Life of David Hume, Esq., Written by Himself*, and *Two Essays* (on suicide, and on immortality). The *Dialogues concerning Natural Religion* followed in 1779. Various minor unpublished texts have been edited by E. C. Mossner: see *MP* xxxix, 1942, and xlv, 1947; *JHI* ix, 1948 (early memoranda, 1729–40). J. M. Keynes and P. Sraffa edited (Cambridge, 1938) *An Abstract of a Treatise of Human Nature*, 1740, and E. C.

Mossner and J. V. Price (Edinburgh, 1967) *A Letter from a Gentleman*, Edinburgh, 1745, two unsigned pamphlets by Hume defending the *Treatise*.

Hume's letters were edited by J. Y. T. Greig, 2 vols., Oxford, 1932, and a volume of new letters has been added by R. Klibansky and E. C. Mossner, Oxford, 1954. Two sets of letters have been published in *TSLL*: ii, 1960 (ed. G. Hunter) and iv, 1962 (ed. E. C. Mossner). Another set is in *Revue philosophique* clvi, 1966 (ed. H. David).

The most reliable text of the philosophical works is still that by T. H. Green and T. H. Grose, 4 vols., 1874–5. The annotations of the *Treatise of Human Nature* in the edition by L. A. Selby-Bigge (1888, often reprinted) are useful; see also the edition by E. C. Mossner, Harmondsworth, 1969. For the *Enquiries*, see the edition by L. A. Selby-Bigge, 1894, rev. P. H. Nidditch, Oxford, 1975. There are good texts of *The Natural History of Religion*, edited by A. W. Colver, and of *Dialogues concerning Natural Religion*, edited by J. V. Price (Oxford, 1976). N. Kemp Smith's edition of the *Dialogues* (Oxford, 1935) has an important introductory essay. Some of the essays have been collected by J. W. Lenz, in *Of the Standard of Taste and Other Essays*, Indianapolis, 1965, and there is a complete text of them in *WC*.

For most purposes, T. E. Jessop's *Bibliography of David Hume and of Scottish Philosophy*, 1938, reissued New York, 1966, is invaluable, but a more detailed account of early editions is provided by W. B. Todd in the 'preliminary bibliography' contributed to *Hume and the Enlightenment*, ed. W. B. Todd, Edinburgh, 1974. See also R. Hall, *A Hume Bibliography from 1930*, Heslington, York, 1971.

No attempt can be made here to indicate the scope of works on Hume as a philosopher in the strict sense, but the interested reader will find much to help him in C. W. Hendel's *Studies in the Philosophy of David Hume*, Princeton, 1925. This has been revised, New York, 1963, with a 'Review of Hume Scholarship since 1925' which includes some interesting pages on *Dialogues concerning Natural Religion*. On these dialogues, see also the analysis developed by A. Jeffner in *Butler and Hume on Religion*, Stockholm, 1966, and by M. Morrisroe, Jr., in *TSLL* xi, 1969 ('Hume's Rhetorical Strategy'). Morrisroe contributes a suggestive essay, 'Linguistic Analysis as Rhetorical Pattern in David Hume', to *Hume and the Enlightenment*, ed. W. B. Todd, Edinburgh,

1974. Among the standard works on Hume may be mentioned N. Kemp Smith, *The Philosophy of David Hume*, 1941, D. G. C. MacNabb, *David Hume: his Theory of Knowledge and Morality*, 1954, Oxford, 1970, and J. B. Stewart, *The Moral and Political Philosophy of David Hume*, New York, 1963. What one may call the temper of Hume's mind is discussed by B. Willey in a chapter of *The English Moralists*, 1964, and by R. Williams in 'David Hume: Reasoning and Experience', *The English Mind*, ed. H. S. Davies and G. Watson, Cambridge, 1964.

The standard biography is by E. C. Mossner, Austin, 1954, Oxford, 1970. Even more important for the literary student is E. C. Mossner's earlier biographical volume, *The Forgotten Hume: le bon David*, New York, 1943. There is a good survey by J. V. Price, New York, 1969, and the same author has an admirable study of Hume as a man of letters, *The Ironic Hume*, Austin, 1965.

Hume's criticism is discussed by, among others, M. Kallich, 'The Associationist Criticism of Francis Hutcheson and David Hume', *SP* xliii, 1946 (reprinted in *The Association of Ideas and Critical Theory in Eighteenth-Century England*, The Hague, 1970); T. Brunius, *David Hume on Taste*, Uppsala, 1952; R. Cohen in two essays: 'David Hume's Experimental Method and the Theory of Taste', *ELH* xxv, 1958, and 'The Transformation of Passion; a Study of Hume's Theories of Tragedy', *PQ* xli, 1962; and E. C. Mossner, 'Hume's "Of Criticism"', *S. H. Monk Festschrift* 1967. There is a large study of Hume's aesthetics, O. Brunet, *Philosophie et esthétique chez David Hume*, Paris, 1965.

On Hume's political attitudes there are useful studies by G. Giarrizzo, *David Hume, politico e istorico*, Turin, 1962; L. L. Bongie, *David Hume: Prophet of the Counter-revolution*, Oxford, 1965; and D. Forbes, *Hume's Philosophical Politics*, Cambridge, 1975. E. C. Mossner has written two important essays on Hume as historian, *PMLA* lvi, 1941, and *JHI* ii, 1941 ('Was Hume a Tory Historian?'). See also the two essays by C. N. Stockton, one in *Studies in History and Society* iii, 1971, the other in *ECS* iv, 1971 ('Historian of the English Constitution'). There is a chapter on Hume in J. B. Black's *The Art of History*, 1926, and L. Braudy deals with him at length in *Narrative Form in History and Fiction*, Princeton, 1970. D. F. Norton and R. H. Popkin have edited, with introductory essays, a volume of extracts: *David Hume: Philosophical Historian*, New York, 1965.

HURD, RICHARD, 1720–1808

Hurd produced an edition of Horace's *Ars Poetica* in 1749, and of the *Epistle to Augustus* in 1751. For this second work he wrote 'A Discourse concerning Poetical Imitation'. Subsequent editions added a dissertation 'On the Provinces of Drama', 1753, and 'A Letter to Mr. Mason, on the Marks of Imitation', 1757. 'A Dissertation on the Idea of Universal Poetry' was added in 1766.

Moral and Political Dialogues appeared in 1759. An edition in 3 vols., 1765, includes *Letters on Chivalry and Romance* (first published in 1762), and *Dialogues on the Uses of Foreign Travel* (first published in Cambridge, 1764). It also has a 'Preface on the Manner of Writing Dialogue'.

Hurd published *An Introduction to the Study of the Prophecies concerning the Christian Church*, 1772, and various sermons. His works were collected in 8 vols., 1811.

His correspondence with William Mason and Thomas Gray has been edited by E. H. Pearce and L. Whibley, Cambridge, 1932. See also J. Nankivell, *MLR* xlv, 1950.

The *Memoir* by F. Kilvert, 1860, is the main authority for the life of Hurd. See also A. W. Evans, *Warburton and the Warburtonians*, Oxford, 1932. H. Trowbridge has an important essay, 'Bishop Hurd: a Reinterpretation', *PMLA* lviii, 1943. He also edited *Letters on Chivalry and Romance*, Los Angeles, 1963 (*ARS*). There is an earlier edition by E. J. Morley, 1911. See also two studies by S. J. Curry: 'The Use of History in Bishop Hurd's Literary Criticism', *Transactions of the Wisconsin Academy of Sciences, Arts, and Letters* liv, 1965; and 'Richard Hurd's Genre Criticism', *TSLL* viii, 1966.

JAGO, RICHARD, 1715–81

Edge-Hill, or the Rural Prospect Delineated and Moralised: a Poem appeared in 1767. *Labor and Genius, a Fable* followed in 1768. Some poems may also be found in Dodsley's *Collection* iv and v, 1755–8. His poems are in Anderson xi and Chalmers xvii.

Jago was a friend and correspondent of Shenstone. See *The Letters of William Shenstone*, ed. M. Williams, Oxford, 1939. There is a study by I. D. Lind, *Richard Jago: a Study in Eighteenth-Century Localism*, Philadelphia, 1945.

JOHNSON, SAMUEL, 1709–84

Much of Johnson's writing was published anonymously, and the full extent of his work is difficult to establish. The bibliography by W. P. Courtney and D. Nichol Smith, Oxford, 1915, reissued 1925, is being revised by J. D. Fleeman. A 'Supplement to Courtney' by R. W. Chapman and A. T. Hazen appeared in *Proceedings of the Oxford Bibliographical Society* v, 1939. D. J. Greene has given an account of the many works attributed to Johnson in recent years in 'The Development of the Johnson Canon', *A. D. MacKillop Festschrift*, 1963.

A Voyage to Abyssinia, by Father Jerome Lobo, was abridged and translated by Johnson, 1735. His contributions to the *Gentleman's Magazine* began in 1738, and it was here that some of his earlier biographical writings were published. *London: a Poem in Imitation of the Third Satire of Juvenal* appeared in the same year. In 1739 he wrote two political pamphlets, *Marmor Norfolciense* and *A Compleat Vindication of the Licensers of the Stage*. The 'Debates in the Senate of Lilliput' appeared in the *Gentleman's Magazine* between July 1741 and March 1744. His subsequent principal works were published as follows: *An Account of the Life of Mr. Richard Savage*, 1744; *Miscellaneous Observations on the Tragedy of Macbeth*, 1745; *The Plan of a Dictionary of the English Language*, 1747; *The Vanity of Human Wishes: the Tenth Satire of Juvenal, Imitated by Samuel Johnson*, 1749; *Irene: a Tragedy*, 1749; the *Rambler*, 20 March 1750–14 March 1752; *A Dictionary of the English Language*, 2 vols., 1755; *The Prince of Abissinia: a Tale*, 2 vols., 1759 (the title on the first page of the text is *The History of Rasselas, Prince of Abissinia*); the *Idler*, 15 April 1758–5 April 1760, in the *Universal Chronicle*; his edition of *The Plays of William Shakespeare*, 8 vols., 1765; his four later political pamphlets, *The False Alarm*, 1770, *Thoughts on the late Transactions respecting Falkland's Islands*, 1771, *The Patriot*, 1774, and *Taxation no Tyranny*, 1775; *A Journey to the Western Islands of Scotland*, 1775; *Prefaces, Biographical and Critical, to the Works of the English Poets*, 10 vols., 1779–81; *Prayers and Meditations*, ed. George Strahan, 1785. Johnson's diaries of visits to North Wales and to France appeared in 1816 (ed. R. Duppa) and in 1932 (ed. M. Tyson and H. Guppy) respectively.

The first collected edition of Johnson's writings was undertaken by Sir John Hawkins, 11 vols., 1787. The 'Debates in the

Senate of Lilliput' (2 vols.) were added in the same year, and two further supplementary vols. in 1788 and 1789. A new edition in 12 vols. was published in 1792, with a life by Arthur Murphy. Further material was added by Alexander Chalmers in new editions in 1806, 1816, and 1823. The 1823 edition remained the basis of many subsequent reprints, but is being superseded by the Yale Edition, ed. A. T. Hazen and J. H. Middendorf, 1958– . So far 10 vols. have appeared: 1. *Diaries, Prayers and Annals*, ed. E. L. McAdam, Jr., and D. and M. Hyde, 1958; 2. *The Idler and the Adventurer*, ed. W. J. Bate, J. M. Bullitt, and L. F. Powell, 1963; 3–5. *The Rambler*, ed. W. J. Bate and A. B. Strauss, 1969; 6. *Poems*, ed. E. L. McAdam, Jr., and G. Milne, 1964; 7–8. *Johnson on Shakespeare*, ed. A. Sherbo, 1968; 9. *A Journey to the Western Islands of Scotland*, ed. M. Lascelles, 1971; 10. *Political Writings*, ed. D. J. Greene, 1977.

Johnson's correspondence has been edited by R. W. Chapman, 3 vols., Oxford, 1952. See also M. Hyde's supplementary essay 'Not in Chapman', *L. F. Powell Festschrift*, 1965. There is a selection by R. W. Chapman, 1925, rev. 1951 (*WC*).

Other editions include one of the *Life of Savage*, ed. C. Tracy, Oxford, 1971; several of *Rasselas*, including those by R. W. Chapman, Oxford, 1927, C. Peake, 1967 (with some essays), J. P. Hardy, Oxford, 1968, and G. Tillotson and B. Jenkins, 1971; *The Rambler*, ed. S. C. Roberts, 1953 (*EL*). The 'Preface' to the edition of Shakespeare is included in D. Nichol Smith's *Eighteenth Century Essays on Shakespeare*, Glasgow, 1903, reissued Oxford, 1963, and the notes to the text have been edited for *ARS* by A. Sherbo, 3 vols., 1956–8. See also Sir W. Raleigh, *Johnson on Shakespeare*, 1908, and W. K. Wimsatt, *Samuel Johnson on Shakespeare*, New York, 1960, reissued London, 1969. *A Journey to the Western Islands of Scotland* has been edited by R. W. Chapman, Oxford, 1924 (with Boswell's *Tour*), and *Lives of the Poets* by G. B. Hill, 3 vols., Oxford, 1905. The *Lives* have been reprinted in both *EL* and *WC*. The principal edition of the poems is that by D. Nichol Smith and E. L. McAdam, Jr., Oxford, 1941, rev. 1962, rev. by J. D. Fleeman 1974. J. D. Fleeman's own edition of the poems appeared in 1971. H. H. Naugle has compiled a concordance, Ithaca, 1973.

There are many useful selections from Johnson's writings. *Johnson. Prose and Poetry*, ed. R. W. Chapman, Oxford, 1922, includes Macaulay's *Encyclopaedia Britannica* article on Johnson and Sir Walter Raleigh's Leslie Stephen Lecture (1907). Chapman's later selection, 1955, reissued 1962 (*WC*), is fuller. Also recommended are the Reynard Library *Johnson*, ed. M. Wilson, 1950, rev. 1966, and *A Johnson Reader*, ed. E. L. McAdam, Jr., and G. Milne, New York, 1964.

More specialized collections include *Prefaces and Dedications*, ed. A. T. Hazen, New Haven, 1937; *Political Writings*, ed. J. P. Hardy, 1968; and *Early Biographical Writings*, ed. J. D. Fleeman, Farnborough, 1973. J. E. Brown's *Critical Opinions of Samuel Johnson*, Princeton, 1926, arranges passages from Johnson under topics, and is a convenient work of reference. The selection by J. Wain, *Johnson as Critic*, 1973, serves as a useful introduction for the general reader. E. L. McAdam, Jr., and G. Milne have edited a selection from the *Dictionary*, New York, 1963.

J. D. Fleeman has edited the sale catalogue of Johnson's library, and D. J. Greene has written an annotated guide to it, 2 vols., Victoria, B.C., 1975.

Works on Johnson are listed in *Samuel Johnson. A Survey and Bibliography of Critical Studies*, by J. L. Clifford and D. J. Greene, Minneapolis, 1970. This incorporates and extends two earlier bibliographies, the first by J. L. Clifford, Minneapolis, 1951, the second by J. L. Clifford and D. J. Greene, in *Johnsonian Studies*, ed. M. Wahba, Cairo, 1962.

Of the biographies before Boswell the most important are by Mrs. Piozzi (formerly Mrs. Thrale), *Anecdotes of the Late Samuel Johnson*, 1786, and by Sir John Hawkins, *Life of Samuel Johnson*, 1787. The *Anecdotes* have been edited by S. C. Roberts, Cambridge, 1925, and by A. Sherbo, 1974 (with William Shaw's *Memoirs of the Life and Writings of the Late Dr. Samuel Johnson*, 1785). The Hawkins *Life* has been abridged by B. H. Davis, New York, 1961. Texts of 14 *Early Biographies of Samuel Johnson* are edited by O. M. Brack, Jr., and R. E. Kelley, Iowa City, 1974, and introduced in the same authors' *Samuel Johnson's Early Biographers*, Iowa City, 1971. Much material of this kind is conveniently accessible in *Johnsonian Miscellanies*, ed. G. B. Hill, 2 vols., Oxford, 1897, reissued 1967. An earlier collection, associated with John Wright, *Johnsoniana: or Supplement to Boswell*, 1836, is based on Croker's edition of Boswell's *Life*, and contains some material not in G. B. Hill. It was revised in 1859.

Boswell's *Life of Samuel Johnson, LL.D.* appeared in 2 vols., 1791 (see under James Boswell, p. 569 above). Another early biography of some importance is that by Robert Anderson, in vol. xi of *Works of the British Poets*, 1795. It is assessed by P. J. Korshin, *HLQ* xxxvi, 1973, and the enlarged third edition of 1815 has been reissued by him, Hildesheim, 1973. Much information about Johnson's early life was collected by A. L. Reade and published in his *Johnsonian Gleanings*, 11 pts., 1909–52. The early years have been authoritatively treated by J. L. Clifford in *Young Sam Johnson*, New York, 1955.

Of the many general studies, two that together still provide the best introduction to Johnson are J. W. Krutch, *Samuel Johnson*, New York, 1944, and W. J. Bate, *The Achievement of Samuel Johnson*, New York, 1955. D. J. Greene, *Samuel Johnson*, New York, 1970, is compact and suggestive. B. H. Bronson's two essays 'Johnson Agonistes' and 'The Double Tradition of Dr. Johnson' are also important: the first appeared in *Johnson and Boswell: Three Essays*, University of California Publications in English, iii, 1944, reprinted as *Johnson Agonistes & Other Essays*, Cambridge, 1946; the second appeared in *ELH* xviii, 1951, and was reprinted in *Eighteenth-Century English Literature: Modern Essays in Criticism*, ed. J. L. Clifford, New York, 1959. Among the earlier commentators, Sir Walter Raleigh's *Six Essays on Johnson*, Oxford, 1910, and D. Nichol Smith's chapter on Johnson and Boswell in the *Cambridge History of English Literature*, x, 1913, are still useful. R. W. Chapman's essays are collected in *Johnsonian and Other Essays and Reviews*, Oxford, 1953. S. C. Roberts's writings on Johnson include a short biography, 1935, and a pamphlet in the *Writers and their Work* series, 1954. There is an interesting section on Johnson in W. B. C. Watkins's *Perilous Balance*, Princeton, 1939, and more recent general studies include those by M. J. C. Hodgart, 1962, E. L. McAdam, Jr., Boston, 1969, P. Fussell, New York, 1971, and the biography by J. Wain, 1974.

Among more specialized studies, two are striking contributions to an understanding of Johnson's neuroses: K. C. Balderston, 'Johnson's Vile Melancholy', *C. B. Tinker Festschrift*, 1949, and (more elaborately) G. Irwin, *Samuel Johnson: a Personality in Conflict*, Auckland, 1971. Various aspects of Johnson's thought are considered by R. Voitle, *Samuel Johnson the Moralist*, Cambridge, Mass., 1961; P. K. Alkon, *Samuel Johnson and Moral Discipline*, Evanston, 1967; M. J. Quinlan, *Samuel Johnson: a Layman's Religion*, Madison, 1964; C. F. Chapin, *The Religious*

Thought of Samuel Johnson, Ann Arbor, 1968; J. Gray, *Johnson's Sermons: a Study*, Oxford, 1972; A. Sachs, *Passionate Intelligence: Imagination and Reason in the Work of Samuel Johnson*, Baltimore, 1967; and by R. B. Schwartz, *Samuel Johnson and the New Science*, Madison, 1971. The main study of Johnson's political position is by D. J. Greene, New Haven, 1960. E. L. McAdam, Jr., has contributed an important study of Johnson and English law, Syracuse, N.Y., 1951. Johnson's prose style has been examined in two books by W. K. Wimsatt, Jr., *The Prose Style of Samuel Johnson*, New Haven, 1941, and *Philosophic Words: a Study of Style and Meaning in the 'Rambler' and 'Dictionary' of Samuel Johnson*, New Haven, 1948.

Several collections of essays form notable contributions to the study of Johnson: *The Age of Johnson: Essays Presented to C. B. Tinker*, ed. F. W. Hilles, New Haven, 1949; *New Light on Dr. Johnson*, ed. F. W. Hilles, New Haven, 1959; *Johnsonian Studies*, ed. M. Wahba, Cairo, 1962; *Johnson, Boswell and their Circle: Essays Presented to L. F. Powell*, ed. M. M. Lascelles *et al.*, Oxford, 1965; *Samuel Johnson: a Collection of Critical Essays*, ed. D. J. Greene (Twentieth Century Views), Englewood Cliffs, 1965; and *Eighteenth-Century Studies in Honour of Donald F. Hyde*, ed. W. H. Bond, New York, 1970.

Selections from the earlier critics of Johnson have been made by J. T. Boulton in a volume in the Critical Heritage series, 1971. Articles on Johnson in the *Monthly Review* were reprinted by J. K. Spittal, *Contemporary Criticism of Dr. Samuel Johnson*, 1923.

On the poetry, T. S. Eliot's introduction to *London* and *The Vanity of Human Wishes*, 1930, has been very influential. So too have been F. R. Leavis's two *Scrutiny* articles 'English Poetry in the Eighteenth Century' (reprinted in *Revaluation*, 1936), and 'Johnson as Poet' (reprinted in *The Common Pursuit*, 1952). B. H. Bronson, 'Personification Reconsidered', *ELH* xiv, 1947, and C. F. Chapin, *Personification in Eighteenth-Century English Poetry*, New York, 1955, treat an important aspect of Johnson's work. Imitation is considered by M. Lascelles, 'Johnson and Juvenal', *New Light on Dr. Johnson*, ed. F. W. Hilles, New Haven, 1959, by H. D. Weinbrot, *The Formal Strain: Studies in Augustan Imitation and Satire*, Chicago, 1969, and by R. Selden, 'Dr. Johnson and Juvenal', *Comparative Literature* xxii, 1970. Johnson's satire is discussed in I. Jack's

Augustan Satire, Oxford, 1952, and M. Emslie, 'Johnson's Satires and "The Proper Wit of Poetry" ', *Cambridge Journal* vii, 1954. There is a full and useful chapter in R. Trickett, *The Honest Muse*, Oxford, 1967, and another, on Johnson and the stoicism of Juvenal, in M. Roberts, *The Tradition of Romantic Morality*, 1973.

Irene is discussed by D. Nichol Smith, *E&S* xiv, 1929, by B. H. Bronson, in *Johnson and Boswell: Three Essays* (see above, p. 613), and by M. Waingrow, *F. A. Pottle Festschrift*, 1965.

B. B. Hoover, *Samuel Johnson's Parliamentary Reporting*, Berkeley, 1953, examines the 'Debates in the Senate of Lilliput'. For other aspects of his journalism, see E. A. Bloom, *Samuel Johnson in Grub Street*, Providence, 1957.

The major work on the *Dictionary* is the study by J. H. Sledd and G. J. Kolb, Chicago, 1955, but there are relevant essays in *New Aspects of Lexicography*, ed. H. D. Weinbrot, Carbondale, 1972. See also G. E. Noyes's study of the reception of the *Dictionary* by Johnson's contemporaries, *MP* lii, 1955, and D. McCracken's examination of Johnson's debt to Bailey's *Dictionarium Britannicum*: 'The Drudgery of Defining', *MP* lxvi, 1969.

A. Sherbo's study of Johnson as an editor of Shakespeare, Urbana, 1956, should be read with A. M. Eastman's defence of Johnson in *Shakespeare Quarterly* viii, 1957. A. M. Eastman's two articles on the text of Johnson's Shakespeare are useful, in *PMLA* lxv, 1950, and *JEGP* xlix, 1950. See also R. E. Scholes, 'Dr. Johnson and the Bibliographical Criticism of Shakespeare', *Shakespeare Quarterly* xi, 1960. The 'Preface' has been comprehensively examined by R. D. Stock in *Samuel Johnson and Neoclassical Dramatic Theory: the Intellectual Context of the Preface to Shakespeare*, Lincoln, Nebraska, 1973.

On the periodical essays, besides W. K. Wimsatt's two studies (see above, p. 614), there are helpful articles by A. T. Elder, 'Irony and Humour in the *Rambler*', *University of Toronto Quarterly* xxx, 1960, and 'Thematic Patterning and Development in Johnson's Essays', *SP* lxii, 1965; and by J. C. Riely, 'The Pattern of Imagery in Johnson's Periodical Essays', *ECS* iii, 1970. P. O'Flaherty considers Johnson's *Idler* in 'The Equipment of a Satirist', *ELH* xxxvii, 1970. R. M. Wiles describes how the *Rambler* was distributed, *ECS* ii, 1968.

On *Rasselas*, there is a convenient assessment of critical

opinion by M. Lascelles, 'Rasselas: A Rejoinder', *RES* N.s. xxi, 1970. She directs particular attention to essays by G. J. Kolb, 'The Structure of *Rasselas*', *PMLA* lxvi, 1951; A. Whitley, 'The Comedy of *Rasselas*', *ELH* xxiii, 1956; F. W. Hilles, '*Rasselas*, an "Uninstructive Tale" ', *L. F. Powell Festschrift*, 1965; E. Jones, 'The Artistic Form of *Rasselas*', *RES* N.s. xviii, 1967; and the introduction to J. P. Hardy's edition, 1968. One should now add H. E. Pagliaro's essay 'Structural Patterns of Control in *Rasselas*', *J. L. Clifford Festschrift*, 1971, and C. McIntosh, *The Choice of Life: Samuel Johnson and the World of Fiction*, New Haven, 1973. There are background studies by E. D. Leyburn, *PMLA* lxx, 1955, D. M. Lockhart, *PMLA* lxxviii, 1963, and A. J. Weitzman, *PQ* xlviii, 1969. The collection of *Bicentenary Essays on 'Rasselas'*, ed. M. Wahba, Cairo, 1959, is rather miscellaneous.

J. Hart's discussion of *A Journey to the Western Islands* in *EC* x, 1960, was challenged by a number of critics, in particular by R. K. Kaul, *EC* xiii, 1963, and A. Sherbo, *EC* xvi, 1966. There are good essays by C. Tracy, *Studies on Voltaire and the Eighteenth Century* lviii, 1967, by T. K. Meier, *Studies in Scottish Literature* v, 1968, by F. R. Hart, *ELH* xxxvi, 1969, and by T. R. Preston, *ECS* v, 1972.

Most discussion of Johnson's achievement as a biographer has been in general surveys of his work, but his theory of biography is considered by B. Evans, *RES* x, 1934, and A. J. Tillinghast, *Johnsonian Studies*, ed. M. Wahba, Cairo, 1962. E. L. McAdam, Jr., has considered his methods in the lives of Sarpi, Blake, and Drake, *PMLA* lviii, 1943. The *Life of Savage* has had its literary background explained by B. Boyce, *SP* liii, 1956, and W. Vesterman and J. A. Dussinger discuss its style and intention, *ELH* xxxvi, 1969, and xxxvii 1970.

The most authoritative study of Johnson's criticism is by J. H. Hagstrum: *Samuel Johnson's Literary Criticism*, Minneapolis, 1952. A revised edition, Chicago, 1967, includes a survey of work in the field since 1952. Other books are W. B. C. Watkins, *Johnson and English Poetry before 1660*, Princeton, 1936, and L. Damrosch, *Samuel Johnson and the Tragic Sense*, Princeton, 1972.

W. R. Keast has an influential essay, 'The Theoretical Foundations of Johnson's Criticism', in *Critics and Criticism*, ed. R. S. Crane, Chicago, 1952. J. W. Wright considers Johnson's critical method, *PMLA* lxxxvi, 1971. Other important essays include the one by F. R. Leavis, *Scrutiny* xii, 1944, and R. D. Havens, on Johnson's distrust of the imagination, *ELH* x, 1948. P. K. Alkon examines Johnson's concept of 'admiration', *PQ* xlviii, 1969. His ideas of generality and particularity have been much discussed. G. Tillotson, 'Imlac and the Business of the Poet', *S. H. Monk Festschrift*, 1967, should be consulted along with two essays in *ECS* v, 1971, by L. Basney and H. D. Weinbrot. See also W. Edinger, 'Johnson on Conceit: the Limits of Particularity', *ELH* xxxix, 1972. His criticism of the metaphysical poets is considered by Allen Tate, *Kenyon Review* xi, 1949 (reprinted in his *Collected Essays*, Denver, 1959), and by W. R. Keast, *ELH* xvii, 1950.

JOHNSTONE, CHARLES, ?1719–1800

Chrysal, or the Adventures of a Guinea appeared in 4 vols., 1760–5. *The Reverie; or, a Flight to the Paradise of Fools*, followed, 2 vols., 1762. *The History of Arsaces, Prince of Betlis*, appeared in 2 vols., 1774; *The Pilgrim: or, a Picture of Life*, 2 vols., 1775; and *The History of John Juniper, Esq.*, 3 vols., 1781.

Sir Walter Scott's essay on Johnstone in *The Lives of the Novelists* makes a vivid introduction to *Chrysal*.

JONES, SIR WILLIAM, 1746–94

Jones's translation from the Persian of a history of Nader Shah was first published in French, 1770, and also a *Traité sur la poésie orientale*. In 1772 he published a volume of poems, mainly translations from Asiatic languages, with essays 'On the Poetry of the Eastern Nations' and 'On the Arts commonly called Imitative'. *Poeseos Asiaticae Commentariorum Libri Sex* appeared in 1774, and versions of *The Moallakat*, 1782, and *Sacontala, or the Fatal Ring: an Indian Drama, by Calidas*, 1789. He published a number of important legal works, including a translation of part of the ordinances of Manu, 1796. Much of his later writing on oriental literature and language is in *The Asiatick Miscellany* and *Asiatick Researches*, both published in Calcutta. His poems are collected in Chalmers xviii. An edition of his works appeared in 6 vols., 1799.

Jones's letters have been edited by G. H. Cannon, 2 vols., Oxford, 1970. G. H. Cannon has also compiled a bibliography, Honolulu, 1952.

There are studies by A. J. Arberry, 1946, by G. H. Cannon, New York, 1964, and by S. N. Mukherjee, Cambridge, 1968. R. M. Hewitt examines Jones's poetry in 'Harmonious Jones', *E&S* xxviii, 1942, and G. H. Cannon considers his connection with Johnson's 'Club' in *MP* lxiii, 1965. There is a chapter, 'Sir William Jones and the New Philology', in H. Aarsleff, *The Study of Language in England, 1780–1860*, Princeton, 1967. The indebtedness of his theory of art to empirical psychology is examined by J. S. Malek in *Enlightenment Essays*, i, 1970.

JORTIN, JOHN, 1698–1770

Jortin published *Remarks on Spenser's Poems*, 1734, and a *Letter concerning the Music of the Ancients* (in Charles Avison's *Essay on Musical Expression*, 1753 ed.). *Remarks on Ecclesiastical History* appeared in 5 vols., 1751–73, and his *Life of Erasmus* in 2 vols., 1758–60. A posthumous collection of *Tracts, Philological, Critical and Miscellaneous* was published with a memoir by R. Jortin, 2 vols., 1790.

JUNIUS

Letters addressed to the *Public Advertiser* over the signature of 'Junius' appeared in that newspaper from 21 January 1769 until 21 January 1772. A collected edition, edited by Junius himself, was published the same year. An edition to which were added 63 private letters from Junius to Woodfall, the printer of the *Public Advertiser*, together with other contributions believed to be by the same author, was edited by J. M. Good and Woodfall's son, 3 vols., 1812. Editions have since been published by J. Wade, 2 vols., 1850, and C. W. Everett, 1927.

The *Letters* have been attributed to Burke, Gibbon, the Earl of Shelburne, the Earl of Chesterfield, Laughlin Macleane, Isaac Barré, and many others. The case for the most generally favoured candidate, Sir Philip Francis, has been reinforced by the stylistic evidence presented in two studies by A. Ellegård: *Who was Junius?* and *A Statistical Method for Determining Authorship: the Junius Letters 1769–1772*, both published in Gothenburg, 1962. *Who was Junius?* includes a scrupulously discriminating survey of the nineteenth-century arguments about the identity of Junius.

On the literary qualities of the Junius *Letters*, see in particular

J. T. Boulton, *The Language of Politics in the Age of Wilkes and Burke*, 1963.

There is a bibliographical examination of the earliest editions by T. H. Bowyer, Charlottesville, 1957, and a not altogether trustworthy *Junius Bibliography* by F. Cordasco, New York, 1949.

KAMES, HENRY HOME, LORD, 1696–1782

Although Kames had written extensively on legal subjects, his historical preoccupations became apparent in his *Essays upon Several Subjects concerning British Antiquities*, 1747. He achieved some notoriety with the controversial *Essays on the Principles of Morality and Natural Religion*, 1751. *Historical Law Tracts*, 1758, made as important a contribution to historical method as *Elements of Criticism*, 3 vols., Edinburgh, 1762, did to a psychological literary criticism. His last major work was *Sketches of the History of Man*, 2 vols., 1774. He also wrote on farming and on education.

The study by I. S. Ross, *Lord Kames and the Scotland of his Day*, Oxford, 1972, is particularly recommended, but the survey by A. E. McGuinness, New York, 1970, is useful, and there is much of interest in W. C. Lehmann's book, *Henry Home, Lord Kames, and the Scottish Enlightenment; a Study in National Character and in the History of Ideas*, The Hague, 1971. Kames's criticism is considered by H. W. Randall, *The Critical Theory of Lord Kames*, Northampton, Mass., 1944. See also A. Horn, 'Kames and the Anthropological Approach to Criticism', *PQ* xliv, 1965. Other essays include one by L. R. Shaw, 'Henry Home of Kames: Precursor of Herder', *Germanic Review* xxxv, 1960, and V. M. Bevilacqua, 'Lord Kames's Theory of Rhetoric', *Speech Monographs* xxx, 1963.

KELLY, HUGH, 1739–77

False Delicacy appeared in 1768, *A Word to the Wise* in 1770, *Clementina* in 1771, *The School for Wives* and *The Romance of an Hour* in 1774. Kelly also contributed to newspapers and magazines, and wrote *Thespis*, 2 vols., 1766–7 (a critique of actors), and *Memoirs of a Magdalen, or the History of Louisa Mildmay*, 2 vols., 1767.

The collected edition of his works, 1778, contains a brief biography, and there is also some biographical material in the

European Magazine, November 1793–January 1794. M. Schorer considers Kelly's place in the 'sentimental school', *PQ* xii, 1933, and C. J. Rawson has written a penetrating study, 'Some Remarks on Eighteenth Century "Delicacy", with a note on Hugh Kelly's *False Delicacy*', *JEGP* lxi, 1962.

KING, WILLIAM, 1685–1763

King's mock-heroic poem *The Toast* was published under the pseudonym of 'F. Scheffer', 1736, and his volume of essays, *The Dreamer*, in 1754. Many of his works are in Latin: a collection, Latin and English, appeared in 1760.

KNIGHT, ELLIS CORNELIA, 1758–1837

Dinarbas; a Tale: being a Continuation of Rasselas, Prince of Abissinia appeared in 1790. She was also the author of *Marcus Flaminius, a View of the Military, Social, and Political Life of the Romans*, 1792, and *A Description of Latium*, 1805. Her autobiography was published in 1861, and it has been edited by R. Fulford, 1960.

There is a biography by B. Luttrell, *The Prim Romantic*, 1965. C. J. Rawson has discussed *Dinarbas* in 'The Continuation of *Rasselas*', *Bicentenary Essays on 'Rasselas'*, ed. M. Wahba, Cairo, 1959.

KNOX, VICESIMUS, 1752–1821

Essays, Moral and Literary appeared in 1778, expanded into 2 vols., 1779. *Liberal Education* followed in 1781, and *Winter Evenings, or Lucubrations on Life and Letters* in 1788. He published *Personal Nobility* in 1793, and *Christian Philosophy* in 1795. In the early years of the French Revolutionary war he published a series of pacifist works: *A Narrative of Transactions relative to a Sermon*, 1793, a translation of Erasmus's *Bellum dulce inexpertis*, as *Antipolemus*, 1794, and a tract that may be included among the replies to Burke's *Reflections*, called *The Spirit of Despotism*, 1795. His last publication was a controversial pamphlet, *Remarks on the Tendency of Clauses in a Bill now Pending in Parliament to Degrade Grammar Schools*, 1821.

Knox purged Horace and Juvenal of their indecencies, but achieved his most enduring fame as the editor of *Elegant Extracts*, 2 vols., *c*. 1781, an anthology long used by schools and governesses. His works were collected in 7 vols., 1824.

LANGHORNE, JOHN, 1735–79

Although Langhorne wrote a respectable quantity of verse in his youth, his first publication was *The Death of Adonis, from Bion*, 1759. Many poems followed, of which the best is *The Country Justice*, 1774. He wrote a popular oriental tale, *Solyman and Almena*, 1762, and an even more popular work of sentiment, *The Letters that passed between Theodosius and Constantia*, 1763. He is chiefly remembered for the translation of Plutarch's *Lives* that he undertook with his brother William Langhorne, 6 vols., 1770. Langhorne's poems are collected in Anderson xi and Chalmers xvi

The Country Justice is reprinted in *The Late Augustans. Longer Poems of the Later Eighteenth Century*, ed. D. Davie, 1958. H. Macdonald contributes an essay on Langhorne to the *D. Nichol Smith Festschrift*, 1945.

LENNOX, CHARLOTTE, *née* RAMSAY, 1720–1804

Mrs. Lennox's first publication was *Poems on Several Occasions, written by a Young Lady*, 1747. *The Life of Harriot Stuart* appeared in 2 vols., 1750, *The Female Quixote, or the Adventures of Arabella* in 2 vols., 1752. *Shakespear Illustrated*, a collection of Shakespeare's sources, was published in 3 vols., 1753–4. Her remaining novels were *Henrietta*, 2 vols., 1758; *Sophia*, 2 vols., 1762; *The History of the Marquis of Lussa and Isabella*, 1764; *Euphemia*, 4 vols., 1790; and *The History of Sir George Warrington: or the Political Quixote*, 3 vols., 1797. She also edited *The Lady's Museum*, 1760–1.

The standard life is by M. R. Small, New Haven, 1935, and there is a study by G. H. Maynardier, *The First American Novelist?*, Cambridge, Mass., 1940. K. Young discusses *Shakespear Illustrated* in 'Samuel Johnson on Shakespeare: One Aspect', *University of Wisconsin Studies in Language and Literature* xviii, 1923.

LLOYD, ROBERT, 1733–64

The Actor, a Poetical Epistle appeared in 1760, as did *Shakespeare, an Epistle to Garrick; with an Ode to Genius*, and *The Tears and Triumphs of Parnassus*; also *Two Odes*. In 1761 he published *Arcadia, or the Shepherd's Wedding: a Dramatic Pastoral*, and *An Epistle to Charles Churchill*. He contributed to the *Connoisseur*,

1754–6, and the *North Briton*, 1762–4, and he was the editor of the *St. James's Magazine*, 1762–4. See R. Halsband, 'The Poet of *The North Briton*', *PQ* xvii, 1938.

Lowth, Robert, 1710–87

The *Praelectiones de Sacra Poesi Hebraeorum* were first published in 1753, and translated by G. Gregory as *Lectures on the Sacred Poetry of the Hebrews*, 2 vols., 1787. Lowth also wrote a *Life of William of Wykeham*, 1758, and *A Short Introduction to the English Grammar*, 1762. His translation of Isaiah appeared in 1778.

Lyttelton, George, Baron Lyttelton, 1709–73

See Vol. VII.

Mackenzie, Henry, 1745–1831

The Man of Feeling appeared in 1771, *The Man of the World* in 2 vols., 1773, and *Julia de Roubigné* in 1777. He conducted, and contributed extensively to, the *Mirror*, 1779–80, and the *Lounger*, 1785–7, both published in Edinburgh. He wrote two tragedies, *The Prince of Tunis*, 1773, and *Virginia: or, the Roman Father*, 1820. He was responsible for the Highland Society's *Report* on the authenticity of Macpherson's Ossian, 1805. He also wrote an account of the life and writings of John Home, prefixed to the edition of Home's works, Edinburgh, 1822. His own works were collected in 8 vols., Edinburgh, 1808. Another edition, Edinburgh 1824, includes a 'critical dissertation' by John Galt on Mackenzie's fiction.

Mackenzie's *Anecdotes and Egotisms* were first published by H. W. Thompson, Oxford, 1927. His letters to Elizabeth Rose have been edited by H. W. Drescher, Münster, 1967.

There is a study by H. W. Thompson, *A Scottish Man of Feeling*, 1931 (with bibliography). D. G. Spencer contributes an essay on Mackenzie as a 'practical sentimentalist' to *Papers in Language and Literature* iii, 1967, and there is a chapter on him in M. Gassenmeier's *Der Typus des Man of Feeling*, Tübingen, 1972. D. Kramer has written on the structural unity of *The Man of Feeling*, *Studies in Short Fiction* i, 1964. H. W. Drescher's excellent book, *Themen und Formen des periodischen Essays in späten 18. Jahrhundert*, Frankfurt, 1971, is devoted to the *Mirror* and the *Lounger*.

MACKLIN, CHARLES, ?1697–1797

Macklin's most successful plays were *Love à la Mode*, first performed in 1759, and *The Man of the World*, first performed in Dublin as *The True-born Scotsman*, 1764, and revised for the London stage, with the new title, in 1781. These and two other pieces have been edited by J. O. Bartley, 1968. There is a life by W. W. Appleton, Cambridge, Mass., 1960. R. R. Findlay's two articles should also be consulted: on 'natural' acting, *Educational Theatre Journal* xix, 1967, and on Macklin's comedies as 'dark satire', ibid. xx, 1968.

MACPHERSON, JAMES, 1736–96

The three Ossianic publications are *Fragments of Ancient Poetry, Collected in the Highlands of Scotland, and Translated from the Galic or Erse Language*, 1760; *Fingal, an Ancient Epic Poem, in Six Books: together with several other poems, composed by Ossian the Son of Fingal. Translated from the Galic Language*, 1762; *Temora, an ancient Epic poem, in Eight Books: together with several other Poems, composed by Ossian, the Son of Fingal. Translated from the Galic Language*, 1763. A collected edition was published in 1765. Malcolm Laing's edition, 2 vols., Edinburgh, 1805, has been reprinted, with an introduction by J. MacQueen, Edinburgh, 1971. Macpherson also published *The Highlander. An heroic poem in six cantos*, 1758, a translation of the *Iliad*, 1773, and three historical works: *An Introduction to the History of Great Britain and Ireland*, 1771; *The History of Great Britain from the Restoration to the accession of the House of Hanover*, 2 vols., 1775; *Original papers, containing the secret history of Great Britain from the Restoration to the accession of the House of Hanover*, 2 vols., 1775.

The two principal collections of Ossianic ballads have been translated and edited, *Heroic Poetry from the Book of the Dean of Lismore*, ed. Neil Ross for the Scottish Gaelic Texts Society, 1939, and *Duanaire Finn*, ed. Eoin Mac Neill and G. Murphy for the Irish Texts Society, 3 vols., 1908, 1933, 1938. The third volume contains a valuable study of these poems by G. Murphy, who has also written a good brief sketch, *The Ossianic Lore and Romantic Tales of Medieval Ireland*, 1955. For the work of Jerome Stone (1727–56), see the *Scots Magazine* xviii, 1756, and *Transactions of the Gaelic Society of Inverness* xiv, 1889.

Any account of Macpherson's activities must still be based

upon the evidence collected in the *Report of the Committee of the Highland Society of Scotland, appointed to inquire into the Nature and Authenticity of the Poems of Ossian*, ed. Henry Mackenzie, 1805. There is a bibliography of material relating to the Ossianic controversy in *Bulletin of the New York Public Library* xxx, 1926 (by G. F. Black), with a supplement in lxxv, 1971 (by J. J. Dunn).

The best studies of Macpherson's life and work are still T. B. Saunders, *The Life and Letters of James Macpherson*, 1894, and J. S. Smart, *James Macpherson: an Episode in Literature*, 1905. There is also a good survey by E. D. Snyder, *The Celtic Revival in English Literature 1760–1800*, 1923; but the most valuable work has been done by D. S. Thomson in *The Gaelic Sources of Macpherson's Ossian*, 1952, and ' "Ossian" Macpherson and the Gaelic World of the Eighteenth Century', *Aberdeen University Review* xl, 1963. Hume's attitude to the Ossian controversy is examined by E. C. Mossner in *The Forgotten Hume*, New York, 1943. On Ossian abroad, see R. Tombo, *Ossian in Germany*, New York, 1901; vol. i of P. van Tieghem's *Le Préromantisme*, Paris, 1924; and a fine study by A. Gillies, *Herder und Ossian*, Berlin, 1933. Macpherson's quality as a historian is discussed by D. B. Horn in 'Some Scottish Writers of History in the Eighteenth Century', *Scottish Historical Review* xl, 1961.

MASON, WILLIAM, 1725–97

Mason's principal non-satirical poems are *Musaeus: a Monody to the Memory of Mr. Pope in Imitation of Milton's Lycidas*, 1747; *Odes*, 1756; *Elegies*, 1763; *The English Garden* in four books, 1772, 1777, 1779, 1781. His plays are *Elfrida*, 1752, and *Caractacus*, 1759. His principal satires are *An Heroic Epistle to Sir William Chambers*, 1773; *An Heroic Postscript to the Public*, 1774; *Ode to Mr. Pinchbeck upon his newly invented patent Candle-Snuffers*, 1776; *An Epistle to Dr. Shebbeare*, 1777; *An Ode to Sir Fletcher Norton in Imitation of Horace Ode VIII Book IV*, 1777; *Ode to the Naval Officers of Great Britain*, 1779. Mason also translated Du Fresnoy's *Art of Painting*, 1783, for which Sir Joshua Reynolds furnished notes; edited Gray's poems, 1775, with a memoir of his life which constitutes the first publication of Gray's letters; and performed the same service for William Whitehead, 1788.

Collected editions of the poems appeared in 1764 and subsequent years, and an edition of the *Works* in 4 vols. in 1811. The

Satirical Poems, with Horace Walpole's notes, were edited by P. Toynbee ('with an Exposé of the Mystification'), 1926. Mason's correspondence with Richard Hurd was edited by E. H. Pearce and L. Whibley, 1932, and his correspondence with Horace Walpole, originally published by Mitford, in 1853, forms volumes xxviii and xxix of the Yale Edition of Walpole's Correspondence, 1955.

There is a critical study by J. W. Draper, *William Mason: a Study in Eighteenth-Century Culture*, New York, 1924. Two essays should be mentioned, one by I. Chase, 'William Mason and Sir William Chambers's Gardening Theories', *JEGP* xxxv, 1936; the other by M. S. Day, 'The Influence of Mason's *Heroic Epistle*', *MLQ* xiv, 1953. See also K. Hopkins, *Portraits in Satire*, 1958.

MELMOTH, WILLIAM, 1710–99

The first edition of *Letters on Several Subjects, by Sir Thomas Fitzosborne* appeared in 1748. The 11th edition, 1805, contains a life of Melmoth. He translated the letters of Pliny, 1747, and of Cicero, 1753; also the *Dialogus de Oratoribus* of Tacitus, 1748, and the *De Senectute* of Cicero, 1773.

MICKLE, WILLIAM JULIUS, 1735–88

Mickle's most important publication was his translation of the *Lusiad* of Camoens, Oxford, 1776, but he wrote a considerable quantity of verse, including *The Concubine, a Poem in the Manner of Spenser*, Oxford, 1767.

There is a study by M. E. Taylor, Washington, 1937, and a series of articles, by S. G. West: 'The Work of Mickle, the first Anglo-Portuguese Scholar', *RES* x, 1934; 'Cumnor Hall', *MLR* xxix, 1934 (on contributions to *Evans's Old Ballads*); and 'Mickle's Translation of *Os Lusiados*', *Revue de littérature comparée* xviii, 1938.

MIDDLETON, CONYERS, 1683–1750

The *Letter from Rome* was published in 1729, and *The History of the Life of Cicero* in 2 vols., 1741. Middleton also wrote *A Treatise on the Roman Senate*, 1747, and *A Free Inquiry into the Miraculous Powers which are supposed to have subsisted in the Christian Church*, 1749.

Sir Leslie Stephen assessed Middleton's theological work in his *History of English Thought in the Eighteenth Century*, 1876, chap. iv.

MILLAR, JOHN, 1735–1801

Observations concerning the Distinction of Ranks in Society appeared in 1771. Its third edition, 1779, has a new title: *The Origin of the Distinction of Ranks: or, an Enquiry into the Circumstances which give rise to Influence and Authority in the Different Members of Society.* This was followed by *An Historical View of the English Government*, 1787, enlarged (4 vols.) 1803.

The 1806 edition of *The Origin of the Distinction of Ranks* contains John Craig's account of Millar's life and writings. The standard modern study is by W. C. Lehmann, Cambridge, 1960. He and L. Schneider discuss 'Tension in the Thought of John Millar' in *Studies in Burke and his Time* xiii, 1971–2. There is a good essay by D. Forbes on Adam Smith and John Millar in relation to 'Scientific Whiggism', *Cambridge Journal* vii, 1954.

MONBODDO, JAMES BURNETT, LORD, 1714–99

Of the Origin and Progress of Language was published in 6 vols., Edinburgh, 1773–92; *Antient Metaphysics, or the Science of Universals*, also in 6 vols., Edinburgh 1779–99. His correspondence is published in *Lord Monboddo and some of his Contemporaries*, by W. Knight, 1900. There is a study by E. L. Cloyd, Oxford, 1972. See also A. O. Lovejoy, 'Monboddo and Rousseau', *MP* xxx, 1933 (also in *Essays in the History of Ideas*, Baltimore, 1948), and S. K. Land, *From Signs to Propositions: the Concept of Form in Eighteenth-Century Semantic Theory*, 1974.

MONTAGU, ELIZABETH, 1720–1800

Mrs. Montagu contributed dialogues xxvi–xxviii to Lyttelton's *Dialogues of the Dead*, 1760, and *An Essay on the Writings and Genius of Shakespear*, 1769. Her letters were first collected by M. Montagu, 4 vols., 1809–13, and more recently by E. J. Climenson, 2 vols., 1906 (to 1761), and by R. Blunt, 2 vols., 1923 (1762–1800). There are studies by R. Huchon, 1906, and J. Busse, 1928. K. G. Hornbeak provides 'New Light on Mrs. Montagu' for the *C. B. Tinker Festschrift*, 1949, and there are two articles in *HLQ*: one by W. P. Jones, 'The Romantic Bluestocking: Elizabeth Montagu', xii, 1949; the other by I. Ross, on Mrs. Montagu's 'aesthetic adventures' in Scotland, xxviii, 1965.

MONTAGU, LADY MARY WORTLEY, 1689–1762

See Vol. VII, but the standard edition of her letters is now that edited by R. Halsband, 3 vols., Oxford, 1965–7. See also *Essays and Poems and Simplicity, a Comedy*, edited by R. Halsband and I. Grundy, Oxford, 1977.

MOORE, EDWARD, 1712–57

Fables for the Female Sex appeared in 1744, and the work was often reprinted. *The Foundling, a Comedy* was performed and published in 1748, *The Gamester, a Tragedy* in 1753. Moore was editor of the *World*, 1753–6. His work was collected in 1756, and there is a life prefixed to his *Dramatic Works*, 1788. His poetry is in Anderson x and Chalmers xiv.

There is a study by J. H. Caskey, New Haven, 1927. *The Gamester* has been edited by C. H. Peake and P. R. Wikelund, Los Angeles, 1948 (*ARS*).

MORGANN, MAURICE, 1726–1802

The *Essay on the Dramatic Character of Sir John Falstaff* was published in 1777. It is available in D. Nichol Smith's *Eighteenth Century Essays on Shakespeare*, Glasgow, 1903. The edition by D. A. Fineman, Oxford, 1972 (as *Shakespearian Criticism*) includes much additional material from manuscript.

MURPHY, ARTHUR, 1727–1805

The Way to Keep Him appeared in 1760, *All in the Wrong*, 1761, and *Know your own Mind*, 1777. *The Works of Arthur Murphy* were published in 7 vols. in 1786. This is a collected edition of his plays and his essays, which first appeared in the *Gray's Inn Journal*, 1752–4. There is a selection of his comedies and farces (*The Way to Keep Him, and Five Other Plays*, New York, 1956) edited by J. P. Emery, who has also published a study, Philadelphia, 1946. There is another study by H. H. Dunbar, New York, 1946. The life by Jesse Foot, 1811, is still worth consulting.

The biography that Murphy wrote as a preface to an edition of the works of Fielding (12 vols., 1762) has found few admirers, though S. M. Passler has contributed an essay in its defence to the *New Rambler*, 1973. His *Essay on the Life and Genius of Samuel*

Johnson, LL.D., 1792, is a better performance, and was reprinted as a preface to editions of Johnson's works. His *Life of David Garrick*, 1801, recounts their never very satisfactory relations, also recorded in Garrick's *Correspondence*. Some *New Essays* have been attributed to him by A. Sherbo, East Lansing, 1963: but see the comments on these attributions by H. K. Miller, *Bulletin of the New York Public Library* lxix, 1965. He translated Tacitus, 4 vols., 1793, and Sallust, 1807. Part of the Sallust first appeared in 1795 as *The History of Catiline's Conspiracy*, translated by 'George Frederic Sydney', i.e. Murphy.

The lives of Fielding and Johnson, with some of the essays, have been edited by M. Grace, Gainesville, 1968.

NEVILLE, SYLAS, 1741–1840

His diary (1767–88) has been edited by B. Cozens-Hardy, 1950.

NEWTON, JOHN, 1725–1807

An Authentic Narrative was first published in 1764. Newton wrote some of the *Olney Hymns*, 1779, with William Cowper. His works were collected in 6 vols., 1808. His *Journal* of 1750–4 has been edited by B. Martin and M. Spurrell, 1962, together with a reprint of *Thoughts upon the African Slave Trade*, 1788. There is a modern edition of his letters, 1960. A short study of Newton is included in W. T. Cairns's *The Religion of Dr. Johnson and Other Essays*, 1946, and there is a popular biography by B. Martin, 1950, revised and abridged, 1960.

NICHOLS, JOHN, 1745–1826

Nichols was associated with the *Gentleman's Magazine* from 1778 onwards, and became sole manager and editor in 1792, continuing thus until his death. His principal work, *Literary Anecdotes of the Eighteenth Century* (9 vols.), with its supplementary *Illustrations of the Literary History of the Eighteenth Century* (8 vols.), originated in a single short volume, *Anecdotes, Biographical and Literary, of the Late Mr. William Bowyer*, 1778. This was enlarged in 1782, and reached its final form in 1812–16 (for the *Literary Anecdotes*) and 1817–58 (for the *Illustrations*, which were continued after Nichols's death by his son, J. B. Nichols). Another important work was *Anecdotes of Mr. Hogarth*, 1780, enlarged both in 1781 and in 1808–17 (as *The Genuine Works of William Hogarth*, by Nichols and George Steevens). Various publications about Leicestershire were incorporated in his massive *History and Antiquities of the County of Leicester*, 4 vols. in 8, 1795–1815.

E. L. Hart has edited a selection of Nichols's biographies, *Minor Lives*, Cambridge, Mass., 1971. There is an excellent introduction on the antiquarian and anecdotal movements in Nichols's time.

OGILVIE, JOHN, 1733–1813

Ogilvie wrote a considerable quantity of verse, and *The Day of Judgment*, 1753, was admired by Boswell, though not by Johnson. *Poems on Various Subjects*, with an essay on the lyric poetry of the ancients, appeared in 1762. Among his theological works was *The Theology of Plato, compared with the Principles of Oriental and Grecian Philosophers*, 1793.

Philosophical and Critical Observations on the Nature, Characters, and Various Species of Composition was published in 2 vols., 1774.

OLDYS, WILLIAM, 1696–1761

Oldys contributed biographies to Thomas Birch's *General Dictionary*, 10 vols., 1734–41, and was general editor of the first edition of the *Biographia Britannica*, 6 vols. (in 7), 1747–66. His *Life of Sir Walter Raleigh* was prefixed to the 1736 edition of Raleigh's *History of the World*.

L. Lipking has a good study, 'The Curiosity of William Oldys: An Approach to the Development cf English Literary History', *PQ* xlvi, 1967, reprinted in *The Ordering of the Arts in Eighteenth-Century England*, Princeton, 1970.

PALEY, WILLIAM, 1743–1805

The Principles of Moral and Political Philosophy appeared in 1785; *Horae Paulinae, or the Truth of the Scripture History of St. Paul Evinced* followed in 1790, *A View of the Evidences of Christianity* in 1794, and *Natural Theology* in 1802. His works were collected in 7 vols., 1825.

There is a study by M. L. Clarke, 1974, and a short selection from the *Natural Theology* with a useful introduction by F. Ferré, Indianapolis, 1963.

PALTOCK, ROBERT, 1697–1767

The Life and Adventures of Peter Wilkins, a Cornish Man appeared in 1751. There have been many reprints, including one in *EL*. There is an excellent modern edition by C. Bentley, 1973. The best study of *Peter Wilkins* is in P. B. Gove, *The Imaginary Voyage in Prose Fiction*, New York, 1941. There is a useful section, too, in M. H. Nicolson, *Voyages to the Moon*, 1948.

PARR, SAMUEL, 1747–1825

Parr edited Bellenden's *De Statu Libri Tres* in 1787, and added a long *Praefatio* in 1788. This contains his views on Middleton's use of Bellenden in the *Life of Cicero*. His *Spital Sermon*, 1801, includes an important critique of William Godwin's ideas. Parr also published *Characters of the Late Charles James Fox*, 2 vols., 1809.

There is an excellent life by W. Derry, Oxford, 1966.

PENNANT, THOMAS, 1726–98

A Tour in Scotland appeared in Chester, 1771, and was enlarged as *A Tour in Scotland and Voyage to the Hebrides*, 2 vols., 1774–6. *A Tour in Wales*, 2 vols., followed in 1778–81. The journal of a continental tour was edited by G. R. de Beer, 1948. His other works include *British Zoology*, 4 vols., 1766–70; *Synopsis of Quadrupeds*, Chester, 1771, revised as *History of Quadrupeds*, 2 vols., 1781; and *Arctic Zoology*, 2 vols., 1784–7. He wrote a number of other works of travel and topography, and a *Literary Life of the late Thomas Pennant, Esq. By himself*, 1793.

PERCY, THOMAS, 1729–1811

Percy's principal publications were: *Hau Kiou Choaan, or the Pleasing History. A Translation from the Chinese. To which are added the Argument or Story of a Chinese Play; a Collection of Chinese Proverbs; and Fragments of Chinese Poetry*, 4 vols., 1761; *Miscellaneous Pieces relating to the Chinese*, 2 vols., 1762; *Five Pieces of Runic Poetry translated from the Islandic*, 1763; *The Song of Solomon, newly translated from the Original Hebrew: with a Commentary and Annotations*, 1764; *Reliques of Ancient English Poetry*, 3 vols., 1765, which reached a fourth edition in 1794; *The Household Book of the Earl of Northumberland in 1512*, 1768; and *Northern Antiquities*

. . . *with a Translation of the Edda*, 2 vols., 1770—a translation of Mallet's *Introduction à l'histoire de Dannemarc*.

There is no collected edition of his poetry. Two pieces were included in Dodsley's *Collection*, vol. vi, several were designed for publication in Shenstone's *Miscellany*, and his translations from Spanish ballads were eventually published as *Ancient Songs, chiefly on Moorish subjects*, ed. D. Nichol Smith, 1932. His longest poem, *The Hermit of Warkworth. A Northumberland Ballad. In Three Fits*, appeared in 1771.

In addition Percy planned and brought to various stages of completion editions of *Don Quixote*, the works of the Duke of Buckingham, the poetry of the Earl of Surrey, and the *Spectator*; he also supervised the writing of a memoir of Goldsmith. Some of these projects reached print, but none were published by him.

Bishop Percy's Folio Manuscript (on which the *Reliques* was based) was published at length, ed. J. W. Hales and F. J. Furnivall, 3 vols., 1867. There is another edition by Sir I. Gollancz, 4 vols., 1905. The best edition of the *Reliques* is by H. B. Wheatley, 3 vols., 1876–7. There is also a reprint in 2 vols. in *EL*.

A selection of Percy's voluminous correspondence was printed by J. B. Nichols in *Illustrations of the Literary History of the Eighteenth Century*, vols. vii (1848) and viii (1858). An edition under the general editorship of D. Nichol Smith and C. Brooks includes the following correspondences: i, *Malone*, ed. A. Tillotson, 1944; ii, *Farmer*, ed. C. Brooks, 1946; iii, *Warton*, ed. M. G. Robinson and L. Dennis, 1951; iv, *Hailes*, ed. A. F. Falconer, 1954; v, *Evans*, ed. A. Lewis, 1957; vi, *Paton*, ed. A. F. Falconer, 1961. Vols. i–v were published in Baton Rouge, vol. vi in New Haven.

There is a life of Percy by A. C. C. Gaussen, 1908, but it is not adequate, and no single work surveys his various achievements at any length, but C. Brooks's study 'The Country Parson as Research Scholar', *Publications of the Bibliographical Society of America* liii, 1959, is authoritative and well balanced, and B. H. Bronson surveys his career in a review of the *Letters*, vols. i–v, 'A Sense of the Past', *Sewanee Review* lxvii, 1959, reprinted in his *Facets of the Enlightenment*, Berkeley, 1968. See also the perceptive essay by L. Dennis, 'Thomas Percy: Antiquarian *vs.* Man of Taste', *PMLA* lvii, 1942. On *Hau Kiou Choäan*, see L. F. Powell, *RES* ii, 1926, and T. C. Fan, *RES* xxii, 1946. On the

Reliques, see the work of A. B. Friedman, 'Percy's Folio Manuscript Revalued', *JEGP* liii, 1954; 'The First Draft of Percy's *Reliques*, *PMLA* lxix, 1954; *The Ballad Revival*, Chicago, 1961, especially chapters v–viii; and W. J. Bate, 'Percy's Use of his Folio-Manuscript', *JEGP* xliii, 1944.

PIOZZI, HESTER LYNCH (MRS. THRALE), 1741–1821

Mrs. Thrale's poem 'The Three Warnings' was first published in Anna Williams's *Miscellanies in Prose and Verse*, 1766. She contributed poems and the preface to *The Florence Miscellany*, ed. W. Parsons, Florence, 1785. *Anecdotes of the Late Samuel Johnson, LL.D., during the Last Twenty Years of his Life* appeared in 1786, and *Letters to and from the Late Samuel Johnson, LL.D. to which are added some Poems never before Printed* in 2 vols., 1788. Her *Observations and Reflections made in the Course of a Journey through France, Italy, and Germany* followed in 2 vols., 1789, and *British Synonymy; or an Attempt at Regulating the Choice of Words in Familiar Conversation* in 2 vols., 1794. She published a political pamphlet, *Three Warnings to John Bull before he Dies*, 1798, and a kind of universal history, *Retrospection: or a Review of the Most Striking and Important Events, Characters, Situations, and their Consequences, which the Last Eighteen Hundred Years have presented to the View of Mankind*, 2 vols., 1801.

The *Anecdotes* are available in G. B. Hill's *Johnsonian Miscellanies*, vol. i, Oxford, 1897, and they have been edited by S. C. Roberts, Cambridge, 1925, and by A. Sherbo, 1974.

In 1861 A. Hayward published the *Autobiography, Letters and Literary Remains of Mrs. Piozzi*, 2 vols.; and in 1910 J. H. Lobban reissued this as *Dr. Johnson's Mrs. Thrale*. The journal of her Welsh tour in 1774 was edited by A. M. Broadley, 1910; her correspondence with Penelope Pennington was edited by O. G. Knapp, 1914; the French journal was edited by M. Tyson and H. Guppy, Manchester, 1932. See also the letters to Hester Maria Thrale ('Queeney') in *The Queeney Letters*, ed. the Marquis of Lansdowne, 1934. Most important of all is *Thraliana: the Diary of Mrs. Hester Lynch Thrale*, ed. K. C. Balderston, 2 vols., Oxford, 1942, rev. 1951.

Several collections have been made of Mrs. Piozzi's marginalia: there are a number in E. Mangin's *Piozziana*, 1833, and many in Hayward (above). See also P. Merritt, *Piozzi Marginalia*, Cambridge, Mass., 1925; J. P. Lyell, *Mrs. Piozzi's Isaac*

Watts, 1934; and M. H. Nicolson, 'Thomas Paine, Edward Nares, and Mrs. Piozzi's Marginalia', *Huntington Library Bulletin* x, 1936. See also an edition of Boswell's *Life of Johnson* with Piozzi marginalia, ed. E. G. Fletcher, 3 vols., 1938. For a fuller list, see *NCBEL*.

The standard life is by J. L. Clifford, *Hester Lynch Piozzi*, Oxford, 1941, rev. 1952 and 1968. Her relations with Boswell have been studied by F. A. Pottle and C. H. Bennett, *MP* xxxix, 1942, and by M. Hyde, *The Impossible Friendship*, Cambridge, Mass., 1972. There is an essay on her letters by J. L. Clifford, *D. Nichol Smith Festschrift*, 1945. See also P. M. Spacks, 'Scrapbook of a Self: Mrs. Piozzi's Late Journals', *Huntington Library Bulletin* xviii, 1970.

PORSON, RICHARD, 1759–1808

The *Letters to Mr. Archdeacon Travis*, mentioned in the text, originally appeared in the *Gentleman's Magazine*, 1788–9. Porson edited four plays of Euripides, and undertook much minute textual criticism, some of it published posthumously, beginning with the *Ricardi Porsoni Adversaria*, ed. J. H. Monk and C. J. Blomfield, Cambridge, 1812.

There is an excellent short life by M. L. Clarke, Cambridge, 1937. See also Clarke's *Greek Studies in England 1700–1830*, Cambridge, 1945.

PRATT, SAMUEL JACKSON, 'COURTNEY MELMOTH', 1749–1814

Although he wrote much poetry and several plays (including *The Fair Circassian*, 1781), Pratt's main importance is as a novelist of sensibility. His works include *Liberal Opinions, or the History of Benignus*, 6 vols., 1775–7; *The Pupil of Pleasure*, 2 vols., 1776; *Travels for the Heart, written in France*, 2 vols., 1777; *Shenstone-Green: or the New Paradise Lost*, 3 vols., 1779; *The Tutor of Truth*, 3 vols., 1779; and *Emma Corbett: or the Miseries of Civil War*, Dublin, 1780.

PRIESTLEY, JOSEPH, 1733–1804

Priestley's scientific publications include *The History and Present State of Electricity*, 1767, enlarged in 1769 and 1775; *The History and Present State of Discoveries relating to Vision, Light and Colours*, 2 vols., 1772 and *Experiments and Observations on Different Kinds of Air*, 3 vols., 1774–7. One of his most characteristic theological publications is *An History of the Corruptions of Christianity*, 2 vols., Birmingham, 1782. The range of his other works is indicated by *A Course of Lectures on the Theory of Language and Universal Grammar*, Warrington, 1762; *Essay on a Course of Liberal Education*, 1765; *An Essay on the First Principles of Government*, 1768; *A Course of Lectures on Oratory and Criticism*, 1777; *The Doctrine of Philosophical Necessity*, 1777; *Lectures on History and General Policy*, Birmingham, 1788. The theological and miscellaneous works were edited in 25 vols. by J. T. Rutt, 1817-31.

Priestley's autobiography has been edited by J. Lindsay, Bath, 1970, and there is a useful selection of his writings on philosophy, science, and politics by J. A. Passmore, New York, 1965. There is a bibliography by R. E. Crook, 1966, and studies by J. G. Gilliam, 1954, and F. W. Gibbs, 1965. His writings are discussed in chap. v of A. Lincoln's study, *Some Political and Social Ideas of English Dissent 1763-1800*, Cambridge, 1938.

RAMSAY, ALLAN, 1686-1758

See Vol. VII.

REEVE, CLARA, 1729-1807

Clara Reeve's first publication was a volume of poems, 1769. *The Champion of Virtue. A Gothic Story*, appeared in 1777, and was reprinted in the following year as *The Old English Baron*. She wrote a number of novels subsequently: *The Two Mentors*, 1783; *The Exiles, or Memoirs of the Count de Cronstadt*, 1788; *The School for Widows*, 1791; *Memoirs of Sir Roger de Clarendon*, 1793; and *Destination: or Memoirs of a Private Family*, 1799. Her critical dialogue, *The Progress of Romance*, was published in Colchester, 1785.

There is a modern edition of *The Old English Baron*, ed. J. Trainer, 1967.

REID, THOMAS, 1710-96

An Inquiry into the Human Mind, on the Principles of Common Sense appeared in Edinburgh, 1764. Reid's *Essays on the Intellectual Powers of Man* followed in 1785, and *Essays on the Active Powers of Man* in 1788. His works were edited by Sir William Hamilton, 2 vols., Edinburgh, 1846-63.

Reid's *Lectures on the Fine Arts* have been edited by P. Kivey, The Hague, 1973. Kivey discusses them in *JHI* xxxi, 1970. D. O. Robbins considers Reid's aesthetics in the *Journal of Aesthetics and Art Criticism* v, 1942.

REYNOLDS, SIR JOSHUA, 1723–92

A collected edition of Sir Joshua's writings, edited by Edmond Malone, was published in 2 vols., 1797. This contains the first collected edition of the *Discourses*, which have been reprinted many times, notably with an introduction by Roger Fry, 1905. There is an edition, with his *Idler* papers and an introduction by A. Dobson, in *WC*. The standard edition is by R. R. Wark, 1959. *Portraits by Sir Joshua Reynolds*, i.e. character-sketches of Goldsmith, Johnson, and Garrick, with other papers, ed. F. W. Hilles, was published in 1952. Hilles has also edited Reynolds's *Letters*, 1929, and written a study, *The Literary Career of Sir Joshua Reynolds*, 1936. The standard biography is still the *Life and Times of Sir Joshua Reynolds* by C. R. Leslie and T. Taylor, 2 vols., 1865, but D. Hudson's book, 1958, should also be consulted. The following essays are helpful: J. Burke, *Hogarth and Reynolds, a Contrast in English Art Theory*, 1943; E. H. Gombrich, 'Reynolds's Theory and Practice of Imitation', *Burlington Magazine* lxxx, 1942, reprinted in *Norm and Form: Studies in the Art of the Renaissance*, 1966; W. J. Hipple, Jr., 'General and Particular in the *Discourses* of Sir Joshua Reynolds', *Journal of Aesthetics and Art Criticism* xi, 1953; R. E. Moore, 'Reynolds and the Art of Characterization', in *S. H. Monk Festschrift*, 1967; and H. D. Goldstein, '*Ut Poesis Pictura*: Reynolds on Imitation and Imagination', *ECS* i, 1968.

RICHARDSON, JOHN, 1741–1811

Richardson published *A Specimen of Persian Poetry* (from Hafiz) in 1774, and a *Grammar of the Arabick Language* in 1776. The *Dissertation on the Languages, Literature, and Manners of Eastern Nations* served as a preface to *A Dictionary, Persian, Arabic, and English*, 2 vols., Oxford, 1777, but it was also published separately.

RICHARDSON, SAMUEL, 1689–1761

Richardson's first published work was *The Apprentice's Vade Mecum*, 1734 (see the edition by A. D. McKillop, Los Angeles,

1975, *ARS*). He brought out editions of Aesop's *Fables*, 1740, based on L'Estrange's version, 1692, to which he contributed the preface and moral reflections, and of Sir Thomas Roe's *Negotiations . . . in his Embassy to the Ottoman Porte, from the Year 1624 to 1628 Inclusive*, 1740. The first two volumes of *Pamela* were published in November 1740, and the remaining two (*Pamela II*) followed in December 1741. *Clarissa* appeared in 7 vols., i and ii in December 1747, iii and iv in April 1748, v in October, vi in November, and vii in December. *The History of Sir Charles Grandison* was published in 7 vols., 1753-4. Richardson revised the texts of all his novels in the course of subsequent editions. The revisions of *Pamela* are considered by T. C. D. Eaves and B. D. Kimpel in *Studies in Bibliography* xx, 1967; *Clarissa*, by M. Kinkead-Weekes in '*Clarissa* Restored?', *RES* n.s. x, 1959, and by S. Van Marter, *Studies in Bibliography* xxvi, 1973, and xxviii, 1975; *Sir Charles Grandison*, by R. C. Pierson, *Studies in Bibliography* xxi, 1968.

The standard edition of the novels is the Shakespeare Head Press edition in 18 vols., 1929-31. *Pamela* and *Clarissa* have been reprinted in *EL*, and there is a fine edition of *Sir Charles Grandison*, ed. J. Harris, 3 vols., 1972. *Letters written to and for Particular Friends, on the Most Important Occasions*, 1741, was edited by B. W. Downs, 1928. Richardson also contributed *Rambler* 97 to Johnson's periodical, and helped Young with *Conjectures on Original Composition*, 1759: see A. D. McKillop, *MP* xxii, 1925.

The 6-volume edition of the correspondence, ed. with a life by Mrs. Barbauld, 6 vols., 1804, is no more than a selection from the letters now in the Victoria and Albert Museum, but it is still the standard edition, and has been reprinted, New York, 1968. J. Carroll's *Selected Letters of Samuel Richardson*, Oxford, 1964, is excellent. See also the edition of Richardson's correspondence with his Dutch translator Johannes Stinstra, by W. C. Slattery, Carbondale, 1969.

There is a bibliography by M. W. Sale, New Haven, 1936.

There have been a number of lives of Richardson, of which particular mention should be made of those by B. W. Downs, 1928, A. D. McKillop, Chapel Hill, 1936, and the very full one by T. C. D. Eaves and B. D. Kimpel, Oxford, 1971. Richardson's career as a printer was definitively surveyed by W. M. Sale, Ithaca, 1950. Richardson figures prominently in all surveys of the eighteenth-century novel, but there are particularly important discussions of his work in A. D. McKillop, *The Early Masters of English Fiction*, Lawrence, 1956, and I. Watt, *The Rise of the Novel*, 1957. Two recent studies are outstanding: M. Kinkead-Weekes, *Samuel Richardson, Dramatic Novelist*, 1971, and M. A. Doody, *A Natural Passion. A Study of the Novels of Samuel Richardson*, Oxford, 1974. See also M. Golden's book, *Richardson's Characters*, Ann Arbor, 1963, I. Konigsberg, *Samuel Richardson and the Dramatic Novel*, Lexington, 1968, the elaborate study by C. Pons, *Richardson et la littérature bourgeoise en Angleterre*, Aix-en-Provence, 1968, C. G. Wolff, *Samuel Richardson and the Eighteenth-Century Puritan Character*, Hamden, 1972, and E. B. Brophy, *Samuel Richardson. The Triumph of Craft*, Knoxville, 1974. There is an excellent brief general survey by R. F. Brissenden, 1958.

J. Carroll has collected recent critical essays for the *Twentieth Century Views* series, Englewood Cliffs, 1969, and there is a similar volume, ed. R. Cowler, Englewood Cliffs, 1969, devoted to *Pamela*. On *Pamela* see also B. Kreissman's account of the parodies, *Pamela-Shamela*, Lincoln, Nebr., 1960. On *Clarissa* there is a notable essay by D. Van Ghent in her book *The English Novel, Form and Function*, New York, 1953, and another by C. Hill, 'Clarissa Harlowe and her Times', *EC* v, 1955. See also J. A. Dussinger, 'Conscience and the Pattern of Christian Perfection in *Clarissa*', *PMLA* lxxxi, 1966; F. W. Hilles, 'The Plan of *Clarissa*', *PQ* xlv, 1966; and A. Kearney's short commentary on the novel, 1975 (cf. his essay in *EC* xvi, 1966). Kearney contributes a volume on Richardson to the *Profiles in Literature* series, 1968.

There is an account by J. Carroll of scholarly work on Richardson in *The English Novel. Select Bibliographical Guides*, ed. A. E. Dyson, 1974.

RICHARDSON, WILLIAM, 1743–1814

Richardson's *Anecdotes of the Russian Empire* were published in 1784. There is a section devoted to this work in P. Putnam, *Some Britons in Imperial Russia*, Princeton, 1952.

His Shakespeare criticism may be found in *A Philosophical Analysis and Illustration of some of Shakespeare's Remarkable Characters*, 1774; *Essays on Shakespeare's Dramatic Characters of Richard III, King Lear, and Timon of Athens*, 1784; and *Essays on Shakespeare's Dramatic Character of Falstaff, and his Imitation of Female*

Characters, 1789. There is a study by R. W. Babcock, *JEGP* xxviii, 1929. See also the same author's *Genesis of Shakespeare Idolatry 1766–1799*, Chapel Hill, 1931.

Richardson also published poems and plays.

RIDLEY, JAMES, 1736–65

The Tales of the Genii; or the Delightful Lessons of Horam, the Son of Asmar, were first published in 1764. They were reprinted a number of times, e.g. in *Tales of the East*, ed. H. Weber, vol. iii, Edinburgh, 1812. He also wrote a novel, *The History of James Lovegrove, Esq.*, 2 vols., 1761, and essays: *The Schemer, or Universal Satirist*, 1763.

RIDPATH, GEORGE, 1717–72

Ridpath's diary for the years 1755–61 was edited by J. B. Paul, Edinburgh, 1922. He wrote a *Border-History of England and Scotland*, which was completed by his brother Philip, and published posthumously in 1776.

There is a brief appreciation of the diary in A. Ponsonby's *Scottish and Irish Diaries*, 1927.

ROBERTSON, WILLIAM, 1721–93

The History of Scotland during the Reign of Queen Mary and of King James VI appeared in 2 vols., 1759. *The History of the Reign of the Emperor Charles V* followed in 3 vols., 1769, and *The History of America*, 2 vols., 1777. Histories of Virginia and New England were added to this last work in a posthumous edition, 4 vols., 1800. *An Historical Disquisition concerning the Knowledge which the Ancients had of India* appeared in 1791. There were many collected editions of his work in the early nineteenth century.

The correspondence of Horace Walpole with Robertson appears in vol. xv of the Yale Edition of Walpole's correspondence, ed. W. S. Lewis and others, New Haven, 1952.

'A View of the Progress of Society in Europe', the first part of the *History of Charles V*, has been edited by F. Gilbert, Chicago, 1972.

Dugald Stewart's *Account of the Life and Writings of William Robertson*, Edinburgh, 1801, is indispensable: it often serves as a preface to collected editions. There is an assessment of Robertson's work in J. B. Black, *The Art of History*, 1926, and M. Schlenke has written a study of Robertson as *Geschichtsschreiber des europäischen Staatensystems*, Marburg, 1953. Robertson's role as Principal of Edinburgh University is concisely examined in D. B. Horn's *Short History of the University of Edinburgh*, Edinburgh, 1967.

Ross, Alexander, 1699–1784

The Fortunate Shepherdess: a Pastoral Tale in Three Cantos, in the Scottish Dialect, appeared in Aberdeen, 1768. Ross's works have been collected by M. Wattie, Edinburgh, 1938.

Scott, John, 1730–83

Scott published *Four Elegies: Descriptive and Moral* in 1760, and an *Elegy, Written at Amwell in Hertfordshire* in 1769, but his best-known work was *Amwell: a Descriptive Poem*, 1776. His posthumously published *Critical Essays on Some of the Poems, of Several English Poets*, 1785, interested Wordsworth, and his publications on the improvement of highways won praise from Sidney and Beatrice Webb. He collected his own poems in 1782. His work is in Anderson xi and Chalmers xvii.

Samuel Johnson intended to write Scott's life, but was prevented by his own death from doing so: see H. Liebert, *Johnson's Last Literary Project*, New Haven, 1948. A biography was written by John Hoole and published with the *Critical Essays*. There is a comprehensive study by L. D. Stewart, Berkeley, 1956.

Seward, Anna, 1742–1809

Anna Seward published her *Elegy on Captain Cook*, 1780, and other poems followed. Her poetry was collected by Walter Scott, 3 vols., Edinburgh, 1810. She also wrote *Memoirs* of Erasmus Darwin, 1804. Her letters (1784–1807) were published in 6 vols., Edinburgh, 1811. There is a selection by H. Pearson, 1936. See also J. L. Clifford's essay on the authenticity of her published correspondence, *MP* xxxix, 1942, reprinted in *Studies in the Literature of the Augustan Age*, ed. R. C. Boys, Ann Arbor, 1952.

There is a biography by M. Ashmun, *The Singing Swan: an Account of Anna Seward and her Acquaintance with Dr. Johnson, Boswell, and Others of their Time*, New Haven, 1931. See also R. M. Myers, *Anna Seward; an Eighteenth-Century Handelian*, Williamsburg, 1947. S. H. Monk has written an essay on her relations with the romantic poets, in *Wordsworth and Coleridge: Studies in Honor of G. M. Harper*, Princeton, 1939.

SHARP, SAMUEL, ?1700–78

Apart from the *Letters from Italy, describing the Customs and Manners of that Country*, 1766, Sharp published two works on surgery, 1739 and 1750.

SHEBBEARE, JOHN, 1709–88

The Marriage Act, a novel, appeared in 1754, and *Lydia, or Filial Piety* in 1755. His *Letters on the English Nation*, 'translated' from 'Battista Angeloni', followed in 1756. He wrote numerous political works, of which the most elaborate was *The History of the Excellence and Decline of the Constitution, Religion, Laws, Manners and Genius of the Sumatrans*, 2 vols., 1760.

There is a study by J. R. Foster, 'Smollett's Pamphleteering Foe Shebbeare', *PMLA* lvii, 1942.

SHENSTONE, WILLIAM, 1714–63

Shenstone's earliest publication was *Poems upon Various Occasions*, Oxford, 1737. It was here that the earliest version of 'The School-mistress' appeared, but an extended version was separately published in 1742. The final text appeared in the second edition of vol. i of Dodsley's *Collection of Poems*, 1748. Shenstone contributed many other poems to Dodsley's *Collection*. A 'Miscellany' of poems collected by Shenstone was edited by I. A. Gordon, Oxford, 1952. His *Works in Verse and Prose* were edited by Dodsley, 2 vols., 1764. Vol. ii contains 'Essays on Men, Manners, and Things', including the influential 'Unconnected Thoughts on Gardening'. Havelock Ellis edited a selection from these essays, Waltham St. Lawrence, 1927. His poems are in Anderson ix and Chalmers xiii.

There are two modern editions of the letters, one by D. Mallam, Minneapolis, 1939, the other by M. Williams, Oxford, 1939. Each prints letters not in the other. See also R. Lewis, 'William Shenstone and Edward Knight: Some New Letters', *MLR* xlii, 1947.

Richard Graves wrote a novel, *Columella*, 1779, based on Shenstone's life, and it is discussed by C. J. Hill in *PMLA* xlix, 1934. Graves also wrote a *Recollection* of Shenstone, 1788. There are two modern studies, one by M. Williams, *William*

Shenstone: a Chapter in Eighteenth-Century Taste, Birmingham, 1935, the other by A. R. Humphreys, *William Shenstone: an Eighteenth-Century Portrait*, Cambridge, 1937. There is a bibliography and appreciation by I. A. Williams, *Seven XVIIIth Century Bibliographies*, 1924.

SHERIDAN, FRANCES, 1724–66

Mrs. Sheridan's earliest novel, *Eugenia and Adelaide*, was not published until 1791, and even then it appeared anonymously. *Memoirs of Miss Sidney Bidulph. Extracted from her own Journal* was published in 3 vols., 1761, and expanded into 5 vols., 1767. She wrote three plays: *The Discovery*, 1763, *The Dupe*, 1764, and *A Trip to Bath*, written in 1765, but not published until 1902, in *Sheridan's Plays as he wrote them*, ed. F. Rae. *The History of Nourjahad* appeared in 1767.

There is a life by A. Lefanu, 1824. S. P. Chew has written an account of Prévost's translation of *Sidney Bidulph*, *MLN* liv, 1939.

SHERIDAN, RICHARD BRINSLEY, 1753–1816

The Rivals was first performed and published in 1775. The text of the first performance, which differs substantially from the received printed text, was first published in 1935, ed. R. L. Purdy. *St. Patrick's Day* was performed in the same year, but not published until 1788, in Dublin. *The Duenna* also appeared in 1775, and *A Trip to Scarborough* in 1777 (published 1781). *The School for Scandal* was first performed in 1777 also, and published in Dublin, 1780. *The Critic: or a Tragedy Rehearsed*, was first performed in 1779, published 1781. *Pizarro*, adapted from Kotzebue, appeared in 1799. Many of Sheridan's political speeches were published, notably those delivered in the course of the impeachment of Warren Hastings.

His plays and poems have been edited by R. C. Rhodes, 3 vols., Oxford, 1928, but the standard edition of the plays is by C. Price, 2 vols., Oxford, 1973. Price has also edited the letters, 3 vols., Oxford, 1966.

There is an interesting collection of *Sheridaniana*, 1826. The best biography is by R. C. Rhodes, Oxford, 1933, but for his political career, see the study by M. T. H. Sadleir, Oxford, 1912. There is a study of the comedies by J. Dulck, Paris, 1962, and essays on Sheridan's work include A. Schiller, '*The School for Scandal*: the Restoration Unrestored', *PMLA* lxii, 1956; J. R. de J. Jackson, 'The Importance of Witty Dialogue in *The School for Scandal*', *MLN* lxxvi, 1961; A. C. Sprague, 'In Defence of a Masterpiece: *The School for Scandal* Re-examined', *English Studies Today*, 3rd ser., Edinburgh, 1964; and M. S. Auburn, 'The Pleasures of Sheridan's *The Rivals*: A Critical Study in the Light of Stage History', *MP* lxxii, 1974–5. J. L. Mahoney considers Sheridan's speeches against Hastings in 'The Classical Oration and Eighteenth-Century Politics', *Burke Newsletter* vi, 1965, and J. Loftis relates them to the 'Whig oratory on stage' in *Pizarro*, *ECS* viii, 1975.

The bibliography in *NCBEL* is excellent, but for a fuller description of first editions, see I. A. Williams, *Seven XVIIIth Century Bibliographies*, 1924.

SHERIDAN, THOMAS, 1719–88

British Education: or, the Source of the Disorders of Great Britain, appeared in 1756, *A Course of Lectures on Elocution* in 1762, and *Lectures on the Art of Reading* in 1775. Sheridan also compiled a *General Dictionary of the English Language*, 2 vols., 1780, and an edition of Swift, 18 vols., 1784.

There is an excellent study by E. K. Sheldon, *Thomas Sheridan of Smock Alley*, 1967. His contribution to rhetoric is considered by W. S. Howell in *Eighteenth-Century British Logic and Rhetoric*, Princeton, 1971, and (more sympathetically) by W. Benzie in *The Dublin Orator: Thomas Sheridan's Influence on Eighteenth-Century Rhetoric and Belles Lettres*, Menston, Yorkshire, 1972.

SHERLOCK, MARTIN, ?1750–97

Sherlock's first publication seems to have been his *Consiglio ad un Giovane Poeta*, Naples, 1779. *Lettres d'un Voyageur Anglois* also appeared in 1779, and was translated into English, 1780. *Nouvelles Lettres d'un Voyageur Anglois* followed in 1780, translated 1781. *Letters on Several Subjects* were published in 2 vols., 1781. Part of the *Consiglio* was translated in 1786 under the title of *A Fragment on Shakespeare*. Most of his work is collected in the edition of *Letters from an English Traveller* published in 2 vols., 1802.

Sherlock's work is commented on, unfavourably, by Thomas Carlyle in his *History of Friedrich II, called Frederick the Great*, vol. vi, 1865.

SKINNER, JOHN, 1721–1807

Skinner turned *Chryste-Kirk on the Green* into Latin heroic verses, Aberdeen, 1772. *John o' Badenyon* appeared in Edinburgh, 1776; also *Tullochgorum*. His poems are collected in vol. iii of his works, Edinburgh, 1809. (Vols. i and ii were published in Aberdeen, as *Theological Works*.)

There is a life by W. Walker, 1883.

SMART, CHRISTOPHER, 1722–71

Smart won the Seatonian Prize at Cambridge five times, for poems on various attributes of the Supreme Being, but his first major publication was *Poems on Several Occasions*, 1752, including 'The Hop-Garden'. He published *The Hilliad* (against John Hill) in 1753, and edited (with Richard Rolt) *The Universal Visiter and Memorialist for the Year 1756*. In 1756, too, he published his *Hymn to the Supreme Being on Recovery from a Dangerous Fit of Illness*. *A Song to David* appeared in 1763, and *A Translation of the Psalms of David*, including 'A Song to David', in 1765. In the same year he published *Hymns and Spiritual Songs for the Fasts and Festivals of the Church of England*, and in 1770 (probably) *Hymns for the Amusement of Children*. *Jubilate Agno* (*Rejoice in the Lamb*) was not published until 1939, ed. W. F. Stead. The standard edition is by W. H. Bond, Cambridge, Mass., 1954. Smart also translated Horace, and wrote a number of libretti for oratorios.

The best modern edition of his poetry is by N. Callan, 2 vols., 1949. but the selection by R. Brittain, Princeton, 1950, should also be consulted. The best biography is by A. Sherbo, East Lansing, 1967, but C. Devlin's *Poor Kit Smart*, 1961, develops an interesting view of the poet. There is a study by S. B. Blaydes, *Christopher Smart as a Poet of his Time: a Re-appraisal*, The Hague, 1966. M. Dearnley's *The Poetry of Christopher Smart*, 1968, is full and well organized.

Among shorter studies, there is a useful one by D. J. Greene on the nature of Smart's interest in science: 'Smart, Berkeley, Scientists and Poets', *JHI* xiv, 1953. A. J. Kuhn considers Smart in 'The Poet as Patriot of the Lord', *ELH* xxx, 1963. K. M. Rogers discusses the sources of *A Song to David*, *PQ* xl, 1961, and *Hymns and Spiritual Songs* are considered by K. Williamson, *PQ* xxxviii, 1959. Among the discussions of *Jubilate Agno*, the study by R. P. Fitzgerald of the form of the poem should be mentioned, *SEL* viii, 1968, and the exposition by F. D. Adams, *PQ* xlviii, 1969. See also W. M. Merchant, 'Patterns of Reference in Smart's *Jubilate Agno*', *Huntington Library Bulletin* xiv, 1960; C. Parish, 'Christopher Smart's Knowledge of Hebrew', *SP* liv, 1961; J. B. Friedman, 'The Cosmology of Praise: Smart's *Jubilate Agno*', *PMLA* lxxxii, 1967; and R. P. Parkin on Smart's 'sacramental cat', *TSLL* xi, 1969.

SMITH, ADAM, 1723–90

The Theory of Moral Sentiments appeared in 1759, with a *Dissertation on the Origin of Languages* added to the third edition, 1767. *An Inquiry into the Nature and Causes of the Wealth of Nations* followed in 2 vols., 1776. The volume of *Essays on Philosophical Subjects* was published posthumously, in 1795. It contains the life by Dugald Stewart first published in 1793 in the *Transactions of the Royal Society of Edinburgh*. Texts of two sets of his lectures have been published more recently: those on justice, police, revenue, and arms, ed. E. Cannan, Oxford, 1896, and on rhetoric and belles-lettres, ed. J. M. Lothian, 1963. There is some material also in W. R. Scott's *Adam Smith as Student and Professor. With Unpublished Documents*, Glasgow, 1937. A catalogue of Smith's library was edited by J. Bonar, 1894; H. Mizuta has added a supplement, Cambridge, 1967.

The Glasgow Edition of Smith's works and correspondence is in progress. *The Theory of Moral Sentiments*, ed. D. D. Raphael and A. L. Macfie, and the *Wealth of Nations*, ed. R. H. Campbell, A. S. Skinner, and W. B. Todd, 2 vols., were published in Oxford, 1976. There is an edition of the early writings by J. R. Lindgren, New York, 1967.

The standard life at present is still that by J. Rae, 1895, reissued in 1965 with an introduction by J. Viner; but a substantial new biography by I. S. Ross will be published in connection with the Glasgow Edition of the works. Also connected with the Glasgow Edition is a representative collection of recent essays dealing with every aspect of Smith's work, ed. A. S. Skinner and T. Wilson, Oxford, 1975.

On Smith as a critic, see the assessment of the *Lectures on Rhetoric* by V. M. Bevilacqua in *Studies in Scottish Literature* iii, 1965. Bevilacqua also wrote 'Adam Smith and some Philosophical Origins of Eighteenth-Century Rhetorical Theory',

MLR lxiii, 1968, and there is an essay by J. L. Golden on Smith as a rhetorical theorist and critic, *Costerus* i, 1972. W. S. Howell writes on Smith in his *Eighteenth-Century British Logic and Rhetoric*, Princeton, 1971.

It is not possible here to provide a bibliography of Smith as a philosopher, but three essays may be mentioned as of special interest to literary students: K. MacLean discusses imagination and sympathy in Sterne and Smith, *JHI* x, 1949; R. F. Brissenden examines authority, guilt, and anxiety in *The Theory of Moral Sentiments*, *TSLL* xi, 1969; and A. S. Skinner looks at science and the role of the imagination in Smith, in *Hume and the Enlightenment. Essays presented to E. C. Mossner*, ed. W. B. Todd, Edinburgh, 1974.

SMOLLETT, TOBIAS GEORGE, 1721–71

The Adventures of Roderick Random, 2 vols., has been reprinted in *EL* and *WC*; *The Adventures of Peregrine Pickle*, 4 vols., 1751, is in *EL* and has also been edited by J. L. Clifford, 1964; *The Adventures of Ferdinand Count Fathom*, 2 vols., 1753, has been edited by D. Grant, 1971; *The Adventures of Sir Launcelot Greaves*, first published in serial in the *British Magazine*, 1760–1, and reprinted in 2 vols., 1762, has been edited by D. Evans, 1973; and *The Expedition of Humphry Clinker*, 3 vols., 1771, is in *EL* and *WC* and has been edited by L. M. Knapp, 1966. Smollett's other novel (though his authorship has been disputed), *The History and Adventures of an Atom*, 2 vols., 1769, has only been reprinted in the collected editions of his works, such as the one edited by G. Saintsbury, 12 vols., 1895, and the Shakespeare Head edition, 11 vols., Oxford, 1925–6.

The best edition of *Travels through France and Italy*, 2 vols., 1766, is in *WC*, ed. T. Seccombe. *A Complete History of England*, 4 vols., 1757–8, and its *Continuation*, 4 vols., 1760–1, have been often reprinted with Hume's *History*. His poems (*The Tears of Scotland*, 1746; *Advice, a Satire*, 1746; *Reproof, a Satire*, 1747; *Ode to Independence*, 1773) and plays (*The Regicide*, 1749; *The Reprisal*, 1757), and his *Account of the Expedition against Carthagena*, 1741, which appeared in his *Compendium of Authentic and Entertaining Voyages*, 7 vols., 1756, are reprinted, with the novels and *Travels*, in Roscoe's popular one-volume edition of the *Miscellaneous Works*, 1841. Besides editing the *Critical Review*, 1756–62, and the *British Magazine*, 1760–7, he translated *Gil Blas*, 4 vols., 1749, and *Don Quixote*, 2 vols., 1755, and was partly responsible for a translation of Voltaire with notes, 36 vols., 1761–9. He contributed to the *Modern Universal History*, 44 vols., 1759–66. His only medical publication, *An Essay on the External Use of Water*, 1752, has been edited by C. E. Jones, Baltimore, 1935. E. S. Noyes's edition of Smollett's letters, Cambridge, Mass., 1926, has been superseded by the edition of L. M. Knapp, Oxford, 1970.

The most authoritative account of Smollett's life is by L. M. Knapp, *Tobias Smollett, Doctor of Men and Manners*, Princeton, 1949. G. M. Kahrl's *Tobias Smollett: Traveler-Novelist*, Chicago, 1945, is an attractive study from a single but fruitful approach. L. L. Martz's *Later Career of Tobias Smollett*, New Haven, 1942, discusses the effect upon *Humphry Clinker* of his work as editor and historian. The most substantial critical survey is by P.-G. Boucé, *Les Romans de Smollett*, Paris, 1971, translated by A. White and P.-G. Boucé as *The Novels of Tobias Smollett*, 1976. See also the excellent volume of Smollett bicentennial essays presented to L. M. Knapp, ed. G. S. Rousseau and P.-G. Boucé, New York, 1971. For the general reader, there is a useful short survey by R. D. Spector, New York, 1968.

Books of more specialized interest include H. S. Buck's *A Study of Smollett*, largely concerned with the revision of *Peregrine Pickle*, and F. W. Boege's *Smollett's Reputation as a Novelist*, Princeton, 1947. There are useful discussions of Smollett in R. Alter's *Rogue's Progress: Studies in the Picaresque Novel*, Cambridge, Mass., 1964, and A. A. Parker's *Literature and the Delinquent. The Picaresque Novel in Spain and Europe, 1599–1753*, Edinburgh, 1967. See also the chapters on Smollett in A. D. McKillop, *The Early Masters of English Fiction*, Lawrence, Kansas, 1956, and R. Paulson, *Satire and the Novel in Eighteenth-Century England*, New Haven, 1967.

There are bibliographies by F. Cordasco of Smollett criticism, that for 1770–1924 appearing in Brooklyn, 1948, and for 1925–45, in Brooklyn, 1947. But there are errors and omissions: see the bibliography in P.-G. Boucé's *Novels of Tobias Smollett*, 1976. D. M. Korte supplies *An Annotated Bibliography of Smollett Scholarship* 1946–1968, Toronto, 1969. There is an excellent essay contributed by L. M. Knapp to *The English Novel. Select Bibliographical Guides*, ed. A. E. Dyson, 1974.

SPENCE, JOSEPH, 1699–1768

See Vol. VII, but the best edition of the *Anecdotes* is now *Observations, Anecdotes and Characters of Books and Men. Collected from Conversation*, ed. J. M. Osborn, 2 vols., Oxford, 1966. See also Osborn on Spence's 'Collections relating to the Lives of the Poets', *Huntington Library Bulletin* xvi, 1968.

STERNE, LAURENCE, 1713–68

Sterne's early contributions to newspapers are indicated in L. P. Curtis's book, *The Politicks of Laurence Sterne*, Oxford, 1929, and he had published two sermons in York, 1747 and 1750. *A Political Romance* appeared in York, 1759 (later called *The History of a Good Warm Watch-Coat*), and the first two volumes of *The Life and Opinions of Tristram Shandy, Gentleman*, were also published there in 1760. Vols. iii and iv followed in 1761, v and vi in 1762, vii and viii in 1765, and ix in 1767. *A Sentimental Journey through France and Italy, by Mr. Yorick*, appeared in 2 vols., 1768. 'Mr. Yorick' also published seven volumes of sermons, 1760–9. *Letters from Yorick to Eliza* was published posthumously, in 1773. In 1870, P. Stapfer published the untitled fragment 'to Mr. Cook', in his *Laurence Sterne. Sa personne et ses ouvrages*, Paris. A 'Rabelaisian Fragment' has appeared in *PMLA* lxxxvii, 1972, ed. M. New.

Sterne's works have been edited by W. L. Cross (with a biography), 12 vols., New York, 1904, and in the Shakespeare Head edition, 7 vols., Oxford, 1926–7. There is a good collection of his work in the Reynard Library edition, ed. D. Grant, 1950. The standard edition of *Tristram Shandy* is by J. A. Work, New York, 1940, but the student should also consult the admirably annotated Riverside Edition, ed. I. Watt, Boston, Mass., 1965. The standard edition of *A Sentimental Journey* is by G. D. Stout, Jr., Berkeley, 1967, but the edition by I. Jack, along with the *Journal to Eliza* (i.e. *Letters from Yorick to Eliza*) and *A Political Romance*, is also satisfactory. There is a good edition of the letters by L. P. Curtis, Oxford, 1935.

Apart from the biography by W. L. Cross mentioned above, which reached a third, revised edition in 1929, there is an excellent biographical section in H. Fluchère's *Laurence Sterne, de l'homme à l'œuvre*, Paris, 1961, and A. H. Cash has written an authoritative account of Sterne's early and middle years, 1975.

In *Yorick and the Critics*, New Haven, 1958, A. B. Howes considers Sterne's reputation from 1760 to 1868. He has also edited the Sterne volume in the Critical Heritage series, 1974. More recent criticism is listed by L. Hartley in *Laurence Sterne in the Twentieth Century*, revised edition, Chapel Hill, 1968. There is a useful guide to current scholarship in D. Isles's contribution to *The English Novel. Select Bibliographical Guides*, ed. A. E. Dyson, 1974.

Two collections of critical essays are particularly helpful in illustrating recent discussion of Sterne. J. Traugott's volume in the Twentieth Century Views series, Englewood Cliffs, 1968, includes such items as an essay by the Russian formalist critic V. Shklovsky (on *Tristram Shandy* as a parodying novel), a chapter from A. A. Mendilow's *Time and the Novel*, 1952, and D. W. Jefferson's article on *Tristram Shandy* and the tradition of learned wit, *EC* i, 1951. The papers collected in *The Winged Skull*, ed. A. H. Cash and J. M. Stedmond, 1971, approach Sterne from an even greater variety of points of view, with much clarification and correction of earlier scholarship.

Among the many books that have been published on Sterne, the following are particularly recommended: J. Traugott, *Tristram Shandy's World: Sterne's Philosophical Rhetoric*, Berkeley, 1954; H. Fluchère, *Laurence Sterne, de l'homme à l'œuvre*, Paris, 1961, the critical section of which has been translated by B. Bray as *Laurence Sterne: from Tristram to Yorick, an Interpretation of 'Tristram Shandy'*, 1965; A. H. Cash, *Sterne's Comedy of Moral Sentiments: the Ethical Dimension of the 'Journey'*, Pittsburgh, 1966; J. M. Stedmond, *The Comic Art of Laurence Sterne: Convention and Innovation in 'Tristram Shandy' and 'A Sentimental Journey'*, Toronto, 1967; J. C. T. Oates, *Shandyism and Sentiment, 1760–1800*, Cambridge, 1968; M. New, *Laurence Sterne as Satirist: a Reading of 'Tristram Shandy'*, Gainesville, 1969; and R. A. Lanham, *'Tristram Shandy': the Games of Pleasure*, Berkeley, 1973. Sterne figures prominently in a number of general discussions of the novel, notably in W. C. Booth's *The Rhetoric of Fiction*, Chicago, 1961. (Booth's article, 'Did Sterne complete *Tristram Shandy*?' *MP* xlviii, 1951, should be read with M. Allentuck's 'In Defence of an Unfinished *Tristram Shandy*', in *The Winged Skull*.) See also J. Preston, *The Created Self: the Reader's Role in Eighteenth-Century Fiction*, 1970.

The standard work on the sermons is by L. van der H.

Hammond, New Haven, 1948, but there is also an excellent chapter in J. Downey's *The Eighteenth Century Pulpit*, Oxford, 1969.

STOCKDALE, PERCIVAL, 1736–1811

Stockdale's first publication was *A Poetical Address to the Supreme Being*, Berwick, 1764, and he wrote a fair quantity of verse, collected in 2 vols., 1808. He undertook a number of translations, and published sermons and much miscellaneous prose. *An Inquiry into the Nature and Genuine Laws of Poetry* appeared in 1778; *Lectures on the Truly Eminent English Poets* in 2 vols., 1808. He contributed to the *Critical Review*.

STUART, GILBERT, 1742–86

An Historical Dissertation concerning the Antiquity of the English Constitution was published in Edinburgh, 1768; *A View of Society in Europe, in its Progress from Rudeness to Refinement* followed in 1778, and *Observations concerning the Public Law and the Constitutional History of Scotland* in 1779. He wrote a history of the Reformation in Scotland, 1780, and a defence of Mary Queen of Scots is the main concern of his *History of Scotland*, 2 vols., 1782.

THORNTON, BONNELL, 1724–68

Thornton was chiefly celebrated for his burlesque *Ode on St. Caecilia's Day, adapted to the Antient British Musick: viz. the Salt-Box, the Jews Harp, the Marrow-Bones and Cleavers, the Hum-Strum or Hurdy &c.*, 1763. He also wrote *The Battle of the Wigs*, 1768, a 'continuation' of Garth's *Dispensary*. With George Colman he conducted the *Connoisseur*, 1754–6, and also translated Plautus, 2 vols., 1767.

W. C. Brown has a study of Thornton as 'a belated Augustan', *PQ* xxxiv, 1935.

TUCKER, JOSIAH, 1713–99

Tucker wrote numerous works on trade and commerce, notably *A Brief Essay on the Advantages and Disadvantages which respectively attend France and Great Britain, with regard to Trade*, 1749; *The Elements of Commerce, and Theory of Taxes*, privately printed, 1755; *The case of Going to War for the Sake of . . . Trade, considered in a New Light*, 1763; and *The True Interest of Great*

Britain, set forth in regard to the Colonies, 1774. His *Instructions for Travellers* were privately printed in 1757.

There is a convenient selection from these writings in R. L. Schuyler's *Josiah Tucker*, New York, 1931.

WALPOLE, HORACE, 1711–97

Lessons for the Day. Being the First and Second Chapters of the Book of Preferment, appeared in 1742. Walpole published a number of similar pamphlets, notably *A letter from Xo Ho, a Chinese Philosopher at London,* 1757. In 1747 he published *Aedes Walpolianae: or, a Description of the Collection of Pictures at Houghton-Hall in Norfolk,* and in 1758 *A Catalogue of the Royal and Noble Authors of England,* 2 vols., Strawberry Hill. *Anecdotes of Painting in England* followed in 4 vols., Strawberry Hill, 1762–71. (A fifth vol., New Haven, 1937, was compiled by F. W. Hilles and P. B. Daghlian from Walpole's *Book of Materials.*) *The Castle of Otranto, a story. Translated by William Marshal, Gent. From the Original Italian of Onuphrio Muralto,* was published in 1765; *Historic Doubts on the Life and Reign of King Richard the Third* in 1768. *The Mysterious Mother* was published at Strawberry Hill, 1768, as were the *Letter to the Editor of the Miscellanies of Thomas Chatterton,* 1779, the *Essay on Modern Gardening,* 1785 (reprinted from vol. iv of *Anecdotes of Painting,* 1771), and *Hieroglyphic Tales,* 1785.

Collections of *Fugitive Pieces in Verse and Prose* appeared at Strawberry Hill, 1758 and 1770, and the *Works,* ed. M. Berry, 5 vols., 1798. Vols. vi–ix followed, 1818–25, of which vols. vii and viii were the first publication of *Memoires of the Last Ten Years of the Reign of George the Second,* ed. Lord Holland, 1822. *Memoirs of the Reign of King George the Third,* ed. D. Le Marchant, followed in 4 vols., 1845, and *Journal of the Reign of King George the Third,* ed. J. Doran, 2 vols., 1859. There is a selection from the *Memoirs* by M. J. C. Hodgart, 1963.

A. T. Hazen has compiled bibliographies of Walpole's own works, New Haven 1948, and of the Strawberry Hill Press, New Haven, 1942, reissued with supplement 1973. With W. S. Lewis he has published a catalogue of Walpole's library, New Haven, 1969.

The standard edition of the correspondence is the Yale Edition, ed. W. S. Lewis *et al.,* 1937– . 39 vols. had been published by 1974. The edition by Mrs. P. Toynbee, 16 vols.,

Oxford, 1903–5, with 3 supplementary vols. 1918–25, is convenient. A number of selections have been published, notably that by W. S. Lewis, New Haven, 1973.

The best biography is by R. W. Ketton-Cremer, 1940, rev. 1946, and there is an excellent study by W. S. Lewis, 1961. See also the compact surveys by H. Honour, 1958, and M. Kallich, New York, 1971. I. W. U. Chase has a useful study of Walpole in relation to gardening and landscape architecture, Princeton, 1943. In spite of its excessive length, P. Yvon's study *La Vie d'un dilettante*, Caen, 1924, may still be read with enjoyment. There is much useful material in the 250th Anniversary volume, *Horace Walpole, Writer, Politician, and Connoisseur*, ed. W. H. Smith, New Haven, 1967. On the *Memoirs*, there is a study by G. P. Judd IV, 1960.

WARBURTON, WILLIAM, 1698–1779

Warburton's principal works were *A Critical and Philosophical Enquiry into the Causes of Prodigies and Miracles*, 1727; *The Alliance between Church and State*, 1736; *The Divine Legation of Moses Demonstrated, on the Principles of a Religious Deist*, 2 vols., 1738–41; *A Critical and Philosophical Commentary on Mr. Pope's Essay on Man*, 1742 (originally published in the *History of the Works of the Learned*, 1738–9); *Julian, or, a Discourse concerning the Earthquake and Fiery Eruption which defeated that Emperor's Attempt to rebuild the Temple at Jerusalem*, 1750; *A View of Lord Bolingbroke's Philosophy*, 1754; *Remarks on Mr. David Hume's Essay on the Natural History of Religion*, 1757; *The Doctrine of Grace*, 1762. Warburton also published an edition of Shakespeare in 8 vols., 1747. His preface to Charles Jervas's version of *Don Quixote*, 1742, considering the oriental origins of romance, was influential.

There is a study by A. W. Evans, *Warburton and the Warburtonians*, 1932. Two essays on Warburton as critic should be mentioned: one by S. J. Curry, *ES* xlviii, 1967, the other, by R. M. Ryley, on Warburton as 'new critic', in the *S. H. Monk Festschrift*, 1967.

WARTON, JOSEPH, 1722–1800

The Enthusiast, or the Lover of Nature, appeared in 1744, followed by *Odes on Various Subjects*, 1746. He edited the poems of his father, Thomas Warton the Elder, 1748, adding two odes to them. He published two further odes in 1749. The first volume of *An Essay on the Writings and Genius of Pope* appeared in 1759, the second in 1782. He contributed 24 essays to the *Adventurer*, 1752–4, and edited Virgil and Pope. A selection from his verse is included in *The Three Wartons*, ed. E. Partridge, 1927.

J. Wooll wrote a biography, 1806. Manuscript materials for a biographer are briefly described by B. Martin, 'Some Unpublished *Wartoniana*', *SP* xxix, 1932.

Warton's methods as an editor of his father's poetry are studied in detail by D. Fairer in two articles in *RES*, n.s. xxvi, 1975. His criticism has been discussed from a number of points of view, notably by H. Trowbridge, 'Joseph Warton on the Imagination', *MP* xxxv, 1937, by P. F. Leedy on genres criticism, *JEGP* xlv, 1946, by P. M. Griffith, on his criticism of Shakespeare, *Tulane Studies in English* xiv, 1965, and by J. Pittock, *The Ascendancy of Taste: the Achievement of Joseph and Thomas Warton*, 1973. The relationship between the widely separated volumes of the *Essay on Pope* has been considered by W. D. MacClintock in his 'History' of its 5 editions, Chapel Hill, 1933, by J. Allison in 'Joseph Warton's Reply to Dr. Johnson's *Lives*', *JEGP* li, 1952, and by J. Pittock, 'Joseph Warton and his Second Volume of the *Essay on Pope*', *RES* n.s. xviii, 1967.

Warton's reputation as a poet is admirably surveyed by J. Hysham in *Studies in Romanticism* i, 1962. See also, on the poetry, A. Fenner, 'The Wartons "Romanticize" their Verse', *SP* liii, 1956, and D. B. Morris, 'Joseph Warton's Figure of Virtue: Poetic Indirection in *The Enthusiast*', *PQ* l, 1971.

WARTON, THOMAS, 1728–90

The Pleasures of Melancholy appeared in 1747, *The Triumphs of Isis* in 1749, and *Newmarket, a Satire*, in 1751. *Observations on the Faerie Queene of Spenser* followed in 1754, enlarged in 2 vols., 1762. *The History of English Poetry from the Close of the Eleventh to the Commencement of the Eighteenth Century* was published in 3 vols., 1774–81. Eighty-eight pages of a fourth volume were printed before Warton's death, but not published until R. Price's edition, 4 vols., 1824, where they appear as sections lxii–lxvi. A further continuation was edited by R. M. Baine, Los Angeles, 1953 (*ARS*). Warton also published *An Enquiry into the Authenticity of the Poems attributed to Rowley*, 1782. He collected his own poems in 1777, and published *Verses on Sir Joshua Reynolds's Painted Window at New College, Oxford*, 1782.

Warton edited *The Union, or Select Scots and English Poems*, Edinburgh, 1753; *The Oxford Sausage*, 1764; and *Poems upon Several Occasions* by John Milton, 1785. He also produced editions of the Greek Anthology and of Theocritus, Oxford, 1766 and 1770. He was the author of lives of Ralph Bathurst, 1761, and of Sir Thomas Pope, 1772, and wrote topographical works on Winchester and Oxford. His essay on Gothic architecture was published, with essays by others on the same subject, in 1800.

The basic study of Warton's work remains that by C. Rinaker, Urbana, 1916, although J. Pittock's book, *The Ascendancy of Taste*, 1973, contains much perceptive comment. The best studies of *The History of English Poetry* are chap. vi of R. Wellek's *The Rise of English Literary History*, Chapel Hill, 1941, and chap. xii of L. Lipking's *The Ordering of the Arts in Eighteenth-Century England*, Princeton, 1970. See also R. D. Havens, 'Thomas Warton and the Eighteenth-Century Dilemma', *SP* xxv, 1928 (reprinted in *A. E. Case Festschrift*, 1952), F. S. Miller, 'The Historic Sense of Thomas Warton, Jr.', *ELH* v, 1938, and A. M. Kinghorn, 'Warton's *History* and Early English Poetry', *ES* xliv, 1963. L. C. Martin discusses Warton and the early poems of Milton, *Proceedings of the British Academy* xx, 1934.

WATSON, RICHARD, 1737–1816

Watson was best known for his *Apology for Christianity*, Cambridge, 1776: a reply to Gibbon; and for his *Apology for the Bible*, 1796: a reply to Paine's *Age of Reason*. He published 5 vols. of *Chemical Essays*, 1781–7. A collection of *Miscellaneous Tracts on Religious, Political, and Agricultural Subjects* appeared in 2 vols., 1815. He wrote *Anecdotes* of his own life, published posthumously in 1817.

WESLEY, JOHN, 1703–91 and WESLEY, CHARLES, 1707–88

To appreciate the scope of John Wesley's writings, it is necessary to read through R. Green's bibliography, 1896, rev. 1906. Apart from many sermons and collections of hymns, and a variety of theological publications, he wrote a number of practical treatises, notably his *Primitive Physick*, 1747, and produced educational works like *A Short Roman History*, 1773, and *A Concise History of England*, 4 vols., 1776. He edited Thomas à Kempis, 1735, several selections from William Law, extracts from Young's *Night Thoughts*, 1771, and from Mme. Guyon's

Memoirs, 1776. He abridged Henry Brooke's novel *The Fool of Quality* as *The History of Henry, Earl of Moreland,* 2 vols., 1781. From 1778 onwards he contribufed frequently to the *Arminian Magazine.*

John Wesley produced his first hymn-book, *A Collection of Psalms and Hymns,* in Charleston, S.C., 1737. The only complete edition of the Wesleys' poetry is that by G. Osborn, 11 vols., 1868–71.

The four volumes of sermons regarded as John Wesley's 'standard sermons' were published in 1746, 1748, 1750, and 1760. These have been edited by E. H. Sugden, 2 vols., 1921. The first major collection of his writings was published in 32 vols., Bristol, 1771–4, and an important edition appeared in 14 vols., 1872. There is a new edition in progress, ed. J. D. Quillian *et al.,* of which vol. xi, *The Appeals to men of Reason and Religion,* ed. G. R. Cragg, appeared in Oxford, 1975.

The standard edition of the *Journal* is edited by N. Curnock, 8 vols., 1909–16. *The Narrative of a Remarkable Transaction in the Early Life of John Wesley* first appeared in 1848. It was edited, with an essay on Wesley's marriage and character, by J. A. Leger, 1910, as *John Wesley's Last Love.* Wesley's letters have been edited by J. Telford, 8 vols., 1931. There is a selection by F. C. Gill, 1956.

Of the earlier lives, that by Robert Southey, 2 vols., 1820, is well documented, but L. Tyerman's *Life and Times of John Wesley,* 3 vols., 1871, offers a more sympathetic approach. There are many modern biographies. The short study by B. Dobrée, 1933, reprinted in his *Three Eighteenth Century Figures,* 1962, may be particularly recommended. The earlier years are treated by V. H. H. Green in *The Young Mr. Wesley. A Study of John Wesley and Oxford,* 1961, and there is a perceptive study by J. E. Rattenbury, *The Conversion of the Wesleys,* 1938. The 'theological biography' by M. Schmidt, translated by N. P. Goldhawk, 2 vols. in 3, 1962–73 (from the German edition of 1953–66), is of more specialized interest, but full and thorough. There are useful essays on the two brothers in *A History of the Methodist Church of Great Britain,* ed. R. Davies and G. Rupp, vol. i, 1965. The Wesleys⁴ social significance is assessed by B. Semmel in *The Methodist Revolution,* 1974.

John Wesley's sermons are considered by W. L. Doughty in *John Wesley, Preacher,* 1955, and in J. Downey, *The Eighteenth-*

Century Pulpit, Oxford, 1969. J. L. Golden has written an essay on John Wesley on rhetoric and belles-lettres, *Speech Monographs* xxviii, 1961. There are useful studies by G. Lawton, *John Wesley's English: a Study of his Literary Style*, 1962, and by T. W. Herbert, *John Wesley as Editor and Author*, Princeton, 1940.

H. Bett's book *The Hymns of Methodism*, 1913, rev. 1920, and enlarged again in 1945, provides a useful background for the literary reader. See also J. L. Nuelson, *John Wesley and the German Hymn*, translated by T. Parry *et al.*, Calverley, 1972. There are a few excellent pages on John Wesley in B. H. Bronson's essay, 'Some Aspects of Music and Literature in the Eighteenth Century', in *Stuart and Georgian Moments*, ed. E. Miner, Berkeley, 1972. In *Theology* lxi, 1958, C. B. Freeman gives a reminder of what Charles Wesley in particular has suffered at the hands of hymn-book editors. D. Davie has an interesting chapter in *Purity of Diction in English Verse*, 1952, rev. 1967, on the classicism of Charles Wesley.

WEST, GILBERT, 1703–56

West celebrated the beauties of Lord Cobham's gardens at Stowe in a poem published in 1732. He imitated Spenser in *A Canto of the Faery Queen*, 1739, and *Education, a Poem: in Two Cantos*, 1751. He translated the odes of Pindar, 1747. His poems are collected in Anderson ix and Chalmers xiii, and he is included in Samuel Johnson's *Lives of the Poets*.

WHITE, GILBERT, 1720–93

See Vol. IX.

WHITEFIELD, GEORGE, 1714–70

Whitefield's *Journals* were first published in 7 parts, 1738–41. He published *A Short Account of God's Dealings with George Whitefield* in 1740, *The Full Account* in 1747, and *A Further Account* in the same year. He edited *Hymns for Social Worship* in 1753, often reissued as *A Collection of Hymns for Social Worship*. His works were collected in 6 vols., 1771–2, including 3 vols. of letters.

Six of his sermons have been edited by J. C. Ryle, 1958, and the *Journals* by I. Murray, 1960.

Much characteristic material was collected in *Sketches of the Life and Labours of the Rev. George Whitefield*, Edinburgh, 1849. The biography by L. Tyerman, 2 vols., 1876, is full and interesting. There is a comprehensive modern study in progress by A. A. Dallimore: vol. i was published in 1970. See also the chapter on Whitefield in J. Downey, *The Eighteenth Century Pulpit*, Oxford, 1969.

WHITEHEAD, WILLIAM, 1715–85

The Danger of Writing Verse appeared in 1741, and was reprinted in Dodsley's *Collection of Poems* ii, 1748. A number of poems followed, including a verse *Essay on Ridicule*, 1743. He achieved fame with his tragedy *The Roman Father*, 1750. His other plays were *Creusa, Queen of Athens*, 1754, and *The School for Lovers*, 1762. He also wrote a volume of *Elegies*, 1757, and *Variety, a Tale for Married People*, 1776.

His poems were collected in 3 vols., York, 1786, the third volume including the memoir by William Mason. Here are included his odes as Poet Laureate. His poems are in Anderson xi and Chalmers xvii.

There is a study by A. Bitter, Halle, 1933, and he is included in two books on the poets laureate, one by E. K. Broadus, Oxford, 1921, the other by K. Hopkins, 1954.

WILKES, JOHN, 1727–97

With Charles Churchill, Wilkes conducted the *North Briton*, 1762–3. Extracts from the *Essay on Woman* were read in the House of Lords in 1763, but it had been privately printed earlier. Many of Wilkes's political utterances are collected in *English Liberty: being a Collection of Interesting Tracts*, 2 vols., 1768–70. His *Letters to his Daughter. With a Collection of his Miscellaneous Poems*, ed. Sir W. Rough, with an account of his life, appeared in 4 vols., 1804, and other correspondence was published in 5 vols. by J. Almon, 1805. The correspondence with Churchill was edited by E. H. Weatherly, New York, 1954.

A. Hamilton has edited a facsimile reprint of *The Infamous 'Essay on Woman'; or, John Wilkes seated between Vice and Virtue*, 1972.

There are biographies by H. W. Bleackley, 1917, R. Postgate, 1930, rev. 1956, C. C. Trench, Edinburgh, 1962, and L. Kronenberger, New York, 1974. His political significance is analysed by I. R. Christie in *Wilkes, Wyvill and Reform*, 1962, and by G. Rudé in *Wilkes and Liberty*, Oxford, 1962. See also G. Nobbe, *The*

North Briton: a Study in Political Propaganda, New York, 1939. L. I. Bredvold has a study of *The Contributions of John Wilkes to the 'Gazette littéraire de l'Europe'*, Ann Arbor, 1950.

WILKIE, WILLIAM, 1721–72

The Epigoniad, an epic poem in 9 books, appeared in 1753. There was a second, revised edition in 1759, with which Wilkie published 'A Dream. In the Manner of Spenser'. He also wrote a collection of verse fables, 1768. His poems are included in Chalmers xvi.

David Hume defended *The Epigoniad* in the *Critical Review* vii, 1759. See E. C. Mossner, *The Forgotten Hume*, New York, 1943.

WOLCOT, JOHN, 1738–1819

See Vol. IX. The following are the most important of the 'Peter Pindar' publications that fall within the period covered by this volume: *Lyric Odes to the Royal Academicians*, 1782; *More Lyric Odes to the Royal Academicians*, 1783; *Lyric Odes for the Year 1785*, 1785; *The Lousiad, an Heroi-Comic Poem* in 5 cantos, 1785, 1787, 1791, 1792, 1795; *Bozzy and Piozzi, or the British Biographers. A Town Eclogue*, 1786; *A Poetical and Congratulatory Epistle to James; Boswell Esq. on his Journal of a Tour to the Hebrides with the Celebrated Dr. Johnson*, 1786; *Ode upon Ode; or a Peep at St. James's; or New Year's Day; or What you Will*, 1787; *An Apologetic Postscript to Ode upon Ode*, 1787; *Instructions to a Celebrated Laureat; alias the Progress of Curiosity; alias a Birthday Ode; alias Mr. Whitbread's Brewhouse*, 1787.

There are studies of 'Peter Pindar' by T. Reitterer, Vienna, 1900, by G. Sinko, *John Wolcot and his School: a Chapter from the History of English Satire*, Wroclaw, 1962, and by R. L. Vales, New York, 1973. A selection from his work has been edited by P. M. Zall, Bath, 1972.

WOOD, ROBERT, 1717–71

The Ruins of Palmyra appeared in 1753, and *The Ruins of Balbec* in 1757. Wood published *An Essay on the Original Genius of Homer* in 1767, when it appeared with *A Comparative View of the Antient and Present State of the Troade*.

Wood is discussed by H. Hecht in *T. Percy, R. Wood und J. D. Michaelis. Ein Beitrag zur Literaturgeschichte der Genieperiode*, Stuttgart, 1933.

WOODFORDE, JAMES, 1740–1803

The Diary of a Country Parson, ed. J. Beresford, appeared in 5 vols., Oxford, 1924–31. There is a selection, also by J. Beresford, 1949 (*WC*).

WRAXALL, SIR NATHANIEL WILLIAM, 1751–1831

Although Wraxall wrote books of travels and a history of France, he is chiefly remembered for *Historical Memoirs of my own Time*, 2 vols., 1815, supplemented by *Posthumous Memoirs of his own Time*, 3 vols., 1836. The best edition of these memoirs is by H. B. Wheatley, 5 vols., 1884, but the one-volume edition by R. Askham, 1904, is convenient.

YOUNG, ARTHUR, 1741–1820

Young wrote numerous pamphlets on agricultural and political topics, and contributed frequently to the *Annals of Agriculture* from 1784 onwards. His principal volumes of travels were *A Six Weeks' Tour, through the Southern Counties of England and Wales*, 1768; *A Six Months' Tour through the North of England*, 4 vols., 1770; *The Farmer's Tour through the East of England*, 4 vols., 1771; *A Tour in Ireland*, 2 vols., 1780; *Travels during the Years 1787, 1788 and 1789, undertaken more particularly with a View of ascertaining the Cultivation, Wealth, Resources, and National Prosperity of the Kingdom of France*, 2 vols., Bury St. Edmunds, 1792–4. The *Tour in Ireland* was edited by A. W. Hutton, 1892, and *Travels in France* by M. Betham Edwards, 1889, and C. Maxwell, Cambridge, 1929. There is a useful selection from his writings by G. E. Mingay, *Arthur Young and his Times*, 1975.

There is a full biography by J. G. Gazley in *Memoirs of the American Philosophical Society* xcvii, 1973. It includes a useful bibliography, though the standard listing of Young's writings is that by G. D. Amery in the *Journal of the Royal Agricultural Society* lxxxv, 1924.

YOUNG, EDWARD, 1683–1765

For his earlier writings, see Vol. VII.

The Complaint: or, Night-Thoughts on Life, Death, & Immortality, began publication in 1742. Three 'Nights' were published in that year, two further 'Nights' followed in 1743, two more in 1744, one in 1745, and the ninth and final 'Night' in 1746. *The Works of the Author of the Night-Thoughts* appeared in 4 vols., 1757. His poems appear in Anderson x and Chalmers xiii, and there is a selection by B. Hepworth, Cheadle, 1975.

He also published *The Brothers: a Tragedy*, 1753; an attack on the manners of the age called *The Centaur not Fabulous*, 1755; and *Conjectures on Original Composition*, 1759. The *Conjectures* have been edited by E. J. Morley, Manchester, 1918.

H. Pettit has compiled *A Bibliography of Young's Night-Thoughts*, Boulder, Colorado, 1954.

Young's letters have been edited by H. Pettit, Oxford, 1971. The biography by W. Thomas, *Le Poète Edward Young*, Paris, 1901, is still the best, but H. C. Shelley's slighter work, *The Life and Letters of Edward Young*, 1914, can be helpful.

There is a good general study by C. V. Wicker, *Edward Young and the Fear of Death: a Study in Romantic Melancholy*, Albuquerque, 1952, and another by I. St. John Bliss, New York, 1969. Bliss has also written a useful study relating *Night-Thoughts* to contemporary Christian apologetics, *PMLA* xlix, 1934. Young figures prominently in P. van Tieghem's work *La poésie de la nuit et des tombeaux*, Paris, 1921, reprinted in vol. ii of the same author's *Le Préromantisme*, Paris, 1930. A. F. Potts relates the *Night-Thoughts* to Wordsworth in her study of *The Prelude*, Ithaca, 1953, and D. W. Odell considers *Night-Thoughts* as an answer to Pope's *Essay on Man*, *SEL* xii, 1972. See also H. Pettit, *The English Rejection of Young's Night-Thoughts*, Boulder, Colorado, 1957.

C. A. A. Krebs surveys Young's work as a dramatist, Königsberg, 1905. J. L. Kind has a study of Young's reputation in Germany, New York, 1906, and F. Baldensperger discusses 'Young et ses *Nuits* en France' in his *Études d'histoire littéraire*, Paris, 1907. A. D. McKillop examines the relationship between Young and Samuel Richardson in connection with the *Conjectures*, *MP* xxii, 1925.

INDEX

Writers and artists are listed, together with major topics, but some incidental references have been omitted. Passages where a writer is alluded to are indexed under that writer's name, even when the name itself does not occur in the text. Main entries are in bold figures. An asterisk indicates a biographical footnote. The index excludes the bibliography.